# FOUNDATIONS FOR FINANCIAL MANAGEMENT: A BOOK OF READINGS

# THE IRWIN SERIES IN FINANCE

EDITORS

Myron J. Gordon
*University of Rochester*

Robert W. Johnson
*Purdue University*

DAVIDS (Editor) *Money and Banking Casebook*
COHEN and HAMMER (Editors) *Analytical Methods in Banking*
VAN HORNE (Editor) *Foundations for Financial Management: A Book of Readings*

# Foundations for Financial Management: A Book of Readings

EDITED BY
JAMES VAN HORNE, PH.D.
ASSISTANT PROFESSOR OF FINANCE
GRADUATE SCHOOL OF BUSINESS
STANFORD UNIVERSITY

1966
RICHARD D. IRWIN, INC.
HOMEWOOD, ILLINOIS

*First Printing, August, 1966*

PRINTED IN THE UNITED STATES OF AMERICA

*Library of Congress Catalog Card No. 66–24610*

# *Preface*

THE PURPOSE of this book is two-fold. The first is to provide students of financial management with important materials which, because of the depth of the analysis involved, are not usually found in textbooks. The 34 articles included represent significant contributions in the major areas of financial management—contributions which constitute the foundations for current theory and practice. In this regard, the book can be used either as a primary text or for collateral reading. The second purpose is to provide a reference book for students, teachers, and practitioners. The materials included give rich perspectives and insight into numerous problems of concern to the financial manager.

No area recently has undergone such far-reaching change as that of financial management. It has changed from a field that was largely descriptive to one that encompasses the analytical and conceptual; from a field primarily devoted to the mechanics of procuring funds to one that includes the management of assets and allocation of funds; and from external analysis of the firm to decision-making within the firm. Traditional writers tended to place considerable emphasis on such matters as recapitalization, reorganization, secured lending, and investment banking. Their approach essentially was defensive as they described the instruments and methods by which a corporation obtained funds. The approach today is far from defensive in nature; rather, it is oriented toward dynamic decision-making.

The changes cited above have opened up entirely new dimensions. There has come to be an ever-increasing use of quantitative tools in financial planning and analysis. The treatment of uncertainty and risk has become an important aspect of financial decision-making. There is a growing awareness of the importance of a sound theoretical framework and clear-cut objectives. More and more, we are seeing an integration of the investment, financing, and dividend decisions with respect to their effect on the value of the firm to its shareholders. Many of the materials included in this book portray vividly these new dimensions.

Part I is devoted to readings that deal with financial planning and the management of current assets. The first reading, by Bierman, is concerned with the measurement and analysis of financial liquidity of the firm. In the Jaedicke and Robiechek reading, probability concepts are related to cost-volume-profit analysis in order to take account of the risk dimension. Methods for the management of a company's cash position are discussed by Horn. These include cash planning, conservation of cash, and utilization of excess funds. Jacobs reports on his empirical investigation of short-term investment practices of large corporations and analyzes trends in these practices. This article is followed by Johnson's discussion of the expanding role of trade credit, the use of electronic data processing equipment in credit management, and new opportunities for the credit manager. In the last reading in this section, Snyder presents and analyzes current theories of inventory management and control.

Part II is concerned with short- and intermediate-term financing, including leasing. Unfortunately, a number of important short-term financing methods are not covered in this section, due to the lack of worthwhile articles. Accounts-receivable lending is taken up in the first reading, which appeared in *Business Conditions* of the Federal Reserve Bank of Chicago. Since the article was published, the Uniform Commercial Code has been enacted in most states. While the Code changes many of the legal requirements for an accounts-receivable loan, the basic principles discussed in the article are still applicable. In the next article, Rogers examines various implications of warehouse receipt loans and their use in financing. The article on term lending, by Budzeika, analyzes term loans in general and recent trends in term lending by New York City banks. Gant, in his article, argues that lease financing must be analyzed critically and rationally in order to put it in its proper perspective. An overall framework for evaluating lease financing is set forth. In the last selection of Part II, Vancil proposes a new method for analyzing lease financing and the alternative of borrowing. He proposes the use of a basic interest rate, which is the minimum cost of debt capital, in order to place the two methods of financing on a comparable basis.

Part III is concerned with long-term financing. Donaldson, in the first reading, suggests that current rules for evaluating debt capacity are inadequate and proposes an alternative approach. This method is based on a cash-flow analysis to determine the probability of cash inadequacy and cash insolvency under a wide range of circumstances. In Donaldson's second article, he argues that preferred stock should be compared with the alternative of retained earnings and not with debt. He goes on to examine the merits of preferred stock relative to other sources of funds and proposes a method for deciding whether preferred stock should be retired. In the next reading, Broman reports the results of an empirical study he undertook on convertible subordinated debentures and discusses implications for the use of this instrument. Winn and Hess analyze the development and use of the call privilege and the value of this privilege to the borrower and the lender. Direct placement is taken up in the last reading, which appeared in the *Economic Review* of the Federal Reserve Bank of Cleveland. Since 1961, over one-half of all corporate debt issues have been directly placed. This article examines the growth in volume of direct placements, reasons for this growth, and the characteristics of direct placements.

Part IV deals with capital budgeting. The first reading, by Bailey, analyzes rigorously the theory of optimal investment decisions. Solomon, in the next reading, analyzes the internal rate-of-return and present-value methods for evaluating investment proposals. The problems of selecting investments, capital rationing, and mutually exclusive investment proposals are explored by Lorie and Savage. They also examine weaknesses in the internal rate-of-return method. Hillier develops a probabilistic method for analyzing investment proposals where risk is involved. He considers the situation where future cash flows for each period are comprised of an independent cash flow and a number of distinct cash flows, each of which are perfectly correlated with corresponding cash flows in other periods. In the next reading, Lerner and Carleton construct a model for determining the simultaneous effect of investment and dividend decisions on the market price of the firm's stock and the maximum share price attainable. They use the Gordon stock-valuation model as a point of departure in developing their model. The repurchase of a company's own stock has received a good deal of attention recently as an alternative to employment of funds in investment proposals. Ellis explores this subject and its effect on the market value of the company's stock in the last selection of Part IV.

Part V is concerned with the capital structure of a company, its cost of capital, and its valuation. Ever since the appearance of the Modigliani and Miller article in 1958, there has been widespread interest in the problem of capital structure and its effect on the cost of capital. In their article. Modigliani and Miller argue that a corporation's total market value and its cost of capital are independent of its capital structure. This position is notably in contrast with the traditional view that there is an optimal capital structure with respect to total valuation and the cost of capital. Solomon, in the following reading, takes specific issue with this position and argues that the cost of capital will rise beyond a certain point as debt is added to acquire additional assets. Schwartz presents a theory of capital structure in the traditional vein, taking up many of the basic tenets involving risk. Gordon, in the next reading, presents his stock-valuation model and proceeds to test the model empirically. In this regard, he analyzes the retention rate that maximizes the market price of a stock. Finally, Lintner examines the determination of the optimal size of capital budget, the optimal financing mix of internal funds and debt, and the optimal rate of growth for the corporation.

Part VI involves dividend policy. The first question to be considered is whether dividend policy has an effect on shareholders' wealth. Implied in the resolution of this problem is consideration of what investors evaluate—dividends or earnings. Miller and Modigliani assert that, given a company's investment policy, the dividend-payout ratio in any period is a matter of irrelevance, having no effect on shareholders' wealth. Walter, in the next article, explores the conditions under which dividend policy does not have an effect and concludes that these conditions are not satisfied in the real world. Thus, dividend policy would have an effect on shareholders' wealth. Gordon also contends that Modigliani and Miller are wrong, that investors evaluate dividends, and that there is an optimal dividend policy. In the last article of this section, Friend and Puckett analyze various statistical biases in empirical studies involving the relative importance of dividends and retained earnings. They develop new regression models for evaluating the relative impact of these factors on share price, testing the models empirically.

Part VII deals with mergers, acquisitions, and valuation. In the first article, McCarthy discusses the various factors necessary to consider in analyzing an acquisition or merger; he constructs a framework for this analysis. Crane proposes the use of probabilities for evaluating mergers and acquisitions. Prospective acquisitions are matched against corporate objectives and against various possible conditions of the market. Also considered is an optimum acquisition strategy using game theory. In the last article of this section, Blum and Katz explore the valuation of a company in a legal sense and how depreciation affects this valuation.

The selections in this book do not cover the entire field of financial management. Economies of publishing necessitate the omission of many worthwhile articles, and the readings in this book were chosen so that there would be a minimum of overlap. Additionally, lead-time required for publication necessarily precludes the use of pertinent articles appearing in various journals prior to the time the book is actually published. Nevertheless, it is felt that the readings in this book embody much of the current thinking with respect to financial management.

JAMES VAN HORNE

Stanford, California
*November, 1965*

# *Table of Contents*

## Part I. Financial Planning and Management of Current Assets



## Part II. Short- and Intermediate-Term Financing



## Part III. Long-Term Financing

PAGE

Part I

# Financial Planning and Management of Current Assets

Chapter 1

# Measuring Financial Liquidity*

By Harold Bierman, Jr.

IN RECENT YEARS, financial analysts have tended to focus attention on the income statement and to disregard the statement of financial position. Accounting conventions have implicitly encouraged this point of view by producing a balance sheet which is a residual of accounting procedures rather than a meaningful statement of financial position which interested parties can use for decision making. In turn, distrust of accounting conventions relative to measuring expenses such as depreciation and pension costs has led to the use of the funds statement in conjunction with the income statement. However, the exact use of the funds statement has not been well defined. What is the significance of the funds statement, and how can it be used in financial analysis? Also, can the balance sheet, as presented by the accountant, be employed in a useful manner? It is the author's contention that the financial position of a firm is relevant in making decisions involving an investment in a firm and should be systematically incorporated into any analysis of financial affairs. In this paper, we shall investigate the use of the balance sheet and funds statement to measure the financial liquidity of a firm.

## The Funds Statement

The term "funds statement" means different things to different people. We shall define funds to mean working capital (current assets less current liabilities), and the funds statement to be a statement of sources and applications of working capital. The term "funds" could be used to refer to cash, and it is possible to prepare a statement of sources and

*Reprinted by permission from *Accounting Review,* Vol. XXXV (October, 1960), pp. 628–32.

applications of cash. For internal management purposes, this type of statement may be more useful than a statement explaining the changes of working capital. However, for general financial reporting purposes the statement reporting the changes in working capital is more useful, since it is somewhat less subject to manipulation. For example, the cash balance may be temporarily increased by deferring the payment of accounts payable, but this action does not change the net working capital.

One of the prime sources of funds will be operations. The funds from operations will be equal to the total revenues earned during the period minus the expenses which utilized working capital. We shall include interest charges as an expense, though they could just as well be excluded. An alternative would be to define funds from operations as being the income of the period after deduction of interest charges, plus any expenses which were deducted which did not utilize working capital. Since depreciation is an expense which does not utilize current resources, the depreciation must be added to the income of the period. There are other technical adjustments which may have to be made, but they will not greatly affect the basic analysis.

The primary information obtained from the funds statement is the change in liquidity for a time period, measured in terms of the change in working capital. This is useful in a general way as an indication of the direction that the state of liquidity is taking; but by itself, this measure can give incorrect impressions of what is happening to the liquidity of the firm. For example, an increase in funds may be the result of issuing additional long-term debt or selling long-lived assets. The long-run effect of these actions may actually decrease the liquidity of a firm rather than increase it.

An analysis using only the funds statement is incomplete for several reasons. It is a measure of change from one position to another, but does not directly relate this change to the financial position. To be more useful, the funds statement must be tied to the financial position of the firm at the end of the accounting period. While an estimate of funds to be generated in future time periods would be useful, we shall base our computations on the funds derived from operations of the most recent accounting period.

## *The Computation of Liquidity Measures*

The conventional measures of liquidity are well known, and their uses and limitations will not be repeated or explained here. Let it suffice to say that the use of the quick ratio (liquid assets divided by current liabilities), the current ratio (current assets divided by current liabilities), and the several stock-equity ratios (relationship of long-term debt to long-term debt plus the stockholders' equity) all tend to give static measures and fail to take into account the rate at which funds are being generated. The measures introduced here will have as their objective the combination of these static measures with the measure of a flow of funds, the funds from operations.

Let us first assume that current liabilities are greater than current assets. If we divide the amount the current liabilities exceed the current assets by the funds generated by operations and multiply by 365, we obtain the number of days required to earn enough funds to pay off the net current liabilities.

Required days (to recover current liabilities net of current assets)

$$= \frac{\text{Current liabilities} - \text{Current assets}}{\text{Funds generated by operations}} \times 365$$

Instead of taking the current assets, we may subtract the liquid assets from the current liabilities.

Required days (to recover current liabilities net of quick assets)

$$= \frac{\text{Current liabilities} - \text{Quick assets}}{\text{Funds generated by operations}} \times 365$$

This gives a measure akin to the quick ratio, with the added advantage that the excess of current liabilities over quick assets is being related to the ability of the firm to generate working capital through operations. As of December 31, 1957, the current liabilities of the Ford Motor Company exceeded the $417 million of its liquid assets (cash, government securities, and receivables) by $239 million. This is an impressive amount of money, but the income for 1957 was $283 million, and the amount of funds generated by operations was $669 million.[1] Dividing the $239 by $669, the funds generated, and multiplying by 365 tells us that the excess of current liabilities over liquid assets is equivalent to 130 days of generated funds, based on the rate of fund generation during 1957. This would seem to be much more meaningful than the absolute amount of $239 million or a quick ratio of 64 percent. If the generation of funds had been at a lesser rate, the impact of an excess of current liabilities over liquid assets on liquidity would be greater.

If the current assets (or liquid assets) were greater than the current liabilities, then to divide by the amount of funds generated by operations would be meaningless. A high ratio may indicate either a large excess of current assets (or liquid assets) over current liabilities, indicating a

[1]An alternative computation of funds from operations would give $460 million. The difference, $209 million, is the amortization of commercial special tools.

high liquidity, or a small generation of funds, a symptom of low liquidity. Thus, we must look around for a more significant computation. If the firm has been losing funds instead of generating funds, a division of the net current assets or net liquid assets by the loss of funds multiplied by 365 gives the number of days' supply of short-term assets on hand. Here again, the stock of resources is related to a flow measure in order to increase its significance:

$$\text{Supply of current assets (in days)} = \frac{\text{Current assets} - \text{Current liabilities}}{\text{Funds lost in operations}} \times 365$$

In general, the generation of funds has been positive in recent years, and there is little experience upon which to judge the rate at which funds will flow from a firm during a depressed period. Since most firms have more current assets than current liabilities, the use of the computation involving current assets will be relatively rare. The use of liquid assets only is consistent with the point of view that inventories are working assets, and not available for paying off debts.

## *Long-Term Debt and Liquidity*

The impact of long-term debt on the liquidity of a firm may be of a qualitative nature, including the restriction of management's actions, but we shall focus attention only on the quantitative measures. Long-term debt generally requires current interest payments (which affect the flow of funds from operation) and will require a lump-sum payment when the debt matures.

Because of the consequences of failure to pay interest on the position of stockholders (failure to pay may lead to bankruptcy and loss of the common stockholders' interests), it is important to determine how well the interest payments are protected. A conventional computation is to relate the interest payments to the income before interest charges and compute "times interest earned." Another meaningful computation is to relate the interest payments to the funds generated by operations, where interest is not deducted in computing the funds. This gives the number of times the interest is covered in terms of the funds being generated and gives an indication of the ability of the firm to survive adversity. Relating interest to funds is not only significant to stockholders but also to bondholders, since it gives an indication of the safety of their investment. Two firms may have the same reported income and the same bonded indebtedness but still have different ability to pay interest because of differences in depreciation procedures followed. The use of funds from operations eliminates the need for computing the depreciation of a period.

Frequently, it is implicitly assumed that the bonds will not have to be repaid since additional bonds can be issued. This ability to refund should not be taken for granted. The financial ability of a firm to meet its long-term obligations should be taken into consideration. Several computations are possible, but only one will be described here. Let us first assume that the total liabilities exceed the total liquid assets. This assumption is necessary since if liquid assets exceed the total liabilities, in the presence of funds being generated by operations, than a computation relating the two would not be significant. A high measure might be caused by a large quantity of net liquid assets (great liquidity) or a small amount of funds generated by operations (little liquidity); thus the ratio computations could not be used.

The excess of total liabilities over liquid assets divided by the amount of funds generated by operations gives an indication of the impact of the total debt on the company. It is more meaningful than balance sheet ratios, as it relates the static picture of the balance sheet to the flow of funds into the firm. The magnitude of the net debt has more meaning if it is related to the generation of funds. The 1958 annual report of the United States Steel Corporation shows long-term debt of $488 million ($596 million if some inadequately described reserves are included) and $457 million of total debt in excess of liquid assets. When we note that the generation of funds from operations during 1958 (a relatively bad year for the steel industry) was $506 million, we find that the company is generating more than enough funds in one year of operations (in fact, it would take only 330 days) to pay off the entire debt. Taking into consideration the fact that United States Steel operated at approximately 59 percent of capacity during 1958, we can form a better opinion of the relationship of debts, liquid assets, and funds being generated than without the computation.[2]

## *Analysis of Eight Steel Companies*

Eight steel companies were selected and a comparison made of total debt, net of liquid assets, to funds generated from operations. Similar and equally useful computations might have been made using current assets instead of liquid assets. None of the eight companies had current liabilities in excess of current assets; thus the computation of net cur-

[2]The analysis would give different results if $530 million of government securities, not classified as working capital, were included as liquid assets.

rent liabilities divided by funds from operations was not significant.[3] Reserves which were not clearly of a liability nature were considered to be part of the balance sheet. The companies' classifications of assets were accepted.

TABLE 1

A MEASURE OF LIQUIDITY OF EIGHT STEEL COMPANIES
(Dollar Figures in Millions)

| *Company* | (1) *Total Liabilities* | (2) *Liquid Assets* | (3) *Net Liabilities (Col. 1 − Col. 2)* | (4) *Funds from Operations* | (5) *Number of Days of Fund Generation Required to Cover Net Liabilities (Col. 3 ÷ Col. 4) × 365* |
|---|---|---|---|---|---|
| Armco Steel Corporation | 234 | 237 | (3) | 98 | * |
| Bethlehem Steel Corporation | 538 | 598 | (60) | 246 | * |
| Crucible Steel Company of America | 48 | 33 | 15 | 14 | 391 |
| Granite City Steel Company | 59 | 21 | 38 | 21 | 660 |
| Inland Steel Company | 245 | 88 | 157 | 78 | 735 |
| National Steel Corporation | 197 | 124 | 73 | 75 | 355 |
| Republic Steel Corporation | 220 | 145 | 75 | 95 | 288 |
| United States Steel Corporation | 1,215 | 758 | 457 | 506 | 330 |

*The liquid assets are greater than the total liabilities.

Table 1 clearly shows that the eight companies have different degrees of liquidity. Two of the companies have liquid assets in excess of the total liabilities, so no computation involving funds from operations was made, although the amount of funds generated is disclosed. Three of the remaining six companies have net liabilities which would require fund generation in excess of one year to pay them off, and the remaining three companies would require fund generations of less than one year.

The annual reports for the year 1958 were the basis of the computations, and it should be remembered that 1958 was a year of slack activity for the steel industry. The amount of fund generation should be related to the percent of capacity at which each company operated, and

[3]This points up the limitation of the computations suggested in this paper. Not all the computations may be applied to all situations.

this should be projected into the future in terms of probable operating rates.

Table 1 would seem to add significantly to our knowledge of the eight steel companies. We know more than if we looked only at the income for the year and any of the standard computations of liquidity which ignore the fund generation. The liquidity of the firms can be determined using this one criterion with a fair degree of certainty, since the effect of most arbitrary accounting procedures has been eliminated.

## *Conclusions*

The determination of the degree of liquidity of a firm is no simple task. In the long run the liquidity may depend on the profitability of the firm, but whether or not the firm will ever survive to reach the long run will depend to some extent on its financial structure. In a recession, excessive debt may result in bankruptcy.

On the other hand, the intelligent use of debt may enable a corporation to obtain funds at less cost than by increasing its common stock equity. Thus, it is necessary for both management and investors to make comprehensive computations indicating the degree of liquidity of a firm. These computations should be based not only on the actual results of the most recent accounting periods, but predictions should also be made into the future, and the effect of adverse business conditions should be taken into consideration.

The funds statement is increasingly becoming a part of the annual report of corporations. The next step is to incorporate it systematically into the analysis of liquidity rather than to restrict its function to the explanation of the causes of changes in working capital. This paper has suggested several possible computations which may assist in the appraisal of financial liquidity. It should be noted that these computations may be made if:

1. The funds from operations are positive and the current ratio is less than one. Example:

$$\frac{\text{Current liabilities} - \text{Current assets}}{\text{Funds generated by operations}} \times 365$$

2. The funds from operations are positive and the quick ratio is less than one. Example:

$$\frac{\text{Current liabilities} - \text{Quick assets}}{\text{Funds generated by operations}} \times 365$$

3. The current ratio (or quick ratio) is greater than one and the fund flow is negative. Example:

$$\frac{\text{Current assets} - \text{Current liabilities}}{\text{Funds lost in operations}} \times 365$$

4. The total liabilities net of current assets (or liquid assets) are positive and the fund flow is positive. Example:

$$\frac{\text{Total liabilities} - \text{Current assets}}{\text{Funds generated by operations}} \times 365$$

Chapter 2

# Cost-Volume-Profit Analysis under Conditions of Uncertainty*

By Robert K. Jaedicke and
Alexander A. Robichek

COST-VOLUME-PROFIT analysis is frequently used by management as a basis for choosing among alternatives. Such decisions as (1) the sales volume required to attain a given level of profits and (2) the most profitable combination of products to produce and sell are examples of decision problems where C-V-P analysis is useful. However, the fact that traditional C-V-P analysis does not include adjustments for risk and uncertainty may, in any given instance, severely limit its usefulness. Some of the limitations can be seen from the following example.

Assume that the firm is considering the introduction of two new products, either of which can be produced by using present facilities. Both products require an increase in annual fixed cost of the same amount, say $400,000. Each product has the same selling price and variable cost per unit, say $10 and $8 respectively; and each requires the same amount of capacity. Using these data, the break-even point of either product is 200,000 units. C-V-P analysis helps to establish the break-even volume of each product, but this analysis does not distinguish the relative desirability of the two products for at least two reasons.

The first piece of missing information is the *expected* sales volume of each product. Obviously, if the annual sales of A are expected to be 30,000 units and of B are expected to be 350,000 units, then B is clearly preferred to A so far as the sales expectation is concerned.

However, assume that the expected annual sales of each product is

*Reprinted by permission from *Accounting Review*, Vol. XXXIX (October, 1964), pp. 917–26.

the same, say 300,000 units. Is it right to conclude that management should be indifferent as far as a choice between A and B is concerned? The answer is *no, unless* each sales expectation is certain. If both sales estimates are subject to uncertainty, the decision process will be improved if the relative risk associated with each product can somehow be brought into the analysis. The discussion which follows suggests some changes which might be made in traditional C-V-P analysis so as to make it a more useful tool in analyzing decision problems under uncertainty.

## *Some Probability Concepts Related to C-V-P Analysis*

In the previous section, it was pointed out that the *expected* volume of the annual sales is an important decision variable. Some concepts of probability will be discussed using the example posed earlier.

The four fundamental relationships used in the example were (1) the selling price per unit, (2) the variable cost per unit, (3) the total fixed cost, and (4) the expected sales volume of each product. In any given decision problem, all four of these factors can be uncertain. However, it may be that *relative to* the expected sales quantity, the costs and selling prices are quite certain. That is, for analytical purposes the decision maker may be justified in treating several factors as certainty equivalents. Such a procedure simplifies the analysis and will be followed here as a first approximation. In this section of the paper, sales volume will be treated as the only uncertain quantity. Later, all decision factors in the above example will be treated under conditions of uncertainty.

In the example, sales volume is treated as a *random variable.* A random variable can be thought of as an *unknown quantity*. In this case

TABLE 1

PROBABILITY DISTRIBUTION FOR PRODUCTS A AND B

| *Events (Units Demanded)* | *Probability Distribution (Product A)* | *Probability Distribution (Product B)* |
|---|---|---|
| 50,000 | ... | 0.1 |
| 100,000 | 0.1 | 0.1 |
| 200,000 | 0.2 | 0.1 |
| 300,000 | 0.4 | 0.2 |
| 400,000 | 0.2 | 0.4 |
| 500,000 | 0.1 | 0.1 |
| | 1.00 | 1.00 |

the best decision hinges on the value of the random variable, sales volume of each product. One decision approach which allows for uncertainty is to estimate, for each random variable, the likelihood that the random variable will take on various possible values. Such an estimate is called a subjective probability distribution. The decision would then be made by choosing that course of action which has the highest *expected monetary value*. This approach is illustrated in Table 1.

The expected value of the random variables, sales demand for each product, is calculated by weighting the possible conditional values by their respective probabilities. In other words, the expected value is a weighted average. The calculation is given in Table 2.

Based on an expected value approach, the firm should select product B rather than A. The expected profits of each possible action are as follows:

Product A:
$2(300,000 units) − $400,000 = $200,000

Product B:
$2(305,000 units) − $400,000 = $210,000

TABLE 2

EXPECTED VALUE OF SALES DEMAND FOR PRODUCTS A AND B

| *(1)* *Event* | *(2)* *P(A)* | *(1 × 2)* | *(3)* *P(B)* | *(1 × 3)* |
|---|---|---|---|---|
| 50,000.......... | ... | ....... | 0.1 | 5,000 |
| 100,000.......... | 0.1 | 10,000 | 0.1 | 10,000 |
| 200,000.......... | 0.2 | 40,000 | 0.1 | 20,000 |
| 300,000.......... | 0.4 | 120,000 | 0.2 | 60,000 |
| 400,000.......... | 0.2 | 80,000 | 0.4 | 160,000 |
| 500,000.......... | 0.1 | 50,000 | 0.1 | 50,000 |
| | 1.00 | | 1.00 | |
| Expected value.... | | 300,000 units | | 305,000 units |

Several observations are appropriate at this point. First, the respective probabilities for each product, used in Table 1, add to 1.00. Furthermore, the possible demand levels (events) are assumed to be mutually exclusive and also exhaustive. That is, the listing is done in such a way that no two events can happen simultaneously, and any events *not* listed are assumed to have a zero probability of occurring. Herein are three important (basic) concepts of probability analyses.

Secondly, the probability distributions may have been assigned by using historical demand data on similar products, or the weights may be purely subjective in the sense that there are no historical data available. Even if the probability distributions are entirely subjective, this approach still has merit. It allows the estimator to express his uncertainty about the sales estimate. An estimate of sales is necessary to make a decision. Hence the question is *not* whether an estimate must be made; it is simply a question of the best way to make and express the estimate.

Now, suppose that the expected value of sales for each product is 300,000, as shown in Table 3. In this example, it is easy to see that the firm would *not* be indifferent between products A and B, even though the expected value of sales is 300,000 units in both cases. In the case of product A, for example, there is a 0.1 chance that sales will be only 100,000 units, and in that case a loss of $200,000 would be incurred

TABLE 3

| *Demand* | *P(A)* | *Expected Value (A)* | *P(B)* | *Expected Value (B)* |
|---|---|---|---|---|
| 100,000 units.......... | 0.1 | 10,000 | .... | ....... |
| 200,000 units.......... | 0.2 | 40,000 | .... | ....... |
| 300,000 units.......... | 0.4 | 120,000 | 1.00 | 300,000 |
| 400,000 units.......... | 0.2 | 80,000 | .... | ....... |
| 500,000 units.......... | 0.1 | 50,000 | .... | ....... |
| | 1.00 | | 1.00 | |
| Expected sales demand......... | | 300,000 | | 300,000 |

(i.e., $2 × 100,000 units – $400,000). On the other hand, there is a 0.3 chance that sales will be above 300,000 units; and if this is the case, higher profits are possible with product A than with product B. Hence the firm's attitude toward risk becomes important. The expected value (or the mean of the distribution) is important, but so is the "spread" in the distribution. Typically, the greater the spread, the greater the risk involved. A quantitative measure of the spread is available in the form of the standard deviation of the distribution, and this concept and its application will be refined later in the paper.

## *The Normal Probability Distribution*

The preceding examples were highly simplified, and yet the calculations are relatively long and cumbersome. The possible sales volumes were few in number, and the probability distribution was discrete; that is, a sales volume of 205,762 units was considered an impossible event.

The use of a continuous probability distribution is desirable not only because the calculation will usually be simplified but because the distribution may also be a more realistic description of the uncertainty aspects of the situation. The normal probability distribution will be introduced and used in the following analysis, which illustrates the methodology involved. This distribution, although widely used, is not appropriate in all situations. The appropriate distribution depends on the decision problem and should, of course, be selected accordingly.

The normal probability distribution is a smooth, symmetric, continuous, bell-shaped curve as shown in Figure 1. The area under the curve sums to one. The curve reaches a maximum at the mean of the distribution, and one half the area lies on either side of the mean.

On the horizontal axis are plotted the values of the appropriate unknown quantity or random variable; in the examples used here, the unknown quantity is the sales for the coming periods.

FIGURE 1

THE NORMAL PROBABILITY DISTRIBUTION

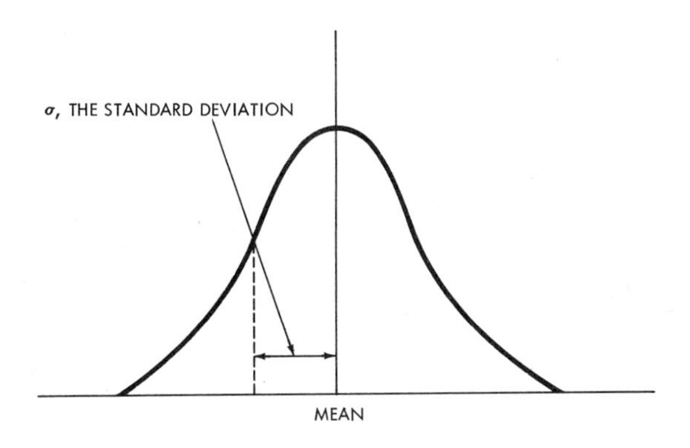


A particular normal probability distribution can be completely determined if its mean and its standard deviation, $\sigma$, are known. The standard deviation is a measure of the dispersion of the distribution about its mean. The area under any normal distribution is one, but one distribution may be "spread out" more than another distribution. For example, in Figure 2, both normal distributions have the same area and the same mean. However, in one case the $\sigma$ is one and in the other case the $\sigma$ is greater than one. The larger the $\sigma$, the more spread-out is the distribution. It should be noted that the standard deviation is not an area but is a measure of the dispersion of the individual observations about the mean of all the observations: It is a distance.

FIGURE 2

NORMAL PROBABILITY DISTRIBUTIONS WITH DIFFERENT STANDARD DEVIATIONS

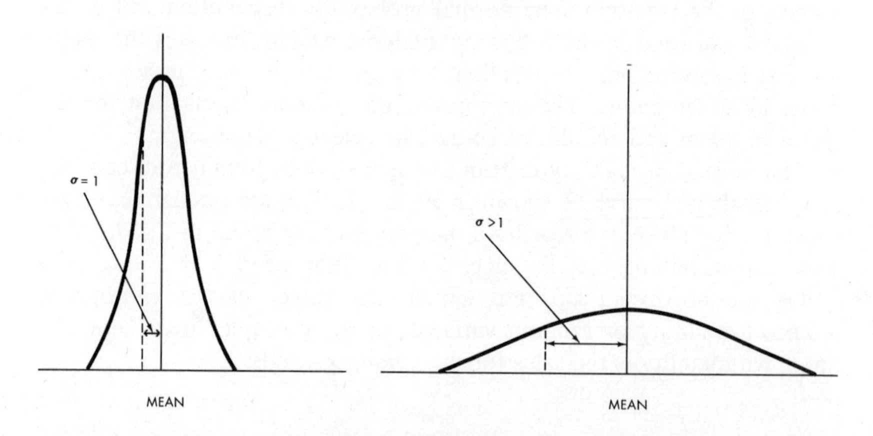


Since the normal probability distribution is continuous rather than discrete, the probability of an event cannot be read directly from the graph. The unknown quantity must be thought of as being in an interval. Assume, for example, that the mean sales for the coming period are

FIGURE 3

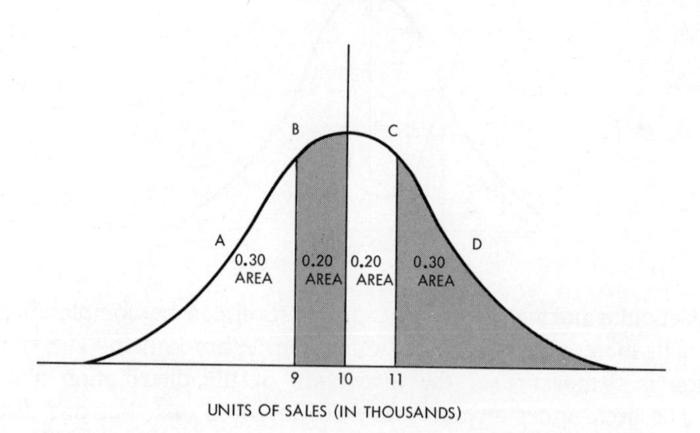


estimated to be 10,000 units and the normal distribution appears as in Figure 3. Given Figure 3, certain probability statements can be made. For example:

1. The probability of the actual sales being between 10,000 and 11,000 units is 0.20. This is shown by area *C*. Because of the symmetry of the curve, the probability of the sales being between 9,000 and 10,000

is also 0.20. This is shown by shaded area *B*. These probabilities can be given a frequency interpretation. That is, area *C* indicates that the actual sales will be between 10,000 and 11,000 units in about 20 percent of the cases.

2. The probability of the actual sales being greater than 11,000 units is 0.30, as shown by area *D*.
3. The probability of the sales being greater than 9,000 units is 0.70, the sum of areas *B*, *C*, and *D*.

Given a specific normal distribution, it is possible to read probabilities of the type described above directly from a normal probability table.

Another important characteristic of any normal distribution is that approximately 0.50 of the area lies within $\pm 0.67$ standard deviations of the mean; about 0.68 of the area lies within $\pm 1.0$ standard deviations of the mean; 0.95 of the area lies within $\pm 1.96$ standard deviations of the mean.

As was mentioned above, normal probabilities can be read from a normal probability table. A partial table of normal probabilities is given in Table 4. This table is the "right tail" of the distribution; that is, probabilities of the unknown quantity being greater than $X$ standard deviations from the mean are given in the table. For example, the probability of the unknown quantity being greater than the mean plus $0.35\sigma$ is 0.3632. The distribution tabulated is a normal distribution with mean zero and standard deviation of one. Such a distribution is known as a standard normal distribution. However, any normal distribution can be standardized; and hence, with proper adjustment, Table 4 will serve for any normal distribution.

For example, consider the earlier case where the mean of the distribution is 10,000 units. The distribution was constructed so that the

TABLE 4

AREA UNDER THE NORMAL PROBABILITY FUNCTION

| *X* | *0.00* | *0.05* |
|---|---|---|
| 0.1 | 0.4602 | 0.4404 |
| 0.3 | 0.3821 | 0.3632 |
| 0.5 | 0.3085 | 0.2912 |
| 0.6 | 0.2743 | 0.2578 |
| 0.7 | 0.2420 | 0.2266 |
| 0.8 | 0.2119 | 0.1977 |
| 0.9 | 0.1841 | 0.1711 |
| 1.0 | 0.1587 | 0.1469 |
| 1.1 | 0.1357 | 0.1251 |
| 1.5 | 0.0668 | 0.0606 |
| 2.0 | 0.0228 | 0.0202 |

standard deviation is about 2,000 units.[1] To standardize the distribution, use the following formula, where $X$ is the number of standard deviations from the mean:

$$X = \frac{\text{Actual sales} - \text{Mean sales}}{\text{Standard deviation of the distribution}}$$

To calculate the probability of the sales being greater than 11,000 units, first standardize the distribution and then use the table:

$$X = \frac{11{,}000 - 10{,}000}{2{,}000} = 0.50 \text{ standard deviations}$$

The probability of being greater than 0.50 standard deviations from the mean, according to Table 4, is 0.3085. This same approximate result is shown by Figure 3; that is, area $D$ is 0.30.

## *The Normal Distribution Used in C-V-P Analysis*

The normal distribution will now be used in a C-V-P analysis problem, assuming that sales quantity is a random variable. Assume that the per unit selling price is $3,000, the fixed cost is $5.8 million, and the variable cost per unit is $1,750. Break-even sales (in units) is calculated as follows:

$$S_B = \frac{\$5{,}800{,}000}{\$3{,}000 - \$1{,}750} = 4{,}640 \text{ units}$$

Furthermore, suppose that the sales manager estimates that the mean expected sales volume is 5,000 units and that it is equally likely that actual sales will be greater or less than the mean of 5,000 units. Furthermore, assume that the sales manager feels that there is roughly a two-thirds (i.e., 0.667) chance that the actual sales will be within 400 units of the mean. These subjective estimates can be expressed by using a normal distribution with mean $E(Q) = 5{,}000$ units and standard deviation $\sigma_q = 400$ units. The reason that $\sigma_q$ is about 400 units is that, as mentioned earlier, about two-thirds of the area under the normal curve (actually 0.68) lies within one standard deviation of the mean. The probability distribution is shown in Figure 4.

The horizontal axis of Figure 4 denotes sales quantity. The probability of an actual sales event taking place is given by the area under

---

[1]To see why this normal distribution has a standard deviation of 2,000 units, remember that the probability of sales being greater than 11,000 units is 0.30. Now, examine Table 4, and it can be seen that the probability of a random variable being greater than 0.50 standard deviations from the mean is 0.3085. Hence, 1,000 units is about the same as 0.50 standard deviations. So 2,000 units is about one standard deviation.

the probability distribution. For example, the probability that the sales quantity will exceed 4,640 units (the break-even point) is the shaded area under the probability distribution (the probability of actual sales exceeding 4,640 units).

The probability distribution of Figure 4 can be superimposed on the profit portion of the traditional C-V-P; this is done in Figure 5. The values for price, fixed costs, and variable costs are presumed to be known with certainty. Expected profit is given by

$$E(Z) = E(Q)(\mathrm{P} - \mathrm{V}) - F = \$450{,}000$$

FIGURE 4

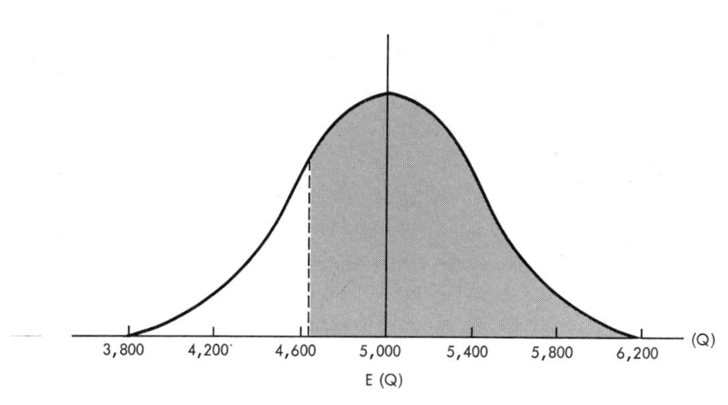


FIGURE 5

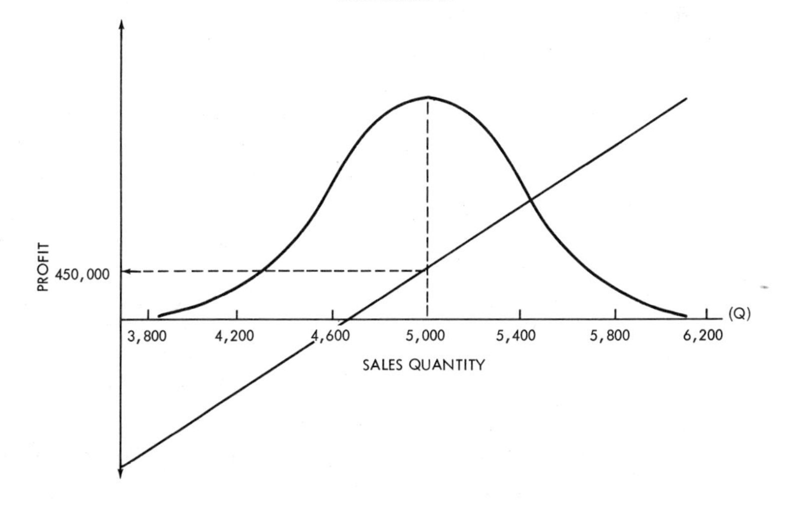

where

$$
\begin{aligned}
E(Z) &= \text{Expected profit} \\
E(Q) &= \text{Expected sales} \\
P &= \text{Price} \\
V &= \text{Variable cost} \\
F &= \text{Fixed cost}
\end{aligned}
$$

The standard deviation of the profit ($\sigma_Z$) is

$$
\begin{aligned}
\sigma_Z &= \sigma_Q \times \$1{,}250 \text{ contribution per unit} \\
&= 400 \; units \times \$1{,}250 = \$500{,}000
\end{aligned}
$$

Since profits are directly related to the volume of sales, and since it is the level of profits which is often the concern of management, it may be desirable to separate the information in Figure 5 which relates to profit. Figure 6 is a graphical illustration of the relationship between

FIGURE 6

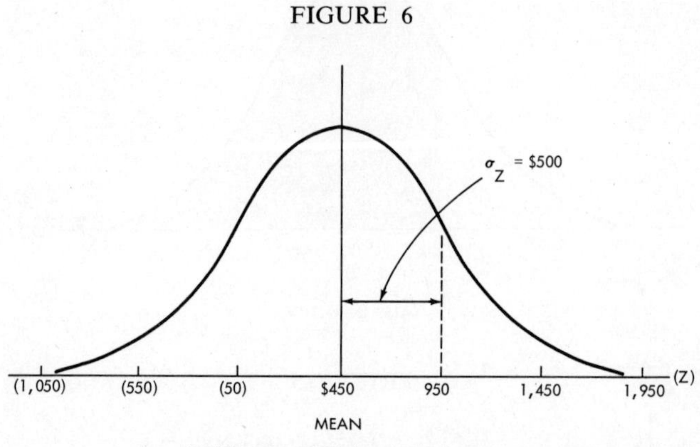


profit level and the probability distribution of the profit level. A number of important relationships can now be obtained in probabilistic terms. Since the probability distribution of sales quantity is normal with a mean of 5,000 units and a standard deviation of 400 units, the probability distribution of profits will also be normal with a mean, as shown earlier, of $450,000 and a standard deviation of $500,000.

Using the probability distribution shown in Figure 6, the following probabilities can be calculated (using Table 4).

1. The probability of at least breaking even: This is the probability of profits being greater than zero and can be calculated by summing the area under the distribution to the right of zero profits. This probability can be calculated as 1 − (the probability of profits being less than

zero). Since the distribution is symmetric, Table 4 can be used to read left-tail as well as right-tail probabilities. Zero profits fall 0.9 standard deviations to the left of the mean, i.e.:

$$\frac{\$450 - 0}{\$500} = 0.9$$

Hence the probability of profits being less than zero is:

$$P \text{ (Profits} < 0.9\sigma \text{ from the mean)} = 0.184$$

Therefore:

$$P \text{ (Profits} > 0) = 1 - 0.184 = 0.816$$

2. The probability of profits being greater than $200,000:

$$\begin{aligned} &P \text{ (Profits} > \$200{,}000) \\ &\quad = 1 - P\left(\text{Profits} < \frac{450 - 200}{500}\sigma \text{ from the mean}\right) \\ &\quad = 1 - P \text{ (Profits} < 0.5\sigma \text{ from the mean)} \\ &\quad = 1 - 0.3085 = 0.692 \end{aligned}$$

3. The probability of the loss being greater than $300,000:

$$\begin{aligned} &P \text{ (Loss} > \$300{,}000) \\ &\quad = P\left(\text{Loss} > \frac{450 - (-300)}{500}, \text{ or } 1.5\sigma \text{ from the mean}\right) \\ &P = 0.067 \end{aligned}$$

The question of how the above information can be used now arises. The manager, in choosing between this product and other products or other lines of activity, can probably improve his decision by considering the risk involved. He knows that the break-even sales are at a level of 4,640 units. He knows that the expected sales are 5,000 units, which would yield a profit of $450,000. Surely, he would benefit from knowing that:

1. The probability of at least reaching break-even sales is 0.816.
2. The probability of making at least $200,000 profit is 0.692.
3. The probability of making at least $450,000 profit is 0.50.
4. The probability of incurring losses, i.e., not achieving the break-even sales volume, is (1.816, or 0.184).
5. The probability of incurring a $300,000 or greater loss is 0.067, etc.

If the manager is comparing this product with other products, probability analysis combined with C-V-P allows a comparison of the risk involved in each product, as well as a comparison of relative break-even points and expected profits. Given the firm's attitude toward and willingness to assume risk (of losses as well as high profits), the decision of choosing among alternatives should be facilitated by the above analysis.

## *Several Relevant Factors Probabilistic*

It is evident from the above discussion that profit, $Z$, is a function of the quantity of sales in units ($Q$), the unit selling price ($P$), the fixed cost ($F$), and the variable cost ($V$). Up to this point, $P$, $F$, and $V$ were considered only as given constants, so that profit was variable only as a function of changes in sales quantity. In the following discussion, $P$, $F$, and $V$ will be treated in a manner similar to $Q$, i.e., as random variables whose probability distribution is known. Continuing the example from the preceding section, assume the data given in Table 5.

TABLE 5

| *Variable* | *Expectation (Mean)* | *Standard Deviation* |
|---|---|---|
| Sales quantity ($Q$)....... | $E(Q') =$ 5,000 units | $\sigma_{Q'} =$ 400 units |
| Selling price ($P$)........ | $E(P') =$ \$3,000* | $\sigma_{P'} =$ \$50* |
| Fixed costs ($F$)......... | $E(F') =$ \$5,800,000* | $\sigma_{F'} =$ \$100,000* |
| Variable costs ($V$)....... | $E(V') =$ \$1,750* | $\sigma_{V'} =$ \$75* |

*The mean and standard deviation for $P$, $F$, and $V$ can be established by using the same method described earlier. That is, the sales manager may estimate a mean selling price of \$3,000 per unit; and given the above information, he should feel that there is roughly a two-thirds probability that the actual sales price per unit will be within \$50 of this mean estimate.

For purposes of illustration, the random variables will be assumed to be independent, so that no correlation exists between events of the different random variables.[2] In this case the expected profit $E(Z')$ and the related standard deviation $\sigma_{Z'}$ can be calculated as follows:

$$E(Z') = E(Q')[E(P') - E(V')] - E(F') = \$450{,}000$$

$$\sigma_{Z'}{}^{3} = \$681{,}500$$

Note that when factors other than sales are treated as random variables, the expected profit is still \$450,000 as in the previous cases. However, the profit's risk as measured by the standard deviation is increased from \$500,000 to \$681,500. The reason for this is that the variability in

[2]This assumption is made to facilitate computation in the example. Where correlation among variables is present, the computational procedure must take into account the values of the respective covariances.

[3]For the case of independent variables given here, $\sigma_{Z'}$ is the solution value in the equation:

$$\sigma_Z = \sqrt{[\sigma_Q{}^2(\sigma_P{}^2 + \sigma_V{}^2) + E(Q')^2(\sigma_V{}^2 + \sigma_V{}^2) + [E(P') - E(V')]^2\sigma_Q{}^2 + \sigma_F{}^2]}$$

all of the components (i.e., sales price, cost, etc.) will add to the variability in the profit. Is this change in the standard deviation significant? The significance of the change is a value judgment based on a comparison of various probabilistic measures and on the firm's attitude toward risk. Using a normal distribution, Table 6 compares expected profits, standard deviations of profits, and select probabilistic measures for three hypothetical products.

TABLE 6

COMPARISON OF EXPECTED PROFITS, STANDARD DEVIATIONS OF PROFITS, AND SELECT PROBABILISTIC MEASURES*

| | *Products* | | |
|---|---|---|---|
| | *(1)* | *(2)* | *(3)* |
| Expected profit | $450,000 | $450,000 | $ 450,000 |
| Standard deviation of profit | $500,000 | $681,500 | $1,253,000 |
| The probability of: | | | |
| *a*) At least breaking even | 0.816 | 0.745 | 0.641 |
| *b*) Profit at least +$250,000 | 0.655 | 0.615 | 0.564 |
| *c*) Profit at least +$600,000 | 0.382 | 0.413 | 0.456 |
| *d*) Loss greater than $300,000 | 0.067 | 0.136 | 0.274 |

*The above probabilities, in some cases, cannot be read from Table 4. However, all probabilities come from a more complete version of Table 4.

In all three situations the proposed products have the same break-even quantity, 4,640 units. The first case is the first example discussed, where sales quantity is the only random variable. The second case is the one just discussed, that is, all factors are probabilistic. In the third case the assumed product has the same expected values for selling price, variable cost, fixed cost, and sales volume, but the standard deviations on each of these random variables have been increased to $\sigma_{Q''} = 600$ (instead of 400 units); $\sigma_{P''} = \$125$ (instead of $50); $\sigma_{F''} = \$200{,}000$ (instead of $100,000); and $\sigma_{V''} = \$150$ (instead of $75).

Table 6 shows the relative "risk" involved in the three new products which have been proposed. The chances of at least breaking even are greatest with product 1. However, even though the standard deviation of the profit on product 3 is over twice that of product 1, the probability of breaking even on product 3 is only 0.17 lower than product 1. Likewise, the probability of earning at least $250,000 profit is higher for product 1 (which has the lowest $\sigma$) than for the other two products.

However, note that the probability of earning profits above the expected value of $450,000 (for each product) is *greater* for products 2 and 3 than for product 1. If the firm is willing to assume some risk, the chances of high profits are improved with product 3, rather than with products 2 and 1. To offset this, however, the chance of loss is also greatest with product 3. This is to be expected, since product 3 has the highest standard deviation (variability) as far as profit is concerned.

The best alternative cannot be chosen without some statement of the firm's attitude toward risk. However, given a certain attitude, the proper choice should be facilitated by using probability information of the type given in Table 6. As an example, suppose that the firm's position is such that any loss at all may have an adverse affect on its ability to stay in business. Some probability criteria can perhaps be established in order to screen proposals for new products. If, for example, the top management feels that any project which is acceptable must have no greater than a 0.30 probability of incurring a loss, then projects 1 or 2 would be acceptable, but project 3 would not.

On the other hand, the firm's attitude toward risk may be such that the possibility of high profit is attractive, provided the probability of losses can be reasonably controlled. In this case, it may be possible to set a range within which acceptable projects must fall. For example, suppose that the firm is willing to accept projects where the probability of profits being greater than $600,000 is at least 0.40, provided that the probability of a loss being greater than $300,000 does not exceed 0.15. In this case, project 2 would be acceptable, but project 3 would not. Given statements of attitude toward risk of this nature, it seems that a probability dimension added to C-V-P analysis would be useful.

## *Summary and Conclusion*

In many cases the choice among alternatives is facilitated greatly by C-V-P analysis. However, traditional C-V-P analysis does not take account of the relative risk of various alternatives. The interaction of costs, selling prices, and volume is important in summarizing the effect of various alternatives on the profits of the firm. The techniques discussed in this paper preserve the traditional analysis but also add another dimension; that is, risk is brought in as another important decision factor. The statement of probabilities with respect to various levels of profits and losses for each alternative should aid the decision maker once his attitude toward risk has been defined.

*Chapter 3*

# *Managing Cash**

By Frederick E. Horn

WHILE THE PRINCIPAL objective of an audit is to enable the certified public accountant to express an opinion that the financial statements present fairly the financial position and results of operations of the client in conformity with generally accepted accounting principles applied on a consistent basis, he should always be aware that there are two collateral objectives which are also important to him and his client during the progress of the examination:

1. To recognize areas in the client's operations, not necessarily limited to accounting, where suggestions for increased efficiences or cost reductions will result in the improvement of certain conditions observed during the audit.
2. To discover opportunities for tax savings through the application of his knowledge of tax accounting to complicated transactions.

This article will deal primarily with these latter objectives; and because of space and time limitations, it is concerned only with a discussion of the ways and mean by which the auditor can assist management in achieving additional economies in its activities through better management of its most liquid asset—cash.

## *Proper Cash Management*

Proper cash management requires the development and application of some practical administrative procedures to accelerate the inflow of cash and to improve the utilization of the excess funds thus generated. These practical administrative procedures include:

---

*Reprinted by permission from *Journal of Accountancy,* Vol. CXVII (April, 1964), pp. 56–62.

1. Proper planning of cash requirements
2. Effective control of cash flow
3. Productive utilization of excess funds

These procedures, properly applied to the cash operations of the company, should give management an additional opportunity to increase the profits of the enterprise. They are discussed in greater detail in the comments that follow.

## *Proper Cash Planning*

In planning its cash requirements and the proper use of the funds subsequently generated through its operations, management should use two tools:

1. A long-range cash projection
2. A short-range forecast of cash position

In making its long-range projections of cash, management must first define the goals it intends to accomplish over the period under consideration—usually a period longer than one year. The basic reports used to define the goals and to make the projections are the pro forma balance sheet, an income statement, and a statement of source and application of funds. The long-range projection does not attempt to show detailed estimates of revenues and expenses. Its purpose is to show whether, over a period of time, money can be generated through working capital growth, when and where funds will be needed, and if they will be available at that time. It also portrays the effect of corporate growth, long-term trends, contemplated acquisitions, the development of new products, any new financing, and other corporate changes over a longer period of time. It is particularly useful in helping management plan the proper financing of capital projects through long-term borrowing or sale of capital stock. This forecast also helps management to make the proper long-range decision—approve, defer, or abandon the various projects which would make borrowing necessary.

The short-range forecast usually takes one of two forms:

1. A cash receipts and disbursements statement showing beginning balances of cash and short-term investments, projected cash receipts for the period, estimated cash disbursements for the period, and the ending balance of cash and short-term investments.
2. A cash flow statement showing the projection of revenues, expenses, and net income adjusted for anticipated changes in noncash items to arrive at estimated income on a cash basis. This statement is usually referred to as the "adjusted net income statement."

Needless to say, there are many variations in these two statements, but the purpose is the same—to project the flow of cash into and out of the company over a regular interval of time—day to day, week to week, monthly, quarterly, semiannually, or even longer periods of time.

The cash receipts and disbursements statement is more often used by those companies which must exercise close control over their cash positions. Its principal advantage is that it traces the flow of cash through each item of revenue and expense. The cash flow statement or "adjusted net income statement" reflects the flow of cash and its impact on working capital. It is more commonly used by the more stable companies with ample cash funds or by companies where cash is not an acute problem.

With the information developed by either statement, management can determine fairly accurately (1) its cash requirements for current operations, (2) its need for short-term financing, if any, and (3) the availability of funds for investment. However, this determination requires the constant attention of management through either frequent conferences and meetings or the delegation of this responsibility to one of the managers who must devote considerable time to this phase of operations. This gives rise to an additional cost which must be considered in the management of cash.

## *Effective Control*

It is obvious that the greater number of times a company can convert its product or its services into cash proceeds in any given period, the less capital it needs to finance a certain volume of business. What means can it employ to accomplish a more frequent turnover? They are only limited by the ingenuity of management; however, the techniques more commonly used today are as follows:

1. Speeding up collections
2. Reducing investment in inventories
3. Improving control over payables and related payments

## *Speeding Up Collections*

In their efforts to speed up the inflow of cash, a number of companies have taken a new look at their collections procedures. In addition to revamping their paper flow systems internally, possibly by automation, to shorten the time lag between shipping, billing, and collection, these companies also are employing other useful tools:

1. Concentration banking
2. Lock box system for collections from customers

Those companies that have adopted "concentration banking" are speeding up their collection processes by establishing strategic collection centers. Collections are made locally by sales offices, divisions, or subsidiaries and then are deposited in local bank accounts. From these local accounts the funds are transferred as rapidly as possible to centralized banks by wire transfers, by drawing drafts, or by the use of imprest or automatic balances. On the basis of reports of daily collections or deposits, management can then transfer any excess funds to wherever they are needed or can use or invest them as it sees fit.

Concentration banking has been found to be effective for speeding up collections for companies with a large number of sales or distribution centers scattered throughout the country and/or when collections are made from a large number of customers remitting relatively small payments. The net result is to reduce the size of the "float" in accounts receivable and bank balances and to make these funds available to the head office several days earlier.

In the "lock box" system (where receipts are mailed by customers to a post office box controlled by the bank), it is also possible to reduce the float in deposits by several days and thereby put the funds thus generated to more productive uses. In the January, 1962, issue of *Fortune,* it was reported that Cerro Corporation's subsidiary in Fairmont, West Virginia, adopted the lock box system and got

> the use for three days of money it formerly lost while checks sent to Fairmont were forwarded to New York to go through the clearing house. Cerro's Vice President Starr estimates that its subsidiary is saving perhaps $2,800 a year by this technique. In addition, Starr has helped the subsidiaries earn more on their surplus cash by having them turn these funds over to the parent company for investment.

Following this thought, it does not take much of a mathematician to determine that if a company has monthly receipts of $600,000, it can recover approximately $100 in interest (at 6 percent per year) for every day it can make its cash tied up in receivables available for investment or other business purposes.

Other advantages of the lock box system are as follows:

1. The number of personnel processing collections may possibly be reduced, since the bank handles the receipts and then records and reports them to its depositor.
2. There may be an improvement in the controls over collections, since only the bank personnel have access to cash receipts.

For some companies, however, the disadvantages listed below may outweigh the advantages described above:

1. Substantial compensating balances may have to be maintained by the company partially to cover the cost of processing the remittances received by the bank.
2. Where compensating balances are not maintained the cost of processing each check (ranging from 10 to 25 cents) may be substantial in the aggregate, depending on services required.[1]
3. There may be a loss of control over credit information due to the fact that the bank processes the checks before the company receives notice of payment and can act on delinquent accounts in dispute.
4. There may be customer resistance, particularly from those who have used the three- to four-day float to their own advantage.

Other procedures which also have been effective in speeding up collections are:

1. Using centralized billing and collection in place of decentralized billing and collection or the lock box system.
2. Reviewing credit procedures to determine the impact on cash of slow-paying customers and bad debt losses. Slow-paying customer accounts are reviewed to determine the extent to which cash is tied up because of disputes which could be avoided. The review also includes an evaluation of credit policies. Perhaps the granting of credit is too strict, thus cutting down on the inflow of cash due to the rejection of sound sales; or on the other hand, perhaps it is too liberal, which could increase the number of slow-paying customers and bad debt losses and thereby decrease the inflow of cash.
3. Shortening credit terms allowed to customers or revising the discounts offered so it would not be profitable for them to use the float to finance their own operations.
4. Determining whether customers can obtain financing elsewhere and then helping them obtain it.
5. Setting up procedures for special handling of extremely large remittances or foreign remittances—expeditors handling government contract reimbursements, personal pickup of large amounts, using airmail and special delivery and similar techniques to speed up collections.

## *Reducing Investment in Inventories*

It is estimated that nearly 30 percent of the working capital of the average company is tied up in inventories; therefore, any means for reducing an investment of cash of this size is worthy of consideration. Space does not permit a thorough discussion of this subject. However,

[1]National Industrial Conference Board, Inc., *Managing Company Cash,* Studies in Business Policy, No. 99 (New York, 1961), p. 77.

the following procedures for reducing the size of the inventory or accelerating its turnover have been employed successfully:

1. Consolidating inventory control records and distribution centers to speed up bookkeeping and the movement of the product to the customer.
2. Planning the flow of raw materials to the plant so they enter production upon arrival, thus minimizing storage, demurrage, and other handling charges and accelerating the conversion process.
3. Preparing reports highlighting the activity of product lines, raw materials, supplies, etc., so attention can be directed to slow-moving and obsolete items. These reports also include the costs involved—acquisition or production, storage, handling, etc.—so that management is fully aware of the amount of money invested in stock which is slow in moving off the shelves or in flowing into the production stream.
4. Establishing budgets and standards of turnover and then making periodic comparisons of actual to budget or to standards and investigating the reason for significant variances.
5. Applying a return-on-investment measure to determine the effectiveness—dollarwise—of inventory management.

Before passing on to the next subject, it is interesting to note that an increasing number of companies are automating their inventory records to obtain better controls over quantities and that they are employing operations research techniques to determine more efficient product distribution. Both techniques also have resulted in lower investments in inventories.

## *Control of Payables and Related Payments*

Procedures employed for maximizing the use of cash through the control of payables and related payments are as follows:

1. Timing payments to vendors so bills are paid only as they fall due.
2. Establishing procedures which will prevent or minimize the loss of discounts.
3. Centralizing payable and disbursement procedures.

In order to increase the company's float in payables and thus use the cash funds available for short-term investment or other corporate purposes, the following payment techniques have been used:

1. Payments have been made very late in the day so cash can be used during the remainder of the day.
2. Payments have been made by bank draft to extend the cash withdrawal period.

3. Arrangements have been made with vendors to set due dates of bills to coincide with the company's period of peak receipts.[2]

Some companies have given considerable attention to speeding up their paper work in order to prevent the loss of discounts. Other companies have set up separate ledger accounts to accumulate discounts lost so they could establish some control over this phase of cash disbursements and thus give management some idea of the money involved and the opportunity to take remedial action. Still other companies have adopted various prepayment procedures. Kaiser Aluminum's system was described in the February 18, 1963, issue of the *Wall Street Journal.* For all purchases under $1,000, which it says include 92 percent of company orders, Kaiser sends with its purchase order a signed blank check good up to $1,000. The check is made out to the vendor, who fills in the correct amount and cashes the check as his payment. By using this system, the manager of plant purchasing services claims that the company has eliminated a lot of clerical work and has just about been able to eliminate the accounts payable department at most of its thirty-one purchasing locations. The new system also has paid off in an increasing number of cash discounts given for early payments.

Centralization of payables and disbursing has the effect of consolidating working funds at the head office and reducing unproductive bank balances in the hands of subsidiaries, divisions, or other offices. It also permits the head office to expedite the paper flow, to schedule payments more effectively, and to invest excess funds generated more productively.

## *Other Areas for Generating Cash Flow*

Before leaving the subject of accelerating the turnover of cash, attention should be given to some other areas which might generate additional cash. These are as follows:

1. Reduction in "compensating balances" on deposit with banks
2. Improving control over intercompany transfers
3. More efficient utilization of facilities
4. More effective use of manpower
5. Strategic tax planning

It behooves management to take a close look at the compensating balances maintained in the company's various bank accounts. Usually the balances requested by the bank average about 20 percent of the loans the bank has agreed to extend to the corporation. In other words, a corporation with a $1 million line of credit is expected to maintain a balance of approximately $200,000. It should be obvious that not

[2] *Ibid,* p. 78.

only are these funds unproductive to the company but they also drain away cash to the extent of the interest payable on the total loan. However, before any action is taken by management to reduce these balances, it should consider what effect such a decision will have on its relations with its bankers, particularly when it expects to obtain additional financing in the future from this source.

Delays in transfers of cash between offices, divisions, subsidiaries, and other locations can also create a needless float. This float can be eliminated if funds are deposited in a central bank account and transfers are made by bookkeeping entries. (This procedure also should eliminate the possibility of a "kiting" operation and give better control over intercompany transactions.)

Most companies have significant investments in plant, property, and equipment; and cash invested in these facilities can only be recovered through the cash flow cycle stretched over a number of years. (However, if one notes the misuse of the cash flow concept in many recent financial reports issued to the public, it is doubtful whether this cash will be recovered for further use in the future.) Because of inflation, obsolescence through automation and other technological improvements, competition at home and abroad, and other factors, alert managements also are concentrating their attention on these investments. Idle capacity in the form of excess plants or buildings is being sold or rented to others, plant layouts are being made more efficient, facilities are being consolidated, and new and better equipment is being installed through either purchase or leasing arrangements.

In the past the sale-leaseback arrangement has been a popular method of financing plant acquisitions, due to the fact that the cash involved in purchasing or constructing the facilities is made available immediately after the sale for financing current and future production. Since more and more companies are entering the leasing markets and are making all kinds of machinery and equipment available, it is advisable that management decide whether it will buy, construct, or lease its new facilities. Here, it must determine which alternative is more profitable by comparing the productivity of the cash invested in a long-term acquisition with that used in current operations over the life of the lease.

Many large companies also are in the process of surveying their manpower needs and are turning to automation to reduce labor costs. Still others are making work measurement studies and are realigning their labor requirements accordingly. These studies have included both direct and indirect labor, and have attained significant savings. The procedures involved can be applied to almost any size company and should result in an additional cash saving.

It has been said that "A fool and his money are soon parted. The rest of us wait until tax time." This need not be so if management uses strategic tax planning to minimize its tax expenditures. Currently, management seems to be employing the following techniques to reduce tax payments:

1. Using accelerated depreciation methods or adopting guide-line depreciation rates, particularly when shorter lives are involved.
2. Using the investment credit to full advantage by strategic acquisitions and dispositions of property, plant, and equipment.
3. Deducting research and development costs and similar expenses in the years the expenditures are made rather than capitalizing them and amortizing such costs over a number of years.
4. Adopting changes in accounting procedures, particularly those initiated by the Internal Revenue Service, or exploiting changes in reporting periods.

Properly planned, these items and others should generate additional cash for the company; on the other hand, however, a lack of knowledge of tax consequences could result in an outflow of cash. For example, a Section 1245 transaction, about which little is written, could create ordinary income when there was no income per books, and thus cash could be siphoned off through an excessive tax payment.

## *Utilization of Excess Funds*

Having reviewed the various ways and means to accelerate the turnover of cash, let us now consider what should be done with the excess funds so generated. A survey of the practices employed to utilize such cash shows that they too are unlimited, but the most common uses of these funds are as follows:

1. Investment in short-term obligations.
2. Application of excess cash to reduce loans outstanding and thereby obtain interest savings.
3. Extension of loans to subsidiaries.
4. Investment of funds through mergers and acquisitions or in new plant facilities in order to earn a higher rate of return.
5. Purchase of own securities to be used in acquisitions, stock option plans, or other payments.
6. Investment of excess funds to develop new products or improve the old ones.
7. Distributions to stockholders.

Due to space limitations, only the first item will be discussed in this section. The other items are more or less self-explanatory.

## *Short-Term Investments*

Today, one finds corporate funds lodged in a multitude of short-term investments—Treasury bills; issues of government-sponsored agencies such as the Federal Home Loan Bank, the Federal Land Banks, etc.; commercial paper and bankers' acceptances; U.S. dollar deposits with Canadian and European banks; and finally, negotiable certificates of deposit. In the past the companies making these investments of their surplus cash seem to have had the following criteria: (1) security, (2) marketability, and (3) yield. However, there now seems to be a trend toward investing more funds in securities carrying larger yields but involving greater risks. In the November 5, 1963, edition of the *Wall Street Journal,* it is reported that corporate treasurers are now investing greater amounts in Mexican commercial paper, in time deposits in Japanese banks, and in preferred stocks of U.S. corporations because of the larger returns received. For a good article on the subject of investments the reader is referred to the May, 1962, issue of *Dun's Review and Modern Industry.*

In the November 5, 1963, issue of the *Wall Street Journal,* additional investment techniques also were described:

1. Corporate savings accounts in savings and loan associations—a deposit earning a higher rate of return.
2. Link financing—an arrangement whereby the borrower seeks a lender through a broker. The lender deposits the money in a bank, which in turn loans the money to the borrower. The lender receives not only the usual time deposit rate from the bank but also a special payment from the borrower, which is forwarded through the broker.
3. Repurchase agreements—the purchase of securities from a dealer with the understanding that he will buy them back within a short period of time. The corporation usually gets a rate of return slightly under what it would have received if it had owned the securities outright.
4. Riding the yield—the corporation buys short-term securities and sells them before maturity in order to make a trading profit in addition to the interest return.

Again, it must be pointed out that the administration of excess funds placed in short-term investments requires the time and attention of some member of management skilled in investment practices or, alternatively, the employment of an investment consultant, each at additional cost.

Typical of the philosophy underlying corporate investment of excess funds in short-term obligations is the following story reported in the August 8, 1962, edition of the *Wall Street Journal.* In the article, M. S.

Mendelsohn, a staff reporter, pointed out that when a western mining company found itself with $500,000 it did not need for the next three days, it put in a quick call to San Francisco's Bank of America, agent for Sears Roebuck Acceptance Corporation, the finance subsidiary of the huge retail and mail-order house. Through the bank the mining company arranged to buy a 2½ percent three-day note from Sears.

By putting the $500,000 to work for the brief period it was not needed, the mining company made a profit of $104.17. Sears, in turn, says it saved a little under $100 by using the mining company's money to reduce a bank loan on which Sears was paying 4½ percent. To each of us the saving might seem to be a small amount and hardly worth the effort; but to Donald W. Hansen, President of the Sears subsidiary, such transactions "are worthwhile when you have a constant stream of them."

On this same subject the January, 1962, issue of *Fortune* pointed out that "one financial man boasted that he had sometimes earned more interest over a long weekend than some of the company's production departments had been able to earn in a week." And in the March 8, 1963, issue of *Time,* it is reported that certificates of deposits "are now bought and sold among treasurers with such frequency that they have practically become a corporate currency."

## *Continuing Study*

As can be seen from the above discussion, managing cash involves (1) the employment of proper forecasting techniques so the company can maintain an adequate cash position, (2) the development of procedures which will insure that cash is handled efficiently from the time it is received from the customer or some other source to the time it flows out in the payment of a bill or for some other expenditure, and (3) the adoption of some program to utilize excess funds generated.

As auditors, we must be constantly aware that the proper utilization of cash by management can bring additional savings to the company. Thus, we should take every opportunity to offer our suggestions for improvements in this area when inefficiences are discovered. In so doing, we must become more knowledgeable about current practices employed in business, and this requires intensive study and continuing research on the subject. It is hoped that this article has piqued the reader's interest sufficiently to do just that.

*Chapter* 4

# *The Marketable Security Portfolios of Nonfinancial Corporations: Investment Practices and Trends**

By Donald P. Jacobs

## *I. Introduction*[1]

DURING THE LAST TWO decades, nonfinancial corporations have become increasingly important suppliers of funds to the money markets. Their holdings of United States government securities increased from $2.2 billion to $16.5 billion between 1939 and 1958. Holdings of other short-term securities are included under "other current assets" in the estimates made by the Securities and Exchange Commission.[2] Although the exact portion of "other current assets" consisting of short-term securities cannot be ascertained, the total of this account increased from $1.4 to $5.9 billion in the 1939–58 period. Because these large amounts of corporate funds are invested in money market securities, changes in the investment practices of nonfinancial corporations influence relative rates of growth in various sectors of the money market.

This study has two purposes: to describe the current short-term investment practices of nonfinancial corporations (Section II) and to indicate significant changes in these practices since 1939 (Section III).

---

*Reprinted by permission from *Journal of Finance,* Vol. XV (September, 1960), pp. 341–52.

[1]The author wishes to express his gratitude and appreciation to the John Evans Foundation of Northwestern University for its financial support of the research underlying this project.

[2]Estimates of nonfinancial corporate holdings of U.S. Treasury securities as well as other current asset items prepared by the Securities and Exchange Commission are available quarterly since 1939 (see "Current Assets and Liabilities of United States Corporations," *Statistical Bulletin* [Washington, D.C.: Securities and Exchange Commission]).

Marketable security portfolios of the largest nonfinancial corporations contain a high proportion of Treasury securities. The yield and other characteristics of alternative investments suggest that this practice sacrifices substantial income. In the past few years an increasing fraction of portfolios has been invested in non-Treasury securities. Data used in this study indicate that this trend may be expected to continue.

## *II. Determinants of Types of Securities Held by Nonfinancial Corporations*

A questionnaire was sent to the financial officers of 250 of the largest nonfinancial corporations. The companies included the 100 largest industrial corporations and 50 of the largest corporations in each of the utility, transportation, and merchandising industries. In all cases, size was measured in terms of total assets.[3]

The following information was requested: a breakdown by type and dollar amount of marketable securities held on December 31, 1957; a statement of any restrictions on the types of securities which may be held and changes in such restrictions during the preceding ten years; and a description of personnel responsible for investment of the corporate portfolio.

Two hundred and nine companies responded to the questionnaire. These companies accounted for 81 percent of the marketable security holdings of all 250 companies in the sample. The 209 corporations held more than 45 percent of all nonfinancial corporate holdings (Table 1). The holdings of each of the asset items of the respondent companies were within the fairly narrow limits of 74–85 percent of the total holdings of the 250 companies.

The holdings of the 250 corporations differ significantly from those of all nonfinancial corporations as estimated by the SEC. The largest

[3]"The *Fortune* Directory for 1956," Supplement to *Fortune Magazine,* July, 1957. In planning the survey, the date for which data would be requested had to be determined. The major advantage of a year-end date is the ability to correlate marketable security data with other financial data contained in the annual reports; furthermore, since year-end data are usually the most readily available, this increases the likelihood of response to the questionnaire. The major drawback of a year-end date is that security holdings at that time may not be typical of the firm's usual portfolio because of seasonal differences in corporate needs, window dressing, or attempts to minimize state and local taxes, which are usually computed on a basis of the year-end statement. It was decided that the advantages of a year-end date far outweighed the disadvantages. The conventional distinction between marketable securities and investments is made in this paper: Marketable securities are short-term holdings designed to earn income directly from otherwise temporarily idle funds; investments are considered relatively more permanent, that is, longer term profit objectives are of primary importance.

corporations held 45 percent of total marketable securities but only 20 percent of total cash. This concentration of holdings of marketable securities is understated, in that, of the 250 companies, 74 did not hold securities on the survey date. Reasons for this concentration may include greater familiarity with money market opportunities among the larger firms and greater incentive to invest when the absolute amounts of cash flow are large.

TABLE 1

BALANCE SHEET DATA (IN BILLIONS OF DOLLARS) OF 250 COMPANIES SURVEYED, COMPANIES SUPPLYING MARKETABLE SECURITIES BREAKDOWNS, AND ALL NONFINANCIAL CORPORATIONS, AS OF DECEMBER 31, 1957

| | *Totals 250 Companies Surveyed** | *Totals 209 Companies Replying†* | *SEC Estimates of All Nonfinancial‡* | *Percent of Companies Replying to 250 Totals§ (Col. 2 − Col. 1)* | *Percent of 250 Total to All Nonfinancial‖ (Col. 1 ÷ Col. 3)* |
|---|---|---|---|---|---|
| | (*1*) | (*2*) | (*3*) | (*4*) | (*5*) |
| Cash | 7.06 | 5.28 | 35.0 | 74.8 | 20.2 |
| Marketable securities | 10.15 | 8.20 | 22.4§ | 80.8 | 45.3 |
| Current assets | 61.06† | 47.66 | 239.9 | 78.0 | 25.5 |
| Total Assets | 196.77† | 167.10 | N.A.‖ | 84.9 | N.A. |

*These data are from Moody's manuals for 1958 and corporate annual reports. In some instances the corporate reporting date was not December 31. Such companies represent a small proportion of the total.

†In many instances, holdings of short-term Treasury securities were used to offset a tax liability or segregated in a reserve fund. When found, these were included in the marketable securities totals and added back to current assets and, where appropriate, to total assets. The additions were $2,147 million to current assets and $1,732 million to total assets.

‡*Statistical Bulletin:* Securities and Exchange Commission estimates for December 31, 1957.

§The SEC categories "government securities" and "other current assets" are added. Since "other current assets" include assets other than marketable securities, this overstates the SEC estimate of marketable securities.

‖Not available on a comparable basis.

Table 2 shows the types and amounts of securities held on the survey date by the 209 respondent firms. Data are classified by type and maturity of securities held.

United States government securities held outright accounted for about 75 percent of total. The proportion increases to 83 percent if securities held under repurchase agreements, which are usually governments, are included.

Probably more than 75 percent of the total portfolio matured within six months. Another 15 percent matured between six months and one year. United States government issues comprised the largest part of the remaining 10 percent maturing in more than one year, but some longer term tax-exempts and railroad equipment trust certificates were held. The maturity breakdown of United States agency securities was not requested; some portion of these holdings, probably very small, may be assumed to have matured in more than one year. Investments in repurchase agreements are usually short-term. Even if the securities held included some of long maturities, the repurchase agreements themselves were almost certainly for a very short period.

TABLE 2

DOLLAR AMOUNTS AND PERCENTAGE DISTRIBUTION OF HOLDINGS OF MARKETABLE SECURITIES OF 209 COMPANIES WHICH REPLIED TO QUESTIONNAIRE AS OF DECEMBER 31, 1957

| *Type of Security* | *Total $(000)* | *Percentage Distribution* |
|---|---|---|
| U.S. Treasury securities, by maturity, held outright: | | |
| Maturing in 1–91 days | 2,174,408 | 26.51 |
| Maturing in 91–180 days | 2,290,944 | 27.93 |
| Maturing in 180 days–1 year | 1,012,677 | 12.34 |
| Maturing in 1–2 years | 415,305 | 5.06 |
| Maturing in 2–3 years | 44,257 | 0.54 |
| Maturing in 3 years or more | 210,277 | 2.56 |
| Total Treasuries Held Outright | 6,147,868 | 74.94 |
| Securities held under repurchase agreements | 696,897 | 8.50 |
| U.S. agency securities | 241,110 | 2.94 |
| Tax-exempt securities, held outright: | | |
| 1. Maturing in 1 year or less | 360,474 | 4.39 |
| 2. Maturing in more than 1 year | 64,970 | 0.79 |
| Foreign government securities | 21,673 | 0.26 |
| Finance company directly placed commercial paper | 539,137 | 6.57 |
| Commercial paper (placed by broker) | 8,267 | 0.10 |
| Railroad equipment trust certificates: | | |
| 1. Maturing in 1 year or less | 5,789 | 0.07 |
| 2. Maturing in more than 1 year | 482 | Nil |
| Other corporate bonds, notes, and marketable securities | 116,863 | 1.42 |
| Total | 8,203,530 | 100.0 |

A portfolio such as shown in Table 2 is almost devoid of risk of default. Some potential loss exists with respect to holdings of tax-exempts, foreign securities, and corporate securities. Although no breakdown of tax-exempt holdings relative to credit rating is available, the extreme conservatism of the rest of the portfolio suggests that most of these are in the highest rated categories. Securities of foreign governments, other than Canadian government obligations, consist mainly of statutory holdings of companies operating abroad and so are not subject to normal investment decisions. In the final category, bankers' acceptances are virtually riskless; corporate stocks and bonds, also included in this category, carry some risk of default. However, the bulk of these is held by railroads and may be more appropriately listed as "investments" than as "marketable securities." An extremely small amount of railroad equipment trust certificates was held by nonfinancial corporations.

The concentration of holdings in short maturities reduces not only the risk of loss through default but also the risk of capital loss through changes in interest rates. A large portion of the portfolio is purchased to be held to maturity; and even if some securities must be sold, extreme interest rate fluctuations could result in only minimum capital losses.

Table 3 presents data on yields available on December 31, 1957, on the important types of securities held.

Repurchase agreements have virtually the same risk of default as Treasury securities. Their yields are negotiated by the purchasing cor-

TABLE 3

SHORT-TERM SECURITY YIELDS, ON DECEMBER 31, 1957

| *Type of Security* | *Yields* |
|---|---|
| U.S. Treasury securities: | |
| 91-day Treasury bills, new issues | 3.102 |
| Maturity of 9–12 months | 3.09 |
| Maturity of 3–5 years | 3.04 |
| U.S. agency securities, 4–6 months' maturity | 3.20* |
| Repurchase agreements with government bond dealers | ⅛ to ¼ percent above yield on security pledged |
| Directly placed commercial paper: | |
| Maturing in 5–29 days | 2.75 |
| Maturing in 30–89 days | 3.38 |
| Maturing in 90–179 days | 3.50 |
| Maturing in 180–265 days | 3.63 |
| Maturing in 270 days | 3.75 |
| Broker-placed commercial paper, 4–6 months' maturity | 3.75–4.13 |

*To compute the yield on 4–6 months' maturity, the offering sheet of C. F. Childs & Company for December 31, 1957, was used. Five types of agency securities were included: Federal Land Bank, Federal Home Loan Bank, Federal National Mortgage Association, Banks for Cooperatives, and Federal Intermediate Credit Banks. Ten quotations were found in the 4–6-month maturity class. Yields after tax were used and then blown up to a pretax basis. This was done because some of the securities were selling at a premium and the capital loss at maturity had important yield effects. The yield shown is the arithmetic mean of the ten quotations.

*Sources.* Treasury securities, *Federal Reserve Bulletin;* United States agency securities, C. F. Childs & Company; repurchase agreements with government bond dealers, C. F. Childs & Company. Directly placed commercial paper, *Wall Street Journal:* broker-placed commercial paper, *Wall Street Journal.*

poration and the selling dealer in Treasury obligations and are usually between one eighth and one fourth of 1 percent above the available yield on a Treasury obligation of similar maturity.

Although United States agency securities are not guaranteed by the United States government, it is widely felt that Congress would feel morally obligated to redeem these issues in the event of imminent default. Five agencies have made substantial public offerings of their securities. Most original offerings are of short or intermediate maturities. Substantial trading is done in the secondary market. Yields of these securities are closest to the yields of Treasury obligations,[4] but the difference of only ten basis points is probably less than usual.

Nine finance companies sell their own commercial paper. Public offerings are made at stated rates of discount, usually in five classes of maturities. Rates are usually graduated one eighth of 1 percent between classes, and yields are one-eighth to one-half percent greater than the yields on similar maturities of Treasury bills. Directly placed commercial paper is sold in any amount from $5,000 to many millions of dollars. The buyer specifies the dollar amount and maturity desired. There is no organized secondary market, but the issuing companies make an "unofficial" commitment to repurchase should the buyer unexpectedly need to liquidate.[5]

Broker commercial paper consists of short-term promissory notes issued by very highly rated companies and sold through brokers. Yields on these notes vary between one eighth and three fourths of 1 percent above those on directly placed commercial paper of the same maturities, depending on the relative credit rating of the issuing company. The notes of individual issues are available only in limited amounts and for stated maturities. Commercial paper of many companies is available at any time, so that the buyer has a wide selection of maturity and issuing companies from which to choose.

It is extremely difficult to compute a representative yield on tax-exempt securities as held by nonfinancial corporations. A large part of these securities is issued with long maturities. Corporate purchases are

---

[4]For a complete discussion of the characteristics of United States government and agency securities, see First Boston Corporation, *Securities of the United States Government* (18th ed.; Boston, 1958).

[5]Additional descriptions of finance company commercial paper, commercial paper sold through brokers, and tax-exempt securities, respectively, are available in Donald P. Jacobs, "Source and Costs of Funds for Large Sales Finance Companies," *Consumer Installment Credit: Conference on Regulation,* Vol. II, No. 1 (Washington, D.C.: Board of Governors of the Federal Reserve System, 1957), pp. 363–79; Herbert V. Prochnow and Roy A. Foulke, *Practical Bank Credit* (2d ed.; New York: Prentice-Hall, Inc., 1950); Roland I. Robinson, *The Post War Market for State and Local Government Securities* (New York: National Bureau of Economic Research, 1960).

mainly in the secondary market of securities near their maturity dates. In recent years, yields on tax-exempts have risen relative to those available in other markets. This has been attributed mainly to the great increase in supply, which has necessitated selling to lenders in lower income tax brackets.[6] The 52 percent income tax rate on corporations indicates that a substantial after-tax yield differential exists between tax-exempts and Treasury bills.

This discussion of characteristics and yields of marketable securities available to managers of corporation portfolios suggests that considerable income was lost as a result of undue conservatism. Holdings of fewer Treasury instruments and larger amounts of alternative money market securities of the same maturities would have substantially increased income derived from the security portfolio of most of the companies included in the 250-firm sample.

A part of the explanation of the extreme conservatism exhibited in corporate short-term investment policy lies in the function of the funds invested in marketable securities. These funds are earmarked for future use or are kept as a liquidity reserve. The expected return in both uses is very high relative to the yields available in the money markets. Moreover, although corporate cash budgeting has made great strides in the past decade, there is much uncertainty as to when substantial portions of the marketable securities portfolio will have to be liquidated.

This cannot be the entire explanation. It may account for the short maturity of the portfolio but not for the preponderance of Treasury issues. Two additional explanations of this conservatism are institutional in nature. The first concerns directives issued to the officers charged with management of the corporation portfolios; the second concerns the training and ability of these officers and the time they are able to devote to this activity.

Replies to the questionnaire concerning restrictions imposed on portfolio managers are tabulated in Table 4. Restrictions refer only to type of security, except that for companies which restrict their purchases to Treasury securities, a breakdown of maturity restrictions is also shown. A large number of companies with broader restrictions on the types of securities that could be purchased also reported maturity restrictions. As shown in Table 4, almost half the respondent companies restrict their investments to Treasury securities. A quarter specified Treasury securities and one or two additional permissible instruments. The remaining quarter had no stated restrictions or enumerated all four major instruments.

Replies to the questionnaire concerning the officer charged with management of the marketable securities portfolio indicated that 122 port-

[6]Robinson, *op. cit.*

TABLE 4

STATED RESTRICTION ON INVESTMENT OF SHORT-TERM EXCESS CASH

| *Type of Security* | *No. of Companies* |
|---|---|
| U.S. Treasury, bills only | 16 |
| Maturing within 1 year | 27 |
| Maturing within 2 years | 4 |
| No maturity restriction | 22 |
| Total U.S. Treasury only | 69 |
| U.S. Treasury and agency securities | 9 |
| Tax-exempts | 4 |
| Directly placed commercial paper | 9 |
| Agency and tax-exempts | 1 |
| Agency and directly placed commercial paper | 6 |
| Tax-exempts and directly placed commercial paper | 9 |
| | 38 |
| No restrictions or all four enumerated types of securities | 39 |
| Total | 146 |

folios were managed by the corporate treasurer, 43 by a specialist or group of specialists, and six by the financial vice president or by action of the board of directors. These data indicate that a large portion of corporate portfolios is managed as a part-time activity of a corporate officer with many additional important duties. He would not have the time to seek out and evaluate investment opportunities as thoroughly as a full-time specialist; but, more important in many instances, the amount of income forgone may not be correctly gaged by an officer with little knowledge of money market opportunities.

## *III. Trend in Corporate Short-Term Investment Practices*

Little is known of the magnitude and composition of marketable security portfolios of nonfinancial corporations during the 1920's and 1930's. In the mid- and late 1920's, nonfinancial corporations held sizable amounts of Treasury securities as well as issues of states, territories, and local political subdivisions.[7] In 1926, nonfinancial corporations held

[7]U.S. Treasury Department *Statistics of Income* (Washington, D.C.). Holdings of these securities by all corporations that file tax returns are shown. Holdings of financial corporations—finance banking, insurance, real estate, holding companies, etc.—are subtracted to derive holdings of nonfinancial corporations.

$2.9 billion of tax-exempt securities, of which $2.3 billion were Treasury securities and $0.5 billion were issued by states, territories, and local governments.[8] After 1926, this detailed breakdown is no longer available; all tax-exempt securities are entered in total. Total holdings of tax-exempt securities reached a peak of $3.4 billion in 1928. Thereafter, they declined irregularly to a low of $1.7 billion in 1940. During the war and postwar years, holdings of Treasury securities increased rapidly. No comparable rise in holdings of tax-exempt securities occurred.

Even less is known of the magnitude of nonfinancial corporate holdings of securities other than tax-exempts during the interwar period. References are made in the literature to purchases of commercial paper[9] and to corporate participation in the supply of funds to the call loan market.[10] Friedrich Lutz has suggested that a large part of marketable securities held by manufacturing corporations during the 1920's was in common stocks.[11]

Holdings of stocks point to the probability that large capital losses were incurred during the 1929–32 period when stock prices fell. Treasury bond prices were relatively stable during 1930 and early 1931; in late 1931, prices dropped and reached their low in February, 1932. Prices of high-grade municipals followed this same pattern, reaching a low in March, 1932.[12] Moreover, defaults and postponed redemptions occurred on many municipal, local improvement, and other types of tax-exempt bonds. It would seem that the bond market became very thin during this period, in which case attempts to liquidate large holdings would have sharply depressed prices. This greatly reduced the liquidity of such holdings.

---

[8]Until December, 1940, all Treasury securities were entirely exempt from normal income tax, and some were also exempt from surtax and excess profits taxes. *Moody's Municipal and Government Manual* describes the exemptions on each issue. Treasury securities without tax exemption were first issued in December, 1940; securities of state and local governments continue exempt from federal taxation.

[9]Roy A. Foulke, *The Commercial Paper Market* (New York: Bankers Publishing Co., 1931), p. 11; Benjamin H. Beckhart, *New York Money Market* (New York: Columbia University Press, 1932), Vol. III, p. 234. Both references state that the amount of commercial paper held by corporations was negligible.

[10]Brokers' loans for the account of others were made in substantial amounts through the 1920's. Although no statistics are available indicating the distribution of loans among nonbank lenders, it is widely believed that nonfinancial corporations supplied a large part of the funds during 1929. For data on outstandings, see Board of Governors of The Federal Reserve System, *Banking and Monetary Statistics* (Washington, D.C., 1943), p. 494. For a discussion of the effects of this movement, see J. Marvin Peterson, "The Customers' Loan Market," *Journal of Political Economy,* Vol. XXX (February 1932), p. 83.

[11]Friedrich A. Lutz, *Corporate Cash Balances, 1914–43* (New York: National Bureau of Economic Research, 1945), p. 56.

[12]Op. cit., *Banking and Monetary Statistics,* (Washington, D.C., 1943), p. 470, shows yields on Treasury bonds and high-grade municipals during this period. Price movements were inferred from the yields.

Thus, at precisely the moment when liquid funds would have been most useful, in light of the decline in prices of real assets and dislocations of credit relationships, large losses and substantial illiquidity developed in corporate assets held to meet these contingencies. Extreme conservatism may have developed from these experiences. Although no direct evidence is available, it is likely that existing restrictions imposed by boards of directors on managers of corporate portfolios are a legacy of this period.

The growth in corporate cash flows during the 1940's and 1950's greatly increased the quantity of corporate cash available for short-term

TABLE 5

COMPOSITE MARKETABLE SECURITY PORTFOLIO OF 100 OF LARGEST NONFINANCIAL CORPORATIONS, DECEMBER 1951, 1954, AND 1957*

| | *Dollar Amounts in $(000) 12/31/51* | *Percent Distribution* | *Dollar Amounts in $(000) 12/31/54* | *Percent Distribution* | *Dollar Amounts in $(000) 12/31/57* | *Percent Distribution* |
|---|---|---|---|---|---|---|
| U.S. government securities | 7,646,018 | 95.68 | 8,069,438 | 92.78 | 5,179,246 | 73.79 |
| Securities held under repurchase agreements with dealers | N.L.† | ...... | N.L. | ...... | 683,897 | 9.75 |
| Directly placed commercial paper | 232,975 | 2.92 | 342,047 | 3.93 | 439,027 | 6.26 |
| Tax-exempt securities | 4,240 | 0.05 | 145,960 | 1.68 | 379,282 | 5.40 |
| U.S. agency securities | 88,600 | 1.08 | 103,290 | 1.19 | 193,150 | 2.75 |
| Broker-placed commercial paper | N.L. | ...... | N.L. | ...... | 18,767 | 0.27 |
| Foreign government securities | 20,631 | 0.26 | N.L. | ...... | 14,122 | 0.20 |
| Railroad equipment trust certificates | 738 | 0.01 | 13,828 | 0.16 | 5,789 | 0.08 |
| Other corporate bonds, notes, marketable securities, N.E.C. | N.L. | ...... | 22,818 | 0.26 | 105,271 | 1.50 |
| Total | 7,991,202 | 100.0 | 8,697,381 | 100.0 | 7,018,551 | 100.0 |

*The 1951 data cover 98 companies, 93 of which responded to the questionnaire. Data for five of the seven companies not responding were obtained from their financial reports and other sources (Sprowls, *op. cit.*, p. 9).

The 100-company list used in the 1951 survey was also used for 1954 and 1957.

The 1954 data cover 96 companies, 82 of which supplied a breakdown in full; data for the additional 14 companies came from published materials (Smith, *op. cit.*, p. 9).

The 1957 data cover six companies which supplied breakdowns of their holdings. No attempt was made to use published materials to supplement the survey data.

†N.L.—Not listed in survey.

*Sources:* 1951 data: John S. Sprowls, "Short-Term Investment Practices of Large Non-financial Corporations" (unpublished MBA essay, University of Pittsburgh, 1953), p. 12; 1954 data: Douglas M. Smith, "Short-Term Investment Policies of Non-financial Corporations" (MBA essay, Graduate School of Banking conducted by the American Bankers Association at Rutgers University), p. 9; 1957 data: derived from the survey reported in Section II of this paper.

investment. Until recently, all but a small fraction of these funds was invested in Treasury securities. Data in Table 5 suggest the beginning of a trend toward investment in non-Treasury issues. Treasury securities, including repurchase agreements, declined from more than 95.7 percent of total holdings in 1951 to 83.5 percent in 1927. Since almost 93 percent of the holdings were in Treasury securities in 1954, the major part of this movement away from Treasury issues took place after 1954.

The increased proportion of non-Treasury securities follows from the growth in holdings of tax-exempts, directly placed commercial paper, and United States agency issues. A possible explanation of this shift is that yield differentials between Treasury and non-Treasury issues may have widened. Table 6 lists annual averages of average monthly yields of Treasury issues and directly placed commercial paper. The data show no trend toward an increasing differential. Moreover, if a relevant measure of the differential is the ratio of the two rates (column 4), the differential has actually narrowed. In the period 1946–57, total outstandings of directly placed commercial paper increased more than

TABLE 6

AVERAGE ANNUAL YIELDS ON TREASURY BILLS AND DIRECTLY PLACED COMMERCIAL PAPER, 1946–57

| | *Average Month-End Yield* | | | | |
|---|---|---|---|---|---|
| *Year* | *Treasury Bills** *(1)* | *Directly Placed† Commercial Paper* *(2)* | *Absolute Differential (Col. 2 — Col. 1)* *(3)* | *Relative Differential Percent (Col. 2 ÷ Col. 1)* *(4)* | *Change in Outstandings (in Millions)* *(5)* |
| 1946...... | 0.375 | 0.781 | 0.41 | 109 | + 56 |
| 1947...... | 0.604 | 0.959 | 0.36 | 60 | + 98 |
| 1948...... | 1.04 | 1.35 | 0.31 | 34 | +183 |
| 1949...... | 1.10 | 1.46 | 0.36 | 33 | +170 |
| 1950...... | 1.22 | 1.42 | 0.20 | 16 | + 6 |
| 1951...... | 1.55 | 1.89 | 0.34 | 22 | +308 |
| 1952...... | 1.77 | 2.16 | 0.39 | 22 | +314 |
| 1953...... | 1.94 | 2.34 | 0.40 | 21 | +187 |
| 1954...... | 0.95 | 1.41 | 0.46 | 48 | −192 |
| 1955...... | 1.75 | 2.03 | 0.29 | 17 | +310 |
| 1956...... | 2.66 | 3.08 | 0.42 | 16 | +150 |
| 1957...... | 3.26 | 3.56 | 0.30 | 9 | +455 |

*Yield on new issues of 91-day Treasury bills.

†Yield offered on 90–179-day commercial paper by the General Motors Acceptance Corporation.

*Source:* Treasury bill yields, *Federal Reserve Bulletin;* commercial paper yields, 1946–55, Donald P. Jacobs, "Source and Costs of Funds for Large Sales Finance Companies," *Consumer Installment Credit: Conference on Regulation*, Vol. II, No. 1 (Washington, D.C.: Board of Governors of the Federal Reserve System, 1957), pp. 410–11; 1956–57, *Wall Street Journal;* directly placed commercial paper outstandings, 1946–55, Jacobs, *op. cit.*, pp. 412–13; 1956–57, *Federal Reserve Bulletin.*

$2 billion. It must therefore be concluded that a widening in the yield differential between these two types of securities cannot explain the relatively large increase in holdings of commercial paper by corporations.

Yield data on other types of short-maturity securities held by nonfinancial corporations are not available. The yield on tax-exempts with twenty years to maturity has increased relative to the yield on Treasury issues of the same maturity. However, it is not certain that a comparable widening has occurred in the yields of securities with one year or less to maturity. The relative rise in yields on tax-exempts, noted above, suggests that some widening has occurred. The prevailing high level of corporate tax rates, however, has probably made these securities attractive during the entire postwar period.

A positive yield differential between Treasury and non-Treasury securities is a necessary condition to any purchase of the latter. Yield data compared with corporate marketable security holdings suggest, however, that during the past few years substantial amounts of corporate funds were transferred from the Treasury to non-Treasury markets with stable absolute yield differentials and falling relative yield differentials.

The discussion in Section II of this paper leads to the suggestion that the major explanation of changes in the composition of corporate portfolios may lie in changes in the attitudes of the managers of these portfolios. The data indicate that corporate investors more and more believe that the existing differential in yields between Treasury and non-Treasury securities is not warranted by differences in risk and liquidity. To some extent, this development is an outgrowth of the large increase in the amounts of funds passing through corporate accounts. This has increased the incentive for management either to place the portfolio in expert hands or to increase the attention devoted to this duty by the responsible corporate officer. There is also some reason to believe that a large part of the change in attitude is attributable to the efforts of the sellers of non-Treasury securities.

Changes in restrictions placed on portfolio managers are an indication of and also contribute to the trend. In most instances, changes are initiated by a request from the financial officer to the board of directors. Of 146 companies responding to the question on restrictions, 23 stated that these had been substantially reduced in the last ten years. Of these, 10 companies are included among those in the sample in Table 5.

It is difficult to forecast how large a portion of nonfinancial corporate marketable securities portfolios will eventually be composed of non-Treasury issues. Data presented in this study suggest that an additional large fraction of the holdings of corporations could profitably be shifted to the non-Treasury markets. Such a shift would not materially alter the existing yield differentials; the supply of these securities is highly elastic.

The growing sophistication of corporate short-term investment portfolios managers is likely to have far-reaching effects on established relationships in the money markets. Corporate portfolio managers have large amounts of funds available for investment. Their growing willingness to purchase non-Treasury securities, as evidenced by the large increase in their holdings of directly placed commercial paper and the growth in the number and value of repurchase agreements with government bond dealers, is certain to entice other issuers of money market securities to tailor offerings to the desires of corporate investors. An indication that such changes are under way is the increase in the number of companies selling their commercial paper directly, changes in the sales procedures of commercial paper houses, and the recent announcement that the Federal National Mortgage Association will sell a short-term security closely resembling directly placed commercial paper.

*Chapter 5*

# *More Scope for Credit Managers**

By Robert W. Johnson

WHAT ACCOUNTS for the phenomenal growth of commercial credit?

What phases of credit management can now be handled by electronic data-processing equipment, and what are the implications for organization and operating policies?

What positive contributions should the credit department be expected to make to the improvement of sales and profits?

How can the modern credit department give valuable support to other corporate functions such as forecasting and financial management?

One of the most important forms of credit in the American economy is commercial, or trade, credit. Yet it has been generally neglected in financial literature and too frequently ignored by top management. Management can no longer afford to overlook the profit potential that often lies dormant in the credit department. Trade credit has grown to a point where it is now one of the most important assets—or developable assets—of a business concern.

Also important, installation of electronic data-processing equipment by progressive companies has forced a reappraisal of the functions of credit management. Freed by the computer from routine tasks, today's credit manager can substantially widen the dimensions of his contributions to top management.

The term *commercial* or *trade credit* refers to short-term credit which

---

*Reprinted by permission from *Harvard Business Review,* Vol. XXXIX (November-December, 1961), pp. 109–20.

is extended by suppliers to commercial buyers for the purchase of goods or services. Thus, this definition excludes consumer credit as well as installment credit for the purchase of machinery and equipment. Possibly one reason that commercial credit has not received adequate attention is that it is so easy to obtain and to grant. It is sometimes referred to as "spontaneous credit," because a very high proportion of outstanding trade credit in the United States is open-book credit. This typical form of commercial credit is evidenced only by purchase orders and sales invoices recorded on the ledgers of sellers. Buyers are not asked to acknowledge their debts by signing promissory notes. The mutual trust that long familiarity with open-book credit has built makes this typs of trade credit available to almost all business concerns.

Although trade credit may appear to be spontaneous, it should *not* arise that way in actuality. The extension of trade credit should rest on sound policies developed by top management and administered by skilled executives in the credit department. To aid top management in formulating basic credit policies that will capitalize on the new potential in trade credit, this study will examine two significant aspects: (1) the growing economic importance of trade credit and (2) the broader contributions to top management that the credit department can begin to make following the installation of electronic data-processing equipment.

## Economic Importance

The very magnitude of commercial credit suggests its importance to the economy and to the business concern. I estimate that at the end of 1960 there was over $100 billion of trade credit outstanding among nonfinancial corporations, nonprofit institutions, unincorporated firms, and farm businesses.[1] This figure considerably exceeded the $85 billion of domestic corporate bonds outstanding or the $56 billion of consumer credit outstanding at the same time. Surprisingly enough, outstanding trade credit even surpassed all forms of commercial bank credit to business concerns; it was considerably more than double the industrial and commercial loans of banks, including open-market paper.[2] Although certain companies rely more heavily on bank credit than on trade credit, the latter is much more universally used. Virtually every business depends on trade credit for a portion of its needs.

---

[1]See "Flow of Funds/Savings," *Federal Reserve Bulletin,* April, 1961, p. 485.
[2]*Ibid.,* p. 434.

## *Rate of Growth*

The growth of accounts receivable in the postwar years has been phenomenal. Accounts receivable of nonfinancial corporations rose by $66.3 billion, or by more than 240 percent from the end of 1946 to the end of 1960 (see Figure 1). In contrast, corporate executives managed

FIGURE 1

GROWTH OF FINANCIAL ASSETS OF NONFINANCIAL CORPORATIONS*

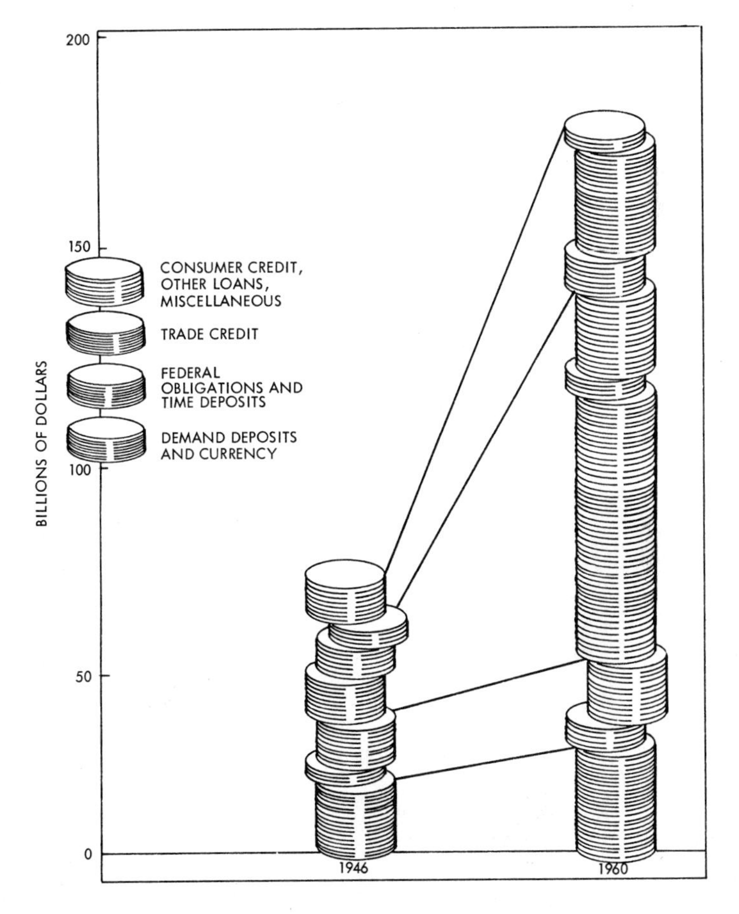


*Nonfinancial corporations are business corporations other than banks, insurance companies, and savings institutions.

*Source:* "Flow of Funds/Savings," *Federal Reserve Bulletin,* August, 1960, p. 942; April, 1961, pp. 476, 480.

to budget cash so that the increase in demand deposits and currency was held to $12.3 billion, or 58 percent, during the same period. As a result of these different rates of growth, the proportion of total financial assets absorbed by trade credit rose from 35 percent at the end of 1946 to 48 percent at the end of 1960. It might be noted that the dollar amount of increase of trade credit considerably exceeded that of consumer credit, although the growth in consumer credit has received a great deal more attention in economic and financial literature.

To a considerable extent, one would expect accounts receivable to increase more rapidly than cash and other financial assets. Accounts receivable are a direct result of sales and rise as unit sales and selling prices grow. Thus a considerable portion of the growth in accounts receivable has resulted from increased dollar sales and not from any specific credit policies of top management.

However, the expansion in receivable cannot be explained entirely on these grounds. A significant part of the expansion evidently has resulted from managements' decision to adopt more lenient credit policies. Although these policies may not have been expressed in stated terms, collections were allowed to lag increasingly behind the growth in sales. As a result, the ratio of receivables to sales has increased over recent

FIGURE 2

RATIO OF RECEIVABLES TO SALES,
U.S. MANUFACTURING CORPORATIONS, 1952–60

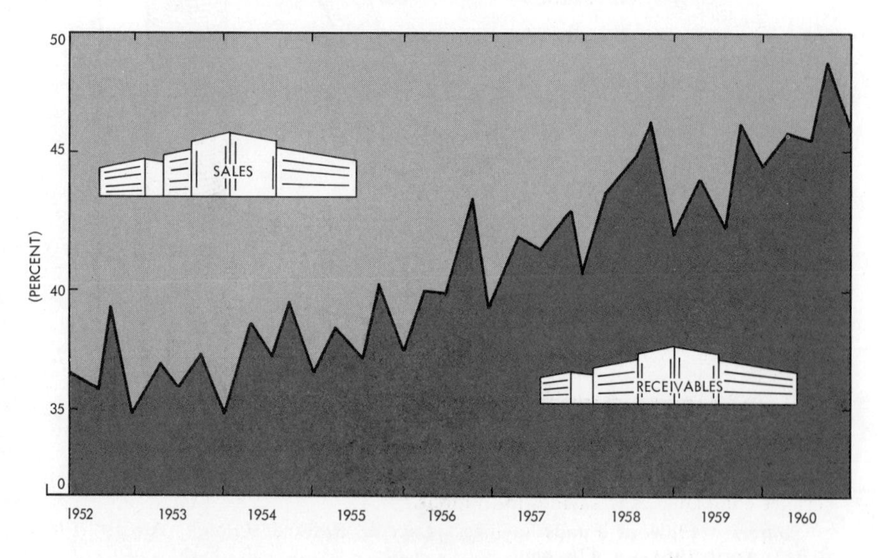


*Source:* Federal Trade Commission and Securities and Exchange Commission, *Quarterly Financial Report for Manufacturing Corporations* (Washington, D.C.: U.S. Government Printing Office, 1952–60).

years, a trend that is readily apparent in data on manufacturing corporations (see Figure 2). The rise in the ratio was particularly marked after 1956. Had the average ratio of receivables to sales that existed in 1952 been characteristic of 1960, receivables of manufacturing corporations in the latter year would have been about $8 billion less than they were.

In part, the rise in the ratio of receivables to sales could have resulted from a change in the mix of manufacturing concerns represented; that is, sales of manufacturers who characteristically grant lengthy credit terms could have increased more rapidly than sales of manufacturers with less lenient terms. However, analysis by industry indicates that such a shift has not been a major factor.[3] Moreover, because receivables were eliminated when transferred to factory-owned finance companies, Figure 2 may actually understate the true rate of growth of the ratio of receivables to sales.

## *Management Attitudes*

Why has top management encouraged, or passively permitted, the expanded use of credit as a sales device, especially in the period 1957–60? One possible reason for such a policy is suggested in a recent study of manufacturing output-capacity relationships:

> In early 1960, when manufacturing production was at a record high, the rate of utilization of manufacturing capacity appeared to be about the same as in early 1957, but it was lower than in earlier periods of high production. . . . In the first quarter of 1961, reflecting the mildness of production curtailments, utilization of manufacturing capacity was higher than in early 1958, but lower than in the 1953–54 recession.[4]

In short, it seems likely that pressure to maintain sales in order to utilize productive capacity has forced management to accept proportionately greater amounts of outstanding receivables. Lengthening of stated terms was likely to be a one-way street. Once terms were extended, it was difficult to retract the action. Competitors followed suit, and a new level of receivables relative to sales was established, only to be raised again by a further easing.

This does not suggest that trade credit is getting out of hand. Indeed, one reason for the expansion of trade credit has been industry's favorable experience with more lenient terms through the early postwar recessions. However, *the growth does emphasize that credit policy is a matter demanding the increased attention of top management.*

---

[3]Federal Reserve Bank of Kansas City, "Forces behind the Growth of Trade Credit," *Monthly Review,* October, 1959, pp. 6–7.

[4]"Upturn in Production," *Federal Reserve Bulletin,* May, 1961, p. 517.

## *Help to Small Business*

Management must also recognize the increasingly important role of the medium-size and large business corporation as a means of channeling funds to small businesses. Throughout the postwar years the accounts receivable in nonfinancial corporations have exceeded their total accounts payable. This gap between receivables and payables may be termed *net* available trade credit.

Although a small portion of the difference is accounted for by trade credit granted to farm businesses, government, and financial concerns, most net available trade credit is granted to unincorporated nonfinancial businesses, usually small companies.

Thus, trade credit serves as a means of channeling borrowed or equity funds from relatively affluent corporations to those business concerns that are most likely to be pressed financially and find it difficult and costly to raise funds. In this sense, business corporations serve as nonfinancial intermediaries in the flow of funds through the money and capital markets.

Net trade credit made available by nonfinancial business corporations rose from $2.9 billion at the end of 1946 to $28.7 billion at the end of 1960.[5] Thus, almost two fifths of the total increase in accounts receivable of these corporations may be attributed primarily to the channeling of funds to unincorporated business firms. If anything, the financial support which large corporations provide to small business firms is understated, since many small business firms are incorporated and the data do not reveal net grants of credit from large to small corporations.

Corporate managers not only have assumed a role of increasing importance as quasi bankers, but they also provide unincorporated customers with an emergency source of funds during periods of recession. In each of the postwar recessions, net trade credit made available by corporations grew at a faster rate than during preceding years of prosperity (see Figure 3). This change was particularly notable in 1954 and in 1958. During the latter year, additional net trade credit made available jumped to a level of $6.4 billion from a rate of only $2 billion during 1957. In contrast, relatively small amounts of additional bank credit were made available to unincorporated businesses during the first three recessions. Banks increased their loans to unincorporated business less rapidly in 1960 than in 1959, while corporations increased net available trade credit even more rapidly in 1960 than in the previous year.

Motives for credit leniency on the part of corporations during periods

[5]"Flow of Funds/Savings," *Federal Reserve Bulletin,* April, 1961, pp. 476, 480.

FIGURE 3

CHANGES IN NET CREDIT EXTENDED TO UNINCORPORATED BUSINESSES BY CORPORATIONS AND BY BANKS

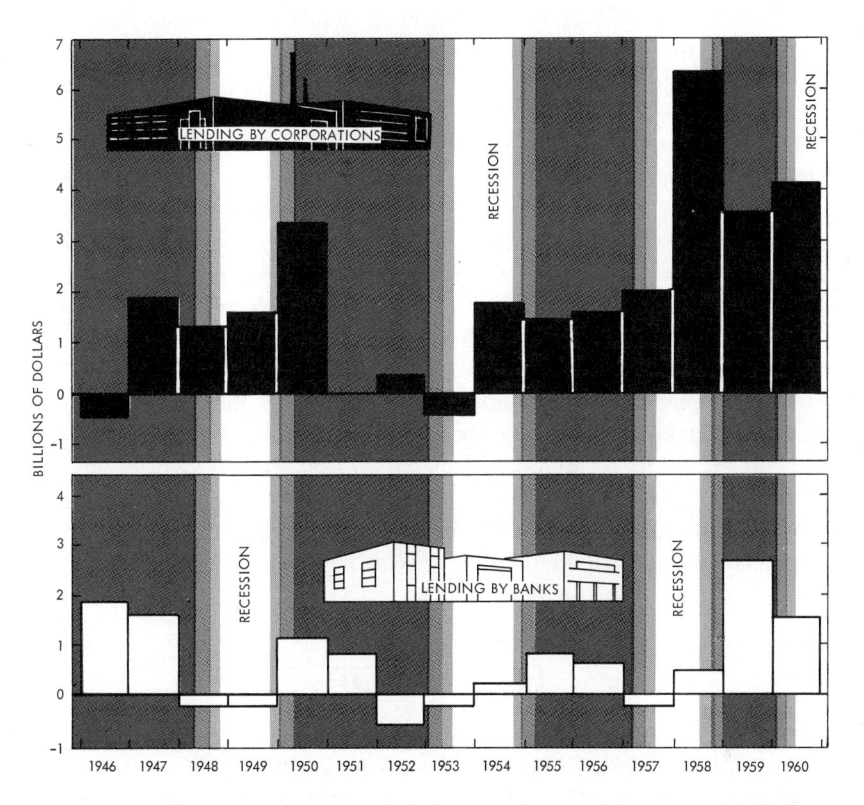


of recession lie not in altruism, but rather in a desire to maintain sales and to help valued customers weather cyclical storms. The very large additional amounts of net trade credit made available during the recessions of 1958 and 1960 suggest that the role of business corporations as nonfinancial intermediaries has become increasingly important. Management must ask itself whether its credit policies and its credit management procedures have progressed as rapidly as have these fundamental changes in the role of trade credit in the economy.

## *Expanding Role*

Although most businessmen are aware that the use of credit can increase sales and that an efficient credit department contributes to the profitability of those sales by improving the flow of cash, these important aspects of credit management are sometimes overlooked in the actions of top executives. Unfortunately, management often becomes concerned with credit only when orders are turned down and when accounts become uncollectible—results that are measurable and easily recognized. Too frequently, management tends to evaluate the performance of the credit department solely in terms of such measures as the ratio of credit losses to sales, percentage of accounts over thirty days past due, and so on.

The fact that the more important contributions of the credit department are often difficult to determine should not lead a company to disregard these contributions. And it is not enough to let support of the sales effort come to management's attention only through chance discussion of particular sales or through the marginal customer who presents a problem. It no longer makes sense to limit the role of credit management to screening credit applicants and to collecting delinquent accounts.

Today the introduction of data-processing equipment (I use the term to refer to punched-card equipment as well as to more sophisticated electronic machines) can free the credit manager from many routine tasks. Indeed, it is fortunate that electronic data-processing equipment became available when it did. Otherwise, credit managers would now be overwhelmed by the conventional tasks of handling the rapid growth of receivables. Let us take a closer look at the way EDP has broadened the dimensions of credit management.

## Effect of EDP

On the one hand, the use of electronic data-processing (EDP) equipment has made information available much faster and has also made new types of information available to top management and the credit manager. On the other hand, some data customarily used in the past are no longer available. The opportunity to gather new data and the threat of loss of old information demand that management examine the true decisional content of the material to be processed. Computers allow a fresh start. But first it is necessary that questions such as the following be answered:

1. What new policies of credit evaluation and credit control must be adopted?
2. What new roles can top management expect of the credit department in view of the new structure of available information?
3. Is management attempting to force EDP equipment to store and produce traditional data and to process it in a traditional manner?
4. Or is top management seizing the opportunity to take a new look at credit management and the greater role it can play in enabling the company to prosper?

## *Extent of Use*

Generally, EDP equipment may be economically applied in the credit department only if it is also used in other phases of the business. Usually, computers are first introduced to perform routine operations, such as the preparation of payrolls and billing. Use of the equipment by the credit department may then absorb time on otherwise idle equipment.

A large number of companies now have the opportunity to let machines handle routine credit operations:

> In July 1960 there were probably about 4,300 general-purpose digital computer installations in American industry, of which 14 per cent were large scale (costing more than $1 million), 20 per cent medium scale (priced between $.5 and $1 million), and 66 per cent small scale but internally programed computers. In addition there were about 6,700 other digital computers, including card-programed calculators.[6]

A survey by the National Office Management Association of 369 installations—excluding punched-card equipment—showed that about half of the companies with small-scale EDP equipment were applying it to accounts receivable, whereas only one third of the companies with large-scale equipment used it for that purpose.[7] Accounts receivable applications are probably found much more frequently among firms with only punched-card equipment.

## *Loss and Gain*

In many instances, EDP equipment is unable to reproduce economically reports which it was customary to prepare in the past. Attempts to force information in traditional form from the machine may be costly and time-consuming. Management must ask why the data are sought and decide whether the report is necessary.

Actually, most business reports provide only partial information because of the expense and time involved in gathering more complete data. The real question becomes whether the computer can economically gather other incomplete data whose informational content for decision making is as good as or better than the incomplete data currently in use.

Suppose that the incomplete information concerns a customer's creditworthiness. On the basis of the available data, we might decide to grant

[6]Einar Hardin, "The Economic Impact of Office Automation," *Michigan Economic Record,* April, 1961, p. 3.

[7]Charles E. Grider, *Why Automation?* November, 1959.

him a line of credit. What is the probability that additional information would change the credit decision? How large is the probable loss that would be avoided if the credit decision were changed? Clearly, if the probability of a change in the decision is low and the expected loss is small, it is uneconomical to incur added expense to obtain more complete information. The available incomplete information tells us all that we can afford to know.

## *Greater Speed*

An excellent illustration of the loss and gain of incomplete information is afforded by the application of EDP equipment to accounts receivable. With automation, the credit manager has lost a record called "ledger experience," but he has gained in return other reports that can serve the same purpose. Thus:

> For many years most companies have maintained a ledger card for every customer showing each of his purchases, each of his payments, and a running total of his unpaid balance. By examining this card, a credit man can quickly determine the highest amount of credit extended at any time during the past several years, the payment habits of the customer, and the amount currently owed.
>
> This ledger experience is viewed as an important source of information concerning the customer's creditworthiness. It is also used, through the facilities of the National Association of Credit Management (NACM), as a basis for replying to credit interchange requests from other credit men. (Indeed, since one of the basic purposes of founding this professional association some sixty-five years ago was to provide rapid and confidential exchange of credit data, automation may force a substantial reappraisal of the content of *Interchange* reports.)
>
> While it would be possible to reproduce the ledger card with EDP equipment, it is usually not economically feasible to do so. The information necessary to reconstruct the ledger card is generally available, but so scattered that it is costly to gather on one record. Loss of ledger experience has sometimes been cited by credit men as a basic objection to the introduction of EDP equipment.
>
> However, the credit men I have interviewed declare that reports generated by the computer do provide an adequate substitute for the ledger experience. For one thing, the computer prepares information much more quickly than before. This information has a "time value," just as money does. If we can speed the preparation of certain reports, the value of their decisional content may be enough to outweigh the value of other information lost in the process of automation.
>
> The substitution of new and more current reports for the old ledger card is illustrated by the experience of a large corporation covered recently in a series of interviews. The corporation, selling on terms of 1/10, net 30 (i.e.,

a 1 percent discount is given if bill is paid within 10 days of date of invoice; otherwise, full amount must be paid within 30 days), no longer obtains ledger experience on its customers. Reports that have been substituted include a record of past-due accounts obtained in the middle of each month and a copy of the customer's statement showing outstanding items at the end of each month. These summaries are available very shortly after the middle and end of each month. If a customer's payments are prompt, his name will of course be absent from the list of past-due accounts.

The amount currently owed by the customer is not readily available on any given day during the month, but his month-end balances are known. Nor is it possible to determine accurately the highest amount of credit granted during the month. Loss of this traditionally important information is not considered by the credit manager to be especially significant, because the month-end balance is regarded as adequate for the purposes of *Credit Interchange* service. Any deficiencies in the content of this information are outweighed by the very current listings of customers who are delinquent.

## *Other Efficiencies*

An important gain from the installation of EDP equipment has been the frequency with which companies can obtain aged trial balances. These are statements showing the amount owed the company that is current, or not past due; the amount that is 0–30 days past due; the amount that is 30–60 days past due; and so on. The report is valuable, both as a means of directing collection activities and as a measure of the credit department's effectiveness. For example, a large corporation which used to obtain aged trial balances twice a year now obtains a trial balance, broken down by regional sales districts, once every three weeks. If necessary, the balance can also be broken down by product line. Here is one positive gain which substantially offsets the loss of detailed ledger experience.

It seems likely that the *Credit Interchange* reports of the NACM will have to be adjusted to show data from aged trial balances when the more traditional information now displayed is not readily available from the computer. For instance, credit managers using EDP equipment may report in response to a credit inquiry that a given customer owed $3,000 on the fifteenth of the month, of which 40 percent was 30 to 60 days past due and 15 percent over 60 days past due. Upon careful analysis, credit managers may find that current information of this kind can be every bit as valuable for credit decisions as the data now requested.

Use of EDP equipment frequently relieves credit men of other routine chores, so that they can concentrate their attention on more important functions. Machines can (1) prepare reminders to customers who fail to take cash discounts and (2) draw up bills for those customers with past-due accounts. Accuracy in posting to accounts receivable is usually increased. Machines can also prepare periodic classifications of accounts by product line, by region, by credit rating. These reports can often be obtained with a reduced number of personnel. One credit executive reported that introduction of EDP equipment enabled a reduction in the number of people in the credit department from 120 to 77, in spite of handling a much larger sales volume. Peak work loads are also handled much more easily.

## *Making Decisions*

Can computers make credit decisions? When a company is selling to a large number of small accounts, it is probably true that a properly programmed computer *can* "make decisions" and thus free credit managers for more important roles in management. An example of application of EDP equipment to routine credit decisions is provided by a large corporation in the Midwest:

> All accounts receivable are assigned a code number and a credit limit by the credit department. On certain accounts, new orders are automatically referred to a credit analyst by the computer. In most cases the accounts are referred to the credit analyst only when the computer notes that a new order would place the account over its assigned credit limit. All other orders, about 70 percent of the total, are "approved" by the computer, which then adds the new order to those already outstanding. Operation of the exception principle through EDP equipment frees credit men for the more important functions of maintaining up-to-date credit files, working with marginal accounts, revising credit limits, reviewing orders referred by the computer, and providing support to the sales effort.
>
> The average amount of credit extended to these accounts is relatively small. Given the low probability of failure on the part of these dealers, the expected loss is small. Under such circumstances, the cost of more careful scrutiny of these accounts would exceed the expected savings that might be obtained if some losses were avoided.

However, when relatively large accounts are involved, it would probably be uneconomical to program a computer to reach credit decisions. Although the probability of a loss on these accounts is less likely than the probability of a loss on smaller accounts, the loss that might occur would be much larger. Consequently, it is important to have current information on any factors that may affect the credit worthiness of medium-size and large accounts. With the need for a more complex credit analysis and the possibility of frequent revision of factors affecting the credit decision, programming changes in the credit rating of individual accounts would be too costly. Instead, the changes are "programmed" into the mind of the credit analyst.

It is revealing that one credit manager, supervising about 9,000 fairly large accounts averaging 125,000 postings per month, commented during my study:

> Last week I had a dealer who took $115,000 of merchandise out of a bonded warehouse without our approval. My opinion of that customer's credit worthiness went way down. How can you have the machine evaluate that? Can it tell me how to handle that account from now on—or what to say to the man when I call him in this week?

## *Introduction of Equipment*

It may be trite to point out the importance of adequate preparation—including attention to the feelings of the human beings concerned—in the introduction of EDP equipment. However, management's failure to observe this elementary point may result in the complete collapse of the installation and the loss of thousands of dollars. Consider the poignant story of one credit manager:

> Management installed a new computer that was supposed to do everything for us but scrub the floors in the evening. However, we were not brought in on the discussions of how it was to be programmed. There was little communication between the credit department and the programmers. They were so sure that it would work that they did not set up any parallel runs. When the day came to go on the computer, we dropped our old system and put all accounts receivable on tape. It developed that the computer was not properly programmed to handle our customers' payments. Only about half of the payments were "hitting"; that is, the computer was matching payment and invoice in only 50 percent of the cases. The remainder had to be matched by hand.
>
> Inside of 40 days, our accounts receivable rose from 24 days to 31 days; this amounted to several million dollars. Somewhere in that mass of whirling tapes there was $63,000 out of balance. Programmers left. We did not get the reports that we had been promised. Finally, we pulled all of the accounts off the computer. It has taken us eight months to work the discrepancy down to $30,000.

The credit department should clearly be involved closely in all stages of planning for the installation of EDP equipment. With the new "common language system" (that is, instructions in English that can be translated by the computer into a program for its use), it is now much easier to program computers. The representative of a large manufacturer of EDP equipment suggested to me: "It is easier to teach a credit man how to program a computer than to teach a programmer how to be a credit man." Adoption of this approach would involve credit men immediately and deeply in the installation of the equipment and avoid some of the dislocations that ensue when professional programmers leave.

## *Impact on Organization*

Management must expect fundamental organizational changes when EDP equipment is introduced into the credit department. In the initial planning stages, there is normally an increased recognition of the interdependence among departments.[8] Bottlenecks become crucial, and a premium is placed on individuals who can adjust to change and work well with representatives of other departments. Thus, EDP equipment becomes a powerful social force that introduces a realignment of power centers within the organization and brings to the fore a somewhat different type of executive from what was characteristic of days when departments operated more independently.

Another trend I have observed is "recentralization," i.e., the drawing-back to the central office of some functions previously performed in regional offices.[9] A function commonly returned (and often the only one) is record keeping. It is one task that almost certainly can be handled more economically on a single, large EDP installation than in smaller divisional offices that are not equipped with large computers and have only local records. Under recentralization, the responsibility for final credit decisions remains with the regional or district credit managers who are located *out* of the central office. New orders are sent to the central office by air mail, and the central office returns regional tabulations of past-due accounts, aged trial balances, and so on.

In contrast, other companies have pulled in from regional offices not only the record-keeping function but the regional credit managers as well. Credit managers of these firms believe that they can make credit decisions centrally as promptly as they could in a decentralized setup. Possibly the exceptional credit refusals needing personal attention occur less frequently in a centralized firm than in a decentralized one.

Finally, installation of EDP equipment seems to have brought about increased participation by top management in the formulation of basic credit policies. Because data are available more quickly, top management can often change the course of events with greater ease. Marginal

---

[8]See Floyd C. Mann and Laurence K. Williams, "Observations on the Dynamics of a Change to Electronic Data-Processing Equipment," *Administrative Science Quarterly,* September, 1960, pp. 217–56.

[9]The term "recentralization" and a broader discussion of its implications appear in Ida Russakoff Hoos, "When the Computer Takes Over the Office," *Harvard Business Review,* Vol. XXXVIII (July-August, 1960), p. 102.

accounts or other exceptional situations can be brought to management's attention more readily. Freed of routine chores, the credit department now has time available to develop more analytical reports to inform top management of recent trends in the credit area.

## Wider Horizons

The more conventional operations of credit that can be turned over to machines, and the greater amount of time that credit managers will thus have to devote to executive rather than clerical duties, the more top management must recognize the need for delegation of authority and responsibility to them. What are the new vistas of credit management? In what areas may top management expect greater contributions from the credit department? What new functions might credit managers assume if given adequate authority and responsibility?

### *Executive Competence*

With the broader responsibilities that will be placed on credit managers in the coming years, management should expect its credit men to develop as executives and to work with others in the field to advance credit management. Facilities are available through the NACM for the promotion of sound credit practices and legislation, exchange of credit information, and improvement of the executive status of credit men.

From the point of view of the greater contributions to management that may be made by credit departments, probably the most important activities of the NACM are its programs of training and research. Every summer since 1952, the association has conducted two graduate schools of credit and financial management, one at Dartmouth College and the other at Stanford University. The association also has a National Institute of Credit, which offers classroom courses through colleges and universities as well as correspondence courses, and a Credit Research Foundation, which promotes and directs credit research. One current research project is an exhaustive study of the applications of EDP equipment to credit management. These are all professional endeavors in which management should encourage its credit men to participate.

### *Support to Sales Effort*

An important phase of modern credit management that can be expanded even further is the assistance given to the sales department with respect to marginal customers and the active support accorded to special sales efforts. To illustrate the contributions that a "sales-oriented" credit manager can make, consider the following situation:

One large manufacturer sold to a parts distributor in a big city. On the basis of traditional credit standards, the account should not have been granted credit. The distributor's balance sheet position would ordinarily call for immediate liquidation to salvage at least a portion of the manufacturer's investment.

However, the sales department pointed out that the distributor was the only outlet currently available to the manufacturer in the city. If he should be forced out of business, dealers would quickly turn to other outlets selling competitors' products, and the company would lose its position in the market. Its national advertising would largely be wasted in that area. Moreover, it would be difficult to persuade a new distributor to take on the company's line in the face of the failure of the other parts distributor.

In cooperation with the sales department the credit department decided to carry the distributor for a year or so until he could be financially rehabilitated or until a buyer could be found for his business. Management felt that the probable loss on the account would be exceeded by the loss of profits that would result from withdrawing credit from the distributor.

Management should encourage the credit department to provide balance to the sales effort. Credit should not operate as an autonomous unit isolated from product development, advertising, and sales. Too often, management views the credit department as a division of the treasurer's office, as solely a financial function. An example of coordination of credit and sales effort is provided in the following illustration:

A manufacturer of a household product planned to saturate a particular market with coupons that permitted consumers to purchase the product at a substantial reduction in price. Normal terms of sale to retailers were 2/10, net 30. Although the merchandise had to be available in the stores prior to the promotion, it would clearly be unwise to expect retailers to pay in 10 days for merchandise they could not sell for 30 days. Therefore the credit department worked out special terms that allowed dealers to pay for the shipments some time after the sales promotion efforts. The obvious result was a direct boost in sales.

Does the company have a "can do" or "can't do" credit department? This is a question for management. Suppose that a customer has had a fire or is moving from one warehouse to another. Will the credit manager aid a dealer during such crises, or does he insist on maintenance of standard terms of payment? Does the credit manager "pull the book" and argue that the Robinson-Patman Act decrees "no favoritism," or does he find a way to see the account through the period of stress? More important, if the credit manager does "pull the book," is this a reflection of his weaknesses, or is it a reflection of top management's? In short, what does top management really expect of the credit manager: a clean bad debt record or a positive contribution to the sales effort?

## *Counsel for Customers*

When a credit manager, having turned over routine tasks to the computer, wants to make a positive contribution, one of the most fruitful fields that he can develop is his role as a financial counselor. Wise counseling may lead to saving many customers and preserving profitable sales. Financial advice also reinforces the role of large corporations as nonfinancial intermediaries in the flow of funds to small firms.

As suggested earlier, small business concerns are notoriously weak in their financial management. It is not enough just to channel funds to these companies via trade credit; they frequently need advice on the proper use of those funds. The manner in which a credit manager may show customers how to conserve working capital is illustrated by the following case:

A large manufacturing company found that one of its distributors was becoming increasingly slow in paying his account. When he was queried, the distributor suggested that the manufacturer renew each month the $10,000 of credit then outstanding, while he made prompt payment on any additional purchases. The credit manager replied that this would be the equivalent of a capital loan, and the manufacturer was not in a position, either financially or legally, to grant capital loans to customers.

The credit manager did not stop with this negative action, however. He visited the distributor and examined his statements. He pointed out that the distributor was giving effective terms of 60–90 days to his dealer accounts, even though his stated terms were "net 30" Since his dealers usually sold the product within a month, they had the use of the distributor's money for an additional 30–60 days.

In short, without realizing it, the distributor was providing interest-free capital loans to his dealers. By tightening his own terms of sale to 30 days, the distributor could put his trade debt on a current basis within eight months. Although such a solution may be readily apparent to men sophisticated in the ways of finance, it had never occurred to the distributor.

The credit manager is in an excellent position to provide this financial advice. For one thing, he is familiar with the financial picture of many other customers in similar lines of business. On the basis of this background and any formal studies he may have made of operating ratios of the industry, he is quick to sense unfavorable developments in customers' financial statements. Often, he recognizes adverse trends before the customer does. He sometimes counsels customers on methods of obtaining bank loans. If a customer is in danger of becoming insolvent, the credit manager may visit him and follow his progress carefully through monthly financial statements in an effort to aid recovery.

An illustration of a well-organized program to give financial counsel to customers is provided by a large eastern manufacturing firm. Here again, many of the routine chores of credit management have been turned over to the company's computer center, and with its newly found freedom the credit department has been able to expand substantially its role as a financial counselor. Although taking care not to impose its financial advice, the department is often called on to offer help to customers with:

1. Analysis of financial statements
2. Record keeping
3. Inventory control
4. Accounts receivable financing control
5. Bank financing
6. Cash budgeting and sales forecasting
7. Expense control
8. Selling on time

In addition, the credit department urges dealers to send in their annual financial statements for analysis and comment. It prepares an annual tabulation of operating and balance sheets statistics with a number of important ratios for different categories of dealers' operations. In addition, dealers are provided with various booklets on financial management, including both material prepared within the department and that developed by outside agencies, such as the Small Business Administration. A joint project of the market research, credit, sales, and advertising departments led to the development of a "dealer's kit," containing full information and numerous aids to retailers who wish to sell to consumers on installment.

It is not entirely surprising that this credit department reports an unusually low delinquency rate, and that the sales department can count on the support of a very loyal group of dealers.

## *Contributions to Finance*

An important and well-known function of credit management, in the words of a job summary for the general credit manager of one large corporation, is to "secure prompt conversion of receivables into cash with a minimum number of past-due balances and bad debt losses." (We have seen that this objective must be tempered by adequate support of the sales effort.) Other contributions to financial management can also be made. For instance, many credit departments aid in the preparation of the cash budget by making estimates of cash collections from receivables. A recent survey by NACM showed that about three fifths of the companies covered prepared cash forecasts, and that the credit department participated in making the forecast in three quarters of those cases.[10] Consider this example of the contribution to cash management by a credit department:

> The credit manager of one large corporation annually makes a long-run forecast of monthly cash collections for the following two years. At the end of each month during the year, he revises his forecast of collections for the next two months. By Monday noon of each week, he makes a forecast of daily collections for the week, and then revises this on Tuesday on the basis of reports of sales during the preceding week. Forecasts of collections are based largely on seasonal adjustments to the percentage of collections of accounts receivable outstanding at the end of each month. Management uses these forecasts to plan short-term purchases of government bills and commercial paper.
>
> The importance placed by management on this function of the credit department is suggested by the remark of the credit manager: "I hear from them when I'm off. They want to know why I missed it." Most of the variations of estimated collections from actual results arise in deviations of actual from budgeted sales. Daily estimates of cash collections seldom vary from actual results by more than a few percentage points. Accuracy of estimates has been noticeably improved by the installation of data-processing equipment, which has speeded the tabulation of daily sales and collections on receivables.

Much more can be done with the help of computers. Given data on recent collection experience, sales forecasts, seasonal patterns in collections, and so on, a properly programmed machine could very rapidly produce estimates of collections on receivables. Many different forecasts based upon various estimates of sales or possible changes in collection experience could be quickly generated. As a result, the credit manager could indicate to the treasurer the limits within which cash receipts might be expected to vary.

Cash flows could also be simulated on the computer under assumptions of significantly different credit terms. Mathematical models could be designed to answer questions such as:

1. If we changed our terms from 2/10, net 30, to 3/10, net 60, what would happen to our daily or weekly collections during the transition period?
2. What would be our eventual investment in accounts receivable?
3. What would happen if we should offer seasonal datings?

---

[10]See also "How Companies Now Use Credit to Protect—and Build—Profits," *Management Methods*, September, 1960, p. 49.

One large manufacturer of consumer goods asked: "If we should form a factory-owned finance company, what would be the required investment?" With the use of his large computer center, the manufacturer was able to judge the month-by-month investment in receivables that would be required under various assumptions as to the proportion of sales made on credit, maturity of contracts written, anticipated collection experience, and so on.

In short, the availability of the computer to credit managers offers exciting new opportunities for significant contributions to the area of financial management.

## *Economic Forecasts*

Probably one of the most overlooked ways in which the credit department may aid top management is assembling timely economic forecasts. Computers offer an opportunity for significant expansion of this function because they can be used to analyze data on sales and collection experience before the information is too ancient to be of value.

One of the indicators that typically leads other indexes of business activity is the series on business failures. Yet a business failure is usually preceded by a credit delinquency. Consequently, in their records of delinquencies, many large corporations have data which, if properly analyzed, might provide worthwhile economic forecasts. Moreover, these data provide very "personalized" forecasts—not of the economy or the industry as a whole, but of the economic outlook for a particular concern.

It might also be possible to gather, through NACM, delinquency reports for trade credit on a national basis in somewhat the same manner that the Instalment Credit Commission of the American Bankers Association now gathers reports on delinquents for various classes of consumer credit. It seems very likely that these figures would provide another useful leading indicator of cyclical economic conditions.

## *Aid to Other Departments*

Imaginative credit policies may lower total operating costs of a company at the expense of a higher investment in accounts receivable. For example, in some lines, seasonal datings allow dealers to order and take delivery on products several months before the selling season, while postponing payment for the goods until funds are realized from sales. Although accounts receivable rise, the manufacturer is enabled to level out his production and to conserve warehouse space. Economies in production and in warehousing may outweigh the added costs associated with the higher receivables. The use of credit to offset shortcomings of a company's distribution system is illustrated as follows:

1. A large breakfast food manufacturer provides prompt shipment to dealers and dates terms of sales (2/10, net 30) from the shipping date. Since the manufacturer has many warehouses located throughout the country, most dealers receive the goods within one or two days from date of shipment and have eight to nine days to make payment in time to earn their cash discount.
2. A competitior, on the other hand, maintains fewer warehouses. If he were to date invoices from date of shipment, dealers some distance from the warehouses might have only four or five days in which to sell the merchandise and pay invoices in time to earn their cash discounts. Consequently, the competitor's invoices are dated from the time dealers receive the merchandise. In effect, the manufacturer substitutes the added expense of carrying higher receivables for the costs of additional warehouses and probably larger inventories.

The credit department may contribute to the performance of other departments as well. For example, it is not uncommon for the credit department to screen suppliers to determine their ability to fulfill contracts. It may also analyze the financial status of prospective carriers for the traffic department and of prospective advertising agencies for the advertising department.

## Conclusion

At a time when commercial, or trade, credit is assuming increased importance on the balance sheets of American corporations, data-processing equipment has taken over much of the burden of handling routine chores of credit management. With adequate delegation of authority and responsibility, credit managers are now in a position to assume a significantly more important role in management. Greater contributions may now be made in the areas of supporting the sales effort, financial counseling to customers, financial management, and economic forecasts.

Frequently, use of the computer will materially aid such activities as the preparation of estimates of cash collections and the simulation of results of changes in basic credit policies. Although the computer scatters data that were previously viewed as essential to credit management, reappraisal of the content of the lost information suggests that the newer and more current reports made possible by EDP equipment are adequate for credit appraisals. The computer does not take away the credit manager's skills or make him technologically unemployed. Instead, it opens new vistas through which dynamic credit management may make substantial contributions to a company's profitability.

*Chapter 6*

# *Principles of Inventory Management**

By Arthur Snyder

## *Introduction*

"WHY ARE WE always out of stock?" Behind this question lies one of the most perplexing problems facing businessmen today. They are confronted with the dilemma of attempting simultaneously (1) to meet ever-increasing demands for improved customer service, (2) to maintain stable production operations, and (3) to keep the investment in inventory at a reasonable level. As a result, during the past decade we have seen a great deal of interest and attention devoted to the subject of inventory management. Unfortunately, considerable doubt and confusion still exist as to what the basic tools of inventory control are, where they come from, and how they should be used.

It is the purpose of this study to analyze the development and application of the principles of inventory control. In discussing these techniques, it is often necessary to use concepts and terminologies which might be foreign to many businessmen. It is impossible, however, to acquire a sound knowledge of these principles without becoming familiar with the fundamental tools upon which they are based.

Hundreds of articles have been written on this subject. Unfortunately, very few provide the reader with anything but generalizations. The contents of this study, therefore, should not be looked upon as either an academic exercise in mathematics or a review of clever clerical devices

---

*Reprinted by permission from *Financial Executive,* Vol. XXXII (April, 1964), pp. 13–21.

which can help shortcut the labyrinth of confusion. Properly understood, these concepts will help the businessman make better policy decisions, which in turn will generate more useful and satisfying procedures. As such, these techniques are worth some time and thought, commensurate with the importance of inventory policy in your business operation.

Included is a new theory on economic ordering quantity *(EOQ)* which shows how the *EOQ* can be interpreted as a quantity range rather than a fixed quantity. It is current practice rigidly to adhere to the specific quantity obtained by using the *EOQ* formula. Deviations are made only under the assumed penalty of increased inventory costs. This myth will be exposed, and it will be shown that the *EOQ* can be interpreted as a quantity range imparting flexibility to the production and inventory control system.

## *Theories of Inventory Control*

Particular attention must be given to acquiring a thorough knowledge of the three fundamental concepts which form the foundation of any sound inventory control system:

1. Classification: What to control
2. Order point: When to make or buy
3. Economic lot size: How much to make or buy

Let us briefly examine each of these concepts to see how it is derived and adapted to practice.

## *Classification: What to Control*

The purpose of classification techniques is to provide a means whereby inventory control efforts can be directed toward those areas in which they can be most effective. On items of small value, it is seldom justifiable to use the same close and detailed control that is applied to high-valued or critical items. If you do, you may be spending more to keep these low-valued items within a prescribed limit than a slight excess in inventory might cost, or you are stealing time from controlling those items that require close policing.

Studies have shown that the average manufacturing company has an inventory which is distributed as to number of items and dollar value as shown in Table 1.

As shown, group A contains only 15 percent of the physical number of items, but represents 70 percent of the total inventory value. It is logical to assume that the more valuable items merit greater attention. This can be accomplished by giving them an *A* rating and reviewing

TABLE 1

| *Group* | *No. of Items* | *Inventory Value* |
|---|---|---|
| A. . . . . . . . . . . . . . . . . . . . . . . . | 15% | 70% |
| B. . . . . . . . . . . . . . . . . . . . . . . . | 30 | 20 |
| C. . . . . . . . . . . . . . . . . . . . . . . . | 55 | 10 |
| | 100% | 100% |

these items more often. This system is often referred to as the *"ABC* analysis of inventory."

Other factors, which are just as important as dollar value, to consider when developing a classification plan include the frequency and quantity of demand for an item, its rate of obsolescence, and whether it is a critical item, the lack of which would create a serious inconvenience to the company or a customer. In short, the development of a sound method of classification and record keeping is the first step toward improved inventory control.

## *Order Point (OP)*

The order point (*OP*) equation is a tool for evaluating the factors affecting the question: "When should I make or buy?" The purpose of the order point is to signal when the inventory level of a particular item has reached the point where, based on forecasted usage, it will be completely exhausted during the time required to manufacture or produce a replenishment stock. The equation is:

$$\text{Order Point } (OP) = S(P - L) + \frac{F}{\sqrt{SQ(P-L)}}$$

$S$ = Sales or usage
$L$ = Lead time
$Q$ = Units per demand
$F$ = Stockout acceptance factor
$P$ = Production or procurement cycle

The definitions of the variables used in the order point equation are included in the Appendix.[1] These schedules should be studied carefully, as it is important that the individuals responsible for the development of an inventory control program thoroughly understand the tools they are about to use.

[1]An analysis of the derivation of the equation, as well as other material, is available in booklet form from the Behr-Manning Company, Troy, N.Y.

It is the function of the order point to optimize the two opposing conditions of minimizing the inventory investment while satisfying demand and reducing the possibility of stockouts to an acceptable level. While, in theory, it is desirable never to have a stockout, for all practical business applications a certain level of stockouts must be planned for and tolerated. Stockouts are the result of fluctuations in usage from the forecasted level. These fluctuations are intensified for those items which have large variations in their usage ($S$) or in the average number of units per demand ($Q$).

In order to allow for these fluctuations in the demand pattern, the order point equation provides for the addition of safety stock. The determination of how much safety stock is required to establish an acceptable stockout level is based on the application of a formula known as the "square root approximation of the Poisson distribution." Statistical studies have shown that there is an acceptable correlation between the fluctuations in an average industrial demand pattern and the Poisson distribution. If the fluctuations for a given industry or product line are abnormal, the formula will break down under testing, and modifications to the value of the stockout acceptance factor ($F$), as it relates to the percentage of stockouts, will be required. These situations can occasionally be anticipated by testing the order point with historical data.

Almost every business requires some safety stock; the amount is largely determined by competitive practices and demands of the trade. Weighing the cost of additional inventory against the loss of a sale and customer goodwill is an important inventory policy decision. It is possible to develop a formula which equates (1) the loss resulting from a stockout in terms of either a lost sale and/or customer goodwill to (2) the cost to carry the additional inventory necessary to prevent the stockout. Such a formula, however, has proven to be quite theoretical and impractical. The problems to resolve are: What portion of the safety stock is responsible for the stockout; what percentage of the stockouts result in an actual lost sale; what is the value of customer goodwill, etc.? The general practice is, or should be, to establish an *OP* using tentatively agreed-upon safety stock limits and adjust the latter based on experience and desired objectives.

A common mistake made in the administration of the *OP* is the practice of releasing a stock replenishment order (when the *OP* is reached) for a lot size as determined by the *EOQ* without giving consideration as to whether or not the remaining stock balance is significantly below the *OP*. For example, an item has a current *OP* of 100 units and an *EOQ* of 50 units. The present stock balance of 140 units is reduced to 80 units by orders for 60 units. Many inventory systems would trigger off a stock replenishment order of 50 units (instead of 70 units), ignoring that 20 units are needed to restore the stock balance to the *OP*.

The result is usually frequent stockouts. To correct this situation, the *OP*'s are raised, which in turn increases the inventory levels. These factors naturally generate dissatisfaction with the system. The practice of rigidly adhering to the *EOQ* is based on the assumption that the *EOQ* is a specific quantity and any deviation will result in increased inventory costs. As will be shown later on, the *EOQ* under most conditions can be interpreted as a rather broad quantity range, thereby imparting flexibility to the inventory control system.

Another implied condition, but worthy of emphasis, is that the administration of the *OP* should carefully distinguish between items "in stock" and items "in process." Using the previous example, after release of a 70-unit stock replenishment order, the 150 units of stock would be distributed as follows: 80 units in stock and 70 units in process. An order for 50 units would reduce the stock balance to the *OP* and require the release of another stock replenishment order. The number of units in stock, however, has been reduced to a dangerously low level of 30 units; and the system should automatically "flag" this condition to permit, if deemed necessary, one of the previous stock orders to be expedited through production to avoid the possibility of a stockout condition. If possible, all in-process orders should show the date released, or the expected date of completion.

## *Economic Ordering Quantity (EOQ)*

The determination of order quantities is primarily a matter of economics. By increasing the size of an order, we reduce the unit cost because we spread the one-time production and/or procurement costs over a larger number of units. On the other hand, there are factors which argue for limiting the lot size, such as the increased inventory investment, higher inventory carrying charges, and a greater risk of obsolescence and spoiled work.

The economic ordering quantity equation (or *EOQ*, as it is more frequently called) provides a means whereby the several factors affecting the cost of a unit can be evaluated simultaneously to determine which lot size will generate the lowest unit cost for a given set of conditions. This familiar equation takes the following form:

$$EOQ = \sqrt{\frac{2SO}{RU} + \frac{PSO}{U} - \frac{O}{U}} \cong \sqrt{\frac{2SO}{RU}}$$

$S$ = Sales or usage
$O$ = Ordering costs

$U$ = Unit costs
$R$ = Investment factor
$P$ = Production or procurement cycle

The simplified version of the *EOQ* formula is sufficiently accurate for most business applications, as the last two functions do not significantly contribute to the final value of the *EOQ*.

As previously emphasized, the development of a sound inventory control program requires that the responsible individuals be thoroughly familiar with the basic theories involved. By itself, the *EOQ* formula is meaningless unless we understand the function of the factors it is based upon and what assumptions are used in its derivation.

## *EOQ Range Theory*

There are two misconceptions concerning the use of the *EOQ* formula for determining economic ordering quantities: (1) that the *EOQ* is a specific quantity and (2) that a small deviation from this specific quantity substantially increases the total cost per unit. The implied inflexibility of the *EOQ* has always been a source of concern to those individuals charged with the responsibility of managing the inventory control system. In actual practice, it is often necessary to release a lot size which is greater or less than the *EOQ*. These deviations from the *EOQ* are usually reluctantly approved because it is believed there will be a significant increase in the total unit cost. We shall show that for all practical purposes the *EOQ* can be interpreted as a quantity range within which can be realized the minimum total unit cost.

## *Advantages of EOQ Range*

The ability to interpret the *EOQ* as a range of quantities, rather than a specific quantity, has many advantages. In general, it imparts flexibility to the inventory and production control system, permitting desired adjustments to the ordering quantity without the fear of increased cost. Deviations from the *EOQ* might be prompted by one of the following reasons:

*Less than EOQ.* The use of ordering quantities less than the *EOQ* is often prompted by conditions such as the desire to reduce work-in-process inventory, fear of product obsolescence when the *EOQ* exceeds more than 6–12 months' supply, conservative adjustment to an optimistic sales forecast, or the desire to smooth out the production load by staggering the release of several small lot sizes.

*More than EOQ.* Those situations which pressure for the release of ordering quantities larger than the *EOQ* are (1) to permit an adjustment of the production load by providing work during a temporary slack period; (2) to build inventory in lieu of anticipated loss of normal capacity due to material shortages, strike, or heavy vacation periods; or (3) to make up for shortages between the stock balance and the *OP*.

Other types of adjustments include the desire to modify the *EOQ* to utilize the full capacity of a machine or to facilitate handling. Whatever the reason may be, there is general agreement that a system which is flexible within controlled limits is preferred over an inflexible system. The latter often creates more problems than it solves.

## *EOQ Formula*

The assumption that the *EOQ* is a specific quantity and any deviation from this quantity increases the total cost per unit stems primarily from the popular concept that cost per unit, plotted as a function of the ordering quantity, results in a curve with a distinct minimum point, as shown in Figure 1. The implied unity of the *EOQ* point is further supported by the *EOQ* formula, which provides only one answer for any given set of data.

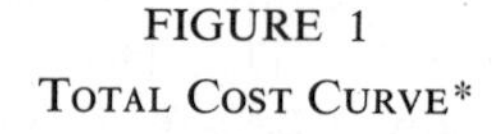

FIGURE 1

TOTAL COST CURVE*

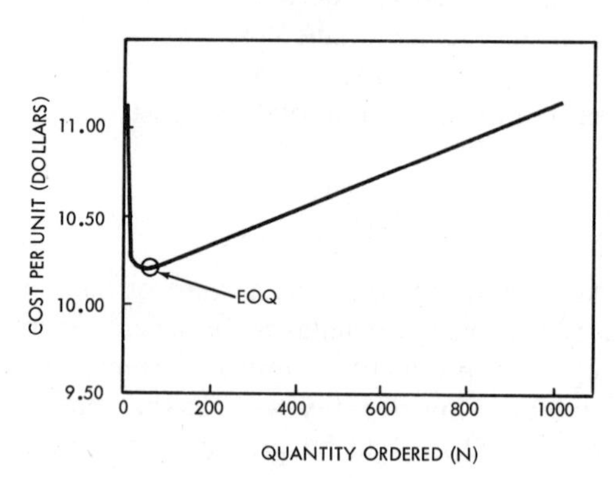


*Data based on Case Problem—Widgets.

Let us direct our attention to Figure 2, which represents an enlargement of the area near the *EOQ* point in Figure 1. Figure 2 shows that what appeared to be a distinct minimum point in Figure 1 is really a flat portion of the curve which extends on either side of the specific *EOQ*

FIGURE 2
ENLARGED SECTION OF TOTAL COST CURVE*

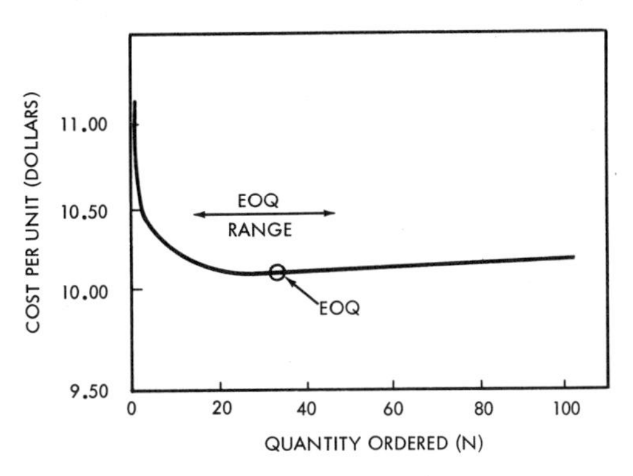


*Data based on Case Problem—Widgets.

point. It will be shown that this condition is the rule and not an exception created by the data chosen for the illustration.

Based on the above example and an understanding of the mathematical derivation of the *EOQ* formula, two observations can be made: (1) The *EOQ* is a precisely determined point on the total cost curve, and (2) this curve has an extremely long and flat portion at the theoretical minimum cost (or *EOQ*) point. What we intend to prove, therefore, is that the *EOQ* is not a specific point, but a section of the total cost curve. This section represents the economic order quantity range which will provide the same minimum total cost per unit as the specific *EOQ*.

## Case Problem

To illustrate this point clearly, let us use a case problem choosing fairly representative data for the variables involved. Suppose the XYZ Company manufactures Widgets and the necessary production and inventory control data for this product are as shown in Table 2.

TABLE 2

| *Symbol* | *Definition* | *Value* |
|---|---|---|
| *S*.................. | Sales volume | 100 per month |
| *P*.................. | Production cycle | 1 month |
| *O*.................. | Ordering costs | \$1 |
| *U*.................. | Unit cost | \$10 each |
| *R*.................. | Investment factor | 24% per year |
| *L*.................. | Lead time | ½ month |
| *Q*.................. | Units per demand | 5 |
| *F*.................. | Stockout acceptance | 10% (1.29) |

Based on the given data and respective formulas, the inventory control procedure for this product would be to establish an order point ($OP$) of 70 units and a lot size ($EOQ$) of 32 units.

$$OP = S(P-L) + F\ \sqrt{SQ(P-L)} = 70 \text{ units}$$

$$EOQ = \sqrt{\frac{2SO}{RU}} = 31.6 \text{ units}$$

We are satisfied with the determination of an order point ($OP$) of 70 units. As explained, the $OP$ is primarily a function of our sales forecast and the production cycle. To the minimum $OP$ of 50 units, we have added a buffer stock of nine units to reduce the probability of stockout to 10 percent and 11 units to adjust the $OP$ for the fact that we average five units per order. We recognize that the latter may have to be adjusted based on actual experience.

The lot size of 32 is interpreted as the most economic manufacturing quantity based on the given values of $S$, $O$, $R$, and $U$. It is implied that a deviation from this quantity will result in a significant increase in the total cost per unit. Rather than accepting this statement, let us actually examine the effect on the total unit cost ($TUC$) as the ordering quantity is increased or decreased from the $EOQ$ of 32 units. The equation for calculating the $TUC$ for a given quantity ($N$) is as follows:

$$TUC = \left[\frac{O}{N} + U\right]\left[1 + \frac{RP}{2} + \frac{RN}{2S} - \frac{R}{2S}\right]$$

Substituting the given data for Widgets, the total cost per unit as a function of the ordering quantity ($N$) simplifies to:

$$TUC = \$10.10 + \frac{\$1.01}{N} + \$0.001\ N$$

Using the above expression, the total cost per unit for lot sizes from one to 1,000 is shown in Table 3. These data were also used for plotting the graphs shown in Figures 1 and 2.

## *EOQ versus Cost*

The function of the $EOQ$ formula is to provide an answer to the question: "What ordering quantity will generate the minimum total cost per unit?" Using the data chosen for our case problem, the $EOQ$ is calculated as 31.6 units, which results in a minimum total cost of $10.16 per unit. If we look at Table 3, however, we find that this is the minimum cost only if we extend the value to four positions after the decimal, or $10.1627. Any lot size between the quantity range of 25–40 has a total variable cost of $10.16 when rounded off to the nearest cent.

This quantity range is not clearly evident if we inspect Figure 1, which represents the universal impression of what the total cost curve looks like. Due to the large quantity range used for the *X* axis, the curve appears to have a distinct minimum point or *EOQ*. As previously discussed, if we enlarge the section of the curve near the *EOQ* as shown in Figure 2, we readily see what the unit cost figures tell us: The curve near the *EOQ* point is almost flat. The *EOQ* is merely the precisely calculated low point of this flat section. Hence, for most conditions the *EOQ* can be considered a range of quantities rather than a specific quantity.

TABLE 3

CASE PROBLEM: TOTAL UNIT COST

| Order Quantity (*N*) | Total Cost per Unit | |
|---|---|---|
| | *Exact* | *Nearest Cent* |
| 1 | $11.1101 | $11.11 |
| 5 | 10.3061 | 10.31 |
| 10 | 10.2101 | 10.21 |
| 15 | 10.1814 | 10.18 |
| 20 | 10.1696 | 10.17 |
| 25 | 10.1645 | 10.16 |
| *EOQ* = 31.6 | 10.1627 | 10.16 |
| 40 | 10.1644 | 10.16 |
| 45 | 10.1665 | 10.17 |
| 55 | 10.1725 | 10.17 |
| 60 | 10.1759 | 10.18 |
| 75 | 10.1876 | 10.19 |
| 100 | 10.2092 | 10.21 |
| 200 | 10.3042 | 10.30 |
| 300 | 10.4025 | 10.40 |
| 500 | 10.6011 | 10.60 |
| 1,000 | 11.1001 | 11.10 |

Let us carry these observations to a further conclusion using our case problems for illustration. The management of the XYZ Company desires to impart flexibility to the ordering quantities of its new product, Widgets. It is agreed that 32 units is the theoretical quantity that will produce the minimum total cost per unit, but it is recognized that the values of the variables chosen for calculating the *EOQ* are not necessarily exact. Management is willing, therefore, to work within an *EOQ* range that does not exceed one half of 1 percent of the theoretical minimum total cost per unit. An increase of one half of 1 percent over the minimum cost of $10.16 would extend the acceptable cost range to $10.21. On this basis, instead of an *EOQ* of 32 units, sales and production management could gear their operations to the release of lot sizes which vary from 10 to 100 units.

## *EOQ versus Cost Ratio*

The *EOQ* formula can be thought of as a function of sales volume ($S$), investment factor ($R$), and cost ($O$, $U$). The equation, when separated in this manner, appears as follows:

$$EOQ = \sqrt{\frac{2SO}{RU}} = \sqrt{S \times \frac{2}{R} \times \frac{O}{U}}$$

When viewed in this manner, it becomes evident that it is the ratio of ordering to unit costs ($O/U$), rather than their absolute values, which determines the *EOQ*. For example, in the case problem we chose a value of $1 for ordering costs and $10 for unit costs, giving a ratio of 1:10. For the same values of $S$ and $R$, any combinations of absolute values for $O$ and $U$ which maintain the same 1:10 ratio will result in the same *EOQ*, as shown in Table 4.

TABLE 4

| | *Examples* | | |
|---|---|---|---|
| *Variable* | *#1* | *#2* | *#3* |
| $S$ (month) | 100 | 100 | 100 |
| $R$ (year) | 24% | 24% | 24% |
| $O$ | $ 1.00 | $ 5.00 | $ 2.20 |
| $U$ | $10.00 | $50.00 | $22.00 |
| $K = O/U$ | 0.1 | 0.1 | 0.1 |
| *EOQ* | 32 | 32 | 32 |

It is often difficult to establish accurate and acceptable ordering and unit costs. The interpretation of these costs as a ratio, rather than as individual absolute amounts, can serve as a very useful approach to handling the cost aspect of the *EOQ* formula. The use of a cost ratio ($O/U$) establishes the proper relationship between the two costs. For instance, if the unit cost for an item is $22, there is no need to fret over whether the ordering cost is $2.00 or $2.20. The effect on the cost ratio, and hence on the *EOQ*, is insignificant. Further, it often simplifies the problem of how much variable overhead cost should be added to each cost. If overhead is a percentage addition to each cost, then it can be ignored, as it will not change the ratio. Another advantage to the cost ratio approach is that it permits products with similar cost ratios to be grouped and handled with the same inventory control charts and procedures.

## *EOQ versus Sales Volume*

Under most conditions, once the cost ratio ($O/U$) and investment factor ($R$) have been determined and agreed upon for a given product, they can be considered constant unless involved in a major cost change. This therefore reduces the *EOQ* formula to the function of one true variable—sales volume.

In the case problem, we chose a sales volume ($S$) of 100 units per month and arrived at an *EOQ* of 32 units and an *EOQ* range of 10–100 units for the control limit of one half of 1 percent increase in minimum total variable cost. Table 5 shows the effect on the *EOQ* and *EOQ* range for changes in the sales volume ($S$) from one to 250 units per month. The *EOQ* was calculated using the standard *EOQ* formula, and the *EOQ* range was determined by substituting the value $T = 0.005$ for the control limit of one half of 1 percent. If a control limit of one tenth of 1 percent were desired, a value of $T = 0.001$ would be used.

TABLE 5

CASE PROBLEM: *EOQ* RANGE

| *Sales Volume* ($S$) | *EOQ* | *EOQ Range* (+ ½%) |
|---|---|---|
| 1 | 3 | 2–5 |
| 5 | 7 | 4–13 |
| 10 | 10 | 4–20 |
| 20 | 14 | 6–32 |
| 30 | 17 | 7–42 |
| 50 | 22 | 8–61 |
| 75 | 28 | 9–86 |
| 100 | 32 | 10–105 |
| 250 | 50 | 12–214 |

Table 5 shows that for the given data of the case problem, the *EOQ* range is significant for all levels of sales volume. When the forecasted sales volume drops to five per month, a quantity range of four to 13 units provides the same minimum cost as the *EOQ* of seven. At a forecasted sales volume of 250 units per month, the *EOQ* is 50 units, but the same minimum cost will be realized for any lot size within the limits of 12 to 214 units. Working within the *EOQ* range, the production control manager could stagger the release of lot sizes to fit a daily, weekly, or monthly schedule if such is desired.

## *Application of EOQ Range Theory*

At this point a criticism could be made by the practitioners of production and inventory control that the availability of an *EOQ* range complicates the problem, as it introduces a decision as to what lot size to use, whereas previously the choice was limited to a specific *EOQ*. If this is a problem, then the solution lies in a well-defined management policy describing the procedure to follow in determining the proper lot size. To explore some of the ways the *EOQ* range can be adapted to practice, let us return to our case problem of Widgets.

FIGURE 3
CASE PROBLEM: *EOQ* RANGE CURVE

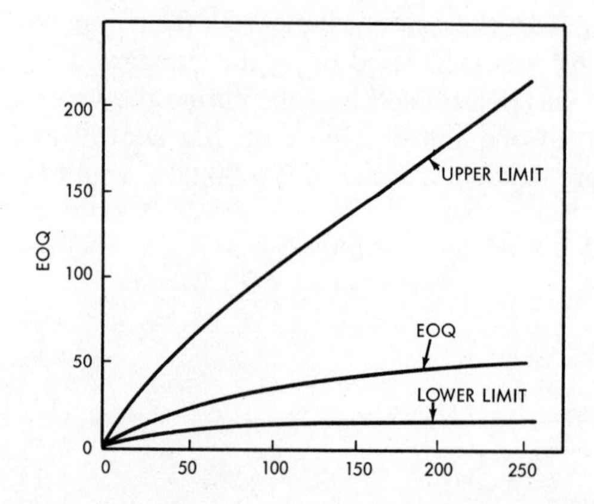


Figure 3 shows one way in which the *EOQ* range, as a function of sales volume, can be represented graphically for easy reference. In a similar manner, Figure 4 shows a graph of the order point as a function of sales volume. The order point is shown with and without the addition of safety stock, the latter being based on a 10 percent stockout acceptance level. Using these graphs, which could be combined, variations in management policy concerning the inventory control of Widgets could be introduced.

1. During the initial stages of introducing the product to the market, the *EOQ* lot size will be standardized at 20 units. The release of small lot sizes is desired by the factory to minimize spoilage usually associated with a new product and reduce the possibility of building excess inventory in case sales do not reach forecasted volumes. An *OP* of 50 units will be established, which represents the order point for sales *(S)* of 100 units per month without the addition of safety stock.

FIGURE 4

CASE PROBLEM: ORDER POINT CURVE

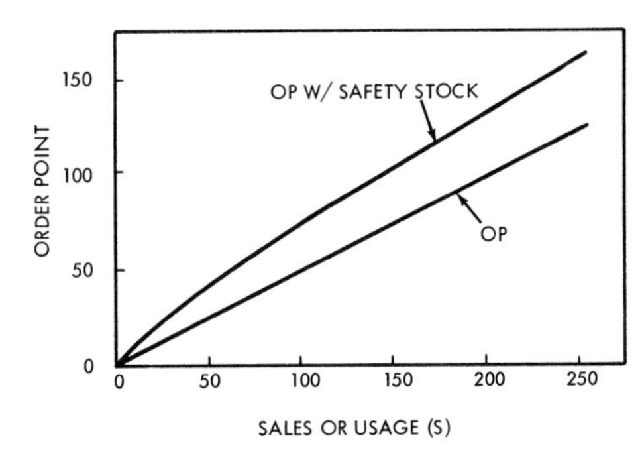


2. After the production "bugs" have been worked out, the *EOQ* will be increased to 50 units and the *OP* to 70 units, provided the forecasted sales volume and buying pattern materialize.
3. Since this is a seasonal item with peak demand during the fourth quarter, additional inventory will be built in the third quarter by increasing the lot size to the maximum level (105 units for forecasted sales of 100 units per month).
4. As the product matures or obsolescence is feared, the *OP* could be reduced by eliminating the safety stock and reducing the lot size to 20 units.

The important conclusion to draw from the above discussion is that management, by reference to charts or graphs of this type, could establish some simple rules which would effectively control the production of this product.

## *Conclusion*

Interpretation of the *EOQ* as a quantity range rather than a specific quantity is an important concept to understand in the formulation of your inventory control program. It will provide the line organization responsible for the day-to-day management of your inventories with the flexibility they must have to meet the demands placed on the system by daily production and sales problems.

## *Purchase Quantity*

Occasionally, you will hear a purchasing agent or distributor ask the question: "The *EOQ* formula is fine for advising the manufacturer how much to make, but can we use it to determine how much to buy?" The answer to this question is a very definitely yes.

$$EOQ = \sqrt{\frac{2SO}{RU}}$$

$S$ = Sales or usage
$R$ = Investment factor
$O$ = Ordering costs
$U$ = Unit costs

The *EOQ* formula shown above is applicable to both manufacturing and purchasing situations. The Appendix provides a thorough analysis of how each variable used in the *EOQ* equation is evaluated, depending upon whether the item is manufactured or purchased.

## *Quantity Discount*

A common practice in industry today is the quantity discount, which is used to encourage buyers to place larger orders. Many suppliers offer a discount schedule wherein the discount increases with the number of units ordered. The result is a variable unit cost for the item which is dependent on the quantity ordered. This problem does not exist for the manufacturer, as his unit cost ($U$), as defined and used in the *EOQ* formula, can usually be considered constant. This brings us to the question: "How are the quantity discount and the resulting variable unit cost recognized in determining the *EOQ* for purchased items?"

The procedure for handling a quantity discount in the *EOQ* formula is not difficult, particularly if we analyze the problem and break it down into its logical components. The effect of a quantity discount is to produce several unit costs for the same item. These unit costs are dependent on the order quantity, which determines the applicable discount. For each unit cost, we can calculate an economic order quantity using the *EOQ* formula. The optimum order quantity will be the largest *EOQ*, provided it falls within the quantity range upon which the unit cost and respective discount are based. Let us use an example to illustrate this.

A company has a monthly usage of 100 units of item A which can be purchased according to the discount schedule shown in Table 6. As-

TABLE 6

| *Purchase Quantity* | *Discount* | *Net Purchase Price per Unit* |
|---|---|---|
| *a*) 1–9 | .... | $10.00 |
| *b*) 10–49 | 10% | 9.00 |
| *c*) 50–99 | 25 | 7.50 |
| *d*) Over 100 | 40 | 6.00 |

sume the company has an established procedure for determining purchase order quantities based on the use of the *EOQ* formula and the following data are applicable to item A:

Investment factor ($R$) = 24% per year
Ordering costs ($O$) = \$1.20 per order
Unit costs ($U$) = Net purchase price per unit *plus* 20% for inventory-carrying costs, taxes, handling, insurance, inspection, etc.

Using the above data and sales ($S$) of 100 units per month, we can calculate the respective *EOQ's* for the four unit costs provided by the discounts schedule (see Table 7).

TABLE 7

| | (*a*) | (*b*) | (*c*) | (*d*) |
|---|---|---|---|---|
| Monthly sales ($S$)........ | 100 | 100 | 100 | 100 |
| Investment factor ($R$).... | 24% | 24% | 24% | 24% |
| Ordering costs ($O$)........ | \$ 1.20 | \$ 1.20 | \$1.20 | \$1.20 |
| Unit costs ($U$)........... | \$12.00 | \$10.80 | \$9.00 | \$7.20 |
| *EOQ*.................... | 32 | 34 | 36 | 41 |
| Purchase quantity*....... | 1–9 | 10–49 | 50–99 | Over 100 |

*Purchase quantity required to obtain net purchase price per unit upon which unit cost ($U$) is based.

As shown in Table 7, the four *EOQ*'s vary from 32 to 41. The optimum *EOQ* is 34, as it is the largest *EOQ* which falls within its respective purchase quantity range (10–49). Theoretically, the *EOQ* of 36 cannot be used, as it is based on a unit cost of \$9.00, which can be realized only if the order quantity is for 50–99 units. For the same reason, the *EOQ* of 41 cannot be used, as its unit cost of \$7.20 requires an order quantity of 100 or more units.

## *Conclusion*

The above procedure is shown for those who wish to apply an exact and rigorous method to the determination of an *EOQ* for purchased items, the net price for which is determined by a quantity discount schedule. Although the above example is based on a single set of conditions, it supports the conclusion that very little is gained by this detailed probing of the problem. All four of the *EOQ*'s, which range from 32 to 41, are within the discount bracket established by a purchase quantity of 10 to 49 units. Based on an expanded series of similar examples, it can be shown that the typical quantity discount schedule has no significant effect on the *EOQ*. At best, recognition of a purchase quantity discount will increase the order quantity only to the next discount bracket.

An easy solution to this problem is to base the purchase order quantity on an evaluation of the *EOQ* range for the item and the respective discount schedule.

Here, then, is another valuable use for the *EOQ* range formula. By interpreting the order quantity as a range rather than a specific amount, judgment can be used in selecting and optimizing an available purchase quantity discount schedule.

## *Summary*

The universal question we all seek to answer is: "What is an optimum inventory level?" The problem of answering this question is compounded by the fact that within a management group there are usually several conflicting opinions. The sales manager will not tolerate stockouts. The factory manager desires long manufacturing runs and stable employment. The treasurer feels that a minimum of working capital should be tied up in inventories.

Many companies blame their inventory problems on a large volume of small orders for diversified products. "We inventory 100,000 items." "Our sales forecasts are too general." "We're really a job shop." Each company feels that its problems in this respect are unusual. Refuge, however, cannot (and should not) be taken behind this smoke screen. These problems are shared by most manufacturers today. If it is not apparent in some companies, perhaps the answer lies in the fact that their managements have been able to minimize the problem.

The key to good inventory control primarily rests in sufficient knowledge of the fundamental techniques to develop enough self-confidence to permit their practical adaptation to the specific needs of the company. Many programs are defeated before they start by imposing upon the group responsible for the execution of the program a "bag of tools" in the guise of mysterious mathematical equations and unique concepts. Seldom is any attempt made first to educate the group on how to use these new tools. The result is distrust of the techniques, poor application, and eventual confusion when things get worse rather than better.

In establishing or improving upon inventory control procedures, it is important to remember that the following fundamentals largely determine the degree of your success:

1. The order point *(OP)* is singularly the most significant factor affecting your inventory control procedure, as it establishes your inventory levels. Hence, it determines your investment in inventories and your

ability to provide satisfactory customer service. Careful attention must be given to the development of your order point procedure. Despite the several factors involved in the formula, remember it is primarily dependent on the accuracy of your sales or usage forecast.

2. The *EOQ* is usually given far too much emphasis; and often a disproportionate amount of time is spent worrying about unit costs, setup costs, and the investment factor. Keep in mind that these factors are not involved in determining your order point. The only factor common to both the *OP* and the *EOQ* is the sales or usage variable. As already shown, the *EOQ* under most conditions can be interpreted as a broad quantity range.

It is perhaps appropriate to close this article with a reminder that regardless of how sophisticated your inventory control techniques, the results will be no better than the day-to-day data fed into the system. Before embarking on any elaborate inventory control program, be sure your accounting and record-keeping procedures can provide the system with current and reliable data. The bottleneck in most inventory control procedures is data input and utilization. It is in this area that we have seen many successful applications of data-processing equipment.

A modern inventory control program affects all phases of your business; therefore, it must be an integral part of your business operation. The degree of success of an inventory program depends largely on how well management conceives the problem, formulates its policy, and executes the program.

*Appendix*

# *Definition of Variables*

This schedule contains a discussion of the eight basic variables used in the ordering point (*OP*) and economic ordering quantity (*EOQ*) equations. In relating specific data to these variables, it is most important to recognize the dimension of these variables as discussed in the last section of this schedule.

## *S = Sales or Usage*

This represents the forecast of future sales or usage. How far into the future the forecast is made is dependent primarily on the production or procurement cycle and the characteristics of the sales pattern. The usual practice is to make a forecast of from three to six months, normally through the projection of historical data. Sales forecasting is at best an inexact science, but every effort should be made to develop the very best possible projections.

## *P = Production or Procurement Cycle*

This is the total elapsed time normally required to procure or manufacture the unit. In determining this time cycle, it should start when the decision is made that additional units are required and end with their delivery to the stockroom or customer. If there are significant fluctuations in the time cycle, the effect on the order point should be tested for the probable extreme ranges of the cycle.

## *O = Ordering Costs*

These are the variable costs associated with the manufacture or procurement of the lot size which are independent of the quantity. A typical list of these costs includes variable labor and expenses for purchasing, receiving, accounting, planning, and manufacturing setup.

### $U$ = *Unit Costs*

This includes the variable costs related to the production or procurement of each unit, such as the manufacturing cost or net purchase price per unit. To this must be added inventory-carrying costs per unit for space, taxes, handling, insurance, inspection, etc.

### $K$ = *Cost Ratio*

$K$ is the ratio of ordering costs ($O$) to unit costs ($U$), or $K = O/U$.

### $R$ = *Investment Factor*

The function of the investment factor is to provide a rate of return on the inventory investment (before taxes) which is commensurate with the risks and costs associated with the business, such as obsolescence, cost of working capital, and spoiled work. In actual application, different interest rates can be used, depending on the degree of risk involved. Factors which should be considered in evaluating the degree of risk are type of product, reliability of the sales or usage forecast, working capital requirements, etc.

### $L$ = *Lead Time*

Lead time can be defined as the average time span between the acceptance of an order and the promised delivery date. For repair parts and critical stock items the lead time is often zero, whereas for a large machine tool the lead time may vary from three to nine months. Lead time is primarily a function of the nature of the product and competitive practices.

### $Q$ = *Units per Demand*

Units per demand refers to the average number of units per order. For instance, an automotive distributor will usually receive orders for spark plugs or valves in six or eight units per demand.

### $F$ = *Stockout Acceptance Factor*

The significance of the stockout acceptance factor ($F$) is discussed in the report under the section "Order Point." The value of $F$ in the order point equation for a given percent stockout level, assuming a Poisson distribution in the demand pattern, can be read from the graph shown in Figure 5.

FIGURE 5

STOCKOUT ACCEPTANCE FACTOR

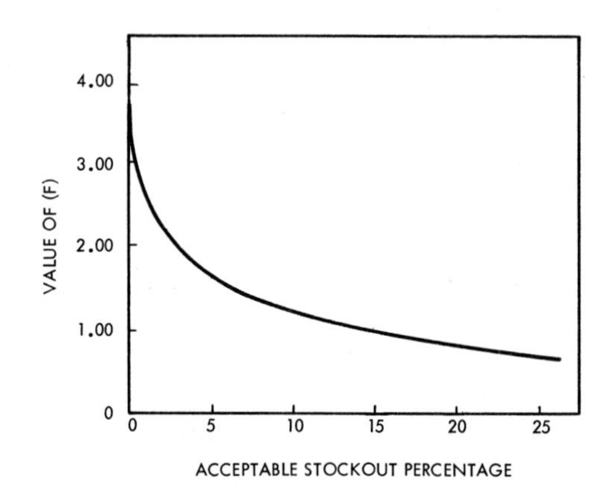


## *T = EOQ Control Limit*

An equation has been developed for the calculation of the *EOQ* range. This function is based on an acceptable percentage increase in the minimum total variable unit cost. The percentage increase is termed the *EOQ* control limit and designated by the letter (*T*).

## *Dimension of the Variables*

In the use of the order point (*OP*), economic order quantity (*EOQ*), and *EOQ* range equations, it is critical that all data be in the same time or units dimension, as shown in Table 8, for example.

TABLE 8

| *Variable* | *Value of Raw Data* | *Formula Value* | |
|---|---|---|---|
| | | *Per Month* | *Per Week* |
| *S* | 200 per month | 200 | 46.2 |
| *P* | 6 weeks | 1.39 | 6 |
| *L* | 1 month | 1 | 4.33 |
| *R* | 24% per year | 0.02 | 0.0046 |
| *O* | \$0.50 per lot | 0.50 | 0.50 |
| *U* | \$3.00 per unit | 3.00 | 3.00 |
| *Q* | 5 per demand | 5 | 5 |
| *F* | 2.06 | 2.06 | 2.06 |
| *T* | ½ of 1% | 0.005 | 0.005 |

Part II

# Short- and Intermediate-Term Financing

*Chapter 7*

# *Accounts Receivable Lending: Credit at the Margin**

FINANCIAL INSTITUTIONS and credit practices are constantly being adapted to service borrowers' needs more effectively. This flexibility is particularly important in the case of marginal business loans in which the adequacy of collateral plays a major role.

Any firm which does not sell on strictly cash terms generates receivables which represent the obligations of its customers. When sales expand, there is a tendency for receivables to grow at the expense of cash, inventory, and, in time, fixed assets. If receivables are not converted into cash with sufficient rapidity, the selling firm may exhaust its credit and find its expansion potential severely limited.

At this point the firm appears "undercapitalized," judged by conservative lending standards. But additional equity capital may be available only at a cost which the owners consider prohibitive in terms of sharing earnings and control with outsiders. One answer to the problem may be secured short-term credit. In many cases the very receivables which are choking off further growth may be the most suitable collateral available.

## *A Self-Liquidating Security*

Receivables which arise out of sales to customers in a sound condition will be paid off in the normal course of business. But until that point, which may be several months away, receivables are, in a sense, frozen assets. A more vigorous attempt to collect from customers may

---

*Reprinted by permission from Federal Reserve Bank of Chicago, *Business Conditions,* March, 1958, pp. 5–12.

require either terms of sale so short as to hamper the competitive position of the firm or the use of costly cash discounts.

A firm's receivables usually include the obligations of a considerable number of customers who may be in differing lines of business, thereby providing diversified security for a loan. Moreover, a firm's customers, on the average, may be in a stronger financial position than the firm itself. As a recent pamphlet of the American Bankers Association states: "Many banks have suddenly realized that the best, and certainly the most liquid, collateral that a borrower has to offer is a portfolio of well diversified self-liquidating, current receivables. . . . "

Commercial banks often engage in lending on assigned accounts receivable. Loans of this type are also offered by a lesser known group of specialized institutions, the commercial finance companies.

## *Wholesalers of Credit*

Commercial finance companies are middlemen in the financial structure. Like sales finance companies, they borrow from the commercial banks and the capital markets and make the funds available to other borrowers. The commercial finance companies lend to business firms engaged in production or distribution of goods and services whose access to primary sources of credit is limited. Typically, the clients of commercial finance companies are those small, growing, or temporarily hard-pressed firms which figure prominently in any discussion of financing problems of undercapitalized or underfinanced business enterprise.

The larger, well-established commercial finance companies are able to keep basic money costs at a minimum. They borrow from commercial banks at the prime rate and obtain funds in the capital markets in competition with large industrial firms. In addition, some of the very large companies, which also operate in the consumer credit field, are able to tap the commercial paper markets at low rates.

At the end of 1956, outstanding commercial loans of all types held by finance companies exceeded $1 billion, equal to about 3 percent of the business loans outstanding at commercial banks. In the two years 1955 and 1956, commercial finance company credits rose by 50 percent, a somewhat greater expansion than for commercial bank business loans. Moreover, the $1 billion of outstandings, assuming a turnover of about ten times a year, indicates total business sales financed in this manner in the neighborhood of $10 billion.

In recent years, commercial finance companies have expanded their operations sharply. New firms have entered the field, and existing organizations have added to their capital by increasing equity funds and by selling long-term debt. When these firms expand their capital base, total resources are increased by a multiple of this amount, since bank borrowings, commercial paper, and unsubordinated debt can be incurred to the extent of two or three times the capital, including equity and subordinated debentures.

## *Types of Lending*

The great bulk of the business lending done by commercial finance companies falls into three classes: (1) accounts receivable financing, which involves the purchase or discounting of receivables generated by firms selling goods and services; (2) other secured lending on inventory, chattels, or even real estate; and (3) time sales financing of equip-

FIGURE 1

OTHER TYPES OF FINANCE COMPANY LENDING

*Time sales financing* is a highly competitive type of lending widely available from banks and manufacturers and their finance subsidiaries, as well as from commercial finance companies. This financing process is similar to that typically used for passenger automobiles. Purchasers of construction machinery, trucks, trailers, and other equipment often buy on time sales contracts.

*Inventories* usually are far less satisfactory security for loans than receivables or equipment. This is because of the sharp price concessions which often are required in the event of forced liquidation. As a result, a loan on inventory is likely to be restricted to a relatively small portion of the cost of the merchandise. Commercial finance companies do make a substantial volume of inventory loans; but almost invariably, this service is offered only as a part of an over-all program of finance for a client. For example, a manufacturer of seasonal merchandise may borrow on inventory until goods are shipped and accounts receivable are generated.

*Chattel mortgages* on equipment granted by commercial finance companies may arise out of the purchase of the equipment itself. The more usual chattel mortgage loan, however, is a secured loan for general working capital purposes. Numerous small finance companies specialize in this type of loan. The amount loaned on equipment in use is ordinarily restricted to its liquidation value. Specialized appraisers are consulted as to the probable value of the equipment "under the hammer," that is, at a fast liquidation, and also the value in an "orderly liquidation." Usually, the former determines the maximum loan value.

ment. The emphasis in this article is upon the first type, the financing of open-book accounts which represent continuing shipments of goods to customers and which do not involve installment notes. Brief descriptions of the other credit services offered by commercial finance companies are provided in Figure 1.

## *Methods of Operation*

Accounts receivable can be converted into cash before maturity in two ways. They can be sold outright, without recourse, to a "factor," or they can be used as collateral for advances from a finance company or a bank. In essence, these devices accomplish much the same purpose; and indeed, both forms are used by a number of companies. But the methods are quite different.

The old-line factor concentrates his attention more upon the financial position of his client's customers, as distinguished from the net worth and solvency of the client himself. This is because he approves the credit before shipment is made and accepts full risk of loss on the resulting receivables. The possibility of substantial returns and allowances sometimes can be handled by advancing less than the full face value of the invoices.

Factoring charges are made up of two components. First, there is a commission charge on all receivables purchased. This usually runs between 1 and 3 percent, depending upon such considerations as the credit standing of the obligor, the total volume of business, the average size of invoice, and the average maturity of the receivables. In addition, there is an interest charge, usually 6 or 7 percent per annum, on funds advanced before the calculated "average due date" on the receivables acquired.

Because of the services performed by the factor, it is difficult to compute an "effective interest rate" so that the cost of this credit service may be compared with other types of financing. Some firms using factors do not take up funds before the due date and so incur no interest charge. Moreover, funds left with the factor after maturity typically draw interest at the same rate charged to borrowers.

Historically, factoring has been associated with the textile industry at the processor stage. In the past thirty years the device has expanded into a variety of other lines, including finished clothing, furniture, shoes, plastics, toys, and a host of other items. However, the great bulk, perhaps 90 percent, of the accounts factored involve textiles.

It would appear that factoring might be an ideal solution to the credit problems of many small firms. It not only provides funds, but also relieves the management of much of its concern over credit and collection problems and allows concentration on sales and production. Nevertheless, relatively little old-line factoring is done in the Midwest. Most of the firms which include the word "factor" in their name do little if any true factoring in the sense defined above. Although the few firms which are engaged in the straight factoring business in this area have been expanding their operations, there are a number of obstacles to a widespread use of the device.

First, there is the problem of notification. Since the receivables become the property of the factor, the customer must know who holds his account and where payment is to be made. Many sellers of goods believe that their customers would object to accounts being assigned to a third party. Such a practice might suggest a shaky financial position, or it could interfere with the flexibility of the seller-buyer relationship.

Second, credits on shipments must be approved by the factor *before* goods are shipped. Otherwise, the client must accept the credit risk himself. Every attempt is made to speed the process of checking credits, but it is apparent that the firm which factors its accounts is at somewhat of a disadvantage in seeking new business, since sales to new accounts must be made subject to a credit check.

Third, many types of business do not generate accounts which are easily factored. This is the case whenever goods are shipped on consignment, where returns are likely to be quite large, or where average invoice size is very small. Receivables of service organizations, for the most part, are difficult to factor because the produce is intangible and the nature of the receivable is less certain than in the case of goods. Construction firm receivables introduce the problem of mechanics' liens and the possibility of nonperformance on the part of contractors.

Fourth, some finance companies have found factoring unprofitable unless a sufficiently large number of clients can be serviced in a given field and the same credit information can be used for more than one account.

## *Nonnotification Financing*

Accounts receivable lending with recourse to the borrower is often called "nonnotification" financing because the purchaser of the goods usually is not informed that his obligation has been assigned to another party.

When a nonnotification deal is arranged, the lender agrees to advance a certain proportion of the face value of the accounts assigned. This proportion may range between 50 and 90 percent of the value, but usually averages around 75 to 80 percent. The proportion depends upon the credit standing of the clients, the financial strength of the borrower, the possibility of returns and allowances, and the cash and trade discounts which are permitted. Usually, the ratio provides for an advance which is no higher than the cost of the goods to the seller.

FIGURE 2

TRADE ACCEPTANCES: PRELUDE TO ACCOUNTS RECEIVABLE FINANCING

Prior to the Civil War, shipments of goods from manufacturers to merchants were accompanied commonly by drafts drawn by the seller upon the purchaser. This instrument was then "accepted" by the purchaser after receipt and approval of the goods and returned to the shipper, who could then discount the obligation with a lender. After the war the practice fell into disuse in favor of open-book credit, partly because of the reduction in the length of terms of trade and partly because the device reduced the flexibility of the seller-buyer relationship. As a result, trade acceptances are rarely used today in domestic transactions.

In the early years of the Federal Reserve System, there was an attempt to revive the trade acceptance. Since these instruments represented "self-liquidating," two-name paper and would tend to rise and fall in volume with the needs of trade, trade acceptances were made eligible for rediscounting at the Federal Reserve banks.

The trade acceptance technique differs from nonnotification accounts receivable financing chiefly in that a negotiable instrument evidences the debt, and in the fact that the purchaser of the goods recognizes that his debt is likely to be assigned to a third party.

Payments by customers are sent to the client, but he forwards these checks to the lender for deposit. The lender endorses the checks in code and credits the client's debt with the amount received. If individual invoices are not paid at maturity or by the expiration of an agreed-upon period past the due date, they must be repurchased by the borrower.

Rates are often cited as a fraction of 1 percent per day. Thus, one twenty-fifth of 1 percent per day is equal to about 15 percent per annum. But rates are also quoted on a per month or per annum basis. The lowest rate charged by finance companies in this area on new business at the present time is about 13 percent per annum. However, business often is done at 18 to 24 percent, and rates sometimes run even higher. Additional service charges, such as charges for audits, are also made in some cases.

In comparing these rates with typical bank charges, it should be kept in mind that accounts receivable financing involves no minimum deposit balance and that collections are credited against outstandings shortly after receipt, so that interest is charged only for the days that funds are actually in use by the borrower. The operation is somewhat similar to the overdraft system used by banks in certain British Commonwealth nations.

## *Checking Up on Clients*

Institutions lending on receivables take a number of precautions to protect themselves against losses. First, it is ascertained that a valid assignment of accounts has been made which will be honored in case of bankruptcy. Second, the percentage of the invoice advanced in cash is held to a point which permits a reasonable margin of safety to cover returns and allowances. Third, over-age accounts are held in a special collateral account or returned to the borrower and exchanged for fresh obligations. Fourth, the lender attempts to assure himself that the receivables are in fact the obligations that they purport to be. Fifth, the lender keeps a watchful eye on the borrower's over-all business conduct to minimize the risk of failure. These "policing" procedures account for the largest share of the expense of receivables lending on a nonnotification basis.

The National Commercial Finance Conference, the industry's trade association, provides a forum for the interchange of ideas and information with regard to financing techniques and the cooperative prevention of fraud. The prudent conduct of this type of financing requires a continuous checking of individual transactions and the over-all condition of borrowers.

Invoices, purchase orders, evidences of shipment and receipt are examined; individual accounts are continuously sampled and verified, using the stationery of a public accounting firm. Finally, surprise audits of the client's books are made frequently, at least every three months. This information helps the lender guard against fraud and improper practices such as excessive cash withdrawals, inventory speculation, or lax accounting procedures. The detailed view of the borrower's business that results may also provide the basis for constructive management advice.

## *Client Characteristics*

The larger commercial financial companies, including the big sales finance companies, which do a commercial finance business, often have branch offices and conduct operations which are national in scope. Subsidiaries may be acquired or created to handle special types of lending or to enable the companies to operate in certain states.

Nevertheless, access to nonnotification accounts receivable financing may be difficult for a smaller firm located a considerable distance from the major business centers. The need to make periodic calls upon clients can easily involve prohibitive expense in the case of small accounts. As in the case of other types of lending operations, large receivables loans can be handled more cheaply in proportion to size than small ones.

The lowest rates charged by large commercial finance companies pertain to clients selling $300,000 to $400,000 of goods annually, at the very least. Those companies which charge only one rate usually will not accept new clients who are not expected to generate business volume of this magnitude. Business firms producing a smaller volume of receivables must seek out or be directed to smaller finance companies.

As finance companies grow and attract larger clients, they often raise their cutoff points on size and reduce their charges, even during periods of rising interest rates.

## *Accounts Receivable Lending by Banks*

Commercial banks have made loans on open-book receivables for more than fifty years. However, it was not until the thirties that banks resorted to this kind of loan in large numbers. In part, this development stemmed from a desire to bolster the holdings of earning assets during a period of depressed business activity and, in part, from an enhanced desire to obtain adequately secured new loans.

Banks which engage in accounts receivable financing almost always use the nonnotification method. There are, however, a few banks which do a factoring business.

Most big city banks will make receivables loans under certain circumstances. A few banks, moreover, have specially trained personnel to handle such lending. Their methods of operation are similar to those of the finance companies. The cost of this type of credit, therefore, usually is higher than that on other bank loans. The effective rate may reflect a service charge similar to a factoring commission.

Even in large cities, there are many bankers who believe accounts receivable lending is not a suitable activity for a commercial bank. However, the number seems to have diminished. Banks commonly lend to commercial financial companies and sometimes participate with them in specified credits. During 1957 the Credit Policy Commission of the American Bankers Association issued a booklet entitled *Accounts Receivable Financing,* explaining the techniques for making receivables loans.

## *Will It Pay?*

Justification for the expense of either factoring or nonnotification accounts receivable financing is found in the effect upon the profits of the client. Aside from the saving in credit and collection expense, the client may be enabled to take cash discounts which he had previously passed up. Borrowing from a supplier on typical 2/10, net 30 terms means that the customer is, in effect, paying 2 percent for twenty days' credit—an effective rate of over 36 percent per annum. Perhaps more important, however, is the opportunity for a client to expand his volume on a small capital base.

Interest charges of any kind have two main components. These are (1) the pure interest rate, which can be represented by the yields on government securities, and (2) the compensation to the lender for exposure to risk. The last can be further divided into expected actual losses and the expense incurred to avoid loss.

The much broader spectrum of interest rates charged by finance companies, as compared with other lenders, is related largely to the expense incurred to avoid loss. Because of the existence of institutions such as commercial finance companies, funds are available to most business borrowers at *some* rate. Aside from the problems of borrower integrity and the possibility of a completely hopeless situation, there is no reason for an interest rate cutoff point on business lending if the cost can be justified on the basis of the borrower's earning potential.

In states where usury laws apply to both corporate and noncorporate business, accounts receivable financing is not done in the nonrecourse form. In such cases, finance companies may resort to outright purchase of the receivables, i.e., factoring, a process not subject to these laws.

Usury laws, nevertheless, limit the expansion of receivables lending. This is particularly true in the case of sole proprietorships and partnerships whose owners may have reasons for not converting to the corporate form.

Another obstacle to accounts receivable financing is present in states where there is legal uncertainty surrounding the making of valid, inequivocal assignments. This is often troublesome when buyers and sellers are located in different states. Even if legal problems do not prevent receivables financing, commercial banks may be deterred from entering the field, and costs of doing business may be increased.

## *A Steady Flow of Funds*

Accounts receivable financing permits undercapitalized business firms to obtain funds on a continuing basis. This money remains available so long as a firm is able to sell goods to customers whose financial standing is sufficiently strong. Ordinary bank loans also are often employed on a fairly permanent basis, if the lender is willing constantly to renew the credit.

The distinction between short- and long-term credit, therefore, is not clear-cut. Nevertheless, it is often maintained that there is an unsatisfied need for longer term loans on the part of smaller firms which are unable to place bonds in the capital markets.

Long-term loans on real estate or equipment are generally obtainable. In the absence of such collateral a request for longer term money must relate to term loans or debentures, instruments employed by firms with excellent credit ratings. Negotiation of unsecured intermediate- or long-term credit ordinarily is preceded by a number of years of successful operation. A relatively new firm or one that is growing rapidly typically faces a highly uncertain future. Injection of long-term funds into situations such as these involves a degree of risk which is usually associated with ownership capital.

Accounts receivable financing may enable a firm to increase its profits by generating a larger volume of sales on its capital investment. These additional earnings can be added to the net worth. Eventually, such an enterprise may qualify for unsecured bank credit. Finance companies expect to lose their more successful clients to the banks in the course of time, and banks which initiate a customer relationship on the security of receivables look forward to the time when the firm's financial position will justify the extension of unsecured credit.

Chapter 8

# Warehouse Receipts and Their Use in Financing*

By Robert W. Rogers

IN DECEMBER, 1957, a speech on "Warehouse Receipts and Their Use in Financing" was given to the Chicago Chapter of Robert Morris Associates and later published in the *Bulletin*. There is presently a great deal of interest in warehouse receipts due to the Salad Oil Scandal. This has resulted in a request to update the article for publication in the present issue of the *Bulletin*. The changes in the concepts for this type of financing since 1957 are minor, most of them being brought about by the adoption of the Uniform Commercial Code in an additional 27 states and the District of Columbia, whereas Pennsylvania was the only code state in 1957. The code is in effect now in 18 states and will be in effect in 10 more by 1965, with other states considering its adoption. However, the code, as it refers to warehousing, basically follows the Uniform Warehouse Receipts Act, adding the possible need for filing, as commented on later.

Warehouse receipts are used by most banks at one time or another; and despite the Salad Oil Scandal, it does not appear that their use will diminish. Warehouse receipts are regularly used in many industries—for example, the grain, butter, and egg businesses. Actually, warehousing of a sort goes back to biblical times, and even the three-ball practitioners might be considered warehouses of a sort.

---

*Reprinted by permission from *Bulletin of the Robert Morris Associates*, Vol. XLVI (April, 1964), pp. 317–27.

# Mechanics behind the Warehouse Receipt: The Warehouse Itself

In setting up the mechanics of a warehouse receipt loan, we must first have a warehouseman. The Uniform Warehouse Receipts Act defines a warehouseman as "a person lawfully engaged in the business of storing goods for profit." The definition by the Uniform Commercial Code is "a person engaged in the business of storing goods for hire." There is no practical difference between the two definitions. The warehouse itself may be organized under state or federal laws. Also, note the phrases "for profit" or "for hire," which will be referred to later.

## *Insurance, or Bonds*

You will often hear the term "bonded warehouse" rather loosely used. for the word "bonded" in itself falsely indicates protection that may not be there. The states and the federal government require warehousemen to carry a "bond" or an equivalent insurance policy, but we do know that some state-bonded warehouses actually are required to put up a bond of only $5,000, despite the fact that such warehouse may be holding goods valued in the hundreds of thousands of dollars. Consequently, the licensing or bonding does not necessarily guarantee the goodness or the validity of a warehouse receipt. Insurance covering both the warehouseman's legal liability and fidelity can be and sometimes is obtained by the warehouseman for protection of the warehouse receipt holder, and such insurance is often referred to as bonds. You should know the extent of such insurance carried by the warehouseman in relation to the total value of the merchandise stored by the warehouseman and the details of such insurance policies. Over the years, insurance companies have been adding exclusions in their policies; hence a certificate of insurance does not, by itself, show whether the warehouseman's liability, is fully covered.

## *Types of Warehouses*

Generally speaking, warehouses can be divided into three classifications, namely, (1) cold storage warehouses, which are for merchandise that must be refrigerated or frozen; (2) general merchandise warehouses, which are for merchandise that can be carried under normal temperature conditions (and this classification would include the well-known grain elevators); and (3) field warehouses, the details of which will be covered later. Certain warehouses under classifications (1) and (2) are under the supervision of a related commodity exchange. Such receipts are "deliverable" on futures contracts of an exchange and should be obtained when loaning on a "hedged" commodity.

The first two types of warehouses, cold storage and general merchandise warehouses, are normally located in population centers and may also be called terminal warehouses. These warehousemen generally own the buildings which constitute the warehouses. Consequently, the merchandise must be moved to these warehouses for storage, and location becomes an important factor in the selection of the warehouse. The first type of warehouse is used quite generally by most companies handling merchandise which needs refrigeration or needs to be kept in a frozen condition. General merchandise warehouses are used by all types of concerns; and generally, location of the warehouse and/or the lack of adequate storage by the owners of the merchandise are influencing factors for their use.

## *Warehouseman's Protection for the Lender*

Since the receipt that the warehouseman issues is no better than the warehouseman himself, it is most important that you have full information on the warehouse company before granting loans against the receipts that such warehouseman may issue. You should determine that it is a bona fide warehouse. It is most important that the management be experienced and have a good record in warehousing operations. It must know how to handle the type of merchandise stored with it. The warehouse company should be in a sound financial condition and, as indicated, should carry adequate warehouseman's legal liability insurance and adequate fidelity bonds on the warehouse employees. Financial information on the warehouse company should be obtained, as well as copies of both types of insurance. The insurance company should be notified that you have an interest in the policy through issuance of a certificate of insurance, so that you will receive prior notice if cancellation of the insurance takes place. If the warehouse should be unable to deliver the merchandise called for under the warehouse receipts, you would then have claim against the warehouseman; and his ability to meet such claim would depend on a combination of his insurance and his own financial position.

This point is well illustrated by the record of a former warehouse company in Florida. This company was originally in the merchandise warehouse business but later set up a field-warehousing operation. The company quoted rates on field-warehousing operations much below the rates of its competitors and thereby obtained a considerable amount of business in the state of Florida. The financial position of the warehouse company was generally satisfactory, although its worth represented only a comparatively small percentage of the many millions of dollars of merchandise against which the company had issued warehouse receipts. Due to low rates charged on field-warehousing operations, the company carried only modest insurance and could afford to make only a very limited number of audits on its various field-warehousing locations. Our bank held its receipts at one time but accepted them only after insisting upon a very substantial increase in its warehouseman's legal liability and its fidelity insurance. A few years later, after we no longer had its receipts and the insurance had reverted to smaller amounts, a citrus operation in Florida became insolvent. A number of banks and industrial concerns held receipts issued by this warehouse for the insolvent concern, and it was found that only a small proportion of the merchandise called for by the receipts was actually in the warehouses. The receipt holders had a claim against the warehouse company; but with woefully inadequate insurance and limited net worth, the ultimate loss to the holders of such warehouse receipts exceeded $750,000.

## *Subsidiary Warehouse Offers No Protection*

There is a type of warehousing known as "subsidiary warehousing." Quite often a subsidiary warehousing operation will be proposed by a borrower who wishes to avoid the relatively moderate costs of outside warehousing. A subsidiary warehouse may well be licensed but actually is owned or controlled by the storer of the merchandise, either as a part of his own operation or as a subsidiary. While the warehouse can be legally licensed, it does not pass the other test of a warehouse, "engaged in the business of storing goods for hire." The subsidiary warehouse is engaged in storing its own goods, and the receipts from such subsidiary warehouses will not protect the lender from third-party claims. In other words, such receipts are worthless as collateral. It is permissible for a bona fide warehouseman to issue receipts against his own commodities, and it is often done in the grain trade. However, such warehouseman must likewise actually store merchandise for others for a fee; and unless the storage of his own merchandise and the issuance of receipts thereon be only a relatively small part of his business, you are exposed to the dangers of subsidiary warehousing. Likewise, you will note that such merchandise is not in the hands of third parties but is under the control of the borrower, eliminating one of the real advantages of legitimate warehousing.

State laws and the supervision given to warehouses by the individual states vary widely. Therefore, it is necessary to know the warehousing laws under which a state-licensed warehouse is organized, the bonds required, and the supervision actually exercised. For example, in an action on a statutory public grain warehouseman's bond, the U.S. Court of Appeals confirmed a judgment in favor of the defendant insurance company, stating that

> holders of warehouse receipts, which were illegal under Illinois law in that they purported to cover grain owned by the warehouseman but did not state on their faces that the grain involved belonged to the warehouseman and was *stored in a separate bin,* were charged with knowledge of such illegality and were not "holders of receipts for such grain" within the provisions of the statutory warehouseman's bond.

Therefore, there was no protection from the issuance for such warehouse receipts.

## *The Field Warehouse Can Be Effective*

The field warehouse is a comparative newcomer to the field, having really come into its own in the last thirty-five years, although it has been in operation for a much longer time. The field warehouse differs from the terminal warehouse in that the warehouse itself is taken to the location of the merchandise. This is accomplished by a field warehouseman selecting a location on or in the borrower's premises, leasing the space, properly recording such lease, and qualifying the location as a public warehouse. Access to the merchandise must be limited to the field warehouseman's representatives; and he must have continuous, exclusive, and notorious possession of the merchandise. This is obtained by segregating the merchandise to be warehoused into the leased space and then keeping the area under lock and key. Signs are posted giving adequate notice to any person visiting the premises that a warehouse of said field warehouse company exists in such space and that the merchandise therein is in the legal possession of the warehouse company. The representative of the field warehouse company on the premises is known as the custodian and is usually a former employee of the borrower who has been taken into the employ of the field warehouse company. While this particular part of the operation was under question at one time, it has since been fully cleared by the courts. The custodian is bonded for fidelity, and the minimum figure for a field warehouse custodian should probably be not less than $100,000. The auditors of the field warehouse make periodic inspections of the warehouse, and the maximum time between such visits is from 60 to 90 days. In addition, the warehouse receipt holder should make his own inspection of the warehouse from time to time to determine that the warehouse is being conducted properly, that the merchandise is properly segregated and actually is the quantity and quality of merchandise "said to be" represented by the warehouse receipt. These operations are bona fide warehouses; and if properly set up and operated, the same protection is afforded the warehouse receipt holder as is provided by any comparable terminal warehouse operation. The well-known field-warehousing companies now operate on a national basis and carry substantial bonds for both warehouseman's legal liability and fidelity. The Salad Oil Scandal has pointed up the need to know the details and the adequacy of insurance to protect against dishonesty of the principal, or so-called "owner," of the merchandise.

The field warehouse has the advantage of being able to operate on the borrower's premises and consequently changes the borrower's operations only slightly. The facilities of the borrower may be used for handling the merchandise, and said merchandise is readily available to the borrower, *subject* to the release of said merchandise by the holder of the receipt. Where nonnegotiable receipts are held, full control over the authority to release the merchandise should be maintained.

Probably the minimum dollar amount which can be economically handled under a field warehouse operation is $25,000. At this level the borrower would be paying the equivalent of 2 percent more for his money as the cost for the warehousing. This gradually reduces to about seven eighths of 1 percent when the value of the merchandise reaches the $1 million level.

## The Warehouse Receipt Itself

Now that we have our warehouse all set up and approved, what about the receipts that are issued? The receipt itself can take literally any form, provided said receipt contains within its printed or written form the nine terms required by the Uniform Warehouse Receipts Act or the same nine terms as required by the Uniform Commercial Code. We have had some queer-looking documents presented to us as warehouse receipts; but on applying the test of these nine terms, they have proven to be true warehouse receipts. I could enumerate these items, but I am sure you would not remember them, and they are available to you in any copy of the Uniform Warehouse Receipts Act or the Uniform Commercial Code.

What value does the warehouse receipt itself provide the lender? The warehouse receipt is a document of title as contrasted to a lien, which, for example, may be obtained through a chattel mortgage. Do not let that document of title mislead you too much, for in the case of trouble you cannot just walk in and take over. However, I know of no case where a warehouse was properly operated in which the courts have not ultimately granted proper rights to the holder of the warehouse receipt. Again, may I point out that by use of a warehouse receipt the merchandise is placed in the hands of a responsible third party, with the exception of certain situations where the warehouseman owns the merchandise himself.

## *The Types of Warehouse Receipts*

There are two types of receipts issued, namely, negotiable and nonnegotiable. A nonnegotiable receipt must have clearly marked on its face the words "nonnegotiable" or "not negotiable," so that the distinction is readily apparent. A negotiable warehouse receipt is, as it implies, a negotiable document and, as such, has the attributes of negotiable paper. However, there is the inherent disadvantage that a negotiable receipt must be presented to the warehouseman before partial or full delivery of the merchandise represented by the receipt can be made. Likewise, it must be as carefully handled as any other negotiable document; and if it is lost, it can be replaced only after an appropriate bond has been posted.

Most of the warehouse receipts issued to banks, outside of receipts representing grain and other hedgable commodities, are nonnegotiable receipts. These receipts are issued in the name of the lender; and while they may be transferred or assigned, they generally are not. They can always be exchanged for a negotiable receipt if one is later desired. A nonnegotiable receipt itself need not be surrendered in case of a partial or full release of the merchandise, but such release is normally made in writing to the warehouseman. The release can also be made verbally in case of emergency with subsequent written confirmation. In view of this, the mechanical handling from the lender's standpoint is greatly simplified.

## *Certain Inherent Weaknesses in Receipts*

The warehouse receipt does have certain weaknesses which must be guarded against, and I should like to point out a few of these. In particular, I should like to emphasize again that the receipt itself is no better than the warehouseman who has issued it. The receipt does not provide insurance for fire, windstorm, and extended coverage unless it is so stated on the face of the receipt itself. For this protection on the merchandise, the borrower normally takes out an insurance policy and provides a loss payable clause in favor of the lender as a rider to the policy. You should realize that all charges of the warehouseman represent a prior lien on the merchandise; and as a consequence, it is important that the warehouse receipt holder knows that the charges of the warehouse are currently paid. The warehouse receipt cannot convey to a holder a title any better than the title held by the storer of the merchandise.

This question of title becomes more important in code states due to the comparative ease with which liens on inventory can be obtained under the code. As a result, there could be more occasions now than formerly in which questions of priority of lien or conflict may arise. Section 7–503(1) of the code does provide some protection for a warehouse receipt holder against a claim of prior lien, but it does not remove the danger. It is our belief that a financing statement should be filed and a security agreement obtained in a code state in all cases where loans are made against the pledge of nonnegotiable warehouse receipts. The state having jurisdiction is determined by the physical location of the merchandise as well as the location of the office of the borrower; and this could result in filing in two or more states. The filing provides several benefits, including avoiding questions of sufficiency of required field warehousemen's "possession" of the goods, assuring notice of later arising liens from "purchase money security interest," and helping solve or avoid questions under Section 7–503.

## *What Does the Receipt Stand for?*

It is most important to realize that the warehouse receipt is a receipt for a specific quantity of items "said to be" or "said to contain." The warehouseman makes no guarantee of the quality or contents of the items and takes no responsibility for the value of the merchandise stored with him. For example, one of the finance companies a few years ago had a loan secured by field warehouse receipts for lumber. The warehouse receipts listed so many board feet of lumber "said to be" No. 2 grade. On the basis of the price for No. 2 lumber, the finance company made a loan of approximately 80 percent of the market. After default by the borrower the finance company learned that the lumber was No. 4 grade rather than No. 2 and its value was only about 50 percent of the amount of the loan. The warehouseman had no responsibility or liability for the difference in the grade of lumber, and the loss was taken by the finance company with no recourse to the warehouseman. This point emphasizes the need for character in your borrower, even though your loans are secured by merchandise represented by warehouse receipts. Cans of oil may be cans of water, or barrels of flour may be barrels of sand. It should now be added that tanks of vegetable oil can be empty or full of salt water. You can protect yourself to a degree by obtaining a grading certificate on the merchandise pledged, by having an expert check the merchandise, or by spot sampling, but these methods still would not be sufficient to protect you from a crook. The so-called "Salad Oil Scandal" has now given full and notorious emphasis to this point.

## The Merchandise Covered by Warehouse Receipts

Now we have a warehouseman, and we know something about the receipts he is going to issue to the lender. What about the merchandise that is to secure the loan? This can be anything, including the proverbial soup to nuts: We have had them both. At one time, forty distinct types of items were identified as having been used as collateral under warehouse receipts for loans from our bank. I am sure the total is higher now.

### *Some Merchandise May Be Hedged*

The type of merchandise pledged can be classified under two general headings, namely, merchandise which may be hedged and all the rest which cannot be hedged. By hedged merchandise, I am referring to the possibility of hedging against the risk of price fluctuations on the futures market for such items as grain, butter, eggs, and cotton. If the merchandise pledged is hedged at all times, the lender can safely advance 85 to 90 percent of the hedge price. Loans of this type have their own special problems and in most larger banks are handled by specialists in that field. Unfortunately, time does not permit going into any detail on this type of warehouse receipt loan; but it should be emphasized that receipts, usually negotiable, which are deliverable on the exchange on which the commodity is hedged are the most desirable to hold as collateral for such loans. Protection is provided by hedging the commodity held under other receipts, but the risks are increased.

### *Usually, It Cannot Be Hedged*

Actually, the lending officers of a bank are most likely to come into contact with loans secured by commodities which cannot be hedged. There are many types of companies which borrow regularly against merchandise that cannot be hedged. The ideal type of borrower in this classification is the seasonal borrower who uses a secured loan because the peak of his needs is high in relation to his financial position but who can pay out annually due to the seasonal swing of inventories. The seasonal food processors or companies manufacturing a Christmas item would come under this category. For growing concerns and for companies whose financial position has deteriorated, the warehouse receipt loan against commodities that cannot be hedged is often used to provide protection for the lender. Such loans can provide satisfactory protection but are not nearly so desirable as the seasonal loans, for the borrowings are liable to become rather permanent in nature.

## *Why Margins Are Necessary*

The question is often asked as to how much may be advanced on a given item which is pledged under warehouse receipts. To answer this, an accurate appraisal of the market for such item must first be made. If your loan is on special tools, their market value in case of failure of your borrower may be only the scrap iron value. However, if the merchandise is a standard, recognized item, such as canned peas, the lender can safely use the quoted market price as the basis for the loan. You must of course know whether or not the market for the item is stable and if it is currently high or low, historically speaking. Depending on the market and other considerations subsequently mentioned, loans on unhedged commodities generally are made from 50 percent to a maximum of 80 percent of the market on which the bank would have to sell the merchandise if it were taken over to satisfy the loan. I might say that an 80 percent loan is on the high side, and the market for the item should be particularly favorable if a loan of that large a percentage is granted.

Why have a margin? You all know that the margin must provide for a market decline in the value of the collateral. We have also noted that warehouse charges are a prior lien against the merchandise, and these warehouse charges will often build up when a borrower gets into financial trouble. Incidentally, to protect against this in the case of a field warehouse company, we ask that copies of the invoices covering warehouse charges be mailed to us. There is another factor which is not quite so generally realized, that is, the amount of money it will cost the lender actually to liquidate the merchandise in case it becomes necessary for the lender to do so. One of the field warehouse companies a few years ago undertook the job of liquidating an inventory of canned foods under ideal conditions; that is, everyone concerned was in agreement and cooperating so that there were no extra legal costs, delays, or other problems. The direct expenses of the warehouse company in liquidating this inventory of canned foods ran just about 10 percent of the sales proceeds. These expenses were for warehouse labor, brokerage, loading merchandise, insurance, and the like. Consequently, in most unhedged items, you can figure that if you are loaning 90 percent of the market, you are actually loaning 100 percent of the net amount you can realize from the sale of the merchandise based on the current market price, and you have no leeway for a decline in the market or for lower prices which usually occur in case of distress selling. Our bank does a great deal of financing in the canning industry, and we customarily advance 60 to 65 percent of the market. This margin has proven sufficient in all cases in which it has been tested to date. In case of financial difficulties of a borrower, it is always desirable to have sufficient margin available to assure full payment of the loan *and* to have some left over for the other creditors. It is amazing what fine cooperation is received from a trustee in bankruptcy and/or from creditors if they can expect to receive something from your collateral after your loan is paid.

## *Guaranteed Markets and Special Handling*

There are situations where a guaranteed market can be obtained or created for the item against which the loan is to be made. With a guaranteed market at a fixed price, up to 90 percent of the established price can be safely advanced, but no more. This guarantee often takes the form of a purchase contract for merchandise produced for a specific buyer. Take, for example, lawn mowers, which are generally sold in a short period of time but may be produced at a lower cost if they can be manufactured over twelve months. Consequently, to benefit from such lower costs, a purchaser of the lawn mowers could guarantee to take said lawn mowers at a specified price and by a specified time, thereby creating for the lender a guaranteed market. A financially responsible buyer is also a necessary ingredient in establishing a good guarantee.

It was mentioned that the warehouse receipt does not guarantee quality, and because of this the lender must know the special storage characteristics of the merchandise to be pledged and how long such merchandise will maintain its quality under those conditions. If you are loaning on frozen foods, you should know that the quality starts to deteriorate in from six months to a year, whereas most canned foods will hold their quality for a number of years. Some items take special handling or controlled humidity as well as temperature. The U.S. government learned about this matter of special handling to its chagrin during World War II when evaporated milk was being stored in government warehouses. The government did not realize that evaporated milk must be turned at least once a month or the fat will separate and solidify. Failure to turn the milk resulted in a large quantity of solidified and spoiled evaporated milk.

## In Conclusion: The Three C's of Credit Are Most Important

In covering some of the high points of warehouse receipt financing, I have made only one mention of the three C's of credit. You must have *character* just as much in this type of loan as in an unsecured credit, and perhaps more so, for the shortage of adequate funds indicated by this type of financing creates additional temptations to a weak character. A dishonest character should be added here to take in the salad oil situation. There must be the *capacity* of the borrower to move the merchandise and therefrom create the cash to pay off the loan; it is much easier to stay in the banking business than it is to get into the merchandising business. There must also be sufficient *capital* supplemented by funds available through the warehouse receipt loan and other sources to carry out the proposed program, or the lender may be faced with increasing his loan, and perhaps the percentage of advance, to an undesirable level in order to avoid closing down an operation in the middle of a season.

Should you ever have occasion to use warehouse receipt financing in your banking career, you will find it an excellent vehicle, provided the loan is set up properly in the first instance and that you know the risks and pitfalls which need to be avoided in this type of financing. Certainly, it is no different in this respect than any other type of loan you may make.

*Chapter 9*

# *Term Lending by New York City Banks**

By George Budzeika

THE GROWTH in term lending to business by commercial banks in recent years has stimulated lively discussion regarding the significance of this practice for the economy and its meaning for the role of commercial banks in the financial structure. In view of this interest, the Federal Reserve Bank of New York in 1960 initiated the gathering of current statistics on the volume of New York City bank term loans, for publication on a weekly basis. The purpose of this article is to describe these statistics and to indicate what they add to our knowedge of term lending.

## *Sources of Statistical Information*

Statistics on the volume and characteristics of term loans have always been rather sketchy. The principal sources of information are the commercial loan surveys conducted by the Federal Reserve System as of a single day in late 1946, 1955, and 1957 and a few earlier surveys of more limited scope conducted by the Federal Reserve and other oganizations. Apart from the new data to be presented here, current information on the volume of term loans is provided only by the *Quarterly Financial Report for Manufacturing Corporations* compiled jointly by the Federal

---

*Reprinted by permission from Federal Reserve Bank of New York, *Essays in Money and Credit* (New York, 1964), pp. 62–66.

This article is reprinted—with certain revisions required to bring it up to date as of April, 1964—from the February, 1961, issue of this Bank's *Monthly Review*.

Trade Commission and the Securities and Exchange Commission from corporate records. Although this *Report* is most valuable for many purposes, it is confined to only one sector of business and contains no information on the volume or structure of term lending by particular categories of banks.

In view of the growing importance of term loans in the lending activities of commercial banks, this bank has for some time been collecting term loan data for New York City banks on a regular basis. Since January 27, 1960, the nine largest New York City banks have been reporting weekly a breakdown of their total volume of business loans outstanding according to the business of the borrower and the maturity of the loan. Loans with an original maturity of one year or under are classified as short-term and those having a maturity of more than one year as term loans. The banks have also been reporting weekly figures for loan extensions and repayments, broken down into the same categories.[1]

## *What Is a "Term" Loan?*

A bank loan has many dimensions, such as purpose, maturity, collateral, method of repayment, type of borrower, etc. Two of these—purpose and maturity—are usually employed to identify term loans. The view underlying the new statistics is that "term" loans are long-term loans to business firms for business purposes; consequently, a loan is recorded as a term loan if it is a business loan with an original maturity longer than one year. This definition, however, does not cover all the types of loans that might be regarded as term loans for particular analytical purposes. The various categories of loans that might be defined as term loans, and the extent to which they are covered by the new statistics, are discussed below.

*Ordinary Term Loans.* These are business loans with an original maturity of more than one year and repayable in a lump sum or in periodic installments. Such loans typically are based on a formal loan agreement containing the terms and conditions of credit extension as well as various provisions regarding the administration of the loan and the financial conduct of the debtor. These loans constitute the bulk of the loans in the "maturity of more than one year" category carried in the new statistics.

---

[1]Reports cover the statement week ended the previous Wednesday and are available each Tuesday morning in the *New York Herald-Tribune.* Loan totals in the release, covering nine banks, differ by small amounts from the business loan totals for the fourteen weekly reporting member banks in New York City that are published in the weekly condition report each Friday morning.

*Bank Credit Extended under Revolving Credit Agreements.* Such loans may technically be classified as short-term business loans, because the notes evidencing the debt are of short-term maturity, typically 90 days. The loan agreement, however, permits the borrower to renew the note at maturity for the next 90-day period, and so on, with the credits remaining on the books for periods as long as two years or more. Since the borrower enjoys a long-term use of credit, such loans therefore might also be classified as term loans.

In the data now being collected for the City banks, bank loans extended under revolving credit agreements are counted as term loans (although it might eventully be desirable to have such loans reported separately). The commercial loan surveys of 1955 and 1957 did not classify revolving credits as term loans unless the original maturity of the note evidencing the debt was more than one year; consequently, the new data are not fully comparable to the loan survey figures.

*Continuously Renewed Short-Term Loans.* As is generally known, many short-term loans are in effect term loans because they are more or less routinely renewed whenever they come to maturity. These loans, therefore, are in some ways similar to loans extended under revolving credit agreements; the major difference is the lack of a formal agreement. Because of the difficulty of segregating continuously renewed short-term loans in bank records, however, these loans are not classified as term loans or otherwise identified in the new statistics on term loans.

*Business Loans Secured by Real Estate.* Business firms often borrow from banks on a pledge of business property. A significant portion of such loans is of long-term maturity, and the proceeds are typically used to finance capital expenditures or additions to permanent working capital. They might, therefore, be regarded as term loans and were so counted in the commercial loan surveys of 1955 and 1957. For call report purposes and in the weekly reporting bank statistics, however, business loans secured by real estate are classified as real estate loans. The new statistics exclude such loans entirely, but this is of minor significance because such loans by New York City banks account for a relatively small proportion of all their business loans.

## *The City Banks and the National Term Loan Market*

Term lending generally plays a more important role at the large New York City banks than at other banks, whether measured by the importance of such loans in loan portfolios or by the share these banks hold of the national term loan market. Term loans presently constitute more than one half of all business loan volume at the New York City banks, while at other member banks the proportion is only about two fifths. Similarly, the share of the City banks in the term loan aggregate for all member banks is roughly one third, although their share in total assets amounts to only about one sixth.

The greater importance of term loans at New York City banks largely reflects the fact that the City banks service large customers located throughout the country and abroad. At all City banks, such large customers account for a significant portion, and at a few of them for the bulk of the bank's business. Since these national business firms have a substantial demand for long-term funds, the City banks with their large capital have wider opportunities, and are under heavier competitive pressure, to extend term loans than many banks located elsewhere.

Another factor that affects the extent of the banks' term lending activities is their preference regarding the types of long-term loans in their portfolios. At the majority of banks outside New York a significant proportion of all assets is invested in real estate loans of medium- or long-term maturity. At the City banks, real estate loans of all kinds are much less significant; they amounted, as of December, 1963, to about 4 percent of total assets for the nine large City banks taken together, compared with about 13 percent at all member banks outside New York.

The composition of liabilities of the City banks may also have a significant impact on their term lending activities. However, the influence of this factor may differ among the banks, reflecting divergences in the composition of their liabilities. Thus, banks that have relatively larger amounts of savings-type deposits might be more inclined to extend term loans. In addition, the large number of checking accounts, business and other, held by some City banks may make them less vulnerable to sharp fluctuations in individual balances and impart a measure of stability and predictability to their reserve positions that may encourage longer term lending. On the other hand, banks whose deposits consist predominantly of the balances of large business firms or correspondent banks, which are considerably more volatile than most other types of deposits, may tend to be more restrained in their term lending activities.

The importance of large borrowers in the New York term loan market is reflected in the heavy concentration of these loans held by a few industry groups. The bulk of City bank term loans (in dollar terms) is extended to borrowers in basic industries characterized by the predominance of relatively large firms, as can be seen in Figure 1. As of April, 1964, the petroleum, chemicals, coal, and rubber industries accounted for about 29 percent of the total; public utilities, 25 percent; and the metals and metal products industries, about 21 percent. The remaining loans were distributed among the various other industries with no significant concentration in any one group. At member banks outside New York City the total share of the three basic borrower groups—petroleum-chemicals, metals, and public utilities—in term loans is only about 40 percent; about 20 percent is accounted for by trade industries, 15 percent by manufacturing industries other than metals and petroleum-chemicals, and the rest by still other borrowers.[2]

FIGURE 1

DISTRIBUTION OF TERM LOANS AT LARGE NEW YORK CITY BANKS, BY INDUSTRY, APRIL 29, 1964

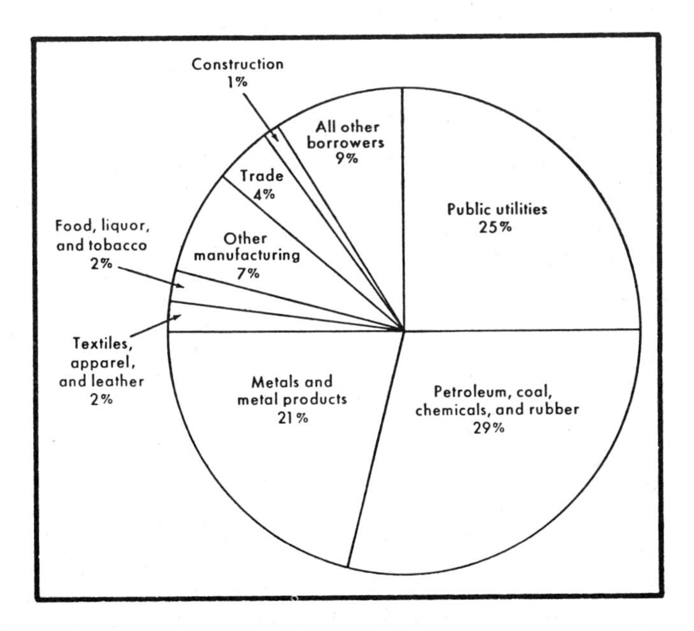


Moreover, the total share of the three major groups in New York City term loans generally tended to increase in the 1955–64 period, mainly reflecting rapid growth in term borrowing by the metals group. Over the same period the volume of loans to some other industry groups actually declined; loans outstanding to the textiles, apparel, and leather group fell by one third between 1957 and 1964.

The concentration of term lending by the City banks is also reflected in the shares of these banks within the national totals for the various

[2]While the figures for outside New York City refer to October, 1957, the latest date for which the national figures are available, it is unlikely that the basic difference in the structure of term lending between New York City and other banks has been significantly affected by subsequent developments.

industries. In October, 1957, the City banks held, for instance, about 60 percent of all member bank term loans to the petroleum-chemicals as well as to the public utilities group, compared with an over-all share of the City banks in member bank term loans of 38 percent. Firms in the textiles, apparel, and leather group also obtain a substantial portion (more than one half in 1957) of their long-term bank funds from the large New York City banks. On the other hand, the City banks' share in nationwide term loans to metal fabricators in 1957 was 39 percent, approximately the same as their share in the over-all total; while the trade, service, construction, and manufacturing industries other than metals, petroleum-chemicals, and textiles obtain in New York only a limited portion of their long-term bank funds—about 20 percent, according to the 1957 data.

## *Trends in New York City Term Loans, 1955–64*

Term loans at New York City banks rose from $3.5 billion in October, 1955, to $6.8 billion in April, 1964. (All such figures collected after January, 1960, are adjusted for seasonal variations.) Most of the rise took place during 1955–57, a period of rapid business expansion; in these two years the dollar volume of term loans rose by about 50 percent. The trend of term lending during the subsequent 1957–58 recession is not clear, because adequate data are not available for these years. Between October, 1957, and February, 1960, however, the City banks' term loans rose from $5.2 billion to $5.7 billion, a rise of roughly 10 percent.[3] Thereafter the volume of term loans leveled off and remained virtually unchanged until October, 1961, when the upward trend was resumed and lasted for more than two years. By April, 1964, the term loan volume at New York City banks had reached $6.8 billion, about 20 percent more than during 1960–61 (see Figure 2).

There is evidence that conversion of short-term loans into formal term loans may have been of importance in the growth of term borrowing by some industries, notably the metals and metal products and the

[3]These figures probably overstate somewhat the actual increase due to differences in the coverage of the commercial loan surveys and the presently collected data on term loans. The latter source includes revolving credits as term loans, while the former does not. An alternative source of information on term loans—long-term bank indebtedness by manufacturing corporations as reported by the FTC-SEC—shows a rise in term loans till March, 1958, followed by a 4 percent drop between March, 1958, and March, 1959, after which the rise resumed. For the late 1957 to early 1960 period, referred to above, there was a 7 percent increase.

FIGURE 2

TERM AND SHORT-TERM LOANS AT LARGE NEW YORK CITY BANKS*

*Data plotted are seasonally adjusted monthly averages of Wednesday figures.

public utilities groups. Thus, term loans to the metals group advanced by $310 million between October, 1957, and October, 1959, a rise of about 40 percent, while short-term loans to this industry declined by about $360 million, or some 30 percent.[4] In the preceding two-year period, from October, 1955, to October, 1957, these short-term loans had more than doubled. A similar pattern in short-term and term loan movements, although much less pronounced, also was observed in borrowings by public utilities.

The shift from short-term to term loans may have happened in two related ways. A number of large corporations are said to have financed their substantial capital expenditures of 1955–57 partially by borrowing from commercial banks with the intention of refinancing later through bond or equity flotations. The available statistics on sources and uses of corporate funds, however, show little evidence of such refinancing, and a substantial part of these term loans may have remained on the books.

[4]The figures for October, 1959, were estimated by extending "backward" the January, 1960, outstandings on the basis of partial loan extension and repayment data available for 1959. The October, 1959, estimates were needed to obtain figures that could be compared with the October, 1957, data, since short-term loans usually show large seasonal fluctuations.

In addition, some short-term loans that were actually "continuous" loans, in practice renewed routinely at maturity, may have been converted into formal term loans.

The leveling-off in term loans of the City banks during 1960–61 appears to reflect at least two major factors. First, there were indications that some City banks deliberately curtailed long-term loan extensions. Second, the demand for such loans apparently declined during 1960, reflecting the easing of business conditions, as well as the accompanying easing of the capital market and liquidity of the corporate sector. The recession-induced leveling-off in term loans during 1960–61 lasted somewhat longer than the recession itself. In fact, the upward trend was not resumed before October, 1961, some eight months after the cyclical upturn in over-all business activity.

As a result of the rise in the City banks' term loans between 1955 and 1964, the share of term loans in the business loan portfolios of these banks has increased significantly (see Table 1). In October, 1955, the City banks' term loans accounted for 47 percent of all their outstanding business loans; but by October, 1957, the ratio had grown to 51 percent. During this period, both term and short-term loans rose substan-

TABLE 1

BUSINESS LOANS AT LARGE NEW YORK CITY BANKS BY MATURITY AND MAJOR BORROWER GROUPS, SELECTED DATES*

| *Type of Loan* | *Oct. 5, 1955* | *Oct. 16, 1957* | *Oct. 14, 1959* | *Oct. 11, 1961* | *Oct. 9, 1963* |
|---|---|---|---|---|---|
| | *In Billions of Dollars* | | | | |
| All business loans | 7.4 | 10.4 | 10.0 | 10.3 | 11.3 |
| Short-term loans | 3.9 | 5.1 | 4.4 | 4.7 | 4.8 |
| Term loans | 3.5 | 5.2 | 5.7 | 5.5 | 6.6 |
| Metals and metal products | 0.4 | 0.8 | 1.1 | 1.1 | 1.3 |
| Petroleum, chemicals, coal, rubber | 1.0 | 1.7 | 1.5 | 1.5 | 2.0 |
| Transportation, communication, and other public utilities | 1.0 | 1.7 | 1.9 | 1.7 | 1.7 |
| All other | 1.0 | 1.2 | 1.3 | 1.3 | 1.6 |
| | *In Percent* | | | | |
| Ratio of term to all classified business loans | 47 | 51 | 57 | 54 | 58 |

*Because of rounding, figures do not necessarily add to totals. Figures for October 14, 1959, are partially estimated. All figures are unadjusted for seasonal variations. The coverage of short-term and term loans for 1959 and thereafter differs from that for 1955 and 1957 (see text). Loans to nonbank financial institutions are excluded from all figures.

*Sources:* Commercial loan surveys, 1955 and 1957; weekly reports to the Federal Reserve Bank of New York, 1959–63.

tially, but the rise in term loans was more rapid. Over the following two-year period, from October, 1957, to October, 1959, the proportion of term loans at City banks grew even faster, to reach an estimated 57 percent of total business loans in October, 1959. This, however, was caused mainly by a decline of 15 percent in short-term loans, while term loans continued to rise (although more slowly than before). The four-year rise in the share of term loans was reversed during 1960, with the proportion of term to total business loans dipping to 54 percent by October, 1961. This reversal, however, was temporary and was followed by a rise that brought the proportion of term loans in the City banks' business loan total to 58 percent by the end of 1963, or one percentage point higher than the 1959 high.

## *Conclusions*

The developments in term lending by banks during 1955–64 provide strong evidence that commercial banks are an important source for long-term funds to finance capital expenditures by industry. Since capital expenditures by business are the major and often also the most volatile factor in the growth of the economy, the commercial banks' ability and willingness to finance these expenditures are important elements to be considered in the analysis of business trends.

Many observers believe that the evolution of the term loan in the past quarter century has filled a real gap in the field of business finance. Term credit is said to be granted in many instances to small businesses that do not have ready access to the capital market. Moreover, for large business firms, borrowing from banks may often be a quicker, cheaper, and more convenient means of raising long-term funds, particularly in the five- to eight-year maturity range, than flotations of bonds or equities in the capital markets. Bank term loans can be tailored to individual borrower needs through direct negotiations with the lending bank, thus giving the borrower more leeway in determining the repayment schedules and permitting more efficient use of the loan proceeds.

The expansion of term loans, however, also entails certain drawbacks. After all, the primary function of commercial banks, whose principal liabilities are deposits withdrawable on demand, remains the meeting of short-term credit needs. For certain types of long-term lending, at least, other lenders (including individual investors) may sometimes be in a better position to judge and carry the risks involved. To the extent, moreover, that individual commercial banks engage in the extension of long-term loans to business firms, they lose a degree of flexibility in the management of their loan and investment portfolios, since term loans are not readily "shiftable." Furthermore, the conversion of a large proportion of business loans into term loans by the commercial banking system as a whole may "freeze" these funds for prolonged periods of time and thereby deprive other borrowers, who may possess no other sources of credit than their banks, of access to short-term funds. The rapid shifting of resources in a dynamic economy, in the course of which new credit demands spring up in unexpected areas, requires that financial institutions preserve some freedom of maneuver in their operations.

Clearly, it would be undesirable for the growth of the share of term loans in total loans to continue indefinitely. On the other hand, there is no single yardstick, such as the ratio of term to all business loans, by which the "appropriate" amount of term lending can be gaged. As mentioned earlier, many other factors, such as the composition of a bank's other assets, the composition and volatility of its deposits, the size of its capital, and the kinds of customers it has, must be considered. The term loan statistics gathered since 1960 will contribute, it is hoped, to increased awareness and understanding of these issues.

*Chapter* 10

# *A Critical Look at Lease Financing**

By Donald R. Gant

LEASE FINANCING has experienced a tremendous growth during the post-war period, not only in terms of volume but also in the diversity of the applications to which the technique of leasing has been adapted. Beginning with the sale and leaseback of real estate, we have more recently witnessed the emergence of equipment leasing on a large scale, giving impetus to the formation of a great number of specialized leasing companies. It seems safe to say that it is now possible for a company of sufficient credit standing to lease literally any type of capital asset it may require.

In fact, there recently appeared an announcement by one company of what it called "a new milestone in American business finance." This turned out to be a program under which qualified applicants can lease money. The announcement pointed out that the major advantage which this program offered over equipment leasing was that the lessee was not restricted to a specific piece of equipment. He could use the leased capital to purchase any item of equipment he wanted, or he could invest it in inventory or receivables.

Now, few readers will see anything "new" in this proposition. Most will have been engaged in this same practice for a long time, but under a different name.

This merely emphasizes the point made earlier—that there is very little that is different or new about lease financing. It represents merely an adaptation of more conventional forms of financing.

---

*Reprinted by permission from *Controller,* Vol. XXIX (June, 1961), pp. 274–77, 311–12.

Before proceeding further, let us establish a common understanding of the types of lease arrangements which this discussion will encompass. The term "leasing" is an extremely broad one which includes a great number of transactions which are outside the scope of these remarks. The type of transactions which they will have reference to come under the heading of "lease financing," since they involve the use of the lease as an alternative method of financing the acquisition of assets where ownership is another practicable alternative.

This would exclude such things as the leasing of office space in metropolitan areas, the leasing of assets for a relatively short period to meet temporary needs, or the full-maintenance leasing of computers and other office equipment where the manufacturer offers protection against obsolescence under a lease arrangement.

The first and most important consideration in the valuation of lease financing is to decide *what* it is, in other words, where it logically fits in the broad spectrum of financing alternatives.

There seems to be a considerable difference of opinion on this score. Some people maintain that financial leases are a form of debt; others say that they are more like preferred stock; still others claim that they are a substitute for, and therefore are comparable to, common stock financing. There is still another school of thought which holds that leasing does not represent a form of capital at all, but instead offers an opportunity to avoid a capital investment by shifting it to someone else.

This is a very fundamental question which must be resolved in order to determine the method of financing to which the cost of leasing should be compared:

*Should it be weighed against debt, preferred stock, or common stock?*

*Or should it be treated in the same way as a "make-or-buy" proposition and compared with the average return on investment?*

Let us take common stock first. No lease has been known to provide that the amount and the payment of rent is to be solely within the discretion of the lessee's board of directors, to be determined in the light of future earnings and the availability of cash. Yet this is generally the extent of a company's obligation to pay common stock dividends.

Preferred stock dividends are fixed in amount, but their payment is left to the discretion of the board of directors. As a result, they can be, and have been, deferred over a period of years. The writer knows of no leases with similar provisions.

## *Features like Debt Instruments*

But when lease obligations are compared to debt instruments, certain striking similarities are apparent. Lease payments are fixed obligations, just as are the interest and sinking fund requirements of a debt issue. As they become due, they are legally enforceable claims, ranking equally with other liabilities.

It is true that there may be a difference in the treatment accorded a lease for real property if the lessee is in bankruptcy. In the event that the trustee rejected the lease, the lessor would be entitled to a maximum claim of one year's rent in bankruptcy and three years' rent in reorganization proceedings. These claims would of course be in addition to the recovery of the leased asset. These statutory limitations apply only to leases for real property, not to chattel leases.

This treatment differs from that accorded a mortgage loan, where the lender would be entitled to a full claim for any deficiency between the realizable value of the asset and the amount owed him. This difference has been cited as an argument against classifying lease obligations as a form of debt, but it seems more a legal distinction than a practical financial one.

For one thing, inability to meet lease payments can lead to financial difficulties just as surely as the inability to meet interest or sinking fund requirements. This is the important thing to the company as well as to the investor, not who gets what after the company is in bankruptcy.

Also, it is quite conceivable that in reorganization a lessor may enjoy a position that is actually senior to that of other creditors. If the leased assets are essential to the continuation of the business, the trustee may be forced to continue the rental payments while other obligations are in default. This is the primary reason that railroads have been able to sell equipment trust certificates, which are based upon leases at attractive rates during periods when there was virtually no interest in general mortgage bonds of the same line.

But in any event, this difference should hardly be a valid consideration to a company in choosing between lease financing and direct borrowing. It seems highly questionable that a company should predicate its financial policy on eventual bankruptcy. A far sounder approach would be to assume that the company intends to stay in business and to meet its obligations; and from this viewpoint, lease obligations have the same impact as debt securities.

## *The Sources of Lease Financing*

Another indication of the similarity between lease financing and direct borrowing can be seen in the general pattern of lease transactions. The principal sources of funds, either directly or indirectly, are insurance companies, banks, pension funds, and other institutional investors. These investors are typically buyers of senior securities involving a minimum of risk. The fact that they are willing to advance funds upon the security of a lease indicates that they consider the lease a general credit obligation which is just as secure as the lessee's ability to pay.

The attitude of financial institutions and analysts toward lease obligations is indicated by the results of a recent survey conducted among the major insurance companies, banks, investment bankers, and rating services. The results were reported in the *Harvard Business Review*.[1]

1. With regard to long-term leases (those with terms of three years or more), 81 percent of the respondents considered them a form of debt, almost all ranking them with senior or secured debt.
2. Regarding shorter term leases, there was somewhat of a divergence of opinion between long-term investors and short-term lenders. Some 69 percent of the commercial banks regarded them as debt, while only half of the insurance companies shared this view. This undoubtedly reflects the basic difference in their points of view, the commercial bank being concerned with the short-term picture and the insurance company taking the longer term view.

A very candid description of the lease financing procedure is found in the following excerpt from a memorandum circulated among prospective underwriters of a stock issue of one of the larger leasing companies:

> The leasing company's contracts are contingent upon its ability, using the lessee's credit, to borrow 100 percent of the funds necessary to purchase the equipment. This method of operation results in an unusual balance sheet. While equipment with a book value of $19 million and liabilities of $20 million are shown, neither the assets nor the liabilities are in reality the leasing company's.

Or consider the following comment from the 1958 *Annual Report* of Booth Leasing Corporation:

> The company is primarily concerned with the credit standing of the lessee and the eligibility of the lessee for the long-term credit implicit in a term lease agreement. It is secondarily concerned with the collateral value of the leased equipment.

All this evidence merely confirms the conviction that a financial lease represents a promise to pay and, as such, qualifies as a general credit obligation. Much of the confusion which surrounds this simple fact arises from the following very interesting phenomenon. If you enter into a contract which reads "I promise to pay *X* dollars a month for a

---

[1]Richard F. Vancil and Robert N. Anthony, "The Financial Community Looks at Leasing," *Harvard Business Review,* Vol. XXXVII (November-December, 1959).

certain period of years," it makes a great deal of difference in an accounting sense whether the title at the top of the page reads "Loan Agreement" or "Lease Agreement."

But the distinction is primarily an accounting one. In an economic sense and from the point of view of corporate financial policy, there is very little difference between the two types of transactions. Lease financing is merely a form of borrowing, and lease obligations represent a form of indebtedness. If this were not true, then leasing would offer virtually unlimited possibilities. In fact, there would appear to be little justification for financing fixed assets by any other means.

## *The Fallacy of Free Choice*

Let us turn now for a moment to the school of thought which holds that leases are not a form of capital at all. This type of reasoning is apparent in the argument which we often hear that leasing frees working capital. By leasing its fixed assets, a company can make the funds which would otherwise be tied up in those assets available for alternative uses such as working capital. The high earning power of working capital is often demonstrated by dividing a company's total income by its working capital, which usually indicates returns of 20 percent or higher.

This type of reasoning is prevalent in the retailing field, where it is frequently argued that companies should stay out of the real estate business and devote all their capital to merchandising activities.

Or we sometimes hear that a company should lease assets which offer a low return, such as warehouses or automotive equipment, and conserve its own capital for higher yielding investments.

The fallacy in this type of reasoning is its underlying premise that a company has a choice as to which of its assets it will finance. Unfortunately, this is rarely the case. There are many factors which determine a company's total capital requirements, but the method of financing employed is not one of them.

The left side of the balance sheet determines the right, and not vice versa. The amount of assets which a business requires is determined by technology and by policy decisions relating to such things as the rate of expansion, the level of inventories to be carried, or the credit terms to be extended.

It is true that these decisions are tempered by financial considerations which balance the return on investment against the cost of capital. But once these decisions are reached, the choice remaining to the financial manager is not whether to finance the required assets but *how* to finance them.

The essential point here is that leasing is not a way of *avoiding* financing. It *is* financing. And it makes no difference whether you own profitable assets and lease unprofitable assets, or vice versa, so long as you require both kinds.

The important question is the cost of leasing relative to other financing alternatives. The introduction of calculations which purport to show the relative profitability of various classes of assets only serves to obscure this basic issue.

After all, by financing the acquisition of assets with borrowed money, a company avoids tying up its present working capital. But suppose that a bank or an insurance company were to solicit loans on the following basis: "Use our money to finance your fixed assets instead of disturbing your own funds. Your money can earn 20 percent in the form of working capital versus the 7 percent you will pay to use ours." I think it would find few takers so long as there were other lenders offering money at 5 percent or 6 percent.

*Why shouldn't the same reasoning apply to lease financing?*

## *A Realistic Basis for Decision*

Now the writer would like to submit an approach which he considers a more realistic basis upon which to evaluate leasing proposals.

Lease financing should be utilized wherever it is financially defensible. By this is meant that it must either:

1. Offer cost savings over direct borrowing, or
2. It must be available where an equivalent amount of debt financing is not available, or
3. It must offer some offsetting advantage which in the opinion of management justifies its higher cost.

Let us examine these three alternatives in order.

The question of relative costs involves the consideration of many factors. Two that come to mind immediately will generally work to the disadvantage of leasing.

One is the fact that investors will normally seek a higher return on funds advanced on the basis of a lease as opposed to a direct loan to the same company. This differential is commonly in the range of from one half of 1 percent to 1 percent. If a leasing company is involved as an intermediary, its charge adds to this differential.

The other involves the disposition of the asset upon the termination of the lease. If the asset is lost to the lessee, or if he must then repurchase it or continue to pay rent for its use, this represents an added element of cost.

Despite these possible disadvantages, there can be offsetting cost savings implicit in a lease arrangement.

For instance, leasing may offer certain tax benefits. This area represents a complex subject which deserves an article in itself. However, possible tax advantages which might be mentioned in passing include the following:

1. The possibility of cash flow advantages through the more rapid write-off of the leased asset. This used to represent a substantial advantage for leasing, but the advantage has been largely nullified by the accelerated depreciation options introduced in the 1954 code.
2. Or the possible advantage of being able to write off land values for tax purposes through leasing. The validity of this advantage depends largely upon the extent to which the lessee discounts the potential value of the land at the expiration of the lease.
3. Finally, there can be advantages in the sale and leaseback of older assets when this will result in a substantial capital loss or capital gain which can be effectively utilized by the company.

All these potential tax savings should be carefully scrutinized in the light of the latest tax rulings, of course. But to the extent that they are valid, they should be taken into consideration in any cost comparison.

Another possible cost advantage of leasing can accrue to companies engaged in production under "cost-plus" government contracts. By leasing equipment under leases tailored to the term of the contract, the company can charge off the full cost of the equipment to the government. If it were owned, the equipment would have to be depreciated over its normal life.

There are other possible cost differentials, such as the savings on the purchasing and disposal of vehicles which the fleet-leasing companies claim they can effect. All these cost factors must be taken into consideration in determining the advisability of financing by means of a lease.

The question of the methodology to be used in making such a comparison is also complex enough to deserve an article in itself. There are several approaches which might be used, but the important thing is that the method take into consideration all the cost differences between leasing and ownership and that it recognize the debt equivalent of the lease. As another writer on the subject has concluded, "the management decision that we are interested in is not an acquisition decision as connoted by the phrase 'lease-or-buy' but rather is a financing decision which might better be termed 'lease-or-borrow.'[2]

[2]Richard F. Vancil, "Lease Financing of Airline Equipment" (unpublished doctoral thesis, Harvard University, 1960).

## *Second Consideration: Availability*

If we turn now to those situations in which the leasing alternative is available to a company that could not borrow an equivalent amount of money, these calculations of relative cost lose much of their significance.

From a theoretical standpoint, it might be expected that these situations would account for the major portion of lease financing. Since leasing is generally a high-cost method of borrowing, it would be logical to assume that it would be used predominately by companies that had exhausted other sources of credit, just as an individual will turn to the pawnbroker only after failing to get a bank loan.

Paradoxically, this is not the case. The great bulk of lease financing is engaged in by companies of high credit standing which have considerable unused borrowing power and companies with weaker credit standing which would welcome the opportunity to lease but often find that the alternative is not available to them.

The reason, of course, is that the investors who finance lease transactions subject the prospective lessee to much the same sort of credit analysis as a prospective borrower. And they will generally refuse to finance a lease transaction for a company to which they would not be willing to lend an equal amount on a direct basis.

There are possible exceptions to this. One is where existing loan agreements or indentures restrict additional borrowing but will permit additional leasing. However, restrictions on lease commitments are now common in loan agreements, and it can be expected that they will become even more common as the use of lease financing becomes more widespread.

Another possibility is that a manufacturer may extend lease terms to a customer whose credit standing would not otherwise justify the amount of debt involved. The manufacturer may be willing to assume the additional credit risk in order to make the sale.

## *Other Possible Advantages*

This brings us to the third consideration in the writer's approach. This is the possibility that even where other forms of borrowing are available at a lower cost, leasing might offer some offsetting advantage which would justify its added cost.

This, of course, is inevitably a matter of judgment for each individual company, depending upon the relative weighting given to certain factors. There are, however, several such possible advantages that might be mentioned.

Probably the most important by far is the so-called "balance sheet advantage" of leasing. We often hear that leasing does not disturb existing credit lines, or that it enhances a company's financial ratios. More to the point, there exists the possibility that since lease obligations do not appear on the balance sheet, their existence will not affect the company's credit standing. As a result, through a combination of leasing and borrowing, a company might be able to secure a greater total amount of credit than it could through borrowing alone.

This possibility raises several important questions. The first, naturally, is whether or not this advantage is a valid one. After all, the same institutions that finance lease deals are also the primary sources of borrowed funds.

*Is it reasonable to expect that these investors will make investments on the strength of lease obligations and then ignore those same obligations in evaluating the lessee's credit standing for other purposes?*

The *Harvard Business Review* survey cited earlier sheds some light on this question. The respondents were asked whether, in making an analysis of a company's credit standing, they took lease obligations into consideration where they were known to be material.

Virtually all the respondents indicated that they did. Some 77 percent of the analysts indicated that they make use of formal techniques in evaluating lease obligations. These include capitalizing lease rentals to obtain an equivalent amount of debt to be added to the balance sheet and adding rentals to interest in computing the coverage of fixed charges. The remaining 23 percent presumably employ informal procedures.

## *Effects on Credit Standing*

There are perhaps some qualifying comments which should be made here with respect to the attitude of the financial community toward lease obligations and to the bearing which this attitude should have upon a company's decision as to whether or not to use lease financing.

First of all, there is strong reason to doubt that the analytical procedures being employed by financial analysts are as comprehensive as the above figures would suggest. A follow-up survey led the authors of the *Harvard Business Review* article to conclude that many of the respondents had indicated what they thought should be done, rather than what they do as routine practice. The writer's own feeling is that the present evaluation of lease obligations in financial analysis is neither as all-inclusive nor as refined as it might be.

Some of the reasons for this are:

1. The lack of adequate information being furnished by companies with regard to their lease commitments.

2. The lack of standardized procedures for evaluating the information that is available.
3. A certain amount of inertia on the part of the analysts.

Another question which might be raised is what effect a moderate amount of leasing will have upon the credit standing of a company which otherwise has a relatively sound and conservative capitalization. The answer is probably no effect whatever. In the first place, most companies have not been required to provide information concerning their lease commitments unless they are considered material, and there has been a great lack of uniformity in applying the tests of materiality.

But regardless of whether such commitments are reported or not, it seems doubtful that they would have any significant effect on an otherwise sound credit standing. After all, the various categories of credit rating are quite broad. It is not a matter of clearly defined ratios, where if you cross a certain dividing line you automatically drop down a notch.

## *Still a Form of Borrowing*

Now, *does this mean that if lease financing is used in moderate amounts, it need not be considered a form of borrowing nor be compared to the cost of debt?*

Not at all. The fact that the amount is not material does not support such a conclusion. Neither would an equivalent amount of debt have a material effect on the company's credit standing, so that the question is still which alternative offers the greatest advantage.

After all, this question of whether lease financing can in fact make a greater amount of credit available is pretty much an academic one for a company whose total debt and lease obligations are within conservative limits. If there is any advantage, it can only accrue to a company that has pushed the total amount of its borrowing above what would be regarded as a sound limit.

This brings up another point with regard to this so-called "balance sheet advantage." It suggests a line of reasoning which goes something like this: The only significance of debt is the effect which it has on the balance sheet appearance and on the opinions which analysts and lenders may have regarding the company.

Except for this, a company would be wise to raise all its capital requirements through various forms of debt and thus obtain the maximum amount of leverage for its common stockholders.

The objective, then, should be to keep conventional borrowing within the limits of certain ratios which analysts like to see, and then circumvent those ratios through various means of off-the-balance-sheet financing, such as leasing.

The soundness of this kind of reasoning is certainly questionable. There is more significance to debt than merely the outward appearance which it gives. If it has implications to financial analysts and lenders, it has even more important implications to the owners of the business, the stockholders whom management represents. For this reason, a sound financial management will impose its own limitation on the amount of fixed obligations it is willing to incur, whether in the form of debt or leases, and whether they appear on the balance sheet or not.

## *Freedom from Restrictions*

There are other more or less intangible factors which might, in the opinion of management, justify the use of lease financing. One is freedom from the restrictive covenants which are customarily imposed by debt agreements. These include limitations on the payment of dividends and the incurring of additional debt, and the required maintenance of a certain minimum amount of working capital. As yet, restrictions of this sort have not made their appearance to any extent in financial leases.

Or leasing might offer a convenient method of financing at the particular time. The amount of capital required may be considered too small to justify a term loan or debt issue, so that leasing might be resorted to in spite of a higher cost.

Along with these offsetting factors which might tip the scales in favor of leasing might be mentioned two possible dangers which it creates.

One is the possibility that leasing can result in a loss of control over capital expenditures. Unless leasing is controlled at the operating level, the result may be that division managers will be able to obtain assets through leasing for which they were denied appropriations in the capital budget. Some companies have recognized this possible danger by instituting a separate leasing budget.

A corollary of this is that leasing may result in distortions in the evaluation of intercompany performance. To the extent that leased assets are used, the comparison of return on invested capital between divisions can be distorted. Some companies have overcome this by capitalizing lease rentals in measuring return on capital investment.

## *Justification by Analysis*

In conclusion, the writer's position might be summarized in the following terms. Lease financing is a perfectly valid method of financing which should be used wherever it can be justified in comparison with other alternatives. However, it has often been justified on the basis of reasoning which will not stand up under any form of logical analysis. The adoption of a rational analytical approach will undoubtedly reveal many situations in which leasing offers definite advantages which would justify its use. However, the writer's own conclusion is that, for companies of sound credit standing with access to the various forms of capital, these opportunities will be relatively limited.

The growth of lease financing has unquestionably introduced many new opportunities in the field of corporate finance. But it has also posed important implications for several groups.

First, for the *public accounting profession*. There seem to be serious deficiencies in the present accounting for lease obligations. The accounting profession has the obligation to see that financial statements portray the actual condition of a business. It is difficult to see how accountants can properly fulfill this obligation so long as they continue to account for fixed assets on the basis of legal form rather than economic substance. It is unreasonable to expect financial analysts and the investing public to reconstruct financial statements on the basis of fragmentary information contained in a footnote.

*Financial analysts* may also have contributed to this situation either by overstressing financial ratios or by creating the impression that ratios play a conclusive role in determining a company's credit standing. After all, ratios are merely analytical tools which are useful in reaching a judgment; but it is the judgment which is significant, not the ratios themselves. This preoccupation with the maintenance of satisfactory ratios may have led some companies to follow practices which have no economic justification.

There is also the possibility that analysts have paid lip service to historical views on debt ratios which are no longer valid, while recognizing the fact that these limits have been evaded through the use of lease financing. Perhaps, for example, the food chains with their inherent stability can support debt ratios similar to those of public utility companies. At any rate, the food chains have achieved this result through the extensive use of lease financing.

And finally, some *corporate financial managers* might well reexamine their policies to determine whether they have made the most effective use of the various financing alternatives available to them.

*Chapter* 11

# *Lease or Borrow: New Method of Analysis**

By Richard F. Vancil

THE CONTROVERSY about lease financing, which has raged for several years now, has been almost exclusively concerned with the accounting treatment of this instrument. Most of the articles that have appeared on the *desirability* of lease financing have either (1) attempted to prove that leasing is "good" or "bad," or (2) dealt with the subject in broad generalities, compiling lists of pros and cons without specifying how these various factors should be combined in order to reach a decision.

The purpose of this article is to fill the analytical gap by describing a procedure for evaluating leasing plans and for comparing them with other methods of acquisition in order to determine the most desirable alternative in any specific situation. As a student of leasing, rather than an advocate or opponent of it, I am not interested in finding one, all-purpose answer to the question of "to lease or not to lease." The pertinent question which I shall try to help management answer is: "Are the costs of a *particular* leasing plan lower than the costs that would be incurred if the asset were owned?"

## Types of Contracts

For purposes of analysis, it is convenient to divide all leasing contracts into two broad categories—financial and operating leases:

A *financial* lease is defined as a contract under which the lessee agrees to make a series of payments to the lessor which, in total, exceed the pur-

*Reprinted by permission from *Harvard Business Review*, Vol. XXXIX (September-October, 1961), pp. 122–36.

chase price of the asset acquired. Typically, payments under a financial lease are spread over a period of time equal to the major portion of the useful life of the asset acquired. During this initial term of the lease, the contract is noncancelable by either party; that is, the lessee is irrevocably committed to continue leasing the asset.

*Operating* leases, on the other hand, may be defined as all other leasing contracts, and typically are cancelable by the lessee upon giving due notice of cancellation to the lessor. Operating leases, therefore, do not involve any fixed future commitment by the lessee, and in this respect are similar to most types of business expenditures. For example, telephone service may be thought of as a periodic payment under an operating lease from the utility providing the service.

In both types of contracts, legal title is, of course, retained by the lessor. But entering into a financial lease does have many of the characteristics of an investment decision, in that once the contract is signed, the stream of payments to be made cannot be changed by management's subsequent decisions.

Most leasing contracts clearly fall into one category or the other. In fact, only two types of agreements may, in practice, be difficult to categorize: (1) certain long-term real estate leases, which may involve a significant future commitment even though the total of all the payments will not exceed the purchase price of the piece of real estate; and (2) a wide variety of leasing plans available for automotive equipment, many of which defy a simple classification as either "operating" or "financial."

I shall ignore both of these important groups of leasing transactions in this article and restrict my examination to transactions involving all other types of industrial equipment. My purpose in so doing is to simplify the development of a sound theoretical solution to leasing decisions. Once the analyst has learned how to evaluate equipment-leasing contracts, he will find that the same principles may be used in the analysis of leasing transactions involving real estate or automotive equipment.

## Services by Lessors

In almost every decision involving a choice between buying or leasing a piece of equipment, a prospective lessee can readily observe that the sum total of all of his payments will probably be greater than the purchase price less the salvage value of the equipment acquired. Nevertheless, many lessees find that leasing is more attractive than purchasing. What are the services performed by a lessor which make leasing more attractive than buying, even though it apparently costs more than buying?

A detailed list of these services might be very long; but in a general way, we can group all of the functions performed by lessors into three broad categories:

1. Allowing the lessee to pay only part of the full purchase price at the time he begins using the equipment—granting credit, in effect.
2. Shouldering part or all of the risk that the equipment will soon become obsolete.
3. "Packaging" a series of legal, administrative, tax, and other expenses and adding them to the price of the lease.

Let us examine each of these services in turn and consider certain of their implications for management. We shall also do well to keep in mind that since the performance of a function by the lessor usually entails a cost for the lessee, we must be sure to recognize what the lessee's direct cost of performing those same functions would be when computing the cost of acquisition by outright purchase.

## *Granting Credit*

The most distinguishing characteristic of a leasing plan is that it permits the lessee to avoid paying the full purchase price of a piece of equipment on the date that it is acquired. Thus, as a minimum, lease payments must provide enough revenue to the lessor to cover not only the cost of the equipment but also the lessor's interest expense while he is waiting to recover his money, and to compensate the lessor for running the risk that he may not be able to collect the amounts due him from the lessee.

The interest charged by the lessor on the money which he has invested in equipment is the main reason that the total of the expected future lease payments exceeds the purchase price of the equipment. But because the lease payments are spread over many future periods, it is misleading to make a comparison such as this; rather, the present value of the future lease payments should be found if such a comparison is to be valid. (By present value, I mean the value today of money due at a future time. "It is the reciprocal of the compound amount, and may also be defined as that sum of money, which, when placed at compound interest for the full number of periods involved, will amount to the given sum."[1] Thus, at a discount rate of 8 percent, $250 to be earned

[1]Jules I. Bogen, *Financial Handbook* (3d ed.; New York: Ronald Press Co., 1948), p. 1181. Also see Robert N. Anthony, *Management Accounting* (Homewood, Ill.: Richard D. Irwin, Inc., 1960), pp. 534–36; and Joel Dean, "Measuring the Productivity of Capital," *Harvard Business Review,* Vol. XXXII (January-February, 1954), pp. 128–29.

a year from now has a value today of $232, and $250 to be earned two years from now has a value today of $214.)

Excluding the impact of income taxes for a moment, and assuming that the lessor performed no services for the lessee other than granting credit, it is easy to visualize a simplified (and obviously fictional) leasing plan in which, if the future lease payments were discounted at the interest rate which the lessor is charging for the use of his capital, the present value of the lease payments made by the lessee would be exactly equal to the purchase price of the equipment. (This is illustrated later, in the example beginning on page 150.)

*Not for Real.* While it is true that the acceptance of a leasing contract always has the effect of supplying capital on credit to the lessee, it is not necessarily true that the function of granting this credit is always performed by the lessor. In a legal sense, of course, the lessor is absorbing the credit risk, since he is the only other party to the leasing contract. In an economic sense, however, there are many situations in which the lessor acts only as an intermediary, receiving his capital from conventional sources and using it to purchase the equipment, which is then turned over to the lessee. As a practical example:

> Many leasing transactions have been arranged in which the lessor is really a "dummy corporation" established by the lessee in order to secure certain incomes tax advantages from leasing an asset rather than owning it. The lessor corporation typically has only a nominal capitalization but is able to borrow large amounts of money from conventional financial institutions by assigning the rental receipts under the lease to the financial institution. The financial institution grants the loan exclusively on the credit qualifications of the lessee, and looks to him for the repayment of its loan even though the loan repayments are nominally in the form of lease payments to the lessor.

Transactions of this type are only possible under a financial lease in which the lessee's obligation to make all of the lease payments is a noncancelable commitment. Obviously, if the lessee firm could cancel its obligations to make the lease payments, then the lending institution would be put in a position of trying to collect the unrecovered balance of its loan from the thinly capitalized lessor corporation, whose only asset would be a piece of used equipment of uncertain value.

It is worth noting that some commercial leasing companies specialize in transactions of this type. These firms may be run as private commercial enterprises rather than as "dummy corporations" owned by the lessee, but they have only a small capitalization and enter into transactions only with the "blue chip" company whose credit standing is high enough to permit it to finance all or practically all of the purchase price of the equipment being leased.

In transactions of the type just described, it seems more realistic to think of the lessor's function as being something other than the entrepreneurial function of absorbing credit risks. But in most leasing transactions the granting of credit to the lessee *is* one of the functions performed by the lessor. Thus:

1. In all operating leases the credit function is performed by the lessor; the very nature of the operating lease contract—its cancelability—reduces its usefulness as a collateral that the lessor can use in obtaining capital. In such situations the lessor may mortgage the equipment as security for his loans; but because financial institutions are usually unwilling to loan 100 percent of the cost of a specific asset, the lessor usually provides the balance of the capital requirements with equity funds.
2. The lessor may also give credit under a financial lease contract in circumstances where the creditworthiness of the lessee is inadequate to support a conventional loan for the full value of the equipment. Here again, the lessor may assign the lease payments to the bank that is supplying a major portion of the capital for the transaction, but the balance of the capital is provided by the lessor's own equity funds.

*Cost of Borrowing.* A careful consideration of the credit-granting function in lease contracts is highly important to a proper analysis in order to resolve the following controversy:

1. Advocates of leasing point out that one of its primary advantages is that it permits the lessee to finance the full purchase price of the asset acquired rather than only 60 to 70 percent of the price, i.e., whatever could be borrowed on a conventional chattel mortgage.
2. But opponents of leasing argue that when the lessee does obtain a 100 percent "loan" through leasing, he is really obtaining an unsecured advance based on his (the lessee's) general creditworthiness, and that such a loan could probably be made directly without the use of the leasing device.

In essence, the difference between these two points of view turns on the question of whether or not the lessor performs a credit-granting function which would not otherwise be available to the lessee. It should be obvious that the controversy cannot be resolved without considering the cost of obtaining money. In many situations, it is true that the lessee can "borrow" money by leasing even though his credit is such that he could not obtain a 6 percent bank loan. But in these cases the interest rate charged by the lessor may be 10 percent or higher; and at that rate the lessee might find that he has several alternative sources of funds, such as commercial credit houses and accounts receivable factors. (There is an important psychological difference here, however, in that the interest rate charged by a lessor may not be explicitly stated, even though the interest cost is built into the lease payments. Thus the lessee may be willing to accept a lease plan at a high interest rate even though unwilling to admit to himself—or to his other creditors—that his credit rating is so poor that he has to pay a premium rate for additional debt-type capital.)

For the sake of our quantitative analysis, let us assume that the alternatives can be stated clearly and that any lessee who is offered an opportunity to lease a piece of equipment could, if he chose to pay a high enough interest rate, borrow a sufficient amount of money to finance the outright purchase of the equipment. This assumption is realistic for most practical situations and has the advantage of permitting us to ignore the distinction made previously between lessors who do perform the credit function and those who do not. We can then go to the heart of the matter and reach this conclusion: In order to compare acquisition alternatives, the lessee *should compare the cost of a leasing plan against the cost of raising the same amount of capital through debt financing at the lowest possible rate available to him.* The analysis should not be influenced by the amount of equity capital that the lessor brings to the transaction.

This method of analyzing a leasing contract has been argued against on the grounds that it is unrealistic to compare the cost of leasing with the cost of debt financing when, in fact, the lessee might really have to resort to equity financing in order to raise the necessary funds for outright purchase, and equity financing is more expensive than debt. But this argument is specious, in my opinion. While it is true that equity funds are very expensive because the investors have claim to the full profits of a business regardless of how large the profits may be, the investors are not *guaranteed* any payment for the use of the funds. Lease payments, which are not contingent upon earnings, carry a contractual cost for the use of capital and in this respect are more closely akin to debt capital. The contractual cost may not be spelled out clearly—it may be more implicit than explicit—but that does not affect its nature.

*BIR Defined.* For purposes of analyzing leasing contracts, therefore, I propose that the first step should be to determine the interest rate at which the prospective lessee could, alternatively, borrow a sufficient amount of money directly to permit him to purchase the equipment. For lack of a better term, I shall refer to this interest rate as the corporation's basic interest rate. I define BIR as the minimum rate that the company would have to pay today in order to secure a given amount of funds from the issuance of the most attractive type of fixed cost (debt) securities that management is in a position to sell. This rate is a market-determined rate and reflects primarily the over-all cost of debt money in the economy at a given point in time, the lender's appraisal of the credit worthiness of the borrower, and the amount of funds that the borrower wishes to raise at this time.

## *Obsolescence Insurance*

A second major function that is often performed by lessors involves another kind of risk taking, this time not the risk of granting credit but the risk of early obsolescence of the equipment. As all businessmen know, one of the most important estimates which is made by a prospective purchaser of a piece of equipment concerns the technological or market life of the equipment. For how long a period will the continued use of the equipment be more advantageous than replacing it or discarding it?

Particularly in industries where the rate of technological change is rapid, the prospective purchaser may feel a great deal of uncertainty about the economic life of the machine that he is considering acquiring. Wrong decisions in this area can be very expensive, and wrong decisions can be made in either of two ways: (1) by failing to acquire a piece of equipment soon enough in the hope that a more advanced model will come out within a short period of time or (2) by acquiring a piece of equipment too soon, only to find that it is shortly rendered obsolete.

Faced with what appears to be a high probability of making the wrong decision, many businessmen prefer not to purchase such equipment outright but to lease it from someone who will absorb the risk of early obsolescence for them. Probably the most familiar example is in data-processing equipment, where the rate of technological change is almost breathtaking and where leasing plans are offered by most of the equipment manufacturers.

The extent to which the risk of obsolescence is absorbed by the lessor is determined by the terms of the lease contract:

1. Some operating leases require only a thirty-day notice of cancellation, and in such circumstances the risk is borne entirely by the lessor. Conceivably, if a more advanced piece of equipment were introduced every month, the lessee could continue to turn in the outdated models each time after having paid only one month's rental, and would always have the advantage of having the most up-to-date equipment available.
2. Other leasing contracts, although still falling within our definition of an operating lease, may not permit the lessee to cancel his obligation during the first year or two, or may specify that notice of cancellation be given six to twelve months in advance. But even in these cases, practically the full burden of the risk of early outmoding falls on the lessor.

*Protection of Lessor.* It should be obvious that when the lessor assumes the burden, he expects to be compensated for it by the lessee. In some respects, this arrangement might be likened to an insurance contract in which the insurer (lessor) collects a premium from each person insured (lessee), and the sum total of all the premiums collected is sufficient to cover the cost of losses (the unrecovered value of the machines rendered obsolete). Like any insurer, the lessor also expects to make a profit for his risk taking, and lessees apparently are willing to permit this profit because it reduces their exposure to a potentially large individual loss.

Actually, in situations in which the lessor is the equipment manufacturer, a good argument can be made that both parties benefit from an *operating* lease under which the equipment manufacturer bears the risk of obsolescence on the ground that the manufacturer is in a better position to estimate when outmoding will occur (and in fact may control when it occurs), and is also in a better position to recondition and dispose of used equipment turned in by the original lessee.

Under *financial* lease contracts the situation is different. The lessee's commitment to make payments that exceed the purchase price of the equipment has the effect of placing on him most of the risk of obsolescence in much the same way as if he had actually purchased the equipment. For instance, financial leases on nonautomotive equipment are seldom less than five years' duration; and if the equipment becomes obsolete during that time, the lessee must continue to make his payments even though he replaces the equipment with an improved model. (Some financial lease contracts permit the lessee to "pay off" the balance of his future lease payments in order that he may acquire title to the obsolete asset and thus dispose of it, usually at a loss, or turn it back to the lessor, who will attempt to dispose of it.) Still, it is possible to have a portion of the risk transferred to the lessor, depending on the terms of the agreement. To illustrate:

The lessor may require lease payments during the initial term of the lease which will just recover the cost of the equipment plus interest, so that his profit will be the residual value of the equipment at the end of the initial term. In such a situation, he is running a risk that he will not be able to realize his profit if the machine becomes obsolete before the end of the initial term, and he may therefore require that the initial term of the lease be relatively short, say five years, so that his uncertainty about the value at the end of the term is not too great.

This also has the effect of reducing the risk borne by the lessee, however, and the total cost of such a contract might be greater than it would be if the lease (1) were for a longer minimum term or (2) contained attractive, i.e., low-priced, renewal or purchase options. Measuring "total cost" in such a situation requires explicit consideration of the expected value of the equipment at the end of the initial term of the lease.

## *Packaging of Costs*

A final function that is performed by all lessors has frequently been overlooked in the analysis of leasing expenditures, but must be specifically dealt with if we are to have a precise analysis. This function might be described as a "packaging" function; it is the function of accumulating into a single total all the costs concerned with a given acquisition and recovering them through the stream of periodic lease payments.

Such costs make up a longer list than might at first be assumed. Included are not only the cost of the equipment and the interest payments on the money provided, but also several auxiliary financing costs, such as:

1. Commitment fees for bank loans arranged in advance of the time the money is required to purchase the equipment.
2. The cost of carrying any compensating balances required by the lender.
3. Legal fees.
4. Administrative and clerical costs.
5. The fee for arranging the transaction, which might be thought of either as the profit for the lessor under a leasing contract or as the fee that might be paid an investment banker for acting as a third party in arranging a piece of financing.

These auxiliary financing costs may be quite small relative to the size of the total transaction; but if the transaction is large enough, they may be too large to ignore. For example, I have estimated that on the leasing of $28 million worth of jet engines from the General Electric Company in 1958, American Airlines agreed under the terms of the lease to pay more than $300,000 over and above the cost of the engines plus interest. This amount was identified in the lease contract as a payment for some of the auxiliary costs listed above and did not include any profit to General Electric as lessor.

*Income Tax Deduction.* Another cost which is implicitly packaged in the terms of any leasing contract is connected with the federal income tax deduction.

One of the frequently claimed advantages for equipment leasing is that a leasing contract permits the lessee to enjoy a more advantageous stream of income tax expense deductions than would be possible if he owned the equipment outright and could only deduct depreciation and interest. In fact, it may be possible to achieve some advantage if the lease payments are scheduled in such a way that they are higher in the earlier years of the lease than the sum of depreciation and interest and, conversely, lower in the later years. When these conditions are prevalent, the present value of the tax deductions received under the lease plan is greater than the present value of the tax deductions under outright ownership.

This same advantage may be achieved in another way under financial leases. The agreement may be drawn to run for a relatively short initial term, say five years. During this time the lessor recovers his entire cost of the equipment, and the lessee can deduct his payments to the lessor as expenses; whereas if the lessee were to purchase the equipment directly, he would have to depreciate it over a longer time span, say seven to ten years.

In order to protect the public from abuses under this potential tax loophole, the Internal Revenue Service promulgated Revenue Ruling No. 55–540 in 1955. The effect of this ruling is to eliminate any tax advantage for leasing contracts which are, in all important respects, really purchase transactions. However, most leasing contracts today can be and are written in such a way that they will qualify for tax treatment as leases. The interesting thing to note here is that drawing the contract in such a way that it is advantageous in terms of income taxes may make it *dis*advantageous in other respects. For example:

1. It may not provide a purchase option, which has the effect of shifting part of the risk of obsolescence to the lessor. This means that the lessor would expect to earn a higher profit on the transaction.
2. The lessor is also a taxpayer and, as owner of the equipment, will be depreciating it in his tax returns. If he is willing to offer the lessee a stream of lease payments which appear advantageous to *him,* but which have the effect of creating more taxable income for the lessor in the early years, the lessor obviously must somehow adjust his lease payments to compensate him for his early tax payments for the benefit of the lessee.

Accordingly, it is probably best to think of income tax deductions as being part of the packaged cost of a lease plan. The mere fact that the lease payments appear to be more advantageous than the tax deductions under ownership does not mean that the *total* cost of the lease plan will be less than the total (after-tax) cost under ownership.

*Varying Importance.* While it is true that all lease payments consist of a "package" of equipment, tax, and financial costs, the function of putting the package together may be a relatively minor one for certain types of leasing contracts. For example, the packaging service is not an important one under most operating leases, which characteristically entail a relatively high cost for shifting the risk of obsolescence from the lessee to the lessor.

On the other hand, there are certain types of financial leases where packaging is the *primary* function performed by the lessor. In such situations the lessor may act very much like an investment banker who arranges a source of funds based on the creditworthiness of the lessee, risks little or none of his own equity capital, and earns a legitimate profit by performing this work for the lessee.

## Operating Lease Decisions

The choice between buying a piece of equipment and acquiring it under an operating lease is essentially an investment decision, and it can be resolved quantitatively using familiar techniques.[2] Viewed in their proper perspective, operating leases pose no problems for the analyst who already has a thorough understanding of the techniques of investment analysis. Financial leases, however, require a different analytical technique. In order to highlight the contrast, let us first look briefly at the reasons why the operating lease decision does not require a special analytical methodology.

### *Lease or Buy?*

A businessman considering the acquisition of a new piece of equipment which can be procured either by purchase or under an operating lease must choose the best of three courses of action: (1) decide against the acquisition and continue the status quo, (2) purchase the equipment, or (3) enter into an operating lease for the equipment. A two-step analysis is necessary before the best course of action can be identified. Specifically:

As a first step, the relevant costs and revenues of continuing the status quo for a while should be compared to the relevant costs and revenues that would obtain if the business had the use of the equipment under an operating lease. This analysis, in most cases, will be quite easy, since there would be no "investment" under either alternative; the better alternative will be the one with the lower annual operating costs or the higher annual net revenues.

If operating costs under the status quo are lower than those under the operating lease, acquisition by means of a lease is not indicated. The second step of the analysis then involves a comparison between the status quo and purchase of the equipment, a routine (though not necessarily easy) type of investment decision using one of the approved analytical procedures. But if operating costs under the lease are lower than those under the status quo,

---

[2]See, for example, John G. McLean, "How to Evaluate New Capital Investments," *Harvard Business Review*, Vol. XXXVI (November-December, 1958), p. 59.

acquisition of the equipment is indicated, and the question becomes whether it would be even more advantageous to purchase the equipment than to lease it. This is also a routine investment decision involving the comparison of the present value of a stream of future annual payments with the cost of purchasing the equipment immediately and thus avoiding the future annual payments.

If we look at the functions performed by the lessor under an operating lease, we see that he is primarily an entrepreneur and that his main function is to absorb the risks that (1) the economic life of the equipment will be less than anticipated and (2) the lessee will not be able to make the required lease payments. But it is hard to separate the two risks because in either event the lessee would stop making lease payments and would return the used equipment to the lessor. (If the lessee's reason for returning the equipment is his inability to make the payments, the lessor's loss will probably not be a serious one since, presumably, the equipment will still have some economic life remaining and can be leased to another party.) Looking at the transaction from the point of view of the lessor, therefore, we see that when he offers to lease a piece of equipment, he is really making an investment decision in reverse; he stands ready to give up a sum certain today (the purchase price of the equipment) in exchange for receiving a stream of payments for an uncertain period into the future.

In broadest terms, the lessee will find an operating lease advantageous in those situations in which:

1. His investment "opportunity rate" (i.e., the discount rate used to reduce the future lease payments to their present value) is higher than the discount rate used by the lessor in establishing the amount of future lease payments.
2. The lessor estimates that the economic life of the equipment is longer, or the residual value is greater, than the estimates made by the lessee.

## Financial Lease Decisions

Having looked briefly at the lease-or-buy decision, we turn now to a problem which can best be phrased as "lease or borrow."

The choice between buying a piece of equipment and acquiring it under a financial lease requires a new analytical technique because management must make a financial decision rather than an investment decision. It is not valid to make a direct comparison between the cash flows under a financial lease and the cash flows under the status quo (or under an operating lease) because in the former case the lessee irrevocably commits himself to make the required payments, while he is not so committed in the latter case. It is because of the contractual nature of financial lease payments that we may say that when a lessee enters into a financial lease, he has, in effect, purchased the equipment just as surely as if he paid cash for it.

The first step in the analysis of financial leases, therefore, is to compare the alternative of purchasing the equipment for cash with the alternative of continuing the status quo. This is another routine investment decision. If purchase does not appear desirable, a financial lease will probably not be desirable either (the only exception being the highly unusual case where the interest rates and other financing terms of the lease are more attractive than the rates and terms the company could arrange for direct debt financing).

Thus the consideration of a financial lease should begin *only after a company has previously decided that the purchase of a piece of equipment is desirable.* This is the most important decision. Having made it, management may then be faced with several alternative methods of financing the acquisition: purchase for cash, purchase on an installment plan or some other method involving debt financing, or acquisition via a financial lease.

## Madison Case

There may be significant cost differences between these alternative methods of financing. To show how the comparison should be made, I shall take a simplified example:

The Madison Company has decided to acquire a piece of equipment with a cash purchase price of $1,000. The management is reasonably sure that the piece of equipment will have a useful life of at least four years, but no longer than five years, at the end of which time the equipment will have a zero scrap value. The company's financial situation is sound; and during the past few years, management has always been able to select new investment projects that had a projected rate of return of at least 10 percent after taxes. Management expects that this investment "opportunity rate" on new projects will continue in the future.

The company's capital structure includes about 35 percent long-term debt. Although the firm has not made much use of short-term debt, its commercial bank has indicated a willingness to loan up to $20,000 at 6 percent interest. Day-to-day operations of the business require the maintenance of sizable cash balances at the bank, so that no additional balance requirements would be imposed by the bank if the amount of any new loan did not exceed $20,000.

In addition to being available for outright purchase, the new machine being acquired by the Madison Company can be financed on either of two conditional sales contracts (plans 1 and 2 in Table 1) or on either of two noncancelable lease agreements (plans 3 and 4).

TABLE 1

ALTERNATIVE FINANCING PLANS

| End of Year | Debt Financing | | Lease Financing | |
|---|---|---|---|---|
| | *Plan 1* | *Plan 2* | *Plan 3* | *Plan 4* |
| 0 | $ 224 | $ 0 | $ 224 | $ 375 |
| 1 | 224 | 237 | 224 | 275 |
| 2 | 224 | 237 | 224 | 200 |
| 3 | 224 | 237 | 224 | 150 |
| 4 | 224 | 237 | 224 | 100 |
| 5 | ...... | 237 | ...... | ...... |
| Total | $1,120 | $1,185 | $1,120 | $1,100 |

*Interest Rate Computations.* The interest rates implicit in each of the financing plans above are computed in Table 2. An interest rate may be said to be implicit in a plan because even though the rate is not stated, the fact that the total payments exceed the purchase price of the equipment means that some interest rate is being charged for the provision of capital, and that once the amount and timing of the payments are known, the implicit interest rate can be found by a trial-and-error process. For example:

Plans 1 and 3 require the same contractual payments and therefore have the same implicit interest rate. This rate is discovered to be 6 percent in Table 2 by discounting each of the future payments at several rates until that rate is found which reduces the $1,120 to a present value of $1,000. In a similar fashion the interest rate on plan 2 is also found to be 6 percent, and the implicit rate on plan 4 is 7½ percent.

One possible decision rule for evaluating financing alternatives would be to compare the interest rates charged by each plan and to pick the one which provides money at the lowest interest rate. If we were to apply this rule to the Madison Company case, we would eliminate plan 4 because it charges a higher rate than the other three, and we would say that the company can be indifferent as to which of the other three plans it selects. This answer, as we shall see, is not correct.

*The Conventional Approach.* Another possible analytical device for comparing financial alternatives would be to discount all future cash flows at some rate representing the utility of funds to the borrower. (I use the phrase "utility of funds" to refer to what the firm could earn after taxes if it reinvested the money in other operations instead of paying it to a bank or lessor for the equipment.) This approach, too, has shortcomings, as we shall see when we apply it to our case situation.

TABLE 2

COMPUTATION OF INTEREST RATES FOR ALTERNATIVE FINANCING PLANS*

| *End of Year* | *Payment* | *Discount Factor*† | *Present Value Amount* |
|---|---|---|---|
| | Plans 1 and 3 | | |
| 0 | $ 224 | 1.0000 | $ 224 |
| 1 | 224 | 0.9434 | 211 |
| 2 | 224 | 0.8900 | 199 |
| 3 | 224 | 0.8396 | 188 |
| 4 | 224 | 0.7921 | 178 |
| Total | $1,120 | | $1,000 |
| | Plan 2 | | |
| 0 | $.... | 1.0000 | $.... |
| 1 | 237 | 0.9434 | 224 |
| 2 | 237 | 0.8900 | 211 |
| 3 | 237 | 0.8396 | 199 |
| 4 | 237 | 0.7921 | 188 |
| 5 | 237 | 0.7473 | 178 |
| Total | $1,185 | | $1,000 |
| | Plan 4 | | |
| 0 | $ 375 | 1.0000 | $ 375 |
| 1 | 275 | 0.9302 | 256 |
| 2 | 200 | 0.8653 | 173 |
| 3 | 150 | 0.8050 | 121 |
| 4 | 100 | 0.7488 | 75 |
| Total | $1,100 | | $1,000 |

*Discount rates (annual receipt and compounding) are taken from *Financial Compound Interest and Annuity Tables* (Boston: Financial Publishing Co., 1942).

†Turns out to be 6 percent for plans 1 and 3; 6 percent for plan 2; and 7½ percent for plan 4.

To begin, let us assume that management uses 10 percent as the rate for reducing future lease payments to their present value; that is, 10 percent is the investment "opportunity rate." Then Table 3 is a computation of the present-value cost of each of the financing alternatives being considered by the Madison Company. An important feature of this calculation is the explicit recognition of the differences in income tax payments under each alternative. The Madison Company is subject to a 52 percent federal income tax and follows the policy of depreciating owned assets by the sum-of-the-years'-digits method. For simplicity, let us assume that the acquisition will occur on January 1, and that tax payments are made on the last day of each calendar year. Lease payments

## TABLE 3

### ANALYSIS OF ALTERNATIVE FINANCING PLANS*

A. Present-Value Cost (after Taxes) of Cash Purchase

| | | | | |
|---|---|---|---|---|
| Purchase price of equipment | | | | $1,000 |
| Present value of tax shield provided by depreciation: | | | | |
| *(1) End of Year* | *(2) Sum-of-the-Digits Depreciation* | *(3) 52% Tax Saving* | *(4) Present Value at 10%* | |
| 1 | $ 333 | $173 | $157 | |
| 2 | 267 | 139 | 115 | |
| 3 | 200 | 104 | 78 | |
| 4 | 133 | 69 | 47 | |
| 5 | 67 | 35 | 22 | |
| Total | $1,000 | $520 | $419 | 419 |
| Net present-value cost after taxes | | | | $581 |

*(Continued on next page)*

TABLE 3 (*Continued*)

B. Present-Value Cost (after Taxes) of Debt Financing on Plan 1

| (1) End of Year | (2) Debt Payments | (3) Principal Balance Outstanding (Previous Balance − Col. 2 + Col. 4) | (4) 6% Interest on Principal (Col. 3 × 6%) | (5) Tax Savings on Interest (Col. 4 × 52%) | (6) Total Tax Savings Depreciation and Interest (Col. 5 + Col. 3 in A) | (7) Net Cash Flows (Col. 2 − 6) | (8) Present Value of Net Flows at 10% |
|---|---|---|---|---|---|---|---|
| 0 | $ 224 | $776 | $ 0 | $.. | $... | $224 | $224 |
| 1 | 224 | 598 | 46 | 24 | 197 | 27 | 25 |
| 2 | 224 | 410 | 36 | 18 | 157 | 67 | 55 |
| 3 | 224 | 211 | 25 | 13 | 117 | 107 | 80 |
| 4 | 224 | 0 | 13 | 7 | 76 | 148 | 101 |
| 5 | ...... | .... | .... | ... | 35 | (35) | (22) |
| Total | $1,120 | | $120 | $62 | $582 | $538 | $463 |

C. Present-Value Cost (after Taxes) of Debt Financing on Plan 2

| End of Year | Debt Payments | Principal Balance Outstanding | 6% Interest on Principal | Tax Savings on Interest | Total Tax Savings Depreciation and Interest | Net Cash Flows | Present Value of Net Flows at 10% |
|---|---|---|---|---|---|---|---|
| 0 | $..... | $1,000 | $... | $.. | $... | $... | $... |
| 1 | 237 | 823 | 60 | 31 | 204 | 33 | 30 |
| 2 | 237 | 635 | 49 | 25 | 164 | 73 | 60 |
| 3 | 237 | 435 | 37 | 19 | 123 | 114 | 86 |
| 4 | 237 | 224 | 26 | 14 | 83 | 154 | 105 |
| 5 | 237 | 0 | 13 | 7 | 42 | 195 | 121 |
| Total | $1,185 | | $185 | $96 | $616 | $569 | $402 |

(*Continued on next page*)

TABLE 3 *(Continued)*

D. Present-Value Cost (after Taxes) of Lease Financing on Plan 3

| *End of Year* | *Lease Payments* | *52% Tax Savings at End of Year* | *Net Cash Flows* | *Present Value of Net Flows at 10%* |
|---|---|---|---|---|
| 0 | $ 224 | $... | $224 | $224 |
| 1 | 224 | 116 | 108 | 98 |
| 2 | 224 | 117 | 107 | 88 |
| 3 | 224 | 116 | 108 | 81 |
| 4 | 224 | 117 | 107 | 73 |
| 5 | ...... | 116 | (116) | (72) |
| Total | $1,120 | $582 | $538 | $492 |

E. Present-Value Cost (after Taxes) of Lease Financing on Plan 4

| *End of Year* | *Lease Payments* | *52% Tax Savings at End of Year* | *Net Cash Flows* | *Present Value of Net Flows at 10%* |
|---|---|---|---|---|
| 0 | $ 375 | $... | $375 | $375 |
| 1 | 275 | 195 | 80 | 73 |
| 2 | 200 | 143 | 57 | 47 |
| 3 | 150 | 104 | 46 | 35 |
| 4 | 100 | 78 | 22 | 15 |
| 5 | ...... | 52 | (52) | (32) |
| Total | $1,100 | $572 | $528 | $513 |

*( ) represent cash inflows rather than cash outflows.

Computing the present-value cost of the cash purchase plan is relatively easy. The full purchase price is paid immediately; and although tax deductions will amount to $520 over the five-year period, the present value of these deductions is only $419, yielding a net present-value cost for this plan of $581.

A comparable computation for debt plan 1 is more complicated, due to the necessity to calculate the amount of deductible interest which is included in each year's installment payment. This is done in the first four columns of Part B of this table. The initial down payment of $224 at the date of acquisition serves to reduce the effective amount of the loan to $776. When the second installment is made at the end of the first year, it can then be identified as $46 of interest (6 percent on the balance of $776 outstanding during the year) and $178 of principal reduction. The principal amount of the loan outstanding during the second year is therefore $598. During the four-year period when some part of the loan is outstanding, a total of $120 of interest will be paid (the total of column 4), while the remaining $1,000 of the total payments is for repayment of the principal. The tax savings on interest (column 5) are then added to the tax savings from depreciation of an owned asset, as determined in column 3 of Part A, to yield the total tax deductions for plan 1 in column 6. These deductions are then netted against the contractual payments to yield net cash flows in column 7, and the present value of these cash flows amounts to $463. A similar computation for plan 2 yields a net present-value cost of $402.

The calculation of present-value cost for the two leasing plans is shown in Parts D and E, and is relatively straightforward. Plan 3 has a net present-value cost of $492, and the cost of plan 4 is $513.

are deductible for income tax purposes in the year in which payments are made. The results of these calculations may be recapped as follows:

| *Acquisition Method* | *Present-Value Cost: 10% Annual Discount* |
|---|---|
| Cash purchase | $581 |
| Debt plan 1 | 463 |
| Debt plan 2 | 402 |
| Lease plan 3 | 492 |
| Lease plan 4 | 513 |

Thus, plan 2 is the alternative that has the lowest present-value cost.

Focusing now on the two debt programs alone, why is plan 2 significantly more attractive than plan 1 when both carry a 6 percent interest charge and result in the same depreciation deductions? The answer is that plan 2 makes more funds available to the company; and since our calculations assume that money can be invested to earn 10 percent after taxes, these additional funds constitute an important advantage.

*Effect of Different Rates.* This assumption about the value of money is important and needs to be examined further:

1. Table 4 is a calculation of the present-value cost of each plan using a variety of assumptions about the utility of investable funds to the Madison Company. The column labeled "Net Flows after Taxes" is drawn from the computations for each plan in Table 3; and these flows are then discounted at 2½ percent, 5 percent, and 7½ percent.
2. Lowering the discount rate has the effect of reducing the present-value cost for the cash purchase alternative because future receipts from income tax deductions are relatively more valuable; and when the present value of these receipts is deducted from the immediate outlay, the net cost under this plan falls as the discount rate falls.
3. Conversely, lowering the discount rate for debt plan 1 raises the present-value cost of that plan, because the effect on the tax deductions is more than offset by the increase in the present-value cost of the installment payments on the debt.
4. The interrelationship between the present-value cost of each plan and the discount rate applied to the net cash flows for that plan can best be seen in a graph such as that shown in Figure 1. Here we see that the cost lines for the debt and cash purchase plans intersect at a discount rate of 2.88 percent; that is, if we apply this discount rate to the cash flows for each plan, we shall find that they all have the same present-value cost of approximately $512. The significant thing is that this intersection point is equivalent to the after-tax interest rate charge on plans 1 and 2 (i.e., 48 percent of 6 percent). If the utility of investable funds were less than 2.88 percent after taxes, the cash purchase plan would be more attractive than either of the debt plans; if the utility rate were greater than 2.88 percent, either of the debt plans would be more attractive than a cash purchase.

TABLE 4

PRESENT VALUE (AFTER TAXES) OF ALTERNATIVE FINANCING PLANS AT VARIOUS DISCOUNT RATES*

| *Plan* | *End of Year* | *Net Flows after Taxes* | *Present Value at 2½%* | *Present Value at 5%* | *Present Value at 7½%* |
|---|---|---|---|---|---|
| Cash purchase.... | 0 | $1,000 | $1,000 | $1,000 | $1,000 |
| | 1 | (173) | (169) | (165) | (161) |
| | 2 | (139) | (132) | (126) | (120) |
| | 3 | (104) | ( 97) | ( 90) | ( 84) |
| | 4 | ( 69) | ( 63) | ( 57) | ( 52) |
| | 5 | ( 35) | ( 31) | ( 27) | ( 24) |
| Total....... | | $ 480 | $ 508 | $ 535 | $ 559 |
| 1............... | 0 | $ 224 | $ 224 | $ 224 | $ 224 |
| | 1 | 27 | 26 | 26 | 25 |
| | 2 | 67 | 64 | 61 | 58 |
| | 3 | 107 | 99 | 92 | 86 |
| | 4 | 148 | 134 | 122 | 111 |
| | 5 | (35) | (31) | (27) | (24) |
| Total........ | | $ 538 | $ 516 | $ 498 | $ 480 |
| 2............... | 0 | $..... | $..... | $..... | $..... |
| | 1 | 33 | 32 | 31 | 31 |
| | 2 | 73 | 69 | 66 | 63 |
| | 3 | 114 | 106 | 98 | 92 |
| | 4 | 154 | 140 | 127 | 115 |
| | 5 | 195 | 172 | 153 | 136 |
| Total........ | | $ 569 | $ 519 | $ 475 | $ 437 |
| 3............... | 0 | $ 224 | $ 224 | $ 224 | $ 224 |
| | 1 | 108 | 105 | 103 | 100 |
| | 2 | 107 | 102 | 97 | 93 |
| | 3 | 108 | 100 | 93 | 87 |
| | 4 | 107 | 97 | 88 | 80 |
| | 5 | (116) | (103) | (91) | (81) |
| Total........ | | $ 538 | $ 525 | $ 514 | $ 503 |
| 4............... | 0 | $ 375 | $ 375 | $ 375 | $ 375 |
| | 1 | 80 | 78 | 76 | 74 |
| | 2 | 57 | 54 | 52 | 49 |
| | 3 | 46 | 43 | 40 | 37 |
| | 4 | 22 | 20 | 18 | 16 |
| | 5 | (52) | (46) | (41) | (36) |
| Total........ | | $ 528 | $ 524 | $ 520 | $ 515 |

*( ) represent cash inflows rather than cash outflows.

FIGURE 1

PRESENT-VALUE COST (AFTER TAXES) OF ALTERNATIVE FINANCING PLANS AT VARIOUS DISCOUNT RATES

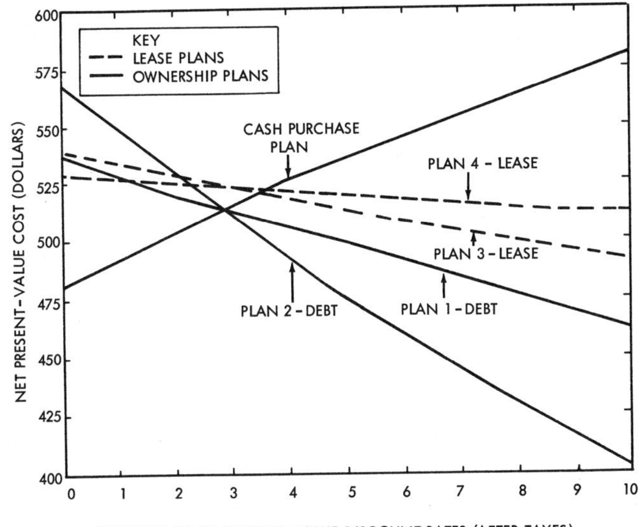


*Making Better Comparisons.* Earlier, I indicated that discounting at the investment "opportunity rate" was a technique with shortcomings. The reason can now be understood. Let us first look at the two debt plans, then at the debt plans as compared with the leasing plans.

The primary difference between plans 1 and 2 is that the Madison Company is always carrying a greater balance of outstanding debt under the second than under the first. But keep in mind that the decision as to the amount of debt to be carried each year should be a conscious one on the part of Madison's management. If the company desires to have a $1,000 loan outstanding during the first year after the asset has been acquired, this can be accomplished *either* by accepting plan 2 *or* by accepting plan 1 and floating a separate loan for $224 repayable in a lump sum at the end of five years with interest payable annually at 6 percent. If this latter course were followed, the amount of debt outstanding at any point of time in each case would be identical.

Management might still have a preference between the two plans, but it should base its preference for, say, plan 2 over plan 1 on the fact that the former provides the desired amount of financing in one transaction rather than in two. Executives should not be fooled into thinking that plan 2 has a cost advantage of $61 at the company's opportunity rate; this advantage could be obtained just as well by raising the same amount of debt funds from other sources at the same interest rate.

The implication of this line of reasoning in the comparison of debt and lease financing is a major one, since one of the important differences that is usually found when comparing any two specific proposals is the amount of financing provided by each. Recognizing that other sources of money are available means that it is desirable to eliminate the difference in the amount of financing provided when comparing specific proposals. For this reason, it is no more possible to compare the present-value cost of plan 3 with the cost of plan 2 than it is to compare the cost of plan 1 with that of plan 2.

It *is* possible, however, to compare plans 1 and 3 directly. Because each involves an identical set of contractual payments, the amount of financing provided by each is the same. Holding constant the amount of financing provided, as is done in these two plans, allows us to isolate one of the most important differences between debt and lease financing: the difference in permissible income tax deductions. *It is this difference, and this difference alone, that makes the present-value cost of plan 1 less than that of plan* 3.

I believe that an effective quantitative method for evaluating financial leases should give proper recognition to income tax differences but should not be influenced by the amount of financing provided by a given plan. Discounting the future cash flows at the investment opportunity rate does not accomplish this because the present-value costs reflect the intermingled effects of tax treatment and the amount of funds provided. For this reason, plan 4 cannot be compared with any of the other plans, and none of the other intersection points in Figure 1 are meaningful.

## *The BIR Method*

A method of analysis which fulfills the criteria just mentioned is one that I shall call the basic interest rate (BIR) method. This approach, in essence, treats the minimum cost of debt capital as an unavoidable cost of any financing plan. Since this cost will not change between alternative plans, it is eliminated from the comparison. Financing plans which charge an interest rate higher than the BIR are penalized to the extent of the *incremental* cost of the higher interest charges.

*Steps in Procedure.* To illustrate how this method of analysis works, let us go back to the case of the Madison Company:

1. We must determine the BIR for the firm. A corporation's BIR is defined as the minimum rate that the company would have to pay today in order to secure a given amount of funds from the issuance of the

most attractive type of fixed rate (debt) securities that the company is in a position to sell. This is a market-determined rate, and it reflects primarily:

*a*) The over-all cost of debt money in the economy at a given point in time.

*b*) The lender's appraisal of the creditworthiness of the borrower.

*c*) The amount of funds that the borrower wishes to raise at this time.

In the simple case of the Madison Company, this rate is assumed to be 6 percent. In the first stage of the analysis, we should discount all contractual (debt-type) payments under any financing plan at this 6 percent rate.

2. Applying the discounting procedure to one of the lease plans available to the Madison Company, we find the present value of the contractual payments on plan 3 to be $1,000. (It is not necessary to begin with any one type of plan. I take plan 3 here because we have already seen that it happens to be comparable to plan 1.) The present-value computations are set forth in Table 5.
3. Next comes the more complicated step of computing the present value of the tax shield on the "equivalent depreciation" element in the lease payments. This is done by first determining an amount of imputed

TABLE 5

ANALYSIS OF LEASE PLAN 3 BY BIR METHOD*

Fixed commitments: Present value at 6% of five annual payments in advance of $224 each. . . $1,000

Less: Tax shield provided by lease payments in excess of 6% interest:

| (1) *End of Year* | (2) *Lease Payment* | (3) *Balance of "Loan" during Year* | (4) *6% Interest on Principal × Balance in Col. 3* | (5) *Noninterest Deductions: Prior Year's Lease Payment (Col. 2) Less Current Interest (Col. 4)* | (6) *52% Tax Savings at End of Year on Noninterest Deductions* | (7) *Present Value of Savings at 10%* | |
|---|---|---|---|---|---|---|---|
| 0. . . . . . . . | $ 224 | $1,000 | $. . . | $. . . . . | $. . . | $. . . | |
| 1. . . . . . . . | 224 | 776 | 46 | 178 | 93 | 85 | |
| 2. . . . . . . . | 224 | 598 | 36 | 188 | 98 | 81 | |
| 3. . . . . . . . | 224 | 410 | 25 | 199 | 103 | 77 | |
| 4. . . . . . . . | 224 | 211 | 13 | 211 | 110 | 75 | |
| 5. . . . . . . . | . . . . . . | 0 | . . . | 224 | 116 | 72 | |
| Total. . | $1,120 | | $120 | $1,000 | $520 | $390 | 390 |

Net present-value cost of plan 3. . . . . . . . . . . . . . . . . . . . . . . . . . . . . . . . . . . . . . . . . . . . . $610

*We are interested here only in the tax shield that will result from the allowable deduction of lease payments. At the end of the first year the Madison Company would be able to deduct $224, the amount of the payment made at the beginning of the year. Since we have identified $46 of this as interest charges for the first year, the remaining $178 is the "equivalent depreciation" deduction. This figure is subtracted from $776 to obtain the loan balance for the second year. By similar calculations for each year, we determine the amount of depreciation deductions during the life of the lease, and this total is $1,000 (column 5).

interest in each lease payment. The amount of this interest is then deducted from the lease payment, and the balance is identified as being equivalent to a depreciation deduction. These deductions for plan 3 amount to $520, the same amount as the total depreciation deductions under ownership. But the *timing* of the deductions is different. When they are discounted at 10 percent, their present value is only $390. Deducting this sum from the present value of the fixed commitments, we may say that the net present-value cost (excluding financing costs) for plan 3 is $610.

4. The cost thus determined for plan 3 is now easily compared to any financing alternative which involves ownership of the asset. The figure that is directly comparable is found in Part A of Table 3, where the present-value cost of a cash purchase is computed as $581. *The reason that the two calculations are directly comparable is that no financing charges are included in either of them.* Thus, we see that plan 3 has a present-value cost that is $29 higher than the cost of any financing plan which involves ownership and which would provide an identical amount of financing at the basic interest rate.

*Advantages of Simplicity.* It should now be clear that all the BIR method really does is eliminate some of the calculations in order to arrive more simply at the same answer that we would get by using the discounted cash flow method to compare lease and debt plans providing the same amount of financing. Actually, we shall never be so fortunate as to have directly comparable financing plans in a practical situation, and we need a device which will allow us to compare many different financing plans, each of which provides a slightly different amount of funds. Here the real advantage of the BIR method comes into play. Since all debt-financing plans can be compared in terms of the interest rate they charge, we do not need to do an analysis such as was done in Parts B and C of Table 3; we need only to realize that our decision is determined by the amount of financing we wish to obtain.

Lease-financing plans, however, need to be examined individually because each provides a unique set of tax deductions for the depreciation of the asset. By washing out the financing charges in a lease plan, as we do in the BIR method, we focus clearly on the depreciation deductions. We can thus compare all of the lease plans with each other, and with the comparable costs under ownership.

Let us turn now to lease plan 4 and examine the results we obtain from a BIR analysis of it (see Table 6). Specifically:

This plan is more realistic than plan 3 because, as is usually the case, the interest rate charged by the lessor is somewhat higher than the corporation's basic interest rate. Discounting the lease payments at the BIR, therefore, yields a present value which exceed the purchase price of the equipment. In plan 4 the amount is $1,017. We shall refer to the extra $17 as the lessor's

## TABLE 6

### ANALYSIS OF LEASE PLAN 4 BY BIR METHOD*

Fixed commitments:

| *End of Year* | *Lease Payments* | *Present Value at 6%* |
|---|---|---|
| 0 | $ 375 | $ 375 |
| 1 | 275 | 259 |
| 2 | 200 | 178 |
| 3 | 150 | 126 |
| 4 | 100 | 79 |
| Total | $1,100 | $1,017 |

Net present-value cost at 6% ........ $1,017

Less: Tax shield provided by lease payments in excess of 6% interest:

| (1) *End of Year* | (2) *Lease Payment* | (3) *Balance of "Loan" during Year* | (4) *6% Interest on Principal × Balance in Col. 3* | (5) *Noninterest Deductions: Prior Year's Lease Payment (Col. 2) Less Current Interest (Col. 4)* | (6) *52% Tax Savings at End of Year on Noninterest Deductions* | (7) *Present Value of Savings at 10%* | |
|---|---|---|---|---|---|---|---|
| 0 | $ 375 | $1,000 | $.. | $..... | $... | $... | |
| 1 | 275 | 625 | 38 | 337 | 175 | 159 | |
| 2 | 200 | 388 | 23 | 252 | 131 | 108 | |
| 3 | 150 | 211 | 13 | 187 | 97 | 73 | |
| 4 | 100 | 74 | 4 | 146 | 76 | 52 | |
| 5 | ...... | 0 | ... | 100 | 52 | 32 | |
| Total | $1,100 | | $78 | $1,022 | $531 | $424 | 424 |

Net present-value cost of lease plan 4 ........ $593

*The imputed interest amounts to only $78 here, and this amount plus the cost of the equipment is $22 less than the total amount of the lease payments. This $22 is the same lessor's premium, but the $17 present-value cost of that premium has grown to $22 by the time we assume it is paid at the end of the fourth year. (Reference to a compound interest table will show that $17 invested for four years at 6 percent, compounded annually, will grow to $22.) We could make a different assumption about the date at which the lessor's premium is paid, but we choose to consider it as being part of the final lease payment so that all of the early lease payments can be used to reduce the balance of the "loan" as rapidly as possible.

"premium"; it is, in effect, a payment to the lessor for assuming the auxiliary financing costs connected with the transaction and for his profit or fee for arranging the transaction.

The tax shield calculation in Table 6 is essentially the same as the calculation in Table 5, but is complicated by the existence of the lessor's premium. The amount of the lessor's premium, when paid, is added to the cost of the equipment to determine the total amount of tax deductions provided by the lease. This amounts to $1,022. The present value of these tax deductions is $424. Therefore the net present-value cost is $593, and this cost is comparable to the $581 cost of the cash purchase found in Part A of Table 3.

Lease plan 4 is thus identified as being $17 cheaper than lease plan 3 and only $12 more expensive than an ownership plan which would provide the same amount of financing at the basic interest rate. Note that this is a different conclusion from the one reached on page 155, where all plans were compared using the discounted cash flow method.

*Choosing between Lease Plans.* In company debt plans 1 and 2, I stated earlier that the cost of the plans was the same, and that the Madison Company should choose the plan that more closely provides the desired amount of financing. But a similar statement can*not* be made about lease plans 3 and 4. Plan 4 provides less financing than plan 3; and even though the interest cost is higher, plan 4 is cheaper because of the more favorable tax deductions provided by the declining-scale lease payments. If the company were to choose plan 3 over plan 4, it would be obtaining greater financing, but at the sacrifice of the more valuable stream of tax deductions provided by the latter. Thus, if the Madison Company wants to use a lease plan, but also wants to obtain more financing than plan 4 provides, the best solution (although not quite as good as either of the debt plans) would be to combine plan 4 with a direct loan for the balance of the money desired.

Generalizing from this, I would say that it is irrational for a company to try to choose between financial leasing plans on the basis of the amount of financing provided, because the tax deductions are directly tied to the rate at which the "loan" is repaid. The best lease is the one which offers the best combination of a low interest rate and rapid tax (and therefore principal) amortization. If a lessee does not take the stream of tax deductions into consideration in his decision, he runs the risk of failing to take advantage of the most important cost saving offered by financial leases.

## Conclusion

The distinction between operating leases and financial leases is an important one, in terms of both the magnitude of the commitment made by the lessee and the method of analysis required to evaluate each type of contract. *Operating* leases can be evaluated by using the now well-developed techniques of capital expenditure analysis. *Financial* leases require a radically different analytical procedure. The most significant new concept in the analysis of financial leases is the recognition that the decision to be made is a financial decision (lease or borrow?), not an investment one (lease or buy?).

Most potential borrowers or lessees will find that there are several available financing alternatives, if they are willing to be realistic about the rate of interest that they may have to pay in order to "borrow" the amount of money they want. In order to compare these alternatives, management must first eliminate any differences between the programs that are due solely to the *amount* and *term* of the funds provided. This is the key to understanding the new approach.

To put the whole procedure in perspective, let us now recapitulate the seven steps involved in the analysis. Management should:

1. Decide whether or not the equipment should be acquired, using the cash purchase price and the company's investment opportunity rate to evaluate the proposed investment.
2. Compute the after-tax cost of a cash purchase by deducting the present value of future tax deductions from the original cost of the equipment.
3. Estimate the company's BIR (basic interest rate), the lowest rate at which it could borrow an amount equal to the purchase price of the equipment. This step prepares the way for a comparison either of debt- and lease-financing plans or of different leasing plans.
4. Discount the future lease payments at the BIR to determine the "equivalent purchase price" of the equipment. Any excess over the actual purchase price is the "lessor's premium."
5. Eliminate an imputed interest charge (at the BIR) from each lease payment. The remainder of each payment is analogous to a depreciation deduction.
6. Subtract the present value of the "equivalent depreciation" deductions (discounted at the opportunity rate) from the "equivalent purchase price" determined in the fourth step. The balance is the after-tax cost of the leasing plan, stated in comparable terms (no financing charges) to the cost of purchasing determined in the second step.
7. Adjust the cost of the leasing plan for (*a*) any auxiliary financing costs that the lessee will avoid and (*b*) the residual value of the equipment which will not be received by the lessee.

## *Other Points to Analyze*

There are many differences between debt and lease financing which can and should be brought into the quantitative analysis before a decision is reached. This article has discussed the two most important factors: interest cost and income tax deductions. Two other factors, whose importance varies according to the specifics of the transaction, are (1) the residual value of the equipment (reflecting the extent to which the lessor absorbs the risk of obsolescence) and (2) the auxiliary financing costs that the lessor must build into the lease payments when he performs the packaging function earlier described.

Part III

# Long-Term Financing

*Chapter* 12

# *New Framework for Corporate Debt Policy**

By Gordon Donaldson

WHY ARE MANY common rules of thumb for evaluating a company's debt capacity misleading and even dangerous?

Why is outside experience and advice of limited value as a guide to top management's thinking about debt capacity?

What approach will enable management to make an independent and realistic appraisal of risk on the basis of data with which it is already familiar and in terms of judgments to which it has long been accustomed?

The problem of deciding whether it is wise and proper for a business corporation to finance long-term capital needs through debt, and, if so, how far it is safe to go, is one which most boards of directors have wrestled with at one time or another. For many companies the debt capacity decision is of critical importance because of its potential impact on margins of profitability and on solvency. For *all* companies, however large and financially sound they may be, the decision is one to be approached with great care. Yet, in spite of its importance, the subject of corporate debt policy has received surprisingly little attention in the literature of business management in recent years. One might infer from this either that business has already developed a reliable means of resolving the question or that progress toward a more adequate solution has been slow. In my opinion, the latter inference is closer to the truth. The debt-equity choice is still a relatively crude art as practiced by a

*Reprinted by permission from *Harvard Business Review,* Vol. XL (March-April, 1962), pp. 117–31.

great many corporate borrowers. It follows that there is a real opportunity for useful refinement in the decision-making process. However, there is little evidence at present of serious dissatisfaction with conventional decision rules on the part of those responsible for making this decision. Over the past three years, I have been engaged in sampling executive opinions on debt policy, and I have found little indication of the same kind of ferment as is going on with regard to capital-budgeting decisions.[1]

The primary purpose of this article, therefore, is to stimulate dissatisfaction with present-day conventions regarding debt capacity and to suggest the direction in which the opportunity for improvement lies. I intend to show that the widely used rules of thumb which evaluate debt capacity in terms of some percentage of balance sheet values or in terms of income statement ratios can be seriously misleading and even dangerous to corporate solvency. I also intend to develop the argument that debt policy in general and debt capacity in particular cannot be prescribed for the individual company by outsiders or by generalized standards; rather, they can and should be determined by management in terms of individual corporate circumstances and objectives and on the basis of the observed behavior of patterns of cash flows.

The question of corporate debt capacity may be looked at from several points of view, e.g., the management of the business concerned, its shareholders or potential shareholders, and, of course, the lender of the debt capital. Because each of these groups may quite properly have a different concept of the wise and proper limit on debt, let me clarify the point of view taken in this article. I intend to discuss the subject from this standpoint of the management of the borrowing corporation, assuming that the board of directors which will make the final decision has the customary mandate from the stockholders to act on all matters concerning the safety and profitability of their investment. For the reader who ordinarily looks at this problem as a lender, potential stockholder, or investment adviser, the analysis described in this article may appear at first sight to have limited application. Hopefully, however, the underlying concepts will be recognized as valid regardless of how one looks at the problem, and they may suggest directions for improvement in the external as well as the internal analysis of the risk of debt.

## Nature of the Risks

In order to set a background for discussing possible improvements, I shall first describe briefly certain aspects of conventional practice

[1]See, for example, *Harvard Business Review's* "Capital Investment Series."

concerning present-day decision rules on long-term debt. These observations were recorded as a part of a research study which sampled practice and opinion in a group of relatively large and mature manufacturing corporations.[2] The nature of this sample must be kept in mind when interpreting the practices described.

## *Hazards of Too Much Debt*

The nature of the incentive to borrow as an alternative to financing through a new issue of stock is common knowledge. Debt capital in the amounts normally approved by established financial institutions is a comparatively cheap source of funds. Whether it is considered the cheapest source depends on whether retained earnings are regarded as "cost-free" or not. In any case, for most companies it is easy to demonstrate that, assuming normal profitability, the combination of moderate interest rates and high levels of corporate income tax enable debt capital to produce significantly better earnings per share than would a comparable amount of capital provided by an issue of either common or preferred stock. In fact, the advantage is so obvious that few companies bother to make the calculation when considering these alternatives.

Under these circumstances, it is apparent that there must be a powerful deterrent which keeps businesses from utilizing this source to the limits of availability. The primary deterrent is, of course, the risks which are inevitability associated with long-term debt servicing. While it is something of an oversimplification to say that the debt decision is a balancing of higher prospective income to the shareholders against greater chance of loss, it is certainly true that this is the heart of the problem.

When the word "risk" is applied to debt, it may refer to a variety of potential penalties; the precise meaning is not always clear when this subject is discussed. To most people, however, risk—so far as debt is concerned—is the chance of running out of cash. This risk is inevitably increased by a legal contract requiring the business to pay fixed sums of cash at predetermined dates in the future regardless of the financial condition at that time. There are, of course, a great many needs for cash —dividends, capital expenditures, research projects, and so on—with respect to which cash balances may prove inadequate at some future point.

---

[2]The complete findings have been published in book form; see Gordon Donaldson, *Corporate Debt Capacity* (Boston: Division of Research, Harvard Business School, 1961).

### *Too Little Cash*

The ultimate hazard of running out of cash, however, and the one which lurks in the background of every debt decision, is the situation where cash is so reduced that legal contracts are defaulted, bankruptcy occurs, and normal operations cease. Since no private enterprise has a guaranteed cash inflow, there must always be *some* risk, however remote, that this event could occur. Consequently, any addition to mandatory cash outflows resulting from new debt or any other act or event must increase that risk. I have chosen to use the term "cash inadequacy" to refer to a whole family of problems involving the inability to make cash payments for any purpose important to the long-term financial health of the business; "cash insolvency" is the extreme case of cash inadequacy. It should be emphasized that although debt necessarily increases the chances of cash inadequacy, this risk exists whether the company has any debt or not, so that the debt-equity choice is not between some risk and no risk, but between more and less.

## Conventional Approaches

Observation of present-day business practice suggests that businessmen commonly draw their concepts of debt capacity from one or more of several sources. Thus, they sometimes:

1. *Seek the counsel of institutional lenders or financial intermediaries (such as investment bankers).* Most corporate borrowers negotiate long-term debt contracts at infrequent intervals, while the lender and the investment banker are constantly involved in loan decisions and so, presumably, have a great deal more experience and better judgment. Further, it is apparent that unless the lender is satisfied on the question of risk, there will be no loan. Finally, banks and insurance companies have a well-established reputation for being conservative; and conservative borrowers will take comfort from the fact that if the lender errs, it will likely be on the safe side.
2. *See what comparable companies are doing in this area of financial management.* Every business has an idea of those other companies in or out of the industry which are most like themselves so far as factors affecting risk are concerned. Since this is an aspect of corporate policy which is public information, it is natural that the debt-equity ratios of competitors will be carefully considered; and lacking more objective guides, there will be a tendency to follow the mode and reject the extremes. This approach has an added practical appeal; group norms are important in the capital market's appraisal of a company's financial strength. If a company is out of line, it may

be penalized, even though the deviation from the average may be perfectly appropriate for this company.

3. *Follow the practices of the past.* There is a very natural tendency to respect the corporation's financial traditions, and this is often apparent with regard to debt policy. Many businesses take considerable pride in "a clean balance sheet," an Aa rating, or a history of borrowing at the prime rate. It would border on sacrilege to propose a departure which would jeopardize these cherished symbols of financial achievement and respectability! The fact that these standards have apparently preserved corporate solvency in the past is a powerful argument for continuing them, particularly if the implications of a change cannot be precisely defined.
4. *Refer to that very elusive authority called "general practice," "industry practice," "common knowledge," or, less respectfully, "financial folklore."* Remarkable as it seems in view of the great diversity among companies classified as industrials, there is widespread acceptance of the belief that an appropriate limit to the long-term borrowing of industrial companies is 30 percent of capitalization (or alternatively, one third). The origin of or rationale for this particular decision rule has been obscured by the passage of time, but there is no doubt that it has become a widely honored rule of thumb in the decisions of both borrowers and lenders.

## *Fallacy of Double Standard*

Without denying the practical significance of some of the considerations which have led businessmen to follow these guides in formulating debt policy, it must be recognized that there are serious limitations inherent in using them (separately or as a group) as the *only* guides to appropriate debt capacity.

First, consider the practice of accepting advice from the lender. As the lender views the individual loan contract, it is one of a large number of investments which make up a constantly changing portfolio. When negotiated, it is only one of a stream of loan proposals which must be acted on promptly and appraised in terms of the limited information to which generalized standards are applied. The nature of the risk to the lender is necessarily influenced by the fact that this loan is only a small fraction of the total sum invested and that intelligent diversification goes a long way to softening the impact of individual default. Further, even when default occurs, all may not be lost; in time, the loan may be "worked out" through reorganization or liquidation.

All this is small comfort to the borrower. The individual loan which goes sour, if it happens to be *his* loan, is a catastrophe. There are few businessmen who can take a lighthearted attitude toward the prospect of default on a legal contract with the associated threat of bankruptcy. To most, this is viewed as the end of the road. Also, it is important to recognize that while the lender need only be concerned about servicing his own (high-priority) claims, the borrower must also consider the needs which go unsatisfied during the period prior to the time of actual default when debt servicing drains off precious cash reserves.

This is not to imply that the lender is insensitive to individual losses and their effect on the business concerned; but it does mean that risk to the lender is not the same thing as risk to the borrower; and consequently, the standards of one are not necessarily appropriate for the other. The lender's standards can at times be too liberal—as well as too conservative—from the borrower's point of view. Some will argue that, as a practical matter, the borrower must accept the debt capacity standards of the lender, else there will be no contract. However, this implies that there is no bargaining over the upper limit of the amount that will be supplied, no differences among lenders, and/or no shopping-around by borrowers. While all institutional lenders do have absolute limits on the risks they will take (even at a premium interest rate), there is often some room for negotiation if the borrower is so disposed. Under some circumstances, there may be valid reasons for probing the upper limits of the lender's willingness to lend.

## *Lessons of Experience*

The second source of guidance mentioned is the observed practices of comparable businesses. This, too, has its obvious limitations. Even assuming strict comparability, which is hard to establish, there is no proof that the companies concerned have arrived at their current debt proportions in a deliberate and rational manner. In view of the wide variations in debt policy within any industry group, there can be little real meaning in an industry average. And what happens if every member of the group looks to the other for guidance? The most that can be said for this approach to debt policy is that the company concerned can avoid the appearance of being atypical in the investment market so far as its capital structure is concerned. But as in most areas of business, there is a *range* of acceptable behavior, and the skill of management comes in identifying and taking advantage of the limits to which it can go without raising too many eyebrows.

Even a company's own direct experience with debt financing has its limitations as a guide to debt capacity. At best, the evidence that a particular debt policy has not been a cause of financial embarrassment in the past may only prove that the policy was on the conservative side.

However, if assurance of adequate conservatism is the primary goal, the only really satisfactory policy is a no-debt policy.

For companies with some debt the experience of past periods of business recession is only partial evidence of the protection a particular policy affords. In most industries the period of the past twenty years has produced a maximum of four or five periods of decline in sales and earnings. This limited recession experience with the behavior of cash flows—the critical consideration where debt servicing is involved—can be misleading, since cash flows are affected by a variety of factors and the actual experience in any single recession is a somewhat unique, combination of events which may not recur in the future. Thus the so-called "test of experience" cannot be taken at face value.

## *Inescapable Responsibility*

In summing up a criticism of the sources from which management commonly derives its debt capacity standard, there are two aspects which must be emphasized. Both of these relate to the practice of relying on the judgment of others in a situation where management alone is best able to appraise the full implications of the problem. The points I have in mind are as follows:

1. In assessing the risks of running out of cash because of excessive fixed cash obligations, the special circumstances of the individual firm are the primary data that the analyst has to work with. Management has obvious advantages over outsiders in using these data because it has free and full access to them, the time and incentive to examine them thoroughly, and a personal stake in making sensible judgments about what it observes. Even the judgments of predecessors in office are judgments made on information which is inadequate when compared to what management now has in its possession, if only because the predecessor's information is now 10 or 20 years old. (Subsequently, we shall consider how management may approach an independent appraisal of risk for the individual business.)
2. The measurement of risk is only one dimension of the debt capacity decision. In a free enterprise society the assumption of risk is a voluntary activity, and no one can properly define the level of risk which another should be willing to bear. The decision to limit debt to 10 percent, 30 percent, or any other percentage of the capital structure reflects (or should reflect) both the magnitude of the risk involved in servicing that amount of debt *and* the willingness of those who bear this risk—the owners or their duly authorized representatives—to accept the hazards involved.

   In the last analysis, this is a subjective decision which management alone can make. Indeed, it may be said that a corporation has defined its debt policy long before a particular financing decision comes to a vote; it has done this in its choice of the men who are to make the decision. The ensuing decisions involving financial risk will reflect their basic attitudes—whether they see a situation as an opportunity to be exploited or a threat to be minimized.

A most interesting and fundamental question comes up here—one that underlies the whole relationship between management and the shareholder; namely, does management determine the attitude toward risk bearing which the stockholders must then adopt, or vice versa? This is part of the broader question of whether management should choose those financial policies which it prefers and attract a like-minded stockholder group (taking the "if they don't like it, they can sell out" approach) or by some means or other determine the attitudes and objectives of its present stockholder group and attempt to translate these into the appropriate action.

I do not propose to pass judgment on this difficult problem in the context of this article. The fact is, by taking one approach or the other—or some blend—management *does* make these decisions. With respect to risk bearing, however, one point is clear: Responsible management should not be dealing with the problem in terms of purely personal risk preferences. I suspect that many top executives have not given this aspect the attention it deserves.

## *Reasons for Current Practice*

Having considered the case for a debt policy which is internally rather than externally generated, we may well ask why so many companies, in deciding how far to go in using OPM (other people's money), lean so heavily on OPA (other people's advice). The answer appears to be threefold:

1. A misunderstanding of the nature of the problem and, in particular, a failure to separate the subjective from the objective elements.
2. The inherent complexity of the objective side—the measurement of risk.
3. The serious inadequacy of conventional debt capacity decision rules as a framework for independent appraisal.

It is obvious that if a business does not have a useful way of assessing the general magnitude of the risks of too much debt in terms of its individual company and industry circumstances, then it will do one of two things. Either it will fall back on generalized (external) concepts of risk for "comparable" companies, or it will make the decision on purely subjective grounds—on how the management "feels" about debt. Thus, in practice, an internally generated debt capacity decision is often based almost entirely on the management's general attitude toward this kind of problem, without regard for how much risk is actually involved and what the potential rewards and penalties from risk bearing happen to be in the specific situation. The most obvious examples are to be found in companies at the extremes of debt policy that follow such rules as "no debt under any circumstances" or "borrow the maximum available." (We must be careful, however, not to assume that if a company has one or another of these policies, it is acting irrationally or emotionally.)

One of the subjects about which we know very little at present is how individual and group attitudes toward risk bearing are formed in practice. It is apparent, however, that there are important differences in this respect among members of any given management team and even for an individual executive with regard to different dimensions of risk within the business. The risk of excessive debt often appears to have a special significance; a man who is a "plunger" on sales policy or research might also be an archconservative with regard to debt. The risk of default on debt is more directly associated with financial ruin, regardless of the fundamental cause of failure, simply because it is generally the last act in a chain of events which follows from a deteriorating cash position.

There are other bits of evidence which are possible explanations for a Jekyll-and-Hyde behavior on risk bearing in business:

1. Debt policy is always decided at the very top of the executive structure, whereas other policies on sales or production involving other dimensions of risk are shaped to some degree at all executive levels. The seniority of the typical board of directors doubtless has some bearing on the comparative conservatism of financial policy, including debt policy.
2. There is also some truth in the generalization that financial officers tend to be more conservative than other executives at the same level in other phases of the business; and to the extent that they influence debt policy, they may tend to prefer to minimize risk per se, regardless of the potential rewards from risk bearing.

## *What Is a Sensible Approach?*

The foregoing is, however, only speculation in an area where real research is necessary. The point of importance here is that whatever the reason may be, it is illogical to base an internal decision on debt policy on attitudes toward risk *alone,* just as it is illogical to believe that corporate debt policy can be properly formulated without taking these individual attitudes into account.

For the purposes of a sensible approach to corporate debt policy, we need not expect management to have a logical explanation for its feelings toward debt, even though this might be theoretically desirable. It is sufficient that managers know how they feel and are able to react to specific risk alternatives. The problem has been that in many cases they have not known in any objective sense what it was that they were reacting to; they have not had a meaningful measure of the specific risk of running out of cash (with or without any given amount of long-term debt).

It is therefore in the formulation of an approach to the measurement of risk in the individual corporation that the hope for an independent appraisal of debt capacity lies.

## Inadequacy of Current Rules

Unfortunately, the conventional form for expressing debt capacity rules is of little or no help in providing the kind of formulation I am urging. Debt capacity is most commonly expressed in terms of the balance sheet relationship between long-term debt and the total of all long-term sources, viz., as some percent of capitalization. A variation of this ratio is often found in debt contracts which limit new long-term borrowing to some percentage of net tangible assets.

The alternative form in which to express the limits of long-term borrowing is in terms of income statement data. This is the *earnings coverage* ratio—the ratio of net income available for debt servicing to the total amount of annual interest plus sinking fund charges. Under such a rule, no new long-term debt would be contemplated unless the net income available for debt servicings is equal to or in excess of some multiple of the debt-servicing charges, say three to one, so that the company can survive a period of decline in sales and earnings and still have enough earnings to cover the fixed charges of debt. As we shall see shortly, this ratio is more meaningful for internal formation of policy but also has its limitations.

Now, let us go on to examine each type of expression more closely.

### *Capitalization Standard*

Consider a company which wishes to formulate its own debt standard as a percent of capitalization. It is apparent that in order to do so, the standard must be expressed in terms of data which can be related to the magnitude of the risk in such a way that changes in the ratio can be translated into changes in the risk of cash inadequacy, and vice versa. But how many executives concerned with this problem today have any real idea of how much the risk of cash inadequacy is increased when the long-term debt of their company is increased from 10 to 20 percent or from 20 to 30 percent of capitalization? Not very many, if my sample of management information in this area has any validity. This is not surprising, however, since the balance sheet data on which the standard is based provide little direct evidence on the question of cash adequacy and may, in fact, be highly unreliable and misleading.

While we do not need to go into a full discussion here of the inadequacies of relating the principal amount of long-term debt to historical asset values as a way of looking at the chances of running out of cash, we should keep in mind the more obvious weaknesses:

1. There is a wide variation in the relation between the principal of the debt and the annual obligation for cash payments under the debt contract. In industrial companies the principal of the debt may be repaid serially over the life of the debt contract, which may vary from 10 years or less to 30 years or more. Thus the annual cash outflow associated with $10 million on the balance sheet may, for example, vary from $500,000 (interest only at 5 percent) to $833,000 (interest plus principal repayable over 30 years) to $1.5 million (interest plus principal repayable over 10 years).
2. As loans are repaid by partial annual payments, as is customary under industrial term loans, the principal amount declines, and the percent-of-capitalization ratio improves, but the annual cash drain for repayment *remains the same* until maturity is reached.
3. There may be subtantial changes in asset values, particularly in connection with inventory valuation and depreciation policies and, as a consequence, changes in the percent-of-capitalization ratio which have no bearing on the capacity to meet fixed cash drains.
4. Certain off-the-balance-sheet factors have an important bearing on cash flows which the conventional ratio takes no cognizance of. One factor of this sort which has been receiving publicity in recent years is the payments under leasing arrangements. (While various authorities have been urging that lease payments be given formal recognition as a liability on balance sheets and in debt capacity calculations, there is no general agreement as to how this should be done. For one thing, there is no obvious answer as to what the capitalization rate should be in order to translate lease payments into balance sheet values. In my opinion, this debate is bound to be an artificial and frustrating experience—and unnecessary for the internal analyst—since, as will be discussed later, it is much more meaningful to deal with leases, as with debt, in terms of the dollars of annual cash outflow rather than in terms of principal amounts. Thus a footnoting of the annual payments under the lease is entirely adequate.)

## *Earnings-Coverage Standard*

The earnings-coverage standard affords, on the surface at least, a better prospect of measuring risk in the individual company in terms of the factors which bear directly on cash adequacy. By relating the total annual cash outflow under all long-term debt contracts to the net earnings available for servicing the debt, it is intended to assure that earnings will be adequate to meet charges at all times. This approach implies that the greater the prospective fluctuation in earnings, the higher is the required ratio (or the larger the "cushion" between normal earnings and debt-servicing charges).

This standard also has limitations as a basis for internal determination of debt capacity:

1. The net earnings figure found in the income statement and derived under normal accounting procedures is *not* the same thing as net cash inflow—an assumption which is implicit in the earnings-coverage standard. Even when adjustments are made for the noncash items on the income statement (depreciation charges), as is commonly done in the more sophisticated applications, this equivalence cannot safely be assumed. The time when it may be roughly true is the time when we are least concerned about the hazards of debt, i.e., when sales are approximately the same from period to period. It is in times of rapid change (including recessions) that we are most concerned about debt burden, and then there *are* likely to be sharp differences between net income and net cash flow.
2. The question of what the *proper* ratio is between earnings and debt servicing is problematical. In a given case, should the ratio be two to one or twenty to one? If we exclude externally derived standards or rules of thumb and insist that a company generate its own ratio in terms of its own circumstances, how does it go about doing it? Perhaps the best that could be done would be to work backward from the data of past recessions, which would indicate the low points of net earnings, toward a ratio between this experience and some measure of "normal" earnings with the intention of assuring a one-to-one relationship between net earnings and debt servicing at all times. However, if this is the way it is to be done, the estimate of minimum net earnings would itself provide the measure of debt capacity, and it would be unnecessary to translate it into a ratio. Further, as already noted, there are hazards in a literal translation of past history as a guide for the future. And what of the case where the company has experienced net losses in the past? Does this mean that it has no long-term debt capacity? If a net loss is possible, *no* ratio between normal net earnings and debt servicing, however large, will assure the desired equality in future recessions.

The earnings-coverage standard does not appear to be widely used by industrial corporate borrowers as a basis for formulating debt policy. Where it is used, it appears either to derive from the advice of institutional lenders or investment bankers, or merely to reflect the borrower's attitude toward risk bearing. Its use does not seem to indicate an attempt to measure individual risk by some objective means.

## A More Useful Approach

Granted the apparent inadequacies of conventional debt capacity decision rules for purposes of internal debt policy, is there a practical alternative? I believe there is, but it must be recognized immediately that it rests on data which are substantially more complex than what the conventional rules require, and involve a considerably larger expenditure of time and effort to obtain and interpret. However, in view of the unquestioned importance of the debt-equity decision to the future of individual businesses, and in view of the fact that, as will be shown later, the data have a usefulness which goes well beyond the debt capacity decision, there is reason to give this alternative serious consideration.

The basic questions in the appraisal of the magnitude of risk associated with long-term debt can be stated with deceptive simplicity: What are the chances of the business running out of cash in the foreseeable future? How are these chances changed by the addition of *X* thousands of dollars of annual interest and sinking fund payments? First, it is necessary to specify whether our concern is with "running out of cash" in an absolute sense (cash insolvency) or merely with the risk of cash inadequacy, i.e., running out of cash for certain purposes considered essential to management (for example, a minimum dividend on common stock). We can consider both of these possibilities; but let us focus for the moment on the ultimate hazard, the one commonly associated with excessive debt—the chance of complete depletion of cash reserves, resulting in default on the bond contract and bankruptcy.

There are, of course, a variety of possible circumstances under which a company might have its cash reserves drained off. However, considering the problem from the point of view of mature, normally profitable, and reasonably well-managed companies, it is fair to say that the primary concern with debt is with what might happen during a general or industry recession when sales and profits are depressed by factors beyond the immediate control of management. Thus, when the experienced business executive wishes to instill the proper respect for the hazards of too much debt in the minds of aggressive young men eager for leverage, he will recount harrowing tales of disaster and near disaster in the early 1930's.

## *Refocusing on Problem*

The data we seek are information on the behavior of cash flows during the recession periods. An internal analysis of risk must therefore concern itself not with balance sheet or income statement ratios but directly with the factors which make for changes in cash inflow and outflow. Further, since we are dealing with the common denominator of all transactions, analysis must inevitably take into account *all* major influences on cash flow behavior. In short, the problem is a company-wide problem. All decisions involving cash should be included; and where cash solvency is at stake, there can be no meaningful boundaries on risk except those imposed by the corporate entity itself.

Therefore, it is somewhat artificial to think in terms of "the cash available for debt servicing," as the earnings-coverage standard does, as if it were an identifiable hoard when a number of needs equally as urgent are competing for a limited cash reserve. Consequently, the problem to which this article was originally addressed—determining the capacity to bear the incremental fixed charges of long-term debt—is in reality a much more general one, viz., the problem of *determining the capacity to bear incremental fixed cash outflows for any purpose whatever.*

## *Assessing Key Factors*

The analysis which is proposed in this article as a way of resolving this problem can only be briefly summarized here.[3] It includes:

1. *Identification.* At the outset, it is important to identify the primary factors which produce major changes in cash flow with particular reference to contractions in cash flow. The most significant factor will be sales volume; many of the other factors will be related in greater or lesser degree to sales. However, to cite the example of another major factor, cash expenditures for raw materials, the relationship to sales volume in a downswing is not at all an automatic one, since it also depends on (*a*) the volume of finished goods inventory on hand at the onset of the recession; (*b*) the working relationship between finished goods on hand, work scheduled into production, and raw materials ordering; (*c*) the level of raw materials inventory; and (*d*) the responses of management at all levels to the observed change in sales.

For most factors affecting cash flow, there will be a degree of interdependence and also a range of independent variation, both of which must be identified for the purpose of the analysis.

---

[3]For a full statement, see chaps. vii–ix of Donaldson, *op. cit.*

2. *Extent of Refinement Desired.* Obviously, the list of factors affecting cash flow which are to be given separate consideration could be lengthy, depending on the degree of refinement desired; and the longer the list, the greater the complexity of the analysis. It is therefore essential to form a judgment in advance as to how far refinement in the analysis can or should be carried in view of the objectives of the analysis. It is possible for this cash flow analysis to range all the way from simple and relatively crude approximations to the other extreme of involved mathematical and statistical formulas and even to the programming of recession cash flows on a computer.

In their simplest form, cash flows can be considered in terms of accounting approximations derived from balance sheet and income statement data. Thus, for example, sales revenues might be adjusted for changes in accounts receivable to derive current cash inflow, and cost of goods sold could be converted into expenditures for goods actually produced by adjusting for changes in inventory levels. However, the hazard of simplification is that important changes may be obscured by combining factors that at one time may "net each other out" and at some other time may reinforce each other. For instance, changes in dollar sales are produced by changes in product mix, physical volume, and price.

Here is where the internal analyst has a major advantage. Experience tells him what factors should be given separate treatment, and he has access to the data behind the financial statements, so he can carry refinement as far as he wishes. Ideally, the analysis should be in terms of cash and not accrual accounting information; that is, it should be in terms of cash receipts (not dollar sales) and cash expenditures for raw materials received (not an accounting allocation for raw materials according to the number of units sold).

3. *Analysis of Behavior.* Given a list of all major factors affecting cash flow, the next step is to observe their *individual* behavior over time and, in particular, during recessions. The objection raised earlier to using historical evidence as a guide to debt capacity was that, as usually employed, it is an observation of the *net* effect of change in all these factors on particular occasions, an effect which can be seriously misleading. But if management takes the individual behavior of these factors into account, the problem is minimized to a point where it can be disregarded.

Past experience in a company with an established position in its industry commonly leads its management to the sensible conclusion that while it is theoretically possible for the physical volume of sales, for example, to contract to zero in a recession period, in practice there are reasons why this is highly unlikely to occur. These reasons relate to fundamental and enduring forces in the economy, the industry, the competitive position of the firm, consumer buying habits, and so on. Thus, past experience will suggest a range of recession behavior which describes the outside limits of what recession can be expected to do in the future. These limits I wish to refer to as the *maximum favorable limit* and the *maximum adverse limit* (referring to the effect on cash flows and the cash position). By combining the evidence contained in historical records and the judgment of management directly involved in the making of this history, we can describe these limits of expected behavior for all factors affecting cash flow. It will be part of our analysis to do so, taking careful account of interdependent variation for reasons given earlier.

4. *Expected Range of Recession Behavior.* On the basis of such informed observation, it may be concluded, for example, that the recession contraction in physical volume of sales is not expected to be less than 5 percent nor more than 25 percent of the sales of the period immediately preceding the recession. These are the maximum favorable and maximum adverse limits of sales for the company in question. It may also be concluded that the recession is not expected to last less than one year nor more than three years and that no more than 40 percent of the contraction will be concentrated in the first year of the recession. Naturally, our interest focuses on the maximum *adverse* limit, since we are attempting to assess the chances of running out of cash. By setting such boundaries on the adverse recession behavior of a major factor influencing cash flows, we are beginning to set similar boundaries on the recession behavior of the cash flows themselves.

At this point a question presents itself which has major implications for the subsequent character of the analysis: Is it possible to say anything meaningful about the behavior of sales volume or any other factor *within* the limits that have just been described?

## Probability Analysis

It is possible that there may be some historical evidence in the company on the comparative chances or probabilities of occurrence of sales contractions of, say, 5–11 percent, 12–18 percent, 19–25 percent (or any other breakdown of the range), but the statistical data are likely to be sketchy. It is perhaps more likely that management might, on the basis of experience, make some judgments such as, for example, that the contraction is most likely—say five chances out of ten—to fall in the 12–18 percent range; that the chances of its falling in the 5–11 percent range are three chances out of ten; and that the chances of falling in the 19–25 percent range are two chances out of ten.

If this kind of information can be generated for all factors affecting cash flow, then it is possible to come up with a range of estimates of the cash flow in future recession periods based on all possible combinations of the several factors, and for each estimate a numerical measure of its probability of occurrence. The whole set collectively will describe all anticipated possibilities. By totaling the separate probabilities of those combinations of events exhausting the initial cash balance, we can describe in quantitative terms the over-all chances of cash insolvency. Ideally, we want to know that the chances of cash insolvency, as described by this process of analysis of cash flows are, say, one in twenty or one in fifty.

## *Problems to Surmount*

However, in order to get such a precise measure of the risk of cash insolvency, we need estimates of probability that are within the expected range of behavior and not just the limits of behavior. There are important practical problems that stand in the way of obtaining this type of information and conducting this type of analysis:

1. Although the analysis suggested above appears relatively simple, in practice it could be quite complex, requiring the guidance of someone experienced in probability theory as well as in financial analysis to steer the study of cash flows around potential pitfalls. The problems center mainly on (*a*) accurately describing patterns of adjustment over time and (*b*) assessing the varying degrees of interdependence among the variables. These difficulties are not insurmountable, however, since statisticians have resolved similar ones in the case of other types of business problems.
2. Past recession periods may not have provided enough experience with respect to the behavior of sales, collections, inventory levels, and so forth, on which to base firm estimates of probabilities over the entire range of possible behavior. Some companies have had only two or three recessions in the past twenty years; and even then, sometimes statistics are lacking (although presumably management will have some impressions about the events). But *some* experience with varying recession circumstances is essential even to make a guess. Speaking generally, this limitation on a comprehensive appraisal of the risk magnitude is far more serious than the one of technical competence mentioned first.
3. Top management will not base critical decisions, such as debt policy, on data which it does not understand and/or in which it does not have confidence. This, I believe, is the primary obstacle which stands in the way of widespread use of a comprehensive cash flow analysis as a basis for risk measurement and the determination of debt capacity at the present time. Because the method is complex (particularly in contrast to the customary rules of thumb), and because the judgments on probabilities and other aspects of the analysis may appear—and may in fact be—tenuous, management may well be unwilling to use the results, particularly when corporate solvency is at stake.

However, when all this is said, the fact remains that much of present-day practice is seriously inadequate, and there is an urgent need for a more meaningful approach to the problem, particularly so far as the borrower is concerned. Thus, there is a strong incentive to explore the opportunities for partial or approximate measures of the risk of cash insolvency within the general framework suggested by the comprehensive analysis. One such approach is that to be described. Its aim is to produce an indicator of risk magnitude which can be derived from more conventional and less complex data in which management has confidence.

## *Analysis of Adverse Limits*

The new approach focuses on the expected *limits* of recession behavior and, in particular, on the maximum adverse limit. It is based on the assumption that while management may be unable to assess with confidence the probabilities within the range, it usually has strong opinions as to the expected limits and would be prepared to base decisions upon such expectations. Thus, to return to the example of the sales contraction, management may be unwilling to assign the "betting odds" to the three intervals between a 5 percent and a 25 percent contraction, but it probably does have strong feelings that 25 percent is the "absolute" limit of adversity within the foreseeable future. This feeling is based not merely on past statistics but on an expert appraisal of all the facts surrounding the customer's buying habits and circumstances, the competitive situation, and so on.

Following this procedure leads to a set of estimates of the maximum adverse limit of recession behavior covering each factor affecting cash flow; and it is a comparatively simple matter then to come up with an estimate of the maximum adverse behavior in any future recession of net cash flow itself—in terms of the minimum dollars of net inflow (or maximum dollars of net outflow), period by period. Making similar judgments as to the maximum adverse conditions immediately preceding the recession, including prerecession cash balances, it is next possible to determine whether, under such maximum assumptions, the company would become insolvent and, if so, how soon and by how much.

This calculation in itself will give management some "feel" for the nearness or remoteness of the event of cash insolvency. It may demonstrate, as I have done in the case of certain companies, that even under these maximum adverse assumptions the company still has a positive cash balance. If this is so, the amount of this minimum balance is an objective judgment of the total amount of incremental fixed cash charges which the company could assume without *any* threat of insolvency. Making some assumptions about the nature and the terms of the debt contract, this figure could be converted into the principal amount of additional debt which could be assumed with the expectation of complete safety.

Suppose, on the other hand, that the maximum adverse assumptions produce a negative cash balance, indicating the possibility of insolvency under certain adverse conditions. This does not mean that the long-term debt is excluded (except for those managements for whom any action which creates or increases the risk of insolvency, no matter how small it may be, is intolerable). The more likely response will be that, provided the chances are "sufficiently remote," the company is fully prepared to run the risk.

Thus, we are back to the problem of assessing the magnitude of the risk and the extent to which it would be increased by any given amount of debt. As a means of gaining a more precise impression of the chances of insolvency at the adverse end of the range of recession behavior, without going through the formal process of assigning probability values, I suggest that a second adverse limit be defined for each of the factors affecting cash flow. This will be called the *most probable adverse limit.* It reflects management's judgment as to the limit of *normal* recession behavior, as opposed to the maximum adverse limit, which includes all possibilities, however remote.

## *Modes and Ranges*

A visual representation of these two adverse limits of behavior is shown in Figure 1. Assuming experience and expected behavior are somewhat normally distributed about a mode (i.e., the value of most frequent occurrence), there will be:

1. A range of values clustered around this point, where most of past experience has been concentrated and where "bets" as to what the future is likely to bring will also be concentrated.
2. Extremes at either end of the range representing events that have a relatively small chance of happening.

It will be seen that the most probable limit cuts off the extreme "tail" of the frequency distribution in a somewhat imprecise and yet meaningful way. In setting the limits of expected sales contractions, for example, management would be saying that while sales *could,* in its judgment, contract as much as 25 percent, a contraction is *not likely* to exceed, say, 20 percent. This 20 percent is then the most probable adverse limit. While my terms may be new to businessmen, the distinction described is one which is commonly made and one on which judgments as to risk are often based.

FIGURE 1

EXAMPLE OF MAXIMUM AND MOST PROBABLE LIMITS OF RECESSION BEHAVIOR

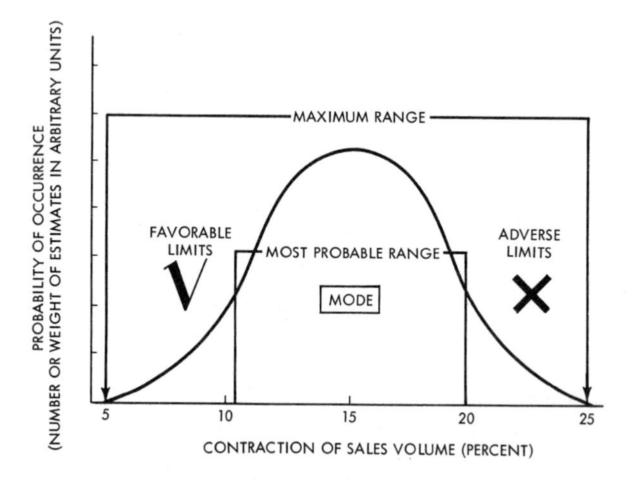


From the data on the most probable adverse limits of the various factors affecting cash flow, the most probable adverse limit of recession *net* cash flows would be calculated and, from this, the most probable minimum recession cash *balance*. This last figure reflects management's best judgment as to the adverse limit of what is "likely to happen" as opposed to what "could happen" to net cash flows.

## *Guide Lines for Policy*

At this point, it should be noted that when considering cash flows from the point of view of solvency, the list of possible expenditures would be stripped down to those which are absolutely essential for continuity of corporate existence and for the generation of current income. (We shall presently bring into consideration other less mandatory expenditures such as dividends and capital expenditures.) Thinking in these terms, suppose the recession cash flow analysis indicates that under the maximum adverse assumptions the minimum cash balance would be negative, say a deficit of $1.5 million. Suppose further that under the most probable adverse assumptions the minimum recession cash balance is a surplus of $3 million. How are these estimates to be interpreted as a guide to corporate debt capacity?

First, it is obvious in this example that management's expectations about the factors governing cash flow include the possibility that the company could become insolvent without any additional debt. However, this possibility is considered to have a relatively remote chance of occurrence, since when the analysis is restricted to the most probable limit of recession behavior, the company is left with a positive minimum cash balance. The amount of this balance is a rough measure of the *total amount of additional fixed cash outflows (e.g., debt charges) which could be incurred without creating the threat of insolvency* in the event of normal recession conditions. Thus:

> If the likely limit of the recession is expected to be two years, the company could stand additional debt servicing of $1.5 million per year of recession. This sum can be readily converted into an equivalent principal amount. Assuming a twenty-year term loan repayable in equal annual installments and bearing 5 percent interest, an additional debt of approximately $15 million could be considered safe under ordinary recession conditions.

Let me emphasize that the cash balance would not be taken as a guide to debt capacity unless management were prepared to live with some chance of insolvency—a chance which would obviously be increased by the new debt. If management were not so inclined, it would reject debt or, alternatively, adopt a debt limit somewhere between zero and $15 million. In any case, management would not increase debt *beyond* $15 million unless it were prepared to accept the chance of insolvency within the most probable range of recession experience. Because of the way the most probable limit has been defined, the chances of insolvency would be expected to increase rapidly and substantially if debt were to exceed $15 million by any significant amount.

There is, of course, nothing sacred about the $15 million limit set by management's judgment on the limits of normal recession experience. There is no reason why some managements would not increase debt capital substantially above this figure, assuming the funds were available. Such a step depends entirely on the willingness to bear the financial risks and on the potential rewards for such risk bearing. The foregoing type of analysis does, however, perform the essential function of alerting management to the range of debt beyond which risks may be expected to increase substantially.

## *Practical Advantages*

It is now apparent that the analytical approach proposed here produces a criterion stated in terms of *the number of dollars of debt servicing* that are acceptable within management's concepts of risk bearing at a given point in time. The criterion is derived entirely from within and is completely independent of external judgments or rules of thumb. While it is admittedly crude and approximate when compared with the theoretical ideal of risk management, I believe it to be meaningful and useful in practice and, in this as in other respects, superior to the conventional forms for expressing debt limits.

It must be added, however, that because the recommended analysis is partial and approximate, those who adopt it must use it as they use current decision rules. That is, they must use it as a general guide and not as a precision instrument. For most managements, this will be entirely adequate.

## Better Decision Making

One of the real advantages of this approach to debt capacity is that it raises—and answers—a much broader question. As previously indicated, the analysis is actually concerned with the capacity to assume additional fixed cash outflows of any kind, and whatever capacity is demonstrated is not confined to debt servicing. Thus, if it is concluded from the example just given that the company in question can stand an additional outflow in recessions totaling $3 million, the first decision to be made by management *is how to use this capacity.*

There are a variety of ways in which the capacity may be used: to cover payments under a lease contract, to maintain a continuous research program, to stabilize employment, to pay a regular dividend in good times and bad, and so on. These are all competing uses for whatever capacity exists. With the information that the cash flow analysis provides, management now can begin to assign priorities and have some idea of how far it can hope to go in realizing its objectives. If debt servicing is given top priority, then the data have been a means of defining debt capacity.

It is because the proposed analysis has much broader significance than the question of debt (important as that question may be) that I believe the expenditure of time, effort, and money required to generate the data needed is well justified for the individual corporation. The analysis provides information which lies at the base of a whole range of financial and other decisions and has continuing significance. Moreover, most corporate treasurers have the staff and the basic data to undertake a careful and detailed study of the behavior of factors affecting cash flow.

### *Testing for Cash Adequacy*

Up to this point the analysis of cash flows has been discussed in terms of cash solvency. As indicated earlier, this means that attention is confined to outflows which are vital to survival. It was also indicated, however, that the risk of insolvency was part of a broader family of risks, described as the risk of cash inadequacy. In discussing the question of solvency with management, we often find that while there are certain expenditures which *could* be slashed to zero in an emergency, there is a reluctance to take action which would put management in a position of having to do so. These are expenditures which must be treated as mandatory for policy reasons, because management believes that to interrupt them would be detrimental to the long-term interest of the corporation. Among the best examples of such expenditures are certain minimum payments for research, for capital assets, and for preferred and common dividends.

This situation can readily be incorporated into the type of analysis outlined earlier. I refer to the method for doing this as the *test for cash adequacy* as opposed to the test for cash solvency. As soon as management has defined the "irreducible minimum" for these expenditures under recession conditions, they are merely added to the outflows of the previous analysis; then the figure generated for the maximum adverse or most probable adverse recession cash balance is the balance which remains over and above such payments. To return to the example previously used:

> The effect would be to wipe out all or some portion of the most probable minimum balance ($3 million) or to add to the maximum adverse deficit ($1.5 million). Thus, if the irreducible minimum is considered to be two years of common dividends at $500,000 a year plus $1 million of minimum capital expenditures, the result would be to cut the most probable balance back to $1 million. The capacity to assume additional fixed cash outflows is thereby substantially reduced. Obviously, management in this case is giving priority to the dividend and capital expenditures over debt leverage—or over any other use for the funds on hand.

One of the benefits of such an analysis is to make management's priorities explicit, to recognize their competing character, and to make possible a reevaluation of their relative importance to the company.

Making separate tests for cash solvency and cash adequacy serves another important purpose. Most discussions of the hazards of debt imply that the danger is the risk of insolvency, and this danger is usually treated with proper respect. However, our analysis may demonstrate that within the range of management's expectations there is little or no risk of insolvency but a substantial risk of cash inadequacy, particularly if large amounts of long-term debt are added. If, in the past, management has been setting limits on debt in terms of an assumed risk of insolvency and now finds that the only significant risk is that of inability to meet certain minimum dividend payments and the like, it may well be disposed to assume a greater magnitude of risk and take on more debt. A management which would reject the risk of insolvency if it exceeded a chance of one in fifty might be prepared to accept a risk of abandoning cash dividends for a year or two if the chance did not exceed, say, one in twenty.

In short, once management knows the *kind* of risk it is taking, it may begin to draw distinctions between one form of contingency and another, and not operate on the general assumption that the only concern is that of possible insolvency. Better information is thus a prerequisite for better decisions.

## *Reappraising Present Rules*

Assuming management can, by the means described, come up with an independent appraisal of its long-term debt capacity, what does this imply for existing decision rules obtained from external sources or inherited from the past? Does it mean that they will be ignored completely? The answer is likely to be no. Debt policy cannot be made in a vacuum. It must take account of the lenders' willingness to lend and also of the reactions of equity investors who make judgments on the risks inherent in the corporation.

One of the first results of the analysis, therefore, is to reappraise existing debt capacity decision rules. To illustrate:

> Suppose a company has been assuming, as many do, that it can safely incur long-term debt up to a maximum of 30 percent of capitalization. This rule can be translated into its equivalent of dollars of annual debt-servicing charges and directly compared with the results of the recession cash flow analysis. In view of the fact that the rule probably has been derived from external sources, it is likely that the annual debt servicing which it permits either exceeds or falls short of the amount of cash flow indicated by the internal analysis.
>
> In view of the approximate nature of the analysis, however, this is not likely to cause a change in debt policy unless the amount of the variation is substantial. It is also possible, of course, that the existing decision rule and the cash flow analysis will produce the same result, in which case the existing rule will appear verified. But this cannot be known in advance of the analysis, and in any case the data have been converted into a form which is much more meaningful for the purposes involved.

Such a comparison gives a measure of management's attitude toward the risk that is implicit in the existing decision rule (although management probably had no clear idea of what the risk magnitude was at the time the rule was established).

The results of the cash flow analysis can also be compared with the lender's concept of debt capacity—if different from that of the corporation. While lenders are often reluctant to make statements on the outside limits of what they will lend, they will, from time to time, give indications of what they consider an appropriate capital structure for a given industry and company. If the borrower's appraisal of his capacity exceeds that of the lender, he may well decide to push the latter to the limit of his willingness to lend. Without good cash flow data, many borrowers appear reluctant to argue their case aggressively, probably because of uncertaintly as to where the safe limit lies.

The results can also be related to other aspects of the debt capacity question, such as the requirements for an A bond rating or the risk expectations of equity investors which appear to be implicit in some price-earnings ratio (assuming this can be determined). Once again, the comparison is between whatever unused debt capacity is indicated by the internal analysis and the standards imposed by external considerations with the aim of probing the acceptable and useful upper limits of long-term debt.

I have carried out this type of analysis for a sample of companies in different industries and made comparisons with existing debt capacity standards of both the corporations themselves and their lending institutions. The data strongly indicate that there are, in fact, major inconsistencies between managements' explicit expectations regarding recession cash flows and the expectations which are implicit in accepted ratios of debt capacity. The evidence is by no means adequate to make any safe or meaningful generalization about the over-all character of industrial debt policy. Nevertheless, among the large and mature corporations which are the basis of the study the evidence seems to suggest:

1. Either the risks of debt have been significantly overrated by a substantial number of firms.
2. Or some managements tend to be unusually conservative toward this aspect of corporate risk.

## Future Trends

The trend of economic events in the past twenty years suggests that there is both a need and an opportunity for a more refined approach to the debt-equity choice in corporate structures. As the specter of the depression of the 1930's has faded into the past and confidence in our capacity to avoid a repetition of extreme economic stagnation has grown, a new generation of corporate executives has shown increasing willingness to use long-term debt financing as a source of funds for consolidation and expansion.

So long as long-term debt is avoided or kept to minor proportions, crude decision rules providing wide margins of safety are quite adequate. As the proportions of debt increase, however, the need for a sharper pencil and a more careful analysis grows. This need is further reinforced by the increase in other kinds of fixed cash commitments such as lease payments and the noncontractual but nonetheless vital steady flows required for research, dividends, and the like. Greater stability in the economy over an extended period is likely to encourage a variety of rigidities in cash outflows, and simple rules of thumb are inadequate to cope with the problems these present.

Along with the increasing need for improved analysis has come a greater capacity to carry out this analysis. This improvement derives both from better data and from improved techniques of processing and analyzing data. Financial executives today have access to far more data on cash flows and the factors behind cash flows than they did twenty years ago—far more, in fact, than many are actually putting to use. They also have access to more sophisticated approaches to the analysis of complex data and to machines which can reduce these data to manageable proportions. As time goes on and financial management becomes increasingly familiar with these tools of analysis and more aware of the opportunities they afford, the current reluctance to adopt a more complex analytical framework is bound to diminish.

But there is one hitch. However sophisticated the financial officer may be in the newer techniques, there is little merit in serving up a diet of financial data to the board of directors, as a basis for the financial decision, which is too rich for their current digestive capacity. It is for this reason that I have not attempted in this article to convert the reader to a full-scale internal analysis of risk and its components. Rather, I have taken on the more modest objectives of alerting top management to four key points bearing on the debt capacity decision:

1. While external sources of advice can and should be consulted as an aid to decision making, the question of debt capacity is essentially an internal one to be settled by management with reference to its individual circumstances and individual preferences.
2. Current rules of thumb regarding debt capacity are seriously inadequate as a framework for this decision.
3. The answer lies in a knowledge of the behavior of cash flows and in having a useful measure of the capacity to assume incremental fixed cash outflows.
4. Management needs approaches that will enable it to approximate its

debt capacity within the context of data with which it is already familiar and in terms of judgments to which it has long been accustomed. The approach described in this article meets these criteria.

By accepting and acting on these points, management would take an important step forward toward debt-equity decisions in which borrowers and lenders alike could have greater confidence.

*Chapter* 13

# *In Defense of Preferred Stock**

By Gordon Donaldson

THE RECORD of corporate financing over the past ten years gives clear evidence that preferred stock has declined substantially in popularity as a source of funds. This change is also reflected in the attitude of those who are discussing and writing about the contractual form of new financing.[1] Their mood of disenchantment with preferred stock commonly arises from a simple and obvious line of reasoning, which runs as follows: In a company that makes a practice of paying dividends on its common stock, the prior claim of a cumulative preferred issue becomes an unavoidable fixed charge on earnings; under such circumstances, the company would be better off paying interest on a bond issue that carries a lower rate and is deductible for purposes of computing the corporate income tax. And the spread between after-tax bond interest and before-tax preferred dividends has been large enough in recent years to convince many companies not only to avoid straight preferred stock in new financing but also to eliminate any preferred stock currently outstanding.

In spite of the popularity of this thesis today, both with businessmen and business educators, I intend in this article to challenge some of the

---

*Reprinted by permission from *Harvard Business Review,* Vol. XL (July-August, 1962), pp. 123–36.

[1]See, for example, Sidney Robbins, "A Bigger Role for Income Bonds," *Harvard Business Review,* Vol. XXXIII (November-December, 1955); Robert W. Johnson, "Subordinated Debentures: Debt That Serves as Equity," *Journal of Finance,* Vol. X (March, 1955); Donald Fergusson, "Recent Developments in Preferred Stock Financing," *Journal of Finance,* Vol. VII (September, 1952).

assumptions on which the reasoning has been based and to question the wisdom of some of the conclusions and action that have followed from it. In particular, I plan to show that:

1. The similarities between preferred stock and debt should not lead to a disregard of important distinctions between the relative risks of financing by these two securities. When the chips are down—when cash inadequacy threatens—these differences can be all-important.
2. Comparisons between the merits of debt and preferred stock tend to mislead and confuse the issue, since it is often true that the surviving permanent source of funds is not debt but common equity (retained earnings).
3. While debt is a cheaper source than preferred, and should be used up to the acceptable limit, the real contest is between preferred stock and retained earnings. A policy which automatically gives priority to retained earnings as a source of funds may be favoring the high-tax-bracket shareholder at the low-tax-bracket shareholder's expense.

## Decline in Popularity

Anyone who is familiar with historical trends in corporate financing knows that the general popularity of the various security types in common use varies from decade to decade in response to numerous influences. It is therefore no surprise to observe a distinct trend in the market for a particular security form, as has been true of straight preferred stock in the post-World War II period. In this instance the trend of popularity so far as *issuers* are concerned (investors may feel quite differently) has been markedly downward, as the statistics on new security issues in Figure 1 suggest.

These data may be explained in part by a tendency for the use of preferred stock to fall off in recession periods. Of particular interest, however, is the fact that since World War II, and especially in the last decade, preferred issues have been held to a relatively small fraction of the new corporate security offerings (an average of 4.2 percent in the years 1957–61). And this is only part of the story. Many corporations with preferred issues outstanding from an earlier period in their financial history have been retiring these issues and substituting either debt or common equity. There has been an absolute decline in the number of preferred issues listed on the New York Stock Exchange—from 461 in 1954 to 402 in 1961.[2] Nor do these statistics adequately reflect the desires of many companies; numerous managements that *would* have eliminated preferred stock have been frustrated by the par-

[2]See Pearson Hunt, Charles M. Williams, and Gordon Donaldson, *Basic Business Finance* (rev. ed.; Homewood, Ill.: Richard D. Irwin, Inc., 1961), p. 368.

ticular terms of their preferred stock contracts (especially the noncallable feature).

FIGURE 1

DECREASING POPULARITY OF PREFERRED STOCK ISSUES

*Source:* Securities and Exchange Commission, *Statistical Bulletin,* February, 1962, p. 4; 1942–60: Department of Commerce, Office of Business Economics, "SEC New Security Issues," *Business Statistics* (Washington, D.C.: U.S. Government Printing Office, 1961), p. 97; 1920–37: Department of Commerce, Office of Business Economics, "Securities Issued," *Survey of Current Business,* 1940 Supplement, p. 68.

## *Reasons for Disfavor*

As a preliminary to a discussion of this trend, it is important to consider the argument against preferred stock in some detail. It runs something like this:

1. Although it is a legal fact that management is not required to pay preferred dividends on a regular basis, as a matter of corporate policy it is necessary for a responsible management to *behave* as if the preferred dividend were a fixed contractual commitment. Companies

which have established a pattern of regular dividends on common stock would do grave damage to the market price of the common if this pattern should be interrupted. It is therefore vital to keep preferred dividends up to date in order to pay something on the common. It would be unwise to formulate and implement financial policy which deliberately ran the risk of suspending preferred dividends.

2. Thus, for all practical purposes, the preferred dividend is like bond interest, but without the advantages that a debt contract provides. Almost invariably, the dividend rate on a preferred issue is significantly higher than the interest rate on a long-term debt issue of the same company; and being a return on equity, it is not deductible for purposes of computing the corporate income tax. For example:

   The after-tax cost of a 5 percent preferred issue would be $5.00 per $100 of new funds, whereas the after-tax cost of an equivalent 3½ percent debt issue would be $1.68 per $100 of new funds. The debt issue reduces taxable income by $3.50 per $100 of new funds and thus reduces the tax by 52 percent of $3.50. The net cost of the debt is therefore $3.50 minus this "tax shield" of $1.82.

   It is this difference in the tax treatment which appears to be the primary explanation for the declining popularity of preferred stock in recent years. Remember that the basic corporate tax rate went from 24 percent in 1940 to 40 percent in 1942 to 52 percent in 1951, not to mention the years of excess profits taxes.

3. If debt is much cheaper than preferred equity capital, and if—*for policy reasons*—preferred dividends must be treated like mandatory bond interest, then it makes sense to substitute debt for preferred wherever possible.

## Debt versus Preferred

So far, the evidence and the arguments look incontrovertible. How is it possible to make a sensible case in favor of the use of straight preferred stock?

As the first step toward answering this, let us consider the decision to retire an outstanding issue of preferred stock as it has appeared to many corporations and indicate how they have handled it. In analyzing the action taken, I propose to show that there are limits to the logic of the argument in favor of eliminating preferred stock and that preferred stock is sometimes underrated as a financing vehicle.

### *Case of Company A*

For the sake of conciseness, let us look at the following example of company A:

As far back as 1947, this company decided to replace its preferred stock with debt. The annual report stated that "in order to take advantage of prevailing (low) interest rates," management had sold $25 million worth of 20-year bonds with a coupon rate of 2⅝ percent, using the proceeds to redeem 250,000 shares of 4½ percent cumulative preferred stock. The annual reduction in cash outflow resulting from this action, measured in after-tax dollars (tax rate of 38 percent), was $718,125. The advantage seemed clear enough.

But was this the end of the analysis? I suggest that it was not. First, let us note that the company could not have taken this action if it had been using its debt capacity to the limit. At the time, it was at least $25 million short of its accepted limit of borrowing, measured by whatever standard the company and its creditors chose to employ. In utilizing this capacity for the purpose of "saving" the preferred dividend charges, the company was precluding the use of this limited financial resource (the power to "trade on the equity") for other purposes. There was, therefore, the real but unrecorded cost of the lost earnings which could have been realized if this money had been put to work elsewhere, say in the acquisition of a new plant facility.

Thus, it can be argued that instead of saving $718,125, the company actually lost money, the amount to be measured by the difference between the 4½ percent preferred dividend and the amount (say 10 percent) that might have been earned by the alternative use of the funds.

But suppose that the company did not have an alternative for this unused debt capacity. The question then arises whether the lack of an alternative use was temporary or long-run. If temporary, then at some later date the decision might have to be made whether to decline an investment opportunity because debt capacity was used up or reissue a new preferred stock, in which case the anticipated savings would have been short-lived.

Actually, the record of corporate finance in recent years suggests that the reissuance of preferred does not often occur in practice and that the kind of action taken by company A is usually intended to eliminate preferred stock from the capital structure permanently. In line with this objective, one often hears the expressed desire of management for a simple capital structure, by which is usually meant a structure that keeps red tape and restraints on management action to a minimum. It is often felt that the legal specifications of a preferred stock issue make life unnecessarily complicated when management contemplates certain moves.

If, then, there is no intention of reissuing preferred stock, we are led to the conclusion either that there are no foreseeable alternative uses for the company's unused debt capacity or that management prefers the "assured" savings of the redemption of the preferred stock ($718,125 in our example) to the less certain 10 percent (or whatever) return on an alternative investment in, say, new productive facilities.

## *Limits on Investment*

At this point, I should like to question an assumption often made in discussion of corporate investment policy. It is the custom among authors in the area of finance, particularly academic people, to assume that companies have an inexhaustible supply of investment opportunities and that they do (or should) take advantage of these opportunities to the limit of available capital—or at least to the point where the net return from the investment over and above the cost of capital no longer compensates adequately for the risks involved. Thus the key factor which restrains further investment is assumed to be financial.

Observation of many of our larger and more mature corporations today suggests that this is not so, at least at their present stage of development. The evidence is simple and obvious. Many of these companies have available to them a variety of capital sources—debt and equity—which they are not using even though the money is available at rates which appear acceptable when compared to the return the company is making on its invested capital. Proof that this situation is common can be found in the records of those companies which over the past twenty years have functioned with near or full independence of the external capital markets in spite of low interest rates and high price-earnings ratios.[3]

This suggests that in practice there are reasons other than the availability of cheap capital which place distinct limits on investment, reasons which may be perfectly valid and rational from an over-all management point of view, such as the limits of managerial or organizational capacity, to name only two. Of course, the matter could be debated at great length; but for the purposes of this article, I shall simply accept as part of reality the fact that nonfinancial restraints on investment decisions are often dominant in many of our leading business corporations. I am also prepared to accept the idea that this situation may be both reasonable and rational. This situation then leads to the possibility that the company may find itself with substantial *unusable* debt capacity for conventional investment purposes over extended periods of time.

Perhaps it would be well to be more specific about the phrase "debt capacity." As I shall use the term, it has these meanings:

1. It expresses the idea that a company desires to limit the threat to the corporate cash position posed by fixed debt-servicing obligations.

[3]For sample data, see Gordon Donaldson, *Corporate Debt Capacity* (Boston: Division of Research, Harvard Business School, 1961).

2. This limit will reflect in part the general financial position of the business and the anticipated fluctuation in cash flows, and in part the subjective attitude of management toward risk bearing.
3. Any new debt will, by the nature of the contract, add to the risk of running out of cash.
4. Up to some point, management will be prepared to add to this risk in the interests of furthering the corporate investment program, and beyond that point the anticipated benefits from added investment will appear inadequate to compensate for the magnitude of the threat that the means of financing poses to the existing investment.
5. At any particular time a company may find itself at this limit to debt capacity, short of it, or even unavoidable beyond it.[4]

### *Substituting Common Equity*

If there is unusable debt capacity for reasons such as those described earlier, then it appears quite appropriate to consider the elimination of preferred stock as a use of this capacity. However, all too frequently the sequence of events is more complicated than this. The debt which is issued to redeem the preferred generally carries a sinking fund provision. Its net effect is to retire the debt over a period of time and ultimately replace preferred equity capital with common equity capital (retained earnings). This process may be slow, as in the case of a twenty-five year debenture, or fast, as in the case of a short-maturity term loan or a convertible debenture. Some companies shortcut the debt vehicle entirely by the use of accumulated cash reserves.

If, then, the ultimate effect (and perhaps intent) of the debt issue is to replace the preferred by common stock or retained earnings, we need to consider whether this result preserves the financial gains that the substitution of debt itself affords. It is true, of course, that if the debt is replaced by retained earnings rather than new common, as is more often the case, the gains *appear* to be enhanced, since the company now "saves" the amount of the bond interest.

## Shareholder Interests

But whether this amount is really a saving depends on one's point of view. Traditionally, commentators on the financial scene have identified themselves with the point of view of the common shareholders as the legal owners of the corporation. Traditionally, management also has identified itself with this point of view, because of the legally de-

[4]For a more detailed discussion, see Gordon Donaldson, "New Framework for Corporate Debt Policy," *Harvard Business Review*, Vol. XL (March-April, 1962), p. 117.

fined chain of authority, and has continued this way of thinking down to the present, at least so far as its public posture on financial matters is concerned. While there are bound to be differences between the best interests of management, the corporation as a permanent business entity, and the common shareholder, these variances need not concern us here. Let us proceed to evaluate policy in terms of what appears best from the point of view of the common shareholders—the basic ownership group which has the residual claim on assets and earnings and which assumes the basic risk—and leave to the reader whatever modifications of this position seem appropriate in an individual case.

## *Who Are the Owners?*

First, the investor in common stocks needs to be characterized. The situation varies greatly from one company to another. In some companies which are closely held, it is possible to get a very precise idea of the shareholders' circumstances and objectives. However, most companies with widely held common stock have only a vague notion of their stockholder group. In the absence of detailed information on the owners of a specific company, we can for purposes of discussion refer to data on all shareholders in the United States:

As Table 1 shows, the various financial intermediaries account for only 8.7 percent of the total. The authors of the study on which Table 1 is based predict that by 1970 this proportion will have increased to 15.5 percent.

TABLE 1

OWNERSHIP OF OUTSTANDING CORPORATE STOCKS IN 1959

| *Owner Category* | *Billions of Dollars* | *Percent* |
|---|---|---|
| Life insurance companies | $ 4.6 | 1.0% |
| Corporate pension funds | 8.4 | 1.9 |
| Fire and casualty insurance companies | 11.5 | 2.6 |
| Investment companies | 13.9 | 3.1 |
| Miscellaneous nonbank institutions | 0.5 | 0.1 |
| Total financial intermediaries | $ 38.9 | 8.7% |
| All other owners | 407.5 | 91.3 |
| Total owners | $446.4 | 100.0% |

*Source:* Robert A. Kavish and Judith Mackey, "A Financial Framework for Economic Growth," *Journal of Finance*, Vol. XVI (May, 1961), pp. 202–25; see, in particular, Table 3, "Ownership of Outstanding Primary Securities, 1959."

Thus the dominant group is and will continue to be "all other owners"; and these are primarily individuals, though charitable organizations and business corporations will account for some of the $407-billion figure. It may be noted in passing, however, that the financial intermediaries undoubtedly have a significant influence on corporate thinking regarding its shareholders, probably out of proportion to their numerical importance. These intermediaries are in general a relatively sophisticated and articulate group, and they make frequent direct contacts with management.

## *Tax Considerations*

As for the circumstances and the objectives of the dominant investor group, the matters of greatest significance to the question of capital structure are (1) the form in which the gain from the investment is to be received, whether dividends or capital gains; and (2) the timing and certainty of these expected gains.

In any shareholder-oriented discussion of corporate financial policy, the question always presented is whether the shareholders are satisfied with the existing mix of dividends and capital gains or whether a different mix involving a larger or smaller payout of earnings would be preferable. Many corporate financial officers assert that in general their shareholders prefer capital gains—because of the favorable tax treatment—and use this as a defense of the policy of financing growth largely or exclusively with retained earnings.

But the tax factor has often been a matter of confusion because of the considerable variations in the personal income and tax brackets of various individual shareholders. Generally, the tax consideration is a minor one for financial intermediaries and other institutional or corporate holders because for them dividend income is either tax-free or subject to low rates. Therefore, it is the large majority of individual stockholders that we must look at. Here, statistics obtained from Internal Revenue Service individual income tax returns are helpful in getting a broad picture of this group. Thus, Table 2 shows:

1. While it is true there is some growth in the holdings of lower income groups, there is little evidence to support the idea that a system of "people's capitalism" is an accomplished fact. It can be seen that 50 percent of the reported dividend income is received by less than 1 percent of the individuals reporting and goes to income brackets in excess of $30,000 a year. For this group the personal income tax rate is in excess of 59 percent. (It is likely that this group is even more influential in matters of corporate policy than the 50 percent of holdings would suggest).
2. As much as 80 percent of the dividend income is received by persons in the income brackets of $10,000 to $20,000 and up, where the in-

TABLE 2

INCOME AND TAX-BRACKET CLASSIFICATION OF U.S. SHAREHOLDERS

| | *Number of Individual Returns* | | *Share of Total Dividend Income* | | *Tax Bracket* | |
|---|---|---|---|---|---|---|
| *Gross Income Class* | *Percent of Total* | *Cumulative* | *Percent of Total* | *Cumulative* | *Average Proportion of Gross Income Taxable* | *Range in Tax Rate* |
| Over $200,000...... | 0.01% | 0.01% | 10% | 10% | 80% | 90–91% |
| $100,000–$200,000.. | 0.04 | 0.05 | 10 | 20 | 80 | 84–90 |
| 45,000– 100,000.. | 0.29 | 0.34 | 20 | 40 | 80 | 65–84 |
| 30,000– 45,000.. | 0.37 | 0.71 | 10 | 50 | 80 | 59–65 |
| 20,000– 30,000.. | 0.58 | 1.29 | 10 | 60 | 77 | 47–59 |
| 10,000– 20,000.. | 7.72 | 9.01 | 20 | 80 | 71 | 34–47 |
| Less than $10,000... | 90.99 | 100.00 | 20 | 100 | 17–63 | 20–30 |
| Weighted average tax range*...... | | | | | | 52–63% |

*Weighted by share of total dividend income.

*Source:* U.S. Treasury Department, *Internal Revenue Service Statistics of Income, 1959 (Preliminary)* (Washington, D.C.: U.S. Government Printing Office, 1960); *Income Tax Returns for 1959* (Washington, D.C.: U.S. Government Printing Office, 1960).

come tax rate is at least 34 percent. This group accounts for less than 10 percent of the individuals reporting.

3. Considering the total group reporting divided income, the average range of personal income tax, weighted by the proportion of total dividend income received per class, is 52 percent to 63 percent.

Whatever the limitations of these statistics, the evidence is clear that capital gains with their maximum tax rate of 25 percent offer a clear advantage, dollar for dollar actually realized, over dividend income to the large majority of shareholders. The figures in Table 2 provide an approximate measure of the amount of the advantage.

With this information about the financial circumstances of a large sample of common shareholders, we can now consider more objectively the desirability of replacing a preferred stock issue with common equity capital, i.e., retained earnings.

## Alternatives Analyzed

*Is* it desirable to retire a company's preferred stock? *Is* it desirable to replace the issues with debt or retained earnings and thus "simplify" the corporate financial structure? To make the discussion of these questions as objective as possible, I shall use, as an up-to-date example, an unnamed but actual corporation. The financial data (rounded to convenient magnitudes) are summarized in Table 3.

TABLE 3

FINANCIAL DATA FOR COMPANY B

|  |  |
|---|---|
| Annual sales volume | $400 million |
| Current book value of assets | $125 million |
| Current long-term capital structure: | |
| Debt (3–4% interest) | 13% |
| Preferred stock (5½% dividend) | 10 |
| Common equity | 77 |
| | 100% |
| Record of investment (past 20 years): | |
| *a*) Average annual rate of growth (percent of net tangible assets) | 15% |
| *b*) Total internally generated funds as a percent of need for new funds for investment | 114% |
| Current market price of common (2 million shares) | $44–$37 |
| Current price-earnings ratio | 10–8.4 |
| Current dividend yield | 5.9% |

Let us assume that this company is considering the retirement of its callable 5½ percent preferred stock. In order to focus sharply on the issue at one point in time, we shall further assume that the funds necessary for this purpose have been accumulated from past earnings and are held in a liquid reserve. Alternatively, we might assume that the retirement could be financed by the use of debt repayable out of earnings over future years, or by the sale of a convertible debenture or of additional common. In each case a replacement by common equity funds is anticipated, but the process may be stretched out over several years and the impact thereby obscured. We also assume that management has in mind no alternative use for the accumulated reserves in the foreseeable future.

Thus, company B's choice is reduced to these three alternatives:

1. Allow the funds to remain invested in low-risk, low-yield, short-term securities.
2. Retire the preferred as proposed.
3. Pay the money out in dividends by declaring an extra dividend or more gradually by a moderate increase in the payout ratio.

It is difficult to defend the first alternative as a permanent use of corporate funds; hence the real choice is between the second and third possibilities. The decision is usually in favor of the second. Management is generally reluctant to raise common dividends for reasons other than a demonstrated increase in long-term earning capacity. It is here that management is likely to plead shareholder preference as a guide to policy. It will commonly argue, in defense of preserving the status quo, that it is easy to increase a dividend but hard to cut it back, and that in any case shareholders would prefer capital gains to dividend income for tax reasons. This latter argument usually goes unchallenged, and the statistics of personal income cited earlier *appear* to support the position. But let us take a look at this alternative in terms of our specific example.

## *Increasing the Dividends*

Suppose that instead of paying back the preferred shareholders, the accumulated earnings are retained as a permanent source of funds, and the $10 million required to retire the preferred issue is paid out instead to the common shareholders. What are the effects of this action on the financial position of the common shareholder as compared to the effects of retiring the preferred?

1. *The money received is going to be taxed, and taxed heavily, as personal income.* In order to give a specific illustration of the effect of taxation, let us assume that the shareholder group of company B is a representative sample of the shareholders described in Table 2. As previously indicated, the weighted average tax bracket (weighted according to concentration of dividend income not numbers of shareholders) comes out as 52–63 percent. Assuming that the $10 million can be distributed so as not to alter substantially the recipients' tax bracket, the shareholders of this company would receive, after taxes, approximately $4.3 million to invest elsewhere (using 57 percent as the midpoint of the range).
2. *The withdrawal of $10 million will affect the market price of the stock.* In theory, one might assume that if $10 million is withdrawn from a corporation, then it is worth $10 million less than before, and the market price should reflect this. However, the actual behavior of the market price, which is more concerned with income than with asset values, does not seem to follow this pattern.

   In general, the market price is primarily influenced by dividends per share and earnings. The increased dividend payments, particularly if spread over several years, would tend to raise market price. As for earnings, since (according to our original assumption) the $10 million is not needed to support the basic earning power of the company, they should not be adversely affected. There would be some loss of income due to the liquidation of dividend-bearing investments, but the rate of return here is low, say 1½ percent after taxes; and in any case, this income would also be lost if management were to retire the preferred stock instead. Any effects on earnings will therefore be ignored in both cases.

## *Value of Holding Preferred*

Thus, we arrive at the conclusion that the common shareholders would, under the dividend distribution alternative, have $4.3 million more in usable funds plus or minus the change in the market price of the common stock of company B due to the change in dividend payout. How does this compare to the plan for retirement of the preferred? The details are:

1. *The earnings on the common shares are increased by the amount of the preferred dividend, $550,000.* The gain to the shareholders should come through the capitalization of this increased earning power; this would be presumably at the prevailing price-earnings ratio. In our example the average price-earnings ratio in the immediate past is 9.2 (based on a range of from 10 to 8.4). Using this rate on $550,000, the total market value should increase by $5.06 million.
2. *There may be some further improvement in the market price.* The elimination of the preferreds' prior claim on earnings makes the common dividend somewhat less risky.
3. *Gains realized are taxed at 25 percent.* In order to convert the market gain into usable funds comparable to the $4.3 million under the cash dividend alternative, the $5.06 million would be subject to a 25 percent capital gains tax, which would reduce it to $3.795 million.

Thus an examination of the primary effects of the two courses of action on the position of the common shareholder suggests that in spite of the heavy tax penalty, the greater benefit would accrue from retaining the preferred and distributing the surplus funds in the form of increased dividends. But of course, one example does not prove the general case. What it does demonstrate is that there are two critical variables which dominate the outcome: (1) the assumed rate of personal income tax taken as representative of the common shareholder group and (2) the anticipated price-earnings ratio of the common stock.

## *Criterion for Decisions*

All this suggests that a simple formula can be developed which will serve executives as a first approximation of the advantage or disadvantage to be derived from the redemption of an outstanding preferred stock. For this purpose, I shall use the following symbols:

$S$ = Sum required for redemption of outstanding preferred stock

$T$ = Rate (percent) of personal income tax assumed to be representative of common shareholders

$P$ = Established (and anticipated) market price of common stock

$E$ = Established (and anticipated) earnings per share

$D$ = Total preferred dividends to be eliminated

Using these symbols, we may say that the preferred stock should be retired *only if:*

$$S\left(1 - \frac{T}{100}\right) < D \times \frac{P}{E} \times 0.75$$

If the left-hand side of this inequality turns out to be *less than* the right-hand side in an individual case, as above, the shareholders will receive more through market appreciation resulting from elimination of the preferred dividend than they would from the alternative of a dividend payout. But if, as in the previous example, the left-hand side had turned out to *exceed* the right-hand side, it would be undesirable to retire the preferred.

I have referred to this formula as a first approximation because it leaves out of consideration the secondary effects of the change on the market price of the stock. I have in mind particularly the effect of increasing the dividend payout and of eliminating a prior (limited) claim on earnings. These effects are more difficult to evaluate, and it is not clear whether the net effect will favor retention or elimination of the preferred stock. However, the *primary* impact of the move will be on the variables included in the formula. If the result shows a clear advantage to one course of action, it is unlikely that the secondary effects will reverse the decision.

Of course, the assumptions are all-important in using the formula, and a slight change in assumptions can make quite a difference (which is one reason why a method of this kind is so useful—to show the effects of different assumptions). A good case in point is the price-earnings ratio, $P/E$. Some readers may be inclined to argue that the ratio in the example is too low to be representative of today's equity market. It is true, of course, that there are many common issues selling at substantially higher ratios; and the higher the ratio, the more attractive the potential gains from eliminating the preferred dividend will appear. If the conditions of company B were changed so as to increase the price-earnings ratio on the common, holding the tax assumption constant, the two alternatives would reach a break-even level at a $P/E$ ratio of 10.4 (instead of 9.2, the average first used); above this figure the redemption alternative would have an advantage.

The question of the price-earnings ratio is, of course, a matter of individual circumstances, and it is not the purpose of this article to make all-inclusive generalizations. The facts of the case will indicate how the decision should go. It is worth noting, however, that the high price-earnings ratios tend to be associated with companies undergoing unusual growth; and the kind of company we have been considering—a company with a substantial amount of unused capital capacity—is almost by definition not a growth company. There is also the question of how permanent these high price-earnings ratios are: The economy and the individual company may not be able to sustain them. The calculations upon which the decision is based should not depend on a ratio which merely reflects a transitory situation.

Before concluding the discussion of this example, we should note that we have assumed the preferred stock is redeemed at book value ($10 million). To the extent that there is a call premium, this will work in favor of the dividend payout alternative, as the proposed formula clearly suggests. This is particularly significant in the case of noncallable preferreds where a substantial premium may have to be paid in order to induce voluntary redemption.

## Should Outstanding Preferred Be Retired?

What can be said by way of summary about the action of companies to redeem their outstanding preferred issues? I think the following conclusion can be reached:

1. The action to eliminate a preferred issue by any means which immediately or ultimately replaces preferred equity capital with common equity capital is subject to serious challenge from the point of view of the common shareholder.
2. An objective test of desirability should be applied, such as described in the preceding text.
3. The circumstances most favorable to the elimination of the preferred are a combination of a high level of personal income tax *and* a high price-earnings ratio. (A high preferred dividend rate also weighs against keeping the preferred.)
4. It should be clearly understood that even where the test of desirability favors the redemption of the preferred, the action results in an advantage to the high-income members of the shareholder group and a *disadvantage to the low-income members.* For example, under the circumstances described in the case of company B, the individual tax bracket would have to exceed 62 percent before the redemption of the preferred becomes the better alternative. Table 2 shows that less than 1 percent of the individuals reporting dividend income have a tax rate above 62 percent, and, more significantly, less than 50 percent of the dividend income is received by persons in these high tax brack-

ets. Such a situation poses a serious problem for management. Which group is it to serve?

## New Financing

Having analyzed the situation in which a corporation is considering the redemption of an outstanding preferred issue, we now turn to the other side of the question—the prospective use of a *new* issue of preferred as a means of financing further growth. To demonstrate that there are circumstances under which a preferred issue should be retained does not necessarily define the circumstances under which this class of security should be used in the future.

There are, of course, different ways to view the capital structure problem. One widely accepted approach is in terms of an ideal or optimum balance of debt and equity sources. Having determined the "right" balance of these sources which limits risk and minimizes cost for the business in question, management proceeds to work toward the desired proportions as new investment and financing permit. For example, it may be determined that the proportions are 25 percent debt, 10 percent preferred stock, and 65 percent common equity. If debt is currently only 15 percent, this will incline the business to use debt for its next financing, so long as it does not increase the proportion above 25 percent. The subsequent financing is then likely to be equity, and so on.

This framework for thinking about sources of funds seems to me best suited to situations of strong and sustained growth over extended periods of time where all sources must be drawn on at one time or another. An example would be public utility financing. Where this is not the case, that is, where growth is modest and/or spasmodic and where all sources are not being utilized at all times, a more useful way of thinking about the problem is in terms of a priority list in which sources are ranked in order of desirability and used as current needs require. Thus, some sources may be used continuously, other sources spasmodically, and still other sources not at all. With this approach, there is no single ideal balance or set of proportions among classes of securities, for the desired mix changes as needs ebb and flow.

### *Usual Priorities Questioned*

This approach is widely used in practice, and it is the one I propose to take here. It is ideally suited to the common situation of fluctuating needs in a highly uncertain future. I do, however, plan to question a particular set of priorities which is frequently used and which ranks the common sources of funds in order of decreasing desirability as follows:

1. Retained earnings
2. Debt
3. New common stock (directly or through conversion)
4. Preferred stock

In some companies the number one position may be given to debt instead of retained earnings, but this does not appear to be the majority choice. Other companies are likely to press debt into the top category if reliance on internal sources for new financing would require a cut in the minimum dividend to which shareholders have become accustomed.

This priority list, despite its wide following in industry, is not the one I shall argue for. From the viewpoint of the common shareholders, at least, the following seems to me to be a better ranking:

1. Debt
2. Preferred stock
3. Retained earnings
4. New common stock (either directly or through conversion)

What are the reasons for ranking the sources in this order?

## Top Priority: Debt

It is generally recognized that debt is a low-cost source of funds, but it is not always recognized that it is the *lowest* cost source for most companies. Many managements behave as if retained earnings were a cheaper source; in fact, some of them would argue that the latter is a no-cost source. From the common shareholders' point of view, however, this is clearly not so. Let me illustrate:

Consider a company requiring $5 million for new investment, with a choice between retained earnings and long-term debt at 4 percent interest as the source of the funds. Suppose this is company B of our earlier example. The retention of earnings in the amount of $5 million would mean that the common shareholders would be out of pocket $2.15 million (assuming the 57 percent personal income tax rate).

By contrast, a debt issue would mean annual interest charges of $200,000 and lowered after-tax earnings for company B of $100,000. Assuming the average price-earnings ratio holds (9.2), this would mean a potential loss in market value of $920,000. But since any capital gain is subject to the capital gains tax, the loss in usable funds to the common shareholder as a result of the interest payments is not $920,000 but 75 percent of this, or $690,000. Obviously, the debt alternative is much to be preferred on an income basis.

There may, again, be secondary effects. It may be argued, in particular, that increased debt means increased risk and that this would depress the price-earnings ratio itself, thus increasing the cost of the debt further. However, I am of the opinion that this is not likely to occur if the debt is kept within what the market considers normal and reasonable bounds. Up to a point, leverage may even improve the price-earnings ratio because of the anticipated positive effect on earnings per share.

As a way of further emphasizing the strong advantage of debt over retained earnings, it can be pointed out that the two alternatives would produce roughly similar effects on the common shareholder *only* if his income tax bracket were approximately 86 percent, and only if the shareholder's tax bracket were above this would the retained earnings alternative be more attractive. Since for the country as a whole less than 20 percent of the dividend income is received by individual shareholders in this high category (see Table 2), it seems unlikely that the widely held corporation can defend a preference for retained earnings over debt of a modest amount unless the risk consideration is overwhelming—in which case long-term debt should not appear on the priority list of sources.

## *Is Preferred Stock "Debt"?*

At this point, it becomes critical to the case for preferred stock to decide whether such stock is significantly different from debt or whether it is in fact simply high-cost debt under the guise of an equity issue. If the latter is true, it seems clear that once debt has been utilized to the acceptable limit of corporate debt capacity, there is no room for additional fixed charges, particularly when these are at a higher rate and not deductible for tax purposes.

Having referred briefly at the outset of this article to a commonly held point of view which equates debt and preferred stock, I should like to outline my reasons for disagreeing with such a position. My whole argument stands on this reasoning.

In setting the limits it wishes to impose on long-term borrowing, management is implicitly or explicity making a choice as to how much risk of running out of cash it is prepared to take. Assume, for example, that a given amount of debt, say 20 percent of the firm's capital structure, will add $1 million of annual debt-servicing charges to a company's cash outflows. Inevitably, these charges increase the chances that at some future date the company will find itself unable to meet all of its cash commitments. This change in risk may be large or small depending on the variability of cash inflows and the magnitude of other fixed cash outflows. Whether it poses a serious threat to the basic solvency of the company (in terms of legal commitments) or merely to certain high-priority expenditures, such as research and engineering, also depends on individual circumstances. In any case, it is clear that debt servicing, once assumed, is an unavoidable outflow.

Thus the decision on debt limits is made in terms of what is likely to happen under conditions of serious adversity and of what avoidable risks, if any, management is willing to assume. The question of preferred stock versus debt is: Faced with some prospect of cash inadequacy or insolvency, does management see any distinction between bond interest and preferred dividends in terms of the risks they impose? My contention is that there is a significant difference between the risk of failing to meet a legal commitment, with the associated chance of becoming insolvent, and the risk of having to suspend a preferred dividend and, along with it, the common dividend. While both events are unpleasant, and while a company may not wish to run a major risk in either event, it may and likely will be willing to run a greater risk of a dividend suspension than it would of default on a legal contract.

If this is so, then there is an important difference between pure debt capacity and debt plus preferred stock capacity. In other words, a concept of debt capacity which drew the line at $1 million annual debt-servicing charges would *not* be the same as, say, $700,000 of debt servicing plus $300,000 of preferred dividend payments. To refer back to the example just used, while management might not want to add debt beyond the amount set by the $1 million servicing limit, it could add preferred stock up to the point where the threat of failure to pay common dividends becomes unacceptably large. For example, another $300,000 of preferred dividends might not, in the judgment of management, raise the chances of suspending common dividends above, say, one chance in twenty, and that may be remote enough to be acceptable.

The specific numbers used here are unimportant. The key point is simply that in anticipating the time when its financial commitments might become critical to the company's future, management will feel more comfortable with preferred dividends than it will with the same amount of bond interest. This should lead it to be willing to add some preferred leverage when the limit of its debt leverage has been reached.

The important distinction between my approach and the view equating debt and preferred stock lies in the circumstances under which the two sources are compared. Under normal, profitable conditions the two commitments do appear roughly similar in urgency. However, the limits on their usage which are intended to contain risk within acceptable bounds are not determined on the assumption of a rosy future. Almost by definition the limits anticipate adversity, and here the difference in the nature of the commitment really counts.

### *What about Income Bonds?*

Should a company which is considering preferred stock also give active consideration to the alternative of income bonds? Such bonds carry a somewhat lower interest rate which is tax-deductible, and the interest need not be paid when not earned. This would seem to reduce the risk differential to which I have referred.

While the risk of cash insolvency in the case of an income bond is less than for a straight bond, there are significant differences which would be important under adversity:

1. The interest *plus sinking fund* on the bond may equal or exceed dividend payments on the preferred stock.
2. There is a difference between earned income and cash flow, so that a company might be liable for income bond interest at a time of zero or negative cash flows.
3. The problem of cash insolvency is not simply that of the condition at the bottom of a recession period, when losses may appear on the income statement. The problem also includes the cash drains of the preceding downswing as well. Then the company may be showing earnings and therefore be required to make payments on the income bonds when it might prefer to reduce or eliminate these payments so as to conserve its cash position.

Thus, I cannot accept the risks of the two securities as being comparable. I conclude that the income bond is not a direct substitute for preferred stock from the risk standpoint.

## Lower Priorities

Having established that there is such a thing as preferred stock capacity as distinct from debt capacity, and having made the assumption that the latter is fully employed, we may turn to the question of the source which should rank second on the priority list.

The choice is between retained earnings and preferred stock. Here the method of analysis is identical to that which was used when redemption of an outstanding preferred was considered:

Continuing the example of company B, assume that the $5 million of new investment, financed by debt, raises the company's annual debt servicing to the limit acceptable to management and that further funds, say $3 million, are needed. Whether this should be obtained from a preferred issue or from retained earnings may be tested by the formula given on page 000. Company circumstances will favor preferred if:

$$S\left(1 - \frac{T}{100}\right) > D \times \frac{P}{E} \times 0.75$$

(Note that the inequality is reversed, and this time the left-hand side is *greater than* the right-hand side.)

In the case of company B, preferred stock should therefore be favored because:

$$\$3{,}000{,}000 \times \left(1 - \frac{57}{100}\right) = \$1{,}290{,}000$$

is greater than

$$\$165{,}000 \times 9.2 \times 0.75 = \$1{,}138{,}500$$

(This assumes a 5.5 percent dividend rate on the new issue.)

What the foregoing says is that the amount of usable funds lost to the common shareholder via the retained earnings route exceeds the amount of usable funds lost via the preferred stock route. Hence the argument for giving preferred stock second position on the priority list of sources *in this case*.

As explained previously, this position could be reversed if the proportion of shareholdings in the higher income tax brackets were significantly greater and/or the price-earnings ratio were higher. Thus, companies could differ in this respect, or the same company could change its position over time. Let me repeat, however, that unless the evidence is strongly in favor of earnings retention, the action to downgrade preferred stock raises the question of favoritism of high-income shareholders over low-income shareholders.

## *Common versus Preferred*

Having now shown that preferred stock is a source of funds which, if not actually superior to retained earnings from the common shareholder's viewpoint is a sufficiently close competitor to warrant a careful comparison of the financial effects, we must go on to consider how preferred stock compares with an issue of common as a source of new funds.

Before doing so, however, we should note what is perhaps obvious to the reader, namely, that retained earnings, to the extent available, are generally preferable to a new issue of common as a source of fresh funds. This is most readily seen in the case of a rights offering to existing shareholders, where the offering is in effect an effort to recapture some of the earnings distributed in the past as cash dividends. Assuming the need for funds can be anticipated by management, it is obviously preferable to the shareholder to have the company retain the funds, so that he can avoid the personal income tax, rather than to have the company pay out the money as a dividend, have it taxed, and then have to match the taxes paid with new money in order to return to the company the equivalent of what was paid out. To put this another way, a rights offering of common by a dividend-paying corporation suggests an error in judgment either (1) by management in anticipating investment needs or (2) by the stockholder in demanding dividends when the funds are needed internally and will be supplied by him in one way or another.

The basic choice between a preferred issue and a common issue of equivalent dollar amount may also be considered in the context of a rights offering in which the existing common shareholders of company B as a group provide the new capital if a preferred issue is not sold:

Assume the need is for $4 million. The sale of additional common to the present shareholders would require the liquidation of another investment of comparable risk—and presumably the loss of comparable earnings of 10.8 percent (the inverse of the 9.2 price-earnings ratio). By this means the company would avoid the reduction of earnings caused by servicing of the preferred stock, but this burden is only 5.5 percent for company B. The net loss to the common shareholder may also be measured in terms of invested dollars: $1.976 million ($4,000,000 − 9.2 × $220,000). Note that here we are comparing invested dollars in both cases, so that no tax factor is involved. In previous examples, we have compared withdrawn or "usable" dollars and in each case had to take the relevant tax rates into account.

It will be obvious from these figures that the company would have to be able to sustain a high price-earnings ratio (in this case a ratio in excess of 18.2) before the substitution of more equity capital from external investments would look attractive as an alternative to an issue of preferred. In any situation comparable to company B's, therefore, there is no question that a common equity issue should rank below retained earnings and preferred stock on the priority list of sources.

## *Use of Convertibles*

The question of issuing senior securities convertible into common stock needs more discussion than we can devote to it here, but a few observations are in order.

First, there is no doubt that convertibles have features which are attractive to the corporate financial officer. The question is *how much* use to make of them. While any unqualified generalization is always dangerous, it does seem to me that when a convertible bond or preferred stock is offered, one of two conditions prevail: Either the company is not yet at the appropriate limit of usage of straight, nonconvertible bonds or preferred, or it is. If it is not at this limit, then a straight bond or straight preferred should be issued and the full leverage obtained.

If, on the other hand, nonconvertible senior securities have been used to the limit that management considers appropriate, and if retained earnings have also been used to the limit, then more common stock is the remaining alternative. Under such circumstances, a convertible issue does offer the prospect of the most favorable pricing for the common (when ultimately converted). However, the fact must be faced that before actual conversion of the senior securities, excessive risks must be assumed. The problem then reduces to the question of whether the prospective gain in pricing of the common is worth the risk which the company runs by exceeding its normal debt limits when the convertibles are issued.

## Policy Guide Lines

If the process of analysis recommended in this article is followed, the individual corporation will have arrived at answers to these two questions:

1. What source or sources of new capital rank ahead of preferred stock on our priority list of sources?
2. When it is issued, how much preferred stock are we prepared to have outstanding in view of the risks involved?

If the circumstances and interests of the common shareholder are fairly considered, there should be a substantial number of companies for which preferred stock is outranked only by long-term debt. Where this is the case, financial policy should be so arranged that both debt and preferred stock will be used as continuously as possible within the limits set by management. This includes, where necessary, an increase in dividend scales so that internally generated funds do not accumulate to the point where reduction or retirement of the senior securities appears the only sensible alternative. Naturally, the timing of preferred issues should be arranged so far as possible to minimize the fixed dividend obligations.

If corporate circumstances are such as to rank preferred stock in third position after retained earnings, then its role is less certain. To review, these are circumstances of high price-earnings ratios *and* high personal income tax brackets for the majority of shareholders. The uncertainty lies in the extent and continuity of the need for funds beyond what can be supplied by long-term debt and retained earnings. Many companies do not need sources other than these when tax and other incentives encourage large-scale retention of internally generated funds, as is the case today.

However, even for the company where the normal rate of growth can generally be sustained by debt plus retained earnings, there are likely to be times when the need for funds temporarily exceeds these sources and a choice must be made between preferred and a new issue of common. The foregoing analysis suggests that at such times, preferred will generally be found to be more desirable than common and should therefore be used up to its appropriate limit. This may mean using preferred stock for a limited period of years, to be redeemed out of the No. 2 source—retained earnings—when the peak need has subsided. It is for this reason that the preferred should always be made callable. It may be expected to come and go in the capital structure with the ebb and flow of fund requirements over the years.

Under circumstances where preferred has a No. 2 position, by contrast, it may be expected to retain a *permanent* position in the capital structure along with long-term debt, with retained earnings taking up variations from year to year.

## *Implications and Questions*

Perhaps the most controversial aspect of what I have written in this article lies in its implications for dividend policy. Many companies today attempt to stabilize dollar dividend payments at a fraction of annual profits. They use the internally generated funds that are left, supplemented when necessary by long-term debt, to finance the varying year-to-year needs for new capital. This policy is the natural and logical application of the traditional priority list cited on page 000.

If management follows the alternative priority list which I believe to be more beneficial to the common shareholder, the effect will be to (1) stabilize the amount of debt and, in some cases, preferred stock at their *maximum* amounts; and (2) shift the impact of year-to-year variations in need to internally generated funds. Assuming that the normal pattern of needs does not change concurrently with the revision of the priority list, it is also to be expected that the new financing policy would lead to a larger payout of dividends over time, with greater year-to-year variability in dividends.

I recognize that this action may have some adverse implications for the market price of the common stock. I would, however, assume that the effects would be temporary. After all, the basic purpose of the change is to create a better over-all utilization of the shareholders' investment; and assuming that my logic is sound and the market is in the long run informed and rational, the ultimate result should be an improvement in the market price. In any case, I see no fundamental reason why common dividends should be stable. Indeed, a fixed common dividend over many years contradicts the basic nature of the common share.

Throughout this discussion, I have held to the single criterion of maximizing the financial interests of the common shareholder. There are, of course, other considerations which will have a bearing on the decision in practice. For instance, availability and flexibility are bound to be powerful factors in influencing the desired priority list of sources; and there are also questions of timing and marketability to consider when an issue of preferred is contemplated. But always the first and most important question to ask is *whether the action would be in the interest of the common shareholder*. If the answer is affirmative, then it is the responsibility of management to use preferred when it can reasonably do so. If it cannot do so, then it should have a clear understanding of the extent to which the stockholder interest is being sacrificed. The "cost" to the common shareholder should be made explicit and weighed before an alternative source is used.

*Chapter* 14

# *The Use of Convertible Subordinated Debentures by Industrial Firms, 1949-59**

By Keith L. Broman

IN MARCH, 1959, the lead article in the *Journal of Finance* concluded with this statement: "In summary, it is contended that the sales finance industry has developed a security which, if properly used, may prove valuable to corporations in many other fields."[1]

Since 1955, it is evident that the subordinated debenture has been used by an increasing number of firms in various classifications of business endeavor. This has been particularly true in the industrial area. The great majority of subordinated debentures have been made convertible into conmmon stock. It is the intention here to review the increasing use of convertible subordinated debentures by industrial firms over the period 1951–59.

Table 1 records the bond issues of this type listed in *Moody's Industrial Manual* as outstanding at the end of the years 1949–59. This paper studies all such bonds over $10 million in issue size which were sold during the period 1951–59. All but two were publicly issued; one was an exchange offer, the other taken wholly by another company.

The 68 convertible subordinated debentures studied were issued by 60 firms.[2] These firms represent many industrial subgroups; and although

---

*Reprinted by permission from *Quarterly Review of Economics and Business,* Vol. III (Spring, 1963), pp. 65–75.

[1]Robert W. Johnson, "Subordinated Debentures: Debt That Serves as Equity," *Journal of Finance,* Vol. X (March, 1955), p. 16.

[2]Allegheny Ludlum Steel, American Machine and Foundry (two issues), Atlantic Refining, Avco Manufacturing, Barium Steel (now Phoenix Steel), Boeing Airplane, Broadway-Hale Stores, Burlington Industries, Burroughs, Carrier, J. I. Case, Celotex, Cerro de Pasco, Champion Paper and Fibre, Chance Vought Air-

*(Continued on next page)*

they vary in size of total assets from over $3.5 billion to less than $50 million, all but eight were reported among the 550 largest American industrial and merchandising corporations in the 1960 *Fortune* directory.

TABLE 1

CONVERTIBLE SUBORDINATED DEBENTURES, 1951–59 INDUSTRIAL ISSUES

| *Outstanding December 31* | *Number** | *Studied*† |
|---|---|---|
| 1949 | 3 | 0 |
| 1950 | 6 | 0 |
| 1951 | 12 | 1 |
| 1952 | 20 | 3 |
| 1953 | 34 | 3 |
| 1954 | 59 | 0 |
| 1955 | 69 | 10 |
| 1956 | 93 | 14 |
| 1957 | 135 | 19 |
| 1958 | 142 | 8 |
| 1959 | 182 | 10 |

*This represents the item count of industrial convertible bonds which are included in the annual issues of Moody and are subordinated; *e.g.*, pp. a132–33, 1959.

†These sixty-eight issues were all of those issued in the indicated years which were over $10 million in issue size.

*Source: Moody's Industrial Manual*, 1950–60, blue page inserts.

Furthermore, these 60 firms represent various stages of economic development: vigorous growth, moderate growth, long-standing stability, and contemporary recession. While the study has been limited to issues of at least $10 million in face value, it represents an analysis of the characteristics and use of this relatively new debt instrument by these

craft, Combustion Engineering, Continental Baking, Douglas Aircraft, Dow Chemical, Dresser Industries, Fairbanks Morse, Food Fair Stores, Fruehauf Trailer (three), Gardner Denver, Garrett, General American Oil (Texas), General American Transportation, General Portland Cement, W. R. Grace, Grand Union, Hooker Chemical (now Hooker Electrochemical), ITE Circuit Breaker, International Minerals and Chemical, Kerr-McGee Oil Industries, Lockheed Aircraft, M. Lowenstein and Sons, R. H. Macy, McDermott, Merritt-Chapman and Scott, National Cash Register, National Cylinder Gas (now Chemstron), National Tea, Northrop (two), Olin Mathieson Chemical (two), Oxford Paper, Pacific Petroleum, Philco, Phillips Petroleum, Radio Corporation of America, Richfield Oil, Shamrock Oil and Gas, Sinclair Oil (two), Spiegel, Sylvania Electric Products (now part of General Telephone and Electronics), Textron American (now Textron), Thompson Products (now Thompson Ramo Wooldridge Products), Union Oil of California (three), United Artists, Vanadium Corporation of America, and Warren Petroleum.

firms, which comprise an important segment of the industrial corporate community.[3]

Traditionally, the convertible bond has been a popular debt instrument during periods of increasing stock market values.[4] And it appears that there is little doubt as to the growing acceptance of the subordinated debenture as an important debt-financing medium.[5] In the convertible subordinated debenture, issuing companies have combined several independently attractive features. First are the regular advantages of debt: trading on the equity, tax deductibility, lower cost of capital, and lower flotation costs. Second is the advantage of subordination, which effectively broadens the financial base for future senior borrowing. Third are the advantages of conversion, which not only add attractiveness to the initial sale of debt but, upon conversion, provide a dollar flow to the company greater than that which would result from direct common stock sale.[6]

## *Characteristics*

Table 2 indicates a tendency to center maturity over a 20- to 25-year term. Inasmuch as 56 of the 68 issues have terms within this period, it appears that the use of a moderately long term has become customary for those firms which utilize this type of security.

There appears to be a further correlation between the maturity of the bond and the strength of the issuer. This relationship is presented in Table 3 in a grouping by bond rating and maturity life of the 68 issues studied. The 20- to 25-year terms, with but two exceptions, were issued

---

[3]It should be noted that 54 percent of a random sample of 196 publicly held industrial bonds listed in investment manuals (1953) were over $10 million in size of issue. See Harry G. Guthmann and Herbert E. Dougall, *Corporate Financial Policy* (3d ed.; New York: Prentice-Hall, Inc., 1955), p. 226.

[4]See George E. Leffler, *The Stock Market* (2d ed.; New York: Ronald Press Co., 1957), p. 381. Also Benjamin Graham and David L. Dodd, *Security Analysis* (3d ed.; New York: McGraw-Hill Book Co., Inc., 1951), p. 529.

[5]*Moody's Bond Survey,* July 18, 1960, pp. 399–402, lists 208 convertible bonds as then outstanding. Of these, all but 36 were subordinated debentures (20 of the 36 were not industrial issues). Fifty-four (all but one still outstanding) of the 68 issues studied were on this list. This monthly listing by Moody apparently combines all convertible issues reported in the separate manuals.

[6]Examine the case of Sinclair Oil Corporation's sale of convertible, subordinated debentures of January 9, 1953. In this instance, 2,312,700 shares of common stock were restricted for conversion purposes at varying conversion values. Most of these shares were issued in exchange for converted bonds before January 3, 1957, when the remainder of the bonds were called and conversion was thus forced. The conversion price was $44 a share, whereas the stock market price at the time of debenture issuance was $41.375. The difference of $2.625 a share provided $4,714,487.50 more than a direct common stock sale at January 9, 1953, would have.

TABLE 2

MATURITIES OF 68 INDUSTRIAL ISSUES

| *Year of Issue* | *Total* | *Years to Maturity from Date of Issue* | | | | | |
|---|---|---|---|---|---|---|---|
| | | *12* | *15* | *20* | *22* | *25* | *30* |
| 1951 | 1 | .. | 1 | .. | .. | .. | .. |
| 1952 | 3 | .. | .. | 1 | .. | 1 | 1 |
| 1953 | 3 | .. | 1 | 1 | .. | .. | 1 |
| 1954 | 0 | .. | .. | .. | .. | .. | .. |
| 1955 | 10 | .. | .. | 6 | .. | 4 | .. |
| 1956 | 14 | .. | 1 | 4 | .. | 8 | 1 |
| 1957 | 19 | 2 | 2 | 8 | .. | 5 | 2 |
| 1958 | 8 | .. | .. | 3 | 1 | 4 | .. |
| 1959 | 10 | .. | .. | 5 | .. | 5 | .. |
| | 68 | 2 | 5 | 28 | 1 | 27 | 5 |

*Sources:* Compiled by author from *Moody's Bond Survey*, prospectuses contained in stock exchange listing agreements, annual reports, and other available public records (cited hereafter as publicly available records).

TABLE 3

RISK GRADE AND MATURITIES OF 68 INDUSTRIAL ISSUES

| *Moody Grade* | *Total* | *Years to Maturity from Date of Issue* | | | | | |
|---|---|---|---|---|---|---|---|
| | | *12* | *15* | *20* | *22* | *25* | *30* |
| A | 4 | .. | .. | .. | .. | .. | 4 |
| Baa | 23 | .. | .. | 8 | .. | 14 | 1 |
| Ba | 37 | .. | 5 | 19 | 1 | 12 | .. |
| B | 2 | 2 | .. | .. | .. | .. | .. |
| Not rated | 2 | .. | .. | 1 | .. | 1 | .. |
| | 68 | 2 | 5 | 28 | 1 | 27 | 5 |

*Sources:* Compiled by author from publicly available records.

by medium (Ba) and upper medium (Baa) rated firms. The five 30-year maturities evidently represent strength of the issuers, as these securities were sold by firms rated by *Moody's Bond Survey* as grade A.[7] Two debentures of 12-year terms were issued by the lower rated firms.

Thus, Table 3 shows a marked correlation between risk rating and term. It seems that the stronger firms have been able to issue longer maturities, the less well regarded have used fairly short terms, and a 20- to 25-year maturity is typical for medium and upper medium rated corporations.

[7]One issue, the first by Sinclair Oil, was rated Baa, but the later issue of the same firm was classed as grade A.

Table 4 presents the issue size of 68 convertible subordinated debentures classified by year of issue. In the more recent years, this security type has been extended to a broad range of issue size in contrast to its initial use by industrial companies.[8] This trend to a broader range of issue size is further emphasized when one considers the large number of issues counted in Table 1 and not included in this study because of

TABLE 4

ISSUE SIZE OF 68 INDUSTRIAL ISSUES

| Year of Issue | *Size of Issue (Millions)* | | | | |
|---|---|---|---|---|---|
| | *$10.0–$14.9* | *$15.0–$19.9* | *$20.0–$49.9* | *$50.0–$99.9* | *$100.0 or More* |
| 1951 | .. | 1 | .. | .. | .. |
| 1952 | .. | .. | 2 | .. | 1 |
| 1953 | 2 | .. | .. | .. | 1 |
| 1954 | .. | .. | .. | .. | .. |
| 1955 | 2 | 2 | 4 | 1 | 1 |
| 1956 | 4 | 2 | 6 | .. | 2 |
| 1957 | 6 | 7 | 3 | 1 | 2 |
| 1958 | 3 | .. | 4 | 1 | .. |
| 1959 | 2 | 2 | 6 | .. | .. |
| | 19 | 14 | 25 | 3 | 7 |

*Sources:* Compiled by author from publicly available records.

TABLE 5

SINKING FUND PROVISIONS IN 65 INDUSTRIAL ISSUES

| Sinking Fund as Percentage of Face Value | Number | *Provision Delay from Issue Date* | | | |
|---|---|---|---|---|---|
| | | *5 Years or Less* | *6 to 10 Years* | *10 Years or More* | *No Delay* |
| 75%–100% | 22 | 3 | 5 | 14 | 0 |
| 50%–74.9% | 39 | 3 | 5 | 30 | 1 |
| Under 50% | 4 | 0 | 0 | 4 | 0 |
| | 65 | 6 | 10 | 48 | 1 |

*Sources:* Compiled by author from publicly available records. Three issues were not tabulated, one because datum was not available and two because of no sinking fund provisions.

[8]Note the five earliest industrial issues (of $10 million or more): October 1, 1951, Warren Petroleum, $15 million; May 7, 1952, Union Oil of California, $35 million; July 15, 1952, Dow Chemical, $100 million; November 13, 1952, International Minerals and Chemical, $20 million; January 9, 1953, Sinclair Oil, $102 million.

size. Tables 1 and 4 record the developing use by industrial companies of this new security type in a broad range of issue size.

Table 5 indicates sinking fund provisions are almost always a part of the convertible subordinated debenture issue. The usual sinking fund provision was less than 100 percent, and all but one provided some delay before their operation commenced. The typical delay in the clauses of those issues studied was for ten or more years. This suggests the expectation of or hope for relatively early conversion.

An analysis of the call provision indicated it to be a universal part of the issues studied. In only three cases was there a provision for a delay in inception. In one instance the delay was three years, and for the other two the delays were two years. With operable call clauses, it is possible for the issuer to force conversion at any desired time. In 1957, by way of contrast, call provisions for nonconvertible issues were often delayed for several years.[9] Thus the conversion clause has apparently provided greater flexibility in financial planning in times of high interest rates in contrast with the record of nonconvertible issues.

## *The Use of Stockholder Rights*

About one third of the issues studied were offered to existing stockholders through privileged subscriptions. In the tables that follow, comparisons are made between stockholder rights and negotiated public offerings.

Table 6 presents underwriting discounts and commissions[10] for 66 con-

---

[9] *Moody's Bond Survey,* February 24, 1958, p. 689. "Every industrial and finance company non-convertible debt issue marketed publicly in 1957 and this year to date incorporated in its terms, for a certain prescribed period, protection against either optional redemption call or refunding with lower interest rate or lower interest call obligations."

[10] The underwriting discounts and commissions, obtained from prospectuses and other publicly available sources, are defined as that percentage of gross proceeds that is paid to the underwriter for services rendered in marketing the issue.

In negotiated public issues the amount is flatly stated; see *Prospectus,* October 2, 1957, Shamrock Oil and Gas Corporation, 5¼ percent convertible subordinated debentures, due 1982, where the underwriting commissions are shown to be 2 percent, or $350,000.

In rights offerings the underwriting compensation is often stated in minimum and maximum amounts; see *Prospectus,* August 12, 1957, Thompson Products, Inc., 4⅞ percent subordinated debentures (convertible), due August, 1982, wherein 1⅛ percent ($211,957) is listed as minimum and 1⅞ percent ($369,928) as maximum underwriting compensation. In this and many other agreements for medium-grade bonds the underwriters have asked for the maximum percentage on the unsubscribed debentures if 10 percent or more of the issue is not taken by the stockholders under the rights offering. This type of agreement was found in 12 rights offerings: American Machine and Foundry (two issues), Boeing, Case, Champion Paper and Fibre, General American Transportation, Grand Union, Macy, National Cash Register, Radio Corporation of America, Thompson Prod-

vertible subordinated debentures. When the issues in total are considered, the percentage of compensation varies inversely with the graded risk of the company. The difference in compensation for all A as contrasted to all Baa issues is slightly more than one fourth of 1 percent. Similarly, the differential between Baa and Ba bonds is nearly three eighths of 1 percent. This rather narrow range, however, is due to the inconsequential differences in compensation for issues sold to stockholders through subscription rights offerings.

TABLE 6

UNDERWRITER COMPENSATION AS PERCENTAGE OF GROSS PROCEEDS IN 66 INDUSTRIAL ISSUES CLASSIFIED BY RISK RATING

| Moody Grade | *Total Offerings* | | *Negotiated Public Offerings* | | *Subscription Offerings* | |
|---|---|---|---|---|---|---|
| | *Issues* | *Compensation* | *Issues* | *Compensation* | *Issues* | *Compensation* |
| A | 4 | 1.219% | 2 | 1.188% | 2 | 1.250% |
| Baa | 24 | 1.401 | 13 | 1.538 | 11 | 1.239 |
| Ba | 35 | 1.774 | 25 | 1.960 | 10 | 1.312 |
| B | 2 | 5.500 | 2 | 5.500 | .. | ..... |
| Not rated | 1 | 2.500 | 1 | 2.500 | .. | ..... |
| | 66 | | 43 | | 23 | |

*Sources:* Compiled by author from publicly available records. Two issues from the study are not included; one was an exchange (Cerro de Pasco), the other taken wholly by another corporation (Union Oil of California, 3¼'s, 1981). Minimum compensation on subscription offerings used in all but one case wherein less than required stockholder participation required the payment of maximum compensation. All averages are simple averages of spreads in each rating group.

The small difference in compensation despite gradation ranges from A to Ba indicates that the investment banker is more inclined to buy debentures on the basis of the value of rights to stockholders than primarily on the quality of the bond. Further evidence that the corporations and the investment bankers believe the stockholders to be the better market is found in the number of companies participating in rights offerings by company choice rather than because of charter or statutory requirement. In fact, of the 23 stockholder rights offerings (21 com-

ucts, and Vanadium Corporation of America. In one case, Food Fair, 8 percent was used instead of 10 percent. In two cases, Hooker and McDermott, all unsubscribed debentures were charged at the maximum rate. In six cases, there was no provision for maximum compensation: Allegheny Ludlum, Avco, Burroughs, Phillips, Richfield, and Sinclair.

In all cases, underwriter participation during rights offerings is quite active. See C. James Pilcher, *Raising Capital with Convertible Securities,* Michigan Business Studies, Vol. XII, No. 2 (Ann Arbor: University of Michigan, Bureau of Business Research, 1955), pp. 106–9.

panies), only 10 firms are listed in *Moody's Industrial Manual* as requiring the use of preemptive rights for convertible debt issues.[11]

In the stockholder rights offerings studied, all but one were subscribed to with positive stockholder action of more than 90 percent (19 by more than 95 percent). In the only poorly subscribed issues (Macy at only 16 percent), the added compensation was one half of 1 percent.

TABLE 7

UNDERWRITER COMPENSATION AS A PERCENTAGE OF GROSS PROCEEDS IN 66 INDUSTRIAL ISSUES CLASSIFIED BY SIZE OF ISSUE

| *Size of Issue (Millions)* | *Total Offerings* | | *Negotiated Public Offerings* | | *Subscription Offerings* | |
|---|---|---|---|---|---|---|
| | *Issues* | *Compensation* | *Issues* | *Compensation* | *Issues* | *Compensation* |
| $10–$19.9.... | 33 | 1.967% | 24 | 2.167% | 9 | 1.431% |
| $20–$49.9.... | 24 | 1.599 | 15 | 1.867 | 9 | 1.153 |
| $50 or more... | 9 | 1.208 | 4 | 1.219 | 5 | 1.200 |

*Sources:* Compiled by author from publicly available records. Two issues excluded for reasons stated in Table 5. Averages as calculated in Table 6.

Table 7, in presenting the percentage of underwriter compensation to gross proceeds for 66 convertible subordinated debentures, clearly indicates a lowered rate of payment for the larger size of issue. This well-established relationship is illustrated in this study with differentials between classes of about three eighths of 1 percent. As the totaled figures disguise an important difference between the two types of offerings, Table 7 is broken down by negotiated public and subscription rights offerings. In the $10–$20 million and $20–$50 million size-of-issue classes, there is a large differential in compensation percentages between the two types of offerings. In 18 subscription offerings within this dollar range, compensation percentages are roughly one third less than for the 39 negotiated public offerings. Once again, the largest class in face value in Table 7, like the highest gradation class in Table 6, shows only a slight and inconsequential difference in compensation percentages.

It appears that important compensation percentage savings have been possible for those stockholder rights offerings of convertible sub-

[11]Preemptive rights required by American Machine and Foundry, Case, Champion Paper and Fibre, Grand Union, Hooker, Macy, National Cash Register, Phillips, Sinclair, and Thompson Products. Preemptive rights not required but rights offerings used by Allegheny Ludlum, Avco, Boeing, Burroughs, Food Fair, General American Transportation, McDermott, Radio Corporation of America, Richfield, Spiegel, and Vanadium Corporation of America.

ordinated debentures with risk grades lower than A and face values below $50 million.

In order to contrast the data from the issues studied with available data for other comparable firms, Table 8 records flotation costs from the Securities and Exchange Commission study on manufacturing companies' public issues of over $10 million in size.[12] While duplication of issues for some of the years exists, it is not likely that the comparison is compromised by this fact. Furthermore, the inclusion of seven non-manufacturing firms in the present study of 68 industrials should not materially alter the comparison.

TABLE 8

COSTS OF FLOTATION AS PERCENTAGE OF GROSS PROCEEDS, MANUFACTURING DEBT ISSUES OFFERED TO THE GENERAL PUBLIC, 1951, 1953, AND 1955

| *Face Value of Issue (Millions)* | *Number* | *Compensation* | *Other Expenses* | *Total Flotation Costs* |
|---|---|---|---|---|
| $10–$19.9 ....... | 10 | 1.70% | 0.65% | 2.35% |
| $20–$49.9 ....... | 16 | 1.30 | 0.40 | 1.70 |
| $50 or more ..... | 5 | 1.02 | 0.28 | 1.30 |

*Source:* Securities and Exchange Commission, *Costs of Flotation of Corporate Securities: 1951, 1953, and 1955* (Washington, D.C.: U.S. Government Printing Office, 1957), Table 2, p. 38.

The rather small difference in underwriter compensation indicates that with the conversion feature, subordinated debentures are not poorly regarded by the underwriter or by the investor despite the subordination agreement and the absence of a particular security pledge.[13]

In further analysis, Table 9 incorporates, to the extent data were available, total costs of flotation for 48 of the issues studied. This was accomplished by adding the "other expenses," as stated in prospectuses, to the underwriting compensation reported earlier.[14]

[12]The SEC study includes 70 percent in number and volume of the total debt issues offered in 1951, 1953, and 1955.

[13]The present acceptance of the debenture and the subordinated debenture follows closely the recommendations for bond investment as stated in Graham and Dodd, *op. cit.*, pp. 284–86. Also note from the same reference, p. 521: "A senior issue may have a speculative feature without being speculative in the sense that it involves an appreciable risk to the buyer. Convertible bonds may theoretically combine adequate safety with an attractive chance for profit."

[14]The "other expenses" of issue are those costs outside of compensation to underwriters which, taken together, make up total costs of flotation. Normally such "other expenses" include printing and engraving; federal revenue stamps; legal, trustee, engineering, and accounting fees; state taxes; and payments to the Securities and Exchange Commission.

TABLE 9

TOTAL FLOTATION COSTS AS PERCENTAGE OF GROSS PROCEEDS, 48 INDUSTRIAL ISSUES CLASSIFIED BY FACE VALUE

| *Face Value of Issue (Millions)* | *Underwriter Compensation* | *Other Expenses* | *Total Flotation Costs* |
|---|---|---|---|
| *$10–$19.9:* | | | |
| 17 negotiated offerings.... | 2.199% | 0.735% | 2.934% |
| 7 stockholder offerings... | 1.268 | 0.967 | 2.235 |
| *$20–$49.9:* | | | |
| 10 negotiated offerings.... | 2.050 | 0.449 | 2.499 |
| 8 stockholder offerings... | 1.141 | 0.731 | 1.872 |
| *$50 or more:* | | | |
| 3 negotiated offerings.... | 1.292 | 0.290 | 1.582 |
| 3 stockholder offerings... | 1.167 | 0.551 | 1.718 |

*Sources:* Compiled by author from prospectuses available for 48 of the issues studied.

The 18 stockholder rights offerings indicated increased cost for "other expenses" as compared with the negotiated public offerings. While this differential varied to some extent by size of issue, it averaged about one fourth of 1 percent. This increased expense relationship is to be expected in view of the added requirements of communication of information to stockholders.

Notwithstanding these increased expenses, the data in Table 9 present a favorable relationship in total flotation costs for these stockholder offerings under $50 million in size. Total costs of flotation for seven $10–$19.9-million stockholder offerings reflect a favorable percentage differential of nearly three-fourths of 1 percent. Similarly, eight $20–$49.9-million stockholder offerings reflect a favorable percentage difference of slightly more than one half of 1 percent.

The convertible subordinated debenture has been successfully marketed in the period 1951 through 1959 at flotation costs not significantly higher than for debt issues of comparable firms. Indeed, through the use of stockholder rights offerings, flotation costs have been most competitive.

Table 10 presents the relationship of market value of stock obtainable through conversion of a bond to the bond face value on original offering date. For broad appeal, it would be expected that the issuer would attempt to set bond conversion prices at a point which would add early equity value to the debt issue. In nearly one half of the cases studied, this was achieved by establishing bond conversion values at discounts of less than 8 percent. The stockholder offerings exhibit a tendency to set conversion prices much closer to original offering price as

TABLE 10

RELATIONSHIP OF MARKET VALUE OF STOCK OBTAINABLE THROUGH CONVERSION OF BOND TO BOND FACE VALUE AT ORIGINAL OFFERING DATE, 66 INDUSTRIAL ISSUES

| *Discount from Market Price* | *Negotiated Offerings* | *Stockholder Offerings* |
|---|---|---|
| 0– 1.9% | 0 | 3 |
| 2– 3.9 | 2 | 2 |
| 4– 5.9 | 5 | 5 |
| 6– 7.9 | 6 | 7 |
| 8– 9.9 | 12 | 1 |
| 10–14.9 | 12 | 4 |
| 15–19.9 | 4 | 0 |
| 20 or more | 3 | 0 |
| | 44 | 22 |

*Sources:* Compiled by author from publicly available records. Two issues, one of each type, were sold with conversion values above stock market price at issuance.

only 5 of 22 stockholder offerings, compared with 31 of 44 negotiated public offerings, involved discounts of 8 percent or more. This difference between offering discounts of the two types suggests that perhaps one reason for the narrow spread in underwriting commission between high and lower rated issues was the absence of risk of nonpurchase by stockholders. Also, the difference in discount between rights and nonrights offerings would support the higher commission for nonrights issues.

## *Conversion of Issues*

The study discloses a pattern of early conversion in several of the issues. Although stock market price increase is certainly the cause, there is some evidence to support the position that early conversion was expected, perhaps planned.

It is customary for convertibles to provide conversion term changes.[15]

[15]Examples of bond conversion changes include (*a*) International Minerals and Chemical, 3.65's, 1977, convertible at $50 through 1957, at $55 through 1962, and at $60 through 1967 when conversion ends; and (*b*) National Cash Register 4½'s, 1981, convertible at $54 through December 15, 1966, and at $5.00 increments each five years threafter until maturity. The first bond was sold when the stock market price was at a discount of more than 20 percent. This stock has never sold above the conversion price. The second bond was sold at a time when the stock market price was at a discount of less than 2 percent. This stock sold

*(Continued on next page)*

Of the 68 issues studied, half had such changes (most commonly at five-year intervals throughout the issue life), whereas the other half provided for no conversion term change. Eight of the former and 15 of the latter terminated conversion prior to the maturity date.

TABLE 11

CONVERSION STATUS OF 68 INDUSTRIAL ISSUES

| *Percentage of Issue Outstanding March 1, 1962** | *Total* | *Year of Issue* | | | | |
|---|---|---|---|---|---|---|
| | | *Prior to 1956* | *1956* | *1957* | *1958* | *1959* |
| 95–100........ | 28 | 0 | 7 | 10 | 5 | 6 |
| 50–94.9....... | 12 | 3 | 1 | 5 | 1 | 2 |
| 25–49.9....... | 5 | 2 | 2 | 0 | 0 | 1 |
| Less than 25... | 3 | 2 | 1 | 0 | 0 | 0 |
| Called........ | 20 | 10 | 3 | 4 | 2 | 1 |
| | — | — | — | — | — | — |
| | 68 | 17 | 14 | 19 | 8 | 10 |

**Moody's Bond Survey*, March 19, 1962, pp. 741–44.

*Sources:* Compiled by author from publicly available records.

Conversion pressures seem to have operated rather fully despite investment advice to the contrary.[16] This information is presented in Table 11, which shows the extent of conversion as of March 1, 1962. Of the 28 issues outstanding in an amount greater than 95 percent of face value,

well above conversion prices, and the bonds were well above face value when they were called on February 9, 1959.

Whereas changing conversion terms will serve to cut down on dilution of equity should conversion take place in later years, it would appear that some firms have sold convertibles at price relationships and with changing conversion terms designed to facilitate early if not forced conversion. See Raymond P. Kent, *Financial Management* (Homewood, Ill.: Richard D. Irwin, Inc., 1960), p. 698.

[16]Graham and Dodd, *op. cit.* p. 528. "In the typical case, a convertible issue should not be converted by the investor. It should be either held or sold." This well-known advice on conversion is set forth by the authors of *Security Analysis* as an "investment rule." They further agree that the investor should sell when the bond price has "passed out of the investment range." When, however, the issuer has announced a call for redemption, or when the investor faces a time limit on conversion or an approaching date of a rising scale of conversion prices, conversion to stock is forced upon some investors, be it the original holder or the one to whom he sells. A typical example is illustrated by the following advice from *Moody's Bond Survey,* January 12, 1959, p. 782. These comments are directed to the holders of four convertible subordinated debentures, two of which are included in the present study (American Machine and Foundry 4½'s, 1981, and National Cash Register 4½'s, 1981.) "As each of the above convertibles has a conversion value well in excess of its indicated redemption basis, it is imperative that commitments in the four issues should either be sold or converted into the applicable common stock on or before the indicated final conversion dates."

11 were issued in the last two years of the study. When it is considered that the typical maturity dates for the issues studied range from 20 to 25 years, it appears likely that the convertible subordinated debenture has been used as a bridge toward equity ownership rather than as a long-term debt issue with added sale inducements. Of course, this period was one characterized by rising dividends, earnings, and stock market values. Over the 1951–60 period the industrial average (Dow Jones) rose 161.6 percent, earnings per share increased 21 percent, and dividends per share increased 30.7 percent.

TABLE 12

PERCENTAGE OF LONG-TERM DEBT TO CAPITAL STRUCTURE, CLASSIFIED BY ASSET SIZE AT TIME OF DEBENTURE ISSUANCE

| | *Asset Size (Millions)* | | | |
|---|---|---|---|---|
| | *$50–$99.9* | *$100–$249.9* | *$250–$999.9* | *$1,000 or More* |
| Long-term debt to capital structure at end of fiscal period in year of issue.... | 40.93% | 36.09% | 36.68% | 30.49% |
| Long-term debt to capital structure, assuming full conversion of issues studied in year of issue...... | 15.09% | 20.32% | 23.23% | 18.06% |
| All manufacturing companies, 4th quarters averaged, 1956–59*.......... | 16.03% | 19.76% | 20.59% | 13.09% |
| Companies studied........ | 15 | 30 | 20 | 3 |

*Federal Trade Commission and Securities and Exchange Commission, *Quarterly Financial Report for Manufacturing Companies*, fourth quarters: 1959, Table 7, pp. 31–33; 1957, Table 5, pp. 25–27. (Washington, D.C.: U.S. Government Printing Office, 1952–60). These figures were adjusted from percentage of total assets to percentage of capital structure and averaged for the four years by the author. Averages are simple averages of percentage for each company in a size class.

*Sources:* Compiled by author from publicly available records.

Table 12 measures the impact upon capital structure of the issuance of convertible subordinated debentures by the 60 firms studied. In this presentation the percentage of all long-term debt to total capital structure (i.e., long-term debt and all equity sources) is shown along with a pro forma capital structure which assumes full conversion of the debentures into common stock. Finally, by comparison, aggregate data for all United States manufacturing corporations are presented.

In Table 12, it must first be noted that long-term debt as a percentage of capital structure is much higher for the 60 firms studied than for the FTC-SEC presentation of aggregate data. Some difference would be expected, since the study data measurement is taken at the issuance of debt, whereas the aggregate data are made up of companies with debt at all stages of retirement plus some companies with no debt at all. Despite this, it appears reasonable to suggest some of the firms studied have pushed debt limits to the extreme. The evidence of this article suggests that the use of this type of security has often been adopted as a means of raising money only temporarily by debt with an intention for bondholder conversion to stock. Thus the pro forma presentation which assumes conversion in full would seem to balance corporate capital structure within limits comparable with aggregate corporate data.

Even though firms issuing convertible subordinated debentures rather than common stock in periods preceding falling rather than rising stock prices would have substantially heavier fixed charge burdens to carry, there appears to be a willingness to bear this risk with the eventual goal of natural or forced conversion. This appears to be further confirmed by the aggressive forced conversion policies of the companies involved in the 20 called issues. Finally, in only 6 of the 60 companies studied was the convertible subordinated debenture the only use of long-term debt. All of the foregoing appears to support the belief that conversion was sought by many of the companies involved.

## *Conclusions*

This study has presented the record of nearly a decade of growth in the use of a relatively new type of security. This security has joined together the subordination and conversion clauses in an unsecured bond. Although its use has certainly been motivated by the desire of corporations to issue securities with tax deductible interest, this study indicates that debt advantages are not as important in the minds of the issuers as an eventual increase in equity ownership at an issue price exceeding that which could be obtained by an immediate sale of stock.

The use of the convertible subordinated debenture has been increasing during the decade. Certainly, rising stock prices are helpful to the sale of any convertible issue; but even during the changing market of 1960, *Moody's Bond Survey* records 27 new convertible subordinated debentures issued by industrial firms through December 31, 1960.

It appears that industrial corporations have made use of a type of security particularly suited to the times and have employed bond clauses in such a way that the movement from bond to stock ownership is common and often rapid. This implies that the historic use of the conversion clause, to "sweeten" an issue, is no longer of singular importance.[17]

---

[17]See Pilcher, *op. cit.*, pp. 60–61. Pilcher's study included this direct question to the presidents of 31 corporations which had issued convertible bonds: "Which played the more important role in the decision by your company to utilize the conversion privilege: the desire to 'sweeten' the senior leverage issue, thereby

Rather, industrial firms have made advantageous use of periods with rising stock market prices so that debt issues will quite often be converted into stock.

The historic hedge of a convertible from the investor standpoint remains, of course, but there appears to be a willingness on the part of the issuer to risk an unbalanced capital structure and the pressure of fixed charges. This tendency toward greater risk in itself is also a phenomenon of the times.

In conclusion, it remains for the future to record the verdict for continued growth in the convertible subordinated debenture. At this moment, however, it is difficult to deny the fact that industrial corporations, with skillful employment of a new debt package, have made effective use of the opportunities presented by the times.

---

making it more attractive to buyers, or the desire to raise common equity on a sort of delayed action basis?" Replies were received from 17 companies issuing subordinated debt. In thirteen cases the latter answer was given, in two cases the former answer was chosen, and in two cases both factors were deemed to be of equal importance.

*Chapter* 15

# *The Value of the Call Privilege**

By Willis J. Winn and Arleigh Hess, Jr.

ONE OF THE most controversial problems in the financial area today pertains to the right of a borrower to repay his debt prior to its contractual maturity. The blood-pressure readings of the interested parties tend to correspond with the general level of interest rates. When rates are high, the value to a borrower of having the right to call the loan to effect interest savings at a later date is increased. At the same time, the value to an investor of the high yield on new issues is increased, and he is eager to protect the maintenance of this income throughout the entire contractual period. On the other hand, when rates decline, the value of the call privilege on new offerings declines because the possibilities of any substantial savings to the borrower from refunding or of loss of income to an investor as a result of redemption prior to maturity is correspondingly reduced. It is the interest saving–interest loss aspects of the controversy on which the arguments have been focused; but strangely enough, in the various resolutions of these conflicts of interest to date, there has been no attempt to measure the relative importance of the factors involved other than by an intuitive approach.[1]

---

*Reprinted by permission from *Journal of Finance,* Vol. XIV (May, 1959), pp. 182–95.

[1]A study is now being completed by the Wharton School, sponsored by the Life Insurance Association of America, in which, for the first time, the value of the call privilege has been quantified. In this study the theory of the value of the call privilege has been developed, and the market experience of various types of issues over the last thirty-two years has been explored, comparing the yields of immediately callable issues with bonds having different degrees of restriction on

The call provision is important to borrower and lender in almost every longe-term loan agreement in the real estate, corporate, or governmental fields, whether the agreement takes the form of a bond issue, mortgage loan, lease, or even a preferred stock offering. For example, the borrower may need or desire to accelerate the payment on his debt if his earnings increase faster than anticipated or if assets are liquidated in the normal course of business and the cash thus accumulated can be used most profitably in the retirement of debt. The borrower may desire or be required to adjust his capital structure to changing business conditions. Changes in the tax structure, in investment preferences and in market prices of securities, in the product mix, and in costs and earnings expectations of the firm also affect the capital requirements and the financial alternatives available to the firm. Sometimes the terms of the loan agreement restrict the capitalization structure, the volume and type of additional debt which can be issued, and the right to sell assets or to buy or merge with other businesses. Any of these developments may make it desirable or necessary to modify the original terms of the agreement or to eliminate the debt prior to the maturity date. Accompanying these considerations and often overshadowing them is the fact that the cost of new money to the firm may be much lower than is currently being paid on outstanding issues, and substantial savings can be effected for protracted periods if the maturity of the debt is extended.

On the other hand, the investor bases his operations upon the expectation that the issue will remain outstanding until maturity. In some instances he, in turn, assumes long-term obligations, and any acceleration in payments poses reinvestment problems. If attractive alternative investments are not immediately available, he may lose income in the temporary use of these funds, or be forced to lower the quality of his holdings. His investment return may be reduced in the long run if the prevailing yields are below the rates paid on the redeemed issue.

Except where yields are above the rate received on the issue being refunded—and experience has shown that this is not likely—prepayment benefits the borrower at the expense of the lender, and callability therefore presents a potential conflict of interest which must be resolved when the security is issued, not at the time when the borrower realizes a need to redeem his debt. If no contractual provision has been made for prepayment, any effort to renegotiate the terms of an outstanding

---

callability. As a result of this study, issuers will be able to estimate in dollar terms just how much the right to call is worth to them under specified conditions; lenders will be able to estimate how much higher a yield they can demand in return for granting the right to call. Preliminary results indicate that the call privilege is a valuable right, which the market has consistently undervalued. This paper, however, is not a summary of the Wharton School study.

obligation may pose virtually insurmountable difficulties, interminable delays, and very heavy expenses for all interested parties.

Consequently, the conditions and terms under which the issuer may repay all or part of his outstanding obligations before maturity are included among the provisions of loan agreements. This provision is often referred to as the "redemption provisions" or the "call privilege." If the price that the issuer must pay to redeem his obligation is above the face value of the obligation, the issue is said to be "callable at a premium"; otherwise, the call price is established at par. Sometimes the issue may be called at any time after date of offering. When the privilege cannot be exercised prior to a specified future date, the issue is said to have a "call deferment." Many issues freely callable at a low premium for most purposes have high premiums and/or call deferments of five or ten years where the purpose of the call is to refund the debt at a lower interest cost.

It is interesting to note the extent to which the desired financial flexibility, blocked by call restrictions, may be obtained through other terms of the agreement. For example, the sinking fund provisions of some outstanding indentures permit the application of the aggregate of these funds from all outstanding issues of the company to any single issue. In other instances the contingent sinking fund provisions permit very rapid debt amortization, while at the same time the issuer may be borrowing to finance his continuing or expanding operations.

The option clauses, particularly in lease agreements, allow far more financial flexibility than is provided concurrently by the call provisions in the same document. While, on the one hand, the transaction cannot be refunded through the exercise of the redemption clause, other clauses relating to sinking funds and purchase of leased property, for example, may be employed to achieve the same result. In still other instances, while the prohibition against refunding specifically states that no bonds may be issued to obtain funds to retire outstanding debt, there is nothing in the agreement, except inferred intent, to prevent the issuer from using bank borrowing, an equity issue, or a sales-leaseback transaction to achieve the same end. The limits on such possibilities are established only by the ingenuity of the legal and financial experts engaged in drawing up, or operating under, the provisions of a specific loan agreement.

The two simplest resolutions of the call problem, at opposite extremes, have been (1) the extension of the right to the issuer to call the loan at par at any time and for any purpose, and (2) the complete prohibition of the right to call for any purpose for the life of the loan. The former solution will give rise to no interest saving or interest loss to borrower and lender if market rates do not fall below the offering yield of the issue before it matures. While this result may actually occur, it is not likely to be anticipated at the time the loan agreement is made. In fact, if the investor were to make this projection of interest rates, it is unlikely that he would enter into the transaction because of the very high probability of realizing increased income through an alternative investment policy. But without the rather extreme assumption about the future level of rates, it is difficult to rationalize the investor's action, since he would not be allowing for, or perhaps not even recognizing, the risk he is assuming in granting the privilege.

On the other hand, implicit in the policy of denying the call privilege for any purpose is the assumption that interest rates, during some period during the life of the loan, will be lower than the prevailing rates. If this is an accurate assessment of the future behavior of rates, the investor clearly desires to protect his commitments made at the prevailing rates. Should he feel that a reduction in rates, particularly during the early life of the loan, is highly probable, he should maximize his commitments with full protection against redemption. Under the same assumptions, the issuer should reexamine his financial planning, with emphasis on the timing of various alternative moves. In the majority of instances, there may be little recognition of the underlying assumptions or any attempt to assess the probabilities of the gains or losses that might accrue to either party. Furthermore, preoccupation with the interest loss aspect of call protection may lead the lender to overlook the rigidity imposed on the issuer, whose operations are restricted by his inability to change his debt structure. Flexibility may be essential if the issuer is to operate successfully. Finally, it is necessary to recognize the psychological value of retaining or denying flexibility, particularly in this world of uncertainty and very rapid change. While complete callability and complete noncallability represent the simplest solutions from the standpoint of the issuer and the investor, respectively, they provide no recognition of the other party's problems resulting from these provisions.

In passing, it may be noted that many problems arising out of the redemption provision would be largely eliminated whenever the interest saving–interest loss issue was not a major consideration, if all obligations were noncallable for any purpose but were freely marketable. An issuer could then repurchase outstanding issues at any time. The problem would be greatly minimized, perhaps, even when the interest rate was the sole consideration, if the security were truly freely marketable. However, this would require a broad distribution of ownership and a trading market for the issue, and neither of these conditions is satisfied in most instances.

An intermediate position is provided by the call deferment. In this category are two approaches based upon different underlying problems.

The first focuses on the offering date of the security and assures that no redemption can be made for several years (three, five, and ten years have been the most common limits), while the second is keyed primarily to the final maturity date. In the second instance the privilege is granted only for a short period prior to maturity (two to five years being most common). This policy is best illustrated by the call provisions on certain government bonds.

The first approach recognizes the problems of the investor. The length of the deferment period has been heavily influenced in practice by the fact that the investor is purchasing the new offerings with the proceeds of a sale of his portfolio holdings at a book loss. The investor is encouraged to make such switches if he is confident that the new acquisitions will provide a sufficient differential in yield for a period long enough to recover the capital loss. The higher the loss, the longer the deferral period must be to achieve this end. Consequently, this approach has focused on increased costs rather than representing an assessment of future fluctuations in interest rates. In other cases, where portfolio items have not been sold, large investors, aware of the probability that rates will decline in the future, have simply demanded call protection as a condition of the loan. However, while they have been concerned about rate changes during the period for which they sought deferment of the call, these investors have largely ignored rate changes beyond the deferment period.

The second approach recognizes the problems which may be encountered by the issuer. In this instance the policy is largely predicated on his need to have some latitude in timing the refinancing of an issue. While some small saving in interest on the maturing issue may be effected, the major concern of the issuer is the yield he will pay on his new issue. If there is, for example, a five-year period prior to the maturity date during which he can refinance, his opportunity to achieve a low cost on the new issue is much greater than if he is required to refund at or near the maturity date. It is of course true that the issuer could engage in anticipatory refinancing or temporize for months at maturity through a roll-over into short-term issues to achieve the same end, but the short-term cost of idle balances or higher short-term rates plus the added financial uncertainties deter such activity.

Another approach to the call problem permits the issuer to call the issue at any time but makes a charge if the privilege is exercised. The most common charge is a three- or five-point premium above par or offering price, or a payment equivalent to the annual coupon rate. This additional payment compensates the investor for some of the costs and possible loss of income entailed in the reinvestment of these funds and, at the same time, reduces the financial gain to the borrower of refinancing at lower rates. If the premium is sufficiently high, it may more than nullify any financial gain to the issuer and therefore discourage calls for rate consideration, but it does not deprive him of financial flexibility. In practice, however, the call price has been established by custom and is not related to the gains or losses realized by either party. The periodic reduction of the premium over the life of the loan suggests an implicit recognition that possible interest gains decrease as an issue nears maturity, but the size of the premium is not related to the magnitude of the potential gain. Finally, the call premium does not represent a charge for the call privilege, since the payment is contingent upon the exercise of the option.

Various combinations or adaptations of the call deferral and call premium are presently used. For example, the privilege to call in order to refund at a lower rate for the life of an issue or for prolonged periods may be denied, while calls for any purpose except refunding may be permitted at any time, or after only a short deferment. Another arrangement has been to establish two different sets of call premiums—one applicable to calls for any purpose, the other a supplemental premium which is added to the first if the call is exercised to refund the issue. In addition, the call privilege may be deferred for a period of time before it becomes effective on a multiple-premium basis. The main difficulty created by the variation in deferments and premiums according to the purpose of the call is that, in any given refunding transaction, the reason for the call may be subject to dispute. Differences in interest rates are rarely the sole consideration, even if they are often the dominating factor, and a question may arise as to which premium to apply or even whether a call is permitted. Thus the groundwork for extensive potential litigation may be laid in some of the more complicated redemption provisions.

A final method of dealing with the problem of callability, but one which is not in current use, is to grant the redemption privilege freely and make a specific charge for this privilege. This charge does not take the form of a contingent fee but is added to the interest rate. Under this approach the issuer is permitted to call his issue at any time for any purpose at par, and for this right he pays a higher interest rate. The charge or compensation differs from the call premium in that the borrower pays whether he exercises the call privilege or not; that is, he pays for the privilege to redeem his bonds rather than for the exercise of the privilege, as in the case of the call premium.

This approach was utilized during the Civil War period when callability was an important issue affecting the market for United States government securities. The terms of the offering were set by Congress, which gave rise to a great deal of criticism by those who felt that members of Congress were not familiar with many of the problems of the securities markets. However, in the late 1860's, Congress moved that there be a sharp differential in yield between callable and noncallable issues, with the higher yields offered on the callable bonds. While there is no indication that this differential was based on anything other than an intuitive feeling, it represented a recognition of the problem. A postscript, however, is in order. The experience with the noncallable issue was far from satisfactory from the issuer's standpoint, since the Treasury was later forced to repurchase the bonds at very substantial premiums, ranging as high as thirty points.

During the last forty years, only a relatively few security offerings other than federal, state, and local government issues have been noncallable. The majority of new issues has been either immediately callable or has had call deferments for three, five, or ten years. In practically every instance a call premium was added which was scaled to zero by the maturity of the issue. In the majority of cases the premium was three or five points, or was made equal to the coupon rate. Finally, an effort was often made to distinguish among call purposes and to apply different restrictions upon each.

During the same period a drastic shift in the ownership of bonds, particularly corporate bonds, has taken place. The individual investor has declined in importance; the institutional investor has grown in size and also changed in type, so that institutional experience with the call problem has encompassed a continually changing group.

The decline in interest rates during the 1930's was accompanied by a rising volume of refundings. This volume increased during the World War II period with the improved financial position of business, the almost complete drying-up of new offerings, and the continued monetary ease. While there was increasing recognition of the call problem, there was little to be gained by the investor in insisting on increased protection on the new and refunding issues. Moreover, new investors, many of whom had little or no experience in this area, were entering the market and were therefore not particularly concerned with problems of callability. Consequently, when interest rates rose, call restrictions were increased only slightly; but within a relatively few months, another wave of refunding at lower rates took place. Since 1956, with the rise in interest rates, there has been a more marked increase in the restrictions imposed upon the call privilege.

It is clear that there has been a growing recognition of the call problem over time by both issuers and investors. The bargaining, however, has focused on the types of restrictions to be imposed upon the right rather than the price to be charged for granting the privilege. In other words, the market has approached the problem of bond redemption largely by determining how far the privilege should extend rather than by granting the privilege and determining how much shall be paid for it. In fact, there is very little evidence that corporate bond issues offered between the end of World War II and the present have reflected in their yields any significant value for the call privilege.

In general, the issues directly placed have had somewhat more restrictive call features than those publicly offered. However, the market for direct placement is dominated by large institutional investors, who, after several adverse investment experiences resulting from an early exercise of the call option, have insisted upon sharp restrictions and even the prohibition of call options for refunding purposes. In fact, some of these investors have stated that they would not buy a freely callable issue at any price. During periods of rapidly rising demand for funds, they have had the bargaining power not only to impose more restrictive call provisions but also to get somewhat higher yields than those obtained on publicly offered issues during the same period. However, since the directly placed issues are not rated, the difference in yield may be attributable in part to quality variations.

This brings us to a consideration of the value of the call privilege. We have seen that free callability has been modified by the use of the call deferment and the call premium, but there is no evidence that the length of deferment or the amount of the premium has been set by any realistic appraisal of the probable gains or losses of either party but rather by custom or habit.

How much should the borrower be willing to pay for the option to call his bonds before they mature? Obviously, the greater the decline in interest rates and the earlier it occurs in the life of the bond, the larger will be his total interest saving. Moreover, the higher the rates at the time the original issue is sold, the more likely is a decline of any magnitude. The three major factors, then—the size, timing, and probability of a decline in rates—determine the minimum value of the call privilege to the borrower.

The borrower may approach the problem of estimating future interest rate changes by examining the variation in rates over the past few decades. He may ascertain the length of time that was required on the average for a drop of 1 or 2 percent from an initial level of 5 or 6 percent, or the average change in rates for a specified period after rates were 5 or 6 percent. Alternatively, he may analyze factors which affect the supply of and demand for loanable funds and estimate how these forces will affect the future movement of interest rates. This method deals more with causes of rate changes, while the former studies effects, namely, the rate changes themselves. The prudent borrower will use both procedures.

Any estimate of future rate changes must be stated in terms of probability, and the probability will vary inversely with the magnitude and the proximity of the change. Therefore, if the issuer decides upon the change which will cause him to refund, he will have to estimate the probabilities (1) that the change will occur in the first year; (2) that it will take place the second year, assuming that it has not already happened; (3) that if it has not previously occurred, the rate will change the third year; and so on, until the final year of the term to maturity. A 20-year bond would require a separate estimate of the probability of a rate reduction of a given magnitude for each of the 20 years (the sum of these twenty values would produce the total probability that the given change will take place sometime within the lifetime of the bond).

The issuer must also compute for each year the present value of total interest savings, after refinancing costs are deducted, which would result if a refunding were effected that year. The present-value computation for each year is multiplied by the probability estimate for the same year, and the sum of these products is the present value to the borrower of the right to refund upon a given decline in rates.

If a different change in rates is assumed, the entire process must be repeated, since the interest savings and presumably the probabilities are different. The borrower can determine by the methods given which combinations of magnitude and probability of decline would produce for him the greatest present value of the refunding privilege.

As we have previously noted, an insurer may want to change his capital structure for reasons not connected with interest saving. Mergers, lengthening of maturities, increasing the size of the debt, shifting to equity securities, paying off the debt with accumulated cash are all goals which may be achieved more readily through the exercise of the redemption option. These objectives do not lend themselves readily to quantitative treatment, however, since the increased earnings which a merger, for example, will produce are difficult if not impossible to estimate. The psychological security which is experienced by the debtor who knows he can redeem his issue for any reason, even if he does not know what some of the reasons may be or when any of them may become important, is a completely subjective matter; but for some debtors, this security may be extremely important.

Since the refunding objective is the only one that lends itself readily to mathematical treatment, we may therefore illustrate the computation of the value of the call privilege on the issuer of the assumption that the call will be exercised only for refinancing to lower interest charges. Let us suppose that a $1,000, immediately callable, twenty-year bond issue with an earliest call premium of 5 percent which declines ¼ percent each year, is offered at 6 percent; that the issuer decides that he will refund his debt if the rates fall to 4 percent; and that the costs of refinancing are equal to 1 percent of the face value of the issue. He estimates on the basis of past movements in interest rates that the probability of a decline in the interest rate from 6 to 4 percent is one in twelve for the first year that the issue is outstanding; one in six for the second year; one in four for the following year; and one in three in each subsequent year. The present value of the call privilege to the borrower at the time his bonds are issued, computed by the method previously described, would be $118, or more than 10 percent of the face value of the bond.

This sum represents the minimum value to the borrower of the right to call. To this, he must add the value of the right to call for purposes other than refunding. He must express these values in money terms, in spite of the fact that they contain subjective elements. The sum of these values sets the upper limit on the price that the borrower will pay for the right to redeem his bonds at par, at any time and for any purpose. Whether he has to pay this maximum value or not will depend, in part, on the lender's evaluation of the redemption option. This leads us to a consideration of the lender's position.

The value of the call privilege to the lender is not the same as its value to the borrower, for several reasons. In the first place, with the exception of the call premium paid for redemption, other costs of the borrower are not income to the lender; and in addition, he must bear the cost of finding a new use for his funds. Interest loss to the lender will be equal to the debtor's interest gain only if the former reinvests at the same rate as that which the latter pays on his new issues. At the time of issue the lender's loss is a matter of uncertainty, and the estimates of the size and probability of this loss by the two parties may not be the same. The gains that the borrower may realize through calling to facilitate a merger, reduce debt, or shift to equity financing need not cause any loss to the lender other than reinvestment costs if interest rates have not fallen since the issue was offered. Both parties may place a value on psychological security, but there is no reason why these values should be equal.

Several federal and state regulatory agencies whose objective it is to "secure economies in the raising of capital" for companies under their jurisdiction have followed a firm policy of requiring these companies to issue bonds which are immediately callable or have short deferment periods and which bear a low call premium. They have asserted that these provisions did not raise offering yields and, furthermore, have implied that they would modify their position if the opposite could be proved. In fact, they have granted waivers or modified their position from time to time, although they have always insisted that the issuer obtain the maximum flexibility feasible under prevailing market conditions.

Some large institutional investors have contended that the policy of the regulatory agencies has forced them to withdraw from the market for utility issues. The portfolios of these investors show that they have in fact withdrawn from these markets when adequate call protection was not granted, but the call issue may not have been the sole reason for this action. The higher yields available on other security offerings, the need for better portfolio balance or diversification, and other investment considerations may have been major reasons for their policy decision. In any case the withdrawal of certain investors from the market has not prevented the utility companies from successfully selling new issues with call options. Moreover, there has been no marked increase in the yields which can be attributed to the call features. Other buyers, such as pension funds and smaller insurance companies, have bought callable issues. However, to the extent that there has been a net reduction in the demand for these issues because of the withdrawal of some investors from this area, interest yields may be higher than they otherwise would have been. This, of course, cannot be measured.

Institutional investors have also criticized the regulatory policy on the ground that it favors the consumer at the expense of the investor. Without going into the philosophy of rate regulation, one may raise the question of the equity of greater government assistance to utility customers than to those providing the capital for the companies. However, if there is no difference in yield which can be attributed to the call option, it is prudent policy from the standpoint of the utility companies to maximize their financial flexibility.

Finally, some critics of the policy of the regulatory agencies have pointed out the inconsistency of the position they have taken on callability for securities offered under their jurisdiction and the call policy that the governments have adopted with respect to their own security issues.

If the market set a value on the call privilege, that is, set a price on it based on the risks assumed by both parties, much of the controversy over the justice of the redemption privilege would disappear. At present, we hear considerable discussion over the ethics of what is termed the "one-way-street" effect of the indenture provision which gives the debtor the right to terminate the loan agreement at his own option, while the creditor has no comparable right. If a proper charge were made for the call privilege, the lender would be compensated, and there would be no "one-way street." In fact, the lender would receive a higher yield for granting callability and might never be called out of his loan, and the borrower would pay for a privilege which he might not exercise.

It is not necessary that the option to call be without any restrictions in order that it be evaluated by the market. An issue can be made callable after a deferment period and would presumably have a lower cost of callability because of the deferment. A premium can be employed, and this should also lower the value of the call right, since it would reduce any gain to the borrower and would offset some or all of the loss to the lender.

We must not claim too much, however, for market valuation of the redemption privilege. It does not solve all the problems faced by the lender. For example, there is still the risk that he will be called out of a loan and have to relend at a lower income. This risk is not reduced at all; instead, he is compensated for assuming it. The borrower, on the other hand, pays for a privilege he may never use. Moreover, since the value of the call privilege is computed on the basis of estimates and probabilities, the realized return to the lender or the borrower from the exercise of the call option may be much different from the price paid for callability.

The only way the lender can protect himself completely against a loss from a refunding call, other than to prohibit it or impose an extremely high call premium, is to require the borrower to pay him the entire savings realized from the refunding for the period of the original issue. This assumes that the lender will relend at the same rate that the borrower obtains on his new issue.

Under this compensating plan, if the borrower called the entire issue which was originally offered on a 6 percent yield basis and replaced it with a 4 percent issue, he would pay the investor 2 percent per year on the face value of the old bonds until their contractual maturity date or a sum equivalent to the present value of such payments. If a bond is retired by the issue of stock, or if the issuer makes a net reduction in his debt, the yields on newly offered bonds of similar rating, term, and size of issue may serve as a basis for computing the loss to the lender. Of course, if these yields are higher than that of the redeemed issue, there would be no loss to the investor.

In effect, then, the issuer would have to pay the offering yield on the original issue until its maturity date, even if the issue were extinguished by call long before its maturity. The investor could reinvest his funds at, or perhaps even above, the rate at which the issuer could refinance; and this, together with the differential in yield that he would receive from the original issue, would assure that his income would not be diminished in spite of the call.

While there would be no reason to call merely for the purpose of reducing the carrying charge for the life of the loan, the issuer might wish to take advantage of attractive market conditions to reset his debt for an extended period of time. Moreover, this arrangement would not restrict a call for any purpose. Neither the issuer nor the investor would have to make any projection of future developments or assume any risk of inflexibility or income loss. No extra premium would be required, and the cost to the issuer would always be directly related to the market conditions prevailing at the time of the refinancing.

This compensating arrangement has one great advantage to the lender which he does not realize from the valuation method, namely, the elimination of interest loss from refunding. If the borrower merely bought the right to refund, he would keep all the interest gain realized from a refunding, and the lender might suffer a loss far in excess of the price he received for granting the call privilege. Since interest loss is avoided by the compensating provision, this arrangement carries no appreciable cost to the lender.

From the borrower's point of view, the compensating procedure has only one important disadvantage; namely, it prevents him from making a purely financial gain through refunding. However, since he can call freely for any purpose, the issuer has complete flexibility, and he can realize any gains, except interest savings, without imposing a cost on the lender.

Presumably, the lender can demand that the borrower pay for this particular type of call privilege, even though the granting of the privilege does not subject the lender to any risk of loss. The value of this particular right to the issuer would be determined by the same procedure as that used to value the unrestricted call privilege, except that there is no interest gain to be considered and therefore no necessity to be concerned about future interest rate changes.

Whether the market places a value on the unrestricted call privilege or on a call provision which incorporates the compensating arrangement, the very act of evaluation would focus attention on the factors which affect the value of the redemption right and would lead issuers and investors to think of the privilege as a vendible good. This attitude might dispense with some of the controversy over the justification of callability and over government regulation of this privilege. Finally, it might lead to some new method of dealing with the call privilege which would be more satisfactory to all parties concerned.

*Chapter* 16

# *Direct Placement of Corporate Debt**

Two basic sources of capital funds are available to corporations. Capital funds may be (1) generated internally or (2) acquired from outside sources. When capital is generated internally, a portion of a corporation's cash flow (net profits and depreciation charges) must be retained. When capital is acquired from external sources, a corporation may choose among alternatives. Thus, funds can be obtained through (1) the sale of equity issues or (2) by borrowing. In either case, there is the further option of making (1) a public offering or (2) a direct placement of securities with large institutional investors.

The raising of long-term external capital by means of a public offering of securities (debt or equity) is a familiar method used by corporation. The offering is handled by an underwriting syndicate which, either by competitive bidding or through negotiation, purchases securities from a borrowing company, and in turn sells the securities to individual and institutional investors. Underwriters assume all of the marketing risk in return for a profit, which is represented by the spread between the price paid *to* the borrowing corporation and the price paid *by* the investor minus underwriting expenses.

The alternative to a public offering is the direct placement of securities with large institutional investors, a method that has assumed growing importance in recent years. Direct placement involves direct negotiation between borrower and lender, and eliminates the underwriting function. In direct placement a prospective borrower investigates, often with the aid of an agent, the possible sale of securities to one or a small group

*Reprinted by permission from Federal Reserve Bank of Cleveland, *Economic Review*, March, 1965, pp. 3–18.

of institutional investors.[1] Terms and conditions of the offering are negotiated by borrower and lender, with the exchange of funds and securities taking place directly.

In recent years, corporate demands for external capital have increased only moderately. As shown in Figure 1, corporate demands have accounted for a progressively smaller share of increasing total net demands for funds in capital markets.[2] In the early part of the period shown (through 1953), corporate demands accounted, on an annual average basis, for about 47 percent of total net funds raised. Since 1954 the annual average has been reduced to 22 percent. During the entire 1946–64 period the ratio of corporate demands to total capital funds raised ranged from a high of 87.5 percent in 1949 to a low of only 8 percent in 1963.

FIGURE 1

NET FUNDS RAISED IN CAPITAL MARKETS

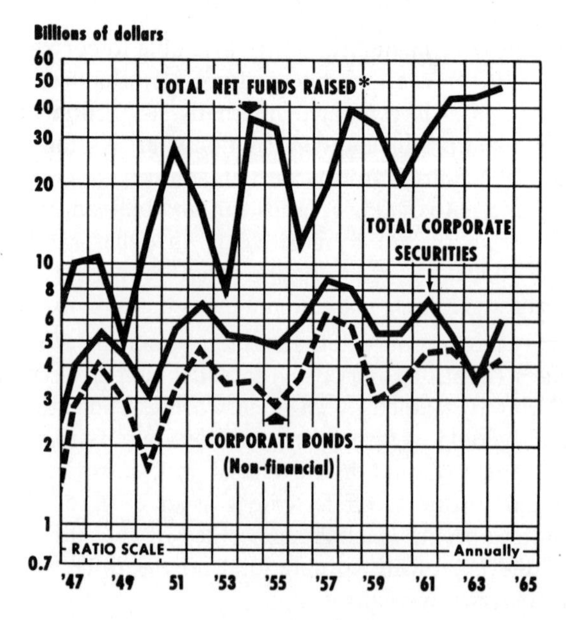


*Long-term securities and mortgages; 1964 estimated.

*Source of data:* Board of Governors of the Federal Reserve System.

[1]An agent (usually a securities underwriter) will often bring borrower and lender together, and assist in negotiating terms and conditions of the offering. The agent receives a fee for these services (usually paid by the borrower).

[2]Net funds raised in capital markets include net long-term borrowing by the U.S. government, state and local governments, nonfinancial corporations, foreigners, and net new mortgage debt.

In contrast, corporate bond offerings have represented a consistently large proportion of total corporate demands for external capital funds, averaging 68 percent per year during the 1946–64 period, and accounting in most years for the swings in total corporate demands. Interestingly, in 1963, as Figure 1 shows, the increase in the volume of corporate bonds actually exceeded that of total corporate funds raised, indicating a net retirement of corporate stock in 1963.

Corporate preference for borrowed funds (as contrasted to equity funds) when raising external capital has principally reflected the availability of larger amounts of corporate funds generated internally. That is to say, the increased availability of internally generated funds—arising from larger depreciation allowances, investment tax credits, and the reduction in corporate tax rates—has contributed importantly to the smaller need for external equity capital. It should also be noted that the internal generation of funds through retained earnings improves the capital base and encourages the use of borrowing to satisfy external financing requirements. In addition, as compared with the cost of equity capital, borrowed funds often provide a less costly source of corporate

TABLE 1

NEW ISSUES OF CORPORATE SECURITIES, 1953–64

| | *Public Offerings and Direct Placements* | | | *Direct Placements of Debt Issues* | | |
|---|---|---|---|---|---|---|
| | | *Debt Issues** | | | | |
| *Year* | *Equity and Debt: Volume (Millions of $'s)* | *Volume (Millions of $'s)* | *As % of Equity and Debt (Col. 1)* | *Volume (Millions of $'s)* | *As % of All Debt Issues (Col. 2)* | *As % of Equity and Debt (Col. 1)* |
| 1953 | $ 8,898 | $ 7,083 | 79.6% | $3,228 | 45.6% | 36.3% |
| 1954 | 9,516 | 7,488 | 78.7 | 3,484 | 46.5 | 36.6 |
| 1955 | 10,240 | 7,420 | 72.5 | 3,301 | 44.5 | 32.7 |
| 1956 | 10,939 | 8,002 | 73.2 | 3,777 | 47.2 | 34.5 |
| 1957 | 12,884 | 9,957 | 77.3 | 3,839 | 38.6 | 30.0 |
| 1958 | 11,558 | 9,653 | 83.5 | 3,320 | 34.4 | 28.7 |
| 1959 | 9,748 | 7,190 | 73.8 | 3,632 | 50.5 | 37.3 |
| 1960 | 10,154 | 8,081 | 79.6 | 3,275 | 40.5 | 32.3 |
| 1961 | 13,165 | 9,420 | 71.6 | 4,720 | 50.1 | 35.9 |
| 1962 | 10,705 | 8,969 | 83.8 | 4,529 | 50.5 | 42.1 |
| 1963 | 12,237 | 10,872 | 88.8 | 6,158 | 56.6 | 50.3 |
| 1964 | 13,381 | 10,300 | 77.0 | 6,900 | 67.0 | 51.6 |
| Average, 1953–64 | ....... | ....... | 78.3% | ...... | 47.7% | 37.4% |

*Debt issues include mortgage bonds, unsecured notes and debentures and convertible bonds, notes and debentures.

*Source:* Securities and Exchange Commission.

working capital, since interest payments on borrowings are a tax-deductible expense. Moreover, a higher proportion of borrowed funds may exert favorable leverage on a corporation's net income.

Growth in the volume of direct placements of debt issues has been impressive, even though corporate reliance on external funds has not increased very much in recent years. Table 1 points up the growing importance of direct placements. A somewhat dramatic comparison is found in the fact that the volume of direct placements (debt issues) in 1964 was 114 percent larger than in 1953. Less dramatic, but nevertheless clearly reflecting the trend toward increased emphasis on direct placement of debt issues, is the fact that the annual average for 1961–64 is substantially greater than for any other four-year period shown in the table. Although not shown in Table 1, it is noteworthy that direct placement of debt issues accounted for nearly 96 percent of all direct placements (equity and debt) in the 1953–64 period.

For 1953–64 as a whole, of all debt issues, direct placements accounted for an average of nearly 48 percent, with the proportion ranging higher in recent years, and reaching 67 percent in 1964. For 1953–64 as a whole, direct placements of debt issues accounted for 37 percent of all corporate securities sold, with this proportion also ranging higher in recent years, and reaching an all-time high in 1964 (see Table 1).

## *Reasons for Growth of Direct Placements*

Why have direct placements of corporate debt increased in importance in recent years? What have been the characteristics of such placements? In the pages that follow, we attempt to answer these questions.

*Initial Costs.* The cost saving to borrowers is perhaps the most frequently mentioned reason for the growing use of direct placements. While supporting data are admittedly fragmentary, there is evidence that costs involved in negotiating direct placements are significantly less than the costs of floating a registered public offering.

Table 2 presents some earlier cost comparisons of public offerings and direct placements.[3] For the time period studied, the data indicate

[3]The data for 1951, 1953, and 1955 are from Securities and Exchange Commission, *Cost of Flotation of Corporate Securities: 1951–55* (Washington, D.C.: U.S. Government Printing Office, 1957). Total costs of public offerings include underwriters' compensation and all other fees and expenses incident to the offering, e.g., legal, printing, accounting, and engineering expenses. Total costs of direct offerings include the fees paid agents or finders and other expenses of the offering.

Data for 1963 on public offerings are from a special study of underwriting spreads on 123 issues of debt securities. See Investment Bankers Association of America, *Statistical Bulletin* (Washington, D.C., June, 1964).

that in all comparable size classes the cost of negotiating a direct placement is significantly less than for floating a public offering. The cost differential (column 8) is particularly large for smaller issues, diminishing gradually as the size of issue increases. A major part of the wide differential is accounted for by the relatively high underwriting cost of public offerings (column 2). Nearly all costs of distribution are avoided in direct placements, with the exception of modest fees paid to agents or "finders." The differential is even wider when the services of an agent are not required.

TABLE 2

COMPARATIVE COSTS OF PUBLIC OFFERINGS AND DIRECT PLACEMENTS OF CORPORATE DEBT SECURITIES

| | 1951–53–55 | | | | | | | 1963 |
|---|---|---|---|---|---|---|---|---|
| | Public Offerings | | | Direct Placements | | | | |
| Size of Issue (Millions of $'s) | Underwriting Spread (as a % of Proceeds) | Other Expenses (as a % of Proceeds) | Total (as a % of Proceeds) | Fees (as a % of Proceeds) | Expenses (as a % of Proceeds) | Total (as a % of Proceeds) | Cost Differential | Underwriting Spread on Public Offerings (as a % of Proceeds) |
| Under 0.3... | .... | .... | ..... | 1.86 | 1.49 | 3.35 | .... | .... |
| 0.3– 0.4.... | .... | .... | ..... | 1.60 | 1.06 | 2.66 | .... | .... |
| 0.5– 0.9.... | 7.53 | 3.96 | 11.49 | 1.31 | 0.83 | 2.14 | 9.35 | 4.73 |
| 1.0– 1.9.... | 5.80 | 2.37 | 8.17 | 0.97 | 0.59 | 1.56 | 6.61 | 7.89 |
| 2.0– 4.9.... | 2.37 | 1.41 | 3.78 | 0.69 | 0.43 | 1.12 | 2.66 | 3.87 |
| 5.0– 9.9.... | 1.01 | 0.82 | 1.83 | 0.49 | 0.34 | 0.83 | 1.00 | 1.61 |
| 10.0–19.9.... | 0.88 | 0.64 | 1.52 | 0.31 | 0.32 | 0.63 | 0.89 | 0.89 |
| 20.0–49.9.... | 0.85 | 0.48 | 1.33 | 0.22* | 0.22 | 0.44 | 0.89 | 0.80 |
| 50.0 and over. | 0.88 | 0.32 | 1.19 | .... | .... | .... | .... | 0.79 |

*Twenty million dollars and over.

*Sources:* Securities and Exchange Commission, and Investment Bankers Association of America

Lack of data prohibits a more up-to-date comparison of costs of public offerings and direct placements, but available evidence indicates that the latter continue to be less costly to arrange. A tabulation of underwriting spreads on public offerings of debt issues in 1963 (last column in Table 2) shows that there have been only minor changes in this expense since the earlier U.S. Securities and Exchange Commission survey. In four of the seven size classes, spreads were higher in 1963 than in the earlier period; while in three size classes, some reduction occurred. If expenses of direct placements and other expenses of public offerings have been essentially unchanged, cost comparisons would continue to favor direct sales, particularly for smaller issues.

*Total Costs.* While direct sales seem to involve lower initial costs to the borrower, the lack of data on costs of public offerings and direct placements over their life span makes it difficult if not impossible to compare total costs of capital raised through the alternative methods. A comparison of this type is important because differential costs of borrowing due to interest costs could appreciably reduce initial advantages.

Some light has been shed on the matter by a study that compared offering yields on public offerings and direct placements of industrial-financial-service (IFS) borrowers, and which showed that yields on direct placements were consistently above yields on public offerings in the 1952–58 period.[4] In that period the annual spread between yields on public offerings and direct placements of IFS debt of $1 million and over averaged 51 basis points, with a high spread of 86 basis points and a low of 30 basis points. While this comparison represents only approximate average yields—due to lack of data on such determinants of yield as quality, maturity, size, and time of offering—it does indicate the magnitude of yield differentials that may exist. To whatever extent a yield differential exists, it will at least partly offset the advantage of lower initial costs of negotiating direct placements.

*Flexibility.* A second important reason cited for the growth of direct placements is the convenience and flexibility provided to both borrower and lender. Because a direct placement involves a limited number of investors (lenders), borrower and lender are closely associated in negotiating terms and conditions of the offering. As a result, terms and conditions can be more precisely tailored to the requirements of both parties.

By paying a small commitment fee, a borrowing corporation can arrange in advance for future capital requirements. An advance commitment provides the issuer some insurance against market uncertainties, while granting the option of canceling the issue if the need for funds does not materialize. An investor is able to earmark funds for future investment and receive an immediate return from the commitment fee. Final negotiations to formulate terms and conditions that best suit the needs of both parties take place at the time of actual takedown.

After an issue has been placed, it is possible to renegotiate terms such as rate and maturity in light of changing requirements of either borrower or lender. Similar flexibility is not possible in widely distributed public offerings.

*Institutional Demand.* Another frequently mentioned reason for growth in direct placements is increased demand for corporate debt securities by institutional investors, which has not been matched by a

---

[4]Avery B. Cohan, *Private Placements and Public Offerings: Market Shares since 1935* (Chapel Hill: University of North Carolina Press, 1961), pp. 16–17.

corresponding increase in supply. As indicated in Figure 2, institutional holdings of corporate bonds more than doubled in the 1945–50 period, while the volume of corporate debt outstanding rose by only 58 percent. Since 1950 the rate of growth in institutional holdings has moderated somewhat, but the increase has more than kept pace with growth in outstanding corporate debt. In the 1945–50 period, corporate bond holdings of life insurance companies and pension funds on average amounted annually to about three fifths of total corporate bonds outstanding; since 1950 the proportion has averaged about three fourths, on an annual basis.

FIGURE 2

FINANCIAL ASSETS OF SELECTED FINANCIAL INSTITUTIONS AND CORPORATE BOND OUTSTANDINGS

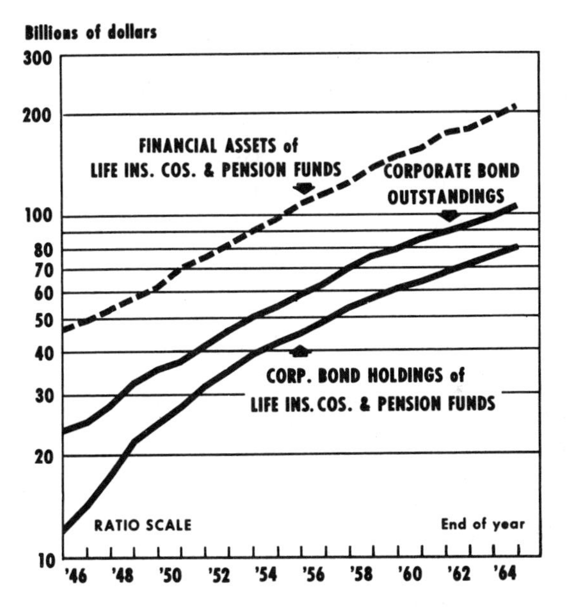


*Source of data:* Board of Governors of the Federal Reserve System.

As total assets of life insurance companies and pension funds have mounted in the postwar period, these institutions have faced the continuing task of employing funds in suitable investments until needed to meet claims. Since 1950, growth of total assets of these institutions has outstripped the growth of corporate bonds, as the stream of premium payments has added considerably more to reserves than is required to meet current claims. Since most claims are long term in nature, investment policy is designed to maximize income, with less emphasis on liquidity and marketability. Corporate debt securities generally are well suited to this purpose, offering acceptable quality and a yield advantage over some other forms of long-term investment.

Institutional preference for corporate bonds is evidenced by the fact that holdings of these securities have constituted a relatively large proportion of the financial assets of life insurance companies and pension funds. For example, corporate bond holdings of life insurance companies and pension funds amounted, on average, to about 41 percent of total assets during 1950–64. Reflecting the slowdown in the rate of growth of corporate bonds outstanding, however, the proportion has declined in each year (with one exception) since 1957. In the way of comparison, the assets of these institutions rose by 67 percent from 1957 through 1964, while the volume of corporate bonds outstanding increased by only 50 percent. Hence, although corporate bond holdings of life insurance companies and pension funds increased at a faster rate than outstandings, the ratio of holdings to total financial assets declined from 43 percent in 1957 to 39 percent in 1964.

*Simplicity.* Another factor that may have stimulated the increased use of direct placements is the burden of registration and disclosure requirements imposed on public offerings by the Securities Act of 1933. Direct placements were exempted from the provisions of the act, thus providing a way by which borrowers could avoid the expense and inconvenience of compliance. While this factor may have been important initially, it is likely that other reasons cited above have been more important to the sustained increase in direct placements.

## *Corporate Debt Issues and Economic Activity*

The pattern of growth in the volume of direct placements (debt issues) in the postwar period has been associated to a large extent with the nation's business and monetary cycles. As indicated in the top panel of Figure 3, direct placements have usually accelerated during periods of business expansion, and levelled off or declined prior to cyclical peaks. This pattern is explained to a large extent by the behavior of debt placements of manufacturing firms, which have historically accounted for a large proportion of direct placements—nearly two fifths of the total during the 1948–64 period.

As indicated in Figure 3, the volume of direct placements of manufacturing firms has increased during the early stages of business expansion, a period usually characterized by interest rates that were either declining or below previous highs (as measured by the rate on Aaa new corporate issues). As the economy has changed direction, with accompanying changes in interest rates, direct placements of manufacturing firms have tended to level off or decline, with the pattern often extending beyond a subsequent reversal in business activity as well as in interest rates. Some of this behavior is of course associated with traditionally early peaks in corporate profits during business expansions, in subsequent cutbacks in capital spending, and in correspondingly smaller needs for borrowed capital.

FIGURE 3

NEW CORPORATE DEBT ISSUES AND RELATED ECONOMIC VARIABLES

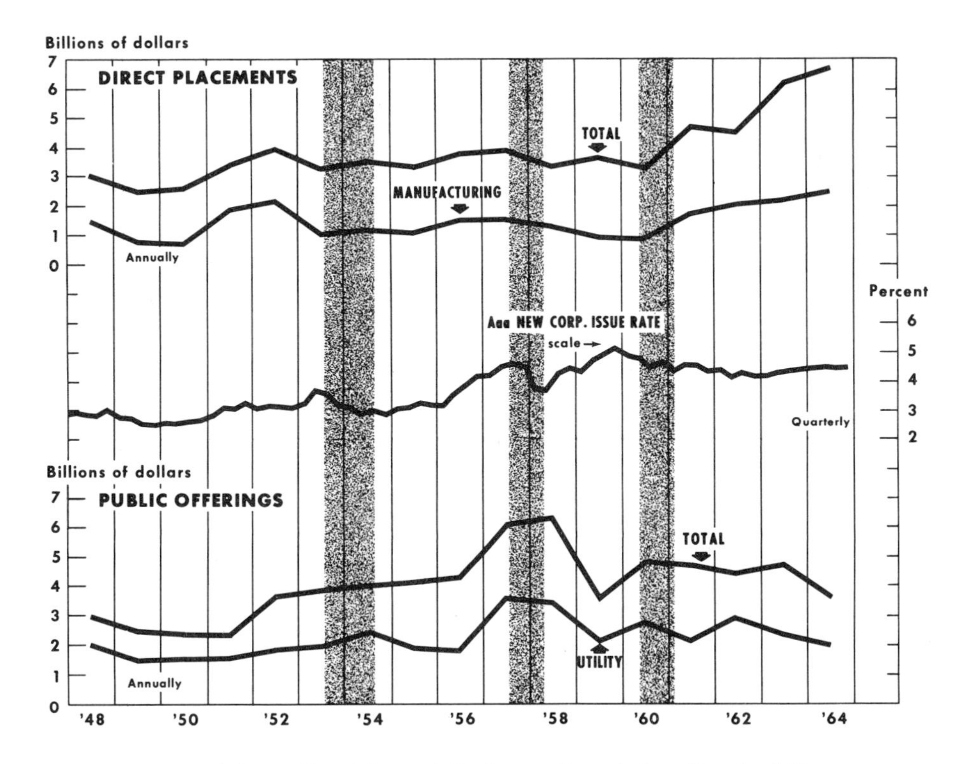


*Sources of data:* Securities and Exchange Commission; Board of Governors of the Federal Reserve System.

The importance of direct placements of manufacturers is suggested by the fact that in the years when the total volume of direct placements (debt issues) was rising—1951–52, 1956–57, and 1961–64—the former accounted for a larger percentage of the total (44 percent) than in years when volume was declining—33 percent in 1949–50, 1953, and 1958–59.

While placements of manufacturing firms have continued to be a major component in the total volume of direct placements, the relative influence has been moderated somewhat in recent years by the growing importance of other types of borrowers (especially real estate and finance firms). For example, while the volume of direct sales by finance and real estate firms accounted for 21 percent of all direct placements in the entire 1948–64 period, the percentage has been on the higher side in each year since 1958, accounting for nearly 29 percent of total placements in 1958–64. Such placements have been particularly significant in the sharp rise in the total volume of direct placements since 1960.

Public offerings of corporate debt securities have shown a somewhat different relationship to monetary and business cycles than have direct placements. As indicated in the lower portion of Figure 3, the volume of public offerings has usually risen markedly in the later stages of business expansion, often continuing at high levels through subsequent recessions.

The pattern of public offerings mainly reflects the behavior of public utility borrowers (gas, electric, water, and communications companies). The volume of offerings of these companies, which accounted for nearly 58 percent of all public offerings in the 1948–64 period, has often expanded during periods when the economy was depressed—in other words, following a peak in business activity. Such periods are usually characterized by improving availability of funds and declining interest rates. The fact that utilities often borrow heavily during periods of depressed economic activity also reflects the stability associated with the demand for utility services as well as the near guarantee of a target rate of return on investment from public utility regulation.[5] An exception to the usual pattern of public utility offerings occurred in 1957, reflecting in large part the capital spending boom which reached a peak in that year. At that time, public offerings (including utility offerings) increased sharply, despite a rapid rise in the level of interest rates.

The predominance of public utility issues among public offerings, as indicated earlier, reflects in part restrictions that require many companies to offer securities at competitive bidding. Moreover, costs of flotation in an underwritten offering of utility debt may be considerably smaller than flotation costs for other types of public offerings. This was clearly evident in the 1951–55 period, for example, according to results of the U.S. Securities and Exchange Commission study of flotation costs (see Table

[5]In most instances, public utilities are not permitted to enter into direct placement agreements. The Public Utility Holding Company Act of 1935 prohibits such agreements by stipulating that specific security issues must be issued via competitive bidding. In addition, many state laws also require public issuance of public utilities securities.

3). The relatively lower flotation costs of public offerings of utility issues reflects the generally higher quality of such offerings and the benefit of smaller underwriting spreads.

TABLE 3

COMPARATIVE COSTS OF PUBLIC OFFERINGS AND DIRECT PLACEMENTS OF CORPORATE DEBT SECURITIES, CLASSIFIED BY SIZE OF ISSUE AND INDUSTRY OF ISSUER, 1951–53–55

| | *Manufacturing* | | | *Utility** | | |
|---|---|---|---|---|---|---|
| *Size of Issue (Millions of $'s)* | *Public (as % of Proceeds)* | *Direct (as % of Proceeds)* | *Cost Differential* | *Public (as % of Proceeds)* | *Direct (as % of Proceeds)* | *Cost Differential* |
| Under 0.3....... | ..... | 2.36 | ..... | .... | 3.46 | .... |
| 0.3– 0.4....... | ..... | 2.37 | ..... | .... | 3.01 | .... |
| 0.5– 0.9....... | 12.12 | 2.07 | 10.05 | .... | 2.30 | .... |
| 1.0– 1.9....... | 9.03 | 1.48 | 7.55 | 5.00 | 1.72 | 3.28 |
| 2.0– 4.9....... | 6.16 | 1.08 | 5.08 | 2.23 | 1.43 | 0.80 |
| 5.0– 9.9....... | 3.47 | 0.71 | 2.76 | 1.52 | 0.93 | 0.59 |
| 10.0–19.9....... | 2.34 | 0.55 | 1.79 | 1.28 | 0.82 | 0.46 |
| 20.0–49.9....... | 1.71 | 0.46† | 1.25 | 1.20 | 0.61† | 0.59 |
| 50.0 and over.... | 1.30 | .... | ..... | 1.15 | .... | .... |

*Includes electric, gas, and water companies.
†Twenty million dollars and over.
*Source:* Securities and Exchange Commission.

As indicated in Table 3, public offerings of manufacturing companies involved higher flotation costs than utility offerings, although the differential narrowed as the size of issue increased. In contrast, costs of direct placements of manufacturers were generally lower than those of direct placements of utility issues. As a result, the differential cost advantage in the use of direct placements was quite sizable for manufacturing issues, although the differential diminished as the size of issue increased.

## *Experience in 1963*

Since the most recent complete data available on the volume of directly placed corporate debt issues are for 1963, a review of the experience during that year is presented here to highlight the major characteristics of direct placements. The volume of direct placements of debt securities of domestic corporations amounted to $6,421 million during 1963, representing a total of 1,217 individual issues.[6] Table 4

[6]See "Corporate Financing Directory," *Investment Dealers' Digest,* Sec. II, July 29, 1963, and February 3, 1964. While totals reported are amounts contracted for in 1963, the latter are taken down over a period of time. For this reason, the

*(Continued on next page)*

summarizes offerings in 1963 and presents a distribution of direct placements by type of borrower, type of issue, and size of issue.

TABLE 4

DIRECT PLACEMENTS OF CORPORATE DEBT SECURITIES, 1963
Distribution by Type of Borrower, Type of Security, and Size of Issue

| | *Number of Issues* | *Percentage Distribution* | *Volume of Issues (Millions of $'s)* | *Percentage Distribution* |
|---|---|---|---|---|
| Type of borrower: | | | | |
| Manufacturing* | 453 | 37.3% | $2,973 | 46.3% |
| Public utility† | 128 | 10.5 | 604 | 9.4 |
| Finance and real estate | 397 | 32.6 | 1,787 | 27.8 |
| All other‡ | 239 | 19.6 | 1,057 | 16.5 |
| Total | 1,217 | 100.0% | $6,421 | 100.0% |
| Type of security: | | | | |
| Mortgage bonds | 46 | 3.8% | $ 194 | 3.0% |
| Other notes and debentures§ | 1,137 | 93.4 | 6,125 | 95.4 |
| Convertible bonds, notes and debentures | 34 | 2.8 | 102 | 1.6 |
| Total | 1,217 | 100.0% | $6,421 | 100.0% |
| Size of issue (in millions of $'s): | | | | |
| Under 0.5 | 244 | 20.0% | $ 62 | 0.9% |
| 0.5– 0.9 | 182 | 15.0 | 120 | 1.9 |
| 1.0– 2.9 | 357 | 29.3 | 594 | 9.2 |
| 3.0– 4.9 | 124 | 10.2 | 455 | 7.1 |
| 5.0– 9.9 | 139 | 11.4 | 883 | 13.8 |
| 10.0–24.9 | 114 | 9.4 | 1,603 | 25.0 |
| 25.0 and over | 57 | 4.7 | 2,704 | 42.1 |
| Total | 1,217 | 100.0% | $6,421 | 100.0% |

*Includes mining and extractive companies.
†Includes electric, gas, water, and communication companies.
‡Includes railroads, other transportation companies, commercial, and other businesses.
§Includes some issues secured by various kinds of collateral other than real estate.
*Source:* *Investment Dealers' Digest.*

In terms of both number of issues and dollar volume, manufacturing industries accounted for the largest share of direct placements in 1963, while companies in the finance and real estate field were second most

total derived for domestic corporate debt issues does not correspond to that reported by the Securities and Exchange Commission. Despite an overstatement of volume, reported characteristics of the issues are revealing. The volume of foreign borrowing is not included.

important. These two categories of borrowers accounted for more than two thirds of the number and nearly three fourths of the dollar volume of direct placements during 1963. Public utilities accounted for only about 10 percent of both the number and the volume of issues, while all other borrowers accounted for less than one fifth of the number of issues and only one sixth of the volume.

The pattern of direct placements is in marked contrast to public offerings in 1963, where public utility issues accounted for slightly more than one half of the dollar volume and manufacturing firms for only one fifth. Offerings by finance and real estate firms and all other borrowers accounted for the remainder of the volume of public offerings.

The summary of direct placements of corporate debt by type of security in Table 4 shows that in 1963 the bulk of both the number and the dollar volume took the form of unsecured borrowing (principally notes and debentures). The relatively small remainder was accounted for by mortgage bonds and debt obligations with some form of conversion privilege.

While relatively small issues accounted for the bulk of the number of placements, dollar volume was centered in a small number of large placements. Placements of more than $10 million constituted about

TABLE 5

DIRECT PLACEMENTS OF CORPORATE DEBT SECURITIES, 1963
Percentage Distribution of Number and Dollar Volume
by Size of Issue and Type of Borrower

| Size of Issue (in Millions of $'s) | *Type of Borrower* | | | | | | | |
|---|---|---|---|---|---|---|---|---|
| | *Manufacturing* | | *Finance and Real Estate* | | *Public Utility* | | *All Other* | |
| | *No.* | *Volume* | *No.* | *Volume* | *No.* | *Volume* | *No.* | *Volume* |
| Under 0.5 | 17.9% | 0.8% | 20.2% | 1.1% | 24.2% | 1.0% | 21.8% | 1.2% |
| 0.5– 0.9 | 13.9 | 1.4 | 16.6 | 2.4 | 10.2 | 1.3 | 16.7 | 2.6 |
| 1.0– 2.9 | 30.9 | 7.8 | 31.2 | 11.6 | 27.3 | 9.1 | 24.3 | 9.4 |
| 3.0– 4.9 | 9.0 | 5.2 | 9.6 | 7.7 | 10.9 | 8.4 | 13.0 | 10.6 |
| 5.0– 9.9 | 11.0 | 11.1 | 11.3 | 15.6 | 14.1 | 17.7 | 10.9 | 16.0 |
| 10.0–24.9 | 11.3 | 25.7 | 6.0 | 16.8 | 10.2 | 31.0 | 10.9 | 33.1 |
| 25.0 and over | 6.0 | 48.0 | 5.1 | 44.8 | 3.1 | 31.5 | 2.4 | 27.1 |
| Total | 100.0% | 100.0% | 100.0% | 100.0% | 100.0% | 100.0% | 100.0% | 100.0% |
| Total number | 453 | ....... | 397 | ....... | 128 | ....... | 239 | ....... |
| Total volume (millions of $'s) | ....... | $2,973 | ....... | $1,787 | ....... | $604 | ....... | $1,057 |

*Source: Investment Dealers' Digest.*

two thirds of the dollar volume but only 14 percent of the number, while placements of less than $3 million accounted for nearly two thirds of the number but only 12 percent of the dollar volume.

Analysis of the size distribution of placements by type of borrower indicates there is no uniform pattern among industry classes (see Table 5). Compared with other industry groups, a larger proportion of the placements of manufacturers was centered in large issues. Large issues (over $10 million) accounted for nearly three fourths of the total dollar volume of placements by manufacturers, compared with an average of about three fifths for the other industry groups. A similar situation existed with respect to number of issues sold.

The dollar volume of issues in the intermediate size class ($3 million to $10 million) represented a fairly uniform proportion of placements of each industry group except manufacturers, where the degree of concentration was somewhat lower. The use of small issues was most prevalent among finance and real estate concerns.

Using maturities and coupon rates as criteria, Table 6 presents a

TABLE 6

DIRECT PLACEMENTS OF CORPORATE DEBT SECURITIES, 1963
Distribution by Maturity and Coupon Rate

| | *Number of Issues* | *Percentage Distribution* | *Volume of Issues (in Millions of $'s)* | *Percentage Distribution* |
|---|---|---|---|---|
| Maturity class: | | | | |
| No maturity reported | 77 | 6.3% | $ 307 | 4.8% |
| Under 5 years | 36 | 3.0 | 141 | 2.2 |
| 5 to less than 10 years | 73 | 6.0 | 233 | 3.6 |
| 10 to less than 15 years | 348 | 28.6 | 688 | 10.7 |
| 15 to less than 20 years | 348 | 28.6 | 1,844 | 28.7 |
| 20 years and over | 335 | 27.5 | 3,208 | 50.0 |
| Total | 1,217 | 100.0% | $6,421 | 100.0% |
| Coupon rates: | | | | |
| No coupon reported | 116 | 9.5% | $ 524 | 8.2% |
| Under 4.00% | 2 | 0.2 | 10 | 0.2 |
| 4.00–4.49% | 31 | 2.5 | 619 | 9.6 |
| 4.50–4.99% | 175 | 14.4 | 1,846 | 28.7 |
| 5.00–5.49% | 231 | 19.0 | 1,480 | 23.0 |
| 5.50–5.99% | 315 | 25.9 | 1,378 | 21.5 |
| 6.00–6.49% | 242 | 19.9 | 354 | 5.5 |
| 6.50% and over | 105 | 8.6 | 210 | 3.3 |
| Total | 1,217 | 100.0% | $6,421 | 100.0% |

*Source: Investment Dealers' Digest.*

summary distribution of direct placements during 1963 (maturity and/or coupon rate were not reported for all offerings). As shown by the table, a large number of issues were uniformly distributed among the three longest maturity classes, with nearly 85 percent of all issues due to mature in more than 10 years from date of issue. The dollar volume of placements was also heavily concentrated in over-10-year maturities, and the bulk of the total dollar volume (one half in 1963) was accounted for by issues maturing in 20 years or longer.

While net interest costs of direct placements cannot be evaluated because of lack of data, the distribution of reported coupon rates does provide an approximation of the range of borrowing costs in 1963 (see

TABLE 7

DIRECT PLACEMENTS OF CORPORATE DEBT SECURITIES, 1963
Percentage Distribution of Number and Dollar Volume by Maturity and Coupon Rate and by Type of Borrower

| | *Type of Borrower* | | | | | | | |
|---|---|---|---|---|---|---|---|---|
| | *Manufacturing* | | *Finance and Real Estate* | | *Public Utility* | | *All Other* | |
| | *No.* | *Volume* | *No.* | *Volume* | *No.* | *Volume* | *No.* | *Volume* |
| Maturity class: | | | | | | | | |
| No maturity reported | 6.6% | 4.2% | 5.8% | 1.9% | 3.9% | 1.0% | 7.9% | 12.6% |
| Under 5 years | 1.4 | 0.7 | 4.7 | 3.5 | 2.3 | 0.2 | 3.4 | 5.5 |
| 5 to less than 10 years | 7.5 | 2.4 | 5.8 | 4.0 | ...... | ...... | 6.7 | 8.5 |
| 10 to less than 15 years | 26.0 | 10.4 | 40.8 | 15.7 | 3.1 | 0.5 | 26.8 | 8.9 |
| 15 to less than 20 years | 38.6 | 37.6 | 22.7 | 23.0 | 9.4 | 6.1 | 29.7 | 27.2 |
| 20 years and over | 19.9 | 44.7 | 20.2 | 51.9 | 81.3 | 92.2 | 25.5 | 37.3 |
| Total | 100.0% | 100.0% | 100.0% | 100.0% | 100.0% | 100.0% | 100.0% | 100.0% |
| Coupon rates: | | | | | | | | |
| No coupon reported | 9.3% | 6.1% | 11.8% | 8.2% | 0.8% | 0.1% | 10.9% | 18.6% |
| Under 4.00% | 0.3 | 0.1 | 0.3 | 0.6 | ...... | ...... | ...... | ...... |
| 4.00–4.49% | 1.3 | 7.5 | 1.3 | 3.8 | 9.4 | 44.7 | 3.3 | 5.4 |
| 4.50–4.99% | 9.7 | 24.5 | 11.8 | 38.3 | 45.3 | 41.2 | 10.9 | 17.6 |
| 5.00–5.49% | 19.2 | 26.8 | 19.9 | 16.9 | 21.1 | 7.8 | 15.9 | 31.4 |
| 5.50–5.99% | 29.8 | 29.8 | 24.4 | 15.9 | 17.2 | 2.2 | 25.5 | 18.3 |
| 6.00–6.49% | 24.7 | 4.7 | 16.9 | 7.7 | 3.9 | 0.5 | 24.3 | 7.1 |
| 6.50% and over | 5.7 | 0.5 | 13.6 | 8.6 | 2.3 | 3.5 | 9.2 | 1.6 |
| Total | 100.0% | 100.0% | 100.0% | 100.0% | 100.0% | 100.0% | 100.0% | 100.0% |
| Total number | 453 | ...... | 397 | ...... | 128 | ...... | 239 | ...... |
| Total volume (in millions of $'s) | ...... | $2,973 | ...... | $1,787 | ...... | $604 | ...... | $1,057 |

*Source: Investment Dealers' Digest.*

Table 6). Nearly three fifths of the number and three quarters of the dollar volume of placements carried coupon rates ranging from 4½ to 6 percent. Placements carrying rates of 4½ to 5 percent accounted for the largest single share of total dollar volume (nearly 29 percent), while the heaviest concentration in number of issues was in the 5½ to 6 percent range (nearly 26 percent). Issues carrying rates in excess of 6 percent accounted for a large share of the number of placements but a small part of the dollar volume.

Data on maturity and coupon rates by type of borrower reveal considerable variation in the distribution of direct placements among several industry groups (see Table 7). For example, public utility borrowing was heavily concentrated in long maturities and relatively low interest rates; the latter reflects the generally high quality of public utility obligations.

While not as heavily concentrated as those of public utilities, placements of manufacturers and finance and real estate firms were also centered largely in longer term maturities. In contrast, offerings of borrowers in the "all other" category were noticeably shorter in maturity than those of other industry groups (possibly due to the relatively high proportion of such placements for which maturity was not reported).

For a relatively high proportion of nonutility placements the coupon rates were not available. Incomplete information indicates, however, that such placements generally carried higher rates than those of public utilities. For example, only 14 percent of the volume of public utility placements carried rates of more than 5 percent, compared with an average of 56 percent of the volume for other industry groups.

## *Yield and Quality Characteristics*

Additional insight into selected characteristics of direct placements of corporate debt is provided in data from the monthly reports of the Life Insurance Association of America. These reports present information on direct placement authorizations of life insurance companies, and are available beginning in 1960.[7] As indicated in Table 8, reporting insurance companies have committed increasing amounts of funds each year to the purchase of corporate bonds that are direct placements. Dur-

[7]Data are from reports of *Average Yields on Directly Placed Corporate Bond Authorizations,* published monthly by the Life Insurance Association of America since January, 1960. The report is a tabulation of statistics on direct placements of corporate debt obligations for which commitments were made during each month by life insurance companies holding approximately two thirds of the assets of all United States life insurance companies. The data cover bonds contracted for but not actually taken down during the months. The data are used here with permission of the Life Insurance Association of America.

TABLE 8

CORPORATE BOND AUTHORIZATIONS, DIRECT PLACEMENTS, REPORTING LIFE INSURANCE COMPANIES

| Year | Total Authorizations (Millions of $'s) | First Quality | | Second Quality | | Third Quality | | Fourth Quality | | Unclassified | |
|---|---|---|---|---|---|---|---|---|---|---|---|
| | | Millions of $'s | % of Total | Millions of $'s | % of Total | Millions of $'s | % of Total | Millions of $'s | % of Total | Millions of $'s | % of Total |
| 1960..... | $2,271 | $16 | 0.7% | $110 | 4.8% | $593 | 26.1% | $ 973 | 42.9% | $579 | 25.5% |
| 1961..... | 2,702 | 30 | 1.1 | 160 | 5.9 | 676 | 25.0 | 1,260 | 46.7 | 576 | 21.3 |
| 1962..... | 3,360 | 7 | 0.2 | 201 | 6.0 | 610 | 18.2 | 1,762 | 52.4 | 780 | 23.2 |
| 1963..... | 3,408 | 18 | 0.5 | 223 | 6.6 | 676 | 19.8 | 1,713 | 50.3 | 778 | 22.8 |
| 1964..... | 3,995 | 60 | 1.5 | 255 | 6.4 | 650 | 16.3 | 2,122 | 53.1 | 908 | 22.7 |

*Source:* Life Insurance Association of America.

ing 1964, commitments totaled nearly $4 billion, or 76 percent more than in 1960. In addition, the table shows that a smaller proportion of recent commitments has been made in direct placements that are in the

FIGURE 4

CORPORATE BOND AUTHORIZATIONS, DIRECT PLACEMENTS, REPORTING LIFE INSURANCE COMPANIES

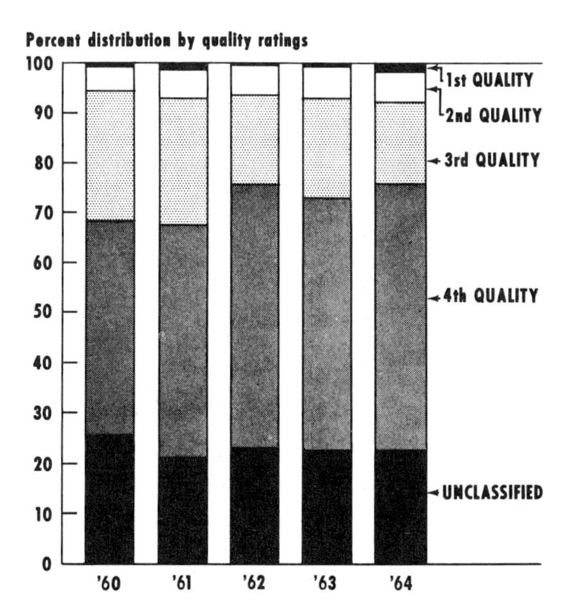


*Source of data:* Life Insurance Association of America.

higher quality grades.[8] The quality distribution of authorizations of direct placements is depicted in Figure 4.

FIGURE 5
CORPORATE BOND YIELDS
Direct Placements and Public Offerings

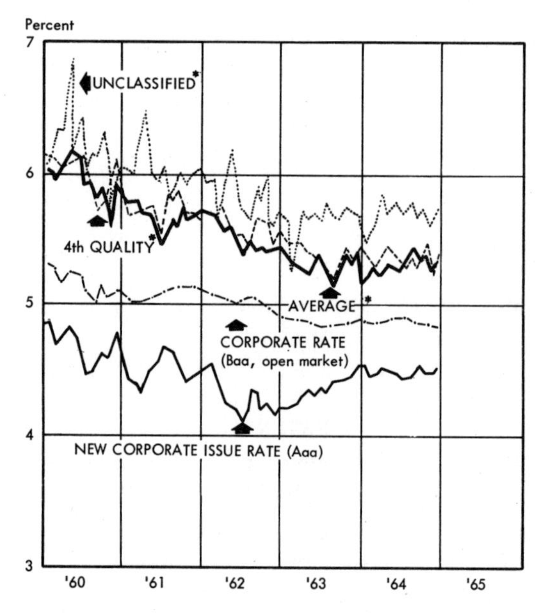


*Yields on direct placements.

*Sources of data:* Life Insurance Association of America; Board of Governors of the Federal Reserve System.

The reduced proportion of commitments in higher quality obligations is at least in part a reflection of the less attractive yields available on these obligations, compared with other issues. It may also reflect the relative shortage of higher quality bond issues. As indicated in Figure 5, average yields on direct placement commitments of life insurance companies were consistently higher than those on both newly offered Aaa corporate bond offerings and outstanding issues of Baa-rated bonds in 1960–64. The differential between the Aaa corporate new issue rate and that on direct placements averaged 1.16 percent during the period.

[8]Monthly volume and yield are reported on the basis of first-, second-, third-, and fourth-quality issues (corresponding to Moody ratings), and issues unclassified as to quality, including those with quality lower than fourth grade, convertible obligations, foreign corporates, oil production loans, and issues with which stocks or warrants are received. Higher quality issues, as used above, refer to those in the first- through third-quality grades.

averaged 0.58 percent in the 1960–64 period). In addition, yields on first-, second-, and third-quality direct placements (not shown in Figure 5) were consistently above the Aaa new corporate issue rate, although the yield differential was considerably smaller.

Although yield comparisons show that yields on direct placements have exceeded rates on public offerings, the differential narrowed considerably in the 1960–64 period. For example, the differential between the average rate on direct placements and the average rate on Aaa new corporate offerings declined from a high of 1.30 percent in 1962 to 0.92 percent in 1964. Compared with yields on Baa-rated corporates, the spread also narrowed, from a high of 0.77 percent in 1960 to 0.53 percent in 1964. A narrowing differential reflects in part increased demand for direct placements, which in turn has exerted downward pressure on interest rates. In addition, increasing institutional acceptance of this type of financing, coupled with ready availability of funds, has resulted in a downward adjustment in the historical relationship between yields on direct placements and on public offerings. The average yield on direct placements of life insurance companies has been in a declining trend throughout the period under review, while the volume of such issues has risen in each year. The yield on direct placements in 1964 averaged 60 basis points less than the average yield in 1960. In contrast, the rate on marketable Aaa new corporate offerings in 1964 was only 24 basis points less than the average yield in 1960.

Part IV

# Capital Budgeting

*Chapter* 17

# *Formal Criteria for Investment Decisions**

By Martin J. Bailey

## I

THIS PAPER attempts to solve certain remaining problems in the theory of optimal investment decisions. It is a formal analysis designed to clarify certain matters on which discussion has remained confused and confusing, without regard to potential practical importance.

The problems to be discussed concern ambiguities and paradoxes connected with the criterion of marginal productivity or rate of return, especially in cases in which the receipts stream of an investment extends over more than two periods. The literature on this subject and present knowledge of it have been summarized by J. Hirshleifer in his recent article, which contains a definitive analysis of the two-period case.[1]

Hirshleifer's analysis is not sufficient to solve the multiperiod case in full generality, since it does not deal adequately with multiperiod investment opportunities. However, since his analysis is applicable as far as it goes, it is useful to review his main conclusions and their direct corollaries. First, when an investment lasts for only two periods—that is, when it is entirely disinvested in the second period—its marginal productivity or rate of return is unambiguously defined. Rates of return may therefore be used to rank different possible two-period investments. Second, if unlimited borrowing and lending are possible at a given rate

*Reprinted from *Journal of Political Economy,* Vol. LXVII (October, 1959), pp. 476–88, by Martin J. Bailey, by permission of the University of Chicago Press. Copyright, 1959, by the University of Chicago.

[1]"On the Theory of Optimal Investment Decision," *Journal of Political Economy,* Vol. LXVI (August, 1958), pp. 329–52.

of interest, the investor should undertake all investments that have a positive present value at that rate of interest (that have a net product not less than that rate of interest), if all investments are independent. If there are mutually exclusive or interdependent investments, he should choose that investment portfolio that has the highest present value at the given rate of interest. In either case, he should then borrow (or lend) the difference between his production plan and his consumption plan. Third, if unlimited borrowing and lending are not possible at a given rate of interest, the investor's investment and borrowing-lending opportunities can be combined into an over-all opportunity set (in a system of coordinates in which one axis represents first-period consumption and the other represents second-period consumption). He should select the point in this set that touches his highest indifference curve. In this case the ranking of investments by their productivity or rate of return is an integral part of the construction of the production-opportunity curve (in the case in which there is no borrowing or lending, this is also the over-all opportunity curve). However, the indiscriminate use of either the rate-of-return criterion or the present-value criterion, as these are ordinarily understood, for determining which investments are selected could in some cases give wrong answers. In the ranking process, mutually exclusive or interdependent investment opportunities give rise to multiple production-opportunity curves; but these have an envelope, which is the interesting curve. These last points are discussed further below.

## II

It is convenient to start the discussion by assuming that all investment options or opportunities are independent of one another, so that simple rate-of-return or present-value reasoning can be applied without difficulty. This will provide the foundation for the more general analysis that follows.

The two-period analysis can be applied as it stands only to the simplest cases of multiple-period investment, such as those in which every investment consists of a single outlay in the first period, followed by a constant perpetual stream of receipts. In this case, all periods after the first can be treated as a single period, and the two-period analysis applies directly.

However, paradoxes and ambiguities arise if one considers investments whose payments streams are not constant after the first period and if one tries to work with a single (perpetual-term) rate of interest. Examples of the difficulties that may arise are given by Hirshleifer.[2] In

[2] *Ibid.*, pp. 346–50.

particular, if the sequence of receipts has any negative terms after the first positive one, an attempt to solve this sequence for its implied over-all rate of return may give multiple solutions or no real solution. These examples have sometimes been cited, along with examples of mutually exclusive opportunities, as qualifications or negations of the rate-of-return concept. As has already been indicated, however, the general solution of the investment decision problem cannot rely solely on either present-value or rate-of-return reasoning.

Recognition of the correct general solution of the investment decision problem has been hindered by the habit of thinking in terms of a single, long-term rate of interest. If writers after Fisher had kept in mind that each period's short-term rate of interest is a separate variable in an over-all opportunity-utility or supply-demand analysis, the confusion would probably have been avoided, even though superficially it complicates matters to deal separately with each short-term rate. For present purposes, it will be sufficient to consider the three-period case, except where otherwise specified. As in the two-period case, the last period may either be the last before the imminent end of the world, or it may be a perpetual period in which everything remains constant.

The key to the solution is to note that any three-period investment can be considered as the outcome of various pairs of two-period investments, where each pair can be obtained by assuming a rate of return for one period's investment and determining what the rate of return for the other period's investment must be to produce the over-all results of the three-period investment. For example, the three-period investment (−1, 1, 1) can be viewed as the outcome of investing $1.00 in the first

TABLE 1

POSSIBLE PAIRS OF ONE-PERIOD INTEREST RATE "SOLUTIONS" FOR THE THREE-PERIOD INVESTMENT ($K = -1, 1, 1$)

| *Hypothetical Second-Period Proceeds of First-Period Investment* | *Second-Period "Reinvestment"* | *Implied Interest Rates (Percent)* $i_1$ | $i_2$ |
|---|---|---|---|
| ∞ | ∞ | ∞ | − 100 |
| 2.0 | 1.0 | 100 | 0 |
| 1.75 | 0.75 | 75 | + 33⅓ |
| 1.618 | 0.618 | 61.8 | + 61.8 |
| 1.50 | 0.50 | 50 | + 100 |
| 1.10 | 0.10 | 10 | +1,000 |
| 1.00 | 0 | 0 | + ∞ |

period to yield a total value of $1.75 in the second period, 75 cents of which are reinvested to yield $1.00 in the third period. Alternatively, it can be viewed as the outcome of investing $1.00 in the first period to yield $1.50 in the second period, 50 cents of which are reinvested to yield $1.00 in the third period.

Table 1 shows a schedule of pairs of one-period interest rates that are possible "solutions" for the assumed investment; that is, these are pairs of interest rates at which the present value of this investment is zero. These rates may be inferred directly from the amount of the assumed reinvested excess over a dollar of the gross return in the second period. For example, the first of the hypothetical pairs of two-period investments mentioned above involves a first-period net rate of return of 75 percent and a second-period net rate of return of 33⅓ percent; the second pair involves a first-period net rate of return of 50 percent and a second-period net rate of return of 100 percent. Another way of representing this three-period investment is to suppose it to be the outcome of a first-period investment of $1.00 yielding a total value of $1.618, of which 61.8 cents are reinvested to yield $1.00. This implies a second-period net rate of return equal to the first at 61.8 percent (approximately). This rate is the implied constant internal rate of return for this investment, on which attention has been focused in previous discussions. As we have seen, this is only *one* element of a continuous sequence of possible pairs of rates of return on two-period investments; other pairs in this sequence are given in Table 1.

As can be seen in Table 1, the possible pairs of short-term interest rates include second-period rates ranging from −100 percent to plus infinity and first-period rates ranging from zero to infinity. These limits are set by the fact that rates below −100 percent are not economically interesting.

Similarly, a three-period investment whose third receipt is *negative* may be represented by a sequence of pairs of short-term interest rates. Table 2 shows the range and some values of such pairs for the investment (−1, 3, −1). The possible first-period rates range from −100 to +200 percent; the second-period rates range from −66⅔ percent to + infinity. In this case the gross product of the first-period investment must be assumed to be less than three, the excess balance being paid for by a negative receipt of a dollar in the third period. For instance, if the first-period rate is assumed to be 100 percent, the one dollar invested in the first period produces two dollars in the second period; all of this is withdrawn from the investment plus an additional dollar, which is paid for by the dollar payment in the third period. This implies a zero second-period interest rate.

TABLE 2

POSSIBLE PAIRS OF ONE-PERIOD INTEREST RATE "SOLUTIONS" FOR THE THREE-PERIOD INVESTMENT ($L = -1, 3, -1$)

| *Hypothetical Second-Period Proceeds of First-Period Investment* | *Second-Period "Disinvestment"* | *Implied Interest Rates (Percent)* $i_1$ | $i_2$ |
|---|---|---|---|
| 0 | 3 | −100 | − 66⅔ |
| 0.382 | 2.618 | − 61.8 | − 61.8 |
| 1.0 | 2 | 0 | − 50 |
| 1.50 | 1.50 | + 50 | − 33⅓ |
| 2.0 | 1 | +100 | 0 |
| 2.50 | 0.50 | +150 | +100 |
| 2.618 | 0.382 | +161.8 | +161.8 |
| 3.0 | 0 | +200 | +∞ |

Within the interesting range of pairs of interest rates by which this investment option can be represented, there are two pairs for which the short-term rates are equal: at −61.8 and at +161.8 percent. This is an example of the "paradox" that has attracted so much attention in connection with investment decision criteria. It should be evident, however, that this paradox is merely an accident of the simplifying device of dealing with a single long-term rate of interest, and that it has no special importance in the more general framework used here. In this more general framework the "solutions" of every three-period investment option are a continuum of pairs of short-term rates of interest, regardless of the form of the receipts stream of that option. As will be shown shortly, the correct procedure in choosing investments involves, in effect, comparing the whole schedule of pairs of short-term rates with the equilibrium pair of short-term rates, regardless of whether the equilibrium rates are equal to each other. The particular pair or pairs of rates equal to each other that may be found on this schedule have no special importance.

There is, however, one very crucial difference between the investment options (−1, 1, 1) and (−1, 3, −1). Calculating the second-period internal rate of return for the first of these options always involves assuming that second-period gross *proceeds* exceed the second-period *withdrawal,* the excess being compared with the third-period return that it hypothetically yields. On the other hand, calculating the second-period return for the second of these options always involves assuming a *withdrawal* in the second period that exceeds the hypothetical gross *proceeds* of the first-period investment, the excess being compared with the third-period payment. If for a moment we regard these hypothetical reinvestments or excess withdrawals, along with the corresponding third-period items, as separate two-period options, we can see that a reinvestment option will be worthwhile if it yields *more* than the going second-period rate of interest, while an excess withdrawal or disinvestment option will be worthwhile if its implied rate of interest is *less* than the going second-period rate of interest.

For example, if the going short rate of interest is 10 percent, an option to pay $1.00 now to receive $1.11 in the next period will be attractive, and so will an option to receive $1.00 now in exchange for paying $1.09 in the next period. Hence, we may say that a three-period investment with a negative third-period receipt will be attractive if it can be represented as a pair of two-period options, the first of which has a rate of return higher than the going first-period rate of interest and the second of which has a rate of return (or more accurately, rate of cost) lower than the going second-period rate of interest.

Since each of the short-term rates in the schedule of pairs is a continuous variable within its permitted range, these criteria can be modified to allow one of the pair to be equal to its corresponding equilibrium rate if the other satisfies the inequality applying to it. Similarly, the criterion for multiperiod investments can center on a single short-term rate where all other short-term rates are assumed to be equal to the equilibrium rates.

These remarks make it clear why the use of a constant, long-term rate of return for judging three-period investments leads to paradoxes. If the third-period receipt of an option is negative, it cannot correctly be said that the solving long-term rate of return for that option should be greater than or less than the equilibrium long-term rate: In fact, only "part of it" should be greater, and "part of it" should be less.

## III

The application of this result to receipt streams of greater length than three periods, in a more general multiperiod model, involves only one further complication of any importance. In dealing with this, it will be helpful to make use of the present-value concept, calculating present values with the short-term rates of interest under consideration. As we shall be directly concerned only with the sign of the present value and not with its magnitude, the point in time for which it is calculated for any given receipt stream is of no concern, except that for present purposes it must be calculated for some point of time within that receipt stream.

Now, consider some receipt stream $(-1, r_2, r_3)$ and a corresponding hypothetical pair of rates of return $(i_1, i_2)$, arranged in appropriate order as column headings, as in Table 3. The body of the table sets out the results so far in schematic form. This scheme represents two propositions: (1) An investment whose receipts are negative, positive or negative, and positive, in that order, is acceptable if it can be represented by a pair of short-term rates both greater than the equilibrium short-term rates. (2) An investment whose receipts are negative, positive, and negative, in that order, is acceptable if it can be represented by a pair of short-term rates the first of which is greater than and the second of which is less than the equilibrium short-term rates.

TABLE 3

SCHEMATIC REPRESENTATION OF ACCEPTABLE INVESTMENTS

| $-1$ | $i_1$ | $r_2$ | $i_2$ | $r_3$ |
|---|---|---|---|---|
| $-$ | $>$ | $\pm$ | $>$ | $+$ |
| $-$ | $>$ | $+$ | $<$ | $-$ |

This scheme has the following interesting characteristic: The "greater than" sign, viewed as an arrowhead, always "points" away from that part of the sequence with a negative present value toward that part of the sequence with a positive present value. Hence the "greater than" sign between the first two periods must point away from the first receipt, which by the definition of an "investment," is always negative and therefore has a negative present value; the other inequality sign will point toward the third receipt if it is positive and away from it if it is negative.

That this manner of characterizing the direction of pointing of the inequality sign should be generally applicable is evident from the preceding discussion. If the first $k$ receipts of a multiperiod stream have a negative present value, calculated, say, at the equilibrium short-term rates of interest for those periods, this negative present value is an investment carried over into and repaid in subsequent periods. In this case, this investment option will be attractive if the $k$th short-term rate of return, implied for the carry-over into the subsequent periods, is *greater* than the corresponding $k$th equilibrium short-term rate. On the other hand, if the first $k$ receipts of the multiperiod stream have a positive present value, the short rate of the $k$th period implied in the option should be *less* than the corresponding equilibrium rate if the over-all option is to be attractive. This is a straightforward application of the ideas developed in connection with three-period investments. However, it is more complicated because in this case, unlike the three-period case, the range of short-term rates assumed for a subset of the periods may legitimately include values that imply either positive or negative present values for that subset of periods. Whether a given short-term rate, assumed as part of a set of such rates representing a given multiperiod option, will have to be greater than or less than the equilibrium short-term rate for that period if the option is to be attractive will therefore depend on the other short-term rates in the assumed set. Subject to this qualification, the propositions arrived at in the analysis of three-period options apply also to multiperiod options. The outcome is still uniquely determined but is more complicated to characterize.

We know merely by looking at the signs of a three-period sequence what the relationship must be between its pairs of rates of return and the equilibrium rates. However, for a multiperiod option, this will be true only at those points at which all the signs in at least one direction are uniform (so that the sign of the present value of the part in that direction is independent of the short-term rates assumed within that part). This, of course, is true at every point in a three-period sequence. In a four-period sequence having receipts of the signs $- + - +$, the first and third rates must be greater than the equilibrium rates, but the corresponding relationship for the second-period rates will depend on the particular first- and third-period rates assumed.

## IV

Up to this point the discussion has relied on the convenient simplification of comparing schedules of pairs (or larger sets, for investments of more than three periods) of short-term rates of interest with a hypothetical equilibrium pair (or set). This determines which investments are worth undertaking at those equilibrium rates but provides no further information on the relative rankings of individual investments. Such information is of course unnecessary if the equilibrium short-term rates are indeed known in advance. In this case, one would undertake those investments whose present values, calculated at the equilibrium rates, are positive and disregard the whole exercise up to this point. What has been done here finds its usefulness in the more complicated cases in which the equilibrium rates are not known in advance and in which the ordering or ranking of individual investments is an essential part of the decision process. The device of referring to hypothetical equilibrium short-term rates must therefore now be dropped, and the ideas so far presented must be reformulated in terms of a ranking scheme.

This reformulation is a straightforward extension of what has been said so far, but the ranking scheme that results will be a little more complicated than one might expect. Consider, first, the schedule of pairs of rates in Table 1 representing the investment (−1, 1, 1). This schedule is shown in Figure 1 as a locus of points in two dimensions, each axis corresponding to one of the short-term interest rates. From what has already been said, we can infer that pairs of rates of interest or rates of return below and to the left of the curve are less attractive than this investment, whereas pairs of rates in the shaded area above the curve are more attractive than this investment. (If the equilibrium rates should turn out to be in the shaded area, this investment would not be undertaken.)

FIGURE 1

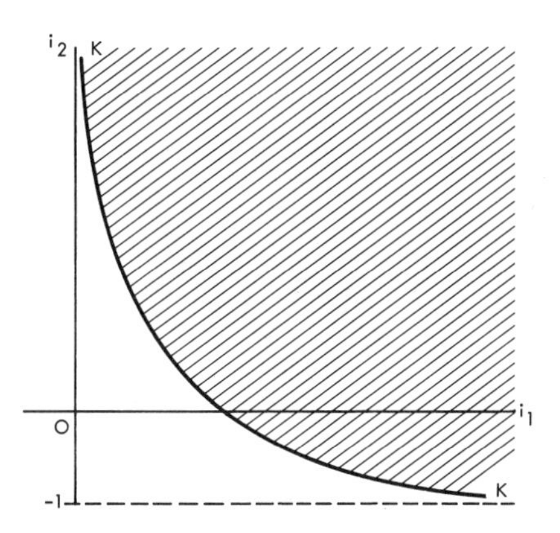


If, like indifference curves, investment curves such as that in Figure 1 never crossed one another, they would provide a simple ranking of investments like that obtainable for independent two-period investments. However, these investment curves do cross, and the ranking scheme must therefore be conceived in two (or more) dimensions rather than in one. In Figure 2, these curves are plotted for both investments considered earlier, investment *K* of Table 1 and investment *L* of Table 2. Rates of return in the doubly shaded area in Figure 2 are more attractive than those obtainable for either of the two investments; rates in the lower singly shaded area are more attractive than *L* but less attractive than *K;* and so on.

Which of these investments is better clearly depends on which part of the figure we are considering. For example, if we consider only positive interest rates, *L* is always superior because in the positive quadrant the curve *LL* is always above the curve *KK*. In general, however, crossings may occur anywhere. Which of any pair of investments is superior may therefore vary according to the values of the two short-term rates of interest. The ranking of any pair of investments is not one-dimensional, but two-dimensional; and all relevant ranking information about all alternative independent three-period investments may be summarized in a graph showing their loci plotted in the manner of the two curves in Figure 2.

FIGURE 2

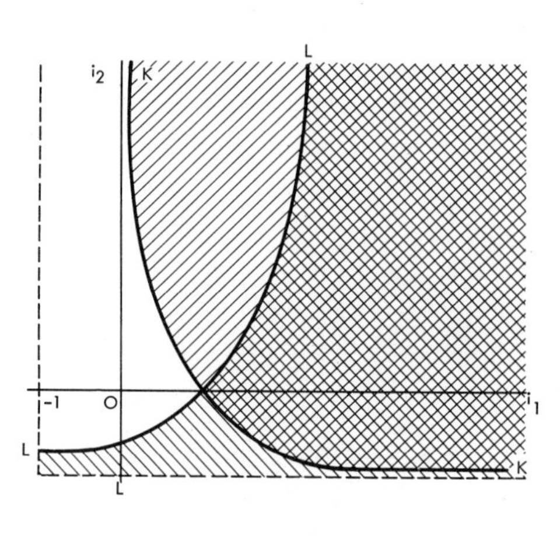


## V

The next step in the generalized investment decision process is to cumulate investment opportunities, appropriately ranked, into an opportunity surface. For the present, I shall continue to assume that all investments are independent, so that only one such surface has to be constructed. This construction is essentially similar to that for an opportunity curve consisting of two-period options, with the number of dimensions increased. In the two-period case the opportunity curve is constructed by placing the investment opportunities end to end in the order of their ranking, in a two-dimensional space representing possible consumptions in the two periods. Similarly, to the two-dimensional ranking of investments in the three-period case there corresponds, a three-dimensional opportunity surface showing the combinations of consumptions in the three periods made possible by the available investments. In this case the investments are encountered on the surface in the (two-dimensional) order implied by the ranking just set out.

The construction of the opportunity surface can be more easily explained if we start by assuming that a large and varied set of two-period investments is available to be started in each of the first two periods. The surface may be tentatively constructed using three opportunities to form it, and we may then see how three-period investments fit into it. Two-period investments starting in the first period will be referred to simply as "first-period investments" and those starting in the second period as "second-period investments."

The preliminary assumption that every investment is independent of every other means that any set of first-period investments may be linked with any set of second-period investments without affecting their respective productivities. But if a particular first-period investment project $I_r$, with rate of return $r$, is in a certain set of first-period investments that are assumed to be undertaken, it is to be taken for granted that every first-period investment of higher productivity is also included in that set. With the term "set" so understood, we must consider as economically interesting the linkage of every possible set of first-period investments with every possible set of second-period investments, subject to the restriction that no second-period set will be considered that invests more than the total resources made available in the second period by the investments of the first.

FIGURE 3

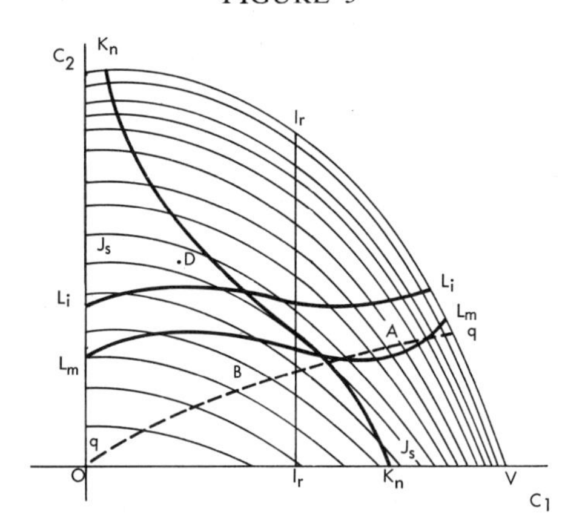


$$I_r\text{:} \quad \triangle C_1 < 0,\ \triangle C_2 = -(1+r)\triangle C_1,\ \triangle C_3 = 0$$

$$J_s\text{:} \cdot \quad \triangle C_1 = 0,\ \triangle C_2 < 0,\ \triangle C_3 = -(1+s)\triangle C_2$$

$$K_n\text{:} \quad \triangle C_1 < 0,\ \triangle C_2 \lesseqgtr 0,\ \triangle C_3 > 0$$

$$\left.\begin{matrix} L_m \\ L_i \end{matrix}\right\} \triangle C_1 < 0,\ \triangle C_2 > 0,\ \triangle C_3 < 0$$

$$L_m \quad (\triangle C_2)^2 > 4\triangle C_1 \triangle C_3$$

$$L_i \quad (\triangle C_2)^2 < 4\triangle C_1 \triangle C_3$$

In Figure 3 the axis $OC_1$ measures production for consumption in the first period, the axis $OC_2$ measures production for consumption in the second period, and the axis that must be imagined perpendicular to the paper measures production for consumption in the third period. The maximum attainable production of goods for consumption in the first period is indicated by $V$ on $OC_1$; if this point is chosen, nothing will be produced in the second and third periods.

A first-period investment opportunity enables us to move away from $V$ to positive second-period production. Such an opportunity will be a vector in the $C_1C_2$ plane, pointing in the direction of less $C_1$ and more $C_2$. If one arrays all such first-period investment vectors end to end in order of declining productivity, one obtains the outermost contour shown in the figure. This contour is an ordinary opportunity curve in two dimensions, showing the maximum combinations of production for consumption attainable in the first two periods when nothing is left over for the third period.

A second-period investment, similarly, is a vector in the direction of more $C_3$ and less $C_2$, without changing $C_1$. At any point on the outermost contour shown, one may move into positive third-period production by undertaking the most productive second-period investment, then a less productive one, and so on, until nothing is left in the second period to reinvest. Any such sequence of second-period investments forms an opportunity curve parallel to the $C_2C_3$ plane, which in the figure is seen edge-on as a line such as that marked $I_r$. The set of all such opportunity curves, starting from all points on the outermost contour shown, forms a three-dimensional surface. Of course, the same surface is "formed" by the sequence of first-period investment opportunity curves (the contours shown in the figure), which are parallel to the $C_1C_2$ plane.

Each of the contours shown corresponds to a constant set of second-period investments all along it, providing a given level of availabilities in the third period (starting with zero at the outermost contour). Therefore, at any point along one of these contours the *next* second-period investment that could be undertaken would always be the same one; and we may refer to the contour as the "location curve" for that second-period investment, such as the investment $J_s$, with a net rate of return $s$. Crossing this location curve (contour) from its outer side implies undertaking the second-period investment to which it corresponds; the point at which it is crossed indicates the amount of first-period investment that is being undertaken.

Similarly, the next first-period investment that could be undertaken would always be the same one along a contour parallel to the $C_2C_3$ plane, such as the line marked $I_r$. This is the location curve for that particular first-period investment; crossing this curve from the viewer's right implies undertaking the first-period investment to which it corresponds. The rate of return $r$ is given, so the slope of every contour at its crossing with $I_r$, given by the vector for that investment, is a constant.

To simplify exposition, it will now be helpful to adopt conventions on the names of these investment "contours" and on their relative positions. One of the curves along which the second-period investments being undertaken is constant will be referred to as a "second-period investment contour." One of these contours lying closer to the origin than another will be referred to as the "higher" of the two, since it corresponds to a higher amount of second-period investment. Similarly, a "curve" along which the first-period investment being undertaken is constant will be referred to as a "first-period investment contour." One of these contours lying to the left of the other, as seen by the viewer, will be referred to as the "higher" of the two, since it corresponds to a higher amount of first-period investment.

The fact that a single investment opportunity appears as a curve (a narrow strip, if the investment is not regarded as infinitesimal) rather than as a point (a short line segment) may seem odd at first sight, because we are more accustomed to the characteristics of two-dimensional opportunity curves. The location of an investment on a two-dimensional curve is the point (or segment) at which the tangent to the curve is a line whose slope is the ratio of changes in the two periods' consumption, $dC_2/dC_1$, given by the investment in question. The changes in consumption given by a two-period investment imply a "slope," or direction, also in three dimensions, of a line touching the opportunity surface wherever the investment is located. Lines of a given set of direction coefficients will touch a curved surface in a whole sequence of points, however, and not merely at a single point. In a two-dimensional (two-period) situation a given investment will be marginal to only a single set of investments, namely, those more productive than it is; hence, it will appear at only one point along a curve constructed from all investments. In a three-dimensional situation a given first-period investment is marginal to a whole sequence of investment combinations, namely, those first-period investments more productive than it is plus a sequence of different total amounts of second-period investment. Hence, it will appear in a curve along the surface corresponding to this sequence of combinations of investments. The same is true, of course, of a second-period investment.

The fact that an investment appears along a curve on the surface is also true of three-period investments, but the curve in this case will not be a contour. Recall that it was shown earlier that a three-period investment may be represented by a sequence of pairs of two-period investments (pairs of rates of return in successive periods). This sequence of pairs includes a whole range of values of each of the two rates of return. In contrast, a genuine pair or combination of which a *two*-period investment is a part includes only one rate of return for the period in which that investment is made, namely, the rate of return on that investment itself. Thus the three-period investments shown in Figure 2 are represented by curves of positive or negative slope, as the case may be, whereas the set of combinations to which a two-period investment is just marginal would be represented by a straight line parallel to one of the axes. A three-period investment curve in Figure 2 has a finite nonzero slope because the set of combinations of two-period investments (among others) to which it is just marginal includes variable sets both of first-period investments and of second-period investments. Hence the location curve of that investment in the opportunity surface (Figure 3) will cut across a series of contours (referred either to the $C_1C_2$ or the $C_2C_3$ plane) rather than coinciding with any of them.[3]

Where the curve representing an investment according to rates of return, as in Figure 2, has a negative slope, the location curve of the investment in the opportunity surface will move from higher to lower second-period investment contours as it moves from the viewer's right to his left, from lower to higher first-period investment contours. The negative slope in Figure 2 is a negative return slope, since rates of return are represented on the axes; and for simplicity, we may therefore say that the corresponding location curve in Figure 3 has a negative return slope. Similarly, when the curve in Figure 2 has a positive slope, the corresponding location curve in Figure 3 moves from *lower to higher* second-period investment contours as it moves from the viewer's right to his left. This type of movement may be referred to as representing a positive return slope. (This does not mean that it necessarily has a positive slope relative to the $C_1$ or $C_2$ axis in Figure 3 but merely that the corresponding curve in Figure 2 has a positive slope.)

## VI

If all investments, whether two- or three-period, are independent of one another, a unique and well-behaved opportunity surface results from the inclusion of all three-period investments along the curves drawn among the two-period investments as just indicated. If no borrowing or lending opportunities exist for the decision maker faced by this investment opportunity surface, his equilibrium position will be found at the tangency of the highest possible indifference surface with this opportunity

[3]As in the case of two-period investments, the set of changes in consumption ($dC_1$, $dC_2$, $dC_3$) given by a three-period investment defines a straight line in three dimensions with direction coefficients proportional to the $dC_i$. (In this case the line will not be parallel to either the $C_1C_2$ plane or the $C_2C_3$ plane, however, as was true of the corresponding line for a two-period investment.) The sequence of points along which this line just touches the opportunity surface is the location curve for the investment.

surface. The existence of borrowing and lending opportunities, whether limited or not, enlarges his effective opportunity surface to an outer envelope inclosing all opportunities, as in the two-period model; and equilibrium is found at the tangency of this enlarged surface with the highest possible indifference surface.

Whether or not an investment has been undertaken in the final equilibrium depends on whether its location curve has been crossed in the movement from $V$, the zero investment point, to the equilibrium point. As some hypothetical lines of movement from $V$ to the equilibrium point will cross an investment's location curve more than once, the rule is that if the curve is crossed an odd number of times, the investment is undertaken, otherwise not. Thus, for example, if the equilibrium is at point $A$, investment $L_m$ will be undertaken, and investment $K_n$ will not. If the equilibrium is at point $B$, $K_n$ will be undertaken, and $L_m$ will not. An equilibrium at point $D$ implies that $K_n$, $L_i$, and $L_m$ will all be undertaken, and so on. As one moves from $V$, one first undertakes the most productive investments, then less productive ones, and so on.

## VII

There remain to be considered the special ranking problems associated with interdependent investment opportunities. However, the difficulties that these present are minimal. The cases of mutually exclusive investments and of interdependent investments in the same period involve exactly the same considerations as in the simpler two-period case. Mutually exclusive investments give rise to dual or multiple opportunity surfaces, each made up of a particular set of independent investments; whichever surface is tangent to the highest indifference surface (or to the relevant borrowing-lending opportunity, as the case may be) indicates the set of investments that will be undertaken and, in particular, indicates which of the mutually exclusive ones is best under the circumstances.

Interdependent investments in the same period occur, for example, where one high-productivity investment can be undertaken only if it is combined with a low-productivity one (but where the latter could be undertaken by itself). Such cases give rise to a multiplicity of opportunity curves or surfaces. This is due to the fact that investments whose productivities are intermediate between those of the two interdependent ones may either precede or follow them in the ranking. Breaking the sequence of such other independent investments at all possible points to insert the interdependent ones gives a corresponding sequence of opportunity curves or surfaces, no one of which is everywhere higher than any other. They therefore form an envelope, the treatment of which is analogous to the case of mutally exclusive investments. This problem is treated no differently in the case of multiperiod investments than in the case of two-period investments.

The final problem case, in which the productivity of a second (or later) period investment depends on whether another investment has been undertaken in a previous period, presents no significant new difficulty. There will be a range of combinations of short-term rates of return over which either these investments will both be undertaken or neither will. Within this range the combination of the two investments will have all the properties of a multiperiod option. That is, they will have a location curve similar to that for a multiperiod option, not following any contour.

Where, at each end, this curve reaches a combination of short-term rates of return at which one of these investments is undertaken but not the other, the two investments part company and have separate curves like those for any independent two-period investments.

In general, all forms of interdependence will involve combinations of the kinds mentioned so far and can be handled similarly in the construction of the opportunity surface. So far as I know, the consideration of multiperiod cases does not involve any new problems not already explicitly or implicitly covered in the preceding analysis.

## VIII

We may now return to the paradoxes mentioned in the rate-of-return–present-value controversies. Consider the reference curve of unit-return slope on the surface in Figure 3, the curve *qq* indicating all the points on the surface at which the first-period rate of return is equal to the second-period rate of return. Along this curve are found the solving rates or constant internal rates of return, if any, implied for three-period investments. An investment such as $K_n$, whose third-period receipt is positive and which therefore has a negative return slope, will cross *qq* only once and hence will have a unique solving rate. An investment with negative third-period receipt, such as $L_i$ or $L_m$ in the figure, will have a positive return slope and can intersect *qq* either not at all or twice, corresponding to imaginary or dual solutions, respectively, of the rate-of-return equations for these investments. The investment $L_i$ might be the investment $(-1, 3, -2\frac{1}{2})$, which would not be undertaken at any rate of interest that remains the same in both periods. It would be undertaken, however, if the second-period rate were sufficiently greater than the first-period rate at equilibrium (as at point $D$).

While the more general framework of analysis used here makes the "solving rate" redundant, at the same time it shows the applicability of the concept of rate of return in such analysis. Of course, the present-value concept retains the virtue of comparative simplicity *for those situations in which it applies.* Generally speaking, it applies whenever unlimited borrowing and lending are possible at known rates of interest, but not otherwise. Present-value calculations are still valid if the rate of interest varies from period to period, as was assumed in the analysis here, so long as unlimited borrowing and lending remain possible.

FIGURE 4

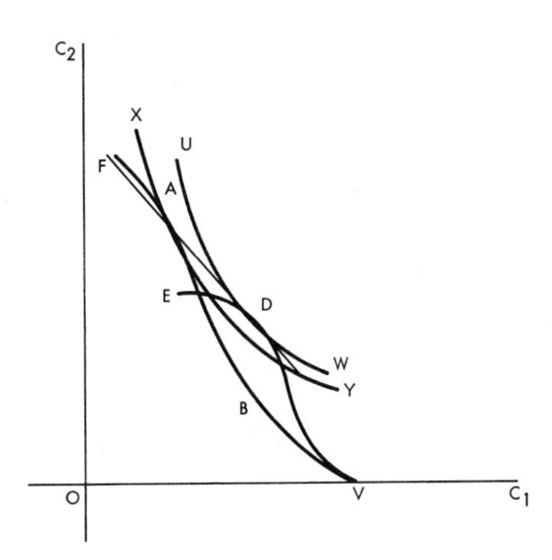


Where borrowing and lending opportunities are effectively limited, so that the equilibrium rates of return are not known until the equilibrium itself is found, the present-value approach is likely to involve the same sort of complexity, at best, as the approach used here. *It can also give wrong answers,* as the following example illustrates. Suppose that a country (or a firm) has borrowed all it can except at prohibitive rates of interest and that it must now balance the value of additional investment projects, over and above those already planned, against the consumption (for the people of the country, or for the firm's owners) that would otherwise be possible. Suppose further that it is considering two mutually exclusive projects, one that can realize its potential only if done on a large scale, the other feasible on a comparatively modest scale. If the modest-scale project is undertaken, the marginal rates of return (and of subjective discounting) at equilibrium might be low enough to show a higher "present value" for the larger investment, yet the larger investment might nevertheless be inferior.

The essentials of such a situation are illustrated in Figure 4, in which the larger investment is represented by the curve *VBA* and the smaller one by the curve *VDE*. (Two-period analysis suffices here.) At the point of tangency *D* between the indifference curve *UW* and *VDE,* the rate of return corresponds to the slope of the line *DF*. Since the point *A* and other higher points on *VBA* lie above *DF,* they have a higher present value than *D* at that rate of return.

On the other hand, a similar line tangent to *VBA* and the indifference curve *XY* at their tangency at *A* would cut below *D,* showing the more modest project to have the higher present value at the rate of return corresponding to this latter line. In other words, applied both ways, *the present-value criterion would give contradictory results in this case.* The correct solution is found only by determining which of the two indifference curves tangent to the two mutually exclusive opportunity curves is higher. In the case illustrated, *UW* is higher, and the more modest project is preferred. The larger project requires too much sacrifice of current consumption to be justified in terms of the tastes of the country (or firm) under consideration.

Evidently, this example has some practical relevance, as does the more general analysis directed primarily at cases in which borrowing opportunities are effectively limited. The apparent simplicity of present-value analysis by itself must therefore be viewed with caution. The only safe general rule is the rule that that investment portfolio should be selected whose corresponding opportunity surface touches the highest possible indifference surface.

*Chapter* 18

# *The Arithmetic of Capital-Budgeting Decisions**

By Ezra Solomon

IN ORDER to make correct capital-expenditure decisions, corporate management needs at least three sets of information. Estimates must be made of net capital outlays required and future cash earnings promised by each proposed project. This is a problem in engineering valuation and market forecasting. Estimates must also be made of the availability and cost of capital to the company. This is a problem in financial analysis. Finally, management needs a correct set of standards by which to select projects for execution so that long-run economic benefits to present owners will be maximized. This is a problem in logic and arithmetic. This paper is concerned exclusively with the last of these three problems.[1]

With respect to the question "Should this investment proposal be accepted or rejected?" the problem of arriving at a correct decision is uncomplicated. Either one of two approaches to measuring the investment worth of a proposal will provide a correct answer.[2] In the usual form in which these approaches are used as capital-rationing criteria, they are:

---

*Reprinted from *Journal of Business,* Vol. XXIX (April, 1956), pp. 124–29, by Ezra Solomon, by permission of the University of Chicago Press. 

[1]For a discussion of the first two problems, see Joel Dean, *Capital Budgeting* (New York: Columbia University Press, 1951); and Ezra Solomon, "Measuring a Company's Cost of Capital," *Journal of Business,* Vol. XXVIII (October, 1955), pp. 240–52.

[2]There are other criteria in use, e.g., determining capital budgets by size of department, by payout period, or by the postponability of projects. It has already been shown that these are at best crude approximations to a correct solution (see Dean, *op. cit.,* chap. ii; and M. J. Gordon, "The Payoff Period and the Rate of Profit," *Journal of Business,* Vol. XXVIII [October, 1955], pp. 253–60).

*The Rate-of-Return Approach.* This approach expresses each project's estimated value as a single over-all "rate of return per annum." This rate is equal to the rate of interest at which the present value of expected capital outlays is exactly equal to the present value of expected cash earnings on that project. The concept is identical with the "effective yield to maturity" on a bond that is purchased at some price other than its par value. It has also been called the "internal rate of profit"[3] or the "marginal efficiency of capital."[4]

If the rate of return on a project is greater than the company's cost of capital (also expressed as a percentage per annum rate), then the project should be accepted.

*The Present-Value Approach.* For each project, find the present value of the expected capital outlays, using the cost of capital as a discount rate. Likewise, find the present value of the expected cash earnings. If the present value of earnings is greater than the present value of outlays, the project should be accepted.

These two approaches give the same results for "accept or reject" decisions. This is so because the computed rate of return on a project will be higher than the cost of capital in all cases for which the present value of earning, discounted at the cost of capital, is greater than the present value of outlays. Or conversely, if a project promises a rate of return greater than the company's cost of capital, then the present value of its earnings, discounted at the cost of capital, will be greater than the present value of its outlays.

For problems which involve more than a simple "accept or reject" decision, the application of these two criteria, as they are generally defined, often yields contradictory or ambiguous results. The purpose of this paper is to explore the reasons for these contradictions or ambiguities and to reformulate this general approach to measuring investment worth so that it always provides a unique and correct basis for decision making.

## *Mutually Exclusive Proposals*

It is often necessary for the management to ask not only "Is this project worth undertaking?" but also "Which of two projects is the better one?" This latter question is crucial whenever two or more projects or proposals are mutually exclusive. For example, the proposals may be alternative ways of doing the same thing. Both might be profitable in an absolute sense. But since only one of the two can be undertaken, the problem is to decide which alternative is the better one.

[3]See Kenneth L. Boulding, *Economic Analysis* (rev. ed.; New York: Harper & Bros., 1948), chaps. xxxv and xxxvi.

[4]See J. M. Keynes, *The General Theory of Employment, Interest, and Money* (New York: Macmillan Co., 1936), pp. 140 ff.

When the *relative* merit of alternative proposals is at issue, the rate-of-return criterion, as defined earlier, and the present-value criterion, as defined, can yield contradictory results. With the increased interest in applying rational approaches to the solution of capital-investment decisions, this possible conflict between the two generally acceptable criteria has received renewed attention. Several recent papers have shown that when projects are ranked by the rate-of-return standard, the results may differ from a ranking of the same projects based on the present-value standard.[5] For analytical purposes, the simplest example of such a conflict will suffice: Assume that there are two investment opportunities available. Both are profitable in an absolute sense, but only one can be undertaken because the two are mutually exclusive.

Project X requires an outlay of $100 now, at time $t_0$, and promises to return $120 exactly one year hence at time $t_1$. Project Y also requires an outlay of $100 now and promises to return $174.90 exactly four years hence at time $t_4$. Assume also that the degree of certainty attaching to each project is identical and that the investor's present "cost of capital" is 10 percent.

The "rate of return" on project X is 20 percent, and on project Y it is 15 percent. The present value of project X, discounted at the cost of capital, is $109.09. For project Y the present value, discounted at the cost of capital, is $119.46. If the two projects are ranked by their rate of return, project X is the better one. If, on the other hand, they are ranked in terms of present value, project Y is the better one. Which should the investor choose?

In order to resolve the problem correctly, it is necessary to isolate the source of the conflict between the two approaches. The easiest way to do this is to compare the two investment proposals in terms of their relative value as of the terminal date ($t_4$) of the longer lived project.[6]

According to the data given, proposal Y will provide the investor with $174.90 at time $t_4$. All we know about proposal X is that it provides $120 at time $t_1$. What happens to these funds between time $t_1$ and $t_4$ is obviously an important piece of necessary information. Neither the rate-of-return approach nor the present-value approach answers this question *explicitly*. But they both answer it *implicitly* and in different ways. This is the source of the conflicting results that they yield.

[5]See James H. Lorie and Leonard J. Savage, "Three Problems in Rationing Capital," *Journal of Business,* Vol. XXVIII (October, 1955), pp. 229–39; George Terborgh, "Some Comments on the Dean-Smith Article on the MAPI Formula," *Journal of Business,* Vol. XXIX (April, 1956), pp. 138–40; and A. A. Alchian, "The Rate of Interest, Fisher's Rate of Return over Costs, and Keynes' Internal Rate of Return," *American Economic Review,* Vol. XLV (December, 1955), pp. 938–42.

[6]The "terminal date" refers to the date at which cash earnings from the longer lived of the two competing projects cease.

Those who use the rate-of-return approach, as it is usually defined, would choose project X over project Y. Hence, they must assume that this choice will yield a larger terminal value than that promised by project Y, i.e., $174.90. This, in turn, implies that the $120 obtained from project X at time $t_1$ can be reinvested between time $t_1$ and $t_4$ at a rate lucrative enough to accumulate to more than $174.90 by time $t_4$. *In general,* the implicit assumption made by the rate-of-return approach is that the reinvestment rate is at least equal to the rate promised by the longer lived of the two projects, in this case, 15 percent.[7]

The present-value approach, as usually defined, assumes that the funds obtained from either project can be reinvested at a rate equal to the company's present cost of capital, i.e., 10 percent. Using this assumption, the investor will end up at time $t_4$ with only $159.72 if he chooses project X. With project Y, he would have $174.90. Thus, according to this approach, project Y is the better choice.

The question of which assumption is likely to be the more justified one is important, but it is not relevant to the argument being made in this paper, namely, that the apparent conflict between the two approaches results only from differing assumptions that each makes about the future. If a common assumption is adopted, both approaches will always rank projects identically.

Let us assume, for example, that the investor can put money to use between time $t_1$ and time $t_4$ at an average return of 12 percent. The following computations and results would ensue:

*Terminal Value.* For project Y, this is $174.90. For project X, we have $120 at time $t_1$, plus interest at 12 percent per annum for three years. This would accumulate to $168.47.

*Rate of Return.* For project Y, this averages 15 percent up to the terminal date at time $t_4$. For project X the rate would be 20 percent for one year and 12 percent for three years—an over-all rate equal to 13.9 percent.

*Present Value.* For project Y, this would be $174.90, discounted from time $t_4$ back to time $t_1$ at 12 percent[8] and back from time $t_1$ to $t_0$ at 10 percent. This gives $113.17. For project X the present value would be $120 discounted from time $t_1$ to time $t_0$ at 10 percent, or $109.09.

All three criteria rank the two projects in the same order. With the particular assumption we used, project Y is the better one by any stan-

[7]For example, if project Z, a third alternative, yielded 15 percent in perpetuity and project X yielded 20 percent, the rate-of-return approach would choose project X over project Z. Hence the approach must assume that funds received from project X can be reinvested at least at 15 percent.

[8]This is the relevant rate because we are assuming that the investor can earn 12 percent on his funds between time $t_1$ and time $t_4$.

dard. Using some other assumption, the ranking might be reversed, but the alternative approaches would still yield identical results.

Our conclusion is that correct and consistent ranking of the investment worth of competing proposals can be obtained only if the following factors are taken into account:

1. The valid comparison is not simply between two projects but between two alternative courses of action. The ultimate criterion is the total wealth that the investor can expect from each alternative by the terminal date of the longer lived project. In order to make a fair comparison, an explicit and common assumption must be made regarding the rate at which funds released by either project can be reinvested up to the terminal date.
2. If the rate of return is to be used as an index of relative profitability, then the relevant rate is the per annum yield promised by each alternative course of action from its inception to a common terminal date in the future (usually the terminal date of the longer lived project).
3. If the present value is to be used as an index of relative profitability, the expected reinvestment rate or set of rates should be used as the discounting factor. These rates will be equal to the company's present cost of capital only by coincidence. When comparing two projects requiring different outlays, it is necessary to compare "present value per dollar of outlay" rather than the absolute present value of the projects.

## *The Problem of "Dual Rates of Return"*

In a recent paper, Lorie and Savage[9] have drawn attention to a second problem involving the arithmetic of capital budgeting. In this paper the authors attempt to show that certain rare and complex investment situations exist which cannot be expressed in terms of a single, unique "rate of return." In such situations the application of the usual prescription for finding *the* rate of return yields two solutions, and thus "the rate-of-return criterion for judging the acceptability of investment proposals, as it has been presented in published works, is ambiguous or anomalous."[10]

In order to understand the problem involved, it is helpful to recognize two basic types of investment situation, classified according to the pattern of estimated cash flows that are projected. In the usual type of situation, which we shall call "pattern A," the stream of net cash inflows promised by a project ends either before or when it reaches that point in time beyond which the value of *net future flows* is negative. In other

---

[9] *Op. cit.*
[10] *Ibid.*, p. 237.

words, the project is assumed to terminate before the stage beyond which its continuation yields a net loss to the investor. The second situation, which we call "pattern B," is a much rarer one. Projects which fall into this category continue beyond the point defined previously, i.e., the terminal section contains a net cash outflow (a net loss). Such a pattern obviously exists only if there are contractual or other compelling reasons which make it impossible for the investor to avoid the terminal losses.

As far as pattern A projects are concerned, it is always possible to express the investment worth of the project as a single, meaningful "rate of return" and hence to make a clear-cut decision on the basis of such a criterion. For pattern B projects the application of the usually prescribed method of finding the appropriate "rate of return" can yield more than one answer.[11]

Let us take a specific example of a pattern B investment project. The proposal being considered is the installation of a larger oil pump that would get a fixed quantity of oil out of the ground more rapidly than the pump that is already in use. Let us assume that by operating the existing pump, the investor can expect $10,000 a year hence and $10,000 two years hence. Let us assume that by installing the larger pump at a net cost of $1,600 now, he can expect $20,000 a year hence and nothing the second year. The installation of the larger pump can be viewed as a project having the cash flow characteristics shown in Table 1.

TABLE 1

| *Time Period* | *Incremental Cash Flow Due to Investment* |
|---|---|
| $t_0$ | −$ 1,600 |
| $t_1$ | + 10,000 |
| $t_2$ | − 10,000 |

The usual prescription for finding the rate of return of a project is to find that rate which makes the discounted value of net cash flows equal to the discounted value of capital outlays. Alternatively—and this amounts to the same thing—find that rate which makes the algebraic sum of the discounted cash outflows and inflows equal to zero. The application of this method to our example will yield two answers, namely, 25 and 400 percent. In other words, using a 25 percent rate, the discounted value of the cash flows is exactly equal to the outlay of $1,600. However, a rate of 400 percent also equates cash flows with

[11]Lorie and Savage explain the general basis for dual rates (*ibid.*, p. 237).

capital outlay. Which of the two "rates" is the correct measure of the investment worth of the project, 25 or 400 percent?

The answer is that neither of these rates is a measure of investment worth, neither has relevance to the profitablility of the project under consideration, and neither, therefore, is correct. The fault lies in the incorrect application of the "usual prescription" for finding the rate of return. A closer look at the implications of defining the rate of return in this context as that rate (or rates) which reduce the discounted cash flows to zero reveals the gross error that such a process entails. In order to find this error, let us vary the net outlay required to install the larger pump (keeping all other cash flows constant) and solve for the "rate of return," using the usual prescription. We get the following absurd results:

1. If the larger pump costs nothing, then the project is worth 0 percent; i.e., at 0 percent, the discounted value of the net cash flows is equal to the value of the outlay.[12]
2. If the larger pump costs $827, the project, according to this method, suddenly becomes quite profitable and is rated at 10 percent; i.e., at a rate of 10 percent, the discounted value of the net cash flows is equal to $827.
3. The more the pump costs, the more "profitable" the project becomes! At a cost of $1,600 the rate of return is 25 percent; at a cost of $2,500, it yields 100 percent. The method would have us believe that the engineer who first thought of the idea of installing the larger pump could have a gold mine if only he could persuade the pump manufacturer to charge him enough for the installation![13]

Needless to say, any definition of "profitability" that leads to these absurd results must itself be in error.

The correct solution for the investment worth of the project is simple and straightforward. But it requires an explicit answer to a relevant question: "What is it worth to the investor to receive $10,000 one year earlier than he would have otherwise received it?" This is actually all that the installation of the larger pump achieves. If the investor expects to be able to put the $10,000 to work at a yield of $x$ percent per annum, then getting the money a year earlier is worth $100$x$. If $x$ is 23 percent, for example, getting $10,000 a year earlier is worth $2,300. In other words, if he spent $1,600 on the larger pump now (at time $t_0$), he would end up at time $t_2$ having $2,300 more than he otherwise would have had. This can be stated as an equivalent "rate of return," which in this case would be about 20 percent ($1,600 at 20 percent per annum would amount to $2,304 at the end of two years). Using this approach, a

[12] Alternatively, one could say that the rate is infinitely large.

[13] This increase in the "rate," as the cost of the pump increases, reaches a maximum level, after which the relationship is reversed.

unique and meaningful rate of return can always be found for any set of cash inflows and outflows.

## *Summary*

The rate of return is a useful concept that enables us to express the profitability of an investment proposal as a single explicit value. This value automatically adjusts for differences in the time pattern of expected cash outflows and inflows. It is also independent of the absolute size of the project. Thus, it provides a useful standard by which all types of projects—large and small, long-run and short-run—can be ranked against each other in relative terms and also against the company's cost of capital, in order to judge their absolute worth. The arithmetic involved in rate-of-return computations is generally straightforward. However, there are two situations in which such computations require a careful consideration of the logic that is involved:

1. When mutually exclusive proposals are being compared, it is necessary to compute the rate on each alternative course of action up to the terminal date of the longer lived alternative. This requires an explicit estimate of the yield to be derived from the cash flows generated by each of the alternatives being considered.
2. When a rate is being computed for complex proposals that have negative terminal values, the usual mechanistic prescription for solving for rates does not apply. This situation also requires an explicit estimate of the yield to be derived from incremental cash flows generated by a project. Given this estimate, the equivalent dollar value of the incremental cash flows can be computed explicitly. A comparison of this value with the outlays required for the project will give a correct and unambiguous measure of the project's rate of return.

If these concepts and methods are used in defining and computing rates of return, this criterion will always provide an unambiguous investment standard, the use of which will lead to a maximization of the investor's net present worth, insofar as the estimates used are accurate.

*Chapter* 19

# *Three Problems in Rationing Capital**

By James H. Lorie and Leonard J. Savage

## I. Introduction

CORPORATE EXECUTIVES face three tasks in achieving good financial management. The first is largely administrative and consists in finding an efficient procedure for preparing and reviewing capital budgets, for delegating authority and fixing responsibility for expenditures, and for finding some means for ultimate evaluation of completed investments. The second task is to forecast correctly the cash flows that can be expected to result from specified investment proposals, as well as the liquid resources that will be available for investment. The third task is to ration available capital or liquid resources among competing investment opportunities. This article is concerned with only this last task; it discusses three problems in the rationing of capital, in the sense of liquid resources.

1. Given a firm's cost of capital and a management policy of using this cost to identify acceptable investment proposals, which group of "independent" investment proposals should the firm accept? In other words, how should the firm's cost of capital be used to distinguish between acceptable and unacceptable investments? This is a problem that is typically faced by top management whenever it reviews and approves a capital budget.

Before presenting the second problem with which this paper deals,

*Reprinted from *Journal of Business,* Vol. XXVIII (October, 1955), pp. 229–39, by James H. Lorie and Leonard J. Savage, by permission of the University of Chicago Press. 

This work was supported in part by the Office of Naval Research and in part by Joel Dean Associates.

the use of the word "independent" in the preceding paragraph should be explained. Investment proposals are termed "independent"—although not completely accurately—when the worth of the individual investment proposal is not profoundly affected by the acceptance of others. For example, a proposal to invest in materials-handling equipment at location A may not profoundly affect the value of a proposal to build a new warehouse in location B. It is clear that the independence is never complete, but the degree of independence is markedly greater than for sets of so-called "mutually exclusive" investment proposals. Acceptance of one proposal in such a set renders all others in the same set clearly unacceptable—or even unthinkable. An example of mutually exclusive proposals would be alternative makes of automotive equipment for the same fleet or alternative warehouse designs for the same site. The choice among mutually exclusive proposals is usually faced later in the process of financial management than is the initial approval of a capital budget. That is, the decision as to which make of automotive equipment to purchase, for example, typically comes later than the decision to purchase some make of equipment.

2. Given a fixed sum of money to be used for capital investment, what group of investment proposals should be undertaken? If a firm pursues a policy of fixing the size of its capital budget in dollars, without explicit cognizance of, or reference to, its cost of capital, how can it best allocate that sum among competing investment proposals? This problem will be considered both for proposals which require net outlays in only one accounting period and for those which require outlays in more than one accounting period. In the latter case, special difficulties arise.

3. How should a firm select the best among mutually exclusive alternatives? That is, when the management of an enterprise, in attempting to make concrete and explicit proposals for expenditures of a type which is included in an approved capital budget, develops more than one plausible way of investing money in conformance with the budget, how can it select the "best" way?

After presenting our solutions to these three problems, we shall discuss the solutions implied by the rate-of-return method of capital budgeting.[1] These solutions are worthy of special attention, since they are based on a different principle from the solutions that we propose, and since the rate-of-return method is the most defensible method heretofore proposed in the business literature for maximizing corporate profits and net worth.

[1]This method was developed by Joel Dean, who has probably done more than anyone else in applying the formal apparatus of economics to the solution of capital-budgeting problems in their business context.

## II. The Three Problems

### *A. Given the cost of Capital, What Group of Investments Should Be Selected?*

The question of determining the cost of capital is difficult, and we, happily, shall not discuss it. Although there may be disagreement about methods of calculating a firm's cost of capital, there is substantial agreement that the cost of capital is the rate at which a firm should discount future cash flows in order to determine their present value.[2] The first problem is to determine how selection should be made among "independent" investment proposals, given this cost or rate.

Assume that the firm's objective is to maximize the value of its net worth—not necessarily as measured by the accountant but rather as measured by the present value of its expected cash flows. This assumption is commonly made by economists and even business practitioners who have spoken on the subject. It is equivalent to asserting that the corporate management's objective is to maximize the value of the owner's equity or, alternatively, the value of the owner's income from the business. Given this objective and agreement about the significance of the firm's cost of capital, the problem of selecting investment proposals becomes trivial in those situations where there is a well-defined cost of capital; namely, proposals should be selected that have positive present values when discounted at the firm's cost of capital. The things to discount are the net cash flows resulting from the investments, and these cash flows should take taxes into account.

There is nothing unusual or original about this proposed solution. It is identical with that proposed by Lutz and Lutz,[3] and is an economic commonplace. Joel Dean in his writings has developed and recommended a method which typically yields the same results for this problem, although the principle of solution is somewhat different, as is discussed later in this article.

The principle of accepting all proposals having positive present value at the firm's cost of capital is obvious, since the failure to do so would

---

[2]One of the difficulties with the concept of cost of capital is that in complicated circumstances there may be no one rate that plays this role. Still worse, the very concept of present value may be obscure.

[3]Friederich Lutz and Vera Lutz, *The Theory of Investment of the Firm* (Princeton: Princeton University Press, 1951). The solution proposed here is identical with the maximization of $V - C$, where $V$ is the present value of future inflows and $C$ is the present value of future outflows. This is discussed in chap. ii of the Lutz book.

clearly mean forgoing an available increment in the present value of the firm's net worth. The principle is discussed here only because it seems a useful introduction to the somewhat more complicated problems that follow. An interesting property of this principle is that adherence to it will result in the present value of the firm's net worth being at a maximum at all points in time.

## *B. Given a Fixed Sum for Capital Investment, What Group of Investment Proposals Should be Undertaken?*

Some business firms—perhaps most—do not use the firm's cost of capital to distinguish between acceptable and unacceptable investments but, instead, determine the magnitude of their capital budget in some other way that results in fixing an absolute dollar limit on capital expenditures. Perhaps, for example, a corporate management may determine for any one year that the capital budget shall not exceed estimated income after taxes plus depreciation allowances, after specified dividend payments. It is probable that the sum fixed as the limit is not radically different from the sum that would be expended if correct and explicit use were made of the firm's cost of capital, since most business firms presumably do not long persist in policies antithetical to the objective of making money. (The profit-maximizing principle is the one that makes use of the firm's cost of capital, as described previously.) Nevertheless, there are probably some differences in the amount that would be invested by a firm if it made correct use of the firm's cost of capital and the amount that would be invested if it fixed its capital budget by other means, expressing the constraint on expenditures as being a maximum outlay. At the very least, the differences in the ways of thinking suggest the usefulness to some firms of a principle that indicates the "best" group of investments that can be made with a fixed sum of money.

The problem is trivial when there are net outlays in only one accounting period—typically, one year. In such cases, investment proposals should be ranked according to their present value—at the firm's cost of capital—per dollar of outlay required. Once investment proposals have been ranked according to this criterion, it is easy to select the best group by starting with the investment proposal having the highest present value per dollar of outlay and proceeding down the list until the fixed sum is exhausted.[4]

The problem can become more difficult when discontinuities are taken

[4]We mention, for completeness, that the outlay or the present value, or both, for a proposal can be negative. Proposals for which the outlay alone is negative—something for nothing—are always desirable but almost never available. Proposals

into account. For large firms the vast majority of investment proposals constitute such a small proportion of their total capital budget that the problems created by discontinuities can be disregarded at only insignificant cost, especially when the imprecision of the estimates of incomes is taken into account. When a project constitutes a large proportion of the capital budget, the problem of discontinuities may become serious, though not necessarily difficult to deal with. This problem can become serious because of the obvious fact that accepting the large proposal because it is "richer" than smaller proposals may preclude the possibility of accepting two or more smaller and less rich proposals which, in combination, have a greater value than the larger proposal. For example, suppose that the total amount available for investment were $1,000 and that only three investment proposals had been made: one requiring a net outlay of $600 and creating an increment in present value of $1,000; and two others, each requiring a net outlay of $500, and each creating an increment in present value of $600. Under these circumstances, the adoption of the richest alternative, the first, would mean forgoing the other two alternatives, even though in combination they would create an increment in present value of $1,200 as compared with the increment of $1,000 resulting from the adoption of the richest investment alternative. Such discontinuities deserve special attention, but the general principles dealing with them will not be worked out here, primarily because we do not know them.

We shall, however, deal with the more serious difficulties created by the necessity to choose among investment proposals, some of which require net cash outlays in more than one accounting period. In such cases a constraint is imposed not only by the fixed sum available for capital investment in the first period but also by the fixed sums available to carry out present commitments in subsequent time periods. Each such investment requires, so to speak, the use of two or more kinds of money—money from the first period and money from each subsequent period in which net outlays are required. We shall discuss only the case of investments requiring net outlays in two periods, for simplicity of exposition and because the principle—although not the mechanics—is the same as for investments requiring net outlays in more than two periods.

Let us start with a very simple case. Suppose that all the available opportunities for investment that yield a positive income can be adopted without exceeding the maximum permitted outlay in either time period 1 or time period 2. Clearly, no better solution can be found, because all desirable opportunities have been exhausted. This simple case is

---

for which both the outlay and the present value are negative can sometimes be acceptable if something sufficiently profitable can be done with ready cash expressed by the negative outlay. The rules which we shall develop can be extended to cover such cases.

mentioned not because of its practical importance, which is admittedly slight, but because it may clarify the more complicated cases that follow.

Next, consider a slightly more complicated case. Suppose that the opportunities available require more funds from either time period 1 or time period 2 than are permitted by the imposed constraints. Under these circumstances, the problem becomes somewhat more complicated, but it still may not be very complicated. It is still relatively simple if (1) the best use of money available in period 1 does not exhaust the money available in period 2 or (2) the best use of money available in period 2 does not exhaust the money available in period 1. In either case the optimum solution—that is, the solution which results in the greatest increment in the net worth of the firm, subject to the two stated constraints—is the one that makes the best possible use of the funds available for investment in one of the two time periods.

This statement is justified by the following reasoning. The imposition of additional restrictions upon the freedom of action of any agency can obviously never increase the value of the best opportunity available to that agency. In the problem at hand, this means that the imposition of an absolute dollar constraint or restriction in time period 2 can never make it possible to make better use of dollars available in time period 1 than would have been possible in the absence of that constraint. Thus, if the best possible use is made of the dollars available in time period 1, the imposition of a restriction relating to time period 2 can never mean increased possibilities of profit from the use of funds available in time period 1. Therefore the maximization of the productivity of dollars available in time period 1 will constitute a maximization of productivity subject to the two constraints as well as to the one constraint. The reasoning is equally valid if we start with the constraint referring to time period 2 and maximize productivity of money available in that time period and then think of the effect of the additional constraint imposed for time period 1.

Unfortunately, typical circumstances will probably make the relatively simple solutions unavailable. The solution to the relatively complex problem will—abstracting from discontinuities—require expending the full amount available for investment in each period. To illustrate how the solution is to be reached, consider the average actual net outlay of the two periods as being an outlay in a single "virtual" period, and consider the average net outlay that is permitted by the constraints as being the average permitted outlay for the "virtual" period. Plan a budget for this "virtual" period according to the method of the one-period problem with which this section begins. That is, ration the capital available in the "virtual" period among the available investment opportunities so as to maximize the firm's net worth according to the principles stated in the discussion of the one period problem. If, by accident, this budget happens to require precisely those outlays which are permitted for the first and second periods, it is easy to see that the problem has been solved. No other budget with a higher present value can be devised within the stated constraints for periods 1 and 2.

Typically, the happy accident referred to in the preceding paragraph will not occur. The optimum use of the average amount available for investment in the two periods will typically result in expending too much in one period and not so much as is permitted in the other. Indeed, the happy accident was mentioned only as a step in explaining one method that will work. Though a simple average will almost never work, there is always some weighted average that will, and it can be found by trial and error. We shall describe in some detail a method that is mathematically equivalent to this method of weighted averages. In this method the solution is found by choosing, for suitable positive constants $p_1$ and $p_2$, those, and only those, proposals for which the following quantity is positive: $(y - p_1c_1 - p_2c_2)$. Here, $y$ is the present value of the proposal; $c_1$ and $c_2$ are the present values of the net outlays required in the first and second periods, respectively; and the multipliers $p_1$ and $p_2$ are auxiliary quantities for which there does not seem to be an immediate interpretation but that nonetheless help in solving the problem.[5]

Initially, the values of $p_1$ and $p_2$ will be determined by judgment. Subsequently, they will be altered by trial and error until the amounts to be expended in the first and second periods, according to the rule just enunciated, are precisely the amounts permitted by the constraints. The initial choice of values for $p_1$ and $p_2$ is not very important, since a graphical process can usually lead rapidly to the correct values.

Certain special possibilities are worth noting. Proposals of positive present value may have negative cost, that is, release cash, for either period. Some proposals of zero or negative present value may be acceptable because they release cash for one period or both. All such possibilities are automatically covered by the rule as stated and by the rules to be given for later problems.

Finding the correct values for $p_1$ and $p_2$ is sometimes not easy—especially when combined with the problem of selecting among mutually exclusive alternatives—but the task is usually as nothing compared to the interests involved or compared to many everyday engineering problems.[6] The following example may clarify the process.

---

[5]The multipliers, $p_1$ and $p_2$, are closely related to what are known in mathematics and in economics as "Lagrange multipliers."

[6]It is true, however, that the numbers in engineering problems are less conjectural; hence the cost of calculation is more likely to be considered worthwhile.

Nine investments have been proposed. The present value of the net outlays required in the first and second time periods and the present values of the investments are as shown in Table 1. The finance committee has stated that $50 and $22 will be available for capital investment in the first and second periods, respectively. We shall consider these amounts to have present values of $50 and $20, respectively. According to the principle stated above, we must now find appropriate multipliers, $p_1$ and $p_2$.

TABLE 1

| *Investment* | *Outlay, Period 1* ($c_1$) | *Outlay, Period 2* ($c_2$) | *Present Value of Investment* |
|---|---|---|---|
| *a* . . . . . . . . . . . . . . . | $12 | $ 3 | $14 |
| *b* . . . . . . . . . . . . . . . | 54 | 7 | 17 |
| *c* . . . . . . . . . . . . . . . | 6 | 6 | 17 |
| *d* . . . . . . . . . . . . . . . | 6 | 2 | 15 |
| *e* . . . . . . . . . . . . . . . | 30 | 35 | 40 |
| *f* . . . . . . . . . . . . . . . | 6 | 6 | 12 |
| *g* . . . . . . . . . . . . . . . | 48 | 4 | 14 |
| *h* . . . . . . . . . . . . . . . | 36 | 3 | 10 |
| *i* . . . . . . . . . . . . . . . | 18 | 3 | 12 |

Multipliers $p_1$ and $p_2$ were initially set at 1 and 3, respectively. With these values, only for investment *d* was the expression $(y - p_1c_1 - p_2c_2)$ positive and therefore acceptable. This would have resulted in net outlays of only $6.00 and $2.00 in periods 1 and 2, respectively. Clearly, the values initially chosen for $p_1$ and $p_2$ were too great. On the other hand, values of 0.1 and 0.5 for $p_1$ and $p_2$, respectively, are too low, resulting in a positive value of $(y - p_1c_1 - p_2c_2)$ for all investments and required outlays in periods 1 and 2 far exceeding the permitted outlays.

Values of 0.33 and 1 for $p_1$ and $p_2$ result in a near-perfect fit. The expression $(y - p_1c_1 - p_2c_2)$ is positive for investments *a, c, d, f,* and *i*. These investments require outlays of $48 and $20 in the first and second periods, as near the permitted outlays of $50 and $20 as discontinuities permit. No other group of investments that is possible within the stated constraints has a greater present value than $70, the present value of this group.[7]

[7]For the three-period problem the relevant quantity is $(y - p_1c_1 - p_2c_2 - p_3c_3)$ rather than $(y - p_1c_1 - p_2c_2)$.

## *C. Selecting the Best among Mutually Exclusive Alternatives*

Before moneys are actually expended in fulfillment of an approved capital budget, the firm usually considers mutually exclusive alternative ways of making the generally described capital investment. When the firm is operating without an absolute limit on the dollars to be invested, the solution to the problem of selecting the best alternative is obvious. (Throughout this article, it is assumed that decisions regarding individual investment proposals do not significantly affect the firm's cost of capital.) The best alternative is the one with the greatest present value at the firm's cost of capital.

When the firm is operating subject to the constraint of an absolute dollar limit on capital expenditures, the problem is more difficult. Consider, first, the case in which there are net outlays in only one time period. The solution is found by the following process:

1. From each set of mutually exclusive alternatives, select that alternative for which the following quantity is a maximum: $(y - pc)$. Here, $y$ is the present value of the alternative, $c$ is the net outlay required, and $p$ is a constant of a magnitude chosen initially according to the judgment of the analyst. (Remember that the alternative of making no investment—that is, accepting $y = 0$ and $c = 0$—is always available, so that the maximum in question is never negative.)
2. Compute the total outlays required to adopt all the investment proposals selected according to the principle just specified.
3. If the total outlay required exceeds the total amount available, $p$ should be increased; if the total amount required is less than the amount available for investment, $p$ should be reduced. By trial and error, a value for $p$ can be found that will equate the amount required for investment with that available for investment.

It should be clear that as the value of $p$ is increased, the importance of the product, $pc$, increases, with a consequent increase in the probability that in each set of mutually exclusive alternatives, an alternative will be selected that requires a smaller net outlay than is required with a smaller value for $p$. Thus, increasing $p$ tends to reduce the total amount required to adopt the investment proposals selected according to the principle indicated in (1) above. Conversely, reducing $p$ tends to increase the outlay required to adopt the investment proposals selected according to this principle.

When there are net outlays in more than one period, the principle of solution is the same. Instead of maximizing the quantity $(y - pc)$, it is necessary to maximize the quantity $(y - p_1c_1 - p_2c_2)$, where again $c_1$ and $c_2$ are the net outlays in the first and second periods and $p_1$ and $p_2$ are auxiliary multipliers.

Up to this point, we have not discussed the problem of rationing capital among both independent investment proposals and sets of mutually exclusive investment proposals. Superficially, this problem seems different from the one of rationing among mutually exclusive proposals only, but in fact the problems are the same. The identity rests upon the fact that each so-called "independent" proposal is and should be considered a member of the set of proposals consisting of the independent proposal and of the always present proposal to do nothing. When independent proposals are viewed in this way, it can be seen that the case of rationing simultaneously among independent proposals and sets of mutually exclusive proposals is really just a special case of rationing among mutually exclusive proposals according to the principles outlined in the preceding paragraph.

The mechanics of solution are easily worked out. All that is required in order to make the solution the same as the solution for what we have called "mutually exclusive" sets of alternatives is that each so-called "independent" proposal be treated as a member of a mutually exclusive set consisting of itself and of the alternative of doing nothing. Once this is done, it is possible to go into the familiar routine of selecting from each set that proposal for which the expression $(y - pc)$, or its appropriate modification to take account of constraints existing in more than one time period, is a maximum. Again, of course, that value of $p$ will have to be found which results in matching as nearly as discontinuities permit the outlays required by the accepted proposals with the outlays permitted by the stated budgetary constraints.

## III. Some Comparisons with the Rate-of-Return Method of Capital Rationing[8]

Since the rate-of-return method of capital rationing is fully described elsewhere, we shall describe it only briefly.[9] As in the methods described previously, attention is focused exclusively on net cash flows rather than

[8]Joel Dean has pioneered in the development of methods of capital rationing that have an understandable relationship to profit maximization, in contrast to methods still quite widely used in business that rely on such criteria as payback, average return on book investment, etc. The method that he advocates is called the "rate-of-return" method.

[9]See Joel Dean, *Capital Budgeting* (New York: Columbia University Press, 1951); "Measuring the Productivity of Capital," *Harvard Business Review,* Vol. XXXII (January-February, 1954).

on the data produced by conventional accounting practices. Investment proposals are ranked according to their "rate of return," defined as that rate of discounting which reduces a stream of cash flows to zero, and selected from this ranking, starting with the highest rate of return.

The rate-of-return solution to the three problems that are the subject of this paper is discussed below.

## *A. Given the cost of Capital, What Group of Investments Should Be Selected?*

The rate-of-return solution to the problem of selecting a group of independent proposals, given the firm's cost of capital, is to accept all investment proposals having a rate of return greater than the firm's cost of capital. This solution is necessarily identical with the solution proposed previously, except when the present value of some of the proposals is other than a steadily decreasing function of the cost of capital. An intuitive substantiation of this statement is achieved by an

FIGURE 1

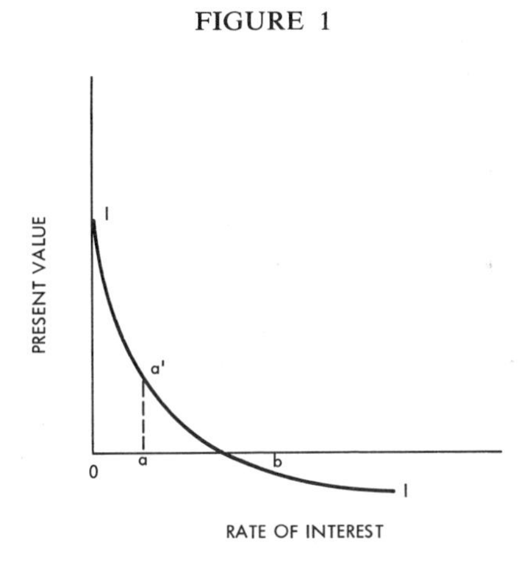


understanding of Figure 1. In Figure 1, *I–I* indicates the present value of an investment at different rates of interest, *Oa* is the firm's cost of capital, *Ob* is the rate of return on the investment, and *aa′* is the present value of the investment at the firm's cost of capital. It should be clear from the diagram that any proposal that has a positive ordinate (present value) at the firm's cost of capital will also have a rate of return (*x*- intercept) greater than the cost of capital. (However, it usually takes a little longer to find an intercept than to determine the value of an ordinate at one point.)

Under what circumstances can the present value of an investment proposal be something other than a steadily decreasing function of the cost of capital? Some investment proposals can intersect the $x$ axis at more than one point. In particular, investment proposals having initial cash outlays, subsequent net cash inflows, and final net cash outlays can intersect the $x$ axis more than once and have, therefore, more than one rate of return. Investments of this nature are rare, but they do occur, especially in the extractive industries. For example, an investment proposal might consist of an investment in an oil pump that gets a fixed quantity of oil out of the ground more rapidly than the pump currently in use. Making this investment would require an initial net outlay (for the new pump), subsequent net incremental cash inflow (larger oil production), and final net incremental cash outlay (the absence of oil production, because of its earlier exhaustion with the use of the higher capacity new pump).[10] The present value of an investment in such a pump could look like Figure 2. In Figure 2, *I–I* indicates the present value of the investment, *Oa* is the firm's cost of capital, *Ob* and *Oc* are the two rates of return on the investment, and *aa′* is the present value of the investment at the firm's cost of capital.

FIGURE 2

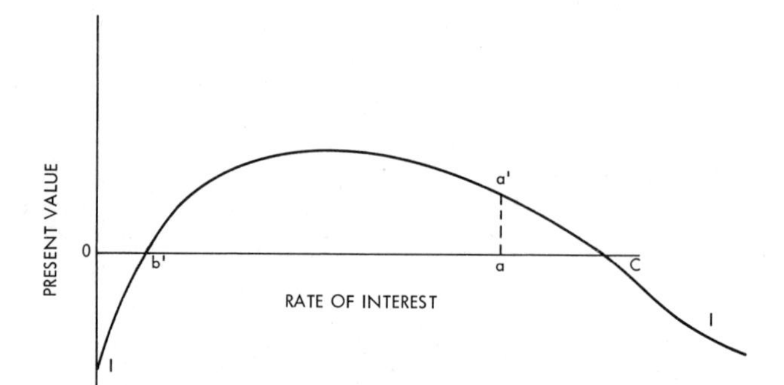


The reasoning behind this apparent paradox of the doublé rate of return is as follows:

1. As the cost of capital of the firm approaches zero, the present value of the investment proposal approaches the algebraic sum of net cash flows and will be negative if this sum is negative.

[10]These incremental flows are measured with reference to the flows that would have resulted from the use of the smaller pump. Thus the final net outlay is not absolute but rather by comparison with oil (money) that would have been produced had the smaller pump been in use.

2. As the cost of capital increases, the present value of the final net cash outflow diminishes in importance relative to the earlier flows, and this diminution can cause the present value of the entire proposal to become positive.
3. If the cost of capital continues to increase, the significance of all future cash flows tend to diminish, causing the present value of the proposal to approach the initial outlay as a limit.

The rate-of-return criterion for judging the acceptability of investment proposals, as it has been presented in published works, is then ambiguous or anomalous. This is in contrast to the clarity and uniform accuracy of the decisions indicated by the principle proposed earlier, which relates to the present value of an investment at the cost of capital rather than to a comparison between the cost of capital and the rate of return.[11]

## *B. Given a Fixed Sum for Capital Investment, What Group of Investment Proposals Should Be Undertaken?*

The rate-of-return solution to the problem of allocating a fixed sum of money—without reference to cost of capital—among competing proposals is to order the proposals according to their rate of return and to proceed down the ladder thus created until the available funds are exhausted. The group of investment proposals selected by the use of this principle can be different, and probably would usually be different, from the group selected when the criterion is present value rather than rate of return. A difference between the two groups would not exist if the available capital funds were just equal to that amount which would permit investment in all those proposals having a rate of return at least equal to the firm's cost of capital, and only those proposals, and if the anomalies mentioned under Section A were not present.

The preceding statements are equivalent to saying that the groups of investments that would be chosen by the use of the two principles or criteria would necessarily be the same only if the fixed sum to be invested happened to be the optimum sum and that investment of any other sum could result in selection of different groups of proposals by use of the two principles. This difference would result from the fact that the different principles can result in a different ranking of proposals within the group that would be accepted if the optimum amount were

[11]The rate-of-return rule could be easily modified to remove this ambiguity or anomaly by specifying that the relevant rate of return is the one at which the investment is a decreasing function of the rate of interest.

invested. Table 2 indicates the validity of the statement that the ordering of two investment proposals according to their rate of return can be contrary to their ordering according to their present value per dollar of outlay.

TABLE 2

| Period | Net Cash Flows | |
|---|---|---|
| | *Investment A* | *Investment B* |
| 0– year | –$ 85 | –$ 90 |
| 0–1 year | + 17 | + 21 |
| 1–2 years | + 35 | + 33 |
| 2–3 years | + 68 | + 57 |
| 3–4 years | + 131 | + 94 |
| 4–5 years | + 216 | + 155 |
| 5–6 years | + 357 | + 255 |
| 6–7 years | + 546 | + 420 |
| 7–8 years | + 555 | + 695 |
| 8–9 years | + 345 | + 1,150 |
| Present value at 20% | + 606 | + 853 |
| Rate of return | 66% | 62% |

The example of Table 2 illustrates that a proposal with a higher rate of return can have a lower present value and that, therefore, the two rules can conflict. The present-value rule maximizes the present value of the firm's net worth—by definition—and the rate-of-return rule therefore may not.

This discrepancy is undoubtedly of small practical significance. In the first place, firms that ration their capital rationally use the firm's cost of capital as the constraint rather than an absolute dollar sum; and under such rational behavior the two rules yield the same results, with the exception noted previously. (Undoubtedly, no firms long persist in setting absolute dollar constraints that differ significantly in their effects from the cost-of-capital constraint.) In the second place, the present values of investment proposals, expressed as functions of the cost of capital, are often thoughtful enough not to intersect above the $x$ axis (the rate-of-interest axis), a necessary condition for a conflict between the rate-of-return and present-value principles.

## *C. Selecting the Best among Mutually Exclusive Alternatives*

The rate-of-return solution to the problem of selecting the "best" among mutually exclusive investment alternatives, although occasionally tricky in practice, is simply explained as follows:

1. Compute the rate of return for that investment proposal, among the set of mutually exclusive proposals, requiring the least initial net outlay.
2. If the rate of return on the investment requiring the smallest outlay exceeds the firm's cost of capital (or other cutoff rate), tentatively accept that investment. Next, compute the rate of return on the incremental outlay needed for the investment requiring the second lowest outlay. If that rate exceeds the firm's cutoff rate, accept the investment requiring the greater outlay in preference to that requiring the lesser. Proceed by such paired comparisons (based on rates of return on incremental outlay) to eliminate all but one investment.
3. If the rate of return on the proposal requiring the least outlay does not exceed the firm's cutoff rate, drop it from further consideration, and compute the rate of return for the proposal requiring the next least outlay. If that rate exceeds the firm's cutoff rate, that investment proposal becomes the bench mark for the first paired comparison. If that rate does not exceed the firm's cutoff rate, drop that proposal from further consideration. The process just described is to be repeated either until a proposal is found with a rate of return exceeding the cost of capital or until all proposals have been eliminated because their rates of return do not exceed the cutoff rate.

The rate-of-return solution to the problem of selecting the best among mutually exclusive investment alternatives is especially subject to the ambiguities and anomalies mentioned under Section A, because the costs and revenues associated with incremental investments required for proposals included in mutually exclusive sets are much more likely to have unusual time shapes and reversals than are the costs and revenues associated with independent investments.

## Summary

We have given solutions to three problems in budgeting capital so as to maximize the net worth of the firm. The solutions that we have given differ in principle from those implied by the rate-of-return method of capital rationing. The difference in principle can lead to differences in behavior. Differences in behavior will be rare in coping with problems of the first and third sorts, and will be relatively frequent for problems of the second sort. When differences do exist, the rate-of-return solution does not result in maximizing the present value of the firm's net worth.

*Chapter* 20

# *The Derivation of Probabilistic Information for the Evaluation of Risky Investments**

By Frederick S. Hillier

## *Introduction*

THE AMOUNT of risk involved is often one of the important considerations in the evaluation of proposed investments. Thus a reasonably safe investment with a certain expected rate of return will often be preferred to a much more risky investment with a somewhat higher expected rate of return. This is especially true when the risky investment is so large that the failure to achieve expectations could significantly affect the financial position of the individual or firm. Moreover, despite theoretical arguments against it, research [8][1] has indicated that many executives maintain this preference even when the personal or corporate resources are more than ample to meet the contingency of adverse events. On the other hand, the prosperity of Las Vegas attests to the fact that some individuals have risk preference rather than risk aversion; i.e., they often select a risky investment with a low or negative expected rate of return because of the possibility of an extremely high return.

Unfortunately, not many expository papers have appeared on practical ways of deriving the type of explicit, well-defined, and comprehensive information that is essential for an accurate appraisal of a risky investment. It is the purpose of this presentation to indicate how, under certain assumptions, such information in the form of the probability

*Reprinted by permission from *Management Science,* Vol. IX (April, 1963), pp. 443–57.

[1]Numbers in brackets refer to publications listed at the end of this paper (p. 326).

distribution of the internal rate of return, present worth, or annual cost of a proposed investment can be derived.

## *Existing Procedures for Considering Risk*

Capital-budgeting literature has not yet given much consideration to the analysis of risk, and such procedures as have been suggested for dealing with risk have tended to be either quite simplified or somewhat theoretical. Thus, either these procedures have tended to provide management with only a portion of the information required for a sound decision, or they have assumed the availability of information which is almost impossible to obtain.

The simplified procedures usually amount to reducing the estimates of the possible values of the prospective cash flow during each time period to a single expected value, in either an intuitive or a statistical sense, and then analyzing the problem as if each of these expected values were certain to occur.[2] Risk is sometimes included in this analysis by using an interest rate appropriate for the associated degree of risk as the standard for the minimum acceptable internal rate of return or for discounting the cash flow for a particular year. These procedures are the ones generally selected for use currently. However, they suffer the disadvantage of suppressing the information regarding the risk of the proposed investment. Thus, while optimistic and pessimistic predictions have both been averaged in to obtain the single measure of the merit of the investment, the executive is not provided with any explicit measure of the risk of the investment. For example, he might be provided with an estimate of the expected rate of return of an investment but not its variance, even though the executive would probably have a distinct preference for an investment with a small variance of the rate of return over another investment with the same expected rate of return and larger variance. As a result, these procedures require the executive to resort to his own intuition for the ultimate consideration of risk.

A useful technique for considering risk which is sometimes used in conjunction with the simplified procedures is sensitivity analysis.[3] This technique involves revising uncertain estimates of prospective cash flows and investigating the sensitivity of the measure of the merit of the investment to such revisions in the estimates. This gives some indication of the effect if one of the original estimates was either too optimistic or too pessimistic. However, sensitivity analysis is quite limited in the amount of information it can provide. For example, it is difficult to draw precise conclusions about the possible effects of combinations of errors

[2]See, for example, [7, chap. xiii]; [2, chap. ix]; [11, pp. 210–13].
[3]See, for example, [7, chap. xiii].

in the estimates, even though this is the typical situation of concern. For statistical reasons, it would usually be misleading to consider the case where all the estimates are too optimistic or where all are too pessimistic. In short, sensitivity analysis is useful, but its conclusions tend to suffer from a lack of conciseness, precision, and comprehensiveness.

A theoretical procedure occasionally suggested would determine the "utility" or degree of merit of each of the possible outcomes of an investment and then determine the expected value of the utility to use as a measure of the merit of the investment.[4] Assuming that valid utilities and associated probabilities are used, this procedure properly weights the merit of both the better and the poorer possible outcomes of an investment so that it accurately and completely takes risk into account. Thus, expected utility is an ideal measure of the merit of an investment from a theoretical point of view. Unfortunately, utility is a subtle concept, so that the measurement of utility is a difficult task. Therefore, it would be extremely difficult to determine explicitly, with the needed precision, the utility to management of all the possible outcomes of an investment. From a practical point of view, management usually would have neither the time nor the inclination to participate in such a monumental task in a formal manner. Another procedure which has been suggested by certain economists [10] involves selecting those investments whose expected rate of return exceeds the firm's average cost of capital, including both stocks and bonds, where this cost is a function of the risk associated with the industry and thus (by implication) the investments. However, practical objections can be made regarding the underlying assumptions, including the premise that executives will act solely in the long-run interests of the stockholders, and the difficulty of determining the prospective rate of return of stock. Another interesting approach to this type of problem has recently been reported [12] in the form of a model for investment in the stock market. However, it does not appear that this approach, involving the maximization of expected monetary gains subject to probabilistic constraints on maximum loss during the various periods, can be extended to the general problem of investment under uncertainty.

Finally, mention should be made of the work of Markowitz [9] concerning the analysis of portfolios containing large numbers of securities. Markowitz shows how to determine the portfolio which provides the most suitable combination of expected rate of return and standard deviation of rate of return. While the nature and scope of this problem differ somewhat from the problem dealt with here, there are similarities in the

---

[4]See, for example, [11, pp. 204–16], and [13, chap. ii].

two approaches to the problem of evaluating risky investments. The primary similarities are in the use of the expected value and standard deviation of rate of return and in the treatment of covariances. Furthermore, [9] contains considerable theoretical material which is relevant to the problem posed here. Especially important is the justification given for the use of both the expected value and the standard deviation of rate of return as decision parameters. For example, it is shown that properly using these decision parameters is essentially equivalent to maximizing a quadratic utility function of rate of return.

## *Comparison of Proposed Procedure with Existing Procedures*

The procedure that will be recommended here is something of a compromise between the simplified procedures and the theoretical procedures described above. While it has some of the same deficiencies, it also enjoys many of the advantages of both types of procedures. It goes beyond the simplified approach to provide additional information, namely, the probability distribution of the selected measure of the merit of the investments. At the same time, this information enables the executive quickly to apply, in an intuitive and implicit sense, the theoretical procedure of evaluating expected utility. Therefore the techniques that will now be developed are actually tools for more clearly exhibiting the risk involved and should complement, rather than supersede, most current procedures for evaluating investments.

## *Formulation of Problems*

Consider an investment which will result in cash flows during at least some of the next $n$ years. Let $X_j$ be the random variable which takes on the value of the net cash flow during the $j$th year, where $j = 0, 1, 2, \ldots, n$. Assume that $X_j$ has a normal distribution with known mean, $\mu_j$, and known standard deviation, $\sigma_j$.

It is recognized that these assumptions regarding $X_j$ will not often be completely justified. In particular, the probability distribution of $X_j$ may not be normal. On the other hand, it would seem that for many types of prospective cash flows, one's best subjective probability distribution would be nearly a symmetrical distribution resembling the normal distribution. Furthermore, by the Central Limit Theorem, the actual distribution of $X_j$ can sometimes deviate considerably from the normal distribution without significantly affecting the final results. More precisely, looking ahead to equation 1, if $X_j/(1 + i)^j$, $j = 0, 1 \ldots, n$, are mutually independent random variables, with finite means and variances, which are either identically distributed or uniformly bounded, then (by the Lindeberg Theorem) the Central Limit Theorem will hold, and the sum of these random variables will be approximately normal if $n$ is large. If this holds, the probability distribution of the measures of the merit of an investment considered in the following sections will be approximately normal, regardless of whether the $X_j$ random variables are normal or not. Finally, even if the $X_j$ random variables are not normal and the Central Limit Theorem is not applicable, all of the subsequent equations (equations 1, 2, . . . , 13) will still hold. Thus the mean and variance of the measures of merit will be the same (or nearly the same in the case of internal rate of return) regardless of the normality of $X_j$. The mean and variance (or standard deviation) of these measures, by themselves, provide a substantial basis for evaluating and comparing prospective investments; furthermore, certain weak probability statements can be made by using the Tchebycheff inequality. The only consequence of nonnormality is that without knowledge of the distribution of the measures of merit, precise probability statements cannot be made.

Regarding the other assumptions, present procedures already assume that some measure of the central tendency of each prospective cash flow is known, since they require a single forecast of the cash flow. This measure usually corresponds roughly either to $\mu_j$ or to the mode ("most likely value"), which, for the normal distribution, equals $\mu_j$. It should not be much more difficult to estimate $\sigma_j$ than $\mu_j$. Merely keep in mind that about 68 percent of the probability distribution will lie within $\mu_j \pm \sigma_j$, about 95 percent within $\mu_j \pm 2\sigma_j$, and about 99.73 percent within $\mu_j \pm 3\sigma_j$. Thus, estimating $\sigma_j$ is just a more definitive version of that aspect of sensitivity analysis involving the investigation of reasonably likely values of $X_j$.

Some assumption needs to be specified regarding the relationship between the $X_j$ random variables for different values of $j$. The two simplest assumptions are that all the $X_j$ random variables are mutually independent or that they are all completely correlated. Actually, there will be many cases where a compromise between these assumptions is needed, since some of the cash flows are reasonably independent, whereas others are closely correlated. Therefore, what will be done is to consider the two cases individually and then show how they can be combined.

The desirability of an investment is not always a question that can be answered entirely independently of other investments. The performance of one investment is, instead, often interrelated with the performance of others. Therefore, for a truly satisfactory investment decision, it would sometimes be desirable to introduce into the analysis some measure or measures of covariance between the investment's merit and that of alternatives or complementary investments. Indeed, Markowitz [9] includes a thorough development of the use of covariance of returns in his analysis. However, this refinement is beyond the scope of this paper. Instead, the problem is confined to describing the desirability of individual prospective investments.

A large number of methods have been advocated for evaluating investments. While it is felt that the approach to be developed here can be applied to most of these methods, only compound interest methods (presently favored by most writers) will be considered. In particular, the three widely advocated discounting procedures—the present worth method, the annual cost method, and the internal-rate-of-return method —as defined by Grant and Ireson [7] will be explored. The objective will be to demonstrate how to obtain a probability distribution for each of these three measures of the merit of an investment.

## *Probability Distribution of Present Worth*

The present worth, $P$, for a proposed productive investment may be defined as:

$$P = \sum_{j=0}^{n} \left[ \frac{X_j}{(1+i)^j} \right] \tag{1}$$

where $i$ is the rate of interest which properly reflects the investor's time value of money. The value of $i$ is often described as the minimum attractive rate of return or the cost of capital.

A more general definition of $P$ is sometimes given by specifying possibly distinct values of $i$ for each of the $n$ periods. The following results can be applied with no increased difficulty to the more general case. However, since uniform values of $i$ are almost always used in actual applications, only this simplest case will be considered, so as to concentrate attention on the new features of the proposed procedure.

It should be recognized that as defined, $P$ is actually a random variable rather than a constant. For purposes of evaluating a proposed investment, the usual procedure is to examine the expected value of $P$:

$$\mu_P = \sum_{j=0}^{n} \left[ \frac{\mu_j}{(1+i)^j} \right] \tag{2}$$

although this is often referred to as "the" present worth. Then, if $\mu_P > 0$, the investment would be made, since this would increase the expected total wealth of the firm more than investing the same money elsewhere at the marginal rate of return $i$. When comparing mutually exclusive alternatives for the same investment funds, the alternative with the largest value of $\mu_P$ would be preferred, assuming no compensating intangible factors.

Assume initially that $X_0, X_1, \ldots, X_n$ are mutually independent. Therefore, it is well known that $P$ would have a normal distribution, where the mean is given by equation 2 and the variance is:

$$\sigma_P^2 = \sum_{j=0}^{n} \frac{\sigma_j^2}{(1+i)^{2j}} \tag{3}$$

Before illustrating the use of this information, other assumptions leading to different variances will be considered. Assume that $X_0, X_1, \ldots, X_n$ are perfectly correlated. That is, if the value that $X_m$ takes on is $\mu_m + C\sigma_m$, then the value that $X_j$ takes on must be $\mu_j + C\sigma_j$ for $j = 0, 1, \ldots, m, \ldots, n$. Thus, this assumption states, in effect, that if circumstances cause the actual net cash flow during one period to deviate from expectations, then these same circumstances will also affect the net cash flow in all other periods in an exactly comparable manner. For this case, it is clear that $P$ has a normal distribution with a mean as given by equation 2 and a standard deviation

$$\sigma_P = \sum_{j=0}^{n} \left[ \frac{\sigma_j}{(1+i)^j} \right] \tag{4}$$

A more realistic model is one which combines the two assumptions considered above. This model would recognize and make allowance for the fact that often some of the cash flows are closely related while the others are reasonably independent. Therefore the assumption is made that $Y_j, Z_j^{(1)}, Z_j^{(2)}, \ldots$, and $Z_j^{(m)}$ are the normally distributed random variables such that

$$X_j = Y_j + Z_j^{(1)} + Z_j^{(2)} + \cdots + Z_j^{(m)} \tag{5}$$

where the new random variables are mutually independent, with the exception that $Z_0^{(k)}, Z_1^{(k)}, \ldots, Z_n^{(k)}$ are perfectly correlated for $k = 1, 2, \ldots, m$. In other words, the net cash flow for each period consists of an independent cash flow plus $m$ distinct cash flows which are each perfectly correlated with the corresponding cash flows in the other periods. Therefore, it follows that $P$ has a normal distribution with

$$\mu_P = \sum_{j=0}^{n} \left[ \frac{\mu_j}{(1+i)^j} \right] = \sum_{j=0}^{n} \frac{E(Y_j) + \sum_{k=1}^{m} E(Z_j^{(k)})}{(1+i)^j} \tag{6}$$

and

$$\sigma_P^2 = \sum_{j=0}^{n} \left[ \frac{\text{Var}\ (Y_j)}{(1+i)^{2j}} \right] + \sum_{k=1}^{m} \left( \sum_{j=0}^{n} \left[ \frac{\sqrt{\text{Var}(Z_j^{(k)})}}{(1+i)^j} \right] \right)^2 \tag{7}$$

It is easily seen that the first two cases treated are actually only special cases of this model combining the two assumptions. The first case of complete independence is obtained by setting $m = 0$. The second case of complete correlation is obtained by setting $m = 1$ and $Y_j = 0$. The essential difference between the various special cases is reflected in equation 7. In particular, given fixed values of $\sigma_j$, $\sigma_P$ is smallest for the case of complete independence and largest for the case of complete correlation.

An even more precise model, from a theoretical point of view, would be one which admitted the possibility of a relationship between random variables which falls somewhere between mutual independence and complete correlation. Ideally, one would be given the covariance matrix for $X_0, X_1, \ldots, X_n$, so that $\mu_P$ would be given by equation 2 and $\sigma_P{}^2$ would be the weighted sum of the elements of the covariance matrix, where $\sigma_{jk}$ is weighted by $(1 + i)^{-(j+k)}$. Unfortunately, it does not yet appear to be realistic to expect investment analysts to develop reliable estimates for covariances. Therefore, attention will be concentrated on the model summarized by equation 5.

Having thus obtained the probability distribution of $P$, this information now provides the executive with some basis for evaluating the risk aspect of the investment decision. For example, suppose that on the basis of the forecasts regarding prospective cash flow from a proposed investment of \$10,000, it is determined that $\mu_P = \$1{,}000$ and $\sigma_P = \$2{,}000$. Ordinarily, the current procedure would be to approve the investment, since $\mu_P > 0$. However, with additional information available ($\sigma_P =$ \$2,000) regarding the considerable risk of the investment, the executive can analyze the situation further. Using widely available tables for the normal distribution, he could note (or be given the information on a drawing of the cumulative distribution function) that the probability that $P < 0$, so that the investment will not pay, is 0.31. Furthermore, the probability is 0.16, 0.023, and 0.0013, respectively, that the investment will lose the present worth equivalent of at least \$1,000, \$3,000, and \$5,000, respectively. Considering the financial status of the firm, the executive can use this and similar information to make his decision. Suppose, instead, that the executive is attempting to choose between this investment and a second investment with $\mu_P = \$500$ and $\sigma_P = \$500$. By conducting a similar analysis for the second investment, the executive can decide whether the greater expected earnings of the first investment justify the greater risk. A useful technique for making this comparison is to superimpose the drawing of the probability distribution of $P$ for the second investment upon the corresponding drawing for the first investment. This same approach generalizes to the comparison of more than two investments.

## *Probability Distribution of Annual Cost*

The equivalent uniform annual cost, $A$, for a proposed investment is shown by Grant and Ireson [7] to be:

$$A = -\sum_{j=1}^{n} \left[\frac{X_j}{(1+i)^j}\right]\left[\frac{i(1+i)^n}{(1+i)^n - 1}\right] = P\left[\frac{i(1+i)^n}{(1+i)^n - 1}\right] \quad (8)$$

Thus, for given values of $i$ and $n$, $A$ differs from $P$ only by a constant factor. Therefore the probability distribution of $A$ is found by finding the probability distribution of $P$, as described above, and then multiplying $P$ by this constant factor. The analysis of the risk would also correspond to the analysis when using the present worth method.

## *Probability Distribution of Internal Rate of Return*

The internal rate of return, $R$, may be defined as that value of $i$ such that $P = 0$. It is used as a measure of the merit of proposed investments. The highest priority is given to those investments with the highest values of $R$. If adequate funds are available, an established minimum attractive rate of return is often used as a standard for comparison, proposed investments being approved only if their value of $R$ exceeds this standard.

Several writers, including Bernhard [1] and Bierman and Smidt [2], have recently voiced their opinion that the internal-rate-of-return method is inferior to the present worth method. This article is intended to be an introductory exposition of a specific technique for evaluating risk, so the issues raised by these writers will be ignored. Thus, it will be assumed that the circumstances are appropriate for the use of the internal-rate-of-return method, so that, for example, there is a unique value for $R$ with probability essentially one.

The proposed procedure for finding the probability distribution of $R$ is a relatively straightforward one. It involves finding the probability distribution of $P$ for various values of $i$ in order to find the cumulative distribution function of $R$ and then, if desired, deriving the probability density function of $R$ from its cumulative distribution function. This procedure will now be outlined.

Selecting an arbitrary value of $i$, find the probability distribution of $P$ as described previously. Find the probability that $P < 0$. Then, except under unusual circumstances such as [1] discusses, this is just the probability that $R < i$. This result should be readily apparent, since $R = i$

only if $P = 0$, and $R$ normally increases as $P$ increases for a given investment and a fixed value of $i$. Summarizing in equation form:

$$\text{Prob}\ \{R < i\} = \text{Prob}\ \{P < 0 \mid i\} \tag{9}$$

Therefore, to find the cumulative distribution function of $R$, one need merely repeat the calculation of Prob $\{P < 0 \mid i\}$ for as many values of $i$ as desired. The calculation of these values provides the basis for a graphical presentation of the cumulative distribution function of $R$. This procedure for deriving the probability distribution of $R$ is illustrated by the example of the following section.

The cumulative distribution function of $R$ can readily be used directly for evaluating an investment. It has a meaningful, yet simple, interpretation which is well suited for this purpose. However, if desired, the cumulative distribution function can be transformed into the probability density function. Simply recall that the value of the probability density function at a certain $i$ is just the first derivative of the cumulative distribution function at that value of $i$. Alternatively, since the probability distribution of R will usually approximate the normal distribution, the normal curve can be used as an approximate probability density function, where the mean and the standard deviation would be estimated from an examination of the cumulative distribution function.

The assertion that under the prevailing assumption of the normality of $P$, the probability distribution of $R$ will usually approximate the normal distribution is supported by the following argument. Assume the usual situation that $\mu_0 < 0$ and $\mu_j > 0$ for $j = 1, 2, \ldots, n$. Therefore, the first derivative of $\mu_P$ with respect to $i$, $\mu'_P$, is obviously negative (see equation 6). Assume, as an approximation, that $\mu'_P$ and $\sigma_P$ are constants for all values of $i$. Then, for any numbers, $\triangle$ and $i_0$:

$$\text{Prob}\ \{P < -\mu'_P \Delta \mid i = i_0\} = \text{Prob}\ \{P < 0 \mid i = i_0 + \Delta\}$$

and therefore:

$$\text{Prob}\ \{R < i_0 + \Delta\} = \text{Prob}\ \{P < -\mu'_P \Delta \mid i = i_0\}$$

Hence, $R$ and $P$ are identically distributed except for the location and scale parameters, mean and standard deviation. Since $P$ is normal, it now follows that the probability distribution of $R$ is the normal distribution. The one shortcoming in this argument is that, in fact, $\mu'_P$ and $\sigma_P$ are not constants. However, the fact that $\mu''_P > 0$, whereas $\sigma'_P < 0$, means that these two discrepancies tend to cancel each other out.

It would be sometimes desirable, when comparing mutually exclusive investments requiring differing amounts of investment funds, to determine the probability distribution of the internal rate of return on each increment in investment. To illustrate how this would be done, consider two such mutually exclusive investments which can be described by the model involving equation 5. Let $P(S)$, $P(L)$, and $P(\triangle)$ denote the present worths of the smaller investment, the larger investment, and the incremental investment, respectively. Let $R(\triangle)$ denote the internal rate of return on the incremental investment. Assume that $P(S)$ and $P(L)$ are mutually independent. Therefore, since

$$P(\Delta) = P(L) - P(S) \tag{10}$$

it is clear that $P(\triangle)$ has a normal distribution with

$$E\{P(\Delta)\} = E\{P(L)\} - E\{P(S)\} \tag{11}$$

and

$$\text{Var}\ \{P(\Delta)\} = \text{Var}\ \{P(L)\} + \text{Var}\ \{P(S)\} \tag{12}$$

Thus, just as before:

$$\text{Prob}\ \{R(\Delta) < i\} = \text{Prob}\ \{P(\Delta) < 0 \mid i\} \tag{13}$$

so that the same procedure is now used for finding the probability distribution of $R(\triangle)$ as for $R$.

## *Example*

The XYZ Company is primarily engaged in the manufacture of cameras. The company will soon be discontinuing the production of one of its older models, and it is now investigating what should be done with the extra productive capacity that will consequently become available. Two attractive alternatives appear to be available. The first alternative is to expand the production of model A, one of the firm's latest and most popular models. This model was initially marketed last year, and its successful reception plus favorable marketing research indicates that there is and will continue to be a market for this extra production. The second alternative is to initiate the production of model B. Model B would involve a number of revolutionary changes which the research department has developed. While no comparable model is now on the market, rumors in the industry indicate that a number of other companies might now have similar models on their drawing boards. Marketing research indicates an exciting but uncertain potential for such a model. Uncertainty regarding the reliability of the proposed new devices, lack of production experience on such a model, and the possibility that the market might be vigorously invaded by competing models at any time all add to the risk involved in this alternative. In short, the decision is between the safe, conservative investment in model A or the risky but promising investment in model B. It is felt that both of these models will be marketable for the next five years. Due to a lack of investment funds and productive capacity, it has been decided that only one of these alternatives can be selected. It is assumed that the production of model B would not affect the market for the presently scheduled production of model A.

Detailed studies have been made regarding the after-tax cash flow consequences of the two alternatives. The analysis of the investment required in model A indicates that considerable new equipment, tooling, and modification of existing production processes will be needed. It was estimated that the difference in the immediate cash flow because of the investment in model A would be −$400,000. However, it is recognized that this estimate is only approximate, so that it is appropriate to estimate the standard deviation for this cash flow. Recalling that the probability is 0.6827, 0.9545, and 0.9973, respectively, that the actual cash flow will be within one, two, and three standard deviations, respectively, of the expected cash flow, it was decided that an estimate of $20,000 was the most appropriate one. In other words, the judgment was that, letting $Y_0$ be the cash flow:

$$\text{Prob}\ \{-\$400{,}000 - \sigma \leqq Y_0 \leqq -\$400{,}000 + \sigma\} = 0.6827$$

$$\text{Prob}\ \{-\$400{,}000 - 2\sigma \leqq Y_0 \leqq -\$400{,}000 + 2\sigma\} = 0.9545$$

$$\text{Prob}\ \{-\$400{,}000 - 3\sigma \leqq Y_0 \leqq -\$400{,}000 + 3\sigma\} = 0.9973$$

most actually reflects the estimator's subjective probabilities if $\sigma$ is chosen as $20,000.

Proceeding with a similar analysis, the expected values and standard deviations of the net cash flows for each of the next five years were estimated. Due to the previous experience with model A, these standard deviations were considered to be small. The variation that does exist largely arises from the variation in the production costs, such as maintenance, equipment replacement, and rework costs, and in the state of the economy. Since these conditions tend to vary randomly from year to year, it was decided that the appropriate assumption is that the net cash flows in the various years are mutually independent. One special problem was encountered in determining the standard deviation for the fifth year, since this net cash flow combines the regular cash flow for the fifth year plus the effective salvage value of the equipment being used. This standard deviation was obtained by assuming independence, so that the variance of the sum equals the sum of the variances of these cash flows. Thus, even though the standard deviation for the salvage value was estimated at $30,000 and the standard deviation for the rest of the net cash flow at $40,000, the estimated standard deviation of the total net cash flow for the fifth year is $50,000.

Table 1 summarizes the results of the estimating process for model A.

TABLE 1

ESTIMATED NET CASH FLOW DATA IN THOUSANDS OF DOLLARS FOR MODEL A

| *Year* | *Corresponding Symbol in Equation 5* | *Expected Value* | *Standard Deviation* |
|---|---|---|---|
| 0 | $Y_0$ | −400 | 20 |
| 1 | $Y_1$ | +120 | 10 |
| 2 | $Y_2$ | +120 | 15 |
| 3 | $Y_3$ | +120 | 20 |
| 4 | $Y_4$ | +110 | 30 |
| 5 | $Y_5$ | +200 | 50 |

The procedure for describing the investment in model B was similar. The primary difference was that this investment was considered to generate both a series of correlated cash flows and a series of independent cash flows. Thus, in equation 5, $m = 1$, instead of $m = 0$ as for the investment in model A. This difference arose because of the uncertainty regarding the reception of model B on the market. Thus, it was felt that if the reception exceeded expectations during the first year or two, it would continue to exceed present expectations thereafter, and vice versa. The resulting conclusion was that the net marketing cash flow, i.e., the net cash flow resulting from the sales income minus the expenses due to the marketing effort and advertising required, for each of the five years should be assumed to be perfectly correlated. On the other hand, it was felt the analysis of the production expenses involved was sufficiently reliable that any deviation from expectations for a given year would be primarily attributable to random fluctuations in production costs, especially in such irregular items as maintenance costs. Therefore, it was concluded that the net production cash flow for each of the five years should be assumed to be mutually independent. The effective equipment salvage value, being essentially independent of the other cash flows, was included in the net production cash flow for the fifth year.

Detailed analyses of the various components of total cash flow led, as for model A, to the desired estimates of the expectations and standard deviations of net cash flow for marketing and for production for each of the five years, as well as for the immediate investment required. These results are summarized in Table 2.

TABLE 2

ESTIMATED NET CASH FLOW DATA IN THOUSANDS OF DOLLARS FOR MODEL B

| *Year* | *Source of Cash Flow* | *Corresponding Symbol in Equation 5* | *Expected Value* | *Standard Deviation* |
|---|---|---|---|---|
| 0...... | Initial investment | $Y_0$ | −600 | 50 |
| 1...... | Production | $Y_1$ | −250 | 20 |
| 2...... | Production | $Y_2$ | −200 | 10 |
| 3...... | Production | $Y_3$ | −200 | 10 |
| 4...... | Production | $Y_4$ | −200 | 10 |
| 5...... | Production; salvage value | $Y_5$ | −100 | $10\sqrt{10}$ |
| 1...... | Marketing | $Z_1^{(1)}$ | +300 | 50 |
| 2...... | Marketing | $Z_2^{(1)}$ | +600 | 100 |
| 3...... | Marketing | $Z_3^{(1)}$ | +500 | 100 |
| 4...... | Marketing | $Z_4^{(1)}$ | +400 | 100 |
| 5...... | Marketing | $Z_5^{(1)}$ | +300 | 100 |

The procedure for using these data to derive the probability distribution of present worth will now be illustrated. For this particular company the appropriate value of $i$ is considered to be $i = 10$ percent.

For the investment in model A, equations 6 and 7 indicate that, since $m = 0$:

$$\mu_P = \sum_{j=0}^{5} \frac{E(Y_j)}{(1.1)^j} = -400 + \cdots + \frac{200}{(1.1)^5} = +95$$

$$\sigma_P^2 = \sum_{j=0}^{5} \frac{\text{Var }(Y_j)}{(1.1)^{2j}} = (20)^2 + \cdots + \frac{(50)^2}{(1.1)^{10}} = 2247$$

so that $\sigma_P = 47.4$. Therefore the probability distribution of present worth of the investment in model A is a normal distribution with a mean of 95 and a standard deviation of 47.4 (in units of thousands of dollars). Thus, referring to probability tables for the normal distribution to find what proportion of the population is less than the mean minus 95/47.4 standard deviations, it is concluded that:

$$\text{Prob }\{P < 0 \mid i = 10\%\} = 0.023$$

Proceeding similarly for the investment in model B, equations 6 and 7 indicate that since $m = 1$:

$$\mu_P = \sum_{j=0}^{5} \frac{E(Y_j) + E(Z_j^{(1)})}{(1.1)^j} = -600 + \frac{50}{1.1} + \cdots + \frac{200}{(1.1)^5} = +262$$

$$\sigma_P{}^2 = \sum_{j=0}^{5} \frac{\text{Var}\ (Y_j)}{(1.1)^{2j}} + \left(\sum_{j=0}^{5}\left[\frac{\sqrt{\text{Var}\ (Z_j^{(1)})}}{(1.1)^j}\right]\right)^2$$

$$= 2500 + \cdots + \frac{1000}{(1.1)^{10}} + \left(\frac{50}{1.1} + \cdots + \frac{100}{(1.1)^5}\right)^2$$

$$= 114{,}700$$

so that $\sigma_P = 339$. Therefore:

$$\text{Prob}\ \{P < 0 \mid i = 10\%\} = 0.22$$

This information regarding the probability distribution of present worth permits a precise probabilistic comparison of the two alternative investments. In order to facilitate this comparison, it is sometimes useful to superimpose the two normal curves) or the corresponding cumulative distribution functions) on the same graph.

If the company had desired to use the internal-rate-of-return criterion, the procedure would have been a straightforward extension of the above procedure for present worth. Thus, given the preceding information regarding present worth, equation 9 immediately indicates that for the investment in model A:

$$\text{Prob}\ \{R < 10\%\} = 0.023$$

and for the investment in model B:

$$\text{Prob}\ \{R < 10\%\} = 0.22$$

Using the same procedure for various other values of $i$, the cumulative distribution function of $R$ can be obtained for each of the investments. They are presented subsequently in Figure 1. Comparing these cumulative distribution functions with the cumulative distribution function for the normal distribution, a close similarity is noticed. Thus a brief examination reveals that for the investment in model A, the distribution of $R$ is approximately normal with a mean of about 18.5 percent and a standard deviation of about 4 percent. For the investment in model B

FIGURE 1

COMPARISON OF THE CUMULATIVE DISTRIBUTION FUNCTIONS OF $R$ FOR THE INVESTMENTS IN MODEL A AND IN MODEL B

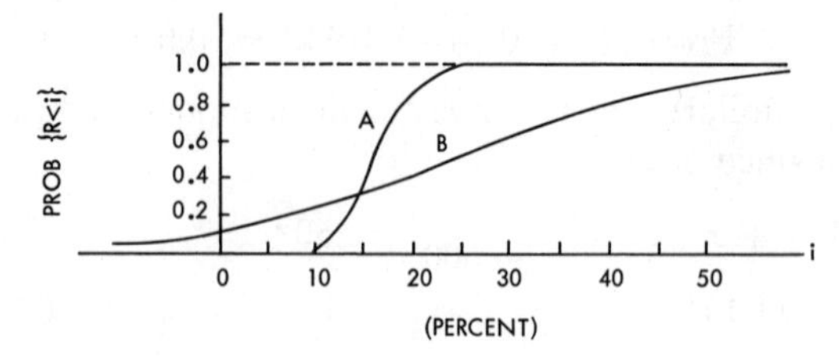

the distribution of $R$ is approximately normal with a mean of about 25 percent and a standard deviation of about 20 percent. This leads to the normal curves given in Figure 2 as the approximate probability density functions of $R$ for the two investments.

FIGURE 2

COMPARISON OF THE APPROXIMATE PROBABILITY DENSITY FUNCTIONS OF $R$ FOR THE INVESTMENTS IN MODEL A AND IN MODEL B

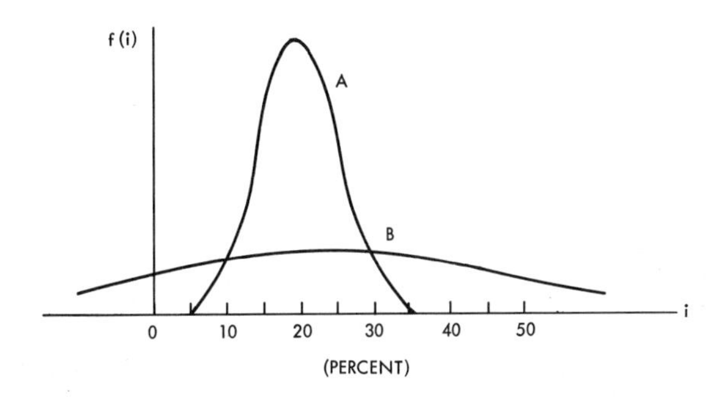


Figure 2, or a reasonable facsimile, could also have been obtained directly by determining the slope of the corresponding curves in Figure 1.

If desired, similar information regarding the incremental investment could have been derived from equations 10, 11, 12, and 13.

The impressive feature of this example is that the decision between the two investments is not an easy one. This is true despite the fact that there is a difference of about $167,000 in the expected present worth and of about 6.5 percent in the expected rate of return. The great difference in the risk involved compels management to examine carefully the financial position of the firm and evaluate the seriousness of the consequences should the riskier investment fail to achieve expectations. Then, considering the probabilities involved, management would, in effect, implicitly assign utilities to the possible outcomes of the investments and select the investment with the larger expected utility.

## *Conclusions*

The risk factor is often an important consideration in the evaluation of a proposed investment. Unfortunately, present procedures for considering risk have not been entirely satisfactory. They have tended either to provide insufficient information or to require the use of essentially unobtainable information. The procedure proposed here appears largely to avoid both of these pitfalls while simultaneously retaining some of the best features of these two types of existing procedures. It requires only that in addition to an estimate of the expected value of a prospective cash flow, the inexactitude of the estimate be described by an estimate of the standard deviation. On this basis, it then generates an explicit and complete description of the risk involved in terms of the probability distribution of the internal rate of return, present worth, or annual cost. This information then permits management to weigh precisely the possible consequences of the proposed investment and thereby make a sound decision regarding the proposal.

## References


1. BERNHARD, RICHARD H. "Discount Methods for Expenditure Evaluation—A Clarification of Their Assumptions," *Journal of Industrial Engineering,* January-February, 1962, pp. 19–27.
2. BIERMAN, HAROLD, JR., and SMIDT, SEYMOUR. *The Capital Budgeting Decision.* New York: Macmillan Co., 1960.
3. BOWKER, ALBERT H., and LIEBERMAN, GERALD J. *Engineering Statistics.* Englewood Cliffs, N.J.: Prentice-Hall, Inc., 1959.
4. DEGARMO, E. PAUL. *Engineering Economy.* 3d ed. New York: Macmillan Co., 1960.
5. ENGLISH, J. MORLEY. "New Approaches to Economic Comparison for Engineering Projects," *Journal of Industrial Engineering,* November-December, 1961, pp. 375–78.
6. GORDON, MYRON J., and SHAPIRO, ELI. "Capital Equipment Analysis: The Required Rate of Profit," *Management Science,* Vol. III (October, 1956), pp. 102–10.
7. GRANT, EUGENE L., and IRESON, W. GRANT. *Principles of Engineering Economy.* 4th ed. New York: Ronald Press Co., 1960.
8. GREEN, PAUL E. "The Derivation of Utility Functions in a Large Industrial Firm," paper given at the First Joint National Meeting of the Operations Research Society of America and the Institute of Management Sciences, 1961.
9. MARKOWITZ, HARRY M. *Portfolio Selection.* New York: John Wiley & Sons, Inc., 1959.
10. MODIGLIANI, FRANCO, and MILLER, MERTON H. "The Cost of Capital, Corporation Finance and the Theory of Investment," *American Economic Review,* Vol. XLVIII, (June, 1958).
11. MORRIS, WILLIAM T. *Engineering Economy.* Homewood, Ill.: Richard D. Irwin, Inc., 1960.
12. NASLUND, BERTIL, and WHINSTON, ANDREW. "A Model of Multi-period Investment under Uncertainty," *Management Science,* Vol. IIX (January, 1962), pp. 184–200.
13. SCHLAIFER, ROBERT. *Probability and Statistics for Business Decisions.* New York: McGraw-Hill Book Co., Inc., 1959.

*Chapter 21*

# *The Integration of Capital Budgeting and Stock Valuation**

By Eugene M. Lerner and Willard T. Carleton

IT IS WIDELY recognized that a corporation's cost of capital cannot be determined until an analysis is made of how the market values the firm's common stock [5, p. 423] [6, p. 143].[1] There is, however, no widely accepted theoretical apparatus linking the market valuation of common stock to a corporation's investment-opportunities schedule, dividend payout function, and capital structure.

It is the position of this paper that a fundamental reason for the current stalemate over the theoretical apparatus is the single-equation nature of recent capital-budgeting and security valuation models [3] [7] [11]. Since one equation can determine at most one unknown, manipulation of these models has, for the generation of results, necessitated a variety of ad hoc restrictions to reduce each equation to a relationship between *two* variables only—as, for example, between share price and capital structure.[2] Two consequences emerge: (1) Since there is no consensus, such restrictions tend to be different. (2) More impor-

---

*Reprinted by permission from *American Economic Review*, Vol. LIV (September, 1964), pp. 683–702.

The authors wish to express their appreciation to Arnold Sametz and the members of the Investments Workshop for many helpful comments and criticisms; and to Howard Hendrickson, who assisted in the design and execution of the figures.

[1]Numbers in brackets refer to publications listed at the end of this paper (p. 346).

[2]For example, see Lintner [7, pp. 250–51]. In order to generate the conclusion that investors will be indifferent to substitutions between elements in a corporation's time vector of dividends, it is necessary for Lintner to assume (among other things) given time vectors of earnings, capital budgets, and market discount rates.

tantly, such variables as share price, capital budget, dividend payout, and capital structure are in the real world jointly determined, and the suppression of this dependency unnecessarily limits the relevance of any theoretical results. That is, whether the problem is simply simultaneous determination of all the variables or maximization of one (e.g., share price) subject to one or more constraints, enumeration of the relevant relationships contained in the budgeting-valuation nexus must be explicit.

In this paper, we depart from the single-equation convention and explicitly introduce two equations: an investment-opportunities (or capital-budgeting) schedule and a stock valuation equation. Under reasonable assumptions, these two equations are shown to determine simultaneously a corporation's internal rate of return, the percentage of earnings that it retains and the percentage that it distributes in dividends, and the price of its common stock. Furthermore, if the stock valuation equation is treated as the corporation's objective function and the capital-budgeting equation as an internal constraint, we show that a unique maximum price can be found as a tangency solution.

The article falls into three major parts. Section I analyzes and modifies in two respects the stock valuation model made popular by Myron J. Gordon in his *The Investment, Financing, and Valuation of the Corporation* [3]. The Gordon model treats the price of a corporation's common stock as the present value of the expected future dividends, discounted at some given rate, $k$. Under the condition that the firm engages in no outside financing, retained earnings are reinvested by definition, so that a fixed relationship between dividend payout and capital budget emerges. A major difficulty of this model is that it generates unacceptable results when it is used as the sole determinant of the retention (hence payout) rate which maximizes the value of the common stock. For example, the conclusion is reached that the corporation should retain and reinvest until the point at which the market value of stock equals book, or asset, value. The reason for anomalies of this sort is shown to be the implicit suppression of the mutual interaction within the firm of rate of return and size of capital budget. When a price map is drawn illustrating the substitutability of rate of return and dividend payout for shareholders at a given discount rate, the need for further specification of shareholder and corporation behavior becomes manifest. However, it is shown that even when $k$ is treated as an increasing linear function of expected growth (in recognition of the growth stock paradox) and the corporation's capital structure is formally introduced into the price model, the problem of what capital budget maximizes share price remains indeterminate.

Section II introduces an investment-opportunities schedule, positing the traditional inverse relationship between capital budget size and internal rate of return. It then becomes obvious that there are two sets of rate-of-return and retention rate expectations, one for the corporation and one for the shareholders. Under the necessary equilibrium condition that these two sets of expectations be equal, share price, dividend payout rate (and by construction, retention rate and capital budget), and internal rate of return are simultaneously determined. Finally, we demonstrate that there is a unique maximum share price attainable at some point along the corporation's investment-opportunities schedule. The more important implications of this tangency solution are: (1) A firm should not, in general, invest until internal rate of return equals the market discount rate; (2) most capital-budgeting "rules of thumb" are likely to be suboptimal; and (3) the consequences of changing the dividend payout rate depend upon whether the firm is operating above or below the point of tangency.

Finally, in Section III the obtained results are evaluated in an equilibrium economics context, subject to amendment in a dynamic framework. In particular, the implied prescription that the corporation adopt shareholders' risk preferences is not unreasonable when the problem of disappointed expectations is suppressed (as is necessary in comparative statics). Such a decision rule might need to be modified for a dynamic world. Also, the introduction of capital structure as a variable to be determined is shown to require another equation, perhaps linking capital financing to dividend payout. The most reasonable context in which to do this may turn out to be an adjustment model in which expectations are generated over time.

## I. The Stock Valuation Equation

### *The Gordon Model*

The basic ingredients of any stock valuation formula include the particular stream of returns which is to be capitalized plus any time-dependent characteristics, such as a growth rate, that the stream possesses; the capitalization period (or investor time horizon); and the discount rate, or function. Academic debate over the proper definition of these ingredients has been exhaustive in recent years without being conclusive. The unfortunate fact is that normative results for corporate management depend rather strongly upon what definitions are adopted —whether the investor horizon is short-run or essentially infinite, for example. Rather than entering this terminological debate, we simply choose as a point of departure Myron Gordon's stock valuation model [3, chap. iv], which is a particularly well-developed and internally consistent approach to the valuation problem. Gordon defines investors' returns to be a growing stream of dividends, the market horizon as infinite, and the discount rate as a function, variously specified. He assumes no outside financing in his basic model, so that the establishment of a dividend payout automatically determines the capital budget as retained earnings.

Proceeding formally, assume that the corporation's dividends are expected to grow at a rate proportional to their present level:

$$\frac{dD}{dt} = gD \tag{1.1}$$

and that a time 0 the dividend payment is $D_0$. (Because new equity financing is excluded, $D$ in the subsequent development can be thought of in terms of either a per share or a firm basis.)

Assume further that the value of a dividend stream decays at a rate proportional to its existing value:

$$\frac{dV}{dt} = -kV \tag{1.2}$$

and that at time 0 the value of the stream is $V_0 = 1$; $k$ can be taken as the market rate of discount.

The solutions of these two differential equations are:

$$D_t = D_0 e^{gt} \tag{1.1$'$}$$

$$V_t = V_0 e^{-kt} \tag{1.2$'$}$$

Since the price of a share is equal to the present value of the stream of all future dividends, equations 1.1′ and 1.2′ can be combined as follows:

$$P_0 = \int_0^\infty D_0 e^{gt} e^{-kt} dt \tag{1.3}$$

where $t = 0$ is now the date of valuation. A necessary condition for performing the integration is that $k>g$, for if $k \leq g$, the value of the expression equals infinity, the well-known problem of growth stock valuation [2].

Solving equation 1.3 yields:

$$P_0 = \frac{D_0}{k - g} \tag{1.4}$$

The assumption that dividends grow at a constant rate is itself based on two assumed expectations: first, that the corporation is expected to earn a constant rate of return, $r$, on assets; and second, that the corporation is expected to retain a constant percentage, $b$, of its income.

With the assumption that there is no debt in the capital structure of the corporation and that all growth of future dividends must come via retained earnings, equation 1.4 can then be rewritten in the form that Gordon gave it:

$$P_0 = \frac{(1 - b)\ Y_0}{k - rb} \tag{1.4'}$$

where $Y$ stands for income and $g = rb$, or as:[3]

$$P_0 = \frac{(1 - b)rA_0}{k - rb} \tag{1.4''}$$

where $A_0$ stands for total assets.

## *The "Optimum" Retention Rate*

The model described in equations 1.4 and 1.4′ suggested ways in which the question of the optimum dividend rate (or optimum retention rate) could be approached. Assume $r$ is fixed, for clearly it is not independent of $b$. If the partial derivative of $P$ with respect to $b$ is set at zero, the price of the stock will be at a maximum if the second derivative is negative at this value. Taking the first partial derivative, it can be seen that $\delta P/\delta b = 0$ when $r$, the internal rate of return on assets, equals $k$, the market rate of discount. Upon taking the second derivative, however it is seen that $P/\delta b>0$ only where $r>k$, and $\delta B/\delta b<0$ only where $r<k$. Stated differently, where the first-order condition, $\delta P/\delta b = 0$, is satisfied, the second-order condition cannot be because the second and higher derivatives disappear. Therefore the conclusion is reached that if $r$ is greater (less) than $k$, the price of the stock rises (falls) with a rise in retained earnings.[4]

---

[3]There is an implicit assumption that $g \geq 0$ and hence $rb \geq 0$. Negative values of $g$, the expected rate of growth of dividends, are possible, but they contradict the assumption either of a constant rate of growth or of no outside financing. For example, consider a $g<0$. This means that $r<0$, since $0 \leq b < 1$. However, $r<0$ implies a constant rate of deficit. $(1 - b)$ times a deficit is a negative expected dividend, or forced capital subscription, which contradicts the outside financing assumption. To allow outside financing only of this sort does not enhance the realism of the model. A heuristic resolution of the problem might be that the infinite horizon model is an approximation, that the expectation of constant $r$ and $b$ is approximate, and that temporary negative $r$ (and therefore $g$) for a going concern is possible.

[4]Gordon proceeded in this manner and went on to state: "A moment's reflection on the conclusion just reached with respect to the variation in share price with $b$ reveals that a corporation should retain all of its income or liquidate depending on whether $r \lesseqgtr k$" [3, p. 48]. He then speculated that this curious result probably stemmed from the assumption of independence of $r$ and $b$; but with only one equation, he was unable to follow the implications of this insight.

Further implications can be derived from this unsuccessful attempt to find the optimum retention rate. Substituting $k$ for $r$,[5] its value when $\delta P/\delta b = 0$, in the denominator of equation 1.4′ yields:

$$P = \frac{(1-b)\,Y}{k - kb} = \frac{Y}{k} \tag{1.5}$$

Thus, in a single-equation valuation model such as 1.4″, the capitalized value of a corporation's dividend stream equals the capitalized value of its earnings stream if the corporation continues to invest until the rate of return on assets equals the market rate of discount.

This should not be considered a surprising result, considering the fixed definitional relationship between earnings and dividends. That an earnings model and a dividend model may lead to identical valuation of share prices has been demonstrated by Gordon [3, chap. v], Lintner [7, p. 256], and Miller and Modigliani [5][6] under various conditions and with different purposes in mind. What is significant is that $P$ in equation 1.5 does not depend upon $b$, nor in fact does it depend upon $r$ or $k$. If $r$ is substituted for $k$ in equation 1.4″, then at the point where $\delta P/\delta b = 0$:

$$P = \frac{(1-b)rA_0}{r - rb} = A_0 \tag{1.5′}$$

or the price of the stock equals the book value of the corporation (since the assumption of no debt was made). With $r$ held constant and greater than $k$, the price of the stock commands a premium over book value and rises as $b$ increases. If $k$ is greater than a constant $r$, the price of the stock is less than book value and falls with a rise in $b$. While intuitively reasonable, the applicability of these results is limited because the manner in which they could be reached is unspecified. That is, if the retention rate is viewed as the firm's decision variable, it is reasonable to suppose that the value of the firm's stock would rise with an increase in its retention rate if internal opportunities remain greater than the shareholders' capitalization rate. On the other hand, the attempt of corporate management to proceed in its retention policy to the point where $r = k$ yields the unacceptable conclusion of equation 1.5′. The difficulty lies in not spelling out how $r$ and $k$ might, in fact, change with changes in $b$. Plainly, shareholders' discount rate and the rate of return on assets are not invariant with respect to changes in dividends and

---

[5] Having developed present-value valuation, subscripts from this point on refer to different values rather than different time periods.

[6] This study goes on to show that the valuation of shares will be identical not only under a dividend model and an earnings model, but also under a discounted cash flow approach and the current earnings plus future investment-opportunities approach.

reinvestment of earnings. Instead of holding $r$ and $k$ fixed, and then tracing the effects of varying $b$ on $P$, a more useful way of working with equation 1.4″ may be to allow all four variables to change. As a first step, we continue to hold $k$ constant and map the $r$, $b$, and $P$ relationship.

If 1.4″ is written as:

$$r = \frac{Pk}{b(P - A) + A} \qquad (1.4''')$$

isoprice lines can be traced on a graph whose axes are $r$ and $b$.

$P_2$ is higher than $P_1$, and both are greater than the corporation's book value. $P_{-1}$ is higher than $P_{-2}$, and both are less than book value. Figure 1 illustrates that for a given $r$, say $r_0 > k$, the price of the stock rises as $b$ increases from $b_1$ to $b_2$. If $r_0$ were less than $k$, the price would fall with increases in $b$. Moreover, for a given $b$, the price of the stock rises as $r$ increases.

FIGURE 1

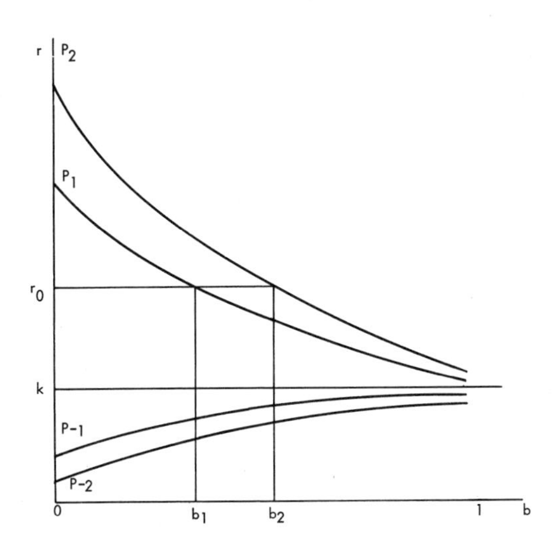


Figure 1 highlights the fact that all the isoprice lines approach $k$ as $b$ approaches one.[7] It therefore follows that a given absolute change in $r$ will lead to a larger price change, the higher the level of $b$. This can be seen analytically by considering $\delta P/\delta r = (1 - b)kA/(k - rb)^2$ in the limiting cases where $b = 0$ and $b$ is close to one. Phrased differently, stocks that have a high retention rate (low dividend payout rate) will

[7] Since $k > rb$ in general, but for $P > A$, $k < r$, it is clear that $b$ can only approach one for $k < r$. The integrability constraint would be violated if this were not the case.

fluctuate more in price for given changes in $r$ than securities with a low retention rate. A similar conclusion was reached by Malkiel [8].

A shift in $k$, the market rate of discount, will change the location of the isoprice lines. For example, if $k$ should fall as a result of a general decline in interest rates, and if $r$ and $b$ remain constant, some isoprice lines that formerly had positive slopes will now acquire negative slopes. Thus, if $k$ changes, the shares of a corporation may sell at a premium over book value (or any other specified price) at one time and at a discount from this price at another, even though the corporation continues to earn the same internal rate of return and follows the same dividend policy. More importantly, a corporation whose present price line shifted from negative to positive slope, say, would find that the consequence of an increase in the retention rate was a fall in share price, whereas formerly a rise would have resulted.

The difficulty with Figure 1 and its supporting equation as they now stand is that no provision is made for $k$ to vary and no bounds are placed on the interaction of $r$ and $b$ within the firm; hence, $P$ is indeterminate. Such also is the type of problem faced in the capital-budgeting decision. In that context, $P$ is usually assumed to be given, and the question is asked: What rate of return must be earned by the corporation if $P$ is to remain at its assumed level? The more relevant question centers on the behavior of $P$ under various combinations of $r$ and $b$[8] and, more specifically, on the capital budget that will make $P$ a maximum. Without internal constraints on the firm or specification of how $k$ depends on $r$ and $b$, the problem cannot be resolved. Our next step is to specify $k$.

## *Specifying k*

Except for the constraint that $k$, the rate of discount, be greater than $rb$, the rate of growth of dividends, $k$ has not been specified. If for no other reason than to avoid the growth stock paradox, $k$ should be related to the firm's expected growth. More importantly from a practical point of view, as indicated above, the suggestion that $k$ is a constant rather than a function leads to unacceptable capital-budgeting decision results.

As a manageable form for such a function, we propose:

$$k = \alpha + \psi rb \tag{1.6}$$

[8]One method of handling this problem was suggested by Cheng and Shelton [1].

where $\alpha$ is the market interest rate on growthless shares[9] and $\psi$ is a risk class specification.[10] $\psi$ is a constant which can assume values between zero and one.[11]

At this stage of the analysis, there is some parallel between Modigliani and Miller's risk class concept and our own. That is, a $\psi$ class would be made up of corporations whose growth rates ($rb$'s) would be discounted in like fashion because in other respects they were similar. Since $\psi$ has not yet been specified (except by its range of possible values), and since debt has not yet been introduced into the capital structure of the firm, principal sources of expected instability in the firm may include previous instability of growth due to industry competition, demand elasticity, vulnerability to technological change, and the like. The greater the degree to which these forces were operative in the past, the more likely, ceteris paribus, they are to be operative in the future. Put slightly differently, when such forces have been significant, there is a greater presumption that they will continue to be so. For example, a high expected growth rate for a firm is more likely to attract competition if barriers to entry have been low, and this possibility creates uncertainty with respect to the mean-value expectation of growth. Since Modigliani and Miller were interested primarily in the effect of leverage on the discount rate, they removed dividend payout from center stage by assuming it already decided in the stockholders' best interests [11, p. 266]. They then defined the discount rate as a linear function of leverage alone, suppressing the growth rate–discount relationship. We prefer to start at a more fundamental level and define $k$ as a linear function of growth even before introducing the leverage problem. At one extreme a $\psi$ value of zero implies the uniform rate of discount we have already discussed. If $\psi = 1$, the rate of discount rises one for one with the expected rate of growth, and stockholders will pay no more for the high-growth company than for the zero-growth firm. As an example of the latter possibility, if the only source of growth was expected inflation of dividend dollars and shareholders insisted on evaluating their prospects in real terms, $\psi$ would equal one.

---

[9]Under the assumption of an infinite stream of returns, yield to maturity equals current yield, a characteristic, for example, of consols. Because the dividend stream in this valuation model is discounted over an infinite horizon, $\alpha$, the market interest rate, is equivalent to a consol yield and might be approximated by the current yield on a growthless long-term security.

[10]Other forms for a risk discount function are of course possible.

[11]This condition gives the limits of $\psi$ when $\alpha = 0$. Since in the real world $\alpha > 0$, equation 1.3 could still be integrated for some $\psi < 0$. Of course, if $\psi < 0$, this would imply that future dividends are worth more than current dividends. Furthermore, although $rb < 0$ gives rise to the logical problems of negative growth, as discussed in n. 3, it is clear that with $0 \leq \psi \leq 1$, integrability conditions are not violated: $k - rb > 0$.

Substituting equation 1.6 into 1.4″ yields:

$$P = \frac{(1 - b)rA}{\alpha + \psi rb - rb} \tag{1.7}$$

The first partial derivative of $P$ with respect to $b$ equals zero when $r = \alpha/(1 - \psi)$, and once again the second derivative will be positive or negative depending upon whether $r(1 - \psi) \gtrless \alpha$.[12] A graph of this expression would be similar to that of Figure 1 above, with the difference that $k$ would be replaced by $\alpha/(1 - \psi)$. Similarly, substituting the value $\alpha$ for $r\ (1 - \psi)$ in equation 1.7 yields:

$$P = \frac{rA}{\alpha} \tag{1.8}$$

Once again, with $r$ a fixed number, there is a point $(\delta P/\delta b = 0)$ at which $P$ is independent of $b$, or the dividend model produces the same price as an earnings model. More importantly, at this point the risk class falls out. This result makes intuitive good sense and justifies the form given the discount function, for if $r$ is fixed and $b$ has been set by differentiation at the point at which it does not influence share price, then growth $(rb)$ does not affect capitalization.

Equation 1.8 can also be rewritten as:

$$r = \frac{\alpha P}{A} \tag{1.8′}$$

In this form the equation focuses attention on the rate of return that a corporation must earn on its assets if its shares are to maintain their existing price. Equation 1.8′ also serves to put to rest the alleged "IBM paradox": Should not a corporation that sells at fifty times earnings invest in any asset yielding over 2 percent? If $\alpha$, the market rate of interest on securities with no growth, equals 4 percent, if the security sells at five times its book value, and if the retention rate is that which makes $\delta P/\delta b = 0$, then the required rate of return necessary to keep the price of the stock at its present level is 20 percent, not any value greater than 2 percent. As indicated earlier, however, equation 1.8′ does not provide an answer to what rate must be earned to maximize $P$, let alone to what happens to $r$ when $b$ is determined.

A further interesting result can be obtained from equation 1.8′. When the firm's capital budget is set at $\delta P/\delta b = 0$, then $\alpha = r(1 - \psi)$, or:

$$\psi = 1 - \frac{\alpha}{r} = 1 - \frac{\alpha A}{Y} \tag{1.9}$$

[12]Again, under the assumption that $dr/db = 0$, or that $r$ is fixed.

Since, under the assumption of an infinite shareholder time horizon, $a$ can be replaced by the current earnings yield, the $\psi$ class of a security when $\delta P/\delta b = 0$ will be given by:

$$\psi = \frac{P - A}{P} \tag{1.10}$$

Note that $\psi = 0$ when the price of the stock equals its book value.[13] As the price rises from book value, $\psi$ increases. Equation 1.10, or some variant, has a long history of use among practitioners of security analysis and portfolio management. In the language of "The Street," risk rises when the security commands a substantial premium over book value. Indeed, one portfolio manager has gone so far as to state that when securities sell for more than six times book value (a $\psi$ class of 0.83 under our assumptions), they no longer belong in a prudent man's portfolio [4].

## *Introduction of Debt into the Capital Structure*

Debt can be formally introduced into the single-equation valuation model as follows:

Let the change in assets in a continuous model be represented by the change in equity plus the change in liabilities:

$$dA = dE + dL \tag{1.11}$$

The change in equity equals retained earnings:

$$dE = Ar_L b \tag{1.12}$$

where $r_L$ is now the levered internal rate of return, or rate of return on assets less interest expenses imposed by the existence of debt. Let the change in debt be represented by $dL = L\mu$ where $\mu$ is some constant. If the ratio of debt to equity is assumed to remain constant,[14] then:

$$\frac{dE}{dL} = \frac{E}{L} = \frac{Ar_L b}{L\mu}$$

Therefore:

$$\mu = \frac{Ar_L b}{E}$$

[13] Since $0 \leq \psi \leq 1$, $P \geq A$, which might seem to be an unnecessarily strong result. On the other hand, if $P < A$ *and* the firm is doing the best it can, then it probably should liquidate. This conclusion is equivalent to Gordon's and follows from essentially the same situation as his case of $r < k$.

[14] For an empirical justification of this assumption, see Lindsay and Sametz [6, chaps. xviii and xix], and Miller [9].

If $z = L/A$:

$$\mu = \frac{Ar_L b}{A - L} = \frac{Ar_L b}{A - A_z} = \frac{r_L b}{1 - z} \tag{1.13}$$

Substituting 1.12 and 1.13 into 1.11:

$$dA = Ar_L b + \frac{L(r_L b)}{(1 - z)}$$

$$= r_L b\left[A + \frac{Az}{1 - z}\right] = \frac{Ar_L b}{1 - z}$$

or

$$\frac{dA}{A} = \frac{r_L b}{1 - z} \tag{1.14}$$

The percentage change in assets is precisely the term we have called $g$ in equation 1.4, by virtue of equation 1.1′ and the assumption that $D = (1 - b)rA$. Substitution of equation 1.14 into 1.4 yields a valuation model for a corporation with a fixed percentage of debt in its capital structure ($k$, however, is unspecified at this point):

$$P = \frac{(1 - b)r_L A}{k - \dfrac{(r_L b)}{(1 - z)}} \tag{1.15}$$

Equation 1.15 suggests the following question: What is the optimum ratio of debt to assets for a corporation, abstracting from taxes? The first derivative of $P$ with respect to $z$ shows that so long as $k(1 - z) > r_L b$, the price of the security will rise with a rise in the ratio of debt to total assets, and as $k(1 - z)$ approaches $r_L b$, the change in price associated with a change in debt approaches infinity. The assumption that $k$ is independent of $z$, however, is not very useful. Indeed, one of the classic controversies in finance centers on the behavior of $k$ over various ranges of $z$. Modigliani and Miller's famous proposition—in terms of equation 1.15—is, of course, that $k$ rises linearly with $z$ so that the average yield of the sum of debt plus equity remains constant. The more conventional position is that $k$ does not change for low levels of $z$; however, as $z$ continues to rise, $k$ rises faster than $r_L b/(1 - z)$. Under this conventional view the price of a stock, therefore, first rises and then falls as progressively larger amounts of debt are introduced into the capital structure.

An alternative behavioral assumption allows $k$ to change with changes in the debt-asset ratio. Such a specification may be given by:

$$k = \alpha + \psi r_L b + \phi z \tag{1.16}$$

where $\phi$ is same constant greater than zero. Substituting equation 1.16 into 1.15 gives a stock valuation model that incorporates debt:

$$P = \frac{(1 - b)r_L A}{\alpha + \psi r_L b + \phi z - \dfrac{(r_L b)}{(1 - z)}} \tag{1.17}$$

For corporations that have no debt, it will be recalled that $\delta P/\delta b = 0$ when $r = \alpha/(1 - \psi)$, where the absence of a subscript means that $r$ is unlevered. The change in $P$ with respect to a change in $b$ for corporations with debt equals zero when:

$$r_L = \frac{(1 - z)\ (\alpha + \phi z)}{1 - \psi + \psi z} \tag{1.18}$$

If $z = 0$, equation 1.18 is identical to the case of a corporation with no debt; $r_L$ is the rate of return after interest that a corporation must earn on assets if the price of the stock is to remain constant with respect to a change in retention rates.

The treatment of debt, however, suffers from being essentially arbitrary. Moreover, the implication of debt in the capital structure has not been carried through to the stream of dividends. Even if these difficulties are accounted for, the retention rate which maximizes $P$ is indeterminate.

## II. A General Model

In Section I, we developed a stock valuation model that specified $k$ and incorporated debt as part of the capital structure. While useful insights are obtained from this model, its usefulness is limited. The principal kinds of questions that can be answered within the model's framework are of the sort: Given a $P$ and a $z$, what is the $b$ which will just maintain the present $P$? Of greater interest is a model which allows more logical "degrees of freedom." In this section, we develop a set of two equations in $r$ and $P$, one of the stock valuation equation, the other an investment-opportunities schedule. Simultaneous solution of these for some $b$ yields $r$ and $P$.

### *The LC Schedule*

The investment-opportunities schedule facing a corporation at a point in time can, with reliance upon traditional economic thinking on the subject, be taken as a function linking inversely the expected rate of return on total assets and size of capital budget.[15]

The development of a stock valuation model invoked shareholders' expectations of $r$ and $b$; the present section deals with management's (expected) constraints on $r$ and $b$. Apart from equilibrium requirements, and undoubtedly in the everyday world, the possibility exists that shareholder and management point estimates of $r$ and $b$ will diverge. It therefore becomes useful to introduce new notation: $r_I$ and $b_I$ to stand for investor (shareholder) expectations of rate of return and retention rate, and $r_C$ and $b_C$ to be expectations of the same variables held by the corporation (management).

With this convention, and recalling that the capital budget is defined identically by the corporation's earnings retention rate,[16] a reasonable form for the investment-opportunity schedule would be:

$$LC(r_C, b_C) = \gamma_0 \geq \frac{r_C}{1 + \gamma_1 b_C} \tag{2.1}$$

where $\gamma_0(\geq 0)$ is the average rate of return expected when retained earnings are zero, and $\gamma_1(<0)$ reflects the declining return associated with movement down an opportunities schedule as $b$ increases. To show the nature of the functional relationship of $r_C$ and $b_C$, inequality 2.1 may be written as:

$$r_C \leq \gamma_0 + \gamma_0 \gamma_1 b_C \tag{2.2}$$

The shaded area in Figure 2 is feasible; for the efficient firm, 2.2 may be written as an equality:

$$r_C = \gamma_0 + \gamma_0 \gamma_1 b_C \tag{2.3}$$

It should be emphasized that this function is a set of equilibrium points, not a demand curve. For the corporation with no debt, no external financing, and no liquidating dividends, the domain of $LC$ is from $b = 0$ to $b = 1$. The choice of $b_C$ (and hence of $r_C$) remains indeterminate for the corporation until it is known which retention rate will in fact maximize share price.

---

[15]The more common statement links the return on the marginal investment to the marginal investment. It is clear that our formulation is consistent, for if $r$, which is the average return on total assets, declines, then so does $r'$, the marginal return. The reason for our formulation rests on the fact that (from the stock valuation equation) $r$ rather than $r'$ is the focus of capital budget decisions designed to maximize share price.

[16]Depreciation is not considered a source of funds because we are interested only in net investment.

FIGURE 2

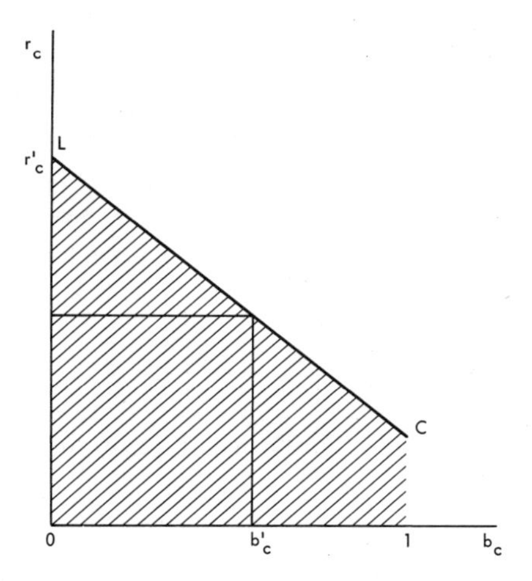


## *The Complete Model*

Recall Figure 1, in which, from equation 1.4″, *r* was expressed as a unique function of *b*, given *P* and *k*. In terms of this section:

$$P = \frac{(1 - b_I)r_I A}{k - r_I b_I} \tag{1.4''}$$

or

$$r_I = \frac{Pk}{b_I(P - A) + A} = \frac{P\alpha}{b_I[P(1 - \psi) - A] + A} \tag{1.4'''}$$

As with equation 2.3, it is clear that the valuation model is incomplete. To state the matter differently, we can fix *P* and $b_I$ and find $r_I$, but how do we arrive at a *P*, much less at a maximum *P*?

The answer lies in the simultaneous solution of equations 2.3 and 1.7. This can most easily be seen by tracing the steps from choice of *b* (the corporation's decision variable) to final determination of *P*. As a first step, it is necessary to impose the equilibrium conditions that:

$$r_C = r_I \tag{2.4}$$

$$b_C = b_I \tag{2.5}$$

in order that there be no divergence in expectations. That is, shareholders accept the firm's retention rate decision and agree with its assessment of the consequences on rate of return (whether or not they like it).

Then it can be seen that with exogenous *A*, $\alpha$, and $\psi$, equation 1.7 expresses share price as a function of *r* and *b* and that equation 2.3 is also a function in the same two variables. Once the firm chooses its retention rate, *b*, then *r* is determined from the latter function. However, substitution of the values for these variables in the stock valuation equation 1.7 produces a unique share price.

The problem of suboptimum price arises in an equilibrium context because although shareholders may agree with the corporation's assessment of its retention policy, they would be better off with some other policy that produced some other return, which might be either higher or lower. Solution of maximum price is somewhat more easily described with equations 1.4‴ and 2.3. The maximum price then is given by the familiar tangency condition:

$$\left(\frac{\delta r}{\delta b}\right)_{eq.\ 1.4'''} = \left(\frac{\delta r}{\delta b}\right)_{eq.\ 2.3} \tag{2.6}$$

Under the conditions assumed, only one $P$, a unique maximum, satisfies the condition that these two slopes be equal:

$$\left(\frac{\delta r}{\delta b}\right)_{eq.\ 2.3} = \gamma_0\gamma_1 < 0$$

and

$$\left(\frac{\delta r}{\delta b}\right)_{eq.\ 1.4'''} < 0 \quad \text{for } P(1 - \psi) > A$$

Furthermore, because the second partial derivative of $r$ with respect to $b$ is zero for the right-hand side and positive for the left-hand side of 2.6, for $P(1 - \psi) > A$,[17] the appropriate convexity of the isoprice lines within the allowable range of the $rb$ plane is satisfied.[18] Figure 3 de-

[17]It may be asked why this statement of a general model was not handled by the more familiar technique of Lagrange multipliers: Maximize equation 1.4 subject to equation 2.1. While such a method yields the same results plus valid economic insights into the nature of the valuation *cum* capital budget problem, a comment is in order. In general $b_c \neq b_i$ and $r_c \neq r_i$. Satisfaction of conditions 2.4 and 2.5 is necessary to secure simultaneous firm and market equilibrium *at any price*. Although the consequences of not meeting these conditions are best dealt with in dynamic models, we prefer not to suppress them this early in the game.

[18]We have drawn the $LC$ function *above* $\alpha/(1 - \psi)$, indicating the firm has opportunity for an average internal return at least equal to the absolute required yield in the market adjusted for risk. For the firm whose $LC$ function is below $\alpha/(1 - \psi)$, the isoprice lines are concave downward, indicating that the best the firm can do is distribute all earnings; retaining and reinvesting serves to lower $P$. As in Gordon's model, however, $b$ can only approach one. For $r > \alpha/(1 - \psi)$, if $b = 1$ the integrability constraint, $r < \alpha/b(1 - \psi)$, is violated. The economic sense of this case—where the tangency is at or beyond the point where $b = 1$—is that a switch to external financing is called for. For $r < \alpha/(1 - \psi)$, any $b > 0$ lowers $P$. Hence the case of $b = 1$ is not meaningful. Satisfaction of the second-order condition is guaranteed by the choice of a downward-sloping linear $LC$ function. It therefore may be argued that our specification of the investment-opportunities schedule is fortuitous. On the other hand, other specifications would produce the same results, and the one chosen is consistent with economic tradition. It is interesting to note that the condition $P(1 - \psi > A$ which is necessary for

scribes the solution of the stock maximization problem, where $b'$ is the solution value of the corporation's decision variable.

The firm faces only one investment-opportunities schedule, downward-sloping, at a point in time, but an entire family of share prices. Without condition 2.6 an infinite number of prices are possible, since the *LC* function intersects infinitely many isoprice lines. Condition 2.6 allows us to find a maximum price, i.e., where the slope of the *LC* function equals the slope of an isoprice line.

FIGURE 3

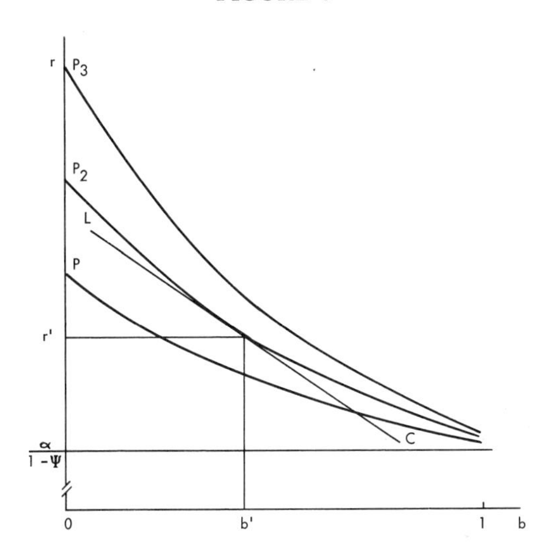


Maximizing profits, that is, carrying on investment projects until $r = \alpha/(1 - \psi)$, is an inadequate criterion for either capital budgeting or dividend payout policy. In the case of Figure 3, investment to the point where $r = \alpha/(1 - \psi)$ (or equivalently until $r = k$) would clearly not be optimal, for once the point of tangency with an isoprice line is passed, movement down the *LC* function toward $b = 1$ produces lower and lower share prices as (implicitly) less profitable projects are undertaken. Such a course would only be another example of the alleged IBM paradox: Investment to the point where $r = \alpha/(1 - \psi)$ or $(r = k)$ represents the undertaking of projects whose returns are not regarded by the market as valuable as using the funds to pay greater dividends.

This conclusion that firms should not in general invest until

negative first derivative and positive second derivative is at variance with the results of equation 1.9 and 1.10 above, in which $P(1 - \psi) = A$ for $\delta P/\delta b = 0$. The reason for this difference is, of course, that the earlier result ignored the $r$, $b$ relationship by considering $r$ to be fixed.

$r = \alpha/(1 - \psi)$ is admittedly at variance with traditional statements on the subject. Such statements have assumed either a single equation which took $P$ as given or an infinitely elastic investment-opportunities schedule. Positing a downward-sloping investment-opportunities schedule and a separate valuation equation leads to the results described above.

Figure 3 and the supporting equations also illustrate the fallacy of the proposition that a firm should retain all earnings or distribute all earnings depending upon whether $r \gtrless \alpha/1 - \psi$. The idea that such a policy could be relevant arises only because the requirements of internal (rate-of-return) and external (share price) equilibrium are not dealt with simultaneously. For the growing firm ($P>A$), equilibrium at a maximum $P$ is obtained only with an $r>\alpha/(1 - \psi)$ (i.e., $r>k$), which could require a $b$ anywhere between zero and one. As discussed in footnote 18, for $r<\alpha/(1 - \psi)$, the maximum obtainable $P$ is at $b = 0$.

This analysis also indicates the limitations of two other "rules of thumb" that allegedly characterize some corporate actions: adopting only those projects that yield more than a given rate of return and paying out a fixed percentage of earnings in dividends. If a corporation rejects all projects that yield less than an arbitrary set $r_0$, a dividend payment is dictated which is likely to be suboptimal with respect to share prices. Similarly, if a corporation adopts a fixed payout (retention) policy, the rate of return that will be earned may not maximize share prices.

A variety of possible situations are manageable within the comparative statics framework of this model. Consider first the effect of an upward shift in $LC$, the investment-opportunities schedule. The result is an increase in $b$ and $P$, and possibly in $r$.

Consider now the selection of a retention rate higher than $b'$. Equilibrium for shareholders is possible now only at a lower $P$ because the exploitation of too many internal opportunities lowers the average rate of return. Similarly, too low a retention rate will not maximize $P$ because dividends are not valued as highly as some margin of the remaining internal opportunities. Securing equilibrium $r$ and $b$ together with a maximum $P$ requires the firm to find a unique retention rate and its associated unique rate of return.

Consider finally the effect of a change in $k$. If, for example, $k$ should rise because of a change in the demand for and supply of loanable funds (equivalently, if $\alpha$ should rise), the isoprice lines will shift so that any given $r$ and $b$ will be associated with lower isoprice lines. With an unchanged $LC$ schedule, the equilibrium $P$ will fall. Moreover, the slopes of the isoprice lines will change for given rates of return. A new price line will now be tangent to the $LC$ function, and only by chance will the point of tangency be the same as where it was before the change in $k$ occurred. The implication of this is that no single capital budget will be optimal under diverse external market circumstances.

## III. Implications for Research

In the previous section, we defined a static equilibrium stock valuation–capital-budgeting model. We demonstrated how $r$ and $b$ must vary if the price of a share is to be optimized under the assumption of a given $k$ function and investment-opportunities schedule. We demonstrated the consequence of a shift in either the $LC$ (investment-opportunities) schedule, or $k$, as well as the consequences of a corporation's choosing an $r$ or $b$ other than the one dictated by the tangency of the $LC$ schedules and an isoprice line.

If the concept of the psi class is introduced into the $k$ function, the essential features of our equilibrium model are not altered. While the location and slope of the particular isoprice lines will change, the price of the security will still be optimized at the point of tangency between the $LC$ function and the isoprice line.

The model assumed no ranking problems for investment projects: Because $r$ is the average return per year on total assets expected by firm and investor and is expected to be a constant, the related problem of finding the marginal profitability of projects having different time streams of returns is suppressed.

Risk was not introduced into the $LC$ function because, arguing heuristically, the risk of the investor's discount function (psi class) is the relevant consideration for firms trying to maximize $P$. Put another way, if firm and investors have the same mean-value forecast of $r$, the risk factor which influences $P$ is that of the investors. Since the model presented in this paper is an equilibrium model, it cannot handle problems in disappointed expectations or consider measured variability as synonymous with risk. In an adjustment model, $\psi$ might best be specified as a function of observed variance around $r$.

The introduction of debt as a variable, however, is more complicated. In this paper, it was handled in an arbitrary manner and not treated as a corporate decision variable. If debt is treated as a variable, another equation, linking debt to the dividend payout, is required. It also may be useful to consider debt in a dynamic context. In an adjustment model, there will be an investor $b$-expectation function such as:

$$b_t^* = b(b_{t-1}, b_{t-2} \cdots).$$

A decline in $b^*$ will tend, ceteris paribus, to lower $P$. The question then arises: Given an investment-opportunities schedule with tangency position at $b > b^*$, should the corporation borrow or reduce dividend payout? Quite possibly the former. Put another way, if investors do not discount increases in leverage too heavily (i.e., if $\phi$ in equation 1.17 is not too large) and the opportunities schedule dictates asset growth, then maximum P suggests both borrowing and paying a $(1 - b^*)$ dividend rate.

## References

1. CHENG, P. L., and SHELTON, J. P. "A Contribution to the Theory of Capital Budgeting—The Multi-investment Case," *Journal of Finance,* Vol. XVIII (December, 1963), pp. 622–37.
2. DURAND, DAVID. "Growth Stocks and the Petersburg Paradox," *Journal of Finance,* Vol. XII (September, 1957), pp. 348–63.
3. GORDON, MYRON J. *The Investment, Financing, and Valuation of the Corporation.* Homewood, Ill.: Richard D. Irwin, Inc., 1962.
4. GUTMAN, W. "Book Value–Market Value Patterns," in LERNER, EUGENE M. (ed.). *Readings in Financial Analysis and Investment Management.* Homewood, Ill.: Richard D. Irwin, Inc., 1963.
5. HUNT, PEARSON; WILLIAMS, CHARLES M.; and DONALDSON, GORDON. *Basic Business Finance,* Rev. ed. Homewood, Ill.: Richard D. Irwin, Inc., 1961.
6. LINDSAY, R., and SAMETZ, A. W. *Financial Management: An Analytical Approach.* Homewood, Ill.: Richard D. Irwin, Inc., 1963.
7. LINTNER, JOHN. "Dividends, Earnings, Leverage, Stock Prices and the Supply of Capital to Corporations," *Review of Economics and Statistics,* Vol. XLIV (August, 1962), pp. 243–69.
8. MALKIEL, B. G. "Equity Yields and the Structure of Share Prices," *American Economic Review,* Vol. LIII (December, 1963), pp. 1004–32.
9. MILLER, MERTON H. "The Corporation Income Tax and Corporate Financial Policy," in COMMISSION ON MONEY AND CREDIT. *Stabilization Policies.* Englewood Cliffs, N.J.: Prentice-Hall, Inc., 1964.
10. MILLER, MERTON, H., and MODIGLIANI, FRANCO. "Dividend Policy, Growth, and the Valuation of Shares," *Journal of Business,* Vol. XXXIV (October, 1961), pp. 411–34.
11. MODIGLIANI, FRANCO, and MILLER, MERTON H. "The Cost of Capital, Corporation Finance and the Theory of Investment," *American Economic Review,* Vol. XLVIII (June, 1958), pp. 261–98.

*Chapter 22*

# *Repurchase Stock to Revitalize Equity**

By Charles D. Ellis

AN IMPORTANT new development is becoming increasingly apparent in the annual reports of a growing number of major industrial corporations: As preferred stock is being retired, as debt capital is being used less and less, and as retained earnings and cash flow rise rapidly, senior capital is being replaced with equity. The result is an unprecedented capital abundance. Is this a generous blessing or a curse in disguise? It all depends on your point of view.

While a plush financial condition allows management to do what it wants to without financial constraints and limitations, plentiful liquid assets and/or limited debt usage usually mean an unnecessarily heavy reliance on stockholders' equity. The evidence may be visible (large nonoperating assets) or invisible (unused debt capacity and redundant working capital). But in either case the result is a needless waste of the potential strength and vitality of the investors' capital. This waste creates a major new problem for the owners and their representatives, the board of directors.

Unless the trend toward increasing dependence on equity capital is reversed, the problem just described will become more acute. The present situation calls for new methods of approach and action; the trends toward the future demand a careful rethinking of that most basic of all corporate money matters, the capitalization of the enterprise.

In this article, I shall assume that the principal objective of capital strategy, particularly the determination of the size and mix of capital,

*Reprinted by permission from *Harvard Business Review,* Vol. XLIII (July-August, 1965), pp. 119–28.

is to maximize the owners' long-term interest as measured by wealth (market value of shares) and income (dividends per share). I shall argue that to accomplish this objective, financial planners should give careful consideration to a flexible and potent, but often overlooked, procedure: buying back common stock.

## Bolder Role Needed

If a corporation is unnecessarily dependent on equity capital, it can advance shareholders' interests significantly by what I like to call "reverse dilution," or the concentration of equity by replacing unnecessary common shares with limited obligation capital such as debt and preferred. This can be seen with simple arithmetic. Suppose a company with $20 million of earnings contracts the equity base from ten million shares to nine million. The effect is as shown in Table 1 assuming income taxes at 50 percent, market value at fifteen times earnings, and debt interest at 5 percent on the purchase cost of $30 million).

TABLE 1

| | *Before* | *After* |
|---|---|---|
| Earnings from operations | $40,000,000 | $40,000,000 |
| Interest on debt | 0 | $750,000 |
| Earnings before taxes | $40,000,000 | $39,250,000 |
| Net income | $20,000,000 | $19,625,000 |
| Outstanding common shares | 10,000,000 | 9,000,000 |
| Earnings per share | $2.00 | $2.18 |
| Dividends (60% of earnings) | $1.20 | $1.31 |
| Market value of 100 shares | $3,000 | $3,270 |

The arithmetic (where applicable) poses a most important but seldom specified challenge to the corporation with excess equity capital: Can the board of directors justify a capital policy which tends to insulate management from the rigors of financial discipline and obliges stockholders to leave unnecessary amounts of equity capital tied up in the enterprise?

Stated as a challenge to present policy, the problem of redundant equity is not limited to shareholders and the directors who represent them, but extends to the management of the corporate entity, which would suffer a reduction in total net assets and income if equity were reduced and debt increased to develop reverse dilution. In a rapidly growing company, reverse dilution can be accomplished over a period of years by increasing the proportionate use of senior capital. But in most cases, reverse dilution must be accomplished by both increasing the use of senior capital and actually reducing the amount of equity. The latter can only be done by repurchasing common shares.

## *Present Practice*

Although no large corporation has as yet fully accepted the broad role of share repurchasing to be proposed in this study, neither has the procedure been wholly ignored. More and more companies are utilizing the repurchase technique.[1] Usually, however, repurchase has been viewed only as a defensive device to avoid dilution. Various reasons are given to justify expenditures on a reacquisition of shares. For instance, it is argued that repurchase will:

1. Avoid diluting earnings per share when stock options are granted and exercised by management.
2. Supply shares for employee stock purchase programs.
3. Obtain shares for common stock bonuses to employees.
4. Provide shares for stock dividends.
5. Avoid diluting earnings per share when convertible securities are changed into common stock.
6. Increase the per share asset value of holding and investment companies when shares sell at a discount in the market.
7. Eliminate small odd-lot holdings, which are inordinately costly to service.
8. Compensate for the diution of earnings per share which is incurred in a merger through exchange of shares.
9. Provide the means to acquire other companies. (It is ironic that many companies are proud of their policy of making acquisitions only with cash, "to avoid equity dilution." Yet, because of the federal tax on capital gains in a cash sale, sellers fare better with exchanges of stock than cash payments, and will usually accept a proportionately lower purchase valuation when these taxes can be avoided. For example, assuming a 25 percent capital gains tax on a cash transaction, and assuming the stock alternative qualifies as nontaxable, $100 in stock may be worth $133 in cash to the seller. Consequently, the acquiring company's stockholders' equity would be far less "diluted" if payment were made in shares previously acquired for this purpose in the open market for only three quarters of the money needed for a cash transaction.)

Repurchase programs which are undertaken for the foregoing reasons occasionally result in a sizeable volume of trading. For instance, General Motors' repurchases in 1964 amounted to 1,136,457 shares, or 10.5 percent of the volume in this stock on the New York Stock Exchange.

[1]See Leo A. Guthart, "More Companies Are Buying Back Their Stock (Thinking Ahead)," *Harvard Business Review,* Vol. XLIII (March-April, 1965), p. 40.

As a rule, however, such reaçquisitions do not lead to significant changes in the number of outstanding shares because purchasing is done specifically for reissue. In a recent study, *Barron's* found only one hundred companies (out of several thousand listed on the major stock exchanges) with more than nominal holdings of their own stock; even in this group, most companies were found to hold less than 3 percent of their total stock and were simply anticipating employee stock options and other similar programs.[2] Although repurchasing is widely accepted for stock options and other minor uses, it is clearly not often used for substantial changes in the equity base.

Later in this article, I hope to show that repurchasing should not be limited to the defensive role of avoiding dilution. I believe many managements should consider a more aggressive role for this approach, using it as a step toward achieving a more rational corporate financial structure in which debt and preferred capital take the place of redundant equity funds.

First, however, let us review the objections to repurchasing common stock.

## Major Objections

There seem to be five main arguments against repurchase. To each of them there is, in my opinion, a good answer.

### *Management Defeatism?*

For some men, buying in common stock has the unfavorable connotation of defeatism and implies that any management not finding new ways to use surplus funds is inept and dull-witted. At present the suggestion that a company "invest in itself" often draws prompt and vigorous criticism. The following statement comes from the president of a medium-sized company with no debt and a portfolio of marketable securities equal to nearly 10 percent of the total market value of the company's stock: "We would never consider buying in our own stock. The task of this management is to invest those funds; and if we can't do it, the directors should bring in a whole new ball team."

This attitude is not justified. Financial annals are replete with case histories of unsuccessful and unprofitable acquisitions and expansion programs. While some managements have avoided the pitfalls attendant to investing in or acquiring other companies, more and more annual reports show that millions of dollars of redundant cash and other liquid assets are being accumulated. It is doubtful that an effort to relinquish

[2] August 17, 1964, p. 9.

this corporate "padding" through repurchasing common stock can logically be considered "going soft" or defeatism.

## *Sign of Deterioration?*

An unfavorable aura surrounds repurchase of common stock in the writings of financial classicists. These writers generally recommend repurchase only as a means of gradually liquidating a deteriorating company or one with wasting assets, and then only when the total market valuation of the common stock is less than net current assets.

In fairness to these traditionalists, the corporate laws of this country appear to be unique among the major capitalist nations in permitting corporations to reacquire their own shares. English law takes the delightful but archaic position that the repurchase of common stock is a constructive fraud against creditors. Canadian law is more moderate but still prohibits repurchase of stocks as an unauthorized reduction of capital.

Needless to say, it is facts, not legends, that we are interested in. The facts, I hope to demonstrate, favor repurchase.

## *Debt Taboo?*

There seems to exist a general management preference for equity and retained earnings rather than debt and preferred capital. For instance, after refinancing a large preferred issue with debt, a large metals company reported with apparent satisfaction that it still had one of the lowest debt radios in its industry. And executives of other companies advertise that their organizations have practically *no* debt.

This antidebt policy apparently arises from the exercise of personal preference by financial managers. There are good reasons to believe that it often conflicts with the interests of stockholders.[3]

## *Abuse of Power?*

In recent years, there have been some abuses of the power of American corporations to repurchase common shares. To illustrate:

1. One company bought out a single large stockholder without making a general tender offer, which would have allowed other shareholders to reduce or liquidate their holdings.
2. Another company sought to increase the marketability of a large shareholder's secondary offering at the then prevailing market price

[3]See Gordon Donaldson, "Financial Goals: Management vs. Stockholders," *Harvard Business Review*, Vol. XLI (May-June, 1963), p. 126.

by using $1 million of company funds to buy a rather large portion of the about-to-be-offered stock for the corporate treasury. This move significantly reduced the number of outstanding shares, increased earnings per share, and lowered the price-earnings ratio to a level more in line with the capitalization rates of similar publicly held companies.

3. Another firm incurred stockholder dismay and anger by acquiring shares on the open market, management's motive apparently being to maintain control over the firm for a particular group of stockholders.

Obviously, repurchases *can* be inappropriate and *can* discriminate unfairly among common shareholders. But such abuses can easily be avoided by corporations willing to make full disclosure of their plans so that all stockholders are treated equitably.

### *Unfair to Stockholders?*

Finally, some have argued that when a corporation repurchases its own common stock, either the sellers or the ramaining holders must be hurt, and that management should not engage in any activity that tends to help some stockholders at the expense of others. Three points should be made clear:

1. A full disclosure of repurchase objectives and plans will enable all shareholders to reappraise the value of their shares and act accordingly.
2. When substantial amounts of stock are to be reacquired, a tender offer will give all shareholders equitable treatment. Such a tender offer should be priced sufficiently above current market levels to balance (*a*) the advantages of the higher present price to those who may wish to sell with (*b*) the advantages of higher future per share earnings and equity values to those who may wish to hold their shares.
3. When relatively small amounts of stock are to be purchased on the stock exchanges, a regular buying program both increases the active demand for and decreases the available supply of the corporation's shares, and consequently tends to increase the price at which the shares will trade to the satisfaction of both holders *and* sellers.

## Possible Alternatives

Thus the standard objections to repurchasing lose their forcefulness when considered carefully, and repurchasing cannot be rejected out of hand. Are there, however, alternatives that management should consider?

## *Distributing Surplus*

When current and anticipated cash inflows exceed present and expected internal cash requirements, an increase in dividend payout is usually appropriate. Such an increase may, however, be an inadequate solution to the problem of surplus cash flows.

Since managers and investors both expect a given level of dividends to be maintained, dividend payments are relatively inflexible; and most managements have been unwilling to commit themselves to a payout rate much above 65 to 70 percent of reported earnings. But since net funds inflows are typically appreciably higher than reported earnings, capital can accumulate rather rapidly, even with a relatively high dividend rate.

Moreover, increasing dividends above a normal payout level implicitly assumes that stockholders prefer more current income to an increasing share of equity in a prosperous and progressive enterprise with the prospect of even higher dividends in the future. This assumption ignores the tax advantages of investing the funds in the corporation.

While higher dividends probably are the most attractive method for distributing a moderately and consistently increasing surplus of cash flow, they are not appropriate when the surplus arises in a sporadic pattern of large amounts. In other cases, when retained earnings have accumulated over a number of years and have become a sizable equity surplus, higher annual dividends would seldom be an acceptable means to most managers of substantially reducing total equity capital.

## *Investment Expansion*

Surplus funds may also be applied toward expansion or modernization, cash acquisitions or investments, and retirement of senior securities. As examples:

1. From 1956 to 1964, R. J. Reynolds Tobacco Company spent $160 million to expand and modernize facilities, increased working capital by $155 million, and reduced senior securities by $85 million. The total program more than doubled book values.
2. Consolidation Coal Company recently bought 7.7 percent of the common stock of Chrysler Corporation for more than $55 million. The market value of this investment has risen since then to over $170 million.

While such investments have worked well for some companies, they often lack appeal for others. Modernization may not be called for. Expanding facilities and production may not be profitable if growth in market demand is limited. Cash acquisitions of attractive and compatible companies may be impracticable or prohibited by antitrust regulation. Investments in other corporations or marketable U.S. Treasury securities usually provide only a modest return on investment.

Consequently, many firms find these methods of exploiting surplus capital either unsatisfactory or unfeasible. Moreover, these procedures may utilize only part of the redundant equity.

Because of the difficulties of profitably employing surplus capital in the company and/or distributing redundant equity funds to stockholders through dividends, a surprisingly large number of corporations have accumulated substantial holdings of marketable short-term securities to absorb redundant capital resources. The roster of such companies includes several having no long-term debt. Table 2 presents data for a few of these companies.

TABLE 2

COMPANIES WITH SUBSTANTIAL HOLDINGS OF SHORT-TERM SECURITIES
(Assets and Debt in Millions of Dollars)

| | | *Nonoperating Assets as a Percent of:* | | |
|---|---|---|---|---|
| | *Nonoperating Assets** | *Net Assets* | *Stock Market Value* | *Debt* |
| Eastman Kodak Company | $ 310.3 | 33.8% | 5.6% | $..... |
| Freeport Sulphur Company | 39.2 | 18.1 | 11.5 | ..... |
| International Nickel Company of Canada, Ltd. | 131.7 | 17.8 | 5.3 | ..... |
| Libby-Owens-Ford Glass Company | 121.7 | 43.5 | 16.5 | ..... |
| Parke, Davis & Company | 55.4 | 30.5 | 12.0 | ..... |
| Phelps Dodge Corporation | 145.4 | 15.2 | 20.5 | ..... |
| General Motors Corporation | 1,010.5 | 13.4 | 3.6 | 132.0 |
| International Business Machines Corporation | 724.0 | 31.4 | 5.0 | 370.4 |
| Kennecott Copper Corporation | 224.7 | 27.4 | 22.0 | 5.2 |
| Minnesota Mining & Manufacturing Company | 57.9 | 10.2 | 2.0 | 8.5 |
| Procter & Gamble Company | 377.9 | 40.2 | 10.6 | 106.9 |

*At year-end 1964 except for Proctor & Gamble, whose assets are listed as of June 30, 1964.

## Reducing the Equity Base

Rather than accumulating liquid assets with only limited returns, financial managers may find that a better case can be made for repurchase of a company's own common stock. For instance:

Following the transfer of its computer division to Bunker-Ramo Corporation, a joint venture with Martin-Marietta, TRW Inc. (formerly Thompson Ramo Wooldridge, Inc.) received $17.4 million, approximately 8 percent of the total market value of its outstanding common stock. The company then made a tender offer for 250,000 of its common shares (7.4 percent) with an expected cost of $14 million. According to Chairman J. D. Wright: "The company now has funds in excess of its operating requirements for the foreseeable future. After considering various alternatives for the use of these funds, we have concluded that the purchase of additional shares of common stock would be more beneficial to shareholders from the standpoint of earnings improvement per share."[4]

For many companies with existing or prospective holdings of low- and fixed-income securities, the repurchase alternative offers significant advantages to the common shareholder. But when managers or investors analyze the choice between expanding the company's operations and reducing its equity base, what standards should they use? I shall develop such a standard in the next section.

To begin, let us specify an ideal. A capital expenditure should:

1. Be of significant size.
2. Utilize the experience and skills of management without making undue demands on executive time and energy.
3. Use existing channels of distribution and serve familiar markets.
4. Require no substantially new technical or production skills.
5. Be based on highly reliable projections of future business developments.
6. Be limited to a specific capital expenditure.
7. Return significant profits quickly.

These "impossible" requirements can often be met, I believe, with repurchase of common shares. To demonstrate this, I shall describe a method of assaying the value of capital expenditures by comparing the benefit to the stockholders of increasing productive assets with the benefit of reducing the equity base. This appraisal index will be called the "stockholder standard."

## *Deriving the Standard*

Table 3 identifies the increase in per share earnings which the management of a hypothetical company obtains by reducing the equity base by repurchasing common stock. It is assumed that $30 million is spent to buy 909,000 shares. For realism, the average cost of shares is assumed to be 110 percent of the prevailing market price. The gain in earnings per share for the present year (1965) is 20 cents. To obtain

[4]*Wall Street Journal,* March 3, 1964.

TABLE 3

FINANCIAL EFFECTS OF BUYING BACK STOCK IN A HYPOTHETICAL CASE

(Assumptions: 5% Trend Growth in Earnings; Market Price is 15 Times Earnings; $30 Million of Available Funds Required to Buy Back 909,000 Shares at 110% of Market Price)

| | *1965* | *1966* | *1967* | *1968* | *1969* | *1970* |
|---|---|---|---|---|---|---|
| Earnings.......... | $20,000,000 | $21,000,000 | $22,100,000 | $23,200,000 | $24,300,000 | $25,500,000 |
| Earnings per share: | | | | | | |
| With 10,000,000 shares...... | 2.00 | 2.10 | 2.21 | 2.32 | 2.43 | 2.55 |
| With 9,091,000 shares...... | 2.20 | 2.31 | 2.44 | 2.56 | 2.68 | 2.80 |
| Dividends (60% of earnings).... | 12,000,000 | 12,600,000 | 13,300,000 | 13,900,000 | 14,600,000 | 15,300,000 |
| Dividends per share: | | | | | | |
| With 10,000,000 shares...... | 1.20 | 1.26 | 1.33 | 1.39 | 1.48 | 1.53 |
| With 9,091,000 shares...... | 1.32 | 1.39 | 1.46 | 1.53 | 1.61 | 1.68 |
| Increase produced by repurchase in: | | | | | | |
| Earnings per share....... | 0.20 | 0.21 | 0.23 | 0.23 | 0.25 | 0.25 |
| Dividends per share....... | 0.12 | 0.13 | 0.13 | 0.14 | 0.15 | 0.15 |

an equal gain in earnings per share by spending the same $30 million on productive facilities would require an after-tax return of 6.7 percent. The calculation is made as follows:

$$\frac{\$0.20 \times 10{,}000{,}000 \text{ shares}}{\$30{,}000{,}000} = 6.7\%$$

Obviously, if the $30 million were spent for new productive facilities, they could not be expected to return profits in the first year; it is highly doubtful that the facilities could even be completed in the first year. Over a period of years, however, an investment in plant and equipment would presumably be profitable; so the entire future stream of profits must be considered. This is done by present-value analysis.

Present-value analysis should also be used to identify the comparable benefits of reducing the equity by repurchasing shares. Unfortunately, profits in the distant future are not susceptible to easy or accurate prediction, and management will wisely avoid making tenuous estimates. However, we can use a reasonable, simple, and more reliable shortcut by estimating the improvement in earnings per share for the fifth year hence (or fourth or sixth year, if management finds a different time period more appropriate), and consider this one year's increase to be equal to the total stream of all future earnings-per-share increases discounted to their present value.

In Table 3 the fifth-year gain in earnings per share is 25 cents, or the equivalent of an 8.3 percent after-tax return (25 cents times 10 million shares, divided by \$30-million investment). Alternative investments can then be appraised by discounting their future after-tax returns by this investment return figure. In effect, 8.3 percent becomes what is often called an "opportunity cost." Its significance is this: If corporate funds spent on the repurchase of common stock return 8.3 percent after taxes, this is a more profitable outlay for shareholders than investments in productive facilities expected to yield a lower present-value return.

The increase in earnings per share is the stockholder standard by which investment opportunities can be judged from the shareholders' point of view. Projects which improve on the stockholder standard should be undertaken when feasible; others should be rejected unless qualitative factors override the mathematical evaluation. When managers deviate from the standard, they should do so explicitly and intentionally.

FIGURE 1

STOCKHOLDERS STANDARDS FOR VARIOUS GROWTH RATES AND PRICE-EARNINGS RATIOS

In Figure 1 the stockholder standard is calculated for a variety of possible growth rates and price-earnings ratios. While these combinations of rates and ratios obviously do not cover all possible circumstances in industry, they do suggest the range in standards for varying situations. Each company should calculate its own stockholder standard using the price-earnings ratio of its own stock and its own expected growth rates.

### *Use and Significance*

A policy of repurchasing stock guided by the stockholder standard has all the advantages of the perfect capital expenditure described previously, but it does have important drawbacks—for some managers. Repurchasing common shares reduces corporate net assets as well as income (earnings and cash flow). Moreover, the stockholder standard is not based on management's principal guide to investment decisions—cash flow. However, if comparing the stockholder standard to present-value cash flow seems like comparing apples and oranges, this incompatibility can be overcome by generating a standard that relates to cash flow rather than to earnings—by substituting the expected increase in cash flow per share for earnings per share in the scheme shown in Table 3.

While the stockholder standard can be a useful guide to managers striving to sustain an efficient use of corporate capital for the long-term benefit of the owners, more powerful measures appear to be warranted before many corporations will be using equity capital efficiently. These are measures that will change the capital structure in a desired way, develop "reverse dilution," and concentrate the power of equity capital by replacing redundant equity funds with fixed cost capital. The next section will be focused on this question.

## Rationalizing Capital

The most important use of common stock repurchases, and the most widely applicable, is the valuable flexibility provided to financial managers who are seeking ways to develop a rational capital structure which will meet the corporation's present and future requirements while optimizing the long-term wealth and income of the owners.

A rational capital structure may be described as one having the size and mix of capital that would be selected if the corporation were being fully recapitalized—if the slate were clean. Such a capital structure would have as its primary objective the long-range enhancement of stockholder wealth and income, and would be based on the internal requirements of the firm after considering developments in the national or world economy, the industry with which the company is associated, and the markets to which it sells its goods and services.

The obvious and substantial differences in existing capital structures of large companies (see Table 4) are too great to be explained away as just differing opinions as to the optimum amount and composition of capital to enhance the stockholders' long-term interests while meeting the present and future requirements of the enterprise. Apparently, customs and traditions are going unchallenged. There seems to be too little awareness of the potentials of revised capital structures.

TABLE 4

VARIATIONS IN DEBT-EQUITY RATIOS IN VARIOUS INDUSTRIES

| Industry | Ratio | Company | Ratio | Company |
|---|---|---|---|---|
| Automobile | 0.0% | (American Motors Corporation) | 21.6% | (Chrysler Corporation) |
| Chemical | 0.0% | (E. I. du Pont de Nemours & Company) | 48.0% | (Air Products & Chemicals, Inc.) |
| Drug | 0.0% | (Parke, Davis & Company) | 48.0% | (Baxter Laboratories, Inc.) |
| Nonferrous metal | 0.0% | (International Nickel Company of Canada, Ltd.) | 15.0% | (Cerro Corporation) |
| Steel | 8.8% | (Bethlehem Steel Corporation) | 32.1% | (Wheeling Steel Corporation) |
| Paper | 0.0% | (International Paper Company) | 23.0% | (Mead Corporation) |
| Oil | 0.1% | (Skelly Oil Company) | 29.0% | (Sinclair Oil Corporation) |

An example of a company that *did* see these potentials is Indian Head Mills:

An unusual, but not unique, opportunity to exploit archaic capitalization were seen by the Indian Head Mills management. President James Robison was determined to create a *rational* capital structure in the equity-dependent textile industry and did so by substituting funded debt and preferred stock for the redundant equity capital in the firms he acquired. These were the exciting results: Per share earnings and dividends rose rapidly; and with a higher price-earnings ratio, the market value of the common equity zoomed tenfold in less than four years!

The changes in capital that can be made by other companies in other industries may not be so dramatic, but nonetheless they can be eminently worthwhile. And effecting these changes does not require unwanted mergers.

## *Cost Analysis*

How far is it profitable to go in buying back stock? Let us begin with a well-known concept in financial management.

The traditional "weighted average" cost-of-capital analysis presupposes the existence of an optimum mix of debt, preferred stock, and common equity such that any change in the amount of one type of capital leads eventually to a proportionately equal change in all. This approach precludes the possibility that changing the capital mix can change the long-term cost of capital except in the special situation where the existing structure is substantially out of proportion to the optimum mix. In this "special" case, realigning the composition of capital *can* change the over-all cost of capital.

The substantial decline in debt and preferred capital in recent years suggests that capital mix has been significantly skewed away from the optimum balance toward heavy equity usage, and that the *special* case in which rearranging the composition of capital will change the over-all cost is actually becoming the *general* case today.

When a corporation has surplus equity capital, the true cost of this capital to the stockholders is the opportunity cost of not repurchasing common shares—the stockholder standard. A comparison of the stockholder standard to the cost of senior capital indicates the degree to which stockholder wealth and income can be advanced by reducing equity and increasing debt and preferred, that is, by moving the capital mix back toward the optimum through "reverse dilution." The point to stop borrowing is when the difference between the debt cost and the return on repurchase becomes narrow and/or the level of future debt charges seems unwise in view of anticipated cash flows.

As we have seen, when the stockholder standard exceeds the after-tax cost of debt and/or preferred stock, equity should be reduced while debt and/or preferred stock are increased. What may startle most readers is this: Even at a very high price-earnings ratio, the stockholder standard can be significantly higher than the cost of either debt or preferred would be. (The situations portrayed in Table 3 illustrate this.) Thus, even in an extreme case, reducing equity by repurchasing shares may well improve the position of the common stockholder.

## *Finding the Optimum*

Identifying the optimum capital structure involves two basic steps:

1. Identifying and comparing relevant costs for debt, preferred, and common stock.
2. Using these costs as guides in determining the most desirable capital mix and the corporation's financial requirements.

While the economics of repurchasing common stock make a good case for maximum use of debt and preferred stock, determination of that maximum can only be made by consideration of the debt capacity of the corporation. Therefore a rational capitalization will be consistent with management requirements (debt not in excess of corporate capacity) and with stockholder objectives (equity not in excess of corporate needs).

Since management should anticipate future changes in the company and its business position, the optimum or "target" capital structure will change. Every shift in either the company or its surroundings offers the possibility that adaptive, responsive adjustments ought to be made in the total amount or the mix of existing capital. Consequently, a regular review which will identify changing financial needs and capacities must be integrated with a continuing program of adaptation to change.

## *Role of Repurchasing*

Repurchasing provides valuable flexibility to managers striving to develop an optimum capital structure. The number of outstanding common shares can be reduced in several ways:

1. *Tender Offers.* For example, American Radiator Company acquired over 10 percent of its common shares through a tender offer in 1963, using a prime rate bank loan of $20 million to provide the necessary funds.[5]
2. *Block Purchases.* In late 1964, General Fireproofing Company purchased 121,558 shares (17 percent) of its own common from Rockwell-Standard Corporation following approval by a special stockholders' meeting.[6]
3. *Regular Purchases in the Open Market.* Amerada Petroleum Corporation had acquired over two million (15.5 percent) of its 12.7 million shares by the end of 1964.[7]
4. *Exchanging Marketable Securities.* During 1964, Emhart Manufacturing Co. exchanged 27,621 shares of its holding in Monsanto Chemical Company for 39,800 of its common shares held by a mutual fund.[8]
5. *Exchanging Senior Securities.* Early in 1964, Ling-Temco-Vought, Inc. offered to exchange a combination of $7.5 million and 500,000 shares of convertible preferred stock for 1.5 million shares of common.[9]

As the foregoing suggests, financial managers have a variety of methods available to them. Equity capital can be reduced considerably and conveniently. It should not be treated as a fixed or inflexible portion of the corporation's capital structure.

[5] *Moody's Industrials,* Sec. I, October 8, 1963, p. 2282.
[6] *Wall Street Journal,* December 22, 1964.
[7] *Barron's,* August 17, 1964, p. 9.
[8] *Business Week,* November 21, 1964, p. 180.
[9] *Wall Street Journal,* May 29, 1964.

## *Market Reaction*

Before embarking on a repurchase program, each management should consider carefully the impact that both the procedure and the objectives of repurchasing are likely to have on the price-earnings ratio of the company's common stock. Although executives may conclude from a brief consideration of repurchasing that the price-earnings ratio will decline if per share earnings growth derives in part from reducing shares rather than wholly from increasingly profitable operations, it seems more likely that if investors and their professional advisers clearly understand the reasons behind a repurchase program, they will look favorably on reacquiring shares either to restructure capitalization or to provide effective discipline for capital expenditures. In fact, the higher rate of earnings-per-share growth resulting from a reduction of the equity base may well increase the market valuation of the company's shares.

Since only knowledgeable investors can react intelligently, management should accept responsibility for educating stockholders as to the objectives of capital policy, and it should inform them regularly of both the practices the company follows and the results achieved.

Prior to implementing a repurchase program, management should seek the advice of legal counsel on such matters as state laws, corporate powers, authorization, and disclosure to the Securities and Exchange Commission and to the stock exchanges. Investment bankers can provide helpful advice to management regarding details of the actual buying program like daily volume limits, pricing, and selection of brokers for continuing open-market purchase programs, or regarding the appropriate terms and procedures for tender offers.

# Conclusion

In recent years, substantial cash flows have altered the capitalization of many corporations and produced an uneconomically high proportion of equity capital. Consequently, reorganizing corporate capital to regain an optimum capital mix will often mean buying back some common stock. This may lead to important improvements in shareholder wealth and income. The stockholder standard described in this article can be a useful guide to appraising capital costs and capital budgeting from the investor's point of view.

Retiring common stock is not so simple or routine as retiring debt and preferred; the acquiring company is dealing with its owners rather than creditors, and equitable treatment must replace the philosophy of caveat emptor. However, the problems are usually not nearly so great as are the potential advantages to the stockholders.

It is widely known that industrial corporations have been "out of the market" for new equity capital for several years because capital requirements have been increasingly supplied by substantial retained earnings. The analysis of this article suggests strongly that many managements should now return to the equity markets, not as sellers but as *buyers* of their common stocks, to eliminate excess equity, to rationalize capitalization, and to discipline capital budgeting. Using repurchasing, managers may be able to find new ways to act in the interest of the long-term common stock investor by revitalizing equity capital.

Part V

# Capital Structure, Cost of Capital, and Valuation of the Corporation

*Chapter 23*

# *The Cost of Capital, Corporation Finance, and the Theory of Investment**

By Franco Modigliani and Merton H. Miller

WHAT IS THE "cost of capital" to a firm in a world in which funds are used to acquire assets whose yields are uncertain, and in which capital can be obtained by many different media, ranging from pure debt instruments, representing money-fixed claims, to pure equity issues, giving holders only the right to a pro rata share in the uncertain venture? This question has vexed at least three classes of economists: (1) the corporation finance specialist concerned with the techniques of financing firms so as to insure their survival and growth; (2) the managerial economist concerned with capital budgeting; and (3) the economic theorist concerned with explaining investment behavior at both the micro and macro levels.[1]

---

*Reprinted by permission from *American Economic Review,* Vol. XLVIII (June, 1958), pp. 261–97.

This article is a revised version of a paper delivered at the annual meeting of the Econometric Society, December, 1956. The authors express thanks for the comments and suggestions made at that time by the discussants of the paper, Evsey Domar, Robert Eisner, and John Lintner, and subsequently by James Duesenberry. They are also greatly indebted to many of their present and former colleagues and students at Carnegie Institute of Technology who served so often and with such remarkable patience as a critical forum for the ideas here presented.

[1]The literature bearing on the cost-of-capital problem is far too extensive for listing here. Numerous references to it will be found throughout the paper, though we make no claim to completeness. One phase of the problem which we do not consider explicitly, but which has a considerable literature of its own, is the relation between the cost of capital and public utility rates. For a recent summary



*(Continued on next page)*

In much of his formal analysis, the economic theorist at least has tended to sidestep the essence of this cost-of-capital problem by proceeding as though physical assets—like bonds—could be regarded as yielding known, sure streams. Given this assumption, the theorist has concluded that the cost of capital to the owners of a firm is simply the rate of interest on bonds; and has derived the familiar proposition that the firm, acting rationally, will tend to push investment to the point where the marginal yield on physical assets is equal to the market rate of interest.[2] This proposition can be shown to follow from either of two criteria of rational decision making which are equivalent under certainty, namely, (1) the maximization of profits and (2) the maximization of market value.

According to the first criterion, a physical asset is worth acquiring if it will increase the net profit of the owners of the firm. But net profit will increase only if the expected rate of return, or yield, of the asset exceeds the rate of interest. According to the second criterion, an asset is worth acquiring if it increases the value of the owners' equity, i.e., if it adds more to the market value of the firm than the costs of acquisition. But what the asset adds is given by capitalizing the stream it generates at the market rate of interest, and this capitalized value will exceed its cost if and only if the yield of the asset exceeds the rate of interest. Note that under either formulation the cost of capital is equal to the rate of interest on bonds, regardless of whether the funds are acquired through debt instruments or through new issues of common stock. Indeed, in a world of sure return the distinction between debt and equity funds reduces largely to one of terminology.

It must be acknowledged that some attempt is usually made in this type of analysis to allow for the existence of uncertainty. This attempt typically takes the form of superimposing on the results of the certainty analysis the notion of a "risk discount" to be subtracted from the expected yield (or a "risk premium" to be added to the market rate of interest). Investment decisions are then supposed to be based on a comparison of this "risk-adjusted" or "certainty-equivalent" yield with the market rate of interest.[3] No satisfactory explanation has yet been pro-

---

of the "cost-of-capital theory" of rate regulation and a brief discussion of some of its implications, the reader may refer to Somers [20].

Numbers in brackets refer to publications listed at the end of this paper (p. 404).

[2]Or more accurately, to the marginal cost of borrowed funds, since it is customary, at least in advanced analysis, to draw the supply curve of borrowed funds to the firm as a rising one. For an advanced treatment of the certainty case, see Lutz [13].

[3]The classic examples of the certainty-equivalent approach are found in Hicks [8] and Lange [11].

vided, however, as to what determines the size of the risk discount and how it varies in response to changes in other variables.

Considered as a convenient approximation, the model of the firm constructed via this certainty—or certainty-equivalent—approach has admittedly been useful in dealing with some of the grosser aspects of the processes of capital accumulation and economic fluctuations. Such a model underlies, for example, the familiar Keynesian aggregate investment function in which aggregate investment is written as a function of the rate of interest—the same riskless rate of interest which appears later in the system in the liquidity-preference equation. Yet few would maintain that this approximation is adequate. At the macroeconomic level, there are ample grounds for doubting that the rate of interest has as large and as direct an influence on the rate of investment as this analysis would lead us to believe. At the microeconomic level the certainty model has little descriptive value and provides no real guidance to the finance specialist or managerial economist, whose main problems cannot be treated in a framework which deals so cavalierly with uncertainty and ignores all forms of financing other than debt issues.[4]

Only recently have economists begun to face up seriously to the problem of the cost of capital *cum* risk. In the process, they have found their interests and endeavors merging with those of the finance specialist and the managerial economist, who have lived with the problem longer and more intimately. In this joint search to establish the principles which govern rational investment and financial policy in a world of uncertainty, two main lines of attack can be discerned. These lines represent, in effect, attempts to extrapolate to the world of uncertainty each of the two criteria—profit maximization and market value maximization—which were seen to have equivalent implications in the special case of certainty. With the recognition of uncertainty, this equivalence vanishes. In fact, the profit maximization criterion is no longer even well defined. Under uncertainty, there corresponds to each decision of the firm not a unique profit outcome, but a plurality of mutually exclusive outcomes which can at best be described by a subjective probability distribution. The profit outcome, in short, has become a random variable; and as such, its maximization no longer has an operational meaning. Nor can this difficulty generally be disposed of by using the mathematical expectation of profits as the variable to be maximized. For decisions which affect the expected value will also tend to affect the dispersion and other characteristics of the distribution of outcomes. In particular, the use of

[4]Those who have taken a "case method" course in finance in recent years will recall in this connection the famous Liquigas case of Hunt and Williams [9, pp. 193–96], a case which is often used to introduce the student to the cost-of-capital problem and to poke a bit of fun at the economist's certainty model.

debt rather than equity funds to finance a given venture may well increase the expected return to the owners, but only at the cost of increased dispersion of the outcomes.

Under these conditions the profit outcomes of alternative investment and financing decisions can be compared and ranked only in terms of a *subjective* "utility function" of the owners which weighs the expected yield against other characteristics of the distribution. Accordingly, the extrapolation of the profit maximization criterion of the certainty model has tended to evolve into utility maximization, sometimes explicitly, more frequently in a qualitative and heuristic form.[5]

The utility approach undoubtedly represents an advance over the certainty or certainty-equivalent approach. It does at least permit us to explore (within limits) some of the implications of different financing arrangements, and it does give some meaning to the "cost" of different types of funds. However, because the cost of capital has become an essentially subjective concept, the utility approach has serious drawbacks for normative as well as analytical purposes. How, for example, is management to ascertain the risk preferences of its stockholders and to compromise among their tastes? And how can the economist build a meaningful investment function in the face of the fact that any given investment opportunity might or might not be worth exploiting, depending on precisely who happen to be the owners of the firm at the moment?

Fortunately, these questions do not have to be answered; for the alternative approach, based on market value maximization, can provide the basis for an operational definition of the cost of capital and a workable theory of investment. Under this approach, any investment project and its concomitant financing plan must pass only the following test: Will the project, as financed, raise the market value of the firm's shares? If so, it is worth undertaking; if not, its return is less than the marginal cost of capital to the firm. Note that such a test is entirely independent of the tastes of the current owners, since market prices will reflect not only their preferences but those of all potential owners as well. If any current stockholder disagrees with management and the market over the valuation of the project, he is free to sell out and reinvest elsewhere, but will still benefit from the capital appreciation resulting from management's decision.

The potential advantages of the market value approach have long been appreciated; yet analytical results have been meager. What appears to be keeping this line of development from achieving its promise is largely the lack of an adequate theory of the effect of financial structure

---

[5]For an attempt at a rigorous explicit development of this line of attack, see Modigliani and Zeman [14].

on market valuations, and of how these effects can be inferred from objective market data. It is with the development of such a theory and of its implications for the cost-of-capital problem that we shall be concerned in this paper.

Our procedure will be to develop in Section I the basic theory itself and to give some brief account of its empirical relevance. In Section II, we show how the theory can be used to answer the cost-of-capital question and how it permits us to develop a theory of investment of the firm under conditions of uncertainty. Throughout these sections the approach is essentially a partial-equilibrium one focusing on the firm and "industry." Accordingly, the "prices" of certain income streams will be treated as constant and given from outside the model, just as in the standard Marshallian analysis of the firm and industry the prices of all inputs and of all other products are taken as given. We have chosen to focus at this level rather than on the economy as a whole because it is at the level of the firm and the industry that the interests of the various specialists concerned with the cost-of-capital problem come most closely together. Although the emphasis has thus been placed on partial-equilibrium analysis, the results obtained also provide the essential building blocks for a general equilibrium model which shows how those prices which are here taken as given are themselves determined. For reasons of space, however, and because the material is of interest in its own right, the presentation of the general-equilibrium model which rounds out the analysis must be deferred to a subsequent paper.

## I. The Valuation of Securities, Leverage, and the Cost of Capital

### *A. The Capitalization Rate for Uncertain Streams*

As a starting point, consider an economy in which all physical assets are owned by corporations. For the moment, assume that these corporations can finance their assets by issuing common stock only; the introduction of bond issues, or their equivalent, as a source of corporate funds is postponed until the next part of this section.

The physical assets held by each firm will yield to the owners of the firm—its stockholders—a stream of "profits" over time; but the elements of this series need not be constant and in any event are uncertain. This stream of income, and hence the stream accruing to any share of common stock, will be regarded as extending indefinitely into the future. We assume, however, that the mean value of the stream over time, or average profit per unit of time, is finite and represents a random variable subject to a (subjective) probability distribution. We shall refer to the average value over time of the stream accruing to a given share as the return of that share, and to the mathematical expectation of this average as the expected return of the share.[6] Although individual investors may have different views as to the shape of the probability distribution of the return of any share, we shall assume for simplicity that they are at least in agreement as to the expected return.[7]

This way of characterizing uncertain streams merits brief comment. Notice first that the stream is a stream of profits, not dividends. As will become clear later, as long as management is presumed to be acting in the best interests of the stockholders, retained earnings can be regarded as equivalent to a fully subscribed, preemptive issue of common stock. Hence, for present purposes the division of the stream between cash dividends and retained earnings in any period is a mere detail. Notice also that the uncertainty attaches to the mean value over time of the stream of profits and should not be confused with variability over time of the successive elements of the stream. That variability and uncertainty are two totally different concepts should be clear from the fact that the elements of a stream can be variable even though known with certainty. It can be shown, furthermore, that whether the elements of a stream are sure or uncertain, the effect of variability per se on the valuation of the stream is at best a second-order one which can safely be neglected for our purposes (and indeed most others, too).[8]

The next assumption plays a strategic role in the rest of the analysis.

---

[6]These propositions can be restated analytically as follows: The assets of the $i$th firm generate a stream

$$X_i(1), X_i(2) \ . \ . \ . \ X_i(T)$$

whose elements are random variables subject to the joint probability distribution

$$x_i[X_i(1), X_i(2) \ . \ . \ . \ X_i(t)]$$

The return to the $i$th firm is defined as

$$X_i = \lim_{T \to \infty} \frac{1}{T} \sum_{t=1}^{T} X_i(t)$$

$X_i$ is itself a random variable with a probability distribution $\Phi_i(X_i)$ whose form is determined uniquely by $\chi_i$. The expected return, $\overline{X}_i$, is defined as $\overline{X}_i, = E(X_i) = \int x_i X_i \Phi_i(X_i) dX_i$. If $N_i$ is the number of shares outstanding, the return of the $i$th share is $x_i = (1/N)X_i$ with probability distribution $\Phi_i(x_i)dx_i = \Phi_i(Nx_i)d(Nx_i)$ and expected value $x_i = (1/N)\overline{X}_i$.

[7]To deal adequately with refinements such as differences among investors in estimates of expected returns would require extensive discussion of the theory of portfolio selection. Brief references to these and related topics will be made in the succeeding article on the general-equilibrium model.

[8]The reader may convince himself of this by asking how much he would be willing to rebate to his employer for the privilege of receiving his annual salary in equal monthly installments rather than in irregular amounts over the year. See also Keynes [10, esp. pp. 53–54].

We shall assume that firms can be divided into "equivalent return" classes such that the return on the shares issued by any firm in any given class is proportional to (and hence perfectly correlated with) the return on the shares issued by any other firm in the same class. This assumption implies that the various shares within the same class differ, at most, by a "scale factor." Accordingly, if we adjust for the difference in scale, by taking the *ratio* of the return to the expected return, the probability distribution of that ratio is identical for all shares in the class. It follows that all relevant properties of a share are uniquely characterized by specifying (1) the class to which it belongs and (2) its expected return.

The significance of this assumption is that it permits us to classify firms into groups within which the shares of different firms are "homogeneous," that is, perfect substitutes for one another. We have thus an analogue to the familiar concept of the industry in which it is the commodity produced by the firms that is taken as homogeneous. To complete this analogy with Marshalian price theory, we shall assume in the analysis to follow that the shares concerned are traded in perfect markets under conditions of atomistic competition.[9]

From our definition of homogeneous classes of stock, it follows that in equilibrium in a perfect capital market the price per dollar's worth of expected return must be the same for all shares of any given class. Or equivalently, in any given class the price of every share must be proportional to its expected return. Let us denote this factor of proportionality for any class, say the $k$th class, by $1/\rho_k$. Then, if $p_j$ denotes the price and $\bar{x}_j$ is the expected return per share of the $j$th firm in class $k$, we must have:

$$p_j = \frac{1}{\rho_k} \bar{x}_j \tag{1}$$

or equivalently:

$$\frac{\bar{x}_j}{p_j} = \rho_k, \text{ a constant for all firms } j \text{ in class } k \tag{2}$$

[9]Just what our classes of stocks contain and how the different classes can be identified by outside observers are empirical questions to which we shall return later. For the present, it is sufficient to observe: (1) Our concept of a class, while not identical to that of the industry, is at least closely related to it. Certainly, the basic characteristics of the probability distributions of the returns on assets will depend to a significant extent on the product sold and the technology used. (2) What are the appropriate class boundaries will depend on the particular problem being studied. An economist concerned with general tendencies in the market, for example, might well be prepared to work with far wider classes than would be appropriate for an investor planning his portfolio, or a firm planning its financial strategy.

The constants $\rho_k$ (one for each of the $k$ classes) can be given several economic interpretations: (1) From equation 2, we see that each $\rho_k$ is the expected rate of return of any share in class $k$. (2) From equation 1, $1/\rho_k$ is the price which an investor has to pay for a dollar's worth of expected return in the class $k$. (3) Again from equation 1, by analogy with the terminology for perpetual bonds, $\rho_k$ can be regarded as the market rate of capitalization for the expected value of the uncertain streams of the kind generated by the $k$th class of firms.[10]

## *B. Debt Financing and Its Effects on Security Prices*

Having developed an apparatus for dealing with uncertain streams, we can now approach the heart of the cost-of-capital problem by dropping the assumption that firms cannot issue bonds. The introduction of debt financing changes the market for shares in a very fundamental way. Because firms may have different proportions of debt in their capital structure, shares of different companies, even in the same class, can give rise to different probability distributions of returns. In the language of finance, the shares will be subject to different degrees of financial risk or "leverage," and hence they will no longer be perfect substitutes for one another.

To exhibit the mechanism determining the relative prices of shares under these conditions, we make the following two assumptions about the nature of bonds and the bond market, though they are actually stronger than is necessary and will be relaxed later: (1) All bonds (including any debts issued by households for the purpose of carrying shares) are assumed to yield a constant income per unit of time, and this income is regarded as certain by all traders regardless of the issuer. (2) Bonds, like stocks, are traded in a perfect market, where the term "perfect" is to be taken in its usual sense as implying that any two commodities which are perfect substitutes for each other must sell, in equilibrium, at the same price. It follows from assumption 1 that all bonds are in fact perfect substitutes up to a scale factor. It follows from assumption 2 that they must all sell at the same price per dollar's worth of return or, what amounts to the same thing, must yield the same rate of return. This rate of return will be denoted by $r$ and referred to as the

[10]We cannot, on the basis of the assumptions so far, make any statements about the relationship or spread between the various $\rho$'s or capitalization rates. Before we could do so, we would have to make further specific assumptions about the way investors believe the probability distributions vary from class to class, as well as assumptions about investors' preferences as between the characteristics of different distributions.

rate of interest or, equivalently, as the capitalization rate for sure streams. We now can derive the following two basic propositions with respect to the valuation of securities in companies with different capital structures:

*Proposition I.* Consider any company $j$ and let $\bar{X}_j$, stand, as before, for the expected return on the assets owned by the company (that is, its expected profit before deduction of interest). Denote by $D_j$ the market value of the debts of the company; by $S_j$ the market value of its common shares; and by $V_j \equiv S_j + D_j$ the market value of all its securities or, as we shall say, the market value of the firm. Then, our Proposition I asserts that we must have in equilibrium:

$$V_j \equiv (S_j + D_j) = \bar{X}_j/\rho_k, \text{ for any firm } j \text{ in class } k \tag{3}$$

That is, the *market value of any firm is independent of its capital structure and is given by capitalizing its expected return at the rate* $\rho_k$ *appropriate to its class.*

This proposition can be stated in an equivalent way in terms of the firm's "average cost of capital," $\bar{X}_j/V_j$, which is the ratio of its expected return to the market value of all its securities. Our proposition then is:

$$\frac{\bar{X}_j}{(S_j + D_j)} \equiv \frac{\bar{X}_j}{V_j} = \rho_k, \text{ for any firm } j \text{ in class } k \tag{4}$$

That is, *the average cost of capital to any firm is completely independent of its capital structure and is equal to the capitalization rate of a pure equity stream of its class.*

To establish Proposition I, we shall show that as long as the relations 3 or 4 do not hold between any pair of firms in a class, arbitrage will take place and restore the stated equalities. We use the term "arbitrage" advisedly. For if Proposition I did not hold, an investor could buy and sell stocks and bonds in such a way as to exchange one income stream for another stream, identical in all relevant respects but selling at a lower price. The exchange would therefore be advantageous to the investor quite independently of his attitudes toward risk.[11] As investors exploit these arbitrage opportunities, the value of the overpriced shares will fall and that of the underpriced shares will rise, thereby tending to eliminate the discrepancy between the market values of the firms.

By way of proof, consider two firms in the same class and assume, for simplicity only, that the expected return, $\bar{X}$, is the same for both firms.

[11]In the language of the theory of choice, the exchanges are movements from inefficient points in the interior to efficient points on the boundary of the investor's opportunity set, and not movements between efficient points along the boundary. Hence, for this part of the analysis, nothing is involved in the way of specific assumptions about investor attitudes or behavior other than that investors behave consistently and prefer more income to less income, ceteris paribus.

Let company 1 be financed entirely with common stock while company 2 has some debt in its capital structure. Suppose first the value of the levered firm, $V_2$, to be larger than that of the unlevered one, $V_1$. Consider an investor holding $s_2$ dollars' worth of the shares of company 2, representing a fraction $\alpha$ of the total outstanding stock, $S_2$. The return from this portfolio, denoted by $Y_2$, will be a fraction $\alpha$ of the income available for the stockholders of company 2, which is equal to the total return, $X_2$, less interest charge, $rD_2$. Since under our assumption of homogeneity the anticipated total return of company 2, $X_2$, is under all circumstances the same as the anticipated total return to company 1, $X_1$, we can hereafter replace $X_2$ and $X_1$ by a common symbol, $X$. Hence the return from the initial portfolio can be written as:

$$Y_2 = \alpha(X - rD_2) \tag{5}$$

Now, suppose the investor sold his $\alpha S_2$ worth of company 2 shares and acquired instead an amount $s_1 = \alpha(S_2 + D_2)$ of the shares of company 1. He could do so by utilizing the amount $\alpha S_2$ realized from the sale of his initial holding and borrowing an additional amount, $\alpha D_2$, on his own credit, pledging his new holdings in company 1 as a collateral. He would thus secure for himself a fraction $s_1/S_1 = \alpha(S_2 + D_2)/S_1$ of the shares and earnings of company 1. Making proper allowance for the interest payments on his personal debt, $\alpha D_2$, the return from the new portfolio, $Y_1$, is given by:

$$Y_1 = \frac{\alpha(S_2 + D_2)}{S_1} X - r\alpha D_2 = \alpha \frac{V_2}{V_1} X - r\alpha D_2 \tag{6}$$

Comparing equation 5 with equation 6, we see that as long as $V_2 > V_1$, we must have $Y_1 > Y_2$, so that it pays owners of company 2's shares to sell their holdings, thereby depressing $S_2$ and hence $V_2$; and to acquire shares of company 1, thereby raising $S_1$ and thus $V_1$. We conclude, therefore, that levered companies cannot command a premium over unlevered companies because investors have the opportunity of putting the equivalent leverage into their portfolio directly by borrowing on personal account.

Consider now the other possibility, namely, that the market value of the levered company, $V_2$, is less than $V_1$. Suppose an investor holds initially an amount $s_1$ of shares of company 1, representing a fraction $\alpha$ of the total outstanding stock, $S_1$. His return from this holding is:

$$Y_1 = \frac{s_1}{S_1} X = \alpha X$$

Suppose he were to exchange this initial holding for another portfolio, also worth $s_1$, but consisting of $s_2$ dollars of stock of company 2 and of $d$ dollars of bonds, where $s_2$ and $d$ are given by:

$$s_2 = \frac{S_2}{V_2} s_1, \qquad d = \frac{D_2}{V_2} s_1 \tag{7}$$

In other words, the new portfolio is to consist of stock of company 2 and of bonds in the proportions $S_2/V_2$ and $D_2/V_2$, respectively. The return from the stock in the new portfolio will be a fraction $s_2/S_2$ of the total return to stockholders of company 2, which is $(X - rD_2)$, and the return from the bonds will be $rd$. Making use of equation 7, the total return from the portfolio, $Y_2$, can be expressed as follows:

$$Y_2 = \frac{s_2}{S_2}(X - rD_2) + rd = \frac{s_1}{V_2}(X - rD_2) + r\frac{D_2}{V_2}s_1 = \frac{s_1}{V_2}X = \alpha\frac{S_1}{V_2}X$$

(since $s_1 = \alpha S_1$). Comparing $Y_2$ with $Y_1$, we see that if $V_2 < S_1 \equiv V_1$, then $Y_2$ will exceed $Y_1$. Hence, it pays the holders of company 1's shares to sell these holdings and replace them with a mixed portfolio containing an appropriate fraction of the shares of company 2.

The acquisition of a mixed portfolio of stock of a levered company, $j$, and of bonds in the proportion $S_j/V_j$ and $D_j/V_j$, respectively, may be regarded as an operation which "undoes" the leverage, giving access to an appropriate fraction of the unlevered return, $X_j$. It is this possibility of undoing leverage which prevents the value of levered firms from being consistently less than those of unlevered firms, or more generally prevents the average cost of capital, $\bar{X}_j/V_j$, from being systematically higher for levered than for nonlevered companies in the same class. Since we have already shown that arbitrage will also prevent $V_2$ from being larger than $V_1$, we can conclude that in equilibrium we must have $V_2 = V_1$, as stated in Proposition I.

*Proposition II.* From Proposition I, we can derive the following proposition concerning the rate of return on common stock in companies whose capital structure includes some debt: The expected rate of return or yield, $i$, on the stock of any company, $j$, belonging to the $k$th class is a linear function of leverage, as follows:

$$i_j = \rho_k + (\rho_k - r)\,D_j/S_j \tag{8}$$

That is, *the expected yield of a share of stock is equal to the appropriate capitalization rate, $\rho_k$, for a pure equity stream in the class, plus a premium related to financial risk equal to the debt-to-equity ratio times the spread between $\rho k$ and $r$.* Or equivalently, the market price of any share of stock is given by capitalizing its expected return at the continuously variable rate, $i_j$, of (8).[12]

[12] To illustrate, suppose $\bar{X} = 1{,}000$, $D = 4{,}000$, $r = 5$ percent, and $\rho_k = 10$ percent. These values imply that $V = 10{,}000$ and $S = 6{,}000$ by virtue of Proposition I. The expected yield or rate of return per share is then:

$$i = \frac{1{,}000 - 200}{6{,}000} = 0.1 + (0.1 - 0.05)\frac{4{,}000}{6{,}000} = 13\tfrac{1}{3} \text{ percent}$$

A number of writers have stated close equivalents of our Proposition I although by appealing to intuition rather than by attempting a proof and only to insist immediately that the results were not applicable to the actual capital markets.[13] Proposition II, however, so far as we have been able to discover, is new.[14] To establish it, we first note that by definition the expected rate of return, $i$, is given by:

$$i_j \equiv \frac{\bar{X}_j - rD_j}{S_j} \tag{9}$$

From Proposition I, equation 3, we know that:

$$\bar{X}_j = \rho_k(S_j + D_j)$$

Substituting in equation 9 and simplifying, we obtain equation 8.

## *C. Some Qualifications and Extensions of the Basic Propositions*

The methods and results developed so far can be extended in a number of useful directions, of which we shall consider here only three: (1) allowing for a corporate profits tax under which interest payments are deductible, (2) recognizing the existence of a multiplicity of bonds and interest rates, and (3) acknowledging the presence of market imperfections which might interfere with the process of arbitrage. The first two will be examined briefly in this section, with some further attention given to the tax problem in Section II. Market imperfections will be discussed in Part D of this section in the course of a comparison of our results with those of received doctrines in the field of finance.

*Effects of the Present Method of Taxing Corporations.* The deduction of interest in computing taxable corporate profits will prevent the arbitrage process from making the value of all firms in a given class proportional to the expected returns generated by their physical assets. Instead, it can be shown (by the same type of proof used for the original

---

[13] See, for example, Williams [21, esp. pp. 72–73]; Durand [3]; and Morton [15]. None of these writers describe in any detail the mechanism which is supposed to keep the average cost of capital constant under changes in capital structure. They seem, however, to be visualizing the equilibrating mechanism in terms of switches by investors between stocks and bonds as the yields of each get out of line with their "riskiness." This is an argument quite different from the pure arbitrage mechanism underlying our proof, and the difference is crucial. Regarding Proposition I as resting on investors' attitudes toward risk leads inevitably to a misunderstanding of many factors influencing relative yields such as, for example, limitations on the portfolio composition of financial institutions. See below, especially Section I(D).

[14] Morton does make reference to a linear yield function but only ". . . for the sake of simplicity and because the particular function used makes no essential difference in my conclusions" [15, p. 443, n. 2].

version of Proposition I) that the market values of firms in each class must be proportional in equilibrium to their expected return net of taxes (that is, to the sum of the interest paid and expected net stockholder income). This means we must replace each $\bar{X}_j$ in the original versions of Propositions I and II with a new variable, $\bar{X}_j^\tau$, representing the total income net of taxes generated by the firm:

$$\bar{X}_j^\tau \equiv (\bar{X}_j - rD_j)(1 - \tau) + rD_j \equiv \bar{\pi}_j^\tau + rD_j \qquad (10)$$

where $\bar{\pi}_j^\tau$ represents the expected net income accruing to the common stockholders and $\tau$ stands for the average rate of corporate income tax.[15]

After making these substitutions, the propositions, when adjusted for taxes, continue to have the same form as their originals. That is, Proposion I becomes:

$$\frac{\bar{X}_j^\tau}{V_j} = \rho_k^\tau, \text{ for any firm in class } k \qquad (11)$$

and Proposition II becomes:

$$i_j \equiv \frac{\bar{\pi}_j^\tau}{S_j} = \rho_j^\tau + (\rho_k^\tau - r)\, D_j/S_j \qquad (12)$$

where $\rho_k^\tau$ is the capitalization rate for income net of taxes in class $k$.

Although the form of the propositions is unaffected, certain interpretations must be changed. In particular, the after-tax capitalization rate $\rho_k^\tau$ can no longer be identified with the "average cost of capital," which is $\rho_k = \bar{X}_j/V_j$. The difference between $\rho_k^\tau$ and the "true" average cost of capital, as we shall see, is a matter of some relevance in connection with investment planning within the firm (Section II). For the description of market behavior, however, which is our immediate concern here, the distinction is not essential. To simplify presentation, therefore, and to preserve continuity with the terminology in the standard literature, we shall continue in this section to refer to $\rho_k^\tau$ as the average cost of capital, though, strictly speaking, this identification is correct only in the absence of taxes.

*Effects of a Plurality of Bonds and Interest Rates.* In existing capital markets, we find not one, but a whole family of interest rates varying with maturity, with the technical provisions of the loan, and, what is most relevant for present purposes, with the financial condition of the borrower.[16] Economic theory and market experience both suggest that

[15]For simplicity, we shall ignore throughout the tiny element of progression in our present corporate tax and treat $\tau$ as a constant independent of $(X_j - rD_j)$.

[16]We shall not consider here the extension of the analysis to encompass the time structure of interest rates. Although some of the problems posed by the time structure can be handled within our comparative statics framework, an adequate discussion would require a separate paper.

the yields demanded by lenders tend to increase with the debt-equity ratio of the borrowing firm or individual). If so, and if we can assume as a first approximation that this yield curve, $r = r\ (D/S)$, whatever its precise form, is the same for all borrowers, then we can readily extend our propositions to the case of a rising supply curve for borrowed funds.[17]

Proposition I is actually unaffected in form and interpretation by the fact that the rate of interest may rise with leverage; while the average cost of *borrowed* funds will tend to increase as debt rises, the average cost of funds from *all* sources will still be independent of leverage (apart from the tax effect). This conclusion follows directly from the ability of those who engage in arbitrage to undo the leverage in any financial structure by acquiring an appropriately mixed portfolio of bonds and stocks. Because of this ability, the ratio of earnings (*before* interest charges) to market value, i.e., the average cost of capital from all sources, must be the same for all firms in a given class.[18] In other words, the increased cost of borrowed funds as leverage increases will tend to be offset by a corresponding reduction in the yield of common stock. This seemingly paradoxical result will be examined more closely below in connection with Proposition II.

A significant modification of Proposition I would be required only if the yield curve $r = r(D/S)$ were different for different borrowers, as might happen if creditors had marked preferences for the securities of a

---

[17]We can also develop a theory of bond valuation along lines essentially parallel to those followed for the case of shares. We conjecture that the curve of bond yields as a function of leverage will turn out to be a nonlinear one in contrast to the linear function of leverage developed for common shares. However, we should also expect that the rate of increase in the yield on new issues would not be substantial in practice. This relatively slow rise would reflect the fact that interest rate increases by themselves can never be completely satisfactory to creditors as compensation for their increased risk. Such increases may simply serve to raise $r$ so high relative to $\rho$ that they become self-defeating by giving rise to a situation in which even normal fluctuations in earnings may force the company into bankruptcy. The difficulty of borrowing more, therefore, tends to show up in the usual case not so much in higher rates as in the form of increasingly stringent restrictions imposed on the company's management and finances by the creditors, and ultimately in a complete inability to obtain new borrowed funds, at least from the institutional investors who normally set the standards in the market for bonds.

[18]One normally minor qualification might be noted. Once we relax the assumption that all bonds have certain yields, our arbitrage operator faces the danger of something comparable to "gambler's ruin." That is, there is always the possibility that an otherwise sound concern—one whose long-run expected income is greater than its interest liability—might be forced into liquidation as a result of a run of temporary losses. Since reorganization generally involves costs, and because the operation of the firm may be hampered during the period of reorganization with lasting unfavorable effects on earnings prospects, we might perhaps expect heavily levered companies to sell at a slight discount relative to less heavily indebted companies of the same class.

particular class of debtors. If, for example, corporations as a class were able to borrow at lower rates than individuals having equivalent personal leverage, then the average cost of capital to corporations might fall slightly, as leverage increased over some range, in reflection of this differential. In evaluating this possibility, however, remember that the relevant interest rate for our arbitage operators is the rate on brokers' loans and, historically, that rate has not been noticeably higher than representative corporate rates.[19] The operations of holding companies and investment trusts which can borrow on terms comparable to operating companies represent still another force which could be expected to wipe out any marked or prolonged advantages from holding levered stocks.[20]

Although Proposition I remains unaffected as long as the yield curve is the same for all borrowers, the relation between common stock yields and leverage will no longer be the strictly linear one given by the original Proposition II. If $r$ increases with leverage, the yield $i$ will still tend to rise as $D/S$ increases, but at a decreasing rather than a constant rate. Beyond some high level of leverage, depending on the exact form of the interest function, the yield may even start to fall.[21] The relation between $i$ and $D/S$ could conceivably take the form indicated by the curve *MD* in Figure 2, although in practice the curvature would be much less pronounced. By contrast, with a constant rate of interest, the relation would be linear throughout, as shown by line *MM′* in Figure 2.

The downward-sloping part of the curve *MD* perhaps requires some comment, since it may be hard to imagine why investors, other than

---

[19]Under normal conditions, moreover, a substantial part of the arbitrage process could be expected to take the form not of having the arbitrage operators go into debt on personal account to put the required leverage into their portfolios but simply of having them reduce the amount of corporate bonds they already hold when they acquire underpriced unlevered stock. Margin requirements are also somewhat less of an obstacle to maintaining any desired degree of leverage in a portfolio than might be thought at first glance. Leverage could be largely restored in the face of higher margin requirements by switching to stocks having more leverage at the corporate level.

[20]An extreme form of inequality between borrowing and lending rates occurs, of course, in the case of preferred stocks, which cannot be directly issued by individuals on personal account. Here again, however, we should expect that the operations of investment corporations plus the ability of arbitrage operators to sell off their holdings of preferred stocks would act to prevent the emergence of any substantial premiums (for this reason) on capital structures containing preferred stocks. Nor are preferred stocks so far removed from bonds as to make it impossible for arbitrage operators to approximate closely the risk and leverage of a corporate preferred stock by incurring a somewhat smaller debt on personal account.

[21]Since new lenders are unlikely to permit this much leverage (cf. n. 17), this range of the curve is likely to be occupied by companies whose earnings prospects have fallen substantially since the time when their debts were issued.

those who like lotteries, would purchase stocks in this range. Remember, however, that the yield curve of Proposition II is a consequence of the more fundamental Proposition I. Should the demand by the risk lovers prove insufficient to keep the market to the perculiar yield curve *MD*, this demand would be reinforced by the action of arbitrage operators. The latter would find it profitable to own a pro rata share of the firm as a whole by holding its stock *and* bonds, the lower yield of the shares being thus offset by the higher return on bonds.

## D. The Relation of Propositions I and II to Current Doctrines

The propositions we have developed with respect to the valuation of firms and shares appear to be substantially at variance with current doctrines in the field of finance. The main differences between our view and the current view are summarized graphically in Figures 1 and 2. Our Proposition I (equation 4) asserts that the average cost of capital, $\overline{X}_j^{\tau}/V_j$, is a constant for all firms *j* in class *k*, independently of their financial structure. This implies that if we were to take a sample of firms in a given class, and if for each firm we were to plot the ratio of expected return to market value against some measure of leverage or financial structure, the points would tend to fall on a horizontal straight line with intercept $\rho_k^{\tau}$, like the solid line *mm'* in Figure 1.[22] From Proposition I, we derived Proposition II (equation 8), which, taking the simplest ver-

FIGURE 1

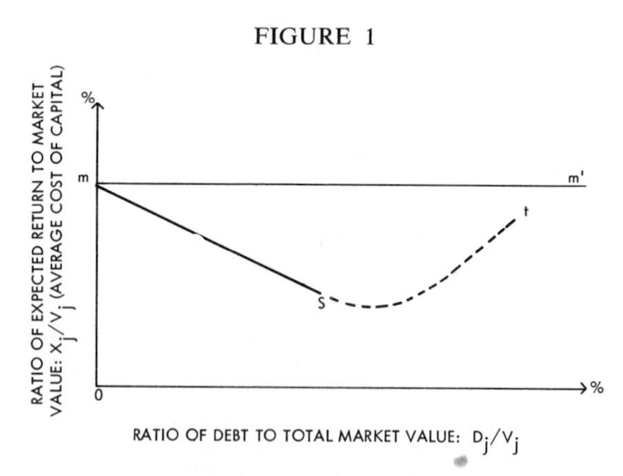


[22]In Figure 1 the measure of leverage used is $D_j/V_j$ (the ratio of debt to market value) rather than $D_j/S_j$ (the ratio of debt to equity), the concept used in the analytical development. The $D_j/V_j$ measure is introduced at this point because it simplifies comparison and contrast of our view with the traditional position.

FIGURE 2

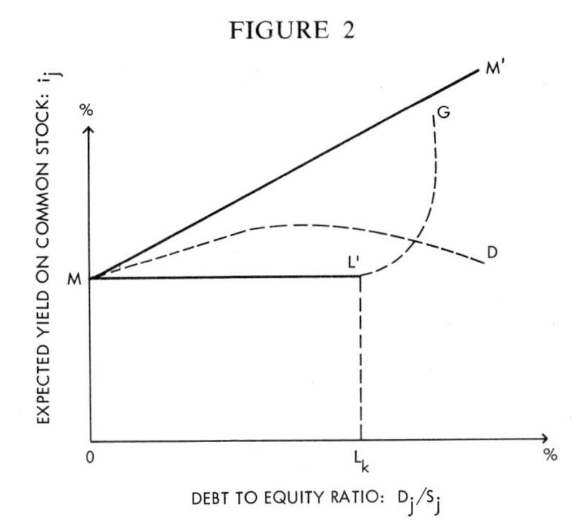


sion with $r$ constant, asserts that for all firms in a class the relation between the yield on common stock and financial structure, measured by $D_j/S_j$, will approximate a straight line with slope $(\rho_k{}^\tau - r)$ and intercept $\rho_k{}^\tau$. This relationship is shown as the solid line $MM'$ in Figure 2, to which reference has been made earlier.[23]

By contrast, the conventional view among finance specialists appears to start from the proposition that, other things equal, the earnings-price ratio (or its reciprocal, the times- earnings multiplier) of a firm's common stock will normally be only slightly affected by "moderate" amounts of debt in the firm's capital structure.[24] Translated into our notation, it asserts that for any firm $j$ in the class $k$:

$$\frac{\bar{X}_j{}^\tau - rD_j}{S_j} \equiv \frac{\bar{\pi}_j{}^\tau}{S_j} = i_k^*, \text{ a constant for } \frac{D_j}{S_j} \leq L_k \qquad (13)$$

or equivalently:

$$S_j = \bar{\pi}_j{}^\tau / i_k^* \qquad (14)$$

Here, $i_k^*$ represents the capitalization rate or earnings-price ratio on the common stock, and $L_k$ denotes some amount of leverage regarded as the maximum "reasonable" amount for firms of the class $k$. This assumed relationship between yield and leverage is the horizontal solid line $ML'$

[23]The line $MM'$ in Figure 2 has been drawn with a positive slope on the assumption that $\rho_k{}^\tau > r$, a condition which will normally obtain. Our Proposition II as given in equation 8 would continue to be valid, of course, even in the unlikely event that $\rho_k{}^\tau < r$, but the slope of $MM'$ would be negative.

[24]See, e.g., Graham and Dodd [6, pp. 464–66]. Without doing violence to this position, we can bring out its implications more sharply by ignoring the qualification and treating the yield as a virtual constant over the relevant range. See in this connection the discussion in Durand [3, esp. pp. 225–37] of what he calls the "net income method" of valuation.

of Figure 2. Beyond $L'$ the yield will presumably rise sharply as the market discounts "excessive" trading on the equity. This possibility of a rising range for high leverages is indicated by the broken-line segment $L'G$ in the figure.[25]

If the value of shares were really given by equation 14, then the over-all market value of the firm must be:

$$V_j \equiv S_j + D_j = \frac{\bar{X}_j^{\tau} - rD_j}{i_k^*} + D_j = \frac{\bar{X}_j^{\tau}}{i_k^*} + \frac{(i_k^* - r)\, D_j}{i_k^*} \quad (16)$$

That is, for any given level of expected total returns after taxes ($\bar{X}_j^{\tau}$), and assuming, as seems natural, that $i_k^* > r$, the value of the firm must tend to *rise* with debt;[26] whereas our Proposition I asserts that the value of the firm is completely independent of the capital structure. Another way of contrasting our position with the traditional one is in terms of the cost of capital. Solving equation 16 for $\bar{X}_j^{\tau}/V_j$ yields:

$$\bar{X}_j^{\tau}/V_j = i_k^* - (i_k^* - r)D_j/V_j \quad (17)$$

According to this equation, the average cost of capital is not independent of capital structure, as we have argued, but should tend to *fall* with increasing leverage, at least within the relevant range of moderate debt ratios, as shown by the line *ms* in Figure 1. Or to put it in more familiar terms, debt financing should be "cheaper" than equity financing if not carried too far.

When we also allow for the possibility of a rising range of stock yields for large values of leverage, we obtain a U-shaped curve like *mst* in Figure 1.[27] That a yield curve for stocks of the form $ML'G$ in Figure 2

[25] To make it easier to see some of the implications of this hypothesis as well as to prepare the ground for later statistical testing, it will be helpful to assume that the notion of a critical limit on leverage beyond which yields rise rapidly can be epitomized by a quadratic relation of the form:

$$(15) \qquad \bar{\pi}_j^{\tau}/S_j = i_k^* + \beta(D_j/S_j) + \alpha(D_j/S_j)^2, \; . \; . \; . \; . \; \alpha > 0$$

[26] For a typical discussion of how a promoter can, supposedly, increase the market value of a firm by recourse to debt issues, see Eiteman [4, esp. pp. 11–13].

[27] The U-shaped nature of the cost-of-capital curve can be exhibited explicitly if the yield curves for shares as a function of leverage can be approximated by equation 15 of n. 25. From that equation, multiplying both sides by $S_j$, we obtain: $\bar{\pi}_j^{\tau} = \bar{X}_j^{\tau} - rD_j = i_k^* S_j + \beta D_j + \alpha D_j^2/S_j$, or, adding and substracting $i_k^* D_k$ from the right-hand side and collecting terms:

$$(18) \qquad \bar{X}_j^{\tau} = i_k^* (S_j + D_j) + (\beta + r - i_k^*)D_j + \alpha D^2_j/S_j$$

Dividing equation 18 by $V_j$ gives an expression for the cost of capital:

(19)

$$\bar{X}_j^{\tau}/V_j = i_k^* - (i_k^* - r - \beta)D_j/V_j + \alpha D_j^2/S_jV_j = i_k^* - (i_k^* - r - \beta)\, D_j/V_j + \alpha(D_j/V_j)^2/(1 - D_j/V_j)$$

which is clearly U-shaped, since $\alpha$ is supposed to be positive.

implies a U-shaped cost-of-capital curve has of course been recognized by many writers. A natural further step has been to suggest that the capital structure corresponding to the trough of the U is an "optimal capital structure" toward which management ought to strive in the best interests of the stockholders.[28] According to our model, by contrast, no such optimal structure exists, all structures being equivalent from the point of view of the cost of capital.

Although the falling, or at least U-shaped, cost-of-capital function is in one form or another the dominant view in the literature, the ultimate rationale of that view is by no means clear. The crucial element in the position—that the expected earnings-price ratio of the stock is largely unaffected by leverage up to some conventional limit—is rarely even regarded as something which requires explanation. It is usually simply taken for granted, or it is merely asserted that this is the way the market behaves.[29] To the extent that the constant earnings-price ratio has a rationale at all, we suspect that it reflects in most cases the feeling that moderate amounts of debt in "sound" corporations do not really add very much to the "riskiness" of the stock. Since the extra risk is slight, it seems natural to suppose that firms will not have to pay noticeably higher yields in order to induce investors to hold the stock.[30]

A more sophisticated line of argument has been advanced by David Durand [3, pp. 231–33]. He suggests that because insurance companies and certain other important institutional investors are restricted to debt securities, nonfinancial corporations are able to borrow from them at interest rates which are lower than would be required to compensate creditors in a free market. Thus, while he would presumably agree with our conclusions that stockholders could not gain from leverage in an unconstrained market, he concludes that they can gain under present institutional arrangements. This gain would arise by virtue of the "safety superpremium" which lenders are willing to pay corporations for the privilege of lending.[31]

---

[28]For a typical statement, see Robbins [16, p. 307]. See also Graham and Dodd [6, pp. 468–74].

[29]See, e.g., Graham and Dodd [6, p. 466].

[30]A typical statement is the following by Guthmann and Dougall [7, p. 245]: "Theoretically it might be argued that the increased hazard from using bonds and preferred stocks would counterbalance this additional income and so prevent the common stock from being more attractive than when it had a lower return but fewer prior obligations. In practice, the extra earnings from 'trading on the equity' are often regarded by investors as more than sufficient to serve as a 'premium for risk' when the proportions of the several securities are judiciously mixed."

[31]Like Durand, Morton [15] contends "that the actual market deviates from [Proposition I] by giving a changing over-all cost of money at different points of the [leverage] scale" (p. 443, n. 2, inserts ours), but the basis for this contention is nowhere clearly stated. Judging by the great emphasis given to the lack of mobility of investment funds between stocks and bonds and to the psychological and

*(Continued on next page)*

The defective link in both the traditional and the Durand version of the argument lies in the confusion between investors' subjective risk preferences and their objective market opportunities. Our Propositions I and II, as noted earlier, do not depend for their validity on any assumption about individual risk preferences. Nor do they involve any assertion as to what is an adequate compensation to investors for assuming a given degree of risk. They rely merely on the fact that a given commodity cannot consistently sell at more than one price in the market or, more precisely, that the price of a commodity representing a "bundle" of two other commodities cannot be consistently different from the weighted average of the prices of the two components (the weights being equal to the proportion of the two commodities in the bundle).

An analogy may be helpful at this point. The relations between $1/\rho_k$, the price per dollar of an unlevered stream in class *k;* $1/r$, the price per dollar of a sure stream; and $1/i_j$, the price per dollar of a levered stream *j*, in the *k*th class, are essentially the same as those between, respectively, the price of whole milk, the price of butterfat, and the price of milk which has been thinned out by skimming off some of the butterfat. Our Proposition I states that a firm cannot reduce the cost of capital—i.e., increase the market value of the stream it generates—by securing part of its capital through the sale of bonds, even though debt money appears to be cheaper. This assertion is equivalent to the proposition that under perfect markets a dairy farmer cannot, in general, earn more for the milk he produces by skimming some of the butterfat and selling it separately, even though butterfat per unit weight sells for more than whole milk. The advantage from skimming the milk rather than selling whole milk would be purely illusory; for what would be gained from selling the high-priced butterfat would be lost in selling the low-priced residue of thinned milk. Similarly, our Proposition II—that the price per dollar of a levered stream falls as leverage increases—is an exact analogue of the statement that the price per gallon of thinned milk falls continuously as more butterfat is skimmed off.[32]

---

institutional pressures toward debt portfolios (see pp. 444–51 and especially his discussion of the optimal capital structure on p. 453), he would seem to be taking a position very similar to that of Durand above.

[32]Let $M$ denote the quantity of whole milk, $B/M$ the proportion of butterfat in the whole milk; and let $p_M$, $p_B$, and $p\alpha$ denote, respectively, the price per unit weight of whole milk, butterfat, and thinned milk from which a fraction $\alpha$ of the butterfat has been skimmed off. We then have the fundamental perfect market relation:

$$(a) \qquad p\alpha(M - \alpha B) + p_B \alpha B = p_M M, \qquad 0 \leq \alpha \leq 1$$

stating that total receipts will be the same amount, $p_M M$, independently of the amount $\alpha B$ of butterfat that may have been sold separately. Since $p_M$ corresponds

It is clear that this last assertion is true as long as butterfat is worth more per unit weight than whole milk; and it holds even if, for many consumers, taking a little cream out of the milk (adding a little leverage to the stock) does not detract noticeably from the taste (does not add noticeably to the risk). Furthermore, the argument remains valid even in the face of institutional limitations of the type envisaged by Durand. For suppose that a large fraction of the population habitually dines in restaurants which are required by law to serve only cream in lieu of milk (entrust their savings to institutional investors who can only buy bonds). To be sure, the price of butterfat will then tend to be higher in relation to that of skimmed milk than in the absence such restrictions (the rate of interest will tend to be lower), and this will benefit people who eat at home and who like skim milk (who managed their own portfolio and are able and willing to take risk). But it will still be the case that a farmer cannot gain by skimming some of the butterfat and selling it separately (a firm cannot reduce the cost of capital by recourse to borrowed funds).[33]

Our propositions can be regarded as the extension of the classical theory of markets to the particular case of the capital markets. Those who hold the current view—whether they realize it or not—must assume not merely that there are lags and frictions in the equilibrating process—a feeling we certainly share,[34] claiming for our propositions

---

to $1/\rho$, $p_B$ to $1/r$, $p_\alpha$ to $1/i$, $M$ to $\overline{X}$, and $\alpha B$ to $rD$, equation $a$ is equivalent to Proposition I, $S + D = \overline{X}/\rho$. From equation $a$, we derive:

$$p\alpha = p_M \frac{M}{M - \alpha B} - p_B \frac{\alpha B}{M - \alpha B} \qquad (b)$$

which gives the price of thinned milk as an explicit function of the proportion of butterfat skimmed off, the function decreasing as long as $p_B > p_M$. From equation $a$ also follows:

$$1/p\alpha = 1/p_M + (1/p_M - 1/p_B) \frac{p_B \alpha B}{p\alpha(M - \alpha B)} \qquad (c)$$

which is the exact analogue of Proposition II, as given by equation 8.

[33]The reader who likes parables will find that the analogy with interrelated commodity markets can be pushed a good deal farther than we have done in the text. For instance, the effect of changes in the market rate of interest on the over-all cost of capital is the same as the effect of a change in the price of butter on the price of whole milk. Similarly, just as the relation between the prices of skim milk and butterfat influences the kind of cows that will be reared, so the relations between $i$ and $r$ influences the kind of ventures that will be undertaken. If people like butter, we shall have Guernseys; if they are willing to pay a high price for safety, this will encourage ventures which promise smaller but less uncertain streams per dollar of physical assets.

[34]Several specific examples of the failure of the arbitrage mechanism can be found in Graham and Dodd [6, e.g., pp. 646–48]. The price discrepancy described on pages 646–47 is particularly curious, since it persists even today despite the fact that a whole generation of security analysts has been brought up on this book!

only that they describe the central tendency around which observations will scatter—but also that there are large and *systematic* imperfections in the market which permanently bias the outcome. This is an assumption that economists, at any rate, will instinctively eye with some skepticism.

In any event, whether such prolonged, systematic departures from equilibrium really exist or whether our propositions are better descriptions of long-run market behavior can be settled only by empirical research. Before going on to the theory of investment, it may be helpful, therefore, to look at the evidence.

## *E. Some Preliminary Evidence on the Basic Propositions*

Unfortunately, the evidence which has been assembled so far is amazingly skimpy. Indeed, we have been able to locate only two recent studies—and these of rather limited scope—which were designed to throw light on the issue. Pending the results of more comprehensive tests which we hope will soon be available, we shall review briefly such evidence as is provided by the two studies in question: (1) an analysis of the relation between security yields and financial structure for some 43 large electric utilities by Allen [1], and (2) a parallel (unpublished) study by Robert Smith [19], for 42 oil companies designed to test whether Allen's rather striking results would be found in an industry with very different characteristics.[35] The Allen study is based on average figures for the years 1947 and 1948, while the Smith study relates to the single year 1953.

*The Effect of Leverage on the Cost of Capital.* According to the received view, as shown in equation 17, the average cost of capital, $\bar{X}^{\tau}/V$, should decline linearly with leverage as measured by the ratio $D/V$, at least through most of the relevant range.[36] According to Proposition I, the average cost of capital within a given class $k$ should tend to have the same value, $\rho_k^{\tau}$, independently of the degree of leverage. A simple test of the merits of the two alternative hypotheses can thus be

[35]We wish to express our thanks to both writers for making available to us some of their original work sheets. In addition to these recent studies, there is a frequently cited (but apparently seldom read) study by the Federal Communications Commission in 1938 [22] which purports to show the existence of an optimal capital structure or range of structures (in the sense defined above) for public utilities in the 1930's. By current standards for statistical investigations, however, this study cannot be regarded as having any real evidential value for the problem at hand.

[36]We shall simplify our notation in this section by dropping the subscript $j$ used to denote a particular firm wherever this will not lead to confusion.

carried out by correlating $\bar{X}^{\tau}/V$ with $D/V$. If the traditional view is correct, the correlation should be significantly negative; if our view represents a better approximation to reality, then the correlation should not be significantly different from zero.

Both studies provide information about the average value of $D$—the market value of bonds and preferred stock—and of $V$—the market value of all securities.[37] From these data, we can readily compute the ratio $D/V$, and this ratio (expressed as a percentage) is represented by the symbol $d$ in the regression equations below. The measurement of the variable $\bar{X}^{\tau}/V$, however, presents serious difficulties. Strictly speaking, the numerator should measure the expected returns net of taxes, but this is a variable on which no direct information is available. As an approximation, we have followed both authors and used (1) the average value of actual net returns in 1947 and 1948 for Allen's utilities and (2) actual net returns in 1953 for Smith's oil companies. Net return is defined in both cases as the sum of interest, preferred dividends, and stockholders' income net of corporate income taxes. Although this approximation to expected returns is undoubtedly very crude, there is no reason to believe that it will systematically bias the test insofar as the sign of the regression coefficient is concerned. The roughness of the approximation, however, will tend to make for a wide scatter. Also contributing to the scatter is the crudeness of the industrial classification, since, especially within the sample of oil companies, the assumption that all the firms belong to the same class, in our sense, is at best only approximately valid.

Denoting by $x$ our approximation to $\bar{X}^{\tau}/V$ (expressed, like $d$, as a percentage), the results of the tests are as follows:

$$\text{Electric utilities:}\quad x = 5.3 + \underset{(\pm\, 0.008)}{0.006d} \qquad r = 0.12$$

$$\text{Oil companies:}\quad x = 8.5 + \underset{(\pm\, 0.024)}{0.006d} \qquad r = 0.04$$

The data underlying these equations are also shown in scatter diagram form in Figures 3 and 4.

[37]Note that for purposes of this test, preferred stocks, since they represent an *expected* fixed obligation, are properly classified with bonds, even though the tax status of preferred dividends is different from that of interest payments, and even though preferred dividends are really fixed only as to their maximum in any year. Some difficulty of classification does arise in the case of convertible preferred stocks (and convertible bonds) selling at a substantial premium; but fortunately, very few such issues were involved for the companies included in the two studies. Smith included bank loans and certain other short-term obligations (at book values) in his data on oil company debts, and this treatment is perhaps open to some question. However, the amounts involved were relatively small, and check computations showed that their elimination would lead to only minor differences in the test results.

The results of these tests are clearly favorable to our hypothesis. Both correlation coefficients are very close to zero and not statistically significant. Furthermore, the implications of the traditional view fail to be supported even with respect to the sign of the correlation. The data, in short, provide no evidence of any tendency for the cost of capital to fall as the debt ratio increases.[38]

It should also be apparent from the scatter diagrams that there is no hint of a curvilinear, U-shaped relation of the kind which is widely be-

FIGURE 3

Cost of Capital in Relation to Financial Structure for 43 Electric Utilities, 1947–48

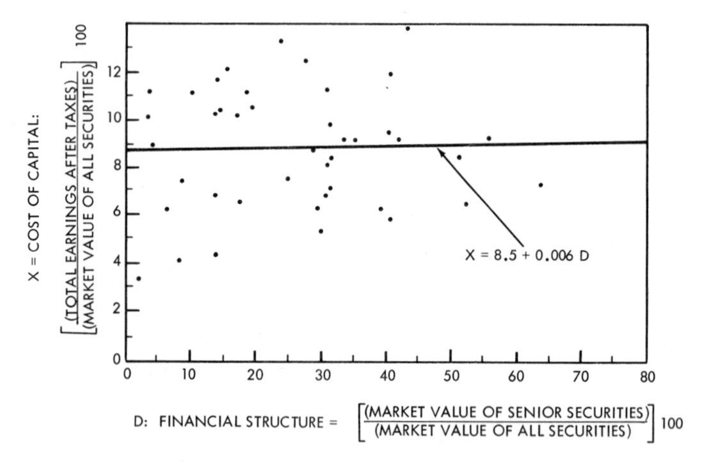


[38]It may be argued that a test of the kind used is biased against the traditional view. The fact that both sides of the regression equation are divided by the variable $V$, which may be subject to random variation, might tend to impart a positive bias to the correlation. As a check on the results presented in the text, we have therefore carried out a supplementary test based on equation 16. This equation shows that if the traditional view is correct, the market value of a company should, for given $\overline{X}^{\tau}$, increase with debt through most of the relevant range; according to our model, the market value should be uncorrelated with $D$, given $\overline{X}^{\tau}$. Because of wide variations in the size of the firms included in our samples, all variables must be divided by a suitable scale factor in order to avoid spurious results in carrying out a test of equation 16. The factor we have used in the book value of the firm denoted by $A$. The hypothesis tested thus takes the specific form:

$$V/A = a + b(\overline{X}^{\tau}/A) + c(D/A)$$

and the numerator of the ratio $X^{\tau}/A$ is again approximated by actual net returns. The partial correlation between $V/A$ and $D/A$ should now be positive according to the traditional view and zero according to our model. Although division by $A$ should, if anything, bias the results in favor of the traditional hypothesis, the partial correlation turns out to be only 0.03 for the oil companies and −0.28 for the electric utilities. Neither of these coefficients is significantly different from zero, and the larger one even has the wrong sign.

lieved to hold between the cost of capital and leverage. This graphical impression was confirmed by statistical tests which showed that for both industries the curvature was not significantly different from zero, its sign actually being opposite to that hypothesized.[39]

FIGURE 4

COST OF CAPITAL IN RELATION TO FINANCIAL STRUCTURE FOR 42 OIL COMPANIES, 1953

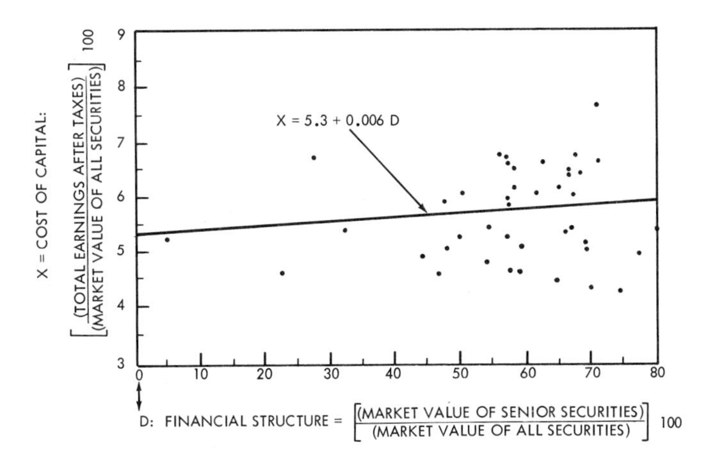


Note also that according to our model, the constant terms of the regression equations are measures of $\rho_k^{\tau}$, the capitalization rates for unlevered streams and hence the average cost of capital in the classes in question. The estimates of 8.5 percent for the oil companies as against 5.3 percent for electric utilities appear to accord well with a priori expectations, both in absolute value and in relative spread.

*The Effect of Leverage on Common Stock Yields.* According to our Proposition II—see equation 12 and Figure 2—the expected yield on common stock, $\bar{\pi}^{\tau}/S$, in any given class, should tend to increase with leverage as measured by the ratio $D/S$. The relation should tend to be linear and with positive slope through most of the relevant range (as in the curve $MM'$ of Figure 2), though it might tend to flatten out if we move far enough to the right (as in the curve $MD'$), to the extent that high leverage tends to drive up the cost of senior capital. According to

[39]The tests consisted of fitting to the data the equation 19 of note 27. As shown there, it follows from the U-shaped hypothesis that the coefficient $\alpha$ of the variable $(D/V)^2/(1-D/V)$, denoted hereafter by $d^*$, should be significant and positive. The following regression equations and partials were obtained:

Electric utilities: $x = 5.0 + 0.017d - 0.003d^*$; $r_{xd^* .d} = -0.15$

Oil companies: $x = 8.0 + 0.05d - 0.03d^*$; $r_{xd^* .d} = -0.14$

the conventional view, the yield curve as a function of leverage should be a horizontal straight line (like $ML'$) through most of the relevant range; far enough to the right, the yield may tend to rise at an increasing rate. Here again, a straightforward correlation—in this case between $\bar{\pi}^{\tau}/S$ and $D/S$—can provide a test of the two positions. If our view is correct, the correlation should be significantly positive; if the traditional view is correct, the correlation should be negligible.

Subject to the same qualifications noted above in connection with $\bar{X}^{\tau}$, we can approximate $\bar{\pi}^{\tau}$ by actual stockholder net income.[40] Letting $z$ denote in each case the approximation to $\bar{\pi}^{\tau}/S$ (expressed as a percentage), and letting $h$ denote the ratio $D/S$ (also in percentage terms), the following results are obtained:

$$\text{Electric utilities:} \quad z = 6.6 + \underset{(+\,0.004)}{0.017h} \qquad r = 0.53$$

$$\text{Oil companies:} \quad z = 8.9 + \underset{(\pm\,0.012)}{0.051h} \qquad r = 0.53$$

These results are shown in scatter diagram form in Figures 5 and 6.

Here again, the implications of our analysis seem to be borne out by the data. Both correlation coefficients are positive and highly significant when account is taken of the substantial sample size. Furthermore, the estimates of the coefficients of the equations seem to accord reasonably well with our hypothesis. According to equation 12, the constant term should be the value of $\rho_k{}^{\tau}$ for the given class, while the slope should be $(\rho_k{}^{\tau} - r)$. From the test of Proposition I, we have seen that for the oil companies the mean value of $\rho_k{}^{\tau}$ could be estimated at around 8.7. Since the average yield of senior capital during the period covered was in the order of 3.5 percent, we should expect a constant term of about 8.7 percent and a slope of just over 5 percent. These values closely approximate the regression estimates of 8.9 percent and 5.1 percent, respectively. For the electric utilities the yield of senior capital was also on the order of 3.5 percent during the test years; but since the estimate

[40] As indicated earlier, Smith's data were for the single year 1953. Since the use of a single year's profits as a measure of expected profits might be open to objection, we collected profit data for 1952 for the same companies and based the computation of $\bar{\pi}^{\tau}/S$ on the average of the two years. The value of $\bar{\pi}^{\tau}/S$ was obtained from the formula:

$$\left(\text{Net earnings in 1952} \cdot \frac{\text{Assets in 1953}}{\text{Assets in 1952}} + \text{Net earnings in 1953}\right)\frac{1}{2} \div (\text{Average market value of common stock in 1953})$$

The asset adjustment was introduced as rough allowance for the effects of possible growth in the size of the firm. It might be added that the correlation computed with $\pi^{\tau}/S$ based on net profits in 1953 alone was found to be only slightly smaller, namely, 0.50.

FIGURE 5

YIELD ON COMMON STOCK IN RELATION TO LEVERAGE FOR 43 ELECTRIC UTILITIES, 1947–48

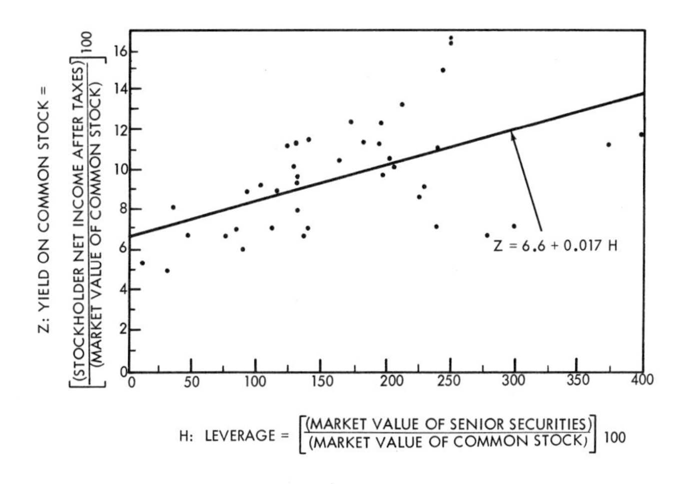


FIGURE 6

YIELD ON COMMON STOCK IN RELATION TO LEVERAGE FOR 42 OIL COMPANIES, 1952–53

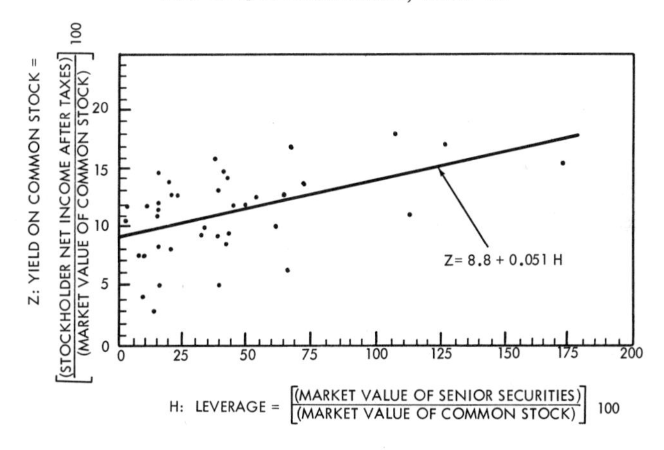


of the mean value of $\rho_k{}^\tau$ from the test of Proposition I was 5.6 percent, the slope should be just above 2 percent. The actual regression estimate for the slope of 1.7 percent is thus somewhat low, but still within one standard error of its theoretical value. Because of this underestimate of the slope, and because of the large mean value of leverage ($\bar{h}=160$ percent), the regression estimate of the constant term, 6.6 percent, is somewhat high, although not significantly different from the value of 5.6 percent obtained in the test of Proposition I.

When we add a square term to the above equations to test for the presence and direction of curvature, we obtain the following etsimates:

$$\text{Electric utilities:} \quad z = 4.6 + 0.004h - 0.007h^2$$

$$\text{Oil companies:} \quad z = 8.5 + 0.072h - 0.016\text{-}h^2$$

For both cases the curvature is negative. In fact, for the electric utilities, where the observations cover a wider range of leverage ratios, the negative coefficient of the square term is actually significant at the 5 percent level. Negative curvature, as we have seen, runs directly counter to the traditional hypothesis, whereas it can be readily accounted for by our model in terms of rising cost of borrowed funds.[41]

In summary, the empirical evidence we have reviewed seems to be broadly consistent with our model and largely inconsistent with traditional views. Needless to say, much more extensive testing will be required before we can firmly conclude that our theory describes market behavior. Caution is indicated especially with regard to our test of Proposition II, partly because of possible statistical pitfalls[42] and partly because not all the factors that might have a systematic effect on stock yields have been considered. In particular, no attempt was made to test the possible influence of the dividend payout ratio, whose role has tended to receive a great deal of attention in current research and thinking. There are two reasons for this omission. First, our main objective has been to assess the prima facie tenability of *our* model; and in this model, based as it is on rational behavior by investors, dividends per se play no role. Second, in a world in which the policy of dividend stabilization is widespread, there is no simple way of disentangling the true effect of dividend payments on stock prices from their apparent effect, the latter reflecting only the role of dividends as a proxy measure of long-term earning anticipations.[43] The difficulties just mentioned are

---

[41]That the yield of senior capital tended to rise for utilities as leverage increased is clearly shown in several of the scatter diagrams presented in the published version of Allen's study. This significant negative curvature between stock yields and leverage for utilities may be partly responsible for the fact, previously noted, that the constant in the linear regression is somewhat higher and the slope somewhat lower than implied by equation 12. Note also in connection with the estimate of $\rho_k{}^T$ that the introduction of the quadratic term reduces the constant considerably, pushing it in fact below the a priori expectation of 5.6, though the difference is again not statistically significant.

[42]In our test, e.g., the two variables $z$ and $h$ are both ratios with $S$ appearing in the denominator, which may tend to impart a positive bias to the correlation (cf. n. 38). Attempts were made to develop alternative tests; but although various possibilities were explored, we have so far been unable to find satisfactory alternatives.

[43]We suggest that failure to appreciate this difficulty is responsible for many fallacious, or at least unwarranted, conclusions about the role of dividends.

further compounded by possible interrelations between dividend policy and leverage.[44]

## II. Implications of the Analysis for the Theory of Investment

### A. *Capital Structure and Investment Policy*

On the basis of our propositions with respect to cost of capital and financial structure (and for the moment neglecting taxes), we can derive the following simple rule for optimal investment policy by the firm:

*Proposition III.* If a firm in class $k$ is acting in the best interest of the stockholders at the time of the decision, it will exploit an investment opportunity if, and only if, the rate of return on the investment, say $\rho^*$, is as large as or larger than $\rho_k$. That is, *the cutoff point for investment in the firm will in all cases be* $\rho_k$ *and will be completely unaffected by the type of security used to finance the investment.* Equivalently, we may say that regardless of the financing used, the marginal cost of capital to a firm is equal to the average cost of capital, which is in turn equal to the capitalization rate for an unlevered stream in the class to which the firms belongs.[45]

To establish this result, we shall consider the three major financing alternatives open to the firm—bonds, retained earnings, and common stock issues—and show that in each case an investment is worth undertaking if, and only if, $\rho^* \geqq \rho_k$.[46]

Consider first the case of an investment financed by the sale of bonds.

---

[44]In the sample of electric utilities, there is a substantial negative correlation between yields and payout ratios, but also between payout ratios and leverage, suggesting that either the association of yields and leverage, or of yields and payout ratios, may be (at least partly) spurious. These difficulties, however, do not arise in the case of the oil industry sample. A preliminary analysis indicates that there is here no significant relation between leverage and payout ratios and also no significant correlation (either gross or partial) between yields and payout ratios.

[45]The analysis developed in this paper is essentially a comparative statics, not a dynamic analysis. This note of caution applies with special force to Proposition III. Such problems as those posed by expected changes in $r$ and $\rho_k$ over time will not be treated here. Although they are in principle amenable to analysis within the general framework we have laid out, such an undertaking is sufficiently complex to deserve separate treatment. Cf. n. 17.

[46]The extension of the proof to other types of financing, such as the sale of preferred stock or the issuance of stock rights, is straightforward.

We know from Proposition I that the market value of the firm before the investment was undertaken was:[47]

$$V_0 = \bar{X}_0/\rho_k \tag{20}$$

and that the value of the common stock was:

$$S_0 = V_0 - D_0 \tag{21}$$

If, now, the firm borrows $I$ dollars to finance an investment yielding $\rho^*$, its market value will become:

$$V_1 = \frac{\bar{X}_0 + \rho^* I}{\rho_k} = V_0 + \frac{\rho^* I}{\rho_k} \tag{22}$$

and the value of its common stock will be:

$$S_1 = V_1 - (D_0 + I) = V_0 + \frac{\rho^* I}{\rho_k} - D_0 - I \tag{23}$$

or, using equation 21:

$$S_1 = S_0 + \frac{\rho^* I}{\rho_k} - I \tag{24}$$

Hence, $S_1 \gtreqless S_0$ *as* $\rho^* \gtreqless \rho_k$.[48]

To illustrate, suppose the capitalization rate for uncertain streams in the *k*th class is 10 percent and the rate of interest is 4 percent. Then, if a given company had an expected income of 1,000, and if it was financed entirely by common stock, we know from Proposition I that the market value of its stock would be 10,000. Assume now that the managers of the firm discover an investment opportunity which will require an outlay of 100 and which is expected to yield 8 percent. At first sight, this might appear to be a profitable opportunity, since the expected return is double the interest cost. If, however, the management borrows the necessary 100 at 4 percent, the total expected income of the company rises to 1,008, and the market value of the firm to 10,080. But the firm now will have 100 of bonds in its capital structure, so that, paradoxically, the market value of the stock must actually be reduced from 10,000 to

[47]Since no confusion is likely to arise, we have again, for simplicity, eliminated the subscripts identifying the firm in the equations to follow. Except for $\rho_k$, the subscripts now refer to time periods.

[48]In the case of bond financing the rate of interest on bonds does not enter explicitly into the decision (assuming the firm borrows at the market rate of interest). This is true, moreover, given the conditions outlined in Section I(C), even though interest rates may be an increasing function of debt outstanding. To the extent that the firm borrowed at a rate other than the market rate, the two $I$'s in equation 24 would no longer be identical; and an additional gain or loss, as the case might be, would accrue to the shareholders. It might also be noted in passing that permitting the two $I$'s in equation 24 to take on different values provides a simple method for introducing underwriting expenses into the analysis.

9,980 as a consequence of this apparently profitable investment. Or to put it another way, the gains from being able to tap cheap, borrowed funds are more than offset for the stockholders by the market's discounting of the stock for the added leverage assumed.

Consider next the case of retained earnings. Suppose that in the course of its operations the firm acquired $I$ dollars of cash (without impairing the earning power of its assets). If the cash is distributed as a dividend to the stockholders, their wealth, $W_0$, after the distribution will be:

$$W_0 = S_0 + I = \frac{\bar{X}_0}{\rho_k} - D_0 + I \tag{25}$$

where $\bar{X}_0$ represents the expected return from the assets exclusive of the amount $I$ in question. If, however, the funds are retained by the company and use to finance new assets whose expected rate of return is $\rho^*$, then the stockholders' wealth would become:

$$W_1 = S_1 = \frac{\bar{X}_0 + \rho^* I}{\rho_k} - D_0 = S_0 + \frac{\rho^* I}{\rho_k} \tag{26}$$

Clearly, $W_1 \gtreqless W_0$ as $\rho^* \gtreqless \rho_k$, so that an investment financed by retained earnings raises the net worth of the owners if, and only if, $\rho^* > \rho_k$.[49]

Consider, finally, the case of common stock financing. Let $P_0$ denote the current market price per share of stock; and assume, for simplicity, that this price reflects currently expected earnings only, that is, it does not reflect any future increase in earnings as a result of the investment under consideration.[50] Then, if $N$ is the original number of shares, the price per share is:

$$P_0 = S_0/N \tag{27}$$

and the number of new shares, $M$, needed to finance an investment of $I$ dollars is given by:

$$M = \frac{I}{P_0} \tag{28}$$

[49]The conclusion that $\rho_k$ is the cutoff point for investments financed from internal funds applies not only to undistributed net profits but to depreciation allowances (and even to the funds represented by the current sale value of any asset or collection of assets). Since the owners can earn $\rho_k$ by investing funds elsewhere in the class, partial or total liquidating distributions should be made whenever the firm cannot achieve a marginal internal rate of return equal to $\rho_k$.

[50]If we assumed that the market price of the stock did reflect the expected higher future earnings (as would be the case if our original set of assumptions above were strictly followed), the analysis would differ slightly in detail but not in essentials. The cutoff point for new investment would still be $\rho_k$; but where $\rho^* > \rho_k$, the gain to the original owners would be larger than if the stock price were based on the preinvestment expectations only.

As a result of the investment, the market value of the stock becomes:

$$S_1 = \frac{\bar{X}_0 + \rho^* I}{\rho_k} - D_0 = S_0 + \frac{\rho^* I}{\rho_k} = NP_0 + \frac{\rho^* I}{\rho_k}$$

and the price per share:

$$P_1 = \frac{S_1}{N + M} = \frac{1}{N + M}\left[NP_0 + \frac{\rho^* I}{\rho_k}\right] \tag{29}$$

Since, by equation 28, $I = MP_0$, we can add $MP_0$ and subtract $I$ from the quantity in bracket, obtaining:

$$P_1 = \frac{1}{N + M}\left[(N + M)P_0 + \frac{\rho^* - \rho_k}{\rho_k} I\right] \tag{30}$$

$$= P_0 + \frac{1}{N + M}\frac{\rho^* - \rho_k}{\rho_k} I > P_0$$

if, and only if, $\rho^* > \rho_k$. Thus an investment financed by common stock is advantageous to the current stockholders if, and only if, its yield exceeds the capitalization rate $\rho_k$.

Once again, a numerical example may help to illustrate the result and make it clear why the relevant cutoff rate is $\rho_k$ and not the current yield on common stock, *i*. Suppose that $\rho_k$ is 10 percent, that *r* is 4 percent, that the original expected income of our company is 1,000, and that management has the opportunity of investing 100, having an expected yield of 12 percent. If the original capital structure is 50 percent debt and 50 percent equity, and 1,000 shares of stock are initially outstanding, then, by Proposition I, the market value of the common stock must be 5,000 or 5 per share. Furthermore, since the interest bill is $0.04 \times 5{,}000 = 200$, the yield on common stock is $800/5{,}000 = 16$ percent. It may then appear that financing the additional investment of 100 by issuing 20 shares to outsiders at 5 per share would dilute the equity of the original owners, since the 100 promises to yield 12 percent, whereas the common stock is currently yielding 16 percent. Actually, however, the income of the company would rise to 1,012, the value of the firm to 10,120, and the value of the common stock to 5,120. Since there are now 1,020 shares, each would be worth 5.02, and the wealth of the original stockholders would thus have been increased. What has happened is that the dilution in expected earnings per share (from 0.80 to 0.796) has been more than offset, in its effect upon the market price of the shares, by the decrease in leverage.

Our conclusion is once again at variance with conventional views,[51]

[51] In the matter of investment policy under uncertainty, there is no single position which represents "accepted" doctrine. For a sample of current formulations, all very different from ours, see Dean [2, esp. chap. iii], Gordon and Shapiro [5], and Roberts [17].

so much so as to be easily misinterpreted. Read hastily, Proposition III seems to imply that the capital structure of a firm is a matter of indifference, and that consequently one of the core problems of corporate finance—the problem of the optimal capital structure for a firm—is no problem at all. It may be helpful, therefore, to clear up such possible misunderstandings.

## *B. Proposition III and Financial Planning by Firms*

Misinterpretation of the scope of Proposition III can be avoided by remembering that this proposition tells us only that the type of instrument used to finance an investment is irrelevant to the question of whether or not the investment is worthwhile. This does not mean that the owners (or the managers) have no grounds whatever for preferring one financing plan to another, or that there are no other policy or technical issues in finance at the level of the firm.

That grounds for preferring one type of financial structure to another will still exist within the framework of our model can readily be seen for the case of common stock financing. In general, except for something like a widely publicized oil strike, we should expect the market to place very heavy weight on current and recent past earnings in forming expectations as to future returns. Hence, if the owners of a firm discovered a major investment opportunity which they felt would yield much more than $\rho_k$, they might well prefer not to finance it via common stock at the then ruling price, because this price may fail to capitalize the new venture. A better course would be a preemptive issue of stock (and in this connection, it should be remembered that stockholders are free to borrow and buy). Another possibility would be to finance the project initially with debt. Once the project had reflected itself in increased actual earnings, the debt could be retired either with an equity issue at much better prices or through retained earnings. Still another possibility along the same lines might be to combine the two steps by means of a convertible debenture or preferred stock, perhaps with a progressively declining conversion rate. Even such a double-stage financing plan may possibly be regarded as yielding too large a share to outsiders, since the new stockholders are in effect being given an interest in any similar opportunities the firm may discover in the future. If there is a reasonable prospect that even larger opportunities may arise in the near future, and if there is some danger that borrowing now would preclude more borrowing later, the owners might find their interests best protected by splitting off the current opportunity into a separate subsidiary with independent financing. Clearly, the problems involved in making the crucial estimates and in planning the optimal financial strategy are by no means trivial, even though they should have no bearing on the basic decision to invest (as long as $\rho^* \geqq \rho_k$).[52]

Another reason why the alternatives in financial plans may not be a matter of indifference arises from the fact that managers are concerned with more than simply furthering the interest of the owners. Such other objectives of the management—which need not be necessarily in conflict with those of the owners—are much more likely to be served by some types of financing arrangements than others. In many forms of borrowing agreements, for example, creditors are able to stipulate terms which the current management may regard as infringing on its prerogatives or restricting its freedom to maneuver. The creditors might even be able to insist on having a direct voice in the formation of policy.[53] To the extent, therefore, that financial policies have these implications for the management of the firm, something like the utility approach described in the introductory section becomes relevant to financial (as opposed to investment) decision making. It is, however, the utility functions of the managers per se and not of the owners that are now involved.[54]

In summary, many of the specific considerations which bulk so large in traditional discussions of corporate finance can readily be superimposed on our simple framework without forcing any drastic (and certainly no systematic) alteration of the conclusion which is our principal concern, namely, that for investment decisions the marginal cost of capital is $\rho_k$.

---

[52]Nor can we rule out the possibility that the existing owners, if unable to use a financing plan which protects their interest, may actually prefer to pass up an otherwise profitable venture rather than give outsiders an "excessive" share of the business. It is presumably in situations of this kind that we could justifiably speak of a shortage of "equity capital," though this kind of market imperfection is likely to be of significance only for small or new firms.

[53]Similar considerations are involved in the matter of dividend policy. Even though the stockholders may be indifferent as to payout policy as long as investment policy is optimal, the management need not be so. Retained earnings involve far fewer threats to control than any of the alternative sources of funds and, of course, involve no underwriting expense or risk. But against these advantages, management must balance the fact that sharp changes in dividend rates, which heavy reliance on retained earnings might imply, may give the impression that a firm's finances are being poorly managed, with consequent threats to the control and professional standing of the management.

[54]In principle, at least, this introduction of management's risk preferences with respect to financing methods would do much to reconcile the apparent conflict between Proposition III and such empirical findings as those of Modigliani and Zeman [14] on the close relation between interest rates and the ratio of new debt to new equity issues; or of Lintner [12] on the considerable stability in target and actual dividend payout ratios.

## *C. The Effect of the Corporate Income Tax on Investment Decisions*

In Section I, it was shown that when an unintegrated corporate income tax is introduced, the original version of our Proposition I,

$$\bar{X}/V = \rho_k = \text{a constant}$$

must be rewritten as:

$$\frac{(\bar{X} - rD)(1 - \tau) + rD}{V} \equiv \frac{\bar{X}^\tau}{V} = \rho_k^{\;\tau} = \text{a constant} \qquad (11)$$

Throughout Section I, we found it convenient to refer to $\bar{X}^\tau/V$ as the cost of capital. The appropriate measure of the cost of capital relevant to investment decisions, however, is the ratio of the expected return *before* taxes to the market value, i.e., $\bar{X}/V$. From equation 11 above, we find:

$$\frac{\bar{X}}{V} = \frac{\rho_k^{\;\tau} - \tau_r(D/V)}{1 - \tau} = \frac{\rho_k^{\;\tau}}{1 - \tau}\left[1 - \frac{\tau r D}{\rho_k^{\;\tau} V}\right] \qquad (31)$$

which shows that the cost of capital now depends on the debt ratio, decreasing, as $D/V$ rises, at the constant rate $\tau r/(1 - \tau)$.[55] Thus, with a corporate income tax under which interest is a deductible expense, gains can accrue to stockholders from having debt in the capital structure, even when capital markets are perfect. The gains, however, are small, as can be seen from equation 31, and as will be shown more explicitly below.

From equation 31, we can develop the tax-adjusted counterpart of Proposition III by interpreting the term $D/V$ in that equation as the proportion of debt used in any additional financing of $V$ dollars. For example, in the case where the financing is entirely by new common

[55]Equation 31 is amenable, in principle, to statistical tests similar to those described in Section I(E). However, we have not made any systematic attempt to carry out such tests so far, because neither the Allen nor the Smith study provides the required information. Actually, Smith's data included a very crude estimate of tax liability; and using this estimate, we did in fact obtain a negative relation between $\bar{X}/V$ and $D/V$. However, the correlation (−0.28) turned out to be significant only at about the 10 percent level. While this result is not conclusive, it should be remembered that according to our theory, the slope of the regression equation should be in any event quite small. In fact, with a value of $\tau$ in the order of 0.5, and values of $\rho_k^{\;\tau}$ and $r$ in the order of 8.5 and 3.5 percent, respectively (cf. Section I(E), an increase in $D/V$ from 0 to 60 percent (which is, approximately, the range of variation of this variable in the sample) should tend to reduce the average cost of capital only from about 17 to about 15 percent.

stock, $D = 0$, and the required rate of return, $\rho_k^S$, on a venture so financed becomes:

$$\rho_k^S = \frac{\rho_k^\tau}{1 - \tau} \tag{32}$$

For the other extreme of pure debt financing, $D = V$, and the required rate of return, $\rho_k^D$, becomes:

$$\rho_k^D = \frac{\rho_k^\tau}{1 - \tau}\left[1 - \tau\frac{r}{\rho_k^\tau}\right] = \rho_k^S\left[1 - \tau\frac{r}{\rho_k^\tau}\right] = \rho_k^S - \frac{\tau}{1 - \tau}r \tag{33}$$

[56]

For investments financed out of retained earnings, the problem of defining the required rate of return is more difficult, since it involves a comparison of the tax consequences to the individual stockholder of receiving a dividend versus having a capital gain. Depending on the time of realization, a capital gain produced by retained earnings may be taxed either at ordinary income tax rates, 50 percent of these rates, 25 percent, or zero, if held till death. The rate on any dividends received in the event of a distribution will also be a variable depending on the amount of other income received by the stockholder, and with the added complications introduced by the current dividend credit provisions. If we assume that the managers proceed on the basis of reasonable estimates as to the average values of the relevant tax rates for the owners, then the required return for retained earnings, $\rho_k^R$, can be shown to be:

$$\rho_k^R = \rho_k^\tau \frac{1}{1 - \tau}\frac{1 - \tau_d}{1 - \tau_g} = \frac{1 - \tau_d}{1 - \tau_g}\rho_k^s \tag{34}$$

where $\tau_d$ is the assumed rate of personal income tax on dividends and $\tau_g$ is the assumed rate of tax on capital gains.

A numerical illustration may perhaps be helpful in clarifying the relationship between these required rates of return. If we take the following round numbers as representative order-of-magnitude values under present conditions: an after-tax capitalization rate, $\rho_k^\tau$, of 10 percent; a rate of interest on bonds of 4 percent; a corporate tax rate of 50 percent; a marginal personal income tax rate on dividends of 40 percent (corresponding to an income of about $25,000 on a joint return); and a capital gains rate of 20 percent (one half the marginal rate on dividends), then the required rates of return would be (1) 20 percent for investments financed entirely by issuance of new common shares, (2) 16 per-

[56] This conclusion does not extend to preferred stocks, even though they have been classed with debt issues previously. Since preferred dividends, except for a portion of those of public utilities, are not in general deductible from the corporate tax, the cutoff point for new financing via preferred stock is exactly the same as that for common stock.

cent for investments financed entirely by new debt, and (3) 15 percent for investments financed wholly from internal funds.

These results would seem to have considerable significance for current discussions of the effect of the corporate income tax on financial policy and on investment. Although we cannot explore the implications of the results in any detail here, we should at least like to call attention to the remarkably small difference between the "cost" of equity funds and debt funds. With the numerical values assumed, equity money turned out to be only 25 percent more expensive than debt money, rather than something on the order of five times as expensive, as is commonly supposed to be the case.[57] The reason for the wide difference is that the traditional view starts from the position that debt funds are several times cheaper than equity funds even in the absence of taxes, with taxes serving simply to magnify the cost ratio in proportion to the corporate rate. By contrast, in our model, in which the repercussions of debt financing on the value of shares are taken into account, the *only* difference in cost is that due to the tax effect, and its magnitude is simply the tax on the "grossed-up" interest payment. Not only is this magnitude likely to be small, but our analysis yields the further paradoxical implication that the stockholders' gain from, and hence incentive to use, debt financing is actually smaller the lower the rate of interest. In the extreme case where the firm could borrow for practically nothing, the advantage of debt financing would also be practically nothing.

## III. Conclusion

With the development of Proposition III the main objectives we outlined in our introductory discussion have been reached. We have in our Propositions I and II at least the foundations of a theory of the valuation of firms and shares in a world of uncertainty. We have shown, moreover, how this theory can lead to an operational definition of the cost of capital and how that concept can be used in turn as a basis for

[57]See, e.g., D. T. Smith [18]. It should also be pointed out that our tax system acts in other ways to reduce the gains from debt financing. Heavy reliance on debt in the capital structure, for example, commits a company to paying out a substantial proportion of its income in the form of interest payments taxable to the owners under the personal income tax. A debt-free company, by contrast, can reinvest in the business all of its (smaller) net income and to this extent subject the owners only to the low capital gains rate (or possibly no tax at all by virtue of the loophole at death). Thus, we should expect a high degree of leverage to be of value to the owners, even in the case of closely held corporations, primarily in cases where their firm was not expected to have much need for additional funds to expand assets and earnings in the future. To the extent that opportunities for growth were available, as they presumably would be for most successful corporations, the interest of the stockholders would tend to be better served by a structure which permitted maximum use of retained earnings.

rational investment decision making within the firm. Needless to say, however, much remains to be done before the cost of capital can be put away on the shelf among the solved problems. Our approach has been that of static, partial-equilibrium analysis. It has assumed, among other things, a state of atomistic completition in the capital markets and an ease of access to those markets which only a relatively small (though important) group of firms even come close to possessing. These and other drastic simplifications have been necessary in order to come to grips with the problem at all. Having served their purpose, they can now be relaxed in the direction of greater realism and relevance, a task in which we hope others interested in this area will wish to share.

## References


1. ALLEN, F. B. "Does Going into Debt Lower the 'Cost of Capital?'" *Analysts Journal,* Vol. X (August, 1954), pp. 57–61.
2. DEAN, JOEL. *Capital Budgeting.* New York: Columbia University Press, 1951.
3. DURAND, DAVID. "Costs of Debt and Equity Funds for Business: Trends and Problems of Measurement," in NATIONAL BUREAU OF ECONOMIC RESEARCH. *Conference on Research in Business Finance,* pp. 215–47. New York, 1952.
4. EITEMAN, W. J. "Financial Aspects of Promotion," in WATERFORD, M. W., and EITEMAN, W. J. *Essays on Business Finance,* pp. 1–17. Ann Arbor: University of Michigan Press, 1952.
5. GORDON, MYRON J., and SHAPIRO, ELI. "Capital Equipment Analysis: The Required Rate of Profit," *Management Science,* Vol. III (October, 1956), pp. 102–10.
6. GRAHAM, BENJAMIN, and DODD, DAVID L. *Security Analysis.* 3d ed. New York: McGraw-Hill Book Co., Inc., 1951.
7. GUTHMANN, HARRY G. and DOUGALL, HERBERT E. *Corporate Financial Policy.* 3d ed. New York: Prentice-Hall Inc., 1955.
8. HICKS, J. R. *Value and Capital.* 2d ed. Oxford: Oxford University Press, 1946.
9. HUNT, PEARSON, and WILLIAMS, CHARLES M. *Case Problems in Finance.* Rev. ed. Homewood, Ill.: Richard D. Irwin, Inc., 1954.
10. KEYNES, J. M. *The General Theory of Employment, Interest, and Money.* New York: Macmillan Co., 1936.
11. LANGE, O. *Price Flexibility and Employment.* Bloomington: University of Indiana Press, 1944.
12. LINTNER, JOHN. "Distribution of Incomes of Corporations among Dividends, Retained Earnings and Taxes," *American Economic Review,* Vol. XLVI (May, 1956), pp. 97–113.

13. LUTZ, FRIEDERICH, and LUTZ, VERA. *The Theory of Investment of the Firm.* Princeton: Princeton University Press, 1951.

14. MODIGLIANI, FRANCO, and ZEMAN, MORTON. "The Effect of the Availability of Funds, and the Terms Thereof, on Business Investment," in NATIONAL BUREAU OF ECONOMIC RESEARCH. *Conference on Research in Business Finance,* pp. 263–309. New York, 1952.

15. MORTON, W. A. "The Structure of the Capital Market and the Price of Money," *American Economic Review,* Vol. XLIV (May, 1954), pp. 440–54.

16. ROBBINS, S. M. *Managing Securities.* Boston: Graduate School of Business Administration, Harvard University, 1954.

17. ROBERTS, H. V. "Current Problems in the Economics of Capital Budgeting," *Journal of Business,* Vol. XXX (January, 1957), pp. 12–16.

18. SMITH, D. T. *Effects of Taxation on Corporate Financial Policy.* Boston: Graduate School of Business Administration, Harvard University, 1952.

19. SMITH, ROBERT. "Cost of Capital in the Oil Industry" (hectograph). Pittsburgh: Carnegie Institute of Technology, 1955.

20. SOMERS, H. M. " 'Cost of Money' as the Determinant of Public Utility Rates," *Buffalo Law Review,* Vol. IV (Spring, 1955), pp. 1–28.

21. WILLIAMS, JOHN B. *The Theory of Investment Value.* Cambridge: Harvard University Press, 1938.

22. FEDERAL COMMUNICATIONS COMMISSION. *The Problem of the "Rate of Return" in Public Utility Regulation.* Washington, D.C.: U.S. Government Printing Office, 1938.

*Chapter* 24

# *Leverage and the Cost of Capital**

By Ezra Solomon

THE PROPER USE OF debt financing is one of the major decision areas of corporate financial management. My paper confines itself to just one facet of the many considerations which jointly determine the optimal use of debt—namely, the effect that a change in financial leverage has, or can be assumed to have, on a company's cost of capital. In particular, it addresses itself to the thesis put forward by Modigliani and Miller that, apart from a tax effect, a company's cost of capital is independent of the degree of leverage in its financial structure.[1]

## I

To isolate the effect of leverage alone from the many other factors that may be involved in using debt wisely, it is useful to conduct the analysis in terms of the following simplified model:

Let X be a company which holds or acquires only one kind of asset. Each dollar invested in these assets generates a flow of operating earnings, before taxes, which provides a rate of return of $k$ per annum of a given quality with respect to the certainty or uncertainty with which it can be expected to occur. We shall assume that this company may use any mixture of only two kinds of financing—pure, externally derived:

---

*Reprinted by permission from *Journal of Finance,* Vol. XVIII (May, 1963), pp. 273–79.

[1]Franco Modigliani and Merton H. Miller, "The Cost of Capital, Corporation Finance and the Theory of Investment," *American Economic Review,* Vol. XLVIII (June, 1958).

equity, on the one hand, and pure debt, on the other. Third, we assume that the structure of market capitalization rates is given and that this *structure* does not change over time.

The following notation will be used:

Total market value of company's securities . . . . . . . . . . . . $V$
Market value of bonds . . . . . . . . . . . . . . . . . . . . . . . . . . . . . . $B$
Market value of stock . . . . . . . . . . . . . . . . . . . . . . . . . . . . . . $S$
Leverage . . . . . . . . . . . . . . . . . . . . . . . . . . . . . . . . . . . . . . . $L = B/S$
Operating earnings (before taxes or interest) . . . . . . . . . . . $O$
Debt charges . . . . . . . . . . . . . . . . . . . . . . . . . . . . . . . . . . . . $F$
Residual earnings on equity (before taxes) . . . . . . . . . . . . . $E = O - F$
Rate of return on investment . . . . . . . . . . . . . . . . . . . . . . . . $k$
Pretax over-all capitalization rate (cost of capital) . . . . . . $k_0 = Q/V$
Pretax equity capitalization rate (cost of equity capital) . . . $k_e = E/S$
Pretax debt capitalization rate (cost of debt capital) . . . . $k_i = F/B$
Pretax marginal cost of borrowing . . . . . . . . . . . . . . . . . . . . $m = \Delta F/\Delta B$

For the all-equity case, we have $k_e = k_0 = k$. When debt is used, we have $k_e > k_0$. Specifically, regardless of the valuation theory one embraces, the relationship $k_e = k_0 + (k_0 - k_i)\ B/S$ and $k_0 = k_eS + k_iB)$ must hold.[2] The heart of the leverage question can now be stated as follows: What happens to $V$ and $k_0$ as we increase the degree of leverage (other things remaining unchanged) from $L = 0$ to $L \to \infty$?

For the purpose of analysis, there are two ways in which leverage can be altered in the model. We can assume that company X *substitutes* debt for equity in its capital structure; i.e., it issues debt and uses the proceeds to redeem outstanding stock. This model has the virtue that it keeps the asset structure constant as leverage changes and therefore permits a direct comparison of $V$ at one level of leverage with $V$ at other levels. But it does not allow for the easy identification of the marginal cost of debt as this is generally measured. As we shall see, this variable is an important key to the entire leverage question.

An alternative model for analyzing changes in leverage is to permit

[2]These two relationships are derived as follows:

*a)* Since $k_e = E/S = O - F/S$ and $O = k_oV = k_o\ (B + S)$ and $F = k_iB$, we have:

$$k_e = \frac{k_0\ (B + S)\ - k_iB}{S}$$

$$= k_0 + (k_0 - k_i)B/S$$

*b)* Since $k_o = O/V = (E + F)/(B + S)$ and $E = k_e\ S$ and $F = k_iB$, we have:

$$k_0 = \frac{k_eS + k_iB}{B + S}$$

company X to expand, i.e., to issue more and more debt, using the proceeds to acquire additional assets. This permits an easy identification of the marginal cost of each increment of debt. However, in order not to contaminate the leverage effect, it is necessary to assume that each new asset acquired generates operating earnings, before tax, of the same size and quality as those produced by existing assets.

On the whole, the latter model is more convenient for present purposes, and we shall use it. Modigliani and Miller have generally used the former model in their illustrations, but it is relatively easy to restate their conclusions and arguments in terms of the latter.

Introducing positive amounts of debt into the model introduces the problem of corporate income and the complication that interest payments are deductible in computing taxes. However, everybody agrees that the tax effect factor does tend to lower the over-all cost of capital of a more highly levered company relative to a less levered company, and we can conveniently ignore the tax effect in addressing ourselves to the more controversial issues.

## II

Ignoring the tax effect, the Modigliani-Miller position is that company X's over-all cost of capital, $k_0$, is constant for all levels of leverage from $L = O$ to $L \rightarrow \infty$. If $k_0{}^*$ is used to represent the over-all cost of capital for a more levered company and $k_0$ to represent the over-all cost of capital for a less levered company in the same risk class, their basic thesis is that, except for the tax effect, $k_0{}^* = k_0$ for any and all levels of leverage.

It is useful to divide their basic thesis into two component statements. Still ignoring the tax effect, these are: (1) An increase in borrowing (and hence in leverage), no matter how moderate or "judicious," can never lower a company's cost of capital; (2) an increase in borrowing (and hence in leverage), no matter how immoderate or "excessive," can never raise a company's cost of capital.

Almost all the analytical controversy generated thus far by the Modigliani-Miller thesis seems to have centered on the first of these two component statements and on the proof put forward on its behalf by its proponents. The proof offered by Modigliani and Miller is that a process akin to arbitrage, in which individual investors engage in "home-made" leverage as a substitute for corporate leverage will keep $k_0{}^*$, the capitalization rate for the more levered situation, equal to $k_0$, the capitalization rate for the less levered situation.

The traditional position is that even if the tax effect of leverage is ignored, moderate leverage can lower $k_0$* relative to $k_0$.[3] The traditionalists' counterargument to Modigliani and Miller's arbitrage model is that homemade leverage is not a perfect substitute for corporate leverage and that the equilibrating mechanism posited in the arbitrage model may not fully erase the tendency for $k_0$* to fall below $k_0$.

While this aspect of the controversy is an interesting one, it is not of great practical consequence for the issue at hand. Whether, in a tax-free world, the traditional view that $k_0$ does fall is correct, or whether the Modigliani-Miller argument that $k_0$ does not fall is correct, in a world of taxable corporate incomes in which interest payments are tax-deductible, everybody agrees that up to a certain "judicious" limit of debt, $k_0$ declines as leverage is increased.

The really crucial part of the Modigliani-Miller thesis is their second statement, namely, that $k_0$ will not *rise,* no matter how far the use of leverage is carried. This conclusion might hold if we assume that the rate of interest paid on debt does not rise as leverage is increased. At least it is possible, given this assumption, to invoke the "arbitrage" argument in order to show that it *should* hold if investors behave rationally.

But in practice, $k_i$, the average rate of interest paid on debt, must rise as leverage is increased. For extreme leverage positions, i.e., as the company approaches an all-debt situation, it its clear that $k_i$ will be at least equal to $k_0$. Given the general attitude of bondholders and bond-rating agencies, it is highly likely that $k_i$ will be *above* $k_0$ for positions of extreme leverage.

Now, as $k_i$, the average cost of debt, rises, the marginal cost of borrowing, $m = \Delta F/\Delta B$, must be above $k_i$. Therefore, there is some point of leverage at which company X finds that $m$, the marginal cost of more debt, is *higher* than its average cost of capital, $k_0$. Again taking into account the general attitudes of those who supply debt funds, this point is likely to be reached quite rapidly if leverage is increased beyond levels acceptable to the debt markets.

For all practical purposes, the point at which a company finds that $m \geqq k_0$ represents the maximum use of leverage, for it can be argued that no rational company will finance with more pure debt if it can do so more cheaply by using a mixture of debt and equity similar to that outstanding in its existing structure. If this fact is accepted, then the argument between Modigliani and Miller and the traditional posi-

[3]For an explicit statement of the traditional position, see Harry G. Guthmann and Herbert E. Dougall, *Corporate Financial Policy* (3d ed.; Englewood Cliffs, N.J.: Prentice-Hall, Inc., 1955), p. 245.

tion vanishes. Both would agree that leverage is clearly excessive if carried beyond the point at which the rising marginal cost-of-debt curve intersects the over-all cost of capital at that point.

## III

Assuming that the straightforward logic of this argument is accepted, what we are left with is something very similar to the U-shaped $k_0$ curve envisaged by traditional theory. This is outlined in Figure 1. In the early or moderate phases of leverage, $k_0$ declines, possibly because of market imperfections but at the very least because of the tax effect factor. As leverage reaches and then exceeds the limits acceptable to the debt markets, $m$ rises rapidly, and the tax advantage of even more leverage is offset by the rising cost of each further increment of debt. When $m$ rises above $k_0$, any further increase in leverage will bring about a rise in $k_0$. We thus have a clearly determinate point or range of optimal leverage.

FIGURE 1

LEVERAGE AND CAPITALIZATION RATES (TAX EFFECT INCLUDED): TRADITIONAL VERSION

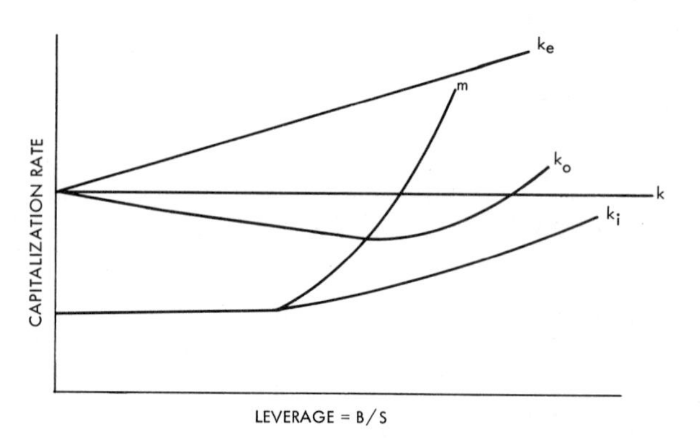


Unfortunately, Modigliani and Miller have not been willing to accept this conclusion. Instead, they argue that $k_0$ remains constant even when leverage is increased beyond the point at which $m > k_0$. According to them, what brings about this startling and wholly illogical result is that $k_e$, the cost of equity capital, *falls* as leverage is increased through the use of increments of debt which cost more than $k_0$. The behavior of the capitalization rates, as they view it, is outlined in Figure 2.

This device of having $k_e$ fall as leverage is increased leads squarely into a second dilemma. We now have to assume that rational investors in the equity markets capitalize a more uncertain stream of residual earnings at a *lower* $k_e$ than they capitalize a less uncertain stream.

It is difficult to reconcile this assumption with Modigliani and Miller's own assumptions about rational investor behavior and reasonably perfect markets. The only explanation they offer in support of a $k_e$ curve that falls as leverage is increased is as follows: "Should demand by risk-lovers prove insuffìcent to keep the market to this peculiar yield-curve, this demand would be reinforced by the action of arbitrage operators."[4]

FIGURE 2

LEVERAGE AND CAPITALIZATION RATES (TAX EFFECT INCLUDED): MODIGLIANI AND MILLER VERSION

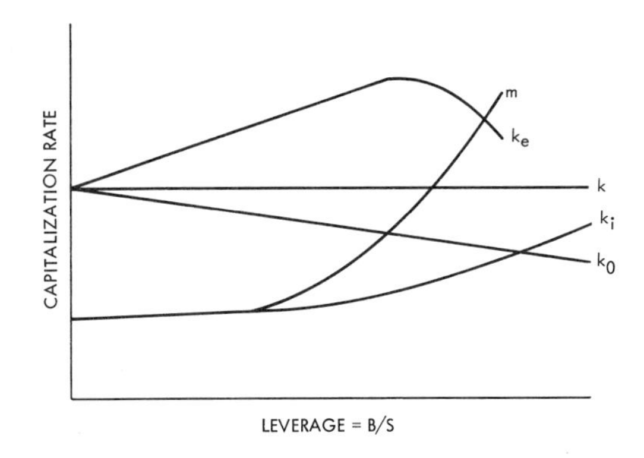


The introduction of subjective risk preference as a major determinant of equity prices just for this phase of the leverage argument is hardly admissible unless one is also prepared to accept it for other phases of leverage.

As a last line of defense in support of a constant $k_0$, even under these circumstances, Modigliani and Miller simply assert that arbitrage will see to it that $k_e{}^*$, the equity capitalization rate for the overly levered stream of net earnings, is kept sufficiently *below* $k_e$, the rate for the less levered stream, so as to maintain an equality between $k_0{}^*$ and $k_0$. If we examine the relationships between the various capitalization rates for situations in which $m > k_0$, we find that this assertion is not justified. Indeed, the opposite is true. Rational investor behavior, including the equilibrating process envisaged in their arbitrage model, will push $k_e{}^*$ *above* $k_e$ and $k_0{}^*$ above $k_0$.

[4] *Op. cit.*, p. 276.

## IV

There is, therefore, no legitimate basis for assuming that $k_e$ will *fall* as leverage is increased and hence no basis for assuming that $k_0$ can remain constant as leverage is increased through the use of debt issues which involve a marginal cost higher than $k_0$. Given this conclusion, it must follow that the cost of capital, $k_0$, rises with increased leverage whenever $m > k_0$.

In short, the thesis that a company's cost of capital is independent of its financial structure is not valid. As far as the leverage effect *alone* is concerned (and ignoring all the other considerations that might influence the choice between debt and equity), there does exist a clearly definable optimum position—namely, the point at which the marginal cost of more debt is equal to, or greater than, a company's average cost of capital.

*Chapter 25*

# *Theory of the Capital Structure of the Firm**

By Eli Schwartz

## *I. Introduction*

IN BOTH ECONOMICS and finance, there hardly exists a complete model of the optimum capital structure of the firm. Many of the concepts needed to construct such a model are available in the literature, but in most cases the authors have been content to set up and use only such partial constructs as would serve their larger purposes.[1] The present article is an attempt to develop a self-contained theory of the financial structure of the individual firm.

---

*Reprinted by permission from *Journal of Finance,* Vol. XIV (March, 1959), pp. 18–39.

The author is indebted to Professor Elmer C. Bratt for valuable criticism on an earlier draft of this paper. He is very grateful to Professor Herbert Fraser of Muhlenberg College for many helpful and fertile suggestions.

[1]M. Kalecki, "The Principle of Increasing Risk," *Economica,* Vol. IV (N.S.), No. 16 (November, 1937); R. G. Hawtrey, "The Trade Cycle and Capital Intensity," *Economica,* Vol. VII (N.S.), No. 24 (1940); Hyman P. Minsky, "Induced Investment and the Business Cycle" (unpublished doctoral dissertation, Harvard University, 1954), especially chap. vi; Sidney Weintraub, *Price Theory* (New York, Pitman Pub. Corp., 1949), pp. 366–71; Friedrich Lutz, and Vera Lutz, *The Theory of Investment of the Firm* (Princeton: Princeton University Press, 1951), chap. xvi; David Durand, "Cost of Debt and Equity Funds for Business: Trends and Problems of Measurement," discussions by Clay J. Anderson and Martin W. Davenport, in National Bureau of Economic Research, *Conference on Research in Business Finance* (New York, 1952). In the same volume, Franco Modigliani and Morton Zeman, "The Effect of the Availability of Funds, and the Terms Thereof, on Business Investment," discussions by Lawrence R. Klein and George L. Bach. A more recent article by Franco Modigliani and Merton H. Miller, "The Cost of Capital, Corporation Finance and the Theory of Investment," appeared in *American Economic Review,* Vol. XLVIII (June, 1958). Both the Modigliani articles are, however, confined to the relationships between stocks and bonds, and give little explicit consideration to the gains that a firm might acquire through the development of a complex financial structure discriminating among many possible sources of financing.

It has been said that the problem of the capital or financial structure is a firm, not a plant, decision. The underlying notion is that whereas the optimum output (a plant function) is uniquely determined if demand and costs are known, financing is, in large part, a matter of the individual taste for risk and is therefore an ownership or firm decision, for which a unique solution may not be possible. I should like to present the contrary view that there is perhaps a single optimum capital structure for any given firm or that, at the least, the range of rational capital structures is narrowly bounded. In the real world, uncertainty and lack of knowledge as to the relevant variables may make this optimum solution a difficult achievement. Under certain simplifying assumptions, however, a theoretical model of the relevant variables and functions can be constructed which does result in a single best financial structure. The usefulness of such a model is in the simplifying insights it may give us into the complexities of reality.

For many writers on corporation finance the term "the capital structure of the firm" seems to include only those sources of funds which are represented by securities.[2] This is too narrow a definition. It leaves one at a loss as to what to make of bank term loans, long-term insurance loans, and current liabilities. In its arbitrary distinction, it implies that the borrower's risk involved in securing funds through fixed debt is somehow greater than borrowing on current account.[3] (The reverse is likely to be true.) The narrow definition of the financial structure—restricted essentially to stocks and bonds—ignores the large measure of substitutability existing between the various forms of external debt.[4] For purposes of this article the terms "capital structure" and "financial structure" are to be considered interchangeable. The phrase "the capital structure of the firm" means the total of all liabilities and ownership claims—the sum of what is usually the credit side of the balance sheet. The adoption of this broader definition of financial structure, i.e., the liability net worth side of the balance sheet, allows us to concentrate on what is recognized as the best single measure of gross risk—the ratio of total debt (including current items) to net worth.[5]

---

[2]See, for example, Harry G. Guthmann and Herbert E. Dougall, *Corporate Financial Policy* (3d ed.; New York: Prentice-Hall, Inc., 1955), pp. 213–90 and *passim*.

[3]If the usual financial definition is followed, then, for example, a bank would never have any capital structure problems.

[4]About two years ago the General Electric Company floated a debenture issue partly to secure net working capital; i.e., it used proceeds from long-term debt to reduce its reliance on current liabilities.

[5]Of course, a more refined judgment of risk entails a thorough study of the composition of the debt structure. There is also the problem of such financing devices as preferred stocks, which are an element of risk as far as the common

## *II. Basic Assumptions*

It is well known that firms in various industries have developed typically different asset structures and that the composition of these asset structures must necessarily help determine the financing of the firm. It is, however, outside the scope of the present paper to discuss the economic rationale and development of optimum asset holdings. Thus the optimum asset structure of the firm is taken as one of the parameters in the development of the argument, although its effect is explicitly recognized as constituting one of the factors contributing to the external risk of the firm and thus influencing its financing. Given this limitation, the following are the basic operating assumptions of the analysis:

1. The individual firm is confronted by two types of risks. One type we might call the "external risk," the other type the "internal" or "financial risk."[6]

2. The external risks are a composite of the *stability of earnings,* or cash flow of the firm, and the liquidity, safety, and marketability of the assets typically held by the firm.[7] This external risk is in large part dictated by the nature of the industry in which the firm is engaged and is not subject to any great extent to the control of the financial decision makers.

3. The internal risk of the firm is the financial risk of its capital structure. It is set by the types of liabilities (whether short-term or funded) that the firm carries and the amounts of these liabilities in proportion to the ownership or equity capital committed to the firm. These factors, together constituting the capital structure, can be varied considerably by the financial management.

4. The two types of risks together are the sum of the hazards to which the owners and creditors of the firm may be subjected. The approach taken in this article is to consider the *external risks as a parameter* given by the nature of the industry; however, these external risks are borne in mind by both borrowers and lenders, and necessarily influence the optimum financial risk that different types of firms will carry.

5. An optimum capital structure for any widely held company is one which maximizes the long-run value per share of the common stock

---

stockholder is concerned but an element of safety from the viewpoint of the creditors. In this article, for purposes of simplicity, "ownership" or "equity" capital refers only to the common shares.

[6]The financial risk was divided into borrower's risk and lender's risk by J. M. Keynes in *The General Theory of Employment, Interest, and Money* (New York: Macmillan Co., 1936), pp. 144–45.

[7]Risk may be held to a minimum by a stable cash flow, as is true of utilities, or by the safety and liquidity of the assets, as is true of banks. In both cases the typical firm in these industries can afford relatively risky capital structures.

on the markets.[8] This is not quite the same as asserting that the optimum capital structure is one which will maximize profit or earnings per share. For both the earnings per share of stock and the *rate at which they are capitalized* must be considered. The amount of financial risk that a firm carries helps set the capitalization rate. If a firm's financial structure carries too much borrowers' risk, the market may set a lower price for the shares than it would give for similar shares with perhaps somewhat smaller earnings but less financial risk.

In order to maximize the *long-run* value of the common stock, the financial decision makers—the management—will in general develop that financial framework which will cause the common shares to sell at the highest price on the present market.[9] However, the security markets are notoriously volatile and perhaps subject to irrational pressures; therefore the financial managers are not guided solely by immediate market prices because they may remember or be aware that the discount rate for risk and liquidity is subject to extreme psychological shifts and that the costs and difficulties of reconstructing the financial structure might make survival difficult for any firm which adapted too uncritically to immediate market conditions.

Nevertheless, existing prices exert the major force in the making of financial decisions. For although every spot price contains within it some element which is a forecast of future prices, the financial markets, which are not burdened by transportation or storage costs or hindered by physical interruptions of supply, are supposed to be especially adept at discounting anticipations. The prices prevailing in the security markets are the *most important* guides to financial management because, supposedly, changes in future prices have already been discounted.

## *III. Solving Certain Problems of the Capital Structure under the Simplifying Assumption of a Fixed Amount of Ownership Capital*

Before proceeding to a general solution of the problem of the optimum financial structure, it may be useful to illustrate the process of

[8]This should perhaps be amended to read: Given any number of shares, the per share value should be maximized. Obviously, this criterion is not affected by such matters as stock splits, stock dividends, etc.

[9]This implies that the management and common stockholders' interests run parallel. This is of course not always true. However, it may not be too amiss to suggest that, in general, the area of common interest is greater than the area of possible conflict; it is likely that, by and large, the income and prestige of the management rises with the economic satisfaction of the stockholders.

discriminating against the supply of external funds by starting with a simplified model employing the major restraints that the firm has a fixed supply of equity capital and wishes mainly to maximize profit without regard to owners' risk. These assumptions are relaxed in Section IV.

Figures 1*A*, 1*B*, 1*C*, and 2*A*, 2*B* each illustrate possible earning and financial supply functions facing various firms. The horizontal axis

FIGURE 1

FIRMS WHOSE SUPPLY OF OUTSIDE CAPITAL IS DISCONTINUOUS DERIVED MAINLY FROM TRADE CREDITORS

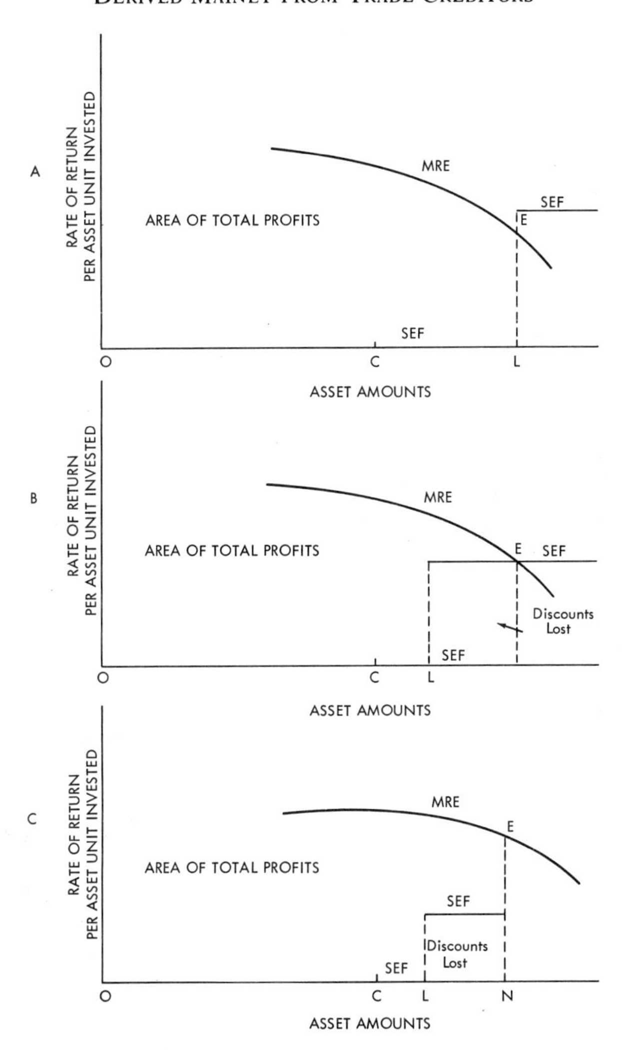

FIGURE 2*A*

EQUILIBRIUM FINANCIAL STRUCTURE SOLUTION FOR A FIRM WHOSE SUPPLY OF OUTSIDE CAPITAL APPROACHES CONTINUITY UNDER CONDITIONS WHERE DISCRIMINATION IS UNFEASIBLE

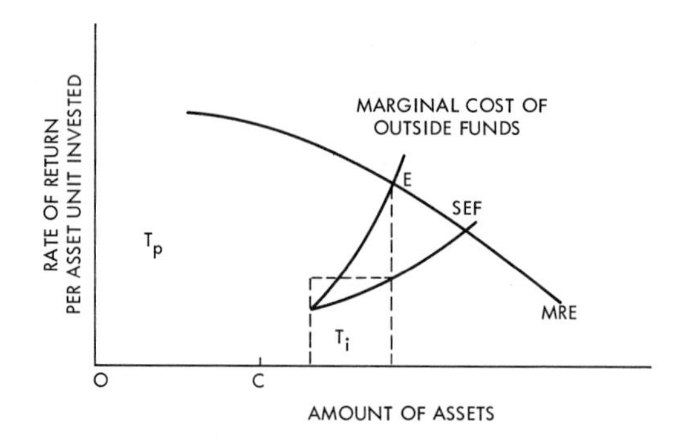


measures the amount of assets that might be employed. The vertical axis measures gross yield or rates of return. The line *MRE* in every case designates the marginal rate of earnings for the corresponding volume of assets; it represents the incremental rate of return that can be obtained by adding additional assets to the firm; the area under the curve (the integral) represents the total earnings for those assets.[10] Of course, given uncertainty, the theoretical *MRE* curve has just a probability location, with a potential dispersion of outcome greater for some firms than for others.

The *MRE* curve has been drawn with a downward slope. This assumes limitations to managerial talent or organizational ability and the

[10]The *MRE* is based on internal rates of return for successive incremental bundles of assets.

$$C = \frac{q^1}{(1+r)} + \frac{q^2}{(1+r)^2} + \dots \frac{q_n}{(1+r)^n} + \frac{S_n}{(1+r)^n}$$

where $C$ stands for the cost of the assets; $q$, the annual net returns; $S$, the scrap value or remaining value of the assets after a given number of years; and $r$, the unknown rate of return that brings about the equality. Perhaps the internal rate of return is not the best method of ranking investment possibilities when the firm is faced with exclusive alternatives and when the time periods of two investments differ (see A. A. Alchian, "The Rate of Interest, Fisher's Rate of Return over Costs, and Keynes' Internal Rate of Return," *American Economic Review,* Vol. XLV [December, 1955]; and James H. Lorie and Leonard J. Savage, "Three Problems in Rationing Capital," *Journal of Business,* Vol. XXVIII [October, 1955]). However, if we consider that the use of the assets will be more or less renewable at similar rates of earnings, the internal rate of return may serve quite well to rank opportunities for a "going concern" (thus, see Romney Robinson, "Interest-Return over Cost or Internal Rates: Comment," *American Economic Review,* Vol. XLVI [December, 1956]).

possible existence of competitive or physical difficulties which at any point of time preclude the assimilation of continual increments of assets at the same rate of profits.

Figures 1*A*, 1*B*, 1*C*, and 2*A*, 2*B* also depict the supply curve of outside funds, given the restraint of a fixed amount of ownership capital. Line *OC* represents the given amount of equity or ownership capital. From this point on, the *SEF* curve is drawn to represent the supply of external funds, facing firms of diverse *asset structure, inherent risks,* and *given different initial amounts of equity capital.*

FIGURE 2*B*

EQUILIBRIUM FINANCIAL STRUCTURE SOLUTION FOR A FIRM WHICH FINDS IT FEASIBLE TO ACT AS DISCRIMINATING MONOPSONIST AGAINST ITS SUPPLY OF EXTERNAL FUNDS*

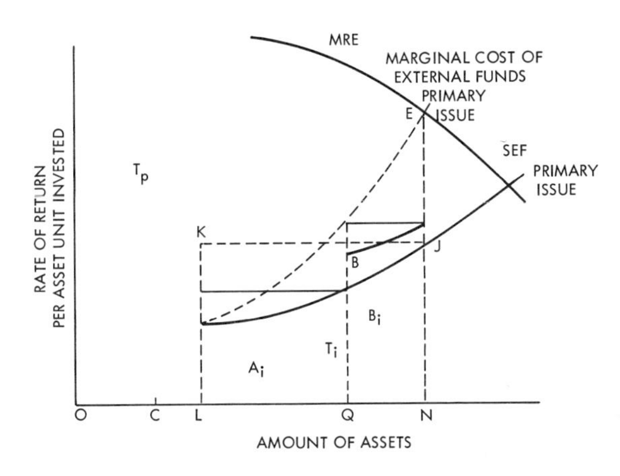


*As in Figure 2*A*, the amount of equity capital is held constant.

Figures 1*A*, 1*B*, and 1*C* are hypothetical examples of three firms relying basically on book credit for their external funds. In these cases the SEF curve is discontinuous; it starts out along the axis for some distance before breaking and continuing at a higher level. The first segment represents the amount of trade or current account credit usually available free or without explicit cost to any given firm. The first plateau represents the situation when all discounts are no longer met; then the use of trade credit becomes quite costly, i.e., the lost discounts, representing 12–30 percent a year, are considered a financial expense. At some point, as various financial ratios deteriorate, further extension of trade credit may cease; this is shown by the discontinuity in the plateau representing the final amount of assets that the firm is likely to acquire.

Under our restricted assumptions, point *E* represents the equilibrium size—the total amount of assets acquired—and the total liability and equity of the firm. Since for firms relying on trade credit the average cost and the marginal costs of outside funds are the same, point *E* is placed where the *SEF* curve intersects the *MRE* curve. Firm A then illustrates a company whose equity relative to its asset structure and earning potential is large enough that it never has to forgo trade discounts; firm B loses some discounts in order to obtain additional earning assets; and firm C is a company which faces Hawtrey's "wall"; it has used up its ration of trade credit entirely.

For firms of somewhat larger size and more complex structure, other types of credit besides accounts payable enter the *SEF* function, bank credit becomes available at a lower rate than nondiscounted trade credit, and various other types of long- and short-term credit may be tapped. In the case of the large company which can draw its fund from many sources, although always at increasing risk for each category of loan, the *SEF* function may begin to assume a smooth shape. Thus, for theoretical and expository purposes in Figures 2*A* and 2*B*, we constructed the *SEF* function as a continuous curve.

Given a fixed ownership capital base, the characteristic supply function of external funds will vary for firms with different typical asset structures and external risk. Those firms in which the dispersion of the return outcomes is great or those having more assets of specialized nature will have steeper supply curves of external funds (i.e., relatively inelastic) with a shorter stretch of free book credit. Those firms in which the risk of the rate-of-return fluctuation is less will have an *SEF* curve which contains more trade credit and runs almost horizontally (i.e., is relatively elastic) over a considerable range. The point to be noted is that the supply price of outside capital rises individually to each firm, since as long as the amount of equity is unchanged, there is an increasing risk to both the owners and the creditors as more liability funds are offered. Thus, each firm is in a monopsonistic position relative to its supply of lender's capital.

On all charts the equilibrium position of the firm has been indicated at point *E*. The area *Ti* surrounding the *SEF* curve up to point *E* represents the total financial changes that would have to be paid for outside funds. All the rest of the area (*Tp*) under the *MRE* curve represents the accounting profits that accrue to the owners.

In those cases where the *SEF* function was discontinuous (Figures 1*A*, 1*B*, and 1*C*), the equilibrium position (*E*) was found rather simply at the intersection of the *SEF* and *MRE* curves. Where, however, the *SEF* curve is more complex and takes the shape of a smooth curve, the equilibrium position is influenced by how effectively the firm can discriminate against the supply curve of capital.[11] If the firm cannot economically and feasibly break its borrowing into independent categories, it must consider the cost of its total borrowing as it obtains more outside funds. In this case the optimum position is determined by taking a marginal cost curve of borrowing from the *SEF* function. The intersection of this marginal cost curve and the *MRE* curve determines the equilibrium position and the amount of assets used. The amount of outside funds actually used and the rate paid for these outside funds are obtained by dropping down to the appropriate position on the *SEF* curve (see Figure 2*A*).

The firms (illustrated in Figure 2*A*) which use the nondiscriminating monopsonist solution are probably those in which there is some instability in the rate of earnings over time. Because the risk of both lenders and borrowers rises rather sharply with increased debt, the *SEF* curve is relatively inelastic. It is difficult under these circumstances to break the capital structure into separate categories. Nevertheless, such a firm does not equate the marginal return on its assets with a final average interest rate but finds a greater total profit by borrowing less and paying a lower rate for the total funds.

The concept of using a curve marginal to the *SEF* curve to obtain a maximum position might give an explanation for certain observed financial phenomena. For example, a well-known rule-of-thumb measure of the margin of safety existing for the use of outside funds is the "times-interest-earned" ratio. This is usually stated as the figure obtained by dividing annual interest charges into total earnings before taxes and interest. As long as a considerable portion of equity capital exists in the financial structure and the intramarginal assets earn more for the firm than the interest charges, in normal periods at least, this ratio will be greater than one. It would seem that the times-interest-earned ratio is a measure of average safety and should *not affect marginal financing decisions*. Nevertheless, even an incremental investment project may not obtain managerial approval unless the proposal has a prospective return *considerably* in excess of the immediate cost of the funds to be used; for the firm may consider that the incremental borrowing may cause the price on all previous borrowings to rise.[12]

---

[11]The idea that a complex capital structure represents an attempt by the firm to discriminate against the rising supply price of loan capital may be found in J. R. Hicks, *Value and Capital* (2d ed.; Oxford: Oxford University Press, 1946), p. 144 n.

[12]Additional borrowing cannot change the present rate on previously borrowed funds, but it may raise the rate when the firm enters the market for refinancing. In any case the notion that the firm must reckon not merely with the market interest rate but with a rising marginal cost of funds probably makes the level of the interest rate a much more important factor in firm decisions than many economists

*(Continued on next page)*

Figure 2*B* illustrates the case in which the supply of funds to the firm is capable of segmentation; i.e., different bargains can be made with various classes of lenders, each having a different preference for and each assuming a different degree of risk. This firm is able to discriminate more effectively against its *SEF* function than the firm illustrated in Figure 2*A* and can obtain as additional profits for its stockholders some of the area between the *SEF* curve and the final equilibrium position (*E*) on the *MRE* curve.

In Figure 2*B* the nondiscriminatory solution is superimposed on the discriminatory solution. The *SEF* curve for a single primary issue is indicated as the lowest supply curve. If the firm followed the nondiscriminatory solution, it would halt its borrowing where the marginal cost of this borrowing equaled the marginal return on its assets, point *E*, and borrow on this issue the amount *LN*, paying the rate *LK* and a total charge for outside funds indicated by *Ti* (or rectangle *LKJN*). By discriminating, it is able to borrow amount *LQ* on issue A at the prime rate for such issues, and then borrow amount *QN* on issue B at a higher rate. The total amount borrowed is *LN*, but the total charges paid are the summation of rectangles $A_i$ and $B_i$. The necessary condition for the superiority of the discriminating solution is that the area $A_i$ plus $B_i$ be less than *Ti* (rectangle *LKJN*).[13]

The possible profitability of discrimination can be illustrated alternatively by simple arithmetic. For example, the financing charges to a firm which used a single prime issue of $80 million at an effective rate of 4½ percent ($3.6 million annual charge) would be $200,000 more expensive than the same amount of financing through the use of two issues —a prime security of $60 million at 4 percent ($2.4 million annual charge) and a subordinate issue of $20 million at 5 percent ($1 million annual charge; total charges $3.4 million).

---

have thought. In an over-all sense, it may mean that monetary policy has considerable efficacy in the "normal" economy.

[13]It should be noted that the supply curve for secondary issue B is drawn above the *SEF* curve that would exist on a primary issue. One reason for this is the extra fixed costs that a firm will have to meet if it floats an additional issue. However, the supply price for borrowing on subordinated issues would be above the equivalent primary issue rate at the same amount, whether these fixed charges existed or not. This is due to the different risk situation which faces the potential lender. The marginal lender on any issue increases the risk of that entire issue, but he and the other lenders share the same average risk on the whole issue. A new issue, however, opens a new and higher risk category. It is not at all equivalent for a lender to come in on the purchase of an $80-million prime issue or to come in on the purchase of a secondary $20-million issue after $60 million of a *higher priority* issue has already been floated. Owing to the necessity of giving lower protective priority to secondary lenders than to the primary lenders, it is impossible to conceive of a perfect discriminatory solution against the *SEF* curve— at least not under the assumptions upon which this function has been constructed.

Monopsonistic discrimination against the suppliers of funds leads to complex capital structures. It exists whenever the market for funds contains suppliers, institutions or individuals, with different preferences for income and aversions to risk. It would seem to be practicable where the amount of total financing is relatively large, since the fixed costs of moving into a new type of issue are proportionately higher the smaller the issue, and these costs would make this type of discrimination uneconomic where the total sum to be borrowed is relatively small. Furthermore, this type of operation is most feasible where the *MRE* curve is estimated to be relatively stable; for otherwise, the *SEF* function would turn inelastic toward its outer extremity, and the borrower could not discriminate in large enough segments (i.e., float big enough issues of the secondary securities) to make it profitable. The public utilities probably best illustrate the possibility of using a complex financial structure, since they have the necessary characteristics of (1) large total financing and (2) relative stability of earnings.

## IV. *The General Solution: Debt and Equity Both Variable*

In Section III, we considered certain adjustments that the firm might make vis-à-vis its supply of outside funds if its supply of equity capital were fixed and if it were primarily interested in maximizing its return on this capital. These assumptions are unrealistic and are used solely for convenience in illustrating discrimination against the supply of external funds. To solve the general case, the amount of both ownership capital and borrowings must be considered variable and substitutable. But equity capital and loan capital *are not perfect substitutes,* for the factor of increasing risk makes the price of borrowing rise as external funds replace ownership funds. Furthermore, the borrower's (or stockholder's) risk increases with a larger proportion of debt to equity in the capital structure. Thus, as long as the marginal rate of earnings on assets is downward-sloping, these factors make it possible to solve for the optimum capital structure—the amounts of equity and debt which will allow the common shares to obtain the highest price on the market.

The validity of the maximization of the per share price as the criterion of the optimum capital structure is dependent on there being a number of shareholders, each with a limited investment in the firm. Given a definite holding on the part of each stockholder, developing a capital structure which brings the common stock to the highest market price will maximize the position of each individual stockholder. This criterion holds whether we are considering a block of new financing for an old firm or the creation of a new firm *ab nova*. In the case of the new firm, let us imagine a promoter (typically rewarded with a block of stock) and/or a group of initial investors now seeking additional funds in the equity and debt markets. Toward what financial structure should they move? Obviously, toward the one which maximizes the value of the ordinary shares, i.e., the one which also maximizes the value of their holdings.[14] (If blocks of stock are sold over time at different prices, one may conceive of this as a process of discriminating in the market for equity funds.) An established firm in a suboptimum position contemplating new financing for expansion or some other financial change should move to enhance the position of the present shareholders by selecting that financial mix which maximizes the value of the common shares.

FIGURE 3*A*

SUPPLY FUNCTIONS OF OUTSIDE FUNDS WHICH FACE AN INDIVIDUAL FIRM AS THE AMOUNT OF EQUITY CAPITAL IS VARIED

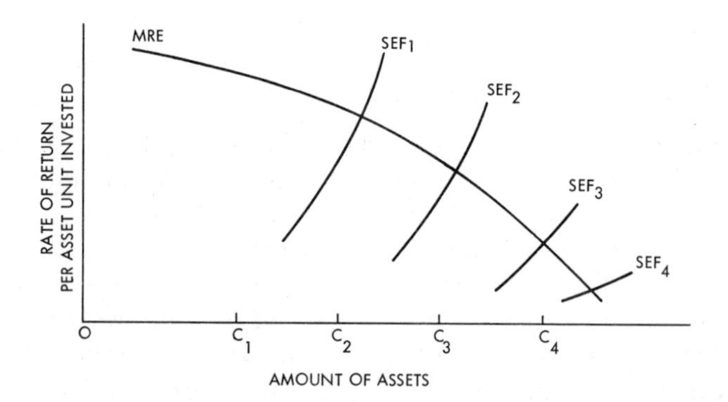


Figure 3*A* is the first step in our general solution of the optimum capital structure; it depicts a hypothetical firm which is faced with a whole set of supply curves of external funds, each curve being pertinent to a particular amount of ownership capital. The variable amounts of ownership capital are represented by stubs, $OC_1$, $OC_2$, etc., and the *SEF* functions which are applicable to these points are labeled $SEF_1$, $SEF_2$, etc. These *SEF* functions have been drawn to conform to the

[14]If the initial group is closely related and has unlimited funds relative to the economic scale of the proposed firm, a different maximand may be postulated. Here the optimum condition may be a maximization of the *difference* between the market value of the *total* equity and the price of the assets invested by the ownership group. This solution would coincide with a maximum per share price only under unlikely conditions of inelasticity—if the issue of more shares should drop the value of all the shares more than proportionately.

notion of increasing lender's risk. The major objective determinant of lender's risk is the debt-to-equity ratio. Each supply of external funds function should be constructed so that at the same interest rate point on each curve the debt-equity ratio is also equal. Since each successive *SEF* function starts out from a larger amount of ownership capital, *equal absolute amounts of borrowing* always represent a lower debt-equity ratio and can be obtained at a lower interest rate. Conversely, a lower interest rate always signifies a lower debt-equity ratio. Thus, for any firm with a given earnings potential, the successive *SEF* curves will start at a lower price (interest rate) and will have a smaller slope.[15]

FIGURE 3*B*

FORMAL SOLUTION OF THE OPTIMUM CAPITAL STRUCTURE OF TWO HYPOTHETICAL FIRMS: FIRM 1

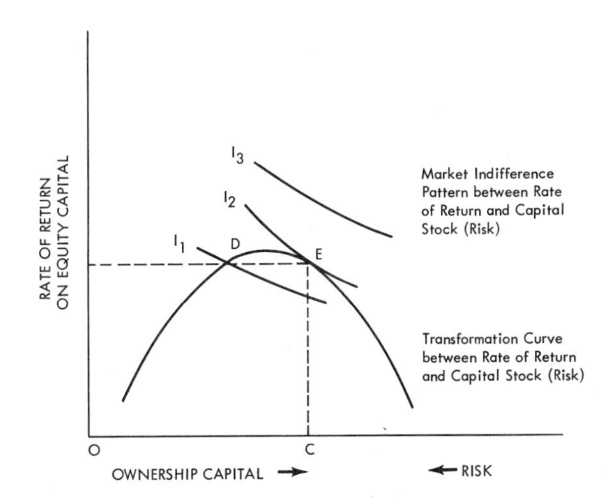


According to the analysis presented in Section III, there exists an optimum amount of borrowing for every amount of equity. Thus, for every firm, given the amount of equity, we can determine (1) the amount of borrowing; (2) the amount of total assets; and (3) the ratio of equity to debt, which decreases for each successive *OC*. What we must find out is the optimum amount of ownership capital.

For every combination of ownership capital and supply of external funds depicted in Figure 3*A*, there exists a total profit or earnings; this is the area under the *MRE* curve extending over the amount of total assets committed, less the financial charges for the optimum amount of

[15]Although the slope of such successive *SEF* functions is less, they would have the same elasticity at each interest rate.

outside funds.[16] In the present context the important consideration is the rate of return per unit of equity capital, and this is easily obtained by dividing the total profit (which is determinant for every capital structure) by the pertinent amounts of equity capital.

Thus the relationships contained in Figure 3*A* can be used to derive another curve whose explicit coordinates are the rate of return on equity capital and the absolute amount of equity capital. Such curves for two hypothetical firms are presented in Figures 3*B* and 3*C*. The other relationships discussed in connection with Figure 3*A* are implicit in the new charts. If the slope of the *MRE* function is negative and the firm operates within the marginal restraints, we can determine the amount of borrowing for each possible amount of ownership capital and also the total assets of the firm. Since a firm can borrow the same proportion of its equity at the same rate, regardless of the amount of equity capital, and since the marginal rate of return on total assets is declining, the interest rate on the optimum borrowings and the debt-equity ratio will be less for successively larger *OC*'s.

FIGURE 3*C*

FORMAL SOLUTION OF THE OPTIMUM CAPITAL STRUCTURE OF TWO HYPOTHETICAL FIRMS: FIRM 2

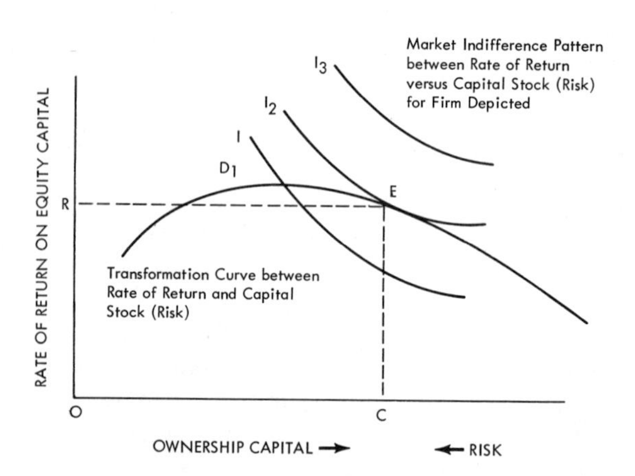


Thus, one other element—the risk factor—is indicated indirectly in Figures 3*B* and 3*C*. As the amount of equity capital increases in a particular firm's capital structure, the debt-equity ratio and the amount of financial risk decrease. The rate of return is depicted as a function of the amount of ownership capital, and the amount of ownership capital

[16]The amount of profit will of course be varied by how effectively the firm can discriminate against a given *SEF* function (see section III).

is an inverse index of risk unique for each particular firm or, perhaps, class of firms.

In Figures 3*B* and 3*C* the segment of the rate-of-return-on-equity function before point *D* (the maximum rate of return) is inoperative for any firm which has open access to a supply of equity funds. For it would seem that up until this point, both the rate of return could be increased and the risk element decreased by putting in more ownership funds. Perhaps a new firm, relatively small and unknown and limited to a small group for its ownership capital, might find itself operating in this area. In such a case the firm would make every attempt to plow back earnings or find other sources of equity capital. A firm which through changes in the economy is now overleveraged might also strive to raise more ownership capital to substitute for debt; however, if earnings on the assets were low, it is possible that the marginal rate of earnings which would be offered in an attempt to secure new equity funds, although higher than the rate the firm was presently earning, still might not be high enough to be competitively attractive.

At any rate, for the firm that has access to the capital market and the ability over time to change the amount of ownership capital, the declining segment of the rate-of-return function is the pertinent one. The exact location that the management would work toward is a question which our initial assumption (i.e., that the management will attempt to maximize the long-run market price of the common shares) may help solve. Let us posit a particular market indifference function representing a choice between profits and more stock (less risk) for a given type of firm.[17] Then the rate-of-return function for a particular firm can be superimposed on this surface. The maximum that will be paid in the market for this stock is shown in Figures 3*B* and 3*C* at the point of tangency, *E*, where the marginal rate of substitution between profit and the risk in the capital structure of this firm is equal to the marginal choice between risk and profit among the investors in the market. This is, of

[17]This indifference curve pattern is unique for each particular firm or type of firm because the functional relationship between risk and earnings and risk and ownership capital—determined as it is by the stability of earnings, the stability of the cash flow, and the liquidity of the asset structure—varies for different firms. We could have constructed a market indifference pattern which was general for risk versus earnings in all investment; but to use it in the analysis, we should have had to construct a pure risk versus rate-of-return transformation function for each firm function. It is better to use the rate-of-return versus ownership capital function because, although risk underlies the investor's choice, it is the debt-equity ratio determined by the amount of ownership capital which is the objective measure of risk. It is to the amount of ownership capital for each firm that the market reacts. By using our method, we shall be able to proceed immediately to the determination of the optimum capital structure for a given firm without tracing our solution back through an intermediate and highly subjective risk function.

course, the point of tangency between the rate-of-return function and the market indifference surface. Past point *E* toward the right, the investors feel that any reduction in the risk of the capital structure does not compensate for the marginal loss in the rate of profits; toward the left, the investors feel that any rise in profits is not worth the additional risk assumed in the financial structure.[18]

To sum up, Figures 3*B* and 3*C* illustrate the equilibrium capital structure for two hypothetical firms. The transformation curve gives the average rate of return for financial structures containing different amounts of ownership capital. It is derived from a chart similar to Figure 3*A* for each firm. Since the amount of ownership capital in proportion to the total assets of the firm is an index of risk, risk is also measured on the horizontal axis as an inverse of the amount of ownership or equity capital. On each chart the tangency point *E* indicates the optimum amount of equity capital and rate of return on equity capital for each firm. In brief, the conditions of the optimum are:

$$\frac{\text{Marginal sacrifice in earnings}}{\text{Marginal decrease in risk}} \quad \text{(Investor's choice)}$$

$$= \frac{\text{Marginal decrease in earnings}}{\text{Marginal increase in ownership capital (decrease risk)}} \quad \text{(in the financial structure of the firm)}$$

The letter *R* indicates the optimum rate of earnings on equity investment and *OC* the optimum amount of equity capital for each firm. If the optimum amount (*OC*) of the ownership capital is carried back to a chart similar to Figure 3*A* for each firm, the corresponding *SEF* function will apply, and the static size of the firm and the whole complex of the firm's capital structure (debt to equity, etc.) are determinate.[19]

[18] The author foresees some objection here. The indifference pattern is only hypothetical; how in actuality would a firm reach the optimum capital structure? The answer is, of course, how all such complicated solutions are reached in practice: by the exercise of the managerial art, by a movement of successive approximations until the best position is bracketed in. It would be expected that in a competitive situation the modal firms would cluster at the optimum solution.

[19] Much of the above discussion can be illustrated very roughly by arithmetic means, as follows: Suppose we have three firms, X, Y, Z, all in the same line of business and almost the same size. Firm X has no debt (leverage) and earns about $2.00 a common share; firm Y has some moderate proportion of debt (leverage) and earns $2.50 a year; whereas firm Z is overly leveraged (has a highly risky capital structure) and earns $3.00 a year per common share. Suppose, further, that in light of firm X's conservative financing, the market gives it a price-earnings ratio of 12 (capitalization rate of 8½ percent); that the market gives firm Y a *P/E* of 10 (capitalization rate of 10 percent); and firm Z's common, because of the high risk, is given a *P/E* of only 8 (capitalization rate of 12½ percent). Then the shares of X will sell for $24, Y for $25, and Z for $24. Company Y may be presumed to have the optimal capital structure of the three (see Benjamin Graham and David L. Dodd, *Security Analysis* [3d ed.; New York: McGraw-Hill Book Co., Inc., 1951], chap. xxxvii).

Having proceeded thus far, what does our model tell us about the typical different capital structures that appear in different industries? In the electric utility industry the cash flow tends to be quite stable, and lender's risk tends to be relatively low. This means that the firm in this industry can borrow a considerable amount on a relatively small equity base without tipping the *SEF* curve sharply upward. The result is that the marginal rate of substitution in the transformation curve between capital stock and earnings is relatively inelastic; i.e., a small cutback in the amount of equity in the capital structure leads to a significant increase in earnings per share. Stated conversely, since an increase in equity will have relatively little effect in lowering the firm's interest rate, the resulting decrease in leverage will reduce the rate of return on equity considerably. Furthermore, the subjective borrowers' risk for potential shareholders is also relatively low—because external risks are low—and the shareholders are willing to shoulder the responsibility for a large volume of debt in exchange for a greater rate of return. In other words, the reaction of both borrowers and lenders of funds to the circumstance of low external risks brings about an optimum capital structure which is relatively heavily leveraged.

Similarly, the asset structure of a bank is so composed that the external risks are considered to be extremely low. The borrowers (shareholders) are therefore willing to give a high capitalization rate to the earnings in spite of what would otherwise appear to be a most risky financial structure.

On the other hand, an industrial firm—facing heavier external risks—is likely to experience a relatively sharp rise in financing charges if its debt-to-equity ratio (leverage) exceeds certain proportions. This means that borrowing beyond a certain point does not bring a proportionate increase in profits; the transformation curve of ownership capital to rate of return is relatively elastic. Moreover, the capitalization rate on equity earnings may drop significantly for firms which are "riskily" financed in the eyes of the stockholders. Thus the typical industrial financial structure would tend to contain a smaller proportion of debt to total financing than either the utility or the bank.

We have attempted to incorporate something of the foregoing discussion in Figures 3*B* and 3*C*, which have been constructed to illustrate differences in financial structure under assumed conditions of varying external risks. Thus, Figure 3*B* might indicate a firm, such as an electric utility, for example, whose stability of earnings would induce the investors to accept a lesser amount of equity capital (i.e., a relatively *larger* amount of financial structure risk), whereas Figure 3*C* would indicate a firm, perhaps a manufacturer, where the investors would prefer relatively less financial structure risk. Thus, we have tried to depict the rate of change between the return on equity and the amount of ownership capital in the financial structure as relatively inelastic in firm B, and somewhat more elastic in firm C.

Reviewing the final solution illustrated in the series under Figures 3*B* and 3*C*, it might be well to discuss the concept of the final equilibrium rate of return or earnings, $R$. Figures 3*B* and 3*C* have been derived from functions similar to those depicted on Figure 3*A*. The basic parameters for all functions are asset values and rates of return on asset values, earnings, or interest expense. Since all the firm functions are in terms of assets, the market indifference curve must also be constructed to give the marginal rate of substitution between earnings and risk in terms of assets. However, the rate of return on market price (let us call this $r$) is implicit in the indifference curves because the condition for the optimum at the point of tangency is that $R/r$ be a maximum, which makes the market price of the shares a maximum. Thus, as Figures 3*B* and 3*C* are constructed, $R$ is not the rate of return on the *market price* of the firm's shares but the optimum return on the reproducible asset value of the equity.[20]

The discounting rate or the return on market price, $r$, is affected by external risks and financing risks. It is competitively determined by the rates prevailing on all other securities. The market price of the shares is derived from the relationship between the rate of earnings on equity and the market discount rate. If $R$ exceeds $r$, the market price of the shares will be greater than the reproducible asset value, and vice versa. However, in industries *which are competitive* the market price of the shares cannot exceed the true or reproducible asset value of the ownership shares without inducing the creation of new firms. *In competitive equilibrium the reproducible asset value of the ownership capital*[21] *and the market valuation of that capital must be equal for all optimally financed firms.* Of course, this need not hold true for firms which may have various competitive advantages or for industries which are adjusting to demand growth or decline or to changes in the production function.

An interesting sidelight may be developed here on the possible difference between competitive and monopolistic financing. For it would seem that the area of financial structure variation is quite narrowly bounded for the competitive firm. Thus, for any firm whose financial structure is heavily cushioned with equity capital in comparison to the

---

[20]To have used the market rate of return at this point would have been to anticipate our solution. We are looking precisely for that rate of earnings per share, given financial risk, which will maximize the market value of the common stock; the rate of return on the market price is thus the final result. For simplicity in exposition, we shall assume some "normal" payout rate of dividends throughout this section.

[21]Obviously, the reproducible asset value must include a charge to cover the costs of obtaining management and of working out the organization of the firm.

production risks it seems to be carrying and whose stock nevertheless seems to sell at a considerable multiple of its asset value, one may be likely on closer examination to discover the possession of some monopolistic advantage. In certain firms which appear to be extremely conservative in their financial structure, the management may have elected to take out some of the monopolistic returns in the form of additional security. And of course, excess security is not as open to criticism as excess profits.

## *V. Adjustments for Growth and Capital Market Changes*

So far, our discussion has been static; we have tried to show how at a given point of time a firm will adjust its capital structure to its earnings potential and supply of available funds. The possibility of growth is, however, a perennially interesting one, and perhaps something should be said on the subject.

Given the model we have used, problems of growth can best be handled through the use of comparative statistics. Firm growth takes place either because the capital market terms change (the supply price of capital falls) or because there is an increase in demand for the firm's products. An increase in the supply of capital is equivalent to a rise in security prices or a fall in the money rates. In general (as is obvious in orthodox theory), such a fall in the money rates will encourage an expansion of the individual firm, since, all other things being constant, a favorable disparity will appear between the earning power of marginal assets and the additional full cost of the funds required to obtain them. It is important to recognize, however, that the *full* cost of the additional funds (including the cost of making changes in the capital mix) must decline in order to bring any expansion through a drop in the supply price of financing. It is possible, for example, for opposing changes in the price of outside funds and the risk preference on shares to take place in a way which would lead only to an offsetting use of one or the other without leading to any increase in the total asset size of the firm. A change would appear in the composition but not the size of the capital structure. It might even be possible that although a drop in market interest rates takes place, a fall in the marginal preference for risk (i.e., a disinclination to borrow) could occur which would exactly offset the effect of the drop in the price of outside funds. In such a case, no net change might occur at all in either the composition or the size of the capital structure.[22]

---

[22]It was perhaps some phenomenon similar to this which militated against the success of monetary policy during the depth of the depression.

A firm may adjust its financial structure for changes in the terms of the financial markets; it may also adjust for growth and declines in the demand for its products. In our model, such changes in demand can be represented by shifts in the *MRE* curve; a shift to the right represents a growth in demand, and to the left, a decline. As a matter of fact, in the real world, such shifts are extremely relevant to the financial managers because the new financial moves called forth by changes in the size of the firm make it easier to adjust the financial structure continually toward equilibrium.

A decline in the demand for the firm's products will release assets and funds which can be applied toward reducing the firm's financial structure. Usually, the funds in such a case will go to repaying debt; but there is no reason why some equity capital may not be repaid, too, through an increase in the dividend payout rate, a payment of dividends from previously accumulated surplus, or, where allowed, through the use of tenders or the repurchase of stock on the open market. Exactly how the adjustment would take place between debt and equity (outside of some institutional problems) would depend on which way the firm must move to obtain an optimum capital structure (between risk and rate of return) for its new size.

The adjustment to an increase in the demand for the products of the firm is perhaps more interesting. An increase in demand for the firm's products is represented by a movement of the *MRE* curve to the right. This means that the marginal rate of earnings on the prevailing volume of assets shifts upward and that more assets could be added to the present firm before the marginal rate of earnings on these assets dropped back to the original level. In order to finance the new assets for expansion, the firm must analyze and explore the supply of funds in the new area. If the firm already has a large equity base (too large for the present optimum structure of the firm), then it may expand and purchase new assets with outside funds; if the firm's present financial structure varies from optimum in the other direction (i.e., the earnings on the ownership capital are overdiscounted because of too much leverage or risk), then the firm should choose to expand through an issue of additional stock or an attempt to build up surplus (retained ownership earnings). A firm which is already in the optimum position[23] will explore the possibilities of adding to both equity and debt. However, this addition does not necessarily have to be in the same proportion as the previous capital structure, for the optimum capital structure of the larger firm may not have the same relative composition as the smaller one.

Thus, growth, perhaps even more readily than decline, gives the

[23]In a sense, this is only a theoretical possibility. In a dynamic economy, no firm at any single point of time is likely to have *the* optimum capital structure.

management an opportunity to recast the financial structure. However, the firm must probably reconsider the financing problem for each step of contemplated growth. Very likely, the stability of the earnings potential of new facilities will be regarded as less certain than on the old assets; and inasmuch as the external risk is greater, the financing may have to be more conservative for the new increment than that which already exists for the rest of the firm.

The necessity of arranging new financing probably constitutes a brake on the time rate of growth of the individual firm. Indeed, Professor Kalecki used as one of his models the large multiplant firm which has no technical limits on its growth, since it is able to invest in any area of the economy which is profitable, i.e., growing, without incurring any increase in risk or decline in earnings. This firm is presumed to have the same opportunities open to it as the general economy, and therefore the only restraint on its rate of growth is the problem of maintaining the proper financing mix between equity and debt.[24] The notion is interesting and quite correct on the basic assumption, except that one may doubt the existence of any significant number of firms that are so diversified and so well balanced in their resources and organization that they are free to enter any area of the economy without suffering a decrease in efficiency.

## *VI. Conclusion*

Under the assumption that firms will attempt to maximize the long-run market value of the ownership shares, there exists an optimum capital structure for each individual firm. This optimum capital structure varies for firms in different industries because the typical asset structures and the stablity of earnings which determine inherent risks vary for different types of production. The theoretical solution of the optimum capital structure is made in a very formal manner, since it must give consideration to many variables—increasing lender's risk, increasing borrower's risk, the interest rate structure, the forecasted earnings function, and the possibility of discriminating against the market supply of outside capital. The limitations of the model are freely admitted; nevertheless, insofar as it casts new light on certain significant relationships—the debt-equity ratio, the stability of earnings, full costs of borrowing, and rates of return versus relative market distastes for risks—the approach seems useful.

[24]Kalecki, op. cit., pp. 440–47; reprinted and revised in the Michal Kalecki *Theory of Economic Fluctuations* (London: G. Allen & Unwin, Ltd.) 1939), pp. 95–106. See also L. Wellisz, "Entrepreneur's Risk, Lender's Risk, and Investment," *Review of Economic Studies,* Vol. XX, No. 52 (1952–55), pp. 105–14.

*Chapter 26*

# *The Savings Investment and Valuation of a Corporation**

By Myron J. Gordon

IN THE neoclassical theory of a firm's investment the objective of the firm is to maximize its value. Its value is a function of its future income, and its future income is a function of its investment. As Lutz and Lutz [8][1] admirably demonstrated in their standard work on the subject, given the behavior postulate and these two functions, the investment and value of a firm may be determined. Unfortunately, however, the numerous models they constructed assume that the future is known with certainty and with minor qualifications that the firm can freely lend or borrow at a given rate of interest. These conditions are not realized in fact, the data of their models cannot be observed, and the models stand as elegant intellectual exercises of limited usefulness.[2] A consequence

*Reprinted by permission of the publishers from Myron J. Gordon, *Review of Economics and Statistics,* Vol. XLIV (February, 1962), pp. 37–51 (Cambridge, Mass.: Harvard University Press). 

The research reported here was supported by a grant from the Sloan Research Fund, School of Industrial Management, Massachusetts Institute of Technology; and the computations were carried out at the Computation Center, MIT. Discussions with Professors Chow, Kuh, and Solow and comments by Professor Modigliani on an earlier draft of this paper have been of considerable assistance to the writer. The advice of Ramesh Gangolli on problems of statistical inference was most helpful. I am especially indebted to Henry Y. Wan, Jr., for his unflagging energy and painstaking care in collecting the data and programming the computations.

[1]Numbers in brackets refer to publications listed on page 455.

[2]In the last half of their book the Lutzes withdraw the assumption that the future is certain, but this material is largely a well-written distillation of the qualitative statements contained in textbooks on finance.

is that the literature concerned with testable propositions on the investment and the valuation of the firm makes little or no reference to the neoclassical theory. Further, empirical theories of investment, for example, those discussed in Meyer and Kuh [10], refer to the valuation of the firm only in passing; and theories of valuation such as Durand [3] make no reference to the investment of the firm. Only the normative literature, including in a sense Modigliani and Miller [11], relates the investment and value of a firm, but this literature continues to provide little empirical information on the investment and financing that maximize the value of a firm.

The purpose of this paper is to present a theory of the investment and valuation of a corporation analogous to the neoclassical theory without the assumptions that the future is certain and that funds are freely available at a given rate of interest. Specifically, the initial statement is that the value of a firm is a function of its expected future income. The future income is then represented by a function of the corporation's investment to obtain an expression in which a share's price is the dependent variable, the investment function provides the independent variables, and the parameters represent the corporation's cost of capital. In general structure the model parallels those of neoclassical theory; and similarly, it may be solved to find the investment that maximizes the value of the firm. The difference is that the variables are observable and the parameters may be estimated from sample data.

The model is developed under restrictive assumptions with respect to the financing policies of corporations and the form of the return-on-investment function. These assumptions are irritating from a theoretical point of view, but they are of limited material significance, as will be evidenced by the empirical results to be presented. Work currently under way and to be reported later, however, will make the model considerably more general.

The theory will be tested here as a valuation model and not as an investment model. That is, the ability of the model to explain the differences in price among common stocks will be tested, and it will be seen that under a variety of considerations the model performs better than previous efforts in this direction. By the statement that the theory will not be tested as an investment model, I mean that no attempt will be made to establish whether or not the investment of the corporation is determined by the objective of maximizing its value.

Under the functional form of the stock price model established, a corporation's cost of capital is an increasing function of the rate of growth in its dividend. An inference from this theorem is that the price of a share is not independent of the distribution of the corporation's income between dividends and retention.[3] Strictly speaking, the statistical findings do not test the theorem. However, the deductive argument leading to its adoption, and the general quality of the empirical results may be considered evidence in support of the theorem. In addition, it will be shown that the theorem is true under a plausible set of assumptions with respect to behavior.

## *The General Theory*

Most of the terms to be used in what follows are defined below:

$Y_t$ = Income a share of stock is expected to earn in period $t$
$D_t$ = Dividend a share of stock is expected to pay in period $t$
$B_t$ = Investment in the corporation or common equity per share of stock at the end of period $t$
$b$ = Fraction of income the corporation is expected to retain

$$b = (Y_t - D_t)/Y_t, \ t = 1, 2, \ldots$$

$r$ = Average return the corporation is expected to earn on the common equity investment of $bY_t$, $t = 1, 2, \ldots$
$P_o$ = The price of a corporation's stock at the end of $t = 0$
k = The rate at which the corporation's future dividends are discounted at the end of $t = 0$ to arrive at their present value

The fundamental proposition of capital theory is that the value of an investment opportunity is the expected future receipts its ownership provides discounted at the rate of profit required on the investment. In the case of a share of stock the expected future receipts are the dividends, so that:

$$P_o = \int_o^\infty D_t e^{-kt} dt \qquad (1)$$

In a system where capital gains are not subject to preferential tax treatment, this statement is true regardless of whether the share is purchased for dividends or for price appreciation, since the price at any future date is expected to be the discounted value of the subsequent dividends.[4] It will be seen shortly that the theory explicitly recognizes

[3]This position is generally rejected by economists. For instance, Modigliani and Miller stated ". . . the division of an income stream between cash dividends and retained earnings in a period is a mere detail" ([11], 266).

[4]It has been widely believed that earnings and not dividends are the relevant variable in the valuation of a share. However, Bodenhorn [1] has shown that the investor does not discount expected future earnings in arriving at the value of a share. It will be shown in what follows that what the advocates of the earnings hypotheses must maintain is that dividends are what investors buy, but the price of a share is independent of the dividend rate.

growth or price appreciation and the market's valuation of it in the price of a share. If capital gains receive preferential tax treatment, the deductive argument and the interpretation of the empirical price model are modified, but the conclusions reached are not materially changed, and the elaboration of the theory on an after-tax basis will not be undertaken here.

It has been shown [4] [6] that if a corporation issues no new shares, maintains a constant debt-equity ratio, retains a fraction $b$ of its income, and earns a rate of return $r$ on investment, then the dividend will grow at a rate $br$. If the initial level of income is $Y_0$, then $D_0 = (1 - b)\ Y_0$, and with continuous growth the dividend in period $t$ will be:

$$D_t = Y_o(1 - b)e^{rbt} \tag{2}$$

Substituting equation 2 for $D_t$ in equation 1 results in:

$$P_o = \int_0^\infty Y_o(1 - b)e^{brt}e^{-kt}dt \tag{3}$$

$P_0$ is finite, and the integration may be carried out if $k > br$. The result is:

$$P_o = \frac{Y_o\,(1 - b)}{k - br} \tag{4}$$

The value of a share is the current dividend divided by the difference between the rate of profit on the stock investors require and the rate of growth in the dividend.

On the four assumptions necessary for equation 4, the first three deal with financing policy. In defense of the first, it is well know that corporations, particularly those engaged in manufacturing, undertake relatively little outside equity financing. On debt financing, a recent study by the writer [5] provides considerable evidence that apart from short-term inventory financing requirements, the maintenance of a stable debt-equity ratio is a widely practiced policy on the part of corporations.[5] To put the matter differently, it is quite reasonable to assume that in estimating a corporation's future dividends, investors do not consider the possible future stock sales by a corporation as being material, and that they expect the corporation to maintain its existing debt-equity ratio.

On the third assumption, it is clear that a corporation will not retain the fraction $b$ of its income in every future period, but we are not really interested in what a corporation actually will do. Rather, what a cor-

[5]Debt is here defined as short-term and long-term liabilities net of monetary-type assets and short-period inventory movements. An increase in debt to finance an increase in government bonds is clearly of no significance for a theory of investment in real assets. For a further discussion of this point, see [5, pp. 476–79].

poration is expected to do by investors is relevant. If investors behave rationally, they estimate what $b$, and $r$ also, will be in the future, or they formulate expectations that contain implicit estimates of $b$ and $r$.[6] Whether or not the expectations are adequately represented by the assumption that $b$ will be the same in every future period is a question of fact that can in part be resolved by the statistical work. Support for the assumption is provided by the work of Lintner [9] and others, which indicates that corporations are widely recognized to follow a policy of paying a stable fraction of their normal income in dividends.

The consequence of these three assumptions is that an investor's estimate of $b$, a corporation's retention rate, implies an estimate of its investment rate. That is, if $q$ is the ratio of a corporation's debt to its equity and $b$ is the fraction of income it retains, $bY_t$ will be the addition to the corporation's equity in period $t$, and $(1 + q)\ bY_t$ will be its investment in the period.

The view that dividend policy is irrelevant to the investment and valuation of a corporation has been so widely accepted that some reflection on the previous argument is desirable. First, we have cited evidence that a very common practice among corporations is to maintain a stable debt-equity ratio. Year-to-year changes cancel out for the most part. Second, we assume that investors estimate a retention rate, $b$, and a debt equity rate, $q$, that they *expect* the corporation to maintain for the indefinite future. Third, the corporation is not expected to engage in outside equity financing. The last two assumptions may not be empirically true, but under them it logically follows that the investment a corporation is expected to undertake in a future period, $t$, is $(1 + q)\ bY_t$. Further, with $q$ given, we may use the terms "investment rate" and "retention rate" interchangeably, since one is a constant multiple of the other.[7]

The last assumption, that a corporation's return on investment is expected to be $r$ in every future period, is probably the most objectionable. The assumption is that, given $b$, the investment rate, investors expect the return on investment to be $r$. It does not exclude the possibility that the value of $r$ expected for a corporation in every future period will vary depending on the value of $b$. It does exclude the case where for a given $b$ $r$, is expected to take on different values over time. Here again, we are not concerned with what the value of the variable actually will be. Our speculation in support of the assumption is, if investors were polled on the change they expect in the rate of profit a corporation will earn,

---

[6] The rational investor values a share on the basis of the future payments it provides, and he therefore performs some operations on the data available to him to arrive at such estimates.

[7] In what follows, we shall assume $q = 0$, but the conclusions reached apply with no qualifications for a corporation with $q \neq 0$.

the typical result will be a frequency distribution with mean zero and a small standard deviation. The quality of the empirical results will turn in large measure on the accuracy of this speculation.

This defense of the four assumptions, of course, does not deny the advantages in theoretical elegance as well as improved accuracy and scope of the empirical findings in having a theory not restricted by the above assumptions. The defense does, I believe, indicate that the assumptions have enough correspondence with reality to justify the empirical investigation of a theory that reflects them.

## *Interpretation and Empirical Formulation of the Theory*

Thus, reviewing the development of equation 4, we began with the statement that the value of a share is the present value of its expected future dividends. It was then shown that under empirically relevant assumptions, this dividend expectation is given by the corporation's current income, $Y_0$, the return on investment the corporation is expected to earn on the common equity investment, and the retention rate, $b$, the corporation is expected to maintain. Given the return on investment investors require, $k$, the value of a share was found to be:

$$P_o = \frac{Y_o\,(1 - b)}{k - br} \tag{4}$$

The model may be used to find the investment rate that maximizes the share's value, with the character of the solution depending on the assumptions with respect to the behavior of $r$ and $k$ as $b$ varies.

For instance, if it is assumed that $r$ and $k$ are independent of $b$, we simply take the derivative of $P$ with respect to $b$ and find that:

$$\frac{\delta P}{\delta b} = (r - k)\,\frac{Y_o}{(k - rb)^2} \tag{5}$$

If $r = k$, $\delta P/\delta b = 0$, or a share's price is independent of the retention rate. If $r$ is greater (less) than $k$, price rises (falls) as $b$ is increased. The important feature of this result is that it agrees perfectly with the conclusions reached by those who maintain that dividend policy per se has no influence on share price.

In the above conclusion, we first assumed that $k$ is a constant. Under this assumption the price of a share is independent of the corporation's retention and investment, if the rate of return the corporation can earn on investment is the same as the rate of return stockholders require. If $r \gtrless k$, the price of the share will rise or fall with $b$, but this is due to the profitability of investment and not the financing of it by retention. The variation in price with $b$ is due simply to the fact that it is the sole method of finance under consideration.

Of course, with $r \gtrless k$, price will not rise or fall indefinitely with $b$, because the rate of return is not a constant. A plausible hypothesis is that $r$ falls; or if there are indivisibilities in the firm's investment opportunities, $r$ rises and then falls as $b$ increases. In this event:

$$\frac{\delta P}{\delta b} = [-k + rb - (1-b)(-r - b\frac{\delta r}{\delta b})]\frac{Y_o}{(k-rb)^2}$$

$$= [r - k + b(1-b)\frac{\delta r}{\delta b}]\frac{Y_o}{(k-rb)^2} \quad (6)$$

This expression yields a maximum price at a finite investment rate. The value of a share is maximized at $b > 0$ if $r > k$ at $b = 0$. As $b$ increases, $r$ falls; and $b(1-\text{b})\ \delta r/\delta b$, which is negative because $\delta r/\delta b$ is negative, increases in absolute amount. Therefore, there is some value of $b$ at which $\delta P/\delta b = 0$, and the price of the share is maximized at this investment rate.

It may be noted that at $b = 1$, we have $P = 0$, regardless of the values of $k$ and $r$. The interpretation of this statement is that regardless of how profitable a corporation is, its stock has a zero value if it is expected that the corporation will never pay a dividend. What this implies is that investors do not believe a corporation will never pay a dividend.[8]

We see, then, that if the management's objective is to maximize the value of a corporation under certain financial constraints, the theory provides a solution to a corporation's investment as well as to its value. To be able to use this solution, however, we must be able to observe the values of the variables in equation 4. For $Y_0$, $r$, and $b$, we may be able to derive estimates from historical data; but what do we do for $k$? Furthermore, can we be sure that $k$ is independent of $r$ and $b$?

If the answer to the last question is in the affirmative, we could proceed as follows. Write equation 4 in the form:

$$\frac{Y_o(1-b)}{P_o} = k - br \quad (7)$$

The left side is $d$, a corporation's dividend yield *based on its current dividend*. Take a sample of corporations that is homogeneous with respect to risk and other attributes that might influence $k$ (the homogeneity

[8]If a corporation has not been paying a dividend, stockholders expect a change in management policy or a change in management. It is evident, however, that our model is not the most effective means of dealing with this type of situation, since stockholders may expect no dividend for a number of years.

achieved by sample selection or the introduction of other variables), and use the sample to estimate the parameters of:

$$d = \alpha_o - \alpha_1 br \qquad (8)$$

$\alpha_0$ is an estimate of $k$, and we would expect to find $\alpha_1 = 1$.

However, $\alpha_1$ would undoubtedly turn out to be significantly less than one.[9] And the more we look at equation 8, the more uncomfortable we get about the assumption that $k$ is independent of $br$. If $k$ is a constant, for a sufficiently high growth rate, $d$ becomes negative, and a share's price goes through infinity.

It may be argued that $br > k$ is unlikely on the following grounds. An extraordinarily high value of $r$ is necessary for $br > k$; but contrary to our assumption, investors are not likely to expect this state to continue forever. Further, a corporation with $r$ very large should undertake additional outside financing. Hence, $br > k$ becomes possible only under the restrictive assumptions of the theory. On the other hand, there are corporations that are expected to earn extraordinary rates of return for a very long time (forever is not necessary with the future discounted), many of them do not engage in other financing, and they still sell at finite prices.

An alternative explanation of why shares sell at finite prices, one that is very attractive empirically, is provided by the assumption that $k$ is an increasing function of $br$. In support of it, common sense as well as the mathematics of our model suggest that as $br$, the rate of growth in the dividend, rises, the required yield based on the current dividend should fall—not in a one-to-one ratio but by decreasing amounts, so that $d$ asymptotically approaches zero. An expression that satisfies this requirement is:

$$d = \alpha_o (1 + br)^{-\alpha_1} \qquad (9)$$

The alternative functions for $d$ are illustrated in Figure 1.

Substituting equation 9 for $k - br = d$ in equation 4, the latter becomes:

$$P = Y_o (1 - b) \frac{1}{\alpha_o} (1 + br)^{\alpha_1} \qquad (10)$$

When $b = 0$, the price of a share is its dividend $Y_0(1 - b)$ multiplied by $1/\alpha_0$. As $b$ increases, the multiplier rises to $(1/\alpha_0)\ (1 + br)\alpha_1$. Given $Y_0(1 - b)$, the current dividend, the larger the value of $br$, its expected rate of growth, the higher the price investors are willing to pay for a share. The only retriction on the parameters of equation 10 is that they be positive.

[9] The empirical work reported in Gordon [4] may be reasonably interpreted to provide evidence in support of this conclusion.

FIGURE 1

VARIATION IN DIVIDEND YIELD WITH EXPECTED RATE OF GROWTH IN THE DIVIDEND

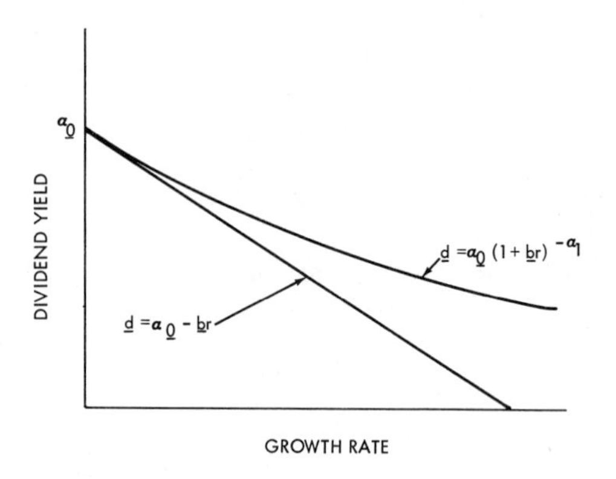


Although equation 10 may be attractive empirically, some may consider its theoretical implications sheer heresy. To justify it theoretically, we must assume that a corporation's cost of capital is an increasing function of the rate of growth in its dividend expectation. To see this, note that:

$$k - br = d = \alpha_o (1 + br)^{-\alpha_1} \tag{11}$$

implies that:

$$k = \alpha_o (1 + br)^{-\alpha_1} + br \tag{12}$$

and:

$$\frac{\delta k}{\delta br} = - \alpha_1 \alpha_o (1 + br)^{-(1+\alpha_1)} + 1$$

$$= 1 - \frac{\alpha_1 \alpha_o}{(1 + br)^{1+\alpha_1}} \tag{13}$$

The product $\alpha_0 \alpha_1$ should be about equal to one.[10] What this means is that if $\alpha_0 \alpha_1 > 1$, $k$ will fall over some interval of $b$ starting with $b = 0$. However, as $b$ and $br$ rise, $\delta k/\delta br$ becomes positive and remains so.

To interpret the definition of $k$ provided by equation 12, $\alpha_0$ is a corporation's cost of capital when $b = 0$. As $br$ rises, the second term on the right side of equation 12 rises, but the first term falls and moderates the rise in $k$ with $br$. Further, the larger the absolute value of $\alpha_1$, the smaller the rise in $k$ with $br$. Hence, $\alpha_1$ may be looked on as the price investors are willing to pay for growth in the dividend. If $\alpha_1$ is large, investors are willing to pay a lot for dividend growth, and vice versa.

[10]Plausible values are $a_0 = 0.08$ and $a_1 = 12$.

What this means is that the value of a share depends on the corporation's dividend and investment rates. The value should of course change with investment due to the return on investment, but we now have an independent influence. Note $k = \alpha_o$ when $br = o$. If we set $r = \alpha_o$, a share's price will change with $b$ because $k$ changes. Formerly, with $k$ a constant and $r = k = \alpha_o$, price was independent of $b$.

An interesting feature of the assumption that $\delta k/\delta br > o$ is that with $r$ a constant, the resultant stock value model yields an optimum price for a finite dividend rate. The optimum dividend or retention rate is found by taking the derivative of equation 10 with respect to $b$ and finding the value of $b$ that satisfied $\delta P/\delta b = o$. If $r$ is independent of $b$, $P_o$ is maximized by the retention rate:

$$b = \frac{\alpha_1}{\alpha_1 + 1} - \frac{1}{r\,(\alpha_1 + 1)} \tag{14}$$

The plausible result is that the optimum retention rate is an increasing function of $r$, the profitability of investment, and of $\alpha_1$, the price the market is willing to pay for growth in the dividend.

It should be noted that having $k$ an increasing function of $br$ does not imply share price is a decreasing function of $br$. Reflection on equation 10 reveals that for given $b$, $P_o$ always rises with $r$; and for given $r$ and $\alpha_1$, $P_o$ rises and then falls with $b$.

## *A Rationale of the Critical Proposition*

The proposition that the rate of profit investors require in placing a value on a dividend expectation is an increasing function of its rate of growth conflicts with widely held views on the cost of capital. Our main defense of the theorem is that a model based on the proposition does a remarkably good job of explaining the valuation of shares by investors. However, before presenting the empirical results, it may be useful to present a theoretical rationale of the proposition. We shall not prove the proposition is true. We shall state a set of assumptions under which the proposition proves to be true. Some may find these assumptions reasonable. More important, this rationale may provide insights for new theorems on observable phenomena that contribute to their explanation and prediction.

The basic postulate of our model is that the price of a share is the present value of its expected future dividend payments. An investor may be *represented* as arriving at the present value of the expected payment in some future period, say $t = n$, by one of two methods. Under the "certainty—equivalent method," he proceeds as follows. Let $D_n$, the dividend during $n$, be a random variable with expected value $\bar{D}_n$ and standard deviation $\sigma_n$. The investor uses $\sigma_n$ as an index of the uncertainty of $D_n$,[11] and he arrives at the certainty equivalent of $D_n$ by multiplying $\overline{D}_n$ by some function of $\sigma_n$. If this function is $f(\sigma_n)$ and $i$ is the pure rate of interest, the present value of the dividend expectation in period $n$ is:

$$PV_n = \frac{\overline{D}_n f\ (\sigma_n)}{(1 + i)^n} \tag{15}$$

Under the "profit rate method," he simply discounts $\overline{D}_n$ at a rate $k_n$ that reflects its risk; that is, $k_n$ is also a function of $\sigma_n$. It is clear that there is some number $k_n$, such that:

$$PV_n = \frac{\overline{D}_n}{(1 + k_n)^n} \tag{16}$$

Both of the above representations of an investor's behavior are plausible, and neither method is inherently superior to the other.

What can we say about the uncertainty of $D_t$ as $t$ goes from one to infinity? If there is no growth expected in the dividend, we might assume that at the end of $t = 0$, $D_0 = \overline{D}_1 = \overline{D}_2 = \ . \ . \ . = \overline{D}_n \ . \ . \ . \ .$ In this event, we should also expect that at the end of $t = n - 1$, $\overline{D}_n = D_{n-1}$. If the variance at the end of $n - 1$ of $D_n - D_{n-1}$ is independent of $n$, equal to $\sigma^2$ say, the successive dividends over time are an additive process with stationary independent increments, and the variance at $t = 0$ of $D_n$ increases with $n$. It is $n\sigma^2$, and the standard deviation of $D_n$ is $\sigma\sqrt{n}$.

The hypothesis that $\overline{D}_t = D_{t-1}$ may not be correct. The entire dividend history may influence $\overline{D}_t$ and subsequent expectations. Regardless of the nature of how expectations are formed, however, it is most likely that the uncertaintly of an intem in a dividend series increases with its time in the future. Hence, we may accept with great confidence that $\sigma_{n+1} > \sigma_n$ and $f(\sigma_{n+1}) < f(\sigma_n)$.

We shall examine now the relation between $k_n$ and $k_{n+1}$ for a dividend expectation with $D_0 = \overline{D}_n = \overline{D}_{n+1}$. Let:

$$PV_n = \frac{\overline{D}_n f\ (\sigma_n)}{(1 + i)^n} = \frac{\overline{D}_n}{(1 + k_n)^n} \tag{17}$$

and

$$PV_{n+1} = \frac{D_{n+1} f\ (\sigma_{n+1})}{(1 + i)^{n+1}} = \frac{\overline{D}_{n+1}}{(1 + k_{n+1})^{n+1}} \tag{18}$$

[11]For some purposes a relative measure of variation should be used, but everything that is established in what follows holds equally when a relative measure such as the coefficient of variation is used.

Dividing $PV_n$ by $PV_{n+1}$, we obtain:

$$\frac{\bar{D}_n f(\sigma_n)(1+i)}{\bar{D}_{n+1} f(\sigma_{n+1})} = \frac{\bar{D}_n (1+k_{n+1})^{n+1}}{\bar{D}_{n+1} (1+k_n)^n} \tag{19}$$

Simplifying, and recalling that $f(\sigma_n) > f(\sigma_{n+1})$, we have:

$$1 < \frac{f(\sigma_n)}{f(\sigma_{n+1})} = \frac{(1+k_{n+1})^{n+1}}{(1+k_n)^n (1+i)} \tag{20}$$

What restrictions does the above equality place on the possible values of $k_n$ and $k_{n+1}$? Absolutely none! Since $i < k_n$, we may have the equality satisfied, given $f(\sigma_n)$ and $f(\sigma_{n+1})$ with $k_n \gtreqless k_{n+1}$. If the uncertainty of the dividend increases only slightly with time, and if aversion to risk is small, $f(\sigma_n)/f(\sigma_{n+1})$ is only slightly greater than one, and $k_{n+1} < k_n$.[12] Under the opposite conditions, $k_{n+1} > k_n$. *The important point to note, however, is that there is nothing to guarantee that $k_t$ is a constant for all values of t.* The behavior of $k_t$ is a question of fact that cannot be settled by deductive argument.

It will be shown next that if it is true that $k_t$ is an increasing function of $t$, a corporation's cost of capital is an increasing function of the rate of growth in its dividend. First, however, let us recall the assumptions which brought us where we are. We assumed only that investors have an aversion to risk and that, other things remaining the same, the uncertainty of each element in a series of payments generated by an asset increases with the payments time in the future. These assumptions seem quite reasonable.

In developing our valuation theory, the value of a share was arrived at by discounting a firm's entire dividend expectation at a single rate $k$. As long as no growth is expected in the dividend and it is an infinite series, this is of no consequence. Nothing is lost by being oblivious of the fact that the single $k$ used to discount the series is in fact an average of the $k_t$

However, this is not true when the dividend is expected to grow. Let $\alpha$ designate a share of stock for which the dividend is expected to grow at the rate $g_\alpha$. At $t = 0$, the expected value of the dividend in $t = n$ is $\bar{D}_{n,\alpha} = D_0 (1 + g_\alpha)^n$. The value of the share is:

$$P_\alpha = D_0 \left[ \frac{1+g_\alpha}{1+k_1} + \frac{(1+g_\alpha)^2}{(1+k_2)^2} + \cdots + \frac{(1+g_\alpha)^n}{(1+k_n)^n} \cdots \right] \tag{21}$$

[12] For example, let $f(\sigma_n) = \mu_0 \sigma_n^{-1/\mu_1}$. If $\mu_1$ is a large number, $f(\sigma_n)$ falls very slowly as $\sigma_n$ increases. If we also have $\sigma_t$ increasing very slowly with $t$, it is likely that $k_t$ falls as $t$ increases.

There is some average of the $k_t$, $\bar{k}_\alpha$ such that the above price

$$P_\alpha = D_o \sum_{t=1}^{\infty} \frac{(1 + g_\alpha)^t}{(1 + \bar{k}_\alpha)^t} \tag{22}$$

Now, let $\beta$ designate another share. $\beta$ has the same initial dividend as $\alpha$, but the dividend on $\beta$ is expected to grow at the rate $g_\beta$, and $g_\beta > g_\alpha$. The two shares have the same degree of risk or relative variance, so that $\bar{D}_{n,\alpha}$ and $\bar{D}_{n,\beta}$ are both discounted at the same rate, $k_n$. Discounting the series $\bar{D}_{t,\beta}$ at the rate $k_t$, $t = 1, 2, \ldots, \infty$, results in a value $P_\beta$ for the share $\beta$. There is some average of the $k_t$, $\bar{k}_\beta$ which satisfies

$$P_\beta = D_o \sum_{t=1}^{\infty} \frac{(1 + g_\beta)^t}{(1 + \bar{k}_\beta)^t} \tag{23}$$

Both $\bar{k}_\alpha$ and $\bar{k}_\beta$ are weighted averages of the same $k_t$ series. However, since $g_\beta > g_\alpha$, the weights of $\bar{k}_\beta$ are relatively greater for the large $k_t$ in the distant future and relatively smaller for the smaller $k_t$ in the near future. The consequence is that $\bar{k}_\beta > \bar{k}_\alpha$ if the $k_t$ increases with $t$.[13] A rigorous proof of this statement has been derived by Ramesh Gangolli and is provided in Appendix A (page 456).

## *Derivation of the Empirical Model*

Our purpose in this section is to arrive at an estimating equation and rules for observing its variables that may be used to establish how well equation 10 explains the differences in price among common stocks.

It is widely accepted that the price an investor is willing to pay for a dividend expectation will vary depending on its uncertainty. As it stands, equation 10 assumes that all corporations have the same degree of risk; and hence, estimates of its parameters from a random sample of corporations would be inefficient. Since risk may vary among industries, there is some advantage in using sample data stratified by industry. With this in mind, samples of 48 food and 48 machinery corporations were used, and sample data were obtained for the years 1954–57.[14] Obtaining

---

[13]It is evident that $P_\beta > P_\alpha$, but the difference is smaller than it would be if $\bar{k}_\beta = \bar{k}_\alpha$ were true.

[14]The corporations included in the sample are from the indicated industry groups of the "Value Line Investment Survey" [13] at the end of 1958. A firm was excluded (*a*) if its dividend and earnings data did not extend back to 1947; (*b*) if there was an abnormal market interest in its shares (e.g., Fairbanks Morse was excluded on the ground that Penn-Texas was buying its stock over most of the period); and (*c*) if its dividend fell below 2 percent of its book value in two or more years of the period 1951–58. The larger sample, 1951–58, is to be used in another study. An objective in these conditions was to include in the sample only those corporations with an historical record that could be interpreted to provide estimates of the corporations' dividend expectation.

sample results for a given industry over a number of years is desirable for reasons that will become evident later.

Within an industry, corporations will differ in risk, and investor evaluation of a corporation's risk should in some measure be related to observable properties of the corporation. Specifically, it may be thought that the more unstable a corporation's past earnings, the more uncertain its future earnings and dividends. Further, stability is associated with size, so that regardless of its actual historical performance, investors may have more confidence in a large than in a small corporation. Accordingly, equation 10, enlarged to recognize the variation in a share's price with these two variables and with $\alpha_5 = 1/\alpha_o$, is:

$$P_o = \alpha_5 Y_o(1 - b)\,(1 + br)^{\alpha_1}\,(1 + u)^{\alpha_2} S^{\alpha_3} \tag{24}$$

$S$ is an index of the corporation's size, and $u$ is an index of the instability of its earnings. When $br = 0$, a corporation's cost of capital is:

$$\alpha_o\,(1 + u)^{-\alpha_2} S^{-\alpha_3} \tag{25}$$

and when $br > 0$, $k$ is obtained by substituting the above expression for $\alpha_o$ in equation 12. We expect $\alpha_2 < 0$ and $\alpha_3 > 0$.

The most difficult problem in testing and using equation 24 is the observation of the variables, particularly $b$ and $r$. They are expectations and not exactly specified historical data. Investors may be presumed to form expectations out of the history available to them, and an essential hypothesis in the empirical formulation of the theory is a statement of how investors arrive at the expectation variables.

We know that earnings, and to a lesser degree dividends, fluctuate from one year to the next, so that the actual values for the current year need not be what an investor considers a suitable basis for formulating expectations. We shall assume that investors take an exponentially weighted average of a corporation's past dividends to arrive at $D'_o$, the normalized current dividend, and of past earnings to arrive at $Y'_o$, the normalized current earnings.[15] Further, it is assumed that the return a corporation is expected to earn on investment is the normalized return it has been earning on its existing assets. Accordingly, the variables of equation 10 are defined as follows:

$$Y_o(1 - b) = D'_o$$

$$r = Y'_o/B_o$$

$$b = 1 - \frac{D'_o}{Y'_o}$$

$$rb = \frac{Y'_o - D'_o}{B}$$

[15]For a discussion of exponentially weighted averages of past values of a variable as an estimate of its normalized value, see Brown [2].

In the above, $B_0$ is the actual net worth or book value per share of stock at the end of $t = 0$.

The two variables introduced in equation 24 are not so important as the others, and their measurement is not so critical. The size, $S$, of a corporation is defined as the sum of its net plant account and working capital.[16] The instability index for a corporation's earnings is an absolute average of the year-to-year difference in the rate of return (earnings divided by book value) from 1947 through the current year. Here, more sophisticated definition and measurement of the variable might materially improve the results, but the computations involved can be quite formidable and were not considered justified at this stage in the empirical work.

Returning to $D'_t$ and $Y'_t$, our definitions of these variables are:

$$D'_t = \beta D_t + (1 - \beta)\, D'_{t-1}$$

and

$$Y'_t = \lambda Y_t + (1 - \lambda)\, Y'_{t-1}$$

$D'_t$ and $Y'_t$ were assigned arbitrary initial values for 1947 equal to 0.05 and 0.08 times the end-of-1947 book value, respectively. The above equations yielded the value in each subsequent year, with the qualification that $D'_t$ was always taken as the higher of the actual dividend or 2 percent of $B_t$.[17]

The final problem to be solved was the values to be assigned to the smoothing constants $\beta$ and $\lambda$. On the basis of an analysis discussed in Appendix B (page 458), the smoothing constants adopted were $\beta = 0.6$ and $\lambda = 0.5$.[18]

## *The Empirical Findings*

In the logs, equation 24 is linear, and least squares estimates of its parameters may be obtained from the expression:

$$\begin{aligned} LnP = {} & ln\ \alpha_5 + \alpha_4\ lnD' + \alpha_1\ ln\ (1 + br) \\ & + \alpha_2\ ln\ (1 + u) + \alpha_3\ lnS \end{aligned} \tag{26}$$

[16]Other definitions such as the market value of its outstanding securities might seem superior on some counts, but the statistical findings should not differ materially.

[17]Also, if inspection of the quarterly dividend payments up through the end of a year indicated a different dividend than that actually paid during the year, the former was used. For instance, if the regular dividend was raised in the second quarter, the higher quarterly figure was annualized in arriving at the figure for the year.

[18]Due to certain computation problems, this was not exactly true for the machinery sample. The variable $br$ was based on the above weights, but $D'$ was determined with $\beta = 0.8$. This undoubtedly did not materially influence the findings.

Notice the form of the model does not force $\alpha_4 = 1$, but obtains an estimate of the coefficient from the sample data.

TABLE 1

STOCK PRICE MODEL VARIABLE AND REGRESSION STATISTICS, FOOD AND MACHINERY SAMPLES, 1954–57

| | *Food Sample* | | | | *Machinery Sample* | | | |
|---|---|---|---|---|---|---|---|---|
| | *1954* | *1955* | *1956* | *1957* | *1954* | *1955* | *1956* | *1957* |
| $LnP$ | 3.70 | 3.69 | 3.59 | 3.54 | 3.53 | 3.62 | 3.67 | 3.36 |
| $S.D.$ | 0.57 | 0.59 | 0.54 | 0.52 | 0.47 | 0.51 | 0.55 | 0.52 |
| $Ln\alpha_5$ | 2.55 | 2.56 | 2.62 | 2.49 | 2.42 | 2.57 | 2.41 | 2.23 |
| $S.E.$ | 0.15 | 0.13 | 0.14 | 0.12 | 0.22 | 0.19 | 0.17 | 0.17 |
| $LnD'$ | 0.671 | 0.672 | 0.654 | 0.600 | 0.609 | 0.619 | 0.553 | 0.557 |
| $S.D.$ | 0.494 | 0.503 | 0.500 | 0.488 | 0.412 | 0.465 | 0.518 | 0.518 |
| $\alpha_1$ | 0.83 | 0.93 | 0.92 | 0.83 | 0.88 | 0.83 | 0.82 | 0.85 |
| $S.E.$ | 0.06 | 0.05 | 0.05 | 0.05 | 0.09 | 0.07 | 0.05 | 0.05 |
| $Ln(1+br)$ | 0.039 | 0.040 | 0.042 | 0.042 | 0.047 | 0.045 | 0.054 | 0.055 |
| $S.D.$ | 0.021 | 0.021 | 0.020 | 0.018 | 0.025 | 0.022 | 0.024 | 0.021 |
| $\alpha_1$ | 11.80 | 9.87 | 8.76 | 9.87 | 4.16 | 6.07 | 7.68 | 3.91 |
| $S.E.$ | 1.49 | 1.29 | 1.34 | 1.25 | 1.32 | 1.39 | 1.12 | 1.25 |
| $Ln(1+u)$ | 0.031 | 0.029 | 0.027 | 0.026 | 0.035 | 0.035 | 0.035 | 0.033 |
| $S.D.$ | 0.024 | 0.022 | 0.020 | 0.019 | 0.023 | 0.020 | 0.019 | 0.017 |
| $\alpha_2$ | −5.49 | −4.28 | −4.44 | −6.21 | −1.97 | −2.32 | −1.77 | −4.52 |
| $S.E.$ | 1.31 | 1.23 | 1.35 | 1.20 | 1.61 | 1.48 | 1.40 | 1.60 |
| $LnS$ | 4.36 | 4.41 | 4.47 | 4.51 | 3.68 | 3.76 | 3.87 | 3.98 |
| $S.D.$ | 0.85 | 0.84 | 0.84 | 0.85 | 0.73 | 0.75 | 0.77 | 0.81 |
| $\alpha_3$ | 0.071 | 0.055 | 0.027 | 0.065 | 0.122 | 0.093 | 0.116 | 0.149 |
| $S.E.$ | 0.036 | 0.032 | 0.032 | 0.026 | 0.045 | 0.039 | 0.034 | 0.033 |
| Mult. Corr. | 0.951 | 0.965 | 0.955 | 0.965 | 0.894 | 0.932 | 0.955 | 0.945 |

Table 1 presents the sample estimates of the parameters, their standard errors, the multiple correlation coefficient, and the means and standard deviations of the variables. The coefficient of the dividend turns out to be very close to one in all eight samples, ranging from 0.82 to 0.93. However, its standard error is so small that it must be considered significantly less than one, particularly since it is below one for every sample. What this means is that a doubling of the dividend with everything else unchanged does not double the price of a share. A possible explanation is that, everything else remaining the same, high-priced shares sell at lower prices (relative to the dividend) than low-priced shares. Another possible explanation is that there is some normal level for the dividend and investors believe a low dividend is more likely to rise than a high dividend.[19] It is also possible that error in the measurement of

[19] Some evidence in support of this hypothesis, with the dividend a percentage of book value as the variable, is presented in Gordon [4].

the dividend has produced some downward bias in the estimate of its coefficient.

The most striking aspect of the statistical findings is the high statistical significance and the small range of fluctuation in successive samples over time in the dividend and the growth rate coefficients. The dividend coefficient, as stated earlier, had a low of 0.82 and a high of 0.93, and it typically is over ten times its standard error. The growth coefficients vary from 8.8 to 11.8 for the food sample and are at least seven times their standard errors. The machinery sample does not perform as well, with a coefficient range of 3.9 to 7.7, but they are all well within the 1 percent level of significance. The somewhat poorer results for the machinery sample might be expected on the ground that investors are less confident that machinery companies will realize the expected rate of growth in their dividends than will food companies. If so, they would pay less for the stock.[20] On the other hand, it may also be true that the historical record is a less reliable source of information on the expected growth rate for machinery companies.

These results are striking by comparison with the results obtained in earlier attempts to explain the variation in price among stocks. Typical practice in these models is to include every variable, particularly dividends, earnings, and book value, that investors are supposed to consider in pricing a share. Due to a number of reasons, including in particular the high intercorrelation among the independent variables, the coefficients have large standard errors and fluctuate violently from one sample to the next. (Cf. Durand [3, p. 53], and Gordon [4, p. 102].) These models do not permit reliable statements on how price will vary with one of the independent variables. The superior results obtained with the present model are in part due to the use of exponentially weighted averages for the independent variables; but averaging has been used with other models, and the results must be attributed in part to the functional form of the relation among price, dividend, earnings, and book value derived from our theory.

Turning to the other two variables, positive results were obtained for them also. The instability of the earnings coefficient is highly significant for every food sample. It is significant at the 5 percent level for only one machinery sample; but in view of the fact that it has the right sign and exceeds its standard error for every sample, it is safe to say that for machinery companies, stock prices vary inversely with earnings instability. The size coefficient behaves like the instability of earnings co-

[20] A result that may or may not be coincidental is that at the end of 1956, a high point in market optimism, the machinery growth coefficient was at its highest, and the food coefficient was at its lowest. The stability of the food industry makes its stocks good defensive issues.

efficient, with the roles of the two industries reversed. The coefficient is highly significant for every machinery sample and fails at the 5 percent level for two food samples. The sign is correct for every food sample.

In the previous discussion the reliability of the coefficient estimates obtained was evaluated by reference to the size of each in relation to its standard error and the variation in a coefficient among samples. Other tests were employed; but before the results of these tests are presented, a methodological observation is in order. When a sample is drawn from a large population, and when the sampling procedure and the data satisfy certain conditions, statistical theory may be used to make probability statements about the population parameters. It is clear, however, that the corporations with the wide investor interest and other attributes necessary for inclusion in an industry category of the "Value Line Investment Survey" do not represent a random sample from a large population. Also, the independent variables are not free of error in the sense, for instance, that we are not certain the value of *br* obtained for a corporation is the value that investors expect. For these and other reasons, the statistical analysis of the sample data, *strictly speaking,* cannot be used to make probability statements about the parameters. It is believed, nonetheless, that such analysis contributes to our knowledge on the performance of the model and the reliability of the coefficient estimates.

When time series data are used to test a theory, the residuals are examined for the presence of serial correlation, since correlation between the residuals in successive periods suggests that a different model may provide a better explanation of the variation in the dependent variable. With cross-section data of the sort used here, the existence of correlation between the squares of the residuals and an independent variable impairs the reliability of the coefficient estimates. For the food samples the correlation between the squares of the residuals and the two important variables, growth rate and dividend, was computed and not found to be significant.

Kuh [7] has shown that when the same sample of firms is used in successive cross sections over time, the residuals may be examined to discover whether "firm effects" influence the determination of the value of the dependent variable. That is, if the average of the residuals for a firm over the *n* cross-section regression equations departs significantly from zero, one or more independent variables excluded from the model and peculiar to the firm in question may have a significant influence on the dependent variable. When firm effects are present, the variance in the estimate of the dependent variable is larger than it otherwise would be, and there is a possibility that the parameter estimates for the included independent variables are biased. The analysis-of-variance test employed by Kuh [7, p. 202] to test the significance of firm effects was used with the food sample, and the firm effect was found to be highly significant. Different measurement rules for the independent variables or the inclusion of additional variables may eliminate the large-firm effects.

Alternatively, it may be possible to deal with them directly, that is, include them among the independent variables in some way. The techniques by which this may be accomplished are still in the exploratory stage, and it would not be appropriate to deal with the problem further in this paper. It will be observed only that the resolution of the problem will result in closer correspondence between actual and predicted value for share prices and possibly in revised estimates of the model's parameters.[21]

## *The Optimum Dividend Rate*

An interesting use of the theory and the data is to examine the quantitative statements they yield with respect to a corporation's optimum dividend rate. Alternative stock price models either exclude the dividend on the ground that it is irrelevant or include it in a manner that implies a share's price is a monotonic increasing function of the dividend with earnings given. The present model states that there is an optimum dividend rate and it is finite.

The theory does more than that. For a corporation that engages in no outside equity financing and maintains a given debt-equity ratio as a matter of policy, the model provides the investment and retention that maximizes the value of its stock. Therefore, we can set up a "representative corporation" and find its optimum retention rate. Most corporations retain between 0.20 and 0.60 of their normal income; and if our representative corporation fell outside of these bounds, we might wonder at the results. If the corporation is representative, possible explanations are that the theory is wrong, that parameter estimates from the sample data are wrong, that corporations do not set their retention rates to maximize the price of their stock, and that the argument underlying this application of the theory is incorrect. If the data indicated that the representative corporation should retain and invest nothing, it would be difficult to reject the suggestion that the theory is wrong or the parameter estimates are seriously in error. On the other hand, the theory would seem to justify further consideration if the normative statements obtained from the parameter estimates proved to be within the bounds of reason.

Our stock price model in its final form is:

$$P = \alpha_5 \left[ Y' (1 - b) \right]^{\alpha_4} (1 + br)^{\alpha_1} (1 + u)^{\alpha_2} S^{\alpha_3} \qquad (27)$$

[21] A paper by Walter [14] presents an approach to the differentiation among shares according to quality, and his approach may be useful for the isolation of the firm effect.

The most plausible assumption with respect to $r$ is that it is a function of $b$; and on the further assumption that indivisibilities in investment opportunities are not important, a simple function we may use is:

$$r = w\ (1 + b)^{-1} \tag{28}$$

When $b = 0$, a corporation's average return on investment is $w$. As $b$ rises, $r$ falls; and for $b = 1$, $r = w/2$. Inspection of the sample data for $b$ and $r$ suggests that $w = 0.20$ is representative of a profitable corporation; $w = 0.15$, of an average corporation; and $w = 0.10$, of an unprofitable one.

To find the retention rate that maximizes the price of a share, we substitute equation 28 for $r$ in equation 27, obtain numerical values for the parameters and the variables, and compute the share's price for various values of $b$. Actually, if we are only interested in the $b$ that maximizes $P$ and not the resultant value of $P$, we need only know $\alpha_1$, $\alpha_4$, and $w$. For the food samples the five-year averages of the parameter estimates are $\alpha_4 = 0.88$ and $\alpha_1 = 10.1$. Using these values, when $w = 0.20$, the price of a share is maximized at $b \sim 0.28$. On the basis of reasonable values for the other variables and parameters and $Y =$ \$2.00, the price of a share is \$25.65 when $b = 0$.[22] By comparison, when $b = 0.28$, $D =$ \$1.44, $r = 0.156$, $br = 0.0437$, and $P =$ \$29.59. With $b = 0.5$, we have $D =$ \$1.00, $r = 0.133$, $br = 0.0667$, and $P =$ \$26.73. Variation in price with the retention rate is both within the bounds of reason and fairly material.

For an average corporation, one with $w = 0.15$, the optimum retention rate falls to $b \sim 0.20$, while for an unprofitable corporation the optimum retention rate barely exceeds $b = 0$. Food corporations typically retain larger fractions of their incomes than our model suggests they should. However, the differences are not alarming. It is possible that maximizing the value of their stock is not the sole concern of these corporations. Also, our parameter estimates may be in error for a number of reasons, among which are errors in the measurement of the independent variables, and the failure of the model to include other forms of financing. However, these empirical findings do not suggest there is something radically wrong with the theory or the data.

Turning to the machinery sample, we have a different story. The sample estimates of $\alpha_1$ vary over such a wide range that there is some question as to whether a meaningful number is obtained by averaging them. Doing so, we have $\alpha_1 = 5.5$ and $\alpha_4 = 0.85$. For a profitable corporation the optimum retention rate is $b \sim 0.10$. Both an average and an unprofitable corporation should at the minimum distribute all of its

[22]We used $ln\alpha_0 = 2.555$, $\alpha_2 = -5$, $ln(1 + u) = 0.028$, $\alpha_3 = 0.05$, and $ln\ S = 4.4$ for the other variables and parameters.

income in dividends. We must conclude that for one reason or another the parameter estimates for the machinery sample are seriously in error.

## *Summary and Conclusions*

Since this paper already is quite long, the summary and conclusion will be brief. Our two fundamental assumptions were (1) that the purchaser of a share of stock buys a dividend expectation; and (2) that in placing a value on the expectation, the rate of profit he requires is an increasing function of the rate of growth in the dividend. The first assumption is quite reasonable, and it has been shown that the second is not beyond the pale of reason. In order to arrive at an operational stock price model, we then made a set of assumptions with respect to investor expectations that are clearly unattractive. Among these assumptions, those that made it possible to ignore a corporation's leverage and outside equity financing are not too serious, in that it is likely that the theory can be enlarged to recognize the variation in the dividend expectation and its valuation with the variables. The more troublesome assumptions were that investors expect a corporation's retention rate and (given its retention rate) its rate of return on investment to be the same in every future period. There are no theoretical problems involved in withdrawing these assumptions, but it is difficult to see how one can have an operational model for explaining stock prices without them. With these assumptions, there are likely to be firms for which the performance of the model is far from satisfactory.

The interesting point is that under the above assumptions, we proceeded directly to an operational stock price model that can be interpreted to yield the functional relation between price and investment rate. The central problem of capital theory on the level of the firm has been to establish the investment that maximizes the value of the firm. Neoclassical theory solved the problem under certainty. In our world of uncertainty, we have three practically independent classes of theories—investment theories, valuation theories, and finance theories—for the guidance of businessmen. The promise of the research described in the preceding pages is an integrated theory of investment, financing, and valuation that can be used to make both normative and descriptive empirical statements on the subject.

Notwithstanding the restrictive nature of the financing and valuation assumptions on which our stock value model was based, it did a very creditable job of explaining the variation in price among common stocks. The significance of these results cannot be emphasized too strongly. They make it very likely that further research will give rise to models that allow very accurate statements on the relations among the variables. Further research will take the form of refinements in the theory to allow withdrawing the restrictive assumptions and improvements in the measurement rules for the variables. The research will benefit from the interaction of theory and evidence due to the operational character of the theory, and it is even possible that the research will modify or disprove the fundamental propositions. For instance, it may turn out that the price of a share is independent of the rate of growth in the corporation's dividend.

## References


1. BODENHORN, DIRAN. "On the Problem of Capital Budgeting," *Journal of Finance,* Vol. XIV (December, 1959), pp. 473–92.
2. BROWN, ROBERT G. *Statistical Forecasting for Inventory Control.* New York, McGraw-Hill Book Co., 1959.
3. DURAND, DAVID. *Bank Stock Prices and the Bank Capital Problem.* Occasional Paper No. 54. New York: National Bureau of Economic Research, 1957.
4. GORDON, MYRON J. "Dividends, Earnings, and Stock Prices," *Review of Economics and Statistics,* Vol. XLI (May, 1959), pp. 99–105.
5. GORDON, MYRON J. "Security and a Financial Theory of Investment," *Quarterly Journal of Economics,* Vol. LXXIV (August, 1960), pp. 472–92.
6. GORDON, MYRON J., and SHAPIRO, ELI. "Capital Equipment Analysis: The Required Rate of Profit," *Management Science,* Vol. III (October, 1956), pp. 102–10.
7. KUH, EDWIN. "The Validity of Cross-Sectionally Estimated Behavior Equations in Time Series Applications," *Econometrica,* Vol. XXVII (April, 1959), pp. 197–214.
8. LUTZ, FRIEDERICH, and LUTZ, VERA. *The Theory of Investment of the Firm.* Princeton: Princeton University Press, 1951.
9. LINTNER, JOHN. "Distribution of Incomes of Corporations among Dividends, Retained Earnings and Taxes," *American Economic Review,* Vol. XLVI (May, 1956), pp. 97–113.
10. MEYER, JOHN R., and KUH, EDWIN. *The Investment Decision: An Empirical Study.* Cambridge: Harvard University Press, 1957.
11. MODIGLIANI, FRANCO, and MILLER, MERTON H. "The Cost of Capital, Corporation Finance and the Theory of Investment," *American Economic Review,* Vol. XLVIII (June, 1958), pp. 261–97.
12. MODIGLIANI, FRANCO, and MILLER, MERTON H. "The Cost of Capital, Corporation Finance and the Theory of Investment: Reply," *American Economic Review,* Vol. XLIX (September, 1959), pp. 655–68.
13. "Value Line Investment Survey." New York: Arnold Bernhard & Co., Inc.
14. WALTER, JAMES E. "A Discriminant Function for Earnings-Price Ratios of Large Industrial Corporations," *Review of Economics and Statistics,* Vol. XLI (February, 1959).

*Appendix* A

# *Variation in a Corporation's Cost of Capital with the Rate of Growth in Its Dividend*

By Ramesh Gangolli

Our purpose is to prove that a corporation's cost of capital, $\bar{k}$, is an increasing function of $g$, the rate at which its dividend is expected to grow. If the current dividend is $D_o$, the price of a share at $t = o$ is:

$$P_o = D_o \left[ \sum_{t=1}^{\infty} \frac{(1+g)^t}{(1+k_t)^t} \right]$$

The $k_i$ are all given with $k_{i+1} > k_i$ for all $i$. To find $\bar{k}$, we have:

$$D_o \sum_{t=1}^{\infty} \left( \frac{1+g}{1+\bar{k}} \right)^t = D_o \sum_{t=1}^{\infty} \frac{(1+g)^t}{(1+k_t)^t}$$

That is:

$$\frac{\dfrac{1+g}{1+\bar{k}}}{1 - \dfrac{1+g}{1+\bar{k}}} = \sum_{t=1}^{\infty} \frac{(1+g)^t}{(1+k_t)^t}$$

or

$$\frac{1+g}{\bar{k}-g} = \sum_{t=1}^{\infty} \frac{(1+g)^t}{(1+k_t)^t}$$

Hence:

$$\bar{k} = \frac{1+g}{\sum_{t=1}^{\infty} \dfrac{(1+g)^t}{(1+k_t)^t}} + g$$

This determines $k$ as a kind of generalized average of the $k_i$'s.

Now, consider the function $k(x)$ defined by:

$$k(x) = \frac{1 + x}{\sum_{t=1}^{\infty} \frac{(1+x)^t}{(1+k_t)^t}} + x$$

If we prove that $k(x)$ is a monotonic strictly increasing function of $x$, we shall be able to say that $\bar{k}$ increases with $g$.

To prove this, we evaluate $k'(x) = \frac{dk(x)}{dx}$. We have:

$$k'(x) = -\frac{\sum_{t=1}^{\infty} (t-1) \frac{(1+x)^t}{(1+k_t)^t}}{\left[\sum_{t=1}^{\infty} \frac{(1+x)^t}{(1+k_t)^t}\right]^2} + 1$$

We now prove a lemma:

*Lemma:* If the sequence $k_t$ is strictly increasing, then:

$$\sum_{t=1}^{\infty} (t-1) \frac{(1+x)^t}{(1+k_t)^t} < \sum_{t=1}^{\infty} \left[\frac{(1+x)^t}{(1+k_t)^t}\right]^2$$

*Proof:* The coefficient $\alpha_n$ of $(1 + x)^n$ in the right member is:

$$a_n = \frac{1}{(1+k_1)} \cdot \frac{1}{(1+k_{n-1})^{n-1}} + \frac{1}{(1+k_2)^2} \cdot \frac{1}{(1+k_{n-2})^{n-2}} \cdots + \frac{1}{(1+k_i)^i} \cdot \frac{1}{(1+k_{n-i})^{n-i}} \cdots + \frac{1}{(1+k_{n-1})^{n-1}} \cdot \frac{1}{(1+k_1)}$$

Now, since $k_t$ increases with $t$:

$$(1+k_i)^i (1+k_{n-i})^{n-i} < (1+k_n)^n \text{ if } i < n$$

Hence:

$$a_n > \frac{1}{(1+k_n)^n} + \frac{1}{(1+k_n)^n} \cdots (n-1) \text{ terms} = \frac{n-1}{(1+k_n)^n}$$

But this is the coefficient of $(1 + x)^n$ in the left member. Hence, our lemma is proved.

Using this lemma, we see that:

$$k'(x) > 0$$

and this implies that $k(x)$ is strictly increasing, or that $k$ is an increasing function of $g$.

*Appendix* B

# *Derivation of Exponential Smoothing Weights*

The following explanation of why the smoothing constants of $\beta = 0.6$ and $\lambda = 0.5$ were used in the measurement of $D'$ and $Y'$ should be of particular interest to anyone considering empirical work on the subject. It was believed that the dividend and in particular the earnings of a corporation experience random disturbances and that investors used normalized rather than actual current values of the variables in placing a value on a share. Exponential smoothing appeared to be a good means of arriving at $D'_t$ and $Y'_t$, and the decision reached was to calculate $D'_t$ and $rb = (Y'_t - D'_t)/B_t$ under the following values of $\beta$ and $\lambda$:

(1) $\beta = 1.0;\ \lambda = 1.0$ (4) $\beta = 0.8;\ \lambda = 0.3$
(2) $\beta = 0.8;\ \lambda = 0.7$ (5) $\beta = 0.6;\ \lambda = 0.5$
(3) $\beta = 0.8;\ \lambda = 0.5$ (6) $\beta = 0.6;\ \lambda = 0.3$

The regression equation

$$ln\ P - ln\ D' = ln\alpha_5 + \alpha_1 ln\ (1 + br) + \alpha_2 ln\ (1 + n) + \alpha_3 ln\ S$$

was used on the sample data with $D'_t$ and $rb$ calculated under each of the above six combinations of $\beta$ and $\lambda$.

Table 2 presents the sample mean values of $ln\ (1+br)$, the estimate of $\alpha_1$, its standard error, and $R$ under each set of weights for each sample year. The striking thing about the data is the rise in $\alpha_1$ both in absolute value and as a multiple of its standard error between the weight set $\beta = \lambda = 1$ and the weight set used. The increase in $\alpha_1$ was by a factor of two or more in over half the samples and by over 50 percent in the others.

The selection of $\beta = 0.6$ and $\lambda = 0.5$ among the alternatives was based on the fact that this set of weights yielded the highest multiple correlation in every sample. In each sample, there was one or more alternative weight set that did not produce a materially smaller value of $R$, but none performed as well consistently.

TABLE 2

MEAN, COEFFICIENT, AND COEFFICIENT STANDARD ERROR OF GROWTH RATE VARIABLE AND MULTIPLE CORRELATION COEFFICIENT UNDER DIFFERENT WEIGHTS, FOOD AND MACHINERY SAMPLES, 1954–57

| *Weights* | | *Food* | | | | *Machinery* | | | |
|---|---|---|---|---|---|---|---|---|---|
| $\beta$ | $\lambda$ | *ln(1+ br)* | $\alpha_1$ | *S.E.*$\alpha_1$ | *R* | *ln(1+ br)* | $\alpha_1$ | *S.E.*$\alpha_1$ | *R* |
| Year 1954: | | | | | | | | | |
| 1.0 | 1.0 | 0.041 | 6.45 | 1.21 | 0.660 | 0.040 | 2.39 | 0.85 | 0.669 |
| 0.8 | 0.7 | 0.040 | 8.81 | 1.28 | 0.745 | 0.045 | 3.65 | 0.98 | 0.689 |
| 0.8 | 0.5 | 0.040 | 10.38 | 1.56 | 0.733 | 0.047 | 4.72 | 1.19 | 0.699 |
| 0.8 | 0.3 | 0.039 | 11.11 | 2.22 | 0.639 | 0.044 | 6.71 | 1.63 | 0.707 |
| 0.6 | 0.5 | 0.039 | 11.01 | 1.51 | 0.765 | 0.047 | 5.14 | 1.14 | 0.715 |
| 0.6 | 0.3 | 0.039 | 12.38 | 2.29 | 0.670 | 0.045 | 7.04 | 1.62 | 0.707 |
| Year 1955: | | | | | | | | | |
| 1.0 | 1.0 | 0.044 | 7.14 | 0.98 | 0.788 | 0.046 | 2.77 | 0.97 | 0.619 |
| 0.8 | 0.7 | 0.042 | 8.49 | 1.03 | 0.819 | 0.045 | 4.89 | 1.14 | 0.690 |
| 0.8 | 0.5 | 0.040 | 9.72 | 1.17 | 0.821 | 0.044 | 6.23 | 1.41 | 0.697 |
| 0.8 | 0.3 | 0.037 | 11.43 | 1.60 | 0.783 | 0.041 | 7.19 | 2.04 | 0.648 |
| 0.6 | 0.5 | 0.040 | 9.97 | 1.13 | 0.836 | 0.045 | 6.85 | 1.34 | 0.724 |
| 0.6 | 0.3 | 0.038 | 11.88 | 1.63 | 0.788 | 0.042 | 8.28 | 1.98 | 0.676 |
| Year 1956: | | | | | | | | | |
| 1.0 | 1.0 | 0.045 | 6.55 | 1.07 | 0.730 | 0.069 | 4.97 | 0.79 | 0.801 |
| 0.8 | 0.7 | 0.043 | 7.72 | 1.11 | 0.767 | 0.060 | 6.61 | 0.96 | 0.810 |
| 0.8 | 0.5 | 0.041 | 8.72 | 1.25 | 0.768 | 0.052 | 8.21 | 1.22 | 0.805 |
| 0.8 | 0.3 | 0.037 | 10.45 | 1.64 | 0.740 | 0.043 | 10.45 | 1.86 | 0.763 |
| 0.6 | 0.5 | 0.042 | 9.13 | 1.17 | 0.797 | 0.054 | 8.88 | 1.19 | 0.818 |
| 0.6 | 0.3 | 0.038 | 11.06 | 1.58 | 0.768 | 0.045 | 11.75 | 1.87 | 0.778 |
| Year 1957: | | | | | | | | | |
| 1.0 | 1.0 | 0.046 | 4.77 | 1.49 | 0.513 | 0.062 | 3.40 | 1.03 | 0.754 |
| 0.8 | 0.7 | 0.044 | 7.96 | 1.45 | 0.681 | 0.059 | 4.54 | 1.17 | 0.763 |
| 0.8 | 0.5 | 0.041 | 9.90 | 1.56 | 0.727 | 0.054 | 5.31 | 1.40 | 0.760 |
| 0.8 | 0.3 | 0.037 | 11.97 | 1.99 | 0.711 | 0.044 | 6.01 | 1.90 | 0.737 |
| 0.6 | 0.5 | 0.042 | 10.56 | 1.42 | 0.776 | 0.055 | 6.05 | 1.36 | 0.788 |
| 0.6 | 0.3 | 0.038 | 12.99 | 1.85 | 0.760 | 0.046 | 7.15 | 1.93 | 0.739 |

A matter of some interest was the change in the values of $ln(1+br)$ as the values of the smoothing constants were reduced. Dividing the sample values of a variable by two doubles its coefficient; and there was some concern that reducing the smoothing constants, particularly the value of $\lambda$ in relation to $\beta$, would produce this result. However, it is clear that the fall in $ln(1+br)$ was slight, particularly for $\beta = 0.6$ and $\lambda = 0.5$. Furthermore, dividing a variable by two doubles not only the coefficient but its standard error as well. Table 2 indicates quite clearly that the change in $\alpha_1$ due to the smoothing constants used cannot be attributed to a change in the scale of the variable.

Chapter 27

# The Cost of Capital and Optimal Financing of Corporate Growth*

By John Lintner

THE INTEREST of professional economists in the theory of corporate finance and capital budgeting has increased markedly within the last decade.[1] Nevertheless, the literature is still marked by confusion and even contradiction: The decision rules which have been proposed for determining the optimal capital budget in a corporation and its optimal capital structure and reliance on different sources of financing are mutually inconsistent in the sense that they would lead to (often substantially) different decisions under given sets of circumstances.

None of the marked differences in decision rules advanced in the literature reviewed here can be attributed to different assumed *goals*, since all the authors to be cited have, explicitly or implicitly, offered their respective criteria as the means to accomplish the same ultimate objective—the greatest satisfaction of common stockholders' preferences. Moreover, since increased current share valuations ceteris paribus obviously increase shareholders' current wealth, which in turn clearly implies greater utility, this criterion of optimizing shareholders' utility has in practice been identified with the maximization of the current market value of the common stock. Further, all authors assumed maximizing

*Reprinted by permission from *Journal of Finance,* Vol. XVIII (May, 1963), pp. 292–310.

[1]This paper is one part of a series of interrelated theoretical and statistical studies of corporate and financial policies being made at the Harvard Business School under a grant of the Rockefeller Foundation for work in the general area of profits in the functioning of the economy. The Foundation's generous support for this work is most gratefully acknowledged. Major parts of this paper are based upon the longer manuscripts [*a*18], [*b*8], [*b*9], and [*b*10].

Numbers in brackets refer to publications listed at the end of this paper (p. 478).

behavior to be universal and financial markets to be purely competitive. *These premises and specifications are accepted without question and maintained throughout the present paper.*

# I. Introduction

## *Disagreements on Optimal Size of Capital Budgets and Cost of Capital*

The seriousness of the conflicts in the literature on the theory of corporate finance and capital budgeting is clearly indicated in the markedly different conclusions offered by eminent economists regarding the determination of the optimal size of capital budgets.

The Lutzes, in their classic study a decade ago [*a*20],[2] concluded that investment within the firm should be increased up to the point where this course no longer added more to the collective stockholders' "net profits prospects" than further outside investment. Cash flows from borrowing and debt service are to be deducted from those of the internal investment plan, the resulting stream of net cash flows is to be discounted at the yield of the preferred maturity of outside riskless investment (government bonds), and internal investments are to be increased only so long as the certainty equivalents of the resulting present values exceed the cost of the investment.

Roberts [*a*28] concurs in the use of the outside lending rate and the netting of cash flows from borrowings and repayments, but argues that the discount rate should be the external yield available on outside investments having (subjectively) similar risk, and he equates this with the *current earnings yield* of the company's own stock.[3] His decision rule is: Investments are to be made so long as the present value of prospective incremental receipts exceeds that of incremental cash outflows, when both flows are discounted at a rate equal to the current earnings yield on the stock. The relevant investment fund flows are the same for the Lutzes and Roberts in any given case; but Roberts' discount rate is much greater, and it has not been shown that this difference offsets the Lutzes' utility adjustment of present values to certainty equivalents.

Dean [*a*4] and, more recently, Modigliani-Miller [*a*23, *a*25], Kuh [*a*16], Benishay [*b*3], and Weston [*a*34, *b*15] have also capitalized

[2]Especially chaps. xiii–xvii.

[3]Spencer and Siegelman [*b*13] have recently advocated the same rule with the proviso that the earnings yield should be measured as it would be "when the firm has what the market considers to be a well-balanced capital structure."

corporate earnings to determine market values and have all argued that the current earnings yield on common stock is the proper discount rate when no debt is outstanding; but otherwise, they urge the use of a *current market value weighted average cost of debt and equity capital* as the proper discount rate. This is often a substantially *lower* figure than the current earnings yield on the equity when debt is outstanding;[4] and these authors do not net debt charges from investment fund flows. For given investment projects the relevant fund flows for these authors are larger than for Lutz and Roberts; their further use of a lower discount rate when debt is outstanding clearly implies acceptance of projects (and thereby extensions of the size of the capital budget) which would not be made under Roberts' rule (and presumably under the Lutzes').

Similarly, Solomon [*a*30], like Roberts, advises netting cash flows due to borrowing from those of individual investment projects, but he substitutes the ratio of "estimated future average earnings per share" to current market price as his recommended discount rate. In growing companies, this is an even *higher* figure than the current earnings yield on equity. For Solomon and Roberts, the relevant investment fund flows from given projects are the same (i.e., both deduct interest costs when debt is used in financing the project), but Solomon's rule will reject projects that Roberts' rule would accept in growth situations because of the latter's lower discount rate.

A still different rule has been advanced by Walter [*a*33], who advocated discounting investment opportunities at the rate at which current and future dividends are capitalized, this rate being defined as "the underlying yield on safe securities (government bonds?) and the required risk premiums."[5] Similarly, Bodenhorn [*a*2] has also urged the use of the market discount rate for comparable risk, and Modigliani and Miller in a new paper [*a*25] have also fixed upon the market discount rate as the proper cost of capital.[6] In some contexts (see below,

---

[4]This is true even when the market value weights urged by Modigliani and Miller are used; further differences are produced by Dean's advocacy of book value weights; but for reasons already clear in the literature, this latter position is invalid.

[5]Since Walter ignores borrowing, strict comparison of his rule with that of other authors can be made only in situations where there is no borrowing; but the conflict in the decisions implied on given sets of data is clear in this class of cases. If different decisions will be made in nonleverage cases, the rules necessarily have different implications in general.

[6]They have thus abandoned the identification of the market discount rate with current earnings yield *in the absence of debt* which provided the decision rule in their earlier paper [*a*23]. In the presence of growth opportunities, they agree with Solomon that the relevant cost of capital is greater than current earnings yields, but their figure is lower (and very much lower in strong growth situations) than his ratio of *future average* earnings to current prices and will thus accept many projects he would reject.

*passim*), growth opportunities will make current earnings yields less than current market discount rates, and these authors' rule would lead to rejection of projects which Roberts' rule would accept, and they would correspondingly reduce the size of capital budgets and the rate of growth below the levels his rule would justify. In other contexts the opposite would occur. The rule advanced by Shapiro and Gordon [*a*14], based upon the sum of the current dividend yield and the expected growth rate, would in general lead to still different decisions; and as our final illustration, we note that Gordon in later writings [*a*11–13, *b*4] has advanced a still different requirement.

So far, we have emphasized differences in rules for accepting investments and setting the optimal size of the capital budget. We should also note that the various authors differ on whether—and how—their respective preferred "cost-of-capital" figure varies as a function of the existing capital structure (primarily the mix of debt and equity capital) and also as a function of the form of the new financing to be used for the capital budget—the proportion of retained earnings, additional debt, and/or new issues of equity capital.

Modigliani-Miller [*a*23 and *a*25] take the limiting position that (apart from the relatively small discrimination in favor of debt financing under the corporate income tax) the cost of capital is *independent* of both the existing capital structure and the mix of new financing, a position apparently also shared by Dean. Others—notably Solomon, Kuh, Weston, Gordon, Duesenberry [*a*6], Schwartz [*b*11], and myself [*a*17, *a*18, and *b*7]—argue that the cost of capital *is* a function of the financing mix, although, once again, there are substantial differences in the exact form of the dependence. Indeed, the rules for decisions regarding *how* the investments should be financed differ as seriously as those for determining the size of the capital budget itself—i.e., those determining the *amount* of finance (whatever the type) to be used.

Since all these authors have defined their optima in terms of maximization of the current market value of existing equity issues, all these differences in the decision rules come down fundamentally either to differences in assumptions regarding the character of the corporations' investment opportunities themselves (to which we revert below) or to differences in the models the various authors have used to explain (1) the determination of stock market prices when their is no debt outstanding and (2) the effects of leverage on those prices. Indeed, in the latter two respects the more significant differences can be traced to the respective author's choice of one of two basic assumptions within each of the two categories just noted: specifically, to whether or not (*a*) (as alleged in "pure earnings" theories), ceteris paribus, the valuation of unlevered equities is determined by (expectational) current earnings *independent* of dividends and (*b*) (as held in "entity value" theories) the market valuation of the corporate entity is independent of its capitalization, apart from corporate tax differentials due to the deductibility of debt interest.

## *Further Context of Present Paper*

In the usual "theory of the firm," there are two separate (or at least separable) parts to the analysis: (1) Given production functions and supply conditions in factor markets, how can the firm minimize the cost of producing each possible quantity of output, and (2) given the results of such isoquant-*cum*-budget-line analysis and specified product market conditions, what *quantity* of output produced and sold will maximize profit? The necessary and sufficient conditions for the validity of the "pure earnings and company investment" and "entity value" theories can best be analyzed under an assumption that time vectors of investment budgets and corporate earnings are fixed throughout all time independent of dividends and the finance mix.

These issues were examined in detail in a previous paper [*b*7]. That analysis corresponded in our financial context to the "theory of the production of a given output" ("output" here being vectors of capital budgets and their associated earnings). Corresponding to the second major problem in the standard theory of the firm, there is the further major issue for the theory of corporate financing and capital budgeting: Given the minimum "cost" (i.e., optimal finance mix) for each possible size of capital budget, what is the optimal size of the capital budget under any given functional relationship between size of budget and corporate earnings? This latter issue is the primary focus of the present paper.

Some of the central results of the previous paper, however, obviously provide an essential basis for the present one: specifically, that both the "pure earnings" theory (investors indifferent to particular dividend vectors) and the "entity value" theory (the sum of market values of equity and debt invariant to debt) *are invalid* even with the time vectors of earnings and investments fixed forevermore *if* the market context involves (1) costs of issuing securities, *or* (2) any personal tax differentials, *or* (3) any lack of prescience *and* identity in investors' subjective probability distributions, *or* (4) any combination of them;[7] that the model making stock prices depend *essentially* upon the (present values of the) time vectors of *cash dividend flows to investors* remains valid

[7]Also, of course, any corporate tax differentials between interest and other income will invalidate the "entity value" theory.

even under these fully generalized neoclassical conditions, while the alternatives are valid *if, and only if,* stated in forms identically reducible to this dividend theory; and that the significance of time vectors of earnings (and of company investments) lies in its implications *for* the prospective stream of dividends, rather than vice versa.

In the present paper, I consequently rely essentially on "present values of dividends models"[8] and, removing the constraint of fixed investment budgets, examine optimal decision rules for the finance mix and size of the capital budget of a corporation and its optimal (expected average) rate of growth over time. Since all these matters depend on the proper determination of the relevant "cost of capital," this issue also provides a common concern throughout the paper.

In keeping with space limitations and the interests of this group, this paper will focus on the important, but necessarily limited, objective of setting forth the essential logic of some of the more fundamental conclusions I have reached on these issues. To this end, I shall outline the basic structure of some of the more useful analytical models I have been developing, present some rigorous proofs, and motivate others. A full set of rigorous mathematical derivations and proofs, and a more complete and general analysis of these and related issues, will be found elsewhere. Among other simplifications, I shall assume throughout this paper that all tax rates are zero; that the (riskless) discount rates, $k_T = k$, are constant over time; and that the variance of profit rates with no growth and no debt, ${\sigma^2}_{p0}$, is given and constant over time.

Finally, two definitions are needed at the outset which, for convenience, are stated in general form to cover uncertainty—certainty being the limiting case for each when all variances approach zero. Specifically, the *marginal cost of* (*a given type of*) *capital* for the corporation is the *minimum* (expectation of) *rate of return required on a marginal investment* for the shareholders to be better off (value of existing equity greater) *with* the incremental investment *cum* this incremental financing *than without either* the increment to the capital budget *or* this financing. Similarly, *corporate earnings* or *profits* (after taxes and interest) for any period are defined to be equal to the maximum cash dividend which (expectationally) *could* be paid in that period consistent with (pro forma) no outside financing *and* with the *expectation* that a similarly large dividend *could* then be paid in future periods subject to the same constraint (this pro forma constraint tying the earnings back to earnings on present assets).[9]

---

[8]See n. 15, p. 469.
[9]See n. 17, p. 250, in [*b*7].

## II. Unlevered Firms under Certainty

Certain issues can most conveniently be handled under the simplifying assumption of certainty. First of all, it can readily be shown that *even in the absence of issue costs, taxes, or uncertainty, the relevant marginal cost of capital for the corporation is not equal to the discount rate* $k$ unless (1) the "investment opportunity" or "profit" function relating the average rate of internal return,[10] $p_t$, per dollar of new investment is *strictly independent* of the amounts of investments made in earlier or subsequent periods, *or* (2) the profit function at every point in time exhibits strictly constant returns to scale *and* these returns, $p_t = k$. The absence of costs, taxes, and uncertainty, together with a profit function $p_t = \psi_t (F_t^* \ldots)$ in which $\psi_t$ is strictly independent of the dollar size of the company's aggregate investments (capital budget), $F_\tau^*$, for all $\tau \neq t$, are *sufficient conditions* to make the discount rate $k$ the appropriate cost of capital because under the fully idealized neoclassical conditions all marginal rates of substitution for all companies and investors are equal to the discount rate $k$ in equilibrium, as demonstrated by Fisher thirty years ago [*a*10].

Under these very restrictive conditions, all investments are perfect substitutes at the margin; and in keeping with standard classical theory, the company should include all increments of investment in each period which have a marginal rate of return $\rho$ on their dollar cost $\geq$ the discount rate $k$. Allowance for issue costs and taxes, however, requires important modifications even under certainty (cf. [*b*7, *a*23, *a*30, and *a*33]), although, with no taxes, the minimum acceptable return $\rho_0 = k$ *so long as* all investments whose $\rho \geq k$ do not exhaust current earnings.[11]

But models based on the profit function $\psi_t$ *restricted* by an independence assumption regarding $F_\tau^*$, $\tau \neq t$, are at based inadequate to handle —and in general[12] are inherently biased with respect to—the essential

---

[10] In this paper, I shall consistently use decision rules in the form of marginal internal rate of return $\geqq$ marginal cost of capital. Under the assumptions made concerning the efficient set of the (portfolio of) investment opportunities facing the firm (and the simplifying assumption of constant discount rates over time), these rules are strictly equivalent to the alternative statement of rules in the form of present values exceeding costs. Cross-sectional nonindependence of investment opportunities is subsumed in the efficient opportunity set; perfect capital markets are assumed throughout; and major lumpiness in discrete investment projects causes no trouble when our assumptions regarding the regularity and smoothness of the envelope of the efficient set are satisfied. Cf. [*b*5 and *b*2].

[11] The reason is that such costs simply insure that new investments in this range, if made, will be financed by retained earnings. See [*b*7].

[12] In this respect, they will be acceptable as a first approximation only for firms selling in markets within which no seller has or creates any significant (product) market power which affects the profitability of future investments, where investments include outlays for product promotion as recognized in Dean [*a*4].

elements and issues of growth and change over time which constitute the primary focus of this paper. For this restriction on $\psi_t$ implies that the (average and marginal) profitability of *any given dollar-sized* capital budget for, say, IBM, du Pont, Avon, or General Motors in 1962 is independent of the capital investments they have made in the last one, three, five, ten, or even twenty years—which is obviously not true. In particular, this restriction on $\psi_t$ ignores the hard fact that—especially in the major oligopolistic industries which account for such large fractions of plant and equipment expenditures and of total equity values, but also quite generally—the position of a firm in its industry and the profitability of further new investments depend heavily upon whether it has led or lagged in the introduction of new products, new capacity, new cost-reducing technologies, research and development, long-range advertising, and other promotion of product-market position, and so on in the recent and more remote past.[13] All this is true not only in the short run but, cumulatively, in the longer run as well.

To encompass the essence of the problems involved in decisions for continuing growth and to incorporate basic determinants of the profit opportunities available to potentially growing firms at given points in time, the function $\psi_t$ must explicitly depend on investments in other periods (or as their surrogate, recent realized—or "normalized"—levels of earnings). The central implications of such dependence are brought out most simply in the profit function originally advanced by Preinreich [*a*27] and Williams [*a*35] a quarter of a century ago and more recently also adopted by Gordon-Shapiro and Gordon in which the function $\psi_t$ is invariant over time when written in the form.

$$p_t = \Psi_t^* (F^*/Y^*, \ldots) = \Psi_t^* (f, \ldots) = p(f, \ldots) = p \text{ constant over time} \quad (1)$$

where $Y^*$ is the corporation's aggregate earnings in the current period, and $f = F^*/Y^*$. Since $p$ will not in general be invariant with respect to $f$, we also have $p'(f) \leq 0$ but constant over time as a function of $f$, and there will be a marginal rate of return, defined as:

$$\rho = \frac{\delta f p(f)}{\delta f} = p(f) + f p'(f) \quad (1a)$$

[13]See Lintner [*a*17], Duesenberry [*a*6], and Meyer-Kuh [*a*22]. The importance of including outlays for advertising, research and development, and other promotion of product-market position in the capital budget, when the outlays are intended to affect receipts in subsequent periods, has been emphasized by Dean.

It should be emphasized that we assume throughout this paper that *financial* markets are strictly and universally *purely competitive* (except for the fact that any given company is the sole issuer of its own securities), but this does not require us to ignore well-known facts of life in the *product*-market place—which do affect in a fundamental way the properties of the firm's profit-opportunity function.

which will also be constant over time for given $f$, with the further property that $\delta p/\delta f \leq 0$.[14]

Since *the criterion* ordering the desirability of alternative outcomes is the market price of the common equity, the profit function (1) must be incorporated into a model of stock price which specifies price as a function of both the profit opportunities of the company and the amounts and types of financing used to finance its internal investments or capital budget. As a first step, note that using continuous compounding for convenience, so that $Y^*_t$ is the instantaneous *rate* of earnings flow, the rate of growth $g^*$ of $Y^*_t$ is:

$$g^* = g^*_{Y_t} = d \log Y^*_t/dt = fp(f) \tag{2}$$

With aggregate dividends determined by $D^*_t = xY^*_t$, where $x$ is the dividend payout ratio, which is a decision variable also assumed to be constant over time, it is clear that the growth rates of dividends and earnings will be equal and that the aggregate dividend distribution at any time $t$ will be:

$$D^*_t = xY^*_t = xY^*_0 e^{g^* t}$$

Stock prices at any given time, however, reflect the values of the streams properly attributable to the *then outstanding* shares of stock. Let $N_t$ be the number of shares at time $t$, and we have $D_t = D^*_t/N_t$ and $Y_t = Y^*_t/N_t$. It follows that if new shares are issued at the relative rate $n = g_{N_t} = d \log N_t/dt$ and we let $g$ without asterisk represent the rate of growth of dividends and earnings on shares outstanding at time $t$, we have:

$$g = d \log D_t/dt = d \log Y_t/dt = d \log D^*_t/dt - d \log N_t/dt = g^* - n \tag{3}$$

so that:

$$D_t = xY_t = xY_0 e^{(g^* - n)t} = xY_0 e^{gt} = D_0 e^{gt} \tag{4}$$

Since the sum of current cash returns (here dividend yields $= D_t/P_t = y_d$) plus rates of growth in own price for all assets must equal the current market rate of discount in equilibrium in perfect markets, the basic *equilibrium price condition* is $y_d + d \log P_t/d_t = k_t$. The solution of this differential equation for market price, recognizing equation 4 and letting $x$ be constant for simplicity, is:

$$P_t = \frac{D_t}{k - g} = \frac{D_0 e^{gt}}{k - g} = \frac{D_0 e^{(g^* - n)t}}{k - (g^* - n)} = \int_t^\infty D_{te}^{-(\tau - t)(k - g)} \, d\tau, \; k > g \tag{5}$$

[14]These latter stipulations incorporate the economist's usual (and seemingly very realistic) assumption that marginal rates of return on investment budgets are not infinitely elastic *as of any given point of time* throughout most of their relevant range; that they become so only with respect to outside investments in the market after all internal investments having higher marginal returns have been exhausted. Cf. Duesenberry [*a*6].

which, by derivation, will satisfy the criterion cross-sectionally over different stocks and securities *and* will do so continuously over time.[15] For the *current* price of the stock, $P_0$, equation 5 reduces to:

$$P_0 = \frac{D_0}{k - g} = \frac{xY_0}{k - g} = \frac{xY_0}{k - (g^* - n)}, \; k > g \tag{5a}$$

Since, in the absence of issue costs, taxes, and uncertainty, all forms of financing are perfect substitutes at the margin, the marginal costs of each are the same. The minimum acceptable marginal rate of return to justify any additional internal investment under these conditions, however financed, can most easily be found for retained earnings. With $n = 0$ and $g^* = g$, and letting the retention ratio $r = 1 - x$:

$$\frac{\delta P_0}{\delta r} = P_0\left[-\frac{1}{x} + \frac{\delta g/\delta r}{k - g}\right] \gtrless 0 \text{ as } \frac{\delta g}{\delta r} = \rho \gtrless \frac{k - g}{x} = Y_0/P_0 = y_e \tag{6}$$

where $y_e$ is the current earnings yield on the stock. The marginal internal rate of return $\rho = \delta g/\delta r$ in this case because $\delta f/\delta r = 1$ and[16] $\rho = \delta f p(f)/\delta f = \delta g/\delta r$.

Under fully idealized neoclassical conditions with opportunities for constant growth forever, the optimizing decision rule is to accept all investments having $\rho \geq y_e$, the current earnings yield.[17] But $y_e$ is equal

---

[15] In [*b*8], we give the more general form of this model in which dividend payouts (earnings) growth rates, rates of issuing new securities, and discount rates are all unique functions, each varying in any way over time, and show that the resulting model also has the properties just stated in the text. A *corollary* of critical importance is that any alternative model of stock prices (such as various models based on earnings) will satisfy this criterion of legitimacy in classical theory *if, and only if,* it is *identically reducible* to the dividend model. (For further elaboration, see Lintner [*b*7].) We consequently do not need to use any such alternatives to dividend models in this paper.

[16] Alternatively, by definition:

$$p(f) = \frac{1}{f}\int_0^f \rho(f)df \text{ or } g = \int_0^f \rho(f)df$$

and the text relation follows by direct differentiation.

[17] This is precisely the rule advanced by Modigliani-Miller in [*a*23], which was derived from a "corporate earnings" model and under essentially static assumptions; but as noted in Lintner [*b*7], for use in dynamic situations, their original definition of "current earnings" must be altered to the more traditional concept in which *current* rates of earnings flows (rather than the undiscounted time average they proposed) are used directly in the numerator of the relevant *current* earnings yield. It is a nice paradox that our model basing values on dividend flows in the steady-growth case under certainty leads to an optimizing rule based on straight *current* earnings yield—which had been advocated by most earnings theorists all along on the basis of a price model which is *not* generally valid in dynamic contexts! (See Lintner [*b*7, p. 249]); that the "market rate" used to discount dividends in these models is seldom the correct cutoff rate; and that the equation of earnings yields to market "discount" rates often presumed holds up in growth situations only on very restrictive additional conditions on profit opportunities.

to the discount rate $k$ *only* in the special case where profit opportunities are infinitely elastic throughout—i.e., strictly constant returns regardless of the size of the investment budget in each period—and at a level equal to $k$.[18] This establishes the second half of the proposition made at the beginning of this section. The extremely unrealistic character of these conditions indicates that the common assertion that optimal investment budgets can be set by equating the corporation's $\rho$ to $k$ is generally in error, even under otherwise idealized conditions, when steady growth is assumed.[19]

Indeed, if the company is operating in the region of diminishing returns, so that $\rho < p$—and this is surely the usual case—then $\rho o < k$ so long as the company is paying any dividends:[20] The minimum marginal return *to the company* which will lead investors under the conditions being assumed to prefer added company investment is necessarily (and often very significantly) *less* than the discount rate $k$, which inter alia reflects returns available on alternative investments.[21] The explanation is that from equation 5, $\delta P/\delta r > 0$ as $x\rho + g \geq k$. The marginal return for the *investor* from added investment within the company is equal to the sum of the dividend payout applied to the marginal internal return within the company *plus* the growth rate on the retention itself; and if this *sum* is greater than the discount rate, he will prefer the retention.[22]

It must be also emphasized that the marginal cost of capital (MCC) is the *current* earnings yield $y_e = Y_0/P_0$, *not* the ratio of future or "average future" earnings to current price, as frequently proposed (e.g., in [$a$30], [$a$23], and [$a$26]). Moreover, the earnings yield *declines*

---

[18]Since $y_e = (k - g)/x = [k - (1 - x)p]/x$, we have $xy_e + (1 - x)p = k$, so that $y_e \gtrless k$ as $p \lessgtr k$, since $0 \leqslant x \leqslant 1$. But $p < k$ can of course be ruled out in any well-manged corporation, and we are left with $y_e \leqslant k$ as $p \geqslant k$.

[19]This error in Gordon and Shapiro's conclusion to this effect [$a$14] has been noted by Bodenhorn [$a$2]. The still more recent paper of Modigliani and Miller [$a$25], however, continues to use the discount rate $k$ as the cost of capital in the "steady-growth" case.

[20]From equation 6, we have $x\rho_0 = k - (1 - x)p$ or $k = p - (p - \rho_0)x$. If $x > 0$ and $\rho_0 < p$, then $p > k$, and the conclusion follows from the second preceding footnote, since $\rho_0 = y_e$.

[21]This is, of course, contrary to the case treated above, where profit opportunities were independent of investment rates in other periods. The reason for the perhaps surprising conclusion that $\rho'_0 < k$ clearly lies in the different assumptions on investment opportunities.

[22]It will be noted that *this result does not depend upon any tax differentials* between ordinary income and capital gains rates such as have been so much emphasized in the literature. The broader significance of the result is to emphasize the importance of the distinction between marginal return requirements *to the company* and marginal returns to investors; for even though $\rho_0 < k$, the investor's return given above *does* meet the opportunity costs of returns on alternative investments reflected in $k$.

with increasing size of capital budget *up to* the optimum scale of investment, since with $y_e = (k - g)/x$, $\delta y_e/\delta r = (y_e - \rho)/x < = > 0$ as $\rho > =$ or $< y_e$: *The act of making appropriate company investments reduces* $y_e$ (= MCC under present assumptions) and does *not* raise it as alleged elsewhere (e.g., [*a*30]); *only improper investment raises* $y_e$.

Before turning to uncertainty, I should also show that the internal returns required to justify expansion financed externally in the face of underpricing and new issue costs are substantially greater than so far recognized. The basic valuation model is still equation 5; but with new stock issues the aggregate size of the capital budget now is $F_t^* = Y_t^* - D_t^* + S_t^*$, where $S_t^*$ is the *net* dollar proceeds to the company from any newly issued shares. Dividing through by $Y_t^*$, we now have $f = r + s$ for use in equations 1 and 1*a*. Differentiating equation 5 partially with respect to $s$ gives:

$$\frac{\delta P_0}{\delta s} = -\frac{P_0\left[\frac{dn}{ds} - \frac{\delta g^*}{\delta s}\right]}{k - g^* + n} \gtreqless 0 \text{ as } \frac{\delta g^*}{\delta s} = \frac{\delta g^*}{\delta f} = \rho \gtrless \frac{dn}{ds} \qquad (7)$$

To relate $s$ to $n$, the relative rate of issuing new shares, first note that in the absence of issue costs, net proceeds to the company are equal to the price to the buyers and also that under classical certainty the aggregate market demand for the company's equity shares is infinitely elastic at the initial (pre-new issue) price earnings ratio, $y_e$.[23] Under *these* conditions,[24] $s = n/y_e$ and $dn/ds = y_e$, so that required returns for "costless" new equity financing are the same as those found above for retained earnings.[25]

[23]This is true under these conditions because aggregate market value (in the absence of debt) is independent of number of shares, so that *both* price per share and earnings per share are rectangular hyperbolas in terms of number of shares, and the ratio is constant at $y_e$. This formulation has also been used by Kuh in [*a*16].

[24]Where $P_t^*$ is the aggregate market value of the stock in the absence of new issues, and $N_t$ the total number of shares outstanding at time $t$, the price per share, $P_t$, in the absence of new issue costs, is determined by $N_t P_t = P_t^*$, where $P_t^*$ is a constant independent of $\Delta N_t = dN_t/dt$, the number of new shares issued in the given time interval. Also, $N_t = N_{t0} + \Delta N_t$, where $N_{t0}$ is the number of shares in the absence of new issues; $S_t^*$, the aggregate net proceeds of the new share issues, will then be:

$$S_t^* = \int_{N\,t0}^{N\,t0+\Delta N\,t} \frac{P_t^*}{N}\, dN = P_t^* \int_0^n dn = P_t^* n$$

Consequently, $s_t = S_t^*/Y_t^* = P_t^* n/Y_t^* = n/y_e$.

[25]The equivalence of required returns when retentions or new stock issues are used *under these conditions* to finance expansion—and hence the indifference of shareholders between more dividends *cum* more new issues versus more retentions *cum* smaller new issues (and so a larger percentage of ownership represented by given initial share holdings)—can also be confirmed by showing that the total differential of $P_0$ in equation 12*a*, with $f$ (and consequently $g^*$) fixed, is equal to zero.

But in real life, there are both fixed and variable costs of issuing new equity securities; and in addition, some "sweetening" in the form of pricing under the current market is usually required to sell new securities.[26] Such overt costs and underpricing can be summarized by making the (average) *net proceeds per share* on the new issue be $p_{t0}\ (a - bn) - c$,[27] so that[28] $s = [n/y_{e0}]\ (a - bn) - c, 0 < a \leq 1, 0 < b < 1, n \geq 0, c > 0$. With these costs recognized, $dn/ds = y_{e0}/(a - 2bn)$, and $\delta P_0/\delta s >$ or $= 0$ only so long as $\rho >$ or $= y_{e0}/(a - 2bn)$, where $t_{e0} = Y_t/P_{t0}$, as defined above. The proper cutoff on new stock issues (even in "growth" situations) is the ratio of the *current* (not future) earnings to the *marginal* net proceeds per share, $P_0\ (a - 2bn)$, of the new stock—and not simply $P_0 a$, as commonly proposed (e.g., in [*a*30]). Moreover, since the return required to justify expansion financed by stock issues in the presence of any unavoidable "underpricing" and of any overt issue costs is greater than that required to finance expansion by retained earnings, there is a vertical shift in the "supply or cost of capital function." Investors will consequently always prefer, in the context of the present model, that investment budgets be financed with retained earnings instead of new stock issues as long as retained earnings are available—i.e., so long as $x > 0$ and $r < 1$. Companies optimizing for shareholders, however, *should* expand capital budgets further by issuing new shares after retentions are exhausted, so long as the stated marginal condition can be satisfied. Finally, it is apparent that the absence of current dividends does not nullify the applicability of our present model based explicitly on dividend flows: The value of *currently* outstanding stock is still simply the present value of the dividends which will be paid in the future on the presently outstanding shares.[29]

[26]Strictly speaking, "underpricing" would never be required in classical markets under certainty, but I have shown in [*b*7] that (*a*) it is unavoidable under uncertainty whenever diverse probability distributions over outcomes are admitted and (*b*) its impact is essentially the same (though different perhaps in degree) as fixed and variable costs under certainty. To save space in the present exposition, the two have been treated together at this point.

[27]The subscript zero refers to values that would have obtained if $n$ were zero; $(1 - a)$ represents the minimum fractional underpricing required to sell *any* new stock, while $b$ covers both the variable cash costs of issuing new securities *and* the *further* underpricing which is dependent on the size of the new issue—the units of both $a$ and $b$ being fractions of $P_{t0}$ as defined; $c$ denotes the *fixed* overt cash cost per share of new issues.

[28]With new issue costs recognized, using symbols defined just above, *aggregate* net proceeds to the company are $S_t^* = P_{t0}^* n(a - bn) - c$; the equation given follows after dividing by $Y_t^*$ when $y_{e0} = Y_t^*/P_{t0}^*$. It should be noted that uncertainties concerning the $b$ or $c$ will further increase the marginal cost of new outside equity relative to that of retained earnings.

[29]Both the latter two points can be nicely illustrated by considering the simple case of a company whose investment opportunities over a period of $m$ years will

## III. Firms under Uncertainty

I now turn to some important general conclusions required by the fact of uncertainty. The first is that, as I pointed out two years ago,[30] while decision rules for determining the optimal size and project composition of capital budgets are generally identical under neoclassical certainty, *they are essentially different under uncertainty: The problem of optimizing the composition of a capital budget of any given size is formally identical with problems of selecting optimal security portfolios.*[31] In the rest of this paper, I shall focus on the optimal determination of the size of the capital budget and the mix of internal funds and debt to be used in its financing, simply assuming that a Markowitz-type "efficient set" analysis has already been made which yields a three-dimensional (per time period) "profit possibility function" relating amount of investment (size of budget), expected average profit rates, and variance of return.

In keeping with our emphasis here on (expectationally) steady growth, however, I assume specifically that $\psi_t(f, p, \delta^2_{p'}) = 0$ is invariant over time, with $f = F^*_t/Y^*_t$ constant at some level to be determined, and that $\delta\hat{p}/\delta f \leq 0$, which is constant over time for any $f$ and $\sigma^2_t$, as is the marginal expected rate of return, $\rho_{\wedge} = \delta f\hat{p}/\delta f$. Also, to simplify the development and concentrate on the budget portfolio returns required in the presence of given company investment risks, I shall assume that the profit rate variance, $\sigma^2_p$, of the budget is fixed or prespecified, that it is invariant over time, and that *it* is also invariant to the size of the budget. Since $\sigma^2_p > 0$ (even when $f = 0$, so that $\hat{g} = 0$), however, and since $g = fp(f)$, in general the variance of the growth rate $\sigma^2_g = (1 +$

---

be so rich that no dividends should be paid during this time, after which its special investment opportunities will be gone and it will pay all subsequent (constant) earnings in dividends. The present value of the stock will be $P_0 = e^{-km}\, Y_m/k$ and $Y_m = Y_0 e^{(g*-n)m}$. Maximizing $P_0$ involves maximizing $Y_m$, which leads immediately to the optimizing rule given above.

[30]In [*a*18]. The final page of Hirschleifer's paper [*b*6] at the same meetings makes the same point. See also my [*b*8] and [*b*9].

[31]As a result, individual investments (projects) may be eminently desirable components of optimizing project portfolio budgets because of low variances and/or covariances with other components (and existing assets) in spite of relatively low expected returns. Also, a project having a large variance in its own quasi rents but low or negative convariances with other existing and future investments will often make a much smaller contribution to company-wide variance (risk) than other projects with low own variances and substantial intercorrelations with other company investments in terms of cash flows. Indeed, many investment proposals are accepted in capital budgets in order to reduce risks and not to raise returns—something incongruous in conventional theoretical contexts of capital budgeting, but surely to be expected in the present framework. It should be clear that, throughout, I take $p$ and $\delta_p^2$ to refer to profit *before* interest.

$a_1 f^2)\ \sigma_p^2$, which does depend on size of budget, although invariant over time for given $f$. Cumulated growth over a period $t$ in length, $\bar{g}t$, is then a random variable with $\sigma^2_{(\bar{g}t)} = t\sigma^2_g$.

In what follows, I examine certain important properties of the *comparative stochastic dynamics* of capital budgeting, corporate financing, and growth, seeking the marginal cost of capital (as previously defined) and the decision rules for the optimal determination of $f$ (and its components, relative rates of retentions, $r$, and borrowing, $\theta$) on the assumption (management's and investor's expectation) that the values of $f$, $r$, and $\theta$ decided upon will be held constant over time.

With the current price of the stock now a random variable, our *criterion* becomes maximization of the expected value of this current market price; and to save space, I shall here simply assume[32] that this expected value is equal to the *present* value (computed essentially at the risk-free discount rate[33]) of the *certainty equivalents* of the uncertain income (dividend) receipts in the stream. I also assume that at the time of the company decision (i.e., on preexisting data and expectations), all investors hold the portfolios they most prefer. Any change in the retention ratio (dividend payout), leverage, or expected growth rate of the *i*th company which increases the present value of its stock will increase its shareholders' wealth and be in their interest.

Our problem essentially involves the terms of trade between expected receipts and varying risks on a given security—"deepening" in Hirschleifer's terminology [*b*6] rather than (or along with) the much simpler "widening" case he examined. It is clear, however, that the functional relation between certainty equivalents, expected returns, and risks must fall between two limiting cases.

On the one hand, in the limit, under the extreme simplifying assumption that all trades are between single-risk assets (or portfolios of fixed

---

[32] Some of the deductive justification is given in Hirschleifer [*b*6] and Smith [*b*12]. See also my [*b*8]. For those who prefer to use the alternative criterion of the certainty equivalent of the probability distribution of the present values of the uncertain streams, I shall simply observe that under a very general set of assumptions otherwise, all the general conclusions drawn below also hold under this alternative criterion where it is viable.

[33] To a reasonably good approximation, these present values can be computed at the risk-free discount rate, $k_0$, for the average or representative company. Provisional present values of all securities computed with discount rates $k_i = k_0$ may, however, lead to switching and other adjustments, which result in changes in (expected) market prices. When all portfolios are in full adjustment on the basis of a given set of underlying expectations, parameter values, supplies of securities, etc., the expected price of any *i*th security can be equated to the present value of its certainty equivalents computed at a discount rate $k_i = k_0 + k_{ci}$, where $k_{ci}$ (either + or −) reflects the impact of changes in share price, $P_i$, due to switches, convariances, etc. In the text, I drop subscripts and implicitly assume $k_{ci}$ to be invariant; but in general, $k_{ci}$ will vary with $\sigma$ and compound to results stated below.

proportions) and *riskless* securities, we know that all investors' marginal rates of substitution are equal in equilibrium to market-determined exchange lines which are linear in expected return and $\delta$ as a measure of risk. But continuing to assume purely competitive markets (as I do throughout), the exchange lines governing expected prices for given expected returns (or expected returns required for given prices), *within the set of risk assets* and when "money illusion" is absent, involve both $\sigma$ and $\sigma^2$. The second limiting case is provided by the observation that market equilibrium with interior solutions requires that the marginal rate of substitution on the latter function not exceed that on investors' utility functions—and in the absence of good viable markets for trading in the relevant disjoint future uncertain receipts, the latter must in themselves provide the certainty equivalents. (See my [b8] and [b9]).

Consider now the second limiting case, letting investors' utility functions, following Tinbergen [b14],[34] be hyperbolic of the form $U(\widetilde{D}_t) = 1 - (C_0/D_t)^{a_1}$, $\alpha > 0$. Then,[35] $E[U(\widetilde{D}_t)] = 1 - (C_0/\check{D}_t)^{a1} = 1 - (C_0/\widetilde{D}_t)^{a_1} = 1 - (C_0/D_0)^{a_1} e^{-a_1 t(\hat{g} - a_1 \sigma_g^2/2)}$, so that the certainty equivalent is $\widetilde{D}_t = D_0 e_t^{(g - a_1 \sigma_{\hat{g}}^2/2)}$, from which the stock price is:

$$P_0 = \int_0^{\infty} D_0 e^{-t[k - g + a_1 \sigma_{\hat{g}}^2/2]}\, dt = \frac{D_0}{k - \hat{g} + a_1 \sigma_g^2/2}, \quad k + a_1 \sigma_g^2/2 > \hat{g} \tag{8}$$

The impact of uncertainty can be clearly seen in the marginal cost of funds for internally financed expansion, which is:

$$\frac{\delta P_0}{\delta r} = P_0 \left[ -\frac{1}{x} + \frac{\rho\wedge - \alpha_1 (\delta \sigma_g^2/\delta r)/2}{k - \hat{g} + \alpha_1 \sigma_g^2/2} \right] \tag{9}$$

$$> 0 \text{ as } \rho\wedge > y_e + \alpha_1 a_1 f \sigma_p^2 = \text{MCC}$$

*Uncertainty, of course, raises the earnings yield,* but the more subtle and far-reaching result is that, *in addition, the marginal cost of capital* (here retained earnings) *is greater than the earnings yield by amounts which vary directly with size of the capital budget f* and the size of the coefficient $a_1$ in $\sigma_{\hat{p}}^2 = (1 + agf^2)\, \sigma_p^2$. (Note also that this result was reached even though the marginal profit variance, $\sigma_p^2$, on the capital budget itself was assumed constant. If $\delta_p^2$ also varies with $f$, the result is compounded.) Moreover, I have shown elsewhere [b8] that these results are quite general. In particular, if viable markets for all future time periods exist which establish exchange lines along which $\hat{g} - \alpha_2$

[34] Quadratic utility functions, however, are patently inappropriate in the context of our concern with long-run growth, even if variances are minimal or zero. A point is soon reached beyond which further increases in dividend (and growth) would *reduce* the utility of the receipt.. The hyperbolic form adopted here is free of this disability and has other important advantages [cf. b8].

[35] Cf. Aitchison and Brown [b1, p.8].

$\sigma^g - a_3\, \sigma^2_g$ are equally valued (the first limiting case above is covered by setting $a_3 = 0$), these same conclusions hold, with the excess of MCC over $y_e$ varying directly with the market exchange coefficients $\alpha_2$ and $\alpha_3$ instead of directly with $\alpha_1$, the coefficient of risk aversion on the utility function itself. Finally (as also shown in [*b*8]), MCC $> y_e$ necessarily, and by amounts that increase essentially exponentially with the size of budget, if, when viewed as of $t_0$, the variance $\sigma^2_{pt}$ of the profitability of new investments to be made at different times in the future is a monotone increasing function of their futurity. With this very plausible and persuasive feature incorporated in the models, the conclusions stated above hold *even if*[36] $a_1 = 0$.

These results lead directly to other fundamental conclusions. Even though leverage per se has not yet been considered explicitly, it necessarily follows from the preceding analysis that *the conventional weighted average cost-of-capital rule is inherently erroneous and down-biased. Even if* a weighted average of equity and debt costs were the proper criterion, the average of earnings yield and interest cost would be *too low* because the relevant marginal cost of retained earnings is *greater* than the earnings yield (and the relevant marginal cost of outside equity still larger). If, for instance, both retained earnings and debt are to be used in financing, standard production theory insures that (1) the optimal *mix* will involve the *equalization of the two* (interdependent) *marginal costs* and (2) the relevant marginal cost of (optimal-mix) finance for any sized budget will be *equal to the* (*equalized*) *marginal costs of each type of finance used.*

Even with quoted interest rates well below equity yields, there is, of course, no problem in having marginal costs of debt equal to marginal equity costs: Not only are marginal interest costs with much use of debt substantially above stated or coupon rates, but—just as nonzero profit rate variances make the *relevant* marginal costs of equity greater than earnings yields—it is reasonable to expect that the *relevant marginal costs of debt will similarly be greater than even the marginal overt interest costs.* And so they are.[37] Although borrowing per se does not affect $\delta^2_p$, the variance of the profit rate before interest, by introducing fixed interest charges, it necessarily increases $\sigma^2_{pa}$, the profit rate variance after interest, and consequently $\sigma^2_g$, which is the variance more directly relevant to the shareholder.[38] Moreover, it does so at every point in

[36]The reason is essentially that increased retentions and growth shift relatively more of the income stream into the further future and thereby increase the relevant weighted average uncertainty of the stream.

[37]This analysis is free of the straitjacket of the "entity value" theory for reasons given in detail in [*b*7].

[38]If $\alpha_1 > 0$, as is surely the usual case, borrowing increases this variance in

time and cumulatively over time—and as interest costs increase with increased borrowing, it does so in necessarily nonlinear fashion even on the standard deviation and a fortiori so on the variance. Such (non-linearly) increasing shareholder risks with increasing corporate borrowing raise the relevant marginal costs of debt (minimum expected marginal returns on investments) *above* its marginal overt interest cost (which is its true marginal cost under certainty)—and by margins which progressively increase with the relative amount of the debt financing—for precisely the same economic reason that any increase in risks in the shareholders' income stream due to added retentions raises *their* true marginal cost above the earnings yield (which would have been their proper marginal cost under certainty).

## IV. Conclusion

In conclusion, it should be emphasized that *so long as* the marginal expected return on the capital budget is > *this* MCC of debt (making full allowance for its risk impact), *debt-financing cum investment raises* the (expected value of) the *current stock price*—and consequently *lowers current earnings yields,* contrary to the common impression. *Only unjustified debt-financed expansion raises current earnings yields.* Of course, $\rho_\wedge <$ MCC (debt) *until* $r$ (or $s$) is substantially positive; but in these models, *after* $r$ and $s$ have been optimized under the constraint of no (permanent)[39] borrowing, $\rho_\wedge$ will often be > MCC (debt), and permanent borrowing is desirable (because it raises share values) up to a well-defined optimum,[40] again contrary to theoretical models now current; alternatively, so long as the equity financing exceeds a certain pace, there is an optimal finance mix involving both equity and debt for each relative size of budget, $f$; and along this finance mix "expansion path," budget size $f$ should be increased until the condition $\rho_\wedge \geq$ MCC is no longer satisfied.[41]

---

compound and nonlinear fashion [since $(1 + a_1 f^2)\sigma^2_{pa}$ is a product]. With borrowing in the picture, $f = r + \theta$, where $\theta$ is the new borrowing and all variables as before as ratios to current earnings.

[39]In view of the emphasis on comparative dynamics, $\theta$ is defined as a fraction of earnings; and with positive growth, total debt grows continuously over time, as in the Domar models. Our $\theta$ does not include temporary borrowing to even out stockastic variations in income flows.

[40]After borrowing is optimized subject to $r$ (or $s$) fixed at *its* optimum, assuming no debt, further retentions will often *become* justified (due to interaction effects between costs of equity and debt capital) and so on interatively to the global optimum.

[41]Depending on parameter values, it is entirely possible (and probably frequent in practice) that $\rho_\wedge <$ MCC (debt) for *all* values of $r$ (and $s$), in which case the optimum borrowing $\theta = 0$ throughout.

## References

*a*1–*a*35. These references refer to the correspondingly numbered items in the Bibliography to item [*b*7] below.

*b*1. AITCHISON, J., and BROWN, J. A. C. *The Lognormal Distribution.* Cambridge: Cambridge University Press, 1957.

*b*2. BAILEY, MARTIN J. "Formal Criteria for Investment Decisions," *Journal of Political Economy,* Vol. LXVII (October, 1959).

*b*3. BENISHAY, HASKEL. "Variability in Earnings-Price Ratios of Corporate Equities," *American Economic Review,* Vol. LI (March, 1961).

*b*4. GORDON, MYRON J. *The Investment, Financing, and Valuation of the Corporation.* Homewood, Ill.: Richard D. Irwin, Inc., 1962.

*b*5. HIRSCHLEIFER, JACK. "On the Theory of Optimal Investment Decision," *Journal of Political Economy,* Vol. LXVI (August, 1958).

*b*6. HIRSCHLEIFER, JACK. "Risk, the Discount Rate, and Investment Decisions," *American Economic Review,* Vol. LI (May, 1961).

*b*7. LINTNER, JOHN. "Dividends, Earnings, Leverage, Stock Prices and the Supply of Capital to Corporations," *Review of Economics and Statistics,* Vol. XLIV (August, 1962).

*b*8. LINTNER, JOHN. "Optimal Dividends and Corporate Growth under Uncertainty," *Quarterly Journal of Economics,* Vol. LXXVII (November, 1963).

*b*9. LINTNER, JOHN. "The Valuation of Risk Assets and the Selection of Risky Investments," *Review of Economics and Statistics,* Vol. XLV (November, 1963).

*b*10. LINTNER, JOHN. "Optimal Risk Bearing, Retentions and Leverage in Corporate Growth," forthcoming.

*b*11. SCHWARTZ, ELI. "Theory of the Capital Structure of the Firm," *Journal of Finance,* Vol. XIV (March, 1959).

*b*12. SMITH, VERNON L. "Comment on Risk, the Discount Rate and Investment Decisions," *American Economic Review,* Vol. LI (May, 1961).

*b*13. SPENCER, MILTON H., and SIEGELMAN, LOUIS. *Managerial Economics.* Homewood, Ill.: Richard D. Irwin, Inc., 1959.

*b*14. TINBERGEN, JAN. "The Optimum Rate of Saving," *Economic Journal,* Vol. LXVI (December, 1956).

*b*15. WESTON, J. FRED. *Managerial Finance.* New York: Holt, Rinehart & Winston, Inc., 1962.

Part VI

# Dividend Policy

*Chapter* 28

# *Dividend Policy, Growth, and the Valuation of Shares**

By Merton H. Miller and Franco Modigliani

THE EFFECT of a firm's dividend policy on the current price of its shares is a matter of considerable importance, not only to the corporate officials who must set the policy but to investors planning portfolios and to economists seeking to understand and appraise the functioning of the capital markets. Do companies with generous distribution policies consistently sell at a premium over those with niggardly payouts? Is the reverse ever true? If so, under what conditions? Is there an optimum payout ratio or range of ratios that maximizes the current worth of the shares?

Although these questions of fact have been the subject of many empirical studies in recent years, no consensus has yet been achieved. One reason appears to be the absence in the literature of a complete and reasonably rigorous statement of those parts of the economic theory of valuation bearing directly on the matter of dividend policy. Lacking such a statement, investigators have not yet been able to frame their tests with sufficient precision to distinguish adequately between the various contending hypotheses. Nor have they been able to give a convincing explanation of what their test results do imply about the underlying process of valuation.

---

*Reprinted from *Journal of Business,* Vol. XXXIV (October, 1961), pp. 411–33, by Merton H. Miller and Franco Modigliani, by permission of the University of Chicago Press. 

The authors wish to express their thanks to all who read and commented on earlier versions of this paper and especially Charles C. Holt, now of the University of Wisconsin, whose suggestions led to considerable simplification of a number of the proofs.

In the hope that it may help to overcome these obstacles to effective empirical testing, this paper will attempt to fill the existing gap in the theoretical literature on valuation. We shall begin in Section I by examining the effects of differences in dividend policy on the current price of shares in an ideal economy characterized by perfect capital markets, rational behavior, and perfect certainty. Still within this convenient analytical framework, we shall go on in Sections II and III to consider certain closely related issues that appear to have been responsible for considerable misunderstanding of the role of dividend policy. In particular, Section II will focus on the long-standing debate about what investors "really" capitalize when they buy shares; and Section III, on the much-mooted relations between price, the rate of growth of profits, and the rate of growth of dividends per share. Once these fundamentals have been established, we shall proceed in Section IV to drop the assumption of certainty and to see the extent to which the earlier conclusions about dividend policy must be modified. Finally, in Section V, we shall briefly examine the implications for the dividend policy problem of certain kinds of market imperfections.

## I. Effect of Dividend Policy with Perfect Markets, Rational Behavior, and Perfect Certainty

### *The Meaning of the Basic Assumptions*

Although the terms "perfect markets," "rational behavior," and "perfect certainty" are widely used throughout economic theory, it may be helpful to start by spelling out the precise meaning of these assumptions in the present context.

1. In "perfect capital markets," no buyer or seller (or issuer) of securities is large enough for his transactions to have an appreciable impact on the then ruling price. All traders have equal and costless access to information about the ruling price and about all other relevant characteristics of shares (to be detailed specifically later). No brokerage fees, transfer taxes, or other transaction costs are incurred when securities are bought, sold, or issued; and there are no tax differentials either between distributed and undistributed profits or between dividends and capital gains.
2. "Rational behavior" means that investors always prefer more wealth to less and are indifferent as to whether a given increment to their

wealth takes the form of cash payments or an increase in the market value of their holdings of shares.

3. "Perfect certainty" implies complete assurance on the part of every investor as to the future investment program and the future profits of every corporation. Because of this assurance, there is, among other things, no need to distinguish between stocks and bonds as sources of funds at this stage of the analysis. We can therefore proceed as if there were only a single type of financial instrument which, for convenience, we shall refer to as shares of stock.

## *The Fundamental Principle of Valuation*

Under these assumptions the evaluation of all shares would be governed by the following fundamental principle: The price of each share must be such that the rate of return (dividends plus capital gains per dollar invested) on every share will be the same throughout the market over any given interval of time. That is, if we let:

$d_j(t) =$ Dividends per share paid by firm $j$ during period $t$
$p_j(t) =$ The price (ex any dividend in $t - 1$) of a share in firm $j$ at the start of period $t$

we must have:

$$\frac{d_j(t) + p_j(t+1) - p_j(t)}{p_j(t)} = \rho(t) \text{ independent of } j \tag{1}$$

or, equivalently:

$$p_j(t) = \frac{1}{1 + \rho(t)} [d_j(t) + p_j(t+1)] \tag{2}$$

for each $j$ and for all $t$. Otherwise, holders of low-return (high-priced) shares could increase their terminal wealth by selling these shares and investing the proceeds in shares offering a higher rate of return. This process would tend to drive down the prices of the low-return shares and drive up the prices of high-return shares until the differential in rates of return had been eliminated.

## *The Effect of Dividend Policy*

The implications of this principle for our problem of dividend policy can be seen somewhat more easily if equation 2 is restated in terms of the value of the enterprise as a whole rather than in terms of the value of an individual share. Dropping the firm subscript $j$, since this will lead to no ambiguity in the present context, and letting:

$n(t) =$ The number of shares of record at the start of $t$

$m(t + 1) =$ The number of new shares (if any) sold during $t$ at the ex-dividend closing price $p(t + 1)$, so that

$$n(t + 1) = n(t) + m(t + 1)$$

$V(t) = n(t)\,p(t) =$ The total value of the enterprise and

$D(t) = n(t)\,d(t) =$ The total dividends paid during $t$ to holders of record at the start of $t$

we can rewrite equation 2:

$$\begin{aligned} V(t) &= \frac{1}{1 + \rho(t)} [D(t) + n(t)p(t + 1)] \\ &= \frac{1}{1 + \rho(t)} [D(t) + V(t + 1) \\ &\qquad - m(t + 1)\,p(t + 1)] \end{aligned} \tag{3}$$

The advantage of restating the fundamental rule in this form is that it brings into sharper focus the three possible routes by which current dividends might affect the current market value of the firm, $V(t)$, or, equivalently, the price of its individual shares, $p(t)$. Current dividends will clearly affect $V(t)$ via the first term in the bracket, $D(t)$. In principle, current dividends might also affect $V(t)$ indirectly via the second term, $V(t + 1)$, the new ex-dividend market value. Since $V(t + 1)$ must depend only on future and not on past events, such could be the case, however, only if both (1) $V(t + 1)$ were a function of future dividend policy and (2) the current distribution, $D(t)$, served to convey some otherwise unavailable information as to what that future dividend policy would be. The first possibility being the relevant one from the standpoint of assessing the effects of dividend policy, it will clarify matters to assume, provisionally, that the future dividend policy of the firm is known and given for $t + 1$ and all subsequent periods and is independent of the actual dividend decision in $t$. Then, $V(t + 1)$ will also be independent of the current dividend decision, though it may very well be effected by $D(t + 1)$ and all subsequent distributions. Finally, current dividends can influence $V(t)$ through the third term, $-m(t + 1)$ $p(t + 1)$, the value of new shares sold to outsiders during the period. For the higher the dividend payout in any period, the more new capital that must be raised from external sources to maintain any desired level of investment.

The fact that the dividend decision affects price not in one but in these two conflicting ways—directly via $D(t)$ and inversely via $-m(t)$ $p(t+1)$—is, of course, precisely why one speaks of there being a dividend policy *problem.* If the firm raises its dividend in $t$, given its investment decision, will the increase in the cash payments to the current holders be more or less than enough to offset their lower share of the terminal value? Which is the better strategy for the firm in financing the investment: to reduce dividends and rely on retained earnings or to raise dividends but float more new shares?

In our ideal world, at least, these and related questions can be simply and immediately answered: The two dividend effects must always exactly cancel out so that the payout policy to be followed in $t$ will have *no* effect on the price at $t$.

We need only express $m(t+1) \cdot p(t+1)$ in terms of $D(t)$ to show that such must indeed be the case. Specifically, if $I(t)$ is the given level of the firm's investment or increase in its holding of physical assets in $t$, and if $X(t)$ is the firm's total net profit for the period, we know that the amount of outside capital required will be:

$$m(t+1)\, p(t+1) = I(t) - [X(t) - D(t)] \tag{4}$$

Substituting expression 4 into 3, the $D(t)$ cancel, and we obtain for the value of the firm as of the start of $t$:

$$V(t) \equiv n(t)\, p(t) = \frac{1}{1+\rho(t)}\,[X(t) - I(t) + V(t+1)] \tag{5}$$

Since $D(t)$ does not appear directly among the arguments, and since $X(t)$, $I(t)$, $V(t+1)$ and $\rho(t)$ are all independent of $D(t)$ (either by their nature or by assumption), it follows that the current value of the firm must be independent of the current dividend decision.

Having established that $V(t)$ is unaffected by the current dividend decision, it is easy to go on to show that $V(t)$ must also be unaffected by any future dividend decisions as well. Such future decisions can influence $V(t)$ only via their effect on $V(t+1)$. But we can repeat the reasoning above and show that $V(t+1)$—and hence $V(t)$—is unaffected by dividend policy in $t+1$; that $V(t+2)$—and hence $V(t+1)$ and $V(t)$—is unaffected by dividend policy in $t+2$; and so on for as far into the future as we care to look. Thus, we may conclude that, given a firm's investment policy, the dividend payout policy it chooses to follow will affect neither the current price of its shares nor the total return to its shareholders.

Like many other propositions in economics, the irrelevance of dividend policy, given investment policy, is "obvious, once you think of it." It is, after all, merely one more instance of the general principle that there are no "financial illusions" in a rational and perfect economic environment. Values there are determined solely by "real" considerations—in this case the earning power of the firm's assets and its investment policy—and not by how the fruits of the earning power are "packaged" for distribution.

Obvious as the proposition may be, however, one finds few references to it in the extensive literature on the problem.[1] It is true that the literature abounds with statements that in some "theoretical" sense, dividend policy ought not to count; but either that sense is not clearly specified, or, more frequently and especially among economists, it is (wrongly) identified with a situation in which the firm's internal rate of return is the same as the external or market rate of return.[2]

A major source of these and related misunderstandings of the role of the dividend policy has been the fruitless concern and controversy over what investors "really" capitalize when they buy shares. We say fruitless because, as we shall now proceed to show, it is actually possible to derive from the basic principle of valuation 1 not merely one, but several valuation formulas each starting from one of the "classical" views of what is being capitalized by investors. Though differing somewhat in outward appearance, the various formulas can be shown to be equivalent in all essential respects, including, of course, their implication that dividend policy is irrelevant. While the controversy itself thus turns out to be an empty one, the different expressions do have some intrinsic interest, since, by highlighting different combinations of variables, they provide additional insights into the process of valuation and open alternative lines of attack on some of the problems of empirical testing.

## II. What Does the Market "Really" Capitalize?

In the literature on valuation, one can find at least the following four more or less distinct approaches to the valuation of shares: (1) the discounted cash flow approach; (2) the current earnings plus future investment opportunities approach; (3) the stream-of-dividends approach; and (4) the stream-of-earnings approach. To demonstrate that these approaches are in fact equivalent, it will be helpful to begin by

[1] Apart from the references to it in our earlier papers, especially [16], the closest approximation seems to be that in Bodenhorn [1, p. 492], but even his treatment of the role of dividend policy is not completely explicit. (The numbers in brackets refer to references listed below, pp. 512–13).

[2] See below, p. 501.

first going back to equation 5 and developing from it a valuation formula to serve as a point of reference and comparison. Specifically, if we assume, for simplicity, that the market rate of yield $\rho\ (t) = \rho$ for all $t$,[3] then, setting $t = 0$, we can rewrite equation 5 as:

$$V(0) = \frac{1}{1+\rho}[X(0) - I(0)] + \frac{1}{1+\rho}V(1) \tag{6}$$

Since equation 5 holds for all $t$, setting $t = 1$ permits us to express $V(1)$ in terms of $V(2)$, which in turn can be expressed in terms of $V(3)$, and so on up to any arbitrary terminal period $T$. Carrying out these substitutions, we obtain:

$$V(0) = \sum_{t=0}^{T-1} \frac{1}{(1+\rho)^{t+1}}[X(t) - I(t)] + \frac{1}{(1+\rho)^{T}}V(T) \tag{7}$$

In general, the remainder term $(1 + \rho)^{-T} \cdot V(T)$ can be expected to approach zero as $T$ approaches infinity,[4] so that equation 7 can be expressed as:

$$V(0) = \lim_{T\to\infty} \sum_{t=0}^{T-1} \frac{1}{(1+\rho)^{t+1}} \times [X(t) - I(t)] \tag{8}$$

which we shall further abbreviate to:

$$V(0) = \sum_{t=0}^{\infty} \frac{1}{(1+\rho)^{t+1}}[X(t) - I(t)] \tag{9}$$

## *The Discounted Cash Flow Approach*

Consider now the so-called "discounted cash flow approach," familiar in discussions of capital budgeting. There, in valuing any specific machine, we discount at the market rate of interest the stream of cash receipts generated by the machine; plus any scrap or terminal value of the machine; and minus the stream of cash outlays for direct labor,

---

[3]More general formulas in which $\rho(t)$ is allowed to vary with time can always be derived from those presented here merely by substituting the cumbersome product

$$\prod_{\tau=0}^{t} [1 + \rho(\tau)]$$

for

$$(1+\rho)^{t+1}$$

[4]The assumption that the remainder vanishes is introduced for the sake of simplicity of exposition only and is in no way essential to the argument. What is essential, of course, is that $V(0)$, i.e., the sum of the two terms in equation 7, be finite, but this can always be safely assumed in economic analysis. See below, n. 14.

materials, repairs, and capital additions. The same approach, of course, can also be applied to the firm as a whole, which may be thought of in this context as simply a large, composite machine.[5] This approach amounts to defining the value of the firm as:

$$V(0) = \sum_{t=0}^{T-1} \frac{1}{(1+\rho)^{t+1}} \times [\Re(t) - \mathcal{O}(t)] + \frac{1}{(1+\rho)^{T}} V(T) \quad (10)$$

where $\Re(t)$ represents the stream of cash receipts and $\mathcal{O}(t)$ of cash outlays, or, abbreviating, as above, to:

$$V(0) = \sum_{t=0}^{\infty} \frac{1}{(1+\rho)^{t+1}} [\Re(t) - \mathcal{O}(t)] \quad (11)$$

But we also know, by definition, that $[X(t) - I(t)] = [\Re(t) - \mathcal{O}(t)]$, since $X(t)$ differs from $\Re(t)$ and $I(t)$ differs from $\mathcal{O}(t)$ merely by the "cost of goods sold" [and also by the depreciation expense if we wish to interpret $X(t)$ and $I(t)$ as net rather than gross profits and investment]. Hence, equation 11 is formally equivalent to equation 9, and the discounted cash flow approach is thus seen to be an implication of the valuation principle for perfect markets given by equation 1.

## *The Investment Opportunities Approach*

Consider next the approach to valuation which would seem most natural from the stand point of an investor proposing to buy out and operate some already going concern. In estimating how much it would be worthwhile to pay for the privilege of operating the firm, the amount of dividends to be paid is clearly not relevant, since the new owner can, within wide limits, make the future dividend stream whatever he pleases. For him, the worth of the enterprise as such will depend only on (1) the "normal" rate of return he can earn by investing his capital in securities (i.e., the market rate of return); (2) the earning power of the physical assets currently held by the firm; and (3) the opportunities, if any, that the firm offers for making additional investments in real assets that will yield more than the "normal" (market) rate of return. The latter opportunities, frequently termed the "goodwill" of the business, may arise, in practice, from any of a number of circumstances (ranging all the way from special locational advantages to patents or other monopolistic advantages).

[5]This is, in fact, the approach to valuation normally taken in economic theory when discussing the value of the *assets* of an enterprise, but much more rarely applied, unfortunately, to the value of the liability side. One of the few to apply the approach to the shares as well as the assets is Bodenhorn in [1], who uses it to derive a formula closely similar to equation 9 above.

To see how these opportunities affect the value of the business, assume that in some future period, $t$, the firm invests $I(t)$ dollars. Suppose further, for simplicity, that starting in the period immediately following the investment of the funds, the projects produce net profits at a constant rate of $\rho^*(t)$ percent of $I(t)$ in each period thereafter.[6] Then the present worth as of $t$ of the (perpetual) stream of profits generated will be $I(t)\ \rho^*(t)/\rho$, and the "goodwill" of the projects (i.e., the difference between worth and cost) will be:

$$I(t)\,\frac{\rho^*(t)}{\rho} - I(t) = I(t)\left[\frac{\rho^*(t) - \rho}{\rho}\right]$$

The present worth as of now of this future "goodwill" is:

$$I(t)\left[\frac{\rho^*(t) - \rho}{\rho}\right](1 + \rho)^{-(t+1)}$$

and the present value of all such future opportunities is simply the sum:

$$\sum_{t=0}^{\infty} I(t)\,\frac{\rho^*(t) - \rho}{\rho}\,(1 + \rho)^{-(t+1)}$$

Adding in the present value of the (uniform perpetual) earnings, $X(0)$, on the assets currently held, we get as an expression for the value of the firm:

$$V(0) = \frac{X(0)}{\rho} + \sum_{t=0}^{\infty} I(t) \times \frac{\rho^*(t) - \rho}{\rho}\,(1 + \rho)^{-(t+1)} \qquad (12)$$

To show that the same formula can be derived from equation 9, note first that our definition of $\rho^*(t)$ implies the following relation between the $X(t)$:

$$X(1) = X(0) + \rho^*(0)\,I(0)$$

. . . . . . . . . . . . . . .

$$X(t) = X(t - 1) + \rho^*(t - 1)\,I(t - 1)$$

and by successive substitution:

$$X(t) = X(0) + \sum_{\tau=0}^{t-1} \rho^*(\tau)\,I(\tau)$$

$$t = 1, 2 \ldots \infty$$

[6]The assumption that $I(t)$ yields a uniform perpetuity is not restrictive in the present certainty context, since it is always possible by means of simple, present-value calculations to find an equivalent uniform perpetuity for any project, whatever the time shape of its actual returns. Note also that $\rho^*(t)$ is the *average* rate of return. If the managers of the firm are behaving rationally, they will of course use $\rho$ as their cutoff criterion (cf. below, p. 491). In this event, we would have $\rho^*(t) \geqq \rho$. The formulas remains valid, however, even where $\rho^*(t) < \rho$.

Substituting the last expression for $X(t)$ in (9) yields:

$$V(0) = [X(0) - I(0)]\,(1+\rho)^{-1} + \sum_{t=1}^{\infty}\left[X(0) + \sum_{\tau=0}^{t-1}\rho^*(\tau)\,I(\tau) - I(t)\right](1+\rho)^{-(t+1)}$$

$$= X(0)\sum_{t=1}^{\infty}(1+\rho)^{-t} - I(0)\,(1+\rho)^{-1} + \sum_{t=1}^{\infty}\left[\sum_{\tau=0}^{t-1}\rho^*(\tau)\,I(\tau) - I(t)\right]\times(1+\rho)^{-(t+1)}$$

$$= X(0)\sum_{t=1}^{\infty}(1+\rho)^{-t} + \sum_{t=1}^{\infty}\left[\sum_{\tau=0}^{t-1}\rho^*(\tau)\,I(\tau) - I(t-1)\times(1+\rho)\right](1+\rho)^{-(t+1)}$$

The first expression is, of course, simply a geometric progression summing to $X(0)/\rho$, which is the first term of equation 12. To simplify the second expression, note that it can be rewritten as:

$$\sum_{t=0}^{\infty} I(t)\left[\rho^*(t)\sum_{\tau=t+2}^{\infty}(1+\rho)^{-\tau} - (1+\rho)^{-(t+1)}\right]$$

Evaluating the summation within the brackets gives:

$$\sum_{t=0}^{\infty} I(t)\left[\rho^*(t)\,\frac{(1+\rho)^{-(t+1)}}{\rho} - (1+\rho)^{-(t+1)}\right] = \sum_{t=0}^{\infty} I(t)\left[\frac{\rho^*(t)-\rho}{\rho}\right](1+\rho)^{-(t+1)}$$

which is precisely the second term of equation 12.

Formula 12 has a number of revealing features and deserves to be more widely used in discussion of valuation.[7] For one thing, it throws considerable light on the meaning of those much abused terms "growth" and "growth stocks." As can readily be seen from equation 12, a corporation does not become a "growth stock" with a high price-earnings ratio merely because its assets and earnings are growing over time. To enter the glamor category, it is also necessary that $\rho^*(t) > \rho$. For if $\rho^*(t) = \rho$, then however large the growth in assets may be, the second term in equation 12 will be zero, and the firm's price-earnings ratio would not rise above a humdrum $1/\rho$. The essence of "growth," in short,

[7] A valuation formula analogous to equation 12, though derived and interpreted in a slightly different way, is found in Bodenhorn [1]. Varients of equation 12 for certain special cases are discussed in Walter [20].

is not expansion but the existence of opportunities to invest significant quantities of funds at higher than "normal" rates of return.

Notice also that if $\rho^*(t) < \rho$, investment in real assets by the firm will actually reduce the current price of the shares. This should help to make clear, among other things, why the "cost of capital" to the firm is the same regardless of how the investments are financed or how fast the firm is growing. The function of the cost of capital in capital budgeting is to provide the "cutoff rate" in the sense of the minimum yield that investment projects must promise to be worth undertaking from the point of view of the current owners. Clearly, no proposed project would be in the interest of the current owners if its yield were expected to be less than $\rho$, since investing in such projects would reduce the value of their shares. In the other direction, every project yielding more than $\rho$ is just as clearly worth undertaking, since it will necessarily enhance the value of the enterprise. Hence the cost of capital or cutoff criterion for investment decisions is simply $\rho$.[8]

Finally, formula 12 serves to emphasize an important deficiency in many recent statistical studies of the effects of dividend policy (such as Walter [19] or Durand [4], [5]. These studies typically involve fitting regression equations in which price is expressed as some function of current earnings and dividends. A finding that the dividend coefficient is significant—as is usually the case—is then interpreted as a rejection of the hypothesis that dividend policy does not affect valuation.

Even without raising questions of bias in the coefficient,[9] it should be apparent that such a conclusion is unwarranted, since formula 12 and the analysis underlying it imply only that dividends will not count given current earnings *and growth potential.* No general prediction is made (or can be made) by the theory about what will happen to the dividend coefficient if the crucial growth term is omitted.[10]

---

[8]The same conclusion could also have been reached, of course, by "costing" each particular source of capital funds. That is, since $\rho$ is the going market rate of return on equity, any new shares floated to finance investment must be priced to yield $\rho$; and withholding funds from the stockholders to finance investment would deprive the holders of the chance to earn $\rho$ on these funds by investing their dividends in other shares. The advantage of thinking in terms of the cost of capital as the cut-off criterion is that it minimizes the danger of confusing "costs" with mere "outlays."

[9]The serious bias problem in tests using current reported earnings as a measure of $X(0)$ was discussed briefly by us in [16].

[10]In suggesting that recent statistical studies have not controlled adequately for growth, we do not mean to exempt Gordon in [8] or [9]. It is true that his tests contain an explicit "growth" variable, but it is essentially nothing more than the ratio of retained earnings to book value. This ratio would not in general provide an acceptable approximation to the "growth" variable of equation 12 in any sample in which firms resorted to external financing. Furthermore, even if by some chance a sample was found in which all firms relied entirely on retained earnings,

*(Continued on next page)*

## *The Stream-of-Dividends Approach*

From the earnings and earnings-opportunities approach, we turn next to the dividend approach, which has, for some reason, been by far the most popular one in the literature of valuation. This approach, too, properly formulated, is an entirely valid one, though of course not the only valid approach as its more enthusiastic proponents frequently suggest.[11] It does, however, have the disadvantage, in contrast with previous approaches, of obscuring the role of dividend policy. In particular, uncritical use of the dividend approach has often led to the unwarranted inference that since the investor is buying dividends, and since dividend policy affects the amount of dividends, then dividend policy must also affect the current price.

Properly formulated, the dividend approach defines the current worth of a share as the discounted value of the stream of dividends to be paid on the share in perpetuity. That is:

$$p(t) = \sum_{\tau=0}^{\infty} \frac{d(t + \tau)}{(1 + \rho)^{\tau+1}} \tag{13}$$

To see the equivalence between this approach and previous ones, let us first restate equation 13 in terms of total market value as:

$$V(t) = \sum_{\tau=0}^{\infty} \frac{D_t(t + \tau)}{(1 + \rho)^{\tau+1}} \tag{14}$$

where $D_t(t + \tau)$ denotes that portion of the total dividends, $D(t + \tau)$, paid during period $t + \tau$, that accrues to the shares of record as of the start of period $t$ (indicated by the subscript). That equation 14 is equivalent to equation 9 and hence also to formula 12 is immediately apparent for the special case in which no outside financing is undertaken after period $t$, for in that case:

$$D_t(t + \tau) = D(t + \tau) = X(t + \tau) - I(t + \tau)$$

---

his tests then could not settle the question of dividend policy. For if all firms financed investment internally (or used external financing only in strict proportion to internal financing, as Gordon assumes in [8], then there would be no way to distinguish between the effects of dividend policy and investment policy (see below, p. 501).

[11]See, e.g., the classic statement of the position in Williams [21]. The equivalence of the dividend approach to many of the other standard approaches is noted to our knowledge only in our [16] and, by implication, in Bodenhorn [1].

To allow for outside financing, note that we can rewrite equation 14 as:

$$V(t) = \frac{1}{1+\rho}\left[D_t(t) + \sum_{\tau=1}^{\infty} \frac{D_t(t+\tau)}{(1+\rho)^{\tau}}\right] \tag{15}$$

$$= \frac{1}{1+\rho}\left[D(t) + \sum_{\tau=0}^{\infty} \frac{D_t(t+\tau+1)}{(1+\rho)^{\tau+1}}\right]$$

The summation term in the last expression can be written as the difference between the stream of dividends accruing to all the shares of record as of $t + 1$ and that portion of the stream that will accrue to the shares newly issued in $t$, that is:

$$\sum_{\tau=0}^{\infty} \frac{D_t(t+\tau+1)}{(1+\rho)^{\tau+1}} = \left(1 - \frac{m(t+1)}{n(t+1)}\right) \times \sum_{\tau=0}^{\infty} \frac{D_{t+1}(t+\tau+1)}{(1+\rho)^{\tau+1}} \tag{16}$$

But from equation 14, we know that the second summation in equation 16 is precisely $V(t + 1)$, so that equation 15 can be reduced to:

$$V(t) = \frac{1}{1+\rho}\left[D(t) + \left(1 - \frac{m(t+1)\,p(t+1)}{n(t+1)\,p(t+1)}\right) \times V(t+1)\right] \tag{17}$$

$$= \frac{1}{1+\rho}[D(t) + V(t+1) - m(t+1)\,p(t+1)]$$

which is equation 3, and which has already been shown to imply both equation 9 and equation 12.[12]

There are, of course, other ways in which the equivalence of the dividend approach to the other approaches might have been established, but the method presented has the advantage, perhaps, of providing some further insight into the reason for the irrelevance of dividend policy. An increase in current dividends, given the firm's investment policy, must necessarily reduce the terminal value of existing shares because part of the future dividend stream that would otherwise have accrued to the existing shares must be diverted to attract the outside capital from which, in effect, the higher current dividends are paid. Under our basic

[12]The statement that equations 9, 12, and 14 are equivalent must be qualified to allow for certain pathological extreme cases, fortunately of no real economic significance. An obvious example of such a case is the legendary company that is expected *never* to pay a dividend. If this were literally true, then the value of the firm by equation 14 would be zero; by equation 9, it would be zero (or possibly negative, since zero dividends rule out $X(t) > I(t)$ but not $X(t) < I(t)$; while by equation 12 the value might still be positive. What is involved here, of course, is nothing more than a discontinuity at zero, since the value under equations 14 and 9 would be positive and the equivalence of both with equation 12 would hold if that value were also positive as long as there was some period $T$, however far in the future, beyond which the firm would pay out $\epsilon > 0$ percent of its earnings, however small the value of $\epsilon$.

assumptions, however, $\rho$ must be the same for all investors, new as well as old. Consequently, the market value of the dividends diverted to the outsiders, which is both the value of their contribution and the reduction in terminal value of the existing shares, must always be precisely the same as the increase in current dividends.

## *The Stream-of-Earnings Approach*

Contrary to widely held views, it is also possible to develop a meaningful and consistent approach to valuation running in terms of the stream of earnings generated by the corporation rather than of the dividend distributions actually made to the shareholders. Unfortunately, it is also extremely easy to mistate or misinterpret the earnings approach, as would be the case if the value of the firm were to be defined as simply the discounted sum of future total earnings.[13] The trouble with such a definition is not, as is often suggested, that it overlooks the fact that the corporation is a separate entity and that these profits cannot freely be withdrawn by the shareholders, but rather that it neglects the fact that additional capital must be acquired at some cost to maintain the future earnings stream at its specified level. The capital to be raised in any future period is, of course, $I(t)$; and its opportunity cost, no matter how financed, is $\rho$ percent per period thereafter. Hence the current value of the firm under the earnings approach must be stated as:

$$V(0) = \sum_{t=0}^{\infty} \frac{1}{(1+\rho)^{t+1}} \times \left[ X(t) - \sum_{\tau=0}^{t} \rho I(\tau) \right] \tag{18}$$

That this version of the earning approach is indeed consistent with our basic assumptions and equivalent to the previous approaches can be seen by regrouping terms and rewriting equation 18 as:

$$\begin{aligned} V(0) &= \sum_{t=0}^{\infty} \frac{1}{(1+\rho)^{t+1}} X(t) - \sum_{t=0}^{\infty} \left( \sum_{\tau=t}^{\infty} \frac{\rho I(t)}{(1+\rho)^{\tau+1}} \right) \\ &= \sum_{t=0}^{\infty} \frac{1}{(1+\rho)^{t+1}} X(t) - \sum_{t=0}^{\infty} \frac{1}{(1+\rho)^{t+1}} \times \left( \sum_{\tau=0}^{\infty} \frac{\rho I(t)}{(1+\rho)^{\tau+1}} \right) \end{aligned} \tag{19}$$

[13] In fairness, we should point out that there is no one, to our knowledge, who has seriously advanced this view. It is a view whose main function seems to be to serve as a "straw man" to be demolished by those supporting the dividend view. See, e.g., Gordon [9, esp. pp. 102–3]. Other writers take as the supposed earnings counterview to the dividend approach not a relation running in terms of the *stream* of earnings but simply the proposition that price is proportional to current earnings, i.e., $V(0) = X(0)/\rho$. The probable origins of this widespread misconception about the earnings approach are discussed further below (p. 501).

Since the last inclosed summation reduces simply to $I(t)$, expression 19 in turn reduces simply to:

$$V(0) = \sum_{t=0}^{\infty} \frac{1}{(1+\rho)^{t+1}} [X(t) - I(t)] \tag{20}$$

which is precisely our earlier equation 9.

Note that the version of the earnings approach presented here does not depend for its validity upon any special assumptions about the time shape of the stream of total profits or the stream of dividends per share. Clearly, however, the time paths of the two streams are closely related to each other (via financial policy) and to the stream of returns derived by holders of the shares. Since these relations are of some interest in their own right, and since misunderstandings about them have contributed to the confusion over the role of dividend policy, it may be worthwhile to examine them briefly before moving on to relax the basic assumptions.

## III. Earnings, Dividends, and Growth Rates

### *The Convenient Case of Constant Growth Rates*

The relation between the stream of earnings of the firm and the stream of dividends and of returns to the stockholders can be brought out most clearly by specializing equation 12 to the case in which investment opportunities are such as to generate a constant rate of growth of profits in perpetuity. Admittedly, this case has little empirical significance, but it is convenient for illustrative purposes and has received much attention in the literature.

Specifically, suppose that in each period $t$ the firm has the opportunity to invest in real assets a sum $I(t)$ that is $k$ percent as large as its total earnings for the period, and that this investment produces a perpetual yield of $\rho^*$ beginning with the next period. Then, by definition:

$$\begin{aligned} X(t) &= X(t-1) + \rho^* I(t-1) \\ &= X(t-1)\,[1 + k\rho^*] \qquad (21) \\ &= X(0)\,[1 + k\rho^*]^t \end{aligned}$$

and $k\rho^*$ is the (constant) rate of growth of total earnings. Substituting from equation 21 into equation 12 for $I(t)$, we obtain:

$$V(0) = \frac{X(0)}{\rho} + \sum_{t=0}^{\infty} \left(\frac{\rho^* - \rho}{\rho}\right) \times kX(0)\,[1 + k\rho^*]^t \times (1 + \rho)^{-(t+1)} \tag{22}$$
$$= \frac{X(0)}{\rho}\left[1 + \frac{k(\rho^* - \rho)}{1 + \rho} \times \sum_{t=0}^{\infty}\left(\frac{1 + k\rho^*}{1 + \rho}\right)^t\right]$$

Evaluating the infinite sum and simplifying, we finally obtain:[14]

$$V(0) = \frac{X(0)}{\rho}\left[1 + \frac{k(\rho^* - \rho)}{\rho - k\rho^*}\right] \tag{23}$$
$$= \frac{X(0)\,(1 - k)}{\rho - k\rho^*}$$

which expresses the value of the firm as a function of its current earnings, the rate of growth of earnings, the internal rate of return, and the market rate of return.[15] Note that equation 23 holds not just for period 0 but for every $t$. Hence, if $X(t)$ is growing at the rate $k\rho^*$, it follows that the value of the enterprise, $V(t)$, also grows at that rate.

---

[14]One advantage of the specialization 23 is that it makes it easy to see what is really involved in the assumption here and throughout the paper that the $V(0)$ given by any of our summation formulas is necessarily finite (cf. above, n. 4). In terms of equation 23 the condition is clearly $k\rho^* < \rho$, i.e., that the rate of growth of the firm be less than market rate of discount. Although the case of (perpetual) growth rates greater than the discount factor is the much-discussed "growth stock paradox" (e.g., [6]), it has no real economic significance, as we pointed out in [16, esp. n. 17, p. 664]. This will be apparent when one recalls that the discount rate $\rho$, though treated as a constant in partial equilibrium (relative price) analysis of the kind presented here, is actually a variable from the standpoint of the system as a whole. That is, if the assumption of finite value for all shares did not hold, because for some shares $k\rho^*$ was (perpetually) greater than $\rho$, then $\rho$ would necessarily rise until an over-all equilibrium in the capital markets had been restored.

[15]An interesting and more realistic variant of equation 22, which also has a number of convenient features from the standpoint of developing empirical tests, can be obtained by assuming that the special investment opportunities are available not in perpetuity but only over some finite interval of $T$ periods. To exhibit the value of the firm for this case, we need only replace the infinite summation in equation 22, with a summation running from $t = 0$ to $t = T - 1$. Evaluating the resulting expression, we obtain:

$$V(0) = \frac{X(0)}{\rho}\left\{1 + \frac{k(\rho^* - \rho)}{\rho - k\rho^*} \times \left[1 - \left(\frac{1 + k\rho^*}{1 + \rho}\right)^T\right]\right\} \tag{22a}$$

Note that equation 22$a$ holds even if $k\rho^* > \rho$, so that the so-called "growth paradox" disappears altogether. If, as we should generally expect $(1 + k\rho^*)/(1 + \rho)$ is close to one, and if $T$ is not too large, the right-hand side of equation 22$a$ admits of a very convenient approximation. In this case, in fact, we can write:

## *The Growth of Dividends and the Growth of Total Profits*

Given that total earnings (and the total value of the firm) are growing at the rate $k\rho^*$, what is the rate of growth of dividends per share and of the price per share? Clearly, the answer will vary depending on whether or not the firm is paying out a high percentage of its earnings and thus relying heavily on outside financing. We can show the nature of this dependence explicitly by making use of the fact that whatever the rate of growth of dividends per share, the present value of the firm by the dividend approach must be the same as by the earnings approach. Thus, let:

$g =$ The rate of growth of dividends per share or, what amounts to the same thing, the rate of growth of dividends accruing to the shares of the current holders (i.e., $D_0(t) = D_0(0)\,[1 + g]^t$)

$k_r =$ The fraction of total profits retained in each period (so that $D(t) = X(0)\,[1 - k_r]$)

$k_e = k - k_r =$ The amount of external capital raised for period, expressed as a fraction of profits in the period

---

$$\left[\frac{1 + k\rho^*}{1 + \rho}\right]^T \cong 1 + T(k\rho^* - \rho)$$

the approximation holding, if, as we should expect, $(1 + k\rho^*)$ and $(1 + \rho)$ are both close to unity. Substituting this approximation into equation 22*a* and simplifying finally yields:

$$V(0) \cong \frac{X(0)}{\rho}\left[1 + \frac{k(\rho^* - \rho)}{\rho - k\rho^*} \times T(\rho - k\rho^*)\right] \qquad (22b)$$

$$= \left[\frac{X(0)}{\rho} + kX(0) \times \left(\frac{\rho^* - \rho}{\rho}\right)T\right]$$

The common sense of equation 22*b* is easy to see. The current value of a firm is given by the value of the earning power of the currently held assets plus the market value of the special earning opportunity multiplied by the number of years for which it is expected to last.

Then the present value of the stream of dividends to the original owners will be:

$$D_0(0) \sum_{t=0}^{\infty} \frac{(1+g)^t}{(1+\rho)^{t+1}} = \frac{D(0)}{\rho - g} = \frac{X(0)[1-k_r]}{\rho - g} \tag{24}$$

By virtue of the dividend approach, we know that equation 24 must be equal to $V(0)$. If, therefore, we equate it to the right-hand side of equation 23, we obtain:

$$\frac{X(0)[1-k_r]}{\rho - g} = \frac{X(0)[1-(k_r+k_e)]}{\rho - k\rho^*}$$

from which it follows that the rate of growth of dividends per share and the rate of growth of the price of a share must be:[16]

$$g = k\rho^* \frac{1-k_r}{1-k} - k_e\rho \frac{1}{1-k} \tag{25}$$

Notice that in the extreme case in which all financing is internal ($k_e = 0$ and $k = k_r$), the second term drops out, and the first becomes simply $k\rho^*$. Hence the growth rate of dividends in that special case is exactly the same as that of total profits and total value, and is proportional to the rate of retention, $k_r$. In all other cases, $g$ is necessarily less than $k\rho^*$ and may even be negative, despite a positive $k\rho^*$, if $\rho^* < \rho$, and if the firm pays out a large fraction of its income in dividends. In the other direction, we see from equation 25 that even if a firm is a "growth" corporation ($\rho^* > \rho$), then the stream of dividends and price per share must grow over time, even though $k_r = 0$, that is, even though it pays out *all* its earnings in dividends.

[16]That $g$ is the rate of price increase per share as well as the rate of growth of dividends per share follows from the fact that by equation 13 and the definition of $g$:

$$\begin{aligned} p(t) &= \sum_{\tau=0}^{\infty} \frac{d(t+\tau)}{(1+\rho)^{\tau+1}} \\ &= \sum_{\tau=0}^{\infty} \frac{d(0)[1+g]^{t+\tau}}{(1+\rho)^{\tau+1}} \\ &= (1+g)^t \sum_{\tau=0}^{\infty} \frac{d(\tau)}{(1+\rho)^{\tau+1}} \\ &= p(0)[1+g]^t \end{aligned}$$

The relation between the growth rate of the firm and the growth rate of dividends under various dividend policies is illustrated graphically in Figure 1, in which for maxium clarity the natural logarithm of profits and dividends have been plotted against time.[17]

FIGURE 1

GROWTH OF DIVIDENDS PER SHARE IN RELATION TO GROWTH IN TOTAL EARNINGS

*A*. Total earnings: $\ln X(t) = \ln X(0) + k\rho^* t$

*B*. Total earnings minus capital invested: $\ln [X(t) - I(t)] = \ln X(0)\ [1 - k] + k\rho^* t$

Dividends per share (all financing internal): $\ln D_0(t) = \ln D(0) + gt = \ln X(0)\ [1 - k] + k\rho^* t$

*C*. Dividends per share (some financing external): $\ln D_0(t) = \ln D(0) + gt$

*D*. Dividends per share (all financing external); $\ln D_0(t) = \ln X(0) + [(k/1 - k)(\rho^* - \rho)]t$

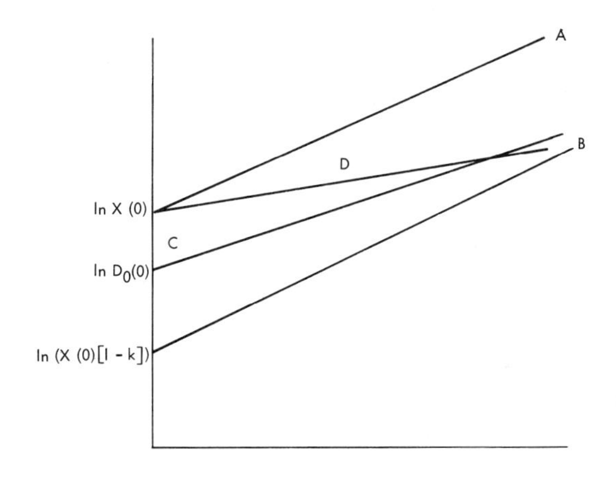


Line *A* shows the total earnings of the firm growing through time at the constant rate $k\rho^*$, the slope of *A*. Line *B* shows the growth of (1) the stream of total earnings minus capital outlays and (2) the stream of dividends to the original owners (or dividends per share) in the special case in which all financing is internal. The slope of *B* is, of course, the same as that of *A*, and the (constant) difference between the curbes is simply $\ln(1 - k)$, the ratio of dividends to profits. Line *C* shows the

[17] That is, we replace each discrete compounding expression such as $X(t) = X(0)\ [1 + k\rho^*]^t$ with its counterpart under continuous discounting, $X(t) = X(0)e^{k\rho^* t}$, which, of course, yields the convenient linear relation $\ln X(t) = \ln X(0) + k\rho^* t$.

growth of dividends per share when the firm uses both internal and external financing. As compared with the pure retention case, the line starts higher but grows more slowly at the rate $g$ given by equation 25. The higher the payout policy, the higher the starting position, and the slower the growth up to the other limiting case of complete external financing, line $D$, which starts at $\ln X(0)$ and grows at a rate of $(k/1 - k) \cdot (\rho^* - \rho)$.

## *The Special Case of Exclusively Internal Financing*

As noted above, the growth rate of dividends per share is not the same as the growth rate of the firm except in the special case in which all financing is internal. This is merely one of a number of peculiarities of this special case on which, unfortunately, many writers have based their entire analysis. The reason for the preoccupation with this special case is far from clear to us. Certainly, no one would suggest that it is the only empirically relevant case. Even if the case were in fact the most common, the theorist would still be under an obligation to consider alternative assumptions. We suspect that in the last analysis the popularity of the internal financing model will be found to reflect little more than its ease of manipulation combined with the failure to push the analysis far enough to disclose how special and how treacherous a case it really is.

In particular, concentration on this special case appears to be largely responsible for the widely held view that even under perfect capital markets, there is an optimum dividend policy for the firm that depends on the internal rate of return. Such a conclusion is almost inevitable if one works exclusively with the assumption, explicit or implicit, that funds for investment come *only* from retained earnings. For in that case, *dividend policy* is indistinguishable from *investment policy;* and there *is* an optimal investment policy which does in general depend on the rate of return.

Notice also from equation 23 that if $\rho^* = \rho$ and $k = k_r$, the term $[1 - k_r]$ can be canceled from both the numerator and the denominator. The value of the firm becomes simply $X(0)/\rho$, the capitalized value of current earnings. Lacking a standard model for valuation more general than the retained earnings case, it has been all too easy for many to conclude that this dropping-out of the payout ratio $[1 - k_r]$ when $\rho^* = \rho$ must be what is meant by their relevance of dividend policy and that $V(0) = X(0)/\rho$ must constitute the "earnings" approach.

Still another example of the pitfalls in basing arguments on this special case is provided by the recent and extensive work on valuation by Gordon.[18] Gordon argues, in essense, that because of increasing uncertainty the discount rate $\hat{\rho}(t)$ applied by an investor to a future dividend payment will rise with $t$, where $t$ denotes not a specific date but rather the distance from the period in which the investor performs the discounting.[19] Hence, when we use a single uniform discount rate, $\rho$, as in equations 22 or 23, this rate should be thought of as really an average of the "true" rates, $\hat{\rho}(t)$, each weighted by the size of the expected dividend payment at time $t$. If the dividend stream is growing exponentially, then such a weighted average, $\rho$, would of course be higher the greater the rate of growth of dividends, $g$, since the greater will then be the portion of the dividend stream arising in the distant as opposed to the near future. But if all financing is assumed to be internal, then $g = k_r\rho^*$, so that, given $\rho^*$, the weighted average discount factor, $\rho$, will be an increasing function of the rate of retention, $k_r$, which would run counter to our conclusion that dividend policy has no effect on the current value of the firm or its cost of capital.

For all its ingenuity, however, and its seeming foundation in uncertainty, the argument clearly suffers fundamentally from the typical confounding of dividend policy with investment policy that so frequently accompanies use of the internal financing model. Had Gordon not confined his attention to this special case (or its equivalent variant), he would have seen that while a change in dividend policy will necessarily affect the size of the expected dividend payment on the share in any future period, it need not, in the general case, affect either the size of the *total* return that the investor expects during that period or the degree of uncertainty attaching to that total return. As should be abundantly clear by now, a change in dividend policy, given investment policy, implies a change only in the distribution of the total return in any period as between dividends and capital gains. If investors behave rationally, such a change cannot affect market valuations. Indeed, if they valued shares according to the Gordon approach and thus paid a premium for higher payout ratios, then holders of the low payout shares would actually

---

[18]See especially [8]. Gordon's views represent the most explicit and sophisticated formulation of what might be called the "bird-in-the-hand" fallacy. For other less elaborate statements of essentially the same position, see, among others, Graham and Dodd [11, p. 433], and Clendenin and Van Cleave [3].

[19]We use the notation $\hat{\rho}(t)$ to avoid any confusion between Gordon's purely subjective discount rate and the objective, market-given yields $\rho(t)$ in Section I above. To attempt to derive valuation formulas under uncertainty from these purely subjective discount factors involves, of course, an error essentially analogous to that of attempting to develop the certainty formulas from "marginal rates of time preference" rather than objective market opportunities.

realize consistently higher returns on their investment over any stated interval of time.[20]

## *Corporate Earnings and Investor Returns*

Knowing the relation of $g$ to $k\rho^*$, we can answer a question of considerable interest to economic theorists, namely: What is the precise relation between the earnings of the corporation in any period $X(t)$ and the total return to the owners of the stock during that period?[21] If we let $G_t(t)$ be the capital gains to the owners during $t$, we know that:

$$D_t(t) + G_t(t) = X(t) \times (1 - k_r) + gV(t) \tag{26}$$

since the rate of growth of price is the same as that of dividends per share. Using equations 25 and 26 to substitute for $g$ and $V(t)$, and simplifying, we find that:

$$D_t(t) + G_t(t) = X(t) \left[ \frac{\rho(1 - k)}{\rho - k\rho^*} \right] \tag{27}$$

The relation between the investors' return and the corporation's profits is thus seen to depend entirely on the relation between $\rho^*$ and $\rho$. If $\rho^* = \rho$ (i.e., the firm has no special "growth" opportunities), then the expression in brackets becomes one, and the investor returns are precisely the same as the corporate profits. If $\rho^* < \rho$, however, the in-

[20]This is not to deny that growth stocks (in our sense) may well be "riskier" than nongrowth stocks. But to the extent that this is true, it will be due to the possibly greater uncertainty attaching to the size and duration of future growth opportunities and hence to the size of the future stream of total returns, quite apart from any questions of dividend policy.

[21]Note also that the above analysis enables us to deal very easily with the familiar issue of whether a firm's cost of equity capital is measured by its earnings-price ratio or by its dividend-price ratio. Clearly, the answer is that it is measured by neither, except under very special circumstances. For from equation 23, we have for the earnings-price ratio:

$$\frac{X(0)}{V(0)} = \frac{\rho - k\rho^*}{1 - k}$$

which is equal to the cost of capital, $\rho$, only if the firm has no growth potential (i.e., $\rho^* = \rho$). And from equation 24, we have for the dividend-price ratio:

$$\frac{D(0)}{V(0)} = \rho - g$$

which is equal to $\rho$ only when $g = 0$; i.e., from equation 25, either when $k = 0$; or if $k > 0$, when $\rho^* < \rho$ and the amount of external financing is precisely

$$k_e = \frac{\rho^*}{\rho} k [1 - k_r]$$

so that the gain from the retention of earnings exactly offsets the loss that would otherwise be occasioned by the unprofitable investment.

vestors' return will be less than the corporate earnings, and in the case of growth corporations the investors' return will actually be greater than the flow of corporate profits over the interval.[22]

## *Some Implications for Constructing Empirical Tests*

Finally, the fact that we have two different (though not independent) measures of growth in $k\rho^*$ and $g$, and two corresponding families of valuation formulas, means, among other things, that we can proceed by either of two routes in empirical studies of valuation. We can follow the standard practice of the security analyst and think in terms of price per share, dividends per share, and the rate of growth of dividends per share; or we can think in terms of the total value of the enterprise, total earnings, and the rate of growth of total earnings. Our own preference happens to be for the second approach, primarily because certain additional variables of interest—such as dividend policy, leverage, and size of firm—can be incorporated more easily and meaningfully into test equations in which the growth term is the growth of total earnings. But this can wait. For present purposes the thing to be stressed is simply

[22]The above relation between earnings per share and dividends plus capital gains also means that there will be a systematic relation between retained earnings and capital gains. The "marginal" relation is easy to see and is always precisely one for one, regardless of growth or financial policy. That is, taking a dollar away from dividends and adding it to retained earnings (all other things equal) means an increase in capital gains of one dollar (or a reduction in capital loss of one dollar). The "average" relation is somewhat more complex. From equations 26 and 27, we can see that:

$$G_t(t) = k_r X(t) + kX(t)\,\frac{\rho^* - \rho}{\rho - k\rho^*}$$

Hence, if $\rho^* = \rho$, the total capital gain received will be exactly the same as the total retained earnings per share. For growth corporations, however, the capital gain will always be greater than the retained earnings (and there will be a capital gain of:

$$kX(t)\left[\frac{\rho^* - \rho}{\rho - k\rho^*}\right]$$

even when all earnings are paid out). For nongrowth corporations the relation between gain and retentions is reversed. Note also that the absolute difference between the total capital gain and the total retained earnings is a constant (given $\rho$, $k$, and $\rho^*$) unaffected by dividend policy. Hence the *ratio* of capital gain to retained earnings will vary directly with the payout ratio for growth corporations (and vice versa, for nongrowth corporations). This means, among other things, that it is dangerous to attempt to draw inferences about the relative growth potential or relative managerial efficiency of corporations solely on the basis of the ratio of capital gains to retained earnings (cf. Harkavy [12, esp. pp. 289–94]).

that two approaches, properly carried through, are in no sense *opposing* views of the valuation process, but rather equivalent views, with the choice between them largely a matter of taste and convenience.

# IV. The Effects of Dividend Policy under Uncertainty

## *Uncertainty and the General Theory of Valuation*

In turning now from the ideal world of certainty to one of uncertainty, our first step, alas, must be to jettison the fundamental valuation principle as given, say, in our equation 3:

$$V(t) = \frac{1}{1 + \rho(t)} [D(t) + n(t)\, p(t + 1)]$$

and from which the irrelevance proposition as well as all the subsequent valuation formulas in Sections II and III were derived. For the terms in the brackets can no longer be regarded as given numbers, but must be recognized as "random variables" from the point of view of the investor as of the start of period $t$. Nor is it at all clear what meaning can be attached to the discount factor, $1/[1 + \rho(t)]$, since what is being discounted is not a given return but at best only a probability distribution of possible returns. We can of course delude ourselves into thinking that we are preserving equation 3 by the simple and popular expedient of drawing a bar over each term and referring to it thereafter as the mathematical expectation of the random variable. But except for the trivial case of universal linear utility functions, we know that $V(t)$ would also be affected, and materially so, by the higher order moments of the distribution of returns. Hence, there is no reason to believe that the discount factor for expected values, $1/[1 + \rho(t)]$, would in fact be the same for any two firms chosen arbitrarily, not to mention that the expected values themselves may well be different for different investors.

All this is not to say, of course, that there are insuperable difficulties in the way of developing a testable theory of rational market valuation under uncertainty.[23] On the contrary, our investigations of the problem

[23]Nor does it mean that all the previous certainty analysis has no relevance whatever in the presence of uncertainty. There are many issues, such as those discussed in Sections I and II, that really relate only to what has been called the pure "futurity" component in valuation. Here, the valuation formulas can still be extremely useful in maintaining the internal consistency of the reasoning and in suggesting (or criticizing) empirical tests of certain classes of hypotheses about valuation, even though the formulas themselves cannot be used to grind out precise numerical values for specific real-world shares.

to date have convinced us that it is indeed possible to construct such a theory—though the construction, as can well be imagined, is a fairly complex and space-consuming task. Fortunately, however, this task need not be undertaken in this paper, which is concerned primarily with the effects of dividend policy on market valuation. For even without a full-fledged theory of what *does* determine market value under uncertainty, we can show that dividend policy, at least, is *not* one of the determinants. To establish this particular generalization of the previous certainty results, we need only invoke a corresponding generalization of the original postulate of rational behavior to allow for the fact that under uncertainty, choices depend on expectations as well as tastes.

## *"Imputed Rationality" and "Symmetric Market Rationality"*

This generalization can be formulated in two steps, as follows: First, we shall say that an individual trader "imputes rationality to the market" or satisfies the postulate of "imputed rationality" if, in forming expectations he assumes that every other trader in the market (1) is rational in the previous sense of preferring more wealth to less, regardless of the form an increment in wealth may take, and (2) imputes rationality to all other traders. Second, we shall say that a market as a whole satisfies the postulate of "symmetric market rationality" if every trader both behaves rationally and imputes rationality to the market.[24]

Notice that this postulate of symmetric market rationality differs from the usual postulate of rational behavior in several important respects. In the first place, the new postulate covers not only the choice behavior of individuals but also their expectations of the choice behavior of others. Second, the postulate is a statement about the market as a whole and not just about individual behavior. Finally, though by no means least, symmetric market rationality cannot be deduced from individual rational behavior in the usual sense, since that sense does not imply imputing rationality to others. It may in fact imply a choice behavior inconsistent with imputed ratonality unless the individual actually believes the market to be symmetrically rational. For if an ordinary rational investor had good reason to believe that other investors would

[24] We offer the term "symmetric market rationality" with considerable diffidence and only after having been assured by game theorists that there is no accepted term for this concept in the literature of that subject even though the postulate itself (or close parallels to it) does appear frequently. In the literature of economics a closely related, but not exact counterpart is Muth's "hypothesis of rational expectations" [18]. Among the more euphonic, though we feel somewhat less revealing, alternatives that have been suggested to us are "putative rationality" (by T. J. Koopmans), "birationality" (by G. L. Thompson), "empathetic rationality" (by Andrea Modigliani), and "panrationality" (by A. Ando).

not behave rationally, then it might well be rational for him to adopt a strategy he would otherwise have rejected as irrational. Our postulate thus rules out, among other things, the possibility of speculative "bubbles," wherein an individually rational investor buys a security he knows to be overpriced (i.e., too expensive in relation to its expected *long-run* return to be attractive as a permanent addition to his portfolio) in the expectation that he can resell it at a still more inflated price before the bubble bursts.[25]

## *The Irrelevance of Dividend Policy despite Uncertainty*

In Section I, we were able to show that, given a firm's investment policy, its dividend policy was irrelevant to its current market valuation. We shall now show that this fundamental conclusion need not be modified merely because of the presence of uncertainty about the future course of profits, investment, or dividends (assuming again, as we have throughout, that investment policy can be regarded as separable from dividend policy). To see that uncertainty about these elements changes nothing essential, consider a case in which current investors believe that the future streams of total earnings and total investment, whatever actual values they may assume at different points in time, will be identical for two firms, 1 and 2.[26] Suppose further, provisionally, that the same is believed to be true of future total dividend payments from period 1 on, so

[25]We recognize, of course, that such speculative bubbles have actually arisen in the past (and will probably continue to do so in the future), so that our postulate can certainly not be taken to be of universal applicability. We feel, however, that it is also not of universal inapplicability, since from our observation, speculative bubbles, though well publicized when they occur, do not seem to us to be a dominant, or even a fundamental, feature of actual market behavior under uncertainty. That is, we would be prepared to argue that as a rule and on the average, markets do not behave in ways which do not obviously contradict the postulate, so that the postulate may still be useful, at least as a first approximation, for the analysis of long-run tendencies in organized capital markets. Needless to say, whether our confidence in the postulate is justified is something that will have to be determined by empirical tests of its implications (such as, of course, the irrelevance of dividend policy).

[26]The assumption of two identical firms is introduced for convenience of exposition only, since it usually is easier to see the implications of rationality when there is an explicit arbitrage mechanism—in this case, switches between the shares of the two firms. The assumption, however, is not necessary; and we can, if we like, think of the two firms as really corresponding to two states of the same firm for an investor performing a series of "mental experiments" on the subject of dividend policy.

that the only way in which the two firms differ is possibly with respect to the prospective dividend in the current period, period 0. In terms of previous notation, we are thus assuming that:

$$\widetilde{X}_1(t) = \widetilde{X}_2(t) \qquad t = 0 \ldots \infty$$
$$\widetilde{I}_1(t) = \widetilde{I}_2(t) \qquad t = 0 \ldots \infty$$
$$\widetilde{D}_1(t) = \widetilde{D}_2(t) \qquad t = 1 \ldots \infty$$

the subscripts indicating the firms and the tildes being added to the variables to indicate that these are to be regarded from the standpoint of current period, not as known numbers but as numbers that will be drawn in the future from the appropriate probability distributions. We may now ask: What will be the return, $\widetilde{R}_1(0)$, to the current shareholders in firm 1 during the current period? Clearly, it will be:

$$\widetilde{R}_1(0) = \widetilde{D}_1(0) + \widetilde{V}_1(1) - \widetilde{m}_1(1)\,\widetilde{p}_1(1) \tag{28}$$

But the relation between $\widetilde{D}_1(0)$ and $\widetilde{m}_1(1)\widetilde{p}_1(1)$ is necessarily still given by equation 4, which is merely an accounting identity, so that we can write:

$$\widetilde{m}_1(1)\,\widetilde{p}_1(1) = \widetilde{I}_1(0) - [\widetilde{X}_1(0) - \widetilde{D}_1(0)] \tag{29}$$

and, on substituting in equation 28, we obtain:

$$\widetilde{R}_1(0) = \widetilde{X}_1(0) - \widetilde{I}_1(0) + \widetilde{V}_1(1) \tag{30}$$

for firm 1. By an exactly parallel process, we can obtain an equivalent expression for $\widetilde{R}_2(0)$.

Let us now compare $\widetilde{R}_1(0)$ with $\widetilde{R}_2(0)$. Note first that by assumption, $\widetilde{X}_1(0) = \widetilde{X}_2(0)$, and $\widetilde{I}_1(0) = \widetilde{I}_2(0)$. Furthermore, with symmetric market rationality the terminal values $\widetilde{V}_i(1)$ can depend only on prospective future earnings, investment, and dividends from period 1 on; and these, too, by assumption, are identical for the two companies. Thus, symmetric rationality implies that every investor must expect $\widetilde{V}_1(1) = \widetilde{V}_2(1)$ and hence finally $\widetilde{R}_1(0) = \widetilde{R}_2(0)$. But if the return to the investors is the same in the two cases, rationality requires that the two firms command the same current value, so that $V_1(0)$ must equal $V_2(0)$ regardless of any difference in dividend payments during period 0. Suppose now that we allow dividends to differ not just in period 0 but in period 1 as well, but still retain the assumption of equal $\widetilde{X}_i(t)$ and $\widetilde{I}_i(t)$ in all periods and of equal $\widetilde{D}_i(t)$ in period 2 and beyond. Clearly, the only way differences in dividends in period 1 can affect $\widetilde{R}_i(0)$ and hence $V_i(0)$ is via $\widetilde{V}_i(1)$. But by the assumption of symmetric market rationality, current investors know that as of the start of period 1 the

then investors will value the two firms rationally, and we have already shown that differences in the current dividend do not affect current value. Thus, we must have $V_1(1) = V_2(1)$—and hence, $V_1(0) = V_2(0)$—regardless of any possible difference in dividend payments during period 1. By an obvious extension of the reasoning to $\tilde{V}_i(2)$, $\tilde{V}_i(3)$, and so on, it must follow that the current valuation is unaffected by differences in dividend payments in *any* future period and thus that dividend policy is irrelevant for the determination of market prices, given investment policy.[27]

## *Dividend Policy and Leverage*

A study of the above line of proof will show it to be essentially analogous to the proof for the certainty world, in which, as we know, firms can have, in effect, only two alternative sources of investment funds: retained earnings or stock issues. In an uncertain world, however, there is the additional financing possibility of debt issues. The question naturally arises, therefore, as to whether the conclusion about irrelevance remains valid even in the presence of debt financing, particularly since there may very well be interactions between debt policy and dividend policy. The answer is that it does, and while a complete demonstration would perhaps be too tedious and repetitious at this point, we can at least readily sketch out the main outlines of how the proof proceeds. We begin, as above, by establishing the conditions from period 1 on that lead to a situation in which $\tilde{V}_1(1)$ must be brought into equality with $\tilde{V}_2(1)$, where the $V$, following the approach in our earlier paper [17], is now to be interpreted as the total market value of the firm, debt plus equity, not merely equity alone. The return to the original investors taken as a whole—and remember that any individual always has the option of buying a proportional share of both the equity and the debt—must correspondingly be broadened to allow for the interest on the debt. There will also be a corresponding broadening of the accounting identity 4 to allow, on the one hand, for the interest return and, on the other, for any debt funds used to finance the investment in whole or in part. The net result is that both the dividend component and the interest component of total earnings will cancel out, making the relevant (total) return, as

[27]We might note that the assumption of symmetric market rationality is sufficient to derive this conclusion but not strictly necessary if we are willing to weaken the irrelevance proposition to one running in terms of long-run average tendencies in the market. Individual rationality alone could conceivably bring about the latter; for over the long pull, rational investors could enforce this result by buying and holding "undervalued" securities because this would insure them higher long-run returns when eventually the prices became the same. They might, however, have a long, long wait.

before, $[X_i(0) - I_i(0) + V_i(1)]$, which is clearly independent of the current dividend. It follows, then, that the value of the firm must also therefore be independent of dividend policy, given investment policy.[28]

## *The Informational Content of Dividends*

To conclude our discussion of dividend policy under uncertainty, we might take note briefly of a common confusion about the meaning of the irrelevance proposition occasioned by the fact that in the real world a change in the dividend rate is often followed by a change in the market price (sometimes spectacularly so), Such a phenomenon would not be incompatible with irrelevance to the extent that it was merely a reflection of what might be called the "informational content" of dividends, an attribute of particular dividend payments hitherto excluded by assumption from the discussion and proofs. That is, where a firm has adopted a policy of dividend stabilization with a long-established and generally appreciated "target payout ratio," investors are likely to (and have good reason to) interpret a change in the dividend rate as a change in management's views of future profit prospects for the firm.[29] The dividend change, in other words, provides the occasion for the price change, though not its cause, the price still being solely a reflection of future earnings and growth opportunities. In any particular instance, of course, the investors might well be mistaken in placing this interpretation on the dividend change, since the management might really only be changing its payout target or possibly even attempting to "manipulate" the price. But this would involve no particular conflict with the irrelevance proposition, unless, of course, the price changes in such cases were not reversed when the unfolding of events had made clear the true nature of the situation.[30]

# V. Dividend Policy and Market Imperfections

To complete the analysis of dividend policy, the logical next step would presumably be to abandon the assumption of perfect capital mar-

[28]This same conclusion must also hold for the current market value of all the shares (and hence for the current price per share), which is equal to the total market value minus the given initially outstanding debt. Needless to say, however, the price per share and the value of the equity at *future* points in time will not be independent of dividend and debt policies in the interim.

[29]For evidence on the prevalence of dividend stabilization and target ratios, see Lintner [15].

[30]For a further discussion of the subject of the informational content of dividents, including its implications for empirical tests of the irrelevance proposition, see Modigliani and Miller [16, pp. 666–68].

kets. This is, however, a good deal easier to say than to do, principally because there is no unique set of circumstances that constitutes "imperfection." We can describe not one but a multitude of possible departures from strict perfection, singly and in combinations. Clearly, to attempt to pursue the implications of each of these would only serve to add inordinately to an already overlong discussion. We shall instead, therefore, limit ourselves in this concluding section to a few brief and general observations about imperfect markets that we hope may prove helpful to those taking up the task of extending the theory of valuation in this direction.

First, it is important to keep in mind that from the standpoint of dividend policy, what counts is not imperfection per se but only imperfection that might lead an investor to have a systematic preference as between a dollar of current dividends and a dollar of current capital gains. Where no such systematic preference is produced, we can subsume the imperfection in the (random) error term always carried along when applying propositions derived from ideal models to real-world events.

Second, even where we do find imperfections that bias individual preferences—such as the existence of brokerage fees which tend to make young "accumulators" prefer low-payout shares and retired persons lean toward "income stocks"—such imperfections are at best only necessary but not sufficient conditions for certain payout policies to command a permanent premium in the market. If, for example, the frequency distribution of corporate payout ratios happened to correspond exactly with the distribution of investor preferences for payout ratios, then the existence of these preferences would clearly lead ultimately to a situation whose implications were different in no fundamental respect from the perfect market case. Each corporation would tend to attract to itself a "clientele" consisting of those preferring its particular payout ratio, but one clientele would be entirely as good as another in terms of the valuation it would imply for the firm. Nor, of course, is it necessary for the distributions to match exactly for this result to occur. Even if there were a "shortage" of some particular payout ratio, investors would still normally have the option of achieving their particular saving objectives without paying a premium for the stocks in short supply simply by buying appropriately weighted combinations of the more plentiful payout ratios. In fact, given the great range of corporate payout ratios known to be available, this process would fail to eliminate permanent premiums and discounts only if the distribution of investor preferences were heavily concentrated at either of the extreme ends of the payout scale.[31]

[31]The above discussion should explain why, among other reasons, it would not be possible to draw any valid inference about the relative preponderance of

Of all the many market imperfections that might be detailed, the only one that would seem to be even remotely capable of producing such a concentration is the substantial advantage accorded to capital gains as compared with dividends under the personal income tax. Strong as this tax push toward capital gains may be for high-income individuals, however, it should be remembered that a substantial (and growing) fraction of total shares outstanding is currently held by investors for whom there is either no tax differential (charitable and educational institutions, foundations, pension trusts, and low-income retired individuals) or where the tax advantage is, if anything, in favor of dividends (casualty insurance companies and taxable corporations generally). Hence, again, the "clientele effect" will be at work. Furthermore, except for taxable individuals in the very top brackets, the required difference in before-tax yields to produce equal after-tax yields is not particularly striking, at least for moderate variations in the composition of returns.[32] All this is not to say, of course, that differences in yields (market values) caused by differences in payout policies should be ignored by managements or investors merely because they may be relatively small. But it may help to keep investigators from being too surprised if it turns out to be hard to measure or even to detect any premium for low-payout shares on the basis of standard statistical techniques.

Finally, we may note that since the tax differential in favor of capital gains is undoubtedly the major *systematic* imperfection in the market, one clearly cannot invoke "imperfections" to account for the difference between our irrelevance proposition and the standard view as to the role of dividend policy found in the literature of finance. For the standard view is not that low-payout companies command a premium but that, in general, they will sell at a discount![33] If such indeed were the case—and we, at least, are not prepared to concede that this has been established—then the analysis presented in this paper suggests there would

---

"accumulators" as opposed to "income" buyers or the strength of their preferences merely from the weight attaching to dividends in a simple cross-sectional regression between value and payouts (as is attempted in Clendenin [2, p. 50] or Durand [5, p. 651]).

[32]For example, if a taxpayer is subject to a marginal rate of 40 percent on dividends and half that, or 20 percent, on long-term capital gains, then a before-tax yield of 6 percent consisting of 40 percent dividends and 60 percent capital gains produces an after-tax yield of 4.32 percent. To net the same after-tax yield on a stock with 60 percent of the return in dividends and only 40 percent in capital gains would require a before-tax yield of 6.37 percent. The difference would be somewhat smaller if we allowed for the present dividend credit, though it should also be kept in mind that the tax on capital gains may be avoided entirely under present arrangements if the gains are not realized during the holder's lifetime.

[33]See, among many, many others, Gordon [8], [9]; Graham and Dodd [11, esp. chaps, xxxiv and xxxvi]; Durand [4], [5]; Hunt, Williams, and Donaldson [13, pp. 647–49]; Fisher [7]; Gordon and Shapiro [10]; Harkavy [12]; Clendenin [2]; Johnson, Shapiro, and O'Meara [14]; and Walter [19].

be only one way to account for it, namely, as the result of systematic irrationality on the part of the investing public.[34]

To say that an observed positive premium on high payouts was due to irrationality would not of course make the phenomenon any less real. But it would at least suggest the need for a certain measure of caution by long-range policy makers. For investors, however, naïve they may be when they enter the market, do sometimes learn from experience and perhaps, occasionally, even from reading articles such as this.

## References

1. BODENHORN, DIRAN. "On the Problem of Capital Budgeting," *Journal of Finance,* Vol. XIV (December, 1959), pp. 473–92.

2. CLENDENIN, JOHN. "What Do Stockholders Like?" *California Management Review,* Vol. I (Fall, 1958, pp. 47–55.

3. CLENDENIN, JOHN, and VAN CLEAVE, M. "Growth and Common Stock Values," *Journal of Finance,* Vol. IX (September, 1954), pp. 365–76.

4. DURAND, DAVID. *Bank Stock Prices and the Bank Capital Problem.* Occasional Paper No. 54. New York: National Bureau of Economic Research, 1957.

5. DURAND, DAVID. "The Cost of Capital, Corporation Finance and the Theory of Investment: Comment," *American Economic Review,* Vol. XLIX (September, 1959), pp. 639–54.

6. DURAND, DAVID. "Growth Stocks and the Petersburg Paradox," *Journal of Finance,* Vol. XII (September, 1957), pp. 348–63.

7. FISHER, G. R. "Some Factors Influencing Share Prices," *Economic Journal,* Vol. LXXI (March, 1961), pp. 121–41.

8. GORDON, MYRON J. "Corporate Saving, Investment and Share Prices," *Review of Economics and Statistics,* Vol. XLIV (February, 1962), pp. 37–51.

9. GORDON, MYRON J. "Dividends, Earnings, and Stock Prices," *Review of Economics and Statistics,* Vol. XLI (May, 1959), pp. 99–105.

10. GORDON, MYRON, J., and SHAPIRO, ELI. "Capital Equipment Analysis: The Required Rate of Profit," *Management Science,* Vol. III (October, 1956), pp. 102–10.

11. GRAHAM, BENJAMIN, and DODD, DAVID L. *Security Analysis.* 3d ed. New York: McGraw-Hill Book Co., Inc., 1951.

12. HARKAVY, OSCAR. "The Relation between Retained Earnings and Common Stock Prices for Large Listed Corporations," *Journal of Finance,* Vol. VIII (September, 1953), pp. 283–97.

---

[34]Or less plausibly, that there is a systematic tendency for external funds to be used more productively than internal funds.

13. HUNT, PEARSON; WILLIAMS, CHARLES M.; and DONALDSON, GORDON. *Basic Business Finance.* Homewood, Ill.: Richard D. Irwin, Inc., 1961.

14. JOHNSON, LYLE R.: SHAPIRO, ELI; and O'MEARA, JOSEPH, JR. "Valuation of Closely Held Stock for Federal Tax Purposes: Approach to an Objective Method," *University of Pennsylvania Law Review,* Vol. C (November, 1951), pp. 166–95.

15. LINTNER, JOHN. "Distribution of Incomes of Corporations among Dividends, Retained Earnings and Taxes," *American Economic Review,* Vol. XLVI (May, 1956), pp. 97–113.

16. MODIGLIANI, FRANCO, and MILLER, MERTON H. "The Cost of Capital, Corporation Finance and the Theory of Investment: Reply," *American Economic Review,* Vol. XLIX (September, 1959), pp. 655–69.

17. MODIGLIANI, FRANCO, and MILLER, MERTON H. "The Cost of Capital, Corporation Finance and the Theory of Investment," *American Economic Review,* Vol. XLVIII (June, 1958), pp. 261–97.

18. MUTH, JOHN F. "Rational Expectations and the Theory of Price Movements," *Econometrica* (forthcoming).

19. WALTER, JAMES E. "A Discriminant Function for Earnings-Price Ratios of Large Industrial Corporations," *Review of Economics and Statistics,* Vol. XLI (February, 1959), pp. 44–52.

20. WALTER, JAMES E. "Dividend Policies and Common Stock Prices," *Journal of Finance,* Vol. XI (March, 1956), pp. 29–41.

21. WILLIAMS, JOHN B. *The Theory of Investment Value.* Cambridge: Harvard University Press, 1938.

*Chapter* 29

# *Dividend Policy: Its Influence on the Value of the Enterprise**

By James E. Walter

THE QUESTION BEFORE the house is whether dividends are in some sense of the word weighted differently from retained earnings at the margin in the minds of marginal investors. As evidenced by the current literature on the subject, the answer is by no means self-evident.

Although the problem that confronts us can be approached in a variety of ways, our preference is to commence with net cash flows from operations and to consider the effect of additions to, and subtractions from, these flows upon stock values.[1] Not only does this starting point bypass certain measurement problems, but it also directs attention to the relevant variables in a manner that other approaches may not.

Net cash flows from operations are available for (1) the payment of interest and principal on debt or the equivalent and (2) capital expenditures and dividend payments. Operating cash flows can of course be supplemented in any period by debt or equity financing. Debt financing creates obligations to pay out cash in future periods and thereby reduces cash flows available for capital expenditures and dividends in those periods. Equity financing, in turn, diminishes the pro rata share of total cash flows available for dividends and reinvestment.

---

*Reprinted by permission from *Journal of Finance,* Vol. XVIII (May, 1963), pp. 280–91.

[1]As a point of departure, *net cash flows from operations* lie somewhere between (*a*) net cash flow and (*b*) net operating income. See, for example, Bodenhorn [1]. For an illustrative breakdown and an explanation of the manner in which net operating cash flows are derived from balance sheets and income statements, refer to chapter xi of Walter [12].

Numbers in brackets refer to publications listed at the end of this paper (p. 524).

The stockholder shares in the operating cash flows of each period to the degree that cash dividends are declared and paid, and in future cash flows insofar as they are reflected in the market price of the stock.[2] In like fashion, the purchaser of a share of stock acquires (1) a finite stream of anticipated cash dividends and (2) an anticipated market price at the end of his holding period. The market price of the stock at any time can be said to be determined by the expectations of marginal investors (as these anticipations pertain to the dividend stream and to the terminal market price) and by their system of weighting the possible outcomes for period and through time.

To focus directly upon the potential influence of variations in dividend policy in this scheme of things, it is useful, first, to draw an analogy to the stream-splitting approach to the cost of capital. Consideration is then afforded (1) the conditions under which adjustments in dividend payout exert no effect upon stock price and (2) the consequences of modifying these conditions to take account of the economic power of large corporations and other aspects of observed behavior. The final item treated in this article is that of statistical testing.

The assumptions that prevailed throughout the analysis are commonplace. One is that the satisfaction which investors derive from owning stock is wholly (or almost wholly) monetary in character. A second is that investors do the best that they can; they operate, however, in a competitive capital market and are unable to stack the results.

Corporate management, we may add, is also keenly aware of the potential impact of its actions upon stock price (if only because of stock options). Management may nonetheless be confronted with such *mixed* motivations as self-preservation and avoidance of antitrust action. The consequence is that maximization of stock price need not be the sole objective.[3]

So far as uncertainty is concerned, it is supposed that unless otherwise stated, people think whatever they think about the future. Whether this assumption is appropriate remains to be seen.

No attempt is made in this treatment of dividend policy to run the gamut from perfect foresight to generalized uncertainty. Papers by Miller and Modigliani [10] and Lintner [7], among others, have already proceeded along these lines. Rather, the intention is to show where dividends fit into the underlying analytical scheme, to spotlight certain as-

---

[2]It almost goes without saying that an existing shareholder periodically compares the objective market price with his subjective version of anticipated dividend streams and terminal prices to determine whether to hold or liquidate. In this respect, his behavior resembles that of a prospective buyer.

[3]For justification, we have only to refer to the statistics on concentration of economic power.

sumptions that underlie recent statements pertaining to the neutrality of dividend policy, and to propose extensions in the theory designed to recognize deficiencies in the perfectly competitive model.

## *Analogy to Cost of Capital*

Before the thrust shifted to dividends, the basic issue in the cost-of-capital discussion was one of dividing the stream of operating cash flows (or some reconcilable variant thereof) between debt and equity in such a manner as to maximize the market value of the enterprise. Modigliani and Miller [8], it may be remembered, dramaticized the stream-splitting aspect by drawing an analogy to the price effect of separating the whole milk into cream and skim milk. Their contention that even in the face of institutional limitations, the farmer cannot gain by splitting the milk stream was subsequently subjected to empirical testing by Durand [3] and shown to be invalid.

When dividends enter the picture, the issue becomes one of dividing the stream of operating cash flows among debt, dividends, and reinvestment in such a way as to achieve the same result. The principal difference in the character of the analysis is that it may no longer be feasible to assume that the size and shape of the stream of operating cash flows is independent of the manner in which it is subdivided.[4]

Much the same as contractual interest payments and other financial outlays, the continuation of cash dividends at their prevailing (or regular) rate can be, and commonly is, assigned a priority by management.[5] In such instances the burden of oscillations in operating cash flows is placed upon lower priority outlays, namely, capital and related expenditures, unless management is both willing and able to compensate by adjusting the level of external financing.[6] Even if management is willing to seek funds outside the firm, moreover, the uncertainties inherent in the terms under which external financing can be obtained in the future reduce the likelihood of such action in the event of operating cash de-

---

[4]Although the milk-separating analogy implies that the dimensions of the stream are unaffected by its division between debt and equity, even this need not be a fundamental difference in character. As evidenced by Donaldson [2], decisions by management to borrow or not to borrow sometimes affect growth, that is, the level of future cash flows.

[5]Cf., for example, Lintner [6], in which observed corporate behavior involves gradual adjustments of dividends to earnings and "greater reluctance to reduce than to raise dividends. . . ."

[6]The term "capital and related expenditures" refers to all outlays that affect operating cash flows over several periods. Either by reason of previous commitments or because of their importance to the continued operation of the business, certain elements of these expenditures may have priorities that equal or exceed those connected with the payment of cash dividends.

ficiencies in any period. The upshot is that current cash dividends may well be capitalized somewhat differently from anticipated future cash flows (net of current dividends, to avoid double counting).

It may be observed that the relative instability of expenditures designed to augment future cash flows shows up even in the aggregate. The change from year to year for new plant and equipment averaged 19 percent for all manufacturing corporations in the postwar period (to 1961), as compared with 9 percent for cash dividends. The maximum declines from one year to the next were 40 percent for new plant and equipment and but 2 percent for dividends.

Again, as in the case of debt versus equity, investor reactions to dividend policy changes can nullify, in whole or in part, their price effect. Whenever the stockholder is dissatisfied with the dividend payout, the balance between present and future income can be redressed by buying or selling shares of stock and perhaps by other means as well (for instance, by "lending" or "borrowing" on the same *risk* terms that cash dividends are paid). If dividends are deemed insufficient, the desired proportion of current income can be obtained by periodically selling part of the shares owned. If current income is too high, cash dividends can be used to acquire additional shares of stock.

The one thing that shareholders cannot do through their purchase and sale transactions is to negate the consequences of investment decisions by management. If, as may well be the case, investment decisions tend to be linked with dividend policy, their neglect in the analysis of dividend effects seems inappropriate.

## Conditions for No-Dividend Effect

The conditions under which changes in dividend payout have minimal influence upon stock values can now be stated. For the most part, they follow from the logics of stream splitting.

1. *Condition No. 1: The Level of Future Cash Flows from Operations (That Is, the Growth Rate) Is Independent of the Dividend Payout Policy.* In essence, this condition implies that the impact of a change in dividend payout upon operating cash flows will be *exactly* offset (or negated) by a corresponding and opposite change in supplemental (or external) financing.

For those who believe that the cost of capital is unaffected by the capital structure, either debt or equity financing is a legitimate means of neutralizing dividend policy changes. For those who believe otherwise, an increase in dividends can be offset only by the sale of equity shares. In the latter instance, then, the capital structure must also be taken as independent of the dividend payout policy.

If attention is confined to offsetting transactions in equity shares for the sake of simplicity and generality, the following result obtains: An increase in dividend payout will leave operating cash flows unchanged in the aggregate, but the share of future cash flows accruing to existing stockholders will decline, since additional stock has to be sold to finance the planned capital outlays. The existing shareholder can of course reconstitute his former pro rata position by purchasing shares in the market with his incremental dividends.

Implicit in these remarks is the presumption that the market completely capitalizes anticipated growth in operating cash flows. New shares are thus acquired at a price that returns new investors *only* the going market rate for the relevant class of risks. The present value of extraordinary returns from investment by the corporation goes to existing stockholders (or whoever was around at the time when the prospect of these returns was first recognized by the market), rather than to new shareholders.

To the degree that the anticipated level of operating cash flows, that is, the growth rate, is connected with the dividend payout for one reason or another, the market value of the firm may be conditioned by variations in dividend payout. The policy changes must of course be unexpected, and their price effect hinges at least partly upon the relation between the *internal* and *market* rates of return. If the former exceeds the latter, the present value of a dollar employed by the firm (other things being equal) will be greater than a dollar of dividends distributed and invested elsewhere. This issue was considered in my 1956 paper [11].

Condition No. 1 can readily be extended to take account of tax differentials. The amended version is that operating cash flows *net* of taxes paid thereon by shareholders are unaffected by the dividend payout. As things stand, this criterion simply does not hold; neither, it might be added, does the corresponding condition hold in the case of debt versus equity.[7]

2. *Condition No. 2: The Weights Employed Are Independent of the Dividend Payout Policy.* In other words, the discount factors or weights, that is, the ratios of indifference values between one period and the next, are invariant with respect to changes in dividend payout.

Gordon [4] argues that the weights employed must also be constant between periods and that such is unlikely to be the case under uncertainty. That is to say, looking forward from period 0, the ratios of the

[7]The price effect of tax differentials may well be less than might be supposed. For example, the marginal tax rates implied in a comparison of recent yields on tax-exempts of high quality with those on United States government securities are on the order of 15–25 percent.

indifference values between periods 0 and 1, 1 and 2, and so on, have to be all the same.

In order to evaluate this possible addition to Condition No. 2, it is pertinent to recall Condition No. 1. If the level of total operating cash flows is unaffected by the policy revision, a change in current cash dividends will alter the stockholder's stake in future cash flows. The gain or loss in current dividends will just equal the gain or loss in the present value of future cash flows (or dividends, if you wish), provided that the system of weights remains unchanged. Gordon's point is thus unacceptable because the firm has to go into the market for funds to replace those paid out in dividends and, in so doing, has to pay the market rate.

Returning to the question of the independence of the weights used from the dividend payout policy, a change in dividend payout undoubtedly disturbs the investors in that stock to some extent unless the modification was anticipated previously. Insofar as costs of one kind or another, indivisibilities, and other factors prevent the shareholders thus activated from completely reconstituting their *old* position and thereby give rise to a new and different equilibrium point, the weights employed will adjust in some measure. The role played by friction in the system is, however, well known, and there is little need to dwell upon this aspect.

More significant, perhaps, is the fact that the substitution of future cash flows for present dividends superimposes an element of market risk upon the basic uncertainty of the operating cash flow stream. As contrasted with cash dividends in which the stockholder receives a dollar for each dollar declared, there is no telling what price the shareholder will realize in the market at any given time for his stake in future cash flows.

It is of course true that the corporation would confront the same market risk if it, rather than the shareholder, were forced to enter the capital market. It is also true that realized prices may average out over a period of time. The fact remains that the firm may well be better able to adjust for—as well as to assume—this class of risk.

Whether further conditions ought to be introduced is a moot point. A recent article by John Lintner [7], for example, concludes that "generalized uncertainty" is itself sufficient to insure that shareholders "will *not* be indifferent to whether cash dividends are increased (or reduced) by substituting new equity issues for retained earnings to finance given capital budgets."

As a generalization, this conclusion is suspect, for it appears to be inconsistent with a logical extension of Lintner's earlier analysis under idealized uncertainty. It is difficult to see why two or two million investors cannot be indifferent at a given price for a variety of reasons. If so, generalized uncertainty can—but perhaps need not—produce the same *surface* result as idealized uncertainty.[8]

In any event, Condition No. 2 is sufficiently broad to embrace the foregoing aspect of the uncertainty issue. To the degree that Lintner's proposition is valid, generalized uncertainty produces an effect that resembles that associated with the presence of costs and frictions in the system.

## *Imperfect Competition, Regulated Enterprise, and Noneconomic Considerations*

That the conditions for no-dividend effect fail to hold in certain important respects has already been established here and elsewhere. At this stage, there is little point in discussing further the consequences of differences in tax treatment, new-issue and other costs associated with external financing, and uncertainty itself (although the *on balance* effect will be considered toward the end of the paper). It is nonetheless relevant, in view of their neglect in the literature, to extend the examination of dividend effects beyond the oft-used competitive model that presupposes rational behavior in the traditional economic sense and to consider the influence of such things as management leeway, economic slack, and intramarginal pricing policies. The following remarks represent a preliminary effort in this direction.

In the bulk of corporations with which it is possible to deal statistically, management has considerable leeway in decision making. Their histories of earnings and dividends, not to mention their economic power, are such that their survival in the foreseeable future seemingly does not hinge upon single modes of behavior. The presence of generalized uncertainty implies, moreover, that there is often no best *visible* course of action.

The frequently observed association between dividend payout policy, capital structure, and rate of growth is a useful case in point; the survival of the corporation ordinarily does not depend, in the short run at least, upon any specific rate of growth. The prime considerations affecting growth, apart from profit opportunities, are (1) the willingness of corporations to go into the public marketplace for additional funds and (2) their attitude toward dividends (including their willingness to return unneeded funds to the investors).

For firms that are reluctant to get involved in external financing (and

---

[8]To add to the confusion, moreover, see note 35 in Lintner [7].

there appear to be many), then, the burden of expansion rests upon residual internal sources, that is, operating cash flows *less* cash dividends and debt servicing *net* of additions to debt. Decisions to increase or decrease dividends thus condition the value of the enterprise as long as the returns on new investments differ from the market rate.

The sword cuts both ways. Wherever the available investment opportunities are unable to earn their keep, the specter of liquidating dividends or repurchase of shares or debt retirement arises. If there is no debt outstanding, and if the repurchase of shares is not contemplated, the burden of liquidation falls upon dividend payout.

The fact that many of the corporations that normally constitute the statistical samples used in testing dividend hypotheses are characterized by negatively sloping demand curves is also worth noting. Suppose, for instance, that such firms do not charge what the traffic will bear in the sense of equating discounted marginal revenues with discontinued marginal costs. Instead, let us assume that they employ some sort of a full-cost pricing policy.

Insofar as these companies assign priorities to the payment of dividends and regard them as a cost (that is, as an obligation of the firm that should be met if possible), the dividend payout policy will affect stock prices. Decisions to alter the dividend payout under the full-costing approach will, sooner or later, be reflected in product prices (although the impact may be barely visible to the naked eye). If the new prices more nearly approach optimum prices from a profit-maximization standpoint, the effect is to increase stock values. If the reverse obtains, values diminish.

The foregoing consideration may be especially significant in the case of regulated companies whose prices are set by edict rather than by competitive forces. The dividends that regulatory bodies explicitly or implicitly permit to be incorporated in the elements that determine product or service prices will be reflected in stock values.

Closely connected with, but extending beyond, the matter of product or service pricing is the question of operating slack. Our experience has been that most profitable firms are able in some measure to curtail their nonoperating and operating outlays without interfering with future cash flows. To the extent that a change in dividend payout policy conditions the amount of slack in the system, the value of the firm is modified by such changes.

The impact of a revision in dividend policy need not show up immediately; it may await a softness in operating cash flows. As mentioned previously, Lintner [6] and others cite evidence that some fraction of cash dividends is commonly placed well up on the priority scale. The upshot is that managements' reactions to unanticipated reductions in operating cash flows may lead not only to the adjustment of lower priority outlays but also to the elimination of slack from the system before dividend payout policies (once established) are altered.

In summary, it is not our purpose to overemphasize the importance of the foregoing extension of the competitive model. The point is simply that hypothesis building in this area has barely begun to scratch the surface. With this in mind, let us turn to the important matter of statistical testing.

## *Statistical Testing*

The woods are currently replete with statistical analyses designed to demonstrate the significance (or nonsignificance) of the diverse factors that may influence stock prices. While it is not our aim to add further to the mounting pile, it is meaningful to mention certain problems of a statistical nature, referred to in the recent literature, that have a bearing on the testing of most hypotheses and, in particular, on the testing of an imperfectly competitive model. Specifically, the comments that follow focus upon the notion of a random variable and collinearity.

In their 1958 article [8], Modigliani and Miller alluded to the peril of relying upon "a single year's profits as a measure of expected profits." Later [9], they argued, as have others, that investors may accept current dividends as an indirect measure of profit expectations.

The difficulties inherent in the use of a random variable to reveal expectations are well known. The realized value of a random variable in any period is ordinarily but one of several values that might have obtained; it may bear little relation, in any visible sense of the word, to the underlying expectation. With this in mind, recent studies have tended to employ averages of one kind or another for the earnings variable. Kolin [5], using an exponential weighting system, has found earnings thus measured to be superior to current dividends in explaining the relative valuation of stocks.

Notwithstanding the fact that current dividends test out more significantly than current earnings, it is important to remember that they, too, are random variables. There is on the surface (apart from their relative stability) little more to recommend current dividends as a measure of expected dividends than there is to presuppose that current earnings adequately reflect anticipated earnings.

Looking to Lintner's earlier work [6], in which dividends were said to adjust gradually to a target payout ratio, an interesting and relevant reversal of the information-content proposition comes to mind. It is entirely possible (as well as quite reasonable) for some weighted average of earnings to be a good surrogate for dividend expectations. In other words, the improved results obtained by Kolin [5] may well be entirely consistent with the *dividend* hypothesis.

In a subsequent piece [10], Miller and Modigliani remarked upon the omission of relevant variables. Pointing a critical finger at certain studies (one of mine and two of Durand were cited!), they stipulated that "no general prediction is made (or can be made) by the theory [i.e., theirs] about what will happen to the dividend coefficient if the crucial growth term is omitted."[9] Except by oblique footnote reference to Gordon's work, however, they neglected to add that specification of the dividend coefficient may be difficult even if a growth term is included.

The issue in question is *collinearity*. In his analysis of a linear function that includes both dividends and earnings, Gordon [4] pointed to the instability present in the coefficients whenever a strong correlation existed between two explanatory variables. His finding was: "They [i.e., the coefficients] vary over a very wide range and they cannot be used to make reliable estimates on the variation in share price with each variable." Kolin [5], in turn, referred to the danger of a "severe loss of accuracy due to near singularity of the correlation matrix of independent variables that would occur if the two highly collinear variables were present in the same regression." His concern was with the stochastic properties that might be introduced by computer programs that treat "all digits of the words that are input to the inversion program as error free digits."

It follows that the correlation between dividend payout and growth (that is, the level of future cash flows), which seems likely to exist in many instances, contributes to the difficulty of interpreting results obtained from regression analyses. At the extreme, as Miller and Modigliani [10] affirmed, there may be "no way to distinguish between the effects of dividend policy and investment policy."

Other pitfalls to statistical testing readily come to mind. Perhaps the most significant (in the context of this paper) is the character of the sample used in relation to the hypothesis being tested. More specifically, it seems incongruous to utilize samples drawn from the universe of either regulated monopolies or very large corporations to test competitive behavior.

## *Conclusions*

The implication of the foregoing treatment is that the choice of dividend policies almost always affects the value of the enterprise. The general conditions for neutrality are simply not satisfied in the world as

[9]Actually, my study should not be castigated on this score, for it incorporated variables that measure both growth and internal rate of return.

we know it. The dimensions of the cash flow stream (both before and after account is taken of taxes imposed on recipients of dividends and capital gains) are conditioned by dividend payout policy; efforts by investors to negate the effects of policy changes are frequently of limited avail; and so on.

In the real world (again, as we know it), it is insufficient to contemplate the effects of dividends under perfectly (or even purely) competitive circumstances. The fact that a great many firms exercise some control over their own destinies deserves to be recognized. Once the possibility of imperfections is admitted, the potential association between dividends and the level of future cash flows, among other things, becomes clear.

Standard objections to dividend neutrality, that is, differences in tax treatment and costs of external financing, ordinarily favor the retention of earnings. Interdependence between dividend payout policy and capital outlays, on the other hand, can work either way; it all depends on the profitability of the enterprise.

Statistical analyses designed to support the "pure earnings" hypothesis—or any other hypothesis, for that matter—remain ambiguous. For one thing, uncertainties exist as to precisely what is being measured. For another, the closer the linkage between dividend policy and dimensions of the total stream, the less meaningful are the coefficients attached to each independent variable.

Be that as it may, we are not opposed to statistical analyses. What we do say, however, is that judgment must ultimately rest on the power of the theory generated.

## References

1. BODENHORN, DIRAN. "On the Problem of Capital Budgeting," *Journal of Finance,* Vol. XIV (December, 1959), pp. 473–92.
2. DONALDSON, GORDON. *Corporate Debt Capacity.* Boston: Division of Research, Harvard Business School, 1961.
3. DURAND, DAVID. "The Cost of Capital in an Imperfect Market: A Reply to Modigliani and Miller," *American Economic Review,* Vol. XLIX (June, 1959).
4. GORDON, MYRON J. *The Investment, Financing, and Valuation of the Corporation.* Homewood, Ill.: Richard D. Irwin, Inc., 1962.
5. KOLIN, MARSHAL. "The Relative Price of Corporate Equity. Boston: Harvard Business School, 1963.
6. LINTNER, JOHN. "Distribution of Incomes of Corporations among Dividends, Retained Earnings and Taxes," *American Economic Review,* Vol. XLVI (May, 1956) pp. 97–113.

7. LINTNER, JOHN. "Dividends, Earnings, Leverage, Stock Prices and the Supply of Capital to Corporations," *Review of Economics and Statistics,* Vol. XLIV (August, 1962), pp. 243–70.

8. MODIGLIANI, FRANCO, and MILLER, MERTON H. "The Cost of Capital, Corporation Finance and the Theory of Investment," *American Economic Review,* Vol. XLVIII (June, 1958), pp. 261–97.

9. MODIGLIANI, FRANCO, and MILLER, MERTON H. "The Cost of Capital, Corporation Finance and the Theory of Investment: Reply," *American Economic Review,* Vol. XLIX (September, 1959), pp. 655–69.

10. MILLER, MERTON H., and MODIGLIANI, FRANCO. "Dividend Policy, Growth, and the Valuation of Shares," *Journal of Business,* Vol. XXXIV (October, 1961), pp. 411–33.

11. WALTER, JAMES E. "Dividend Policies and Common Stock Prices," *Journal of Finance,* Vol. XI (March, 1956), pp. 29–41.

12. WALTER, JAMES E. *The Investment Process* (Boston: Harvard Business School, 1962), chap. xi.

*Chapter* 30

# *Optimal Investment and Financing Policy**

By Myron J. Gordon

IN TWO PAPERS[1] AND IN a recent book,[2] I have presented theory and evidence which lead to the conclusion that a corporation's share price (or its cost of capital) is not independent of the dividend rate. As you may know, MM (Modigliani and Miller) have the opposite view, and they argued their position at some length in a recent paper.[3] Moreover, the tone of their paper made it clear that they saw no reasonable basis on which their conclusion could be questioned. Since they were so sure of their conclusion, it would seem advisable for me to review carefully my thinking on the subject.

## I

Let us begin by examining MM's fundamental proof that the price of a share is independent of its dividend. They defined the value of a share at $t = 0$ as the present value of (1) the dividend it will pay at

*Reprinted by permission from *Journal of Finance,* Vol. XVIII (May, 1963), pp. 264–72.

[1]"Dividends, Earnings, and Stock Prices," *Review of Economics and Statistics,* Vol. XLI (May, 1959), pp. 99–105; "The Savings, Investment and Valuation of the Corporation," *ibid.,* Vol. XLIV (February, 1962), pp. 37–51.

[2]*The Investment, Financing, and Valuation of the Corporation* (Homewood, Ill.: Richard D. Irwin, Inc., 1962).

[3]Merton H. Miller and Franco Modigliani, "Dividend Policy, Growth, and the Valuation of Shares," *Journal of Business,* Vol. XXXIV (October, 1961), pp. 411–33.

the end of the first period, $D_1$, plus (2) the ex-dividend price of the share at the end of the period, $P_1$:

$$P_0 = \frac{1}{1 + k} [D_1 + P_1] \tag{1}$$

They then asked what would happen if the corporation, say, raised its dividend but kept its investment for the period constant by selling the additional number of shares needed to offset the funds lost by the dividend increase. They demonstrated that the ex-dividend price of the stock at the end of the period would go down by exactly the same amount as the increase in the dividend. Since the sum $D_1 + P_1$ remains the same, $P_0$ is unchanged by the change in the dividend.

I shall not review their proof of the theorem in detail because I find nothing wrong with it under the assumption they made that the future is certain. However, after proving the theorem a number of times under different conditions, they withdrew the assumption of certainty and made the dramatic announcement, "our first step, alas, must be to jettison the fundamental valuation equation."[4] Under uncertainty, they continued, it is not "at all clear what meaning can be attached to the discount factor. . . ."[5] The implication which they made explicit in discussing my work is that under uncertainty, we cannot represent investors as using discount rates to arrive at the present value of an expectation of future receipts.

It would seem that all is lost. But no! On the very next page, we are told that their "fundamental conclusion need not be modified merely because of the presence of uncertainty about the future course of profits, investments, or dividends. . . ."[6] By virtue of the postulates of "imputed rationality" and "symmetric market rationality," it remains true that "dividend policy is irrelevant for the determination of market prices."[7]

Their paper continued with a discussion of market imperfections, in which they note that the most important one, the capital gains tax, should create a preference for low payout rates. They concede that it may nevertheless be true that high payout rates sell at a premium, but they found ". . . only one way to account for it, namely, as a result of systematic irrationality on the part of the investing public." They concluded with the hope that ". . . investors, however naïve they may be when they enter the market, do sometimes learn from experience and perhaps, occasionally even from reading articles such as this."[8]

---

[4] *Ibid.*, p. 426.
[5] *Ibid.*, p. 427.
[6] *Ibid.*, p. 428.
[7] *Ibid.*, p. 429.
[8] *Ibid.*, p. 432.

It would seem that under uncertainty, they might have been less sure of their conclusion for two reasons. First, under uncertainty an invester need not be indifferent as to the distribution of the one-period gain on a share between the dividend and price appreciation. Since price appreciation is highly uncertain, an investor may prefer the expectation of a \$5.00 dividend and a \$50 price to a zero dividend and a \$55 price without being irrational. Second, the expectation of a stock issue at $t = 1$ may have a depressing influence on the price at $t = 0$. What MM did was both change the dividend and change the number of new shares issued. Can we be so sure that the price of a share will not change when these two events take place?

## II

Let us turn now to the proof of the MM position on the dividend rate that I presented in my *RES* paper and book. The reasons for presenting this proof will be evident shortly. Consider a corporation that earned $Y_0$ in the period ending at $t = 0$ and paid it all out in dividends. Further, assume that the corporation is expected to continue paying all earnings in dividends and to engage in no outside financing. Under these assumptions the company is expected to earn and pay $Y_0$ in every future period. If the rate of return on investment that investors require on the share is $k$, we may represent the valuation of the share as follows:

$$P_0 = \frac{Y_0}{(1+k)^1} + \frac{Y_0}{(1+k)^2} + \frac{Y_0}{(1+k)^3} + \dots + \frac{Y_0}{(1+k)^t} + \dots \quad (2)$$

We may also say that $k$ is the discount rate that equates the dividend expectation of $Y_0$ in perpetuity with the price $P_0$.

Next, let the corporation announce at $t = 0$ that it will retain and invest $Y_1 = Y_0$ during $t = 1$ and that it expects to earn a rate of return of $k = Y_0/P_0$ on the investment. In each subsequent period, it will pay all earnings out in dividends. Share price is now given by the expression:

$$P_0 = \frac{0}{(1+k)^1} + \frac{Y_0 + kY_0}{(1+k)^2} + \frac{Y_0 + kY_0}{(1+k)^3} + \dots + \frac{Y_0 + kY_0}{(1+k)^t} \quad (3)$$

Notice that the numerator of the first term on the right side is zero. It is the dividend and not the earnings in the period, since the investor is correctly represented as using the dividend expectation in arriving at $P_0$. If he were represented as looking at the earnings expectation, then as Bodenhorn[9] noted, he would be double-counting the first period's earnings.

[9]Diran Bodenhorn, "On the Problem of Capital Budgeting," *Journal of Finance,* Vol. XIV (December, 1959), pp. 473–92.

It is evident that as a result of the corporation's decision, the investor gives up $Y_0$ at the end of $t = 1$ and receives, in its place, $kY_0$ in perpetuity. The distribution of dividends over time has been changed. It is also evident that $kY_0$ in perpetuity discounted at $k$ is exactly equal to $Y_0$. Hence, $P_0$ is unchanged, and the change in the distribution over time of the dividends had no influence on share price. In general, the corporation can be expected to retain and invest any fraction of the income in any period without share price being changed as a consequence, so long as $r$, the return on investment, is equal to $k$. If $r > k$ for any investment, $P_0$ will be increased, but the reason is the profitability of investment and not the change in the time distribution of dividends.

Assume now that when the corporation makes the announcement which changes the dividend expectation from the one given by equation 2 to the one given by equation 3, investors raise the discount rate from $k$ to $k'$. For the moment, let us not wonder why the discount rate is raised from $k$ to $k'$, i.e., why the rate of return investors require on the share is raised as a consequence of the above change in the dividend expectation. If this takes place, equation 3 becomes:

$$P_0' = \frac{0}{(1+k')^1} + \frac{Y_0+kY_0}{(1+k')^2} + \frac{Y_0+kY_0}{(1+k')^3} + \ldots + \frac{Y_0+kY_0}{(1+k')^4} + \ldots \quad (3a)$$

It is clear that with $k' > k$, $P_0' < P_0$.

Let us review what happened. The dividend policy changed: The near dividend was reduced, and the distant dividends were raised. This caused a rise in the discount rate, and the result was a fall in the price of the share. I therefore say that the change in dividend policy changed the share's price.

In response to this argument, MM stated that I fell into "the typical confounding of dividend policy with investment policy."[10] I do not understand their reasoning. It is well known that when the rate of return on investment is set equal to the discount rate, changing the level of investment has no influence on share price. By this means, I neutralized the profitability of investment. It seems to me perfectly clear that I did not confound investment and dividend policy; I changed the discount rate. Share price changed with the dividend rate in the above example because the discount rate was changed. The issue, therefore, is whether the behavior of investors under uncertainty is correctly represented by a model in which the discount rate that equates a dividend expectation with its price is a function of the dividend rate.

I cannot categorically state that $k$ is a function of the rate of growth in the dividend, i.e., the dividend rate, but I can present some theoretical considerations and empirical evidence in support of the theorem. It

[10]Miller and Modigliani, *op. cit.*, p. 425.

seems plausible that (1) investors have an aversion to risk or uncertainty; and (2), given the riskiness of a corporation, the uncertainty of a dividend it is expected to pay increases with the time in the future of the dividend. It follows from these two propositions that an investor may be represented as discounting the dividend expected in period $t$ at a rate of $k_t$, with $k_t$ not independent of $t$. Furthermore, if aversion to risk is large enough and/or risk increases rapidly enough with time, $k_t$ increases with $t$.

It is therefore possible, though not certain, that investor behavior is correctly approximated by the statement that in arriving at the value of a dividend expectation, they discount it at the rates $k_t$ $t = 1, 2 \ldots,$ with $k_t > k_{t-1}$. In this event the single discount rate we use in stock value models is an increasing function of the rate of growth in the dividend. In short, dividend policy influences share price. To illustrate the conclusion, let us rewrite equation 2:

$$P_0 = \frac{Y_0}{(1+k_1)^1} + \frac{Y_0}{(1+k_2)^2} + \frac{Y_0}{(1+k_3)^3} + \ldots \frac{Y_0}{(1+k_t)^t} + \ldots \quad (4)$$

We now look on the $k$ of equation 2 as an average of the $k_t$ of equation 4 such that if the entire dividend expectation is discounted at this single rate, it results in the same share price. The discount rate $k$ is an average of the $k_t$ with $Y_0$, the weight assigned to each item.

Once again, let the corporation retain $Y_1 = Y_0$ and invest it to earn $kY_0$ per period in perpetuity. Using the sequence of discount rates, $k_t$, the same as that appearing in equation 4, the valuation of the new dividend expectation becomes:

$$P_0' = \frac{0}{(1+k_1)^1} + \frac{Y_0+kY_0}{(1+k_2)^2} + \frac{Y_0+kY_0}{(1+k_3)^3} + \ldots + \frac{Y_0=kY_0}{(1+k_t)^t} + \ldots \quad (5)$$

The shareholder gives up $Y_0$ and gets $kY_0$ in perpetuity; but the latter is now discounted at the rates $k_t$, $t = 2 \rightarrow \infty$, and it can be shown that $kY_0$ so discounted is less than $Y_0$. Hence, $P_0' < P_0$, and dividend policy influences share price. It also can be shown that $k'$, the new average of the same $k_t$, is greater than $k$. In general, reducing the near dividends and raising the distant dividends (lowering the dividend rate) changes the weights of the $k_t$ and raises their average.

## III

To summarize the theoretical part of my argument, I started with two assumptions: (1) aversion to risk and (2) increase in the uncertainty of a receipt with its time in the future. From these assumptions,

I proceeded by deductive argument to the proposition that the single discount rate an investor is represented as using to value a share's dividend expectation is an increasing function of the rate of growth in the dividend. The consequence of the theorem is that dividend policy per se influences the value of a share. The assumptions have enough intuitive merit, I believe, that the theorem may in fact be true.

Before proceeding to the empirical evidence, I shall like to comment briefly on two other criticisms MM directed at my argument. First, they differentiated between my "purely subjective discount rate and the objective market-given yields" and stated: "To attempt to derive valuation formulas from these purely subjective discount factors involves, of course, an error. . . ."[11] My assumptions and empirical results may be questioned, but where is the error? Does the theorem fail to follow from the assumptions? Why, as they suggest, is it logically impossible for an investor to arrive at the value of a share by estimating its future dividends and discounting the series at a rate appropriate to its uncertainty?

The following MM criticism of my argument I find even more confusing. They stated: "Indeed if they [investors] valued shares according to the Gordon approach and thus paid a premium for higher payout ratios, then holders of the low payout shares would actually realize consistently higher returns on their investment over any stated interval of time."[12] Under this reasoning, two shares cannot sell at different yields regardless of how much they differ in risk because the holders of the higher yield share would "actually realize consistently higher returns over any stated interval of time." Do MM deny that investors have an aversion to risk?

To test the theorem empirically, I proceeded as follows. The valuation of a share may be represented by the expression:

$$P_0 = \int_0^\infty D_t e^{-kt} dt \qquad (6)$$

where $D_t$ is the dividend expected in period $t$ and $k$ is an operator on the $D_t$ that reduces them to their present value to the investor. Equation 6 is a perfectly general statement that is not open to question. However, to use the equation in empirical work, we must specify how investors arrive at $D_t$ from observable variables. For this, I assumed that investors expect a corporation will (1) retain the fraction $b$ of its income in each future period; (2) earn a rate of return, $r$, on the common equity investment in each future period; (3) maintain the existing debt-equity ratio; and (4) undertake no new outside equity financing. Under

[11] *Ibid.*, p. 424.
[12] *Ibid.*, p. 425.

the above assumptions the current dividend is $D_0 = (1 - b)Y_0$, and its rate of growth is $br$. Further, the entire dividend expectation is represented by these two variables, and equation 6 is equal to:

$$P_0 = \frac{(1 - b)\ Y_0}{k - br} \tag{7}$$

The above four assumptions may be criticized as being too great a simplification of reality. I have admitted their limitations, and I welcome improvement, but I know of no other empirical model that contains as rich and accurate a statement of the dividend expectation provided by a share. Most empirical work, including the published work of MM, represents the investor as expecting that the corporation will pay all earnings in dividends and engage in no outside financing. They therefore also ignore the influence of the profitability of investment on share price. This model incorporates a prediction of the corporation's investment and rate of return on the investment in each future period. The expected investment in period $t$ is the fraction $b$ of the period's income plus the leverage on the retention that maintains the corporation's existing debt-equity ratio. Further, the influence of this retention and borrowing on the dividend expectation is incorporated in the model.

The interesting thing about the model as it stands is that it is consistent with the MM position and should provoke no objection. To see this, let us make their assumption that $k$ is independent of $b$; and to neutralize the profitability of investment, let $r = k$. In this model dividend policy is represented by $b$, the retention rate, so that if we take the derivative of $P_0$ with respect to $b$, we establish the relation between share price and the dividend rate. We find that $\delta P/\delta b = 0$. The value of a share is independent of the dividend rate—exactly what MM argue.

One can use this model in empirical work under the assumption that $k$ is independent of $br$. I did and obtained poor results. Since I found good theoretical grounds for believing that $k$ is an increasing function of $br$, it would seem reasonable to explore the hypothesis, and that is what I did. If $k$ is an increasing function of $br$, we can write equation 7 as

$$P_0 = A_0 [\ (1 - b)\ Y_0]\ [1 + br]^{\alpha_2} \tag{8}$$

In this expression, $A_0$ represents the influence of all variables other than the current dividend, $(1 - b)Y_0$, and its rate of growth, $br$. When $b = \delta$, $P_0$ is the multiple $A_0$ of $Y_0$. As $br$ increases, the dividend, $(1 - b)\ Y_0$, falls and $br$ rises, the former lowering price and the latter raising price. Whether $P_0$ rises or falls with $b$ depends on $r$, the profitability of investment, and on $\alpha_2$. The expression $\alpha_2$ may be looked on as how much investors are willing to pay for growth. Its value depends on how fast the $k_t$ rise with $t$, that is, on how fast uncertainty increases with time and on the degree of investor aversion to risk.

It should be noted that equation 8 is not merely a stock value model. Given the investor's valuation of a share, $A_0$ and $\alpha_2$, and given the profitability of investment, $r$, the model may be used to find the retention rate (equal to the investment rate under our assumptions) that maximizes the value of a share. Extensions of the model developed elsewhere[13] allow its use to find the investment and the financing, retention, debt, and new equity that maximize share price.

The empirical results I obtained with the above model have been published in detail,[14] and all I shall say here is that they are very good. Although the results compare favorably with earlier work, they are not good enough to settle the question. MM[15] and Benishay[16] have pointed out that my independent variables are not free of error, and the consequence is that the parameter estimates have a downward basis. Kolin[17] has reported that his empirical work revealed no relation between dividend policy and share price. As things stand, I should say that the influence of dividend policy on share price is a question that requires further study. The axiomatic basis of the MM position is certainly not so powerful as to force the acceptance of their conclusions.

## IV

I should like to close with a brief comment on the two major camps that are emerging with respect to the theory of corporation finance. In both camps, optimal policy is taken as the policy that maximizes the value of the corporation. Although corporations may not make investment and financing decisions with only this objective in mind, managements are certainly not indifferent to the prices at which their corporations' securities sell. Hence the policy question posed has practical significance.

In one camp, where we find MM, it is argued that a corporation's cost of capital is a constant, i.e., independent of the method and level of financing. Optimal policy is the investment that equates the marginal

[13]Gordon, *The Investment, Financing, and Valuation of the Corporation, op. cit.*

[14]*Ibid.*

[15]Franco Modigliani and Merton H. Miller, "The Cost of Capital, Corporation Finance and the Theory of Investment: Reply," *American Economic Review,* Vol. XLIX (September, 1959), pp. 655–69.

[16]Haskel Benishay, "Variability in Earnings-Price Ratios: Reply," *American Economic Review,* Vol. LII (March, 1962), pp. 209–16.

[17]Marshal, Kolin, *The Relative Price of Corporate Equity,* Boston: Harvard Business School, 1963.

return on investment with this cost of capital. The inescapable conclusion is that financing policy is not a problem. The opposite position is that a corporation's cost of capital varies with the method and level of financing. My judgment is that the theoretical and empirical evidence we have favors this position.

However, regardless of which view prevails, the battle should be lively and productive. For a long time the position that cost of capital is a constant was held almost exclusively by economists, who were sophisticated in methods of theoretical and econometric analysis but knew little of finance. By contrast, the position that the cost of capital is a variable was held by finance men, who were familiar with their subject but not with advanced methods of theoretical and empirical research. People in each group talked only to those who agreed with them; and in consequence, not much was said. The situation has changed, it will change further, and the promise is that the lively debate and active research in progress will advance our knowledge on the subject.

*Chapter* 31

# *Dividends and Stock Prices**

By Irwin Friend and Marshall Puckett

THE RECENT LITERATURE has been characterized by considerable controversy and confusion over the relative importance of dividends and retained earnings in determining the price-earnings ratios of common stocks.[1] The disagreement over theoretical specifications of the expected relationship seems to us to have reached a point of rapidly diminishing returns, with much of the disagreement reflecting differences in interpretation of the questions being raised. However, there do seem to be very real difficulties in the reconciliation of available empirical findings with almost any sensible theory, and in the derivation of more definitive tests to choose among different specifications. This paper, after briefly reviewing the relevant theory and earlier findings, will discuss the limitations of these findings, describe various approaches to avoiding these limitations, and present new results that seem more in accord with theoretical preconceptions.

Relative prices of different issues of stock at a point of time are presumably determined by suitable discounting of expected future returns. These returns may take the form of dividend income or capital gains, both of which, assuming rational behavior, should be estimated on an after-tax basis with a higher average tax applicable to dividend income than to capital gains.[2] The discount factor relevant to these expectations

*Reprinted by permission from *American Economic Review,* Vol. LIV (September, 1964), pp. 656–82.

[1]See Modigliani and Miller [14], Durand's "Comment" [3], and Modigliani and Miller's "Reply" [15]; Gordon [6] [7]; Fisher [4]; Benishay [1]; Miller and Modigliani [13]; Lintner [10]; and Solomon [17].

Numbers in brackets refer to publications listed at the end of this paper (p. 560).

[2]The magnitude of this tax differential is difficult to evaluate, but available evidence indicates it may be smaller than commonly supposed. For instance, past

*(Continued on next page)*

of future return is a function of both the pure rate (or rates) of interest and the degree of risk associated with a particular issue—the evaluation of risk reflecting both the subjective probability distribution of expected return on total capital of the issuer and the degree of financial leverage in the issuer's capital structure.

The fact that investors are willing to hold (or buy) a company's shares at the prevailing price implies that the rate of discount which equates their income expectation with market price constitutes a rate of return at least as high as could be obtained in alternative investments of comparable risk. Now, if these investors are willing to increase their holdings of shares at the same rate of market return, they should also be willing to forgo current dividends insofar as the added equity investment yields this rate. Stated another way, investors should be indifferent if the present value of the additional future returns resulting from earnings retention equals the amount of dividends forgone. Moreover, because increases in present value (market price) are realizable as capital gains, earnings retention carries a tax advantage that lowers the rate of return on corporate investment necessary for shareholder indifference between current dividends and earnings retention.

The influence of earnings retention on share prices should therefore be a function of the profitability of corporate investment opportunities, ceteris paribus, in view of the fact that external equity financing is generally not a completely satisfactory substitute for internal financing. When this corporate rate of profit exceeds the minimum rate required by stockholders, price should increase as the proportion of earnings retained increases (though, since profitability is presumably a decreasing function of the amount of investment, beyond some point increased retention associated with excessive investment may depress the marginal return on investment below the required rate). Conversely, when the corporation's profit rate is less than the market rate, price should decrease with increasing earnings retention.[3]

Despite these theoretical conclusions, empirical findings indicate that

---

yield spreads between institutional-grade corporates and tax-exempt bonds are explained by an investor tax bracket of approximately 20 to 25 percent. However, in view of the institutional forces affecting the corporate bond market, this figure is undoubtedly lower than the tax rate characterizing the marginal investor in the stock market—but we have no idea just how much lower.

[3]As Miller and Modigliani [13] have shown, external equity financing destroys this relationship under conditions of costless flotation and no capital gains tax advantage, if changes in dividends are compensated by changes in external equity financing of equal magnitude and opposite direction (rate of equity investment held constant). However, flotation is not costless, capital gains tax advantages do exist, and the rate of earnings retention is in all likelihood greatly influenced by the rate of investment.

when stock prices are related to current dividends and retained earnings, higher dividend payout is usually associated with higher price-earnings ratios. This result, it might be noted, is found just about as often in highly profitable "growth" industries as it is in less profitable ones. Probably the earliest and best-known observation of this "dividend effect" was made a generation ago by Graham and Dodd [8], who went so far as to assert that a dollar of dividends has four times the average impact on price as does a dollar of retained earnings.[4] More recent statistical studies by Myron J. Gordon, David Durand, and others indicate that the dividend multiplier is still several times the retained earnings multiplier, with Gordon [6] finding little change on the average in the four-to-one ratio of the two multipliers, though the ratio varies widely and inconsistently from industry to industry and from year to year. These statistical results, it might be noted, are based on a large number of cross-section studies utilizing linear and logarithmic (and occasionally even other)[5] relationships between prices and both dividends and retained earnings to explain price variations in samples of companies drawn from particular industries.

Despite the massive array of statistical results tending to confirm the existence of a strong dividend effect, many market analysts have become increasingly skeptical of their validity. With the rise in market emphasis on growth in recent years, and the presumed close relationship between growth and retention of earnings in the minds of investors and managements, it seems strange to many analysts that a dollar of retained earnings (or of total earnings) should be valued so low relative to a dollar of dividends—and even stranger that there seems to have been no substantial shift in the relationship in recent years. Moreover, these doubts are supported quite strongly by several past surveys of shareholder opinion that indicate earnings and capital gains do in fact weigh more heavily than dividends in evaluating the relative desirability of alternative stock investments: "Investors who say a change in corporate earnings would influence their investment decisions outnumber by three to one those who would be influenced by a change in dividends."[6]

The behavioral assumptions necessary for theoretical support of a consistently lower market valuation of retained earnings than of divi-

---

[4]The fourth edition (1962) of this text on security analysis modifies this conclusion only moderately.

[5]See, e.g., Johnson, Shapiro, and O'Meara [9].

[6]Friend and Parker [5]. Also see Merrill Lynch, Pierce, Fenner and Smith [12]: "Just about all surveys of shareholders in recent years show investors are primarily interested in one thing—capital gains—almost two-thirds of our customers placed this at the top of their list. . . . The emphasis on appreciation rises as income rises."

dends are also quite suspect. This lower valuation could exist if any one of the following situations is present: (1) The average holder of common stock possesses, at the *margin* of his portfolio, a very strong preference for current income over future income (a situation which hardly could be expected to persist over time); (2) the expected increase in earnings arising from increased per share investment is viewed as involving a much higher degree of risk than that attaching to earnings on existing corporate assets; (3) the profitability of incremental corporate investment, as viewed by shareholders, is extremely low relative to the competitive yield prevailing in the stock market.

Each of the first two of these assumptions implies high rates of discount on incremental investment which would result in little short-run price appreciation from earnings retention, even though the expected profitability of additional investment may be quite high. However, neither of these assumptions is consistent with observed behavior of the market. Contrary to what might be expected from both of these assumptions, we do not normally witness perceptible drops in the market price level when the aggregate supply of corporate stock is increased by new issues, requiring for their absorption the substitution of current for future income and potentially raising the risk premium demanded by investors; nor do we typically witness sharp drops in per share price when the supply of an individual company's shares is increased. It is possible to infer, of course, that these increases in supply are precisely timed so as to be automatically offset by upward shifts in investor expectations, but this seems completely unrealistic. Thus, both of these first two assumptions can be questioned on the basis of market behavior as well as logical content.

The third assumption—that investors view the profitability of incremental investment as being quite low—also seems highly suspect. Marginal profit rates in a substantial number of industries appear to be quite high, and undue pessimism is hardly consistent with the accepted image of the average shareholder. Moreover, the generally favorable market reaction to new public stock offerings in recent years further belies the prevalence of any pessimistic beliefs about marginal profit rates.

In view of all this, it is our opinion that those statistical studies purporting to show a strong market preference for dividends are in error—especially since the analysis typically employed (described in the following section) includes as a part of the market's valuation of retained earnings the price paid for the relatively high internal rates of return which might be expected to be associated with high retention. Nonetheless, we should still not expect to find a uniform preference for dividends even if internal rates of return were held constant over the sample of companies being examined.[7] We do not, however, deny the existence of instances in which retained earnings are valued less than dividends. Certainly, some companies may be controlled by managements who knowingly do not act in the shareholder's best interest, or there may be sharp disagreement between these two groups over how that interest is defined. However, we feel that these instances are likely to be the exception rather than the rule. Moreover, we should expect that for the average firm, irrespective of investor preferences between dividends and capital gains, payout policies are such that at the margin a dollar of retained earnings should be approximately equal in market value to the dollar of dividends forgone.

## I. Possible Sources of Statistical Bias

In support of our position, we shall now outline a considerable number of reasons why previous statistical studies yielded biased results. These comments are directed in particular at the following regression equation, which is the one most commonly applied to cross-section data, but most of them also apply to past variations in this equation:

$$P_{it} = a + b\,D_{it} + c\,R_{it} + e_{it} \tag{1}$$

Reading from left to right, the variables represent per share price, dividends, and retained earnings. The subscript $i$ denotes the $i$th company in a sample of $n$ companies selected from a particular industry, and all variables are measured in the $t$th time period.

Before discussing the reasons for bias in the application of this relation, we might point out that even those who believe that a higher $b$ than $c$—the typical result— indicates investor preference for dividends seem nonetheless to feel that the optimum earnings payout ratio is normally less than one, which could be regarded as inconsistent with the result obtained. The implicit assumption in the above equation that optimal earnings payout—i.e., that giving rise to the highest price-earnings ratio—is either all, none, or a matter of indifference is, of course, highly questionable. However, even though this equation is quite deficient in that it does not admit of a unique optimum payout between the extremes of zero and 100 percent, it may still be quite useful for estimating price behavior within the observed range of dividend payout.

[7]Lintner [10] maintains that under certain types of uncertainty, retained earnings would be preferred to dividends if the alternative is a new stock issue to finance a given investment. If this is true, though we have some doubts, it would reinforce our argument. On the other hand, again as a result of uncertainty, Lintner argues that for firms with low leverage, investors will prefer higher dividends associated with higher corporate debt to greater retention and lower dividends.

Thus, if the companies in a sample tend, *on the average,* to pay out less than the optimum, $b$ should be greater than $c$; if they pay out more than the optimum, $b$ should be less than $c$; and if they pay just the optimum, regardless of what that optimum is, or if the payout is a matter of indifference, $b$ should equal $c$. Theory would suggest that regardless of the optimum payout for any individual company, at that optimum $1.00 of dividends would on the average have the same effect on stock price as $1.00 of retained earnings.[8] Any difference between the values of $b$ and $c$ therefore represents either a disequilibrium payout position or a statistical limitation of the analysis employed, including most notably a correlation of dividends or retained earnings with omitted factors affecting price. Our analysis will attempt to distinguish between these two possibilities, though the persistence of the relative importance of payout on price, and its apparent invariance to such factors as the rise in market emphasis on growth through earnings retention, argues against the disequilibrium explanation even if this condition is regarded as fairly permanent.

While the linear form used does not provide measures of optimum payout, it can give useful insights into the size of such payout through examination of the residuals over the range of payout experienced. However, an adequate study of the size of optimal payout ratios under varying circumstances requires a more complex statistical analysis, allowing for many more variables than have been incorporated in the framework used in this paper, and will be deferred to a subsequent study. Our analysis in this paper is directed only to an assessment of the general rationality of company payout policy in view of the usual findings (i.e., $b$ systematically higher than $c$), which imply that management typically tends to maintain too low a payout.

It will be noted that the following discussion of regression problems centers exclusively on those encountered in cross-section analysis. While it is possible to work with time-series information, and we shall do so to a limited extent, virtually all of our predecessors used cross-section data in their regression studies, and it is these studies with which we take issue.

## *A. Omitted Variables*

The above equation assumes, among other things, (1) either that risk is held constant by restricting the sample to a particular industry, or else that dividend payout is uncorrelated with risk; and (2) that expectations of growth are determined solely by the relative amount of

[8] This conclusion does not depend on whether, under uncertainty, the relevant discount rate of investors is a function of the dividend rate.

current earnings retention or, alternatively, that growth from other sources is uncorrelated with the relative amount of retention.

With regard to the first of these assumptions, a typical sample of twenty or so companies drawn from industries such as foods, steels, or chemicals contains enormous variations in company size, financial structure, and product mix; therefore, it appears totally unwarranted to assume that risk variations within these industry samples are negligible. In view of what we know about managerial desire to avoid dividend cuts, it certainly seems logical to expect that companies facing greater uncertainty about future profit performance would adopt lower current dividend payout as a means of hedging the risk of being forced to cut their dividend. Thus, high risk may *result* in both low payout and low price-earnings ratios, whereas low risk may *result* in high payout and high price-earnings ratios. Consequently, omission of a risk variable from the regression equation could conceivably impart a substantial upward bias to the dividend coefficient, depending upon both the extent to which risk varies between companies and the strength of risk in determining current payout.

It might be noted that a few previous writers have incorporated a risk variable in the regression equations. However, this variable is usually measured in terms of earnings fluctuations and is heavily influenced by cyclical factors in the company's operating performance. We are inclined to doubt that cyclical earnings variability is a good proxy measure of investor uncertainty about future long-run performance, and therefore are dubious that the problem of risk has been handled properly.

Now, the second assumption—that growth deriving from sources other than earnings retention is either nonexistent or nonbiasing—is equally questionable. Growth in per share earnings, apart from that arising from more efficient use of existing capital, can occur through externally as well as internally financed investment, and there may be a biasing correlation within a sample of companies between internally and externally financed growth. Suppose, for instance, that some companies prefer (or in the case of public utilities, are encouraged by regulatory agencies to have) low earnings retention compensated by large amounts of external financing, whereas other companies prefer high earnings retention and small amounts of external financing. This would impair the relationship between earnings retention and growth, thereby reducing the coefficient on retained earnings when the variable measuring externally financed growth is omitted.[9]

---

[9]If the objective were to arrive at the relative evaluation of dividends and retained earnings *with a given internal rate of return,* then the problem of bias would arise from the omission of the expected growth rate rather than from that of externally financed growth. An analysis which includes past growth rates (as

*(Continued on next page)*

However, it is equally possible that the relationship between internal and external financing could run the other way—that is, that high rates of retention are associated with relatively heavy external financing and low rates of retention with small amounts of external financing. The inherent advantages of retained earnings undoubtedly encourage maximum use of this source of funds before resorting to the capital markets. Thus, external financing may be associated with high earnings retention for companies with abundant investment opportunities, whereas the absence of external financing may be associated with lower earnings retention for other companies. In this case the rate of earnings retention is positively correlated with external financing, and the retained earnings coefficient is biased upward by omission of any consideration of externally financed growth.

In summary, whereas the bias due to omission of a risk variable is reasonably clear in direction (but not in magnitude), the nature of the bias resulting from omission of a variable to take account of externally financed growth is not clear. Nonetheless, both of these variables are potentially too important to be omitted from the regression equation without proof of the negligibility of their influence on regression results.

## *B. Regression Weights*

Contributing to the difficulties imposed by omitted variables is the separate but correlated problem of regression weighting. An individual observation influences regression results according to the extent to which that observation departs from the sample average. Thus, extreme values are much more important in determining regression results than are those values centered more closely about the sample average.

Now, it is a generally accepted fact that high-quality stocks tend to be characterized by high per share values (prices, dividends, and earnings), whereas low-quality stocks are characterized by low per share values. Further, as discussed immediately above, high-quality stocks may tend to pay out a higher proportion of earnings than do the low-quality issues. Thus the association between regression weights and investment quality may exaggerate whatever regression bias exists due to an association between investment quality and dividend payout. This problem of regression weights is reduced when regression variables are converted to logarithms, which was done in some earlier studies.

---

proxies for expected future growth) is Benishay [1], Gordon [7] does introduce both internally and externally financed growth, but the form of the relation he uses does not permit the isolation of dividends from retained earnings effects.

## *C. Random Variations in Income*

The income reported by a corporation in any particular period is subject to a host of short-run economic and accounting factors that render it different from what would have been reported under "normal" conditions. Now, if prices are related to normal rather than reported income, and if the short-run disturbances in reported earnings do not produce equiproportional disturbances in dividends, then a regression equation of the standard form will be biased in favor of dividend payout influences—a point touched upon by earlier writers but in a rather different context. To clarify, companies with above-normal earnings at a point of time will be characterized by both low price-earnings and dividend payout ratios, whereas companies reporting below-normal earnings will be characterized by both high price-earnings and high payout ratios.

The two conditions essential to the above argument are (1) that dividends are a more stable time series than reported earnings and (2) that the elasticity of shareholder expectations with respect to short-run income movements is less than unity. The existence of the first of these conditions has been proved quite conclusively by several studies of corporate dividend payout policy which show a rather slow adaptation of dividends to changes in reported earnings.[10] The second condition has, to our knowledge, not been proved; but in view of the great amount of background data available for the formulation of per share income expectations, it seems reasonable to suppose that expectations are rather insensitive to those short-run movements in relative earnings which are unrelated to fundamental changes in long-run prospects for the economy, the industry, or the company.

## *D. Income Measurement Errors*

The diversity of accounting procedures employed in estimating business earnings gives rise to consistent measurement errors that can bias regression results in favor of dividends on two counts. First, the simple fact that retained earnings are measured imprecisely exerts a downward bias on the coefficient for that variable (dividends are measured precisely, and therefore no such bias exists here). Since retained earnings are generally of the order of magnitude of one third of total earnings, and all of the probably sizable measurement error in total earnings affects the estimate of retained earnings, the downward bias in the re-

[10] See especially Lintner [11], and also Darling [2].

tained earnings coefficient could be quite large.[11] Second, if both prices and dividends are geared to the economically "correct" value of earnings, then firms that employ accounting methods yielding relatively high reported earnings will be characterized by both low payout and low price-earnings ratios compared to the sample average, whereas those firms which maximize current deductions will show both high payout and high price-earnings ratios relative to the sample average. As a result, the retained earnings coefficient is again biased downward relative to the dividends coefficient.

Strictly speaking, the second of these accounting effects could logically have been discussed under the heading "Omitted Variables" above. However, the apparent lack of appreciation for the interrelation between accounting biases in reported earnings and the measured effect of dividends and retained earnings on share prices prompted this separate discussion as a means of drawing attention to what is potentially one of the most glaring weaknesses in those studies. In subsequent discussions of regression models and results, accounting limitations of the type described above will generally be incorporated in the "omitted variable" category.

It might be noted that the above discussion does not include accounting errors of the type that, because of fluctuations in certain costs such as write-offs, advertisement, research and development, etc., would result in random disturbances to an individual company's earnings. These are properly included in the "random income movements" category. We should also mention the problem of general over- or understatement of earnings. While the procedures we shall use do adjust for differences among firms (which are consistent over time) in their reporting of earnings, they do not adjust for any general over- or understatement of earnings because of the formidable conceptual and statistical problems associated with identification and correction of this type of error. We might emphasize, however, that if accounting estimates of earnings are generally less than those "estimated" by investors, the retained earnings coefficient will be biased upward.

## *E. Least Squares Bias*

Assuming that management and shareholder expectations are substantially independent, it is entirely plausible that a price-earnings ratio which is regarded as high by management will result in external stock

[11] See, e.g., Wold [18]. On the other hand, several analyses using average dividends and average retained income as explanatory variables (e.g., see Gordon [6]) attach about the same relative importance to dividends in explaining stock prices, though this use of averages would be expected to reduce the bias in the estimated influence of retained earnings.

financing and high payout, while capitalization ratios regarded as low will result in heavier reliance on internal financing and consequently low payout. Moreover, a similar result would occur if management were motivated only by a desire to maintain dividend-price ratios close to the average for the industry.

If these market relationships are reflected in cross-section data, the standard regression equation will yield results biased in favor of dividend payout because it assumes one-way causality between dividends and prices. That is, the equation fails to take account of the fact that dividend payout differences are, at least in part, the result rather than the cause of differences in price-earnings ratios. Resolution of this problem of dual causality requires the use of a complete model employing both demand and supply schedules for dividends.

## II. Regression Models

The problem of omitted variables could of course be directly handled by expanding the regression equation to include these variables. However, measurement of such slippery concepts as subjective risk evaluation, profitability of investment opportunities, sources of expected future financing, and accounting differences is both difficult and subject to large error. Indirect approaches thus seem particularly attractive.

Theoretically speaking, continuous cross-section techniques are the most appealing of these approaches. If the separate effects on price of all omitted variables are aggregated, and this composite ("company" or "firm") effect given the designation $F_i$, then the basic regression equation 1 can be modified as follows:

$$P_{it} = a_t + b_t D_{it} + c_t R_{it} + F_i + e_{it} \tag{2}$$

The assumption implicit in this equation is that firm effects, which cannot of course be measured directly, are both additive and constant over time. Such firm effects include those relevant to investor assessment of both profit prospects and risk, only some of which (e.g., size of firm and past trend and variability in book earnings) could alternatively be measured directly. Now, if an identical equation is written for an earlier time period, and this last equation is then subtracted from the one above, the following result is achieved:

$$\begin{aligned} P_{it} - P_{i(t-1)} = a_t - a_{t-1} + b_t D_{it} - b_{t-1} D_{i(t-1)} + c_t R_{it} \\ - c_{t-1} R_{i(t-1)} + e_{it} - e_{i(t-1)} \end{aligned} \tag{3}$$

The $F_i$ do not appear in this equation, so the coefficients on dividends and retained earnings ought to be free of the bias due to firm effects.

Despite its theoretical appeal, this procedure runs into two complications: (1) In this particular application the error terms in the continuous cross-section difference equation become quite large; and (2) period-to-period movements in the variables can contain random elements and serial correlations that greatly impair the meaning and reliability of the coefficient.[12] The random movements in earnings are much more likely to be reflected in retained earnings than in dividends or in stock prices, depressing the apparent influence of retained earnings on stock prices. Moreover, the firm effects are more likely to be multiplicative than additive, and continuous cross-section techniques pose special problems in the multiplicative case. Consequently, we feel other approaches are more promising for our purposes, at least at this stage of development of continuous cross-section techniques. In connection with these other approaches, we shall henceforth assume a multiplicative relationship for the firm effects.

Thus, suppose:

$$F_{it} = f_i E_{it} \tag{4}$$

where $f_i$ is now the firm effect "multiplier" and $E$ is per share earnings. The aggregate firm effect ($F_{it}$) for any firm is assumed proportional to its per share earnings, but the factor of proportionality ($f_i$) differs among firms. If it is tentatively assumed that earnings payout effects are negligible, then:

$$P_{it} = (k_t + f_i)E_{it} \tag{5}$$

where $k_t$ is the average price-earnings ratio for the sample. Making the additional assumption that the $f_i$ are constant over any two adjacent time periods:

$$f_{it} = f_{i(t-1)} = \frac{P_{i(t-1)}}{E_{i(t-1)}} - k_{t-1} = (P/E)'_{i(t-1)} \tag{6}$$

Therefore, under the stated assumptions, firm effects can be held constant by introducing into the regression equation a variable $[(P/E)'_{i(t-1)}]$ which measures individual deviations from the sample average price-earnings ratio in the previous time periods; i.e.:

$$P_{it} = a + bD_{it} + cR_{it} + d(P/E)'_{i(t-1)} + e_{it}{}^{13} \tag{7}$$

[12]These complications can be avoided in part by the application of this type of cross-section difference equation to group rather than individual firm data, a procedure which has not been utilized previously and which we plan to experiment with.

[13]In the regressions fitted subsequently, $\left\{\frac{E}{P}\right\}_{i(t-1)}$ is used instead of $\left\{\frac{P}{E}\right\}'_{i(t-1)}$ for statistical reasons. In these regressions, annual data are used as measures of the variables involved, though it can be argued that, at least for earnings, an average over a number of years might be preferable. While this was not tested, it might be pointed out that the use of such averages in another context did not affect the results significantly (see note 11) and that the assumed constancy of the firm effects becomes more tenuous the longer the period covered. Another approach

In this equation (as well as in the continuous cross-section model), firm effects include the profitability of investment opportunities as assessed by the market.

The problem of least squares bias can be handled by specifying a complete model, including a dividend supply function as well as the customary price relation. For instance, let:

$$P_{it} = a + bD_{it} + cR_{it} + d(P/E)'_{i(t-1)} \tag{8}$$

be the relation determining price; and let:

$$D_{it} = e + fE_{it} + gD_{i(t-1)} + h(P/E)'_{i(t-1)} \tag{9}$$

be the dividend supply equation (error terms have been omitted). The dividend supply equation is developed by adding to the best type of relationship developed by previous writers[14] (which stresses the importance of past dividends on current dividends) a variable permitting the firm to adjust its current payout to past market valuation of its future earnings. The system is completed by the identity:

$$E_{it} = D_{it} + R_{it} \tag{10}$$

where $E_{it}$ may be considered exogeneous but, of course, not $D_{it}$ or $R_{it}$. Solving these equations 8, 9, and 10, we have:

$$\begin{aligned} P_{it} = {} & [a + e(b - c)] + [c + f(b - c)]E_{it} + [g(b - c)]D_{i(t-1)} \\ & + [d + h(b - c)]\,(P/E)'_{i(t-1)} \end{aligned} \tag{11}$$

After obtaining the regression coefficients of equations 9 and 11 in the usual manner, the coefficients of equation 8 can be derived and are theoretically free of bias due to effects of price on dividend supply.

Turning to the problem of random income movements, the argument here, it will be recalled, implies that short-term changes in income evoke relatively small short-run changes in relative price. Thus an equation of the form:

$$P_{it} = a + bD_{it} + cR_{it} + dP_{i(t-1)} \tag{12}$$

in which previous expectations, measured by $P_{i(t-1)}$, as well as current dividend and earnings experience, are assumed to determine current price is consistent with this assumption about price behavior. The $b$ and $c$ coefficients in this equation measure the extent of short-run price adjustment to short-run changes in dividends and earnings retention, respectively. Long-run values of these coefficients can, after correcting $d$ for movements in the general market price level, be obtained by dividing

to holding firm effects constant is to substitute equation 6 in equation 5, which results in equation 12, except that theoretically for this purpose the $P_{i(t-1)}$ term in equation 12 should be multiplied by the ratio of $E_{it}$ to $E_{i(t-1)}$.

[14] See Lintner [11].

each through by $1-d$, provided it can be assumed that $d$ measures only the influence of past expectations on current expectations. One of the additional merits of this equation is that lagged price to some extent also holds constant any firm effects that exist; as a result, however, long-run coefficients computed by this method may be somewhat in error.

A more direct approach to the problem of short-run earnings movements lies in the "normalization" of those earnings. Other authors have attempted this—usually by use of centered or weighted averages—but we feel that these methods are somewhat less satisfactory than available alternatives. A simple average of earnings over, say, a three-year period may still contain large short-run components (relative to future expectations) if the adjustment process is slow. The same comment also applies to weighted averages; and in view of the relatively high weight usually given to current earnings, this technique may be even less satisfactory than the use of a simple average.

Of several alternatives available for earnings normalization, an approach that seems especially promising is one in which market estimates are employed. To illustrate, assume that price and dividends are always taken as "normal," and that short-run earnings abnormalities sum to zero over the sample of companies in question (the latter being a reasonable assumption for most industries over most periods if we avoid major cyclical disturbances). Thus the dividend-price ratio is assumed to be always normal, but the earnings-price ratio is subject to short-run fluctuations. Variations about trend values of the ratio $(E/P)_{it}/(E/P)_{kt}$ are, by assumption, due solely to short-run components of the $i$th company's earnings, because the average earnings-price ratio for the sample $[(E/P)_{kt}]$ is defined to be free of earnings disturbances. Examination of the scatter diagrams of the time-series behavior of this "relative earnings yield" ratio failed to indicate any reason for assigning anything other than a linear equation to the underlying time trend. Therefore, on an empirical basis:

$$\frac{(E/P)_{it}}{(E/P)_{kt}} = a_i + b_i t + e_{it} \tag{13}$$

Now, normal value of company earnings-price ratios can be computed as follows (the superscript $n$ denoting normalized value):

$$(E/P)^n_{it} = [a_i + b_i t]\ (E/P)_{kt} \tag{14}$$

Having obtained a normalized value of the earnings-price ratio, normalized earnings are found by simply multiplying this ratio by per share price. Normalized retained earnings are then obtained by subtracting observed dividends from normalized earnings.

The assumptions underlying this approach can of course be questioned—dividends do react to year-to-year fluctuations in earnings, price does contain speculative components, and earnings fluctuations may not sum to zero over the sample. However, dividends are likely to react only to fluctuations in earnings regarded as relatively permanent. Moreover, averaging price over a year should remove most relative speculative components of individual share prices, since, in theory, arbitragers can be expected to hold these to short duration. Any error attaching to the assumption that sample average earnings are normal is likely to be small; and thus, its effect on the regression equation will also be small.[15] Nevertheless, prices, as we measure them, probably do contain individual speculative components of small magnitude. Thus, normal earnings computed from measured prices will contain errors of the same relative magnitude and direction as those contained in price, so that some small bias is probably introduced in favor of the retained earnings coefficient.

All of the statistical models presented earlier can of course be modified to specify normalized values of those variables in which earnings fluctuations play a distorting part. The regression results presented later embody two such modifications.

Finally, the influence of dividend payout on price can be subjected to time-series analysis. For instance, the above equations relating relative earnings yield to time can be compared with regression equations of the following form:

$$\frac{(D/E)_{it}}{(D/E)_{kt}} = a_i + b_i t + e_{it} \tag{15}$$

to ascertain if changes over time in relative earnings-price ratios are consistently associated with changes in relative dividend payout ratios—and if so, the nature of the association. This procedure, it might be noted, involves none of the assumptions necessary for derivation of normalized earnings and hence constitutes an independent check on their validity. Many other time-series tests of the relative importance of dividends and retained earnings are also possible.

## III. Regression Results

For most of our statistical analysis, we worked with five industry samples, viz., chemicals, electronics, electric utilities, foods, and steels, in each of two years, 1956 and 1958. The industries were selected to

[15]This earnings normalization procedure was developed in Marshall Puckett's forthcoming Ph.D. dissertation, and the validity of its assumptions are subjected to critical evaluation in that work. Alternative methods of earnings normalization —for instance, by derivation of a normal dividend payout ratio—are also presented.

permit a distinction to be made between the results for growth and nongrowth industries, and to provide a basis for comparison with results by other authors for earlier years. Both cyclical and noncyclical industries are covered. Ready accessibility of data and resource availability were also factors both in industry and in year selection. An attempt was made to conform to a fairly narrow definition of the industries chosen so that the sample companies would be reasonably homogeneous in industrial composition.[16] The periods covered include a boom year for the economy when stock prices leveled off after a substantial rise (1956) and a somewhat depressed year for the economy when stock prices, however, rose strongly (1958). Originally, we had intended including several earlier years as well, but it was not feasible to do this systematically.

Table 1 presents the usual simple linear relationships between average prices and dividends and retained earnings to show with the data we are using the kinds of results typically obtained, and to provide a basis of comparison with alternative regression models. In this analysis,

TABLE 1

REGRESSION EQUATION: $P_t = a + bD_t + cR_t$*

| Industry (Sample Size) | Regression Coefficients (Standard Errors) | | | | |
|---|---|---|---|---|---|
| | *t* | *a* | *b* | *c* | $\overline{R^2}$ |
| Chemicals ($n$ = 20) | 1956 | −0.86 | +29.94 (3.00) | + 2.91 (4.98) | 0.868 |
| | 1958 | −5.29 | +27.72 (2.22) | +13.15 (5.65) | 0.910 |
| Electronics ($n$ = 20) | 1956 | +7.32 | + 7.27 (9.77) | +17.87 (6.60) | 0.410 |
| | 1958 | +8.53 | +13.56 (12.80) | +26.85 (6.57) | 0.524 |
| Electric utilities ($n$ = 25) | 1956 | +0.85 | +13.86 (2.35) | +14.91 (3.42) | 0.842 |
| | 1958 | +1.11 | +14.29 (3.36) | +18.54 (5.22) | 0.772 |
| Foods ($n$ = 25) | 1956 | +0.78 | +15.56 (1.70) | + 5.23 (1.30) | 0.834 |
| | 1958 | +1.50 | +17.73 (2.10) | + 4.35 (1.56) | 0.805 |
| Steels ($n$ = 20) | 1956 | −2.28 | +17.60 (2.65) | + 2.45 (1.42) | 0.869 |
| | 1958 | +8.55 | +15.23 (1.63) | + 5.98 (2.08) | 0.881 |

*Per share price (average for year), dividends, and retained earnings are represented by $P$, $D$, and $R$, respectively; $t$ designates year; $n$, size of sample; $\overline{R^2}$, coefficient of determination adjusted for degrees of freedom; and standard errors of regression coefficients are indicated under coefficients in parentheses.

[16]A list of the corporations included may be obtained on request to authors.

we find the customary strong dividend and relatively weak retained earnings effect in three of the five industries—i.e., chemicals, foods, and steels. In these three industries, there is little evidence of any significant shift in the relative importance of retained earnings from earlier years as a result of increasing market emphasis on growth.[17] While these results may not be altogether surprising for steels and foods, they seem highly questionable for chemicals, which was probably regarded as a growth industry in this period. Even for steels and foods, the magnitude of the difference between the dividend and retained earnings coefficients seems implausible.

The fact that electric utilities show fully as high a coefficient and electronics a higher coefficient for retained earnings than for dividends is in closer agreement with what might be expected. Unfortunately, we know of no earlier results for electronics that can be used as a basis of comparison.

For electric utilities, there are two earlier analyses that can be compared with our results, though the forms of the relationships used are somewhat different. The first, by Morrissey [16], relates the earnings-price and dividends-price ratios separately to the dividend payout ratios for each of the years 1950–57 and finds that the payout ratio in this industry did affect stock prices significantly in the early part of this period (with higher prices associated with higher payout) but very little in the latter part of this period. Moreover, this study found a steady reduction in the importance of the payout ratio from year to year and some evidence that the direction of its effect had changed by the end of the period, i.e., that higher payout may have been associated with lower prices for given earnings by 1957. These results are consistent with investors' changing evaluations of the growth potential of electric utilities and, for the end of the period covered, with our results in 1956 and 1958. However, the second earlier analysis referred to, which derives a logarithmic relation between the ratio of stock prices to book value and both the ratio of earnings to book value and the payout ratio, yields a different result for utilities in early 1955, showing a positive relation between the price to book ratio and payout.[18]

A recomputation of the electric utilities regressions in Table 1 utilizing logarithms for all the variables again points to a higher dividend than retained earnings effect, unlike the result obtained in the linear form.[19] It is not possible to choose conclusively between the linear and

[17] See, e.g., Gordon [6] for comparable 1951 and 1954 regressions for these industries.

[18] See Durand [3]. It is not clear whether utilities other than electric are included.

[19] The only other industry regressions which were recomputed were for chemicals, and here the logarithmic results were quite close to the linear results.

logarithmic results on statistical or a priori grounds. The logarithmic relations do reduce the problem of regression weights referred to earlier (with a correlation between these weights and investment quality exaggerating any regression bias due to a correlation between quality and dividend payout). However, so do both the ratio relations discussed above and the more complex linear relations in subsequent tables, all of which give the same type of results for the electric utilities as the simple linear relations. Moreover, the ratio and linear regressions, unlike the logarithmic relations, can handle satisfactorily very small and negative retained earnings. We feel that the major difference between the logarithmic and nonlogarithmic regressions may be due to the differing degrees of bias in the regression coefficients produced by short-run income disturbances, and we shall attempt to hold these constant in some of the following statistical analyses.

TABLE 2

REGRESSION EQUATION: $P_t = a + bd_t + cR_t + d(E/P)_{t-1}$*

| *Industry (Sample Size)* | *Regression Coefficients (Standard Errors)* | | | | | |
|---|---|---|---|---|---|---|
| | *t* | *a* | *b* | *c* | *d* | $\bar{R}^2$ |
| Chemicals ($n$ = 20)...... | 1956 | +58.21 | +25.19 | +13.81 | −0.97 | 0.967 |
| | | | (1.69) | (3.00) | (0.14) | |
| | 1958 | +21.75 | +26.93 | +15.20 | −0.45 | 0.959 |
| | | | (1.55) | (3.95) | (0.10) | |
| Electronics ($n$ = 20)..... | 1956 | +32.83 | +15.78 | +19.14 | −0.49 | 0.681 |
| | | | (7.76) | (5.02) | (0.13) | |
| | 1958 | +54.59 | +27.18 | +28.06 | −0.87 | 0.836 |
| | | | (8.14) | (12.60) | (1.57) | |
| Electric utilities ($n$ = 25). | 1956 | +30.26 | +12.42 | +15.50 | −0.41 | 0.892 |
| | | | (2.04) | (2.89) | (0.13) | |
| | 1958 | +41.59 | +13.12 | +14.88 | −0.49 | 0.897 |
| | | | (2.32) | (3.65) | (0.10) | |
| Foods ($n$ = 25)......... | 1956 | +15.66 | +13.68 | + 7.52 | −0.17 | 0.905 |
| | | | (1.44) | (1.16) | (0.04) | |
| | 1958 | +16.93 | +16.75 | + 5.68 | −0.16 | 0.843 |
| | | | (6.27) | (4.91) | (0.07) | |
| Steels ($n$ = 20)......... | 1956 | − 6.39 | +17.85 | + 2.21 | +0.03 | 0.870 |
| | | | (2.78) | (1.55) | (0.07) | |
| | 1958 | + 4.33 | +15.06 | + 5.67 | +0.05 | 0.885 |
| | | | (1.68) | (2.17) | (0.07) | |

*$E$ represents per share earnings. See Table 1 for other symbols.

To summarize the results so far, they provide a little more evidence than has existed heretofore that in growth industries (chemicals, electronics, and electric utilities), more weight relatively is given to retained earnings than in nongrowth industries (steels and foods); but the evidence is not uniform (chemicals), and for one of the two remaining industries (electric utilities) depends partly on the mathematical form of the regression used. In any event, for three of five groups, including one presumably growth industry, we find again the same peculiar result obtained by our numerous predecessors using similar kinds of analysis—i.e., a predominant dividend effect.

TABLE 3

DIVIDEND SUPPLY AND DERIVED PRICE REGRESSIONS, 1958

*Dividend Supply Equation:* $D_t = e + fE_t + gD_{t-1} + h(E/P)_{t-1}$

| Industry (Sample Size) | Parameter Estimates | | | | |
|---|---|---|---|---|---|
| | $e$ | $f$ | $g$ | $h$ | $\bar{R}^2$ |
| Chemicals ($n = 20$)....... | +0.0282 | +0.0850<br>(0.0320) | +0.8334<br>(0.0416) | +0.0007<br>(0.0017) | 0.995 |
| Electric utilities ($n = 25$).. | −0.1163 | +0.1440<br>(0.0326) | +0.7989<br>(0.0502) | +0.0024<br>(0.0018) | 0.989 |
| Foods ($n = 25$).......... | +0.1836 | +0.0735<br>(0.0322) | +0.8435<br>(0.0579) | −0.0004<br>(0.0013) | 0.962 |
| Steels ($n = 20$)........... | +0.6261 | +0.1456<br>(0.0329) | +0.6589<br>(0.0868) | −0.0027<br>(0.0020) | 0.942 |

*Derived Price Equation:* $P_t = a + bD_t + cR_t + d(E/P)_{t-1}$

| Industry (Sample Size) | Parameter Estimates | | | |
|---|---|---|---|---|
| | $a$ | $b$ | $c$ | $d$ |
| Chemicals ($n = 20$)............. | +19.18 | +27.02 | +17.46 | −0.45 |
| Electric utilities ($n = 25$)....... | +41.16 | +11.02 | +18.34 | −0.46 |
| Foods ($n = 25$)............... | +14.31 | +17.65 | + 5.70 | −0.16 |
| Steels ($n = 20$)................ | − 1.06 | +22.41 | +13.81 | +0.07 |

One simple approach to holding firm effects constant (and in the process to reduce the problem of regression weights) is to add a lagged earnings-price ratio to the equations in Table 1. The results presented in Table 2 again indicate that dividends have a predominant influence on stock prices in the same three out of five industries, but the differences between the dividends and retained earnings coefficients are not quite so marked as in the first set of regressions. The dividends and retained earnings coefficients are closer to each other for all industries in both years except for steels in 1956; and the correlations are higher, again except for steels.

These new regressions, however, are not too satisfactory for a variety of reasons, of which the potential bias arising from short-run income disturbances is probably the most important. Moreover, an additional possible source of bias involves another question that was raised previously—i.e., the influence of stock price on dividend payout levels set by managements. Table 3 presents for four industry groups in 1958 the relevant dividend supply equations and the derived price equations obtained from the solution of the complete model, which contains three equations—the price equation (8), the dividend supply equation (9), and the identity (10). The derived price equations show no significant changes from those obtained from the single-equation approach in Table 2, reflecting the fact that stock price, or more accurately the price-earnings ratio, does not seem to have a significant effect on dividend payout. On the other hand, it might be noted that in three of the four cases tested the retained earnings effect is increased relatively, with no change in the fourth case. These results suggest that price effects on dividend supply are probably not a serious source of bias in the customary derivation of dividend and retained earnings effects on stock prices, though such a bias might be masked if the disturbing effects of short-run income movements are sufficiently great.

To provide some direct evidence on the potential bias arising from short-run income movements, the standard linear equation in Table 1 can be modified to include a lagged price variable which allows for slow short-run adjustment in prices to current levels of income. As noted earlier, to some extent the lagged price variable also holds firm effects constant; it also minimizes the problem of regression weights. These results are presented in Table 4.

Examination of this table shows that retained earnings receive greater relative weight than dividends in the majority of cases. The only exceptions are steels and foods in 1958. In all three groups which would normally be considered growth industries (chemicals, electronics, and utilities), the retained earnings effect is larger than the dividend effect for both years covered. For the other two industries (steels and foods), there no longer seem to be any significant systematic differences between the retained earnings and dividend coefficients, though there is some suggestion that dividends became relatively more attractive in 1958 than in 1956, which may not be surprising in view of the possible change in outlook for these industries at that time. This set of regressions has a number of attractive features apart from eliminating the customary anomalous result for dividends and retained earnings. The correlation coefficients as a whole have been substantially improved. The regression coefficients of the constant terms are in general close to zero, which is in accord with the theoretical expectations, and the magnitudes of the lagged price coefficients seem generally sensible. Interestingly also, relationships for earlier years (1949, 1950, and 1952), identical in form to those in Table 4, show relatively weaker retained earnings effects than in the later years, a finding fully in accord with the changing emphasis on growth characteristics of stocks in this period.[20]

TABLE 4

REGRESSION EQUATION: $P_t = a + bD_t + cR_t + dP_{t-1}$

| Industry (Sample Size) | Regression Coefficients (Standard Errors) | | | | | |
|---|---|---|---|---|---|---|
| | *t* | *a* | *b* | *c* | *d* | $\overline{R}^2$ |
| Chemicals ($n$ = 20)..... | 1956 | −1.52 | −2.52 (3.78) | +6.36 (2.10) | +1.06 (0.12) | 0.979 |
| | 1958 | −4.06 | +3.75 (3.23) | +6.45 (2.78) | +0.88 (0.11) | 0.981 |
| Electronics ($n$ = 20).... | 1956 | −4.92 | −7.49 (3.05) | +5.18 (2.14) | +1.27 (0.09) | 0.953 |
| | 1958 | +0.68 | −5.84 (3.02) | +9.20 (1.74) | +1.13 (0.06) | 0.978 |
| Electric utilities ($n$ = 25) | 1956 | +1.62 | −8.19 (3.67) | +2.79 (2.75) | +1.30 (0.20) | 0.947 |
| | 1958 | +2.49 | −1.36 (2.06) | +3.84 (2.59) | +1.11 (0.11) | 0.963 |
| Foods ($n$ = 25)........ | 1956 | +1.74 | +0.31 (1.84) | +2.56 (0.66) | +0.81 (0.09) | 0.967 |
| | 1958 | −1.15 | +1.75 (2.93) | +1.43 (1.08) | +1.08 (0.18) | 0.929 |
| Steels ($n$ = 20)......... | 1956 | +3.89 | −0.17 (4.30) | +3.16 (0.98) | +0.88 (0.19) | 0.943 |
| | 1958 | +0.94 | +7.73 (1.55) | +3.34 (1.26) | +0.55 (0.09) | 0.964 |

However, the regressions in Table 4 also have numerous limitations, including the possibility that the lagged price variable may serve in part as a proxy for dividends. Perhaps as a consequence, the regressions exhibit such undesirable properties as frequently negative dividend coefficients (though these are generally insignificant) and large standard errors for both dividends and retained earnings. These regressions, nevertheless, do seem to point to the weakness of the response of price to

[20]It was possible to derive such regressions in the earlier years for all industry samples except the electronics.

short-run changes in earnings, and to the fact that this response is not greatly affected by whether such changes in earnings are paid out as dividends or retained. There is some indication that retained earnings are more important than dividends (particularly for growth industries); but in half the cases, neither the short-run dividend nor the retained earnings coefficient is significantly different from zero.[21]

Another and independent approach to the problem of short-run income movements which was described earlier is to normalize earnings by deriving time-series regressions of the form of equation 13 for each of the $i$ companies in the $k$th industry group, and obtaining normalized retained earnings by subtracting dividends from normalized earnings, i.e., from $[a_i + b_i t]\ (E/P)_{kt} \cdot P_{it}$. This normalization procedure was based on the period 1950–61, and prices were then related to dividends and normalized retained earnings for chemicals, foods, and steels in 1956

TABLE 5

REGRESSION EQUATION: $P_t = a + bd_t + cR^n{}_t$*

| Industry (Sample Size) | Regression Coefficients (Standard Errors) | | | | |
|---|---|---|---|---|---|
| | $t$ | $a$ | $b$ | $c$ | $\bar{R}^2$ |
| Chemicals ($n$ = 20)......... | 1956 | −6.37 | +27.84 (2.66) | +10.96 (5.22) | 0.89 |
| | 1958 | −5.87 | +25.78 (2.58) | +18.82 (7.46) | 0.91 |
| Foods ($n$ = 25)........... | 1956 | +3.00 | +15.11 (1.28) | + 3.83 (1.46) | 0.93 |
| | 1958 | +2.20 | +15.96 (1.40) | + 4.91 (1.17) | 0.94 |
| Steels ($n$ = 20)............. | 1956 | +0.34 | +15.36 (1.41) | + 4.85 (0.80) | 0.98 |
| | 1958 | +6.11 | +14.37 (1.29) | + 8.24 (1.93) | 0.93 |

*The superscript $n$ denotes normalized value. (See text.)

and 1958, with the results presented in Table 5. Subsequently, the prior year's normalized earnings-price variable was also added to hold firm effects constant; these results are presented in Table 6.

A comparison of the results in Tables 5 and 6 with the corresponding regressions in Tables 1 and 2 shows the significant role of normalized

[21]Logarithmic regressions otherwise identical in form with those in Table 4 were computed for chemicals and electric utilities, and showed very similar results to the linear relations.

TABLE 6

REGRESSION EQUATION: $P_t = a + bD_t + cR^n_t + d(E/P)^n_{t-1}$

| Industry (Sample Size) | Regression Coefficients (Standard Errors) | | | | | |
|---|---|---|---|---|---|---|
| | $t$ | $a$ | $b$ | $c$ | $d$ | $\overline{R}^2$ |
| Chemicals ($n$ = 20)... | 1956 | +37.46 | +25.33 (1.77) | +13.81 (3.62) | −621.53 (137.11) | 0.95 |
| | 1958 | +26.64 | +24.38 (1.95) | +19.29 (5.55) | −605.42 (157.64) | 0.95 |
| Foods ($n$ = 25)...... | 1956 | +21.78 | +13.20 (0.57) | + 9.22 (0.80) | −241.80 (23.51) | 0.98 |
| | 1958 | +23.30 | +13.26 (0.81) | + 8.95 (0.81) | −227.40 (29.57) | 0.97 |
| Steels ($n$ = 20)....... | 1956 | +18.42 | +12.10 (0.90) | + 7.66 (0.70) | −164.26 (34.10) | 0.99 |
| | 1958 | +34.82 | +13.59 (0.87) | +12.19 (1.58) | −353.54 (79.34) | 0.96 |

earnings in eliminating part of the usual understatement of the relative importance of retained earnings, while a comparison of Tables 5 and 6 again indicates the similar role of a device (in this case the normalized price-earnings ratio) holding firm effects constant. An examination of Table 6 shows that for the industry groups covered, most, but not all, of the differences between dividend and retained earnings coefficients disappear when earnings are normalized and firm effects held constant. Similar regressions were not computed for the electronics sample, since a sufficiently long time period for earnings normalization was not available, or for the utilities sample, since a different and more satisfactory sample is being analyzed separately by one of the authors. However, it might be noted that for this somewhat different (and somewhat larger) sample of electric utilities, normalizing earnings and holding firm effects constant reduce the dividend coefficient slightly and increase the retained earnings coefficient fairly markedly.

The results of Table 6 seem considerably more plausible to us than the usual findings for foods and steels, suggesting that in these industries a somewhat (but not drastically) higher investor valuation may be placed on dividends than on retained earnings within the range of payout experienced so that management might be able to increase prices somewhat by raising dividends.[22] However, the regressions for chemicals in the table, though more satisfactory than those customarily obtained,

[22] In this connection, it might be noted that foods and steels are characterized by lower payout than chemicals.

do not seem quite so plausible, since they imply the same type of result as for foods and steels.

A more detailed examination of our chemicals sample disclosed that the results obtained largely reflected the undue regression weighting given the three firms with prices deviating most from the average price in the sample of twenty firms. If these three firms are omitted, the results are changed substantially. As Table 7 indicates, retained earnings now become somewhat more important than dividends as a price determinant (again within the range of payout experienced).

TABLE 7

REGRESSION EQUATIONS FOR 17 CHEMICAL COMPANIES

$$P_t = a + bD_t + cR^n_t$$
$$P_t = a + bD_t + cR^n_t + d(E/P)^n_t$$

| | Regression Coefficients (Standard Errors) | | | | |
|---|---|---|---|---|---|
| *t* | *a* | *b* | *c* | *d* | $\bar{R}^2$ |
| 1956....... | +11.12 | +10.56<br>(4.17) | +14.64<br>(3.79) | .......<br>....... | 0.81 |
| 1958....... | + 6.42 | +11.33<br>(4.28) | +16.63<br>(5.52) | .......<br>....... | 0.79 |
| 1956....... | +39.12 | +12.14<br>(2.40) | +17.23<br>(2.22) | −539.32<br>(313.11) | 0.89 |
| 1958....... | +38.01 | +12.18<br>(1.76) | +18.62<br>(2.27) | −553.87<br>(66.04) | 0.94 |

In view of the possible bias in favor of the retained earnings coefficient that may be introduced by the earnings normalization procedure adopted, it was considered desirable to compare the time-series behavior of the relative earnings yield ratios previously discussed, i.e., equation 13, with that of relative dividend payout ratios obtained by deriving time-series regressions of the form:

$$\frac{(D/E)_{it}}{(D/E)_{kt}} = a_i + b_i t$$

over the same time period. In view of resource limitations, this was done only for chemicals, which is considered the industry for which the customary results are most in question. The results in Table 8 show that in 12 out of 20 cases the time-slope coefficients for the relative earnings yield and relative payout regressions have the same sign, while in eight cases they are of opposite sign. This suggests that as relative payout increases, relative earnings yield increases somewhat more often than otherwise. In other words, the price-earnings ratio may have some tendency to move inversely to the payout ratio in contrast to the customary assertion of a direct relation. The correlation between the two slope coefficients is not very high but is significant ($\bar{R}^2 = 0.543$). This is fairly strong evidence that the customary results are invalid, since the comparison of trends in relative yield and relative payout over time largely avoids both problems of short-run income fluctuations and problems of consistent firm effects. However, it should be noted that one difficulty may remain. If relative earnings yield goes down (i.e., relative price earnings go up) because of a higher prospective rate of return on new corporate investment, the relative payout may go down because lower payout is associated with higher profit prospects, but the decline in payout would have no causative relation to the decline in yield. On the other hand, the customary finding that investors pay a premium for dividends as against retained earnings in the market even when the profitability of corporate investment opportunities is not held constant would still be invalidated.

TABLE 8

TIME-SLOPE COEFFICIENTS FROM RELATIVE EARNINGS YIELD AND RELATIVE PAYOUT REGRESSIONS FOR COMPANIES IN THE CHEMICALS INDUSTRY*

| *Company* | *b* | *b'* |
|---|---|---|
| 1. Du Pont | +0.014 | +0.009 |
| 2. Union Carbide | +0.012 | +0.015 |
| 3. Allied | +0.015 | +0.016 |
| 4. Dow | +0.023 | +0.019 |
| 5. American Cyanamid | +0.031 | +0.036 |
| 6. Monsanto | −0.032 | −0.014 |
| 7. Olin | +0.045 | −0.022 |
| 8. Air Reduction | +0.026 | +0.039 |
| 9. Koppers | +0.037 | +0.039 |
| 10. Hercules | +0.017 | −0.034 |
| 11. Texas Gulf Sulfur | −0.028 | +0.012 |
| 12. Columbian Carbon | −0.038 | +0.020 |
| 13. Hooker | +0.006 | +0.016 |
| 14. Diamond Alkali | −0.010 | +0.005 |
| 15. Pennsalt | −0.013 | +0.002 |
| 16. Atlas Chemical | +0.019 | −0.008 |
| 17. Commercial Solvents | −0.053 | −0.072 |
| 18. Celanese | −0.128 | −0.135 |
| 19. American Potash | +0.046 | −0.002 |
| 20. Imperial Chemical | +0.038 | +0.055 |

* *b* is the time-slope coefficient from the relative earnings yield regressions, and *b'* is the corresponding coefficient from the relative payout regressions. (See text.)

## IV. Some Concluding Remarks

Our analysis suggests that there is little basis for the customary view that in the stock market generally, except for unusual growth stocks, a dollar of dividends has several times the impact on price of a dollar of retained earnings. There is some indication that in nongrowth industries as a whole, a somewhat (but only moderately) higher investor valuation may be placed on dividends than on retained earnings within the range of payout experienced, but that the opposite may be true in growth industries. To the extent that this conclusion is valid, it is possible that management might be able, at least in some measure, to increase stock prices in nongrowth industries by raising dividends, and in growth industries by greater retention. However, the evidence that such possibilities exist to any important degree is rather tenuous, and there is no convincing indication of widespread management irrationality or irresponsibility in payout policy.

Unfortunately, the analysis we have carried out is limited not only in coverage of industries and time periods but also in the linearity assumed. While the latter restriction can be justified on the ground that a major objective was to question as expeditiously as possible the customary—and to us, implausible—results obtained from similar mathematical forms, our results do not go very far in indicating what payout ratios are regarded as optimal by investors for various types of stocks with different profitability of investment opportunities, risk, sources of financing, etc., or even in indicating whether an optimal ratio exists which to some extent is independent of profit prospects. Thus, it would not surprise us if investors as a rule prefer at least a small nonzero (and preferably a stable or rising) payout, even at the cost of forgoing otherwise desirable investment. However, the further study of optimal ratios, while relatively simple in theoretical terms, involves much more complicated empirical analysis than has been attempted here.

## References

1. BENISHAY, HASKEL. "Variability in Earnings-Price Ratios of Corporate Equities," *American Economic Review,* Vol. LI (March, 1961), pp. 81–94.
2. DARLING, PAUL G. "The Influence of Expectations and Liquidity on Dividend Policy," *Journal of Political Economy,* Vol. LXV (June, 1957), pp. 209–24.
3. DURAND, DAVID. "The Cost of Capital, Corporation Finance and the Theory of Investment: Comment," *American Economic Review,* Vol. XLIX (September, 1959), pp. 639–54.

4. FISHER, G. R. "Some Factors Influencing Share Prices," *Economic Journal,* Vol. LXXI (March, 1961), pp. 121–41.

5. FRIEND, IRWIN, and PARKER, SANFORD. "A New Slant on the Stock Market," *Fortune,* September, 1956.

6. GORDON, MYRON J. "Dividends, Earnings, and Stock Prices," *Review of Economics and Statistics,* Vol. XLI (May, 1959), pp. 99–105.

7. GORDON, MYRON J. *The Investment, Financing, and Valuation of the Corporation.* Homewood, Ill.: Richard D. Irwin, Inc., 1962.

8. GRAHAM, BENJAMIN, and DODD, DAVID L. *Security Analysis.* 1st ed. New York: McGraw-Hill Book Co., Inc., 1934.

9. JOHNSON, LYLE R.; SHAPIRO, ELI; and O'MEARA, JOSEPH, JR. "Valuation of Closely Held Stock for Federal Tax Purposes: Approach to an Objective Method," *University of Pennsylvania Law Review,* Vol. C (November, 1951), pp. 166–95.

10. LINTNER, JOHN. "Dividends, Earnings, Leverage, Stock Prices and the Supply of Capital to Corporations," *Review of Economics and Statistics,* Vol. XLIV (August, 1962), pp. 243–69.

11. LINTNER, JOHN. "Distribution of Incomes of Corporations among Dividends, Retained Earnings and Taxes," *American Economic Review,* Vol. XLVI (May, 1956), pp. 97–113.

12. MERRILL LYNCH, PIERCE, FENNER AND SMITH. *Annual Report,* p. 4. New York, 1959.

13. MILLER, MERTON H., and MODIGLIANI, FRANCO. "Dividend Policy, Growth, and the Valuation of Shares," *Journal of Business,* Vol. XXXIV (October, 1961), pp. 411–33.

14. MODIGLIANI, FRANCO, and MILLER, MERTON H. "The Cost of Capital, Corporation Finance and the Theory of Investment," *American Economic Review,* Vol. XLVIII (June, 1958), pp. 261–97.

15. MODIGLIANI, FRANCO, and MILLER, MERTON H. "The Cost of Capital, Corporation Finance and the Theory of Investment: Reply," *American Economic Review,* Vol. XLIX (September, 1959), pp. 655–69.

16. MORRISSEY, FRED P. "Current Aspects of the Cost of Capital to Utilities," *Public Utilities Fortnightly,* April 14, 1958.

17. SOLOMON, EZRA. *The Theory of Financial Management.* New York, 1963.

18. WOLD, HERMAN. *Demand Analysis.* New York: John Wiley & Sons, Inc., 1953.

# *Part* VII

# *Mergers, Acquisitions, and Valuation*

*Chapter* 32

# *Premeditated Merger**

By George D. McCarthy

GENERAL DYNAMICS Corporation increased its sales from $42 million in 1950 to $1.812 million in 1959 largely by acquiring companies in the airplane, guided missile, submarine, nuclear energy, and electronics industries.[1] It accomplished this rapid growth by absorbing large companies in these vital fields while still maintaining its corporate dominance.

Starting in 1957, Philip Morris embarked on a diversification program, and thus far has acquired companies in the flexible packaging, industrial adhesive, and textile fixative fields.[2] Its acquisitions in non-related industries should give it economic protection not available in a one-product enterprise.

At the end of 1958, Studebaker-Packard had a cumulative tax-loss carry-over estimated to be in excess of $120 million. As a result, the company embarked on a program, which recently has been accelerated, to acquire profitable companies in order not to lose the benefit of its tax credits.[3]

The actions taken by these companies illustrate three of the major reasons for the remarkable volume of corporate acquisitions and mergers since World War II: increased sales, profit protection, and financial stability. But this is not all of the merger story, even though it is perhaps the best-known part. Other situations have also prompted mergers or

---

*Reprinted by permission from *Harvard Business Review,* Vol. XXXIX (January-February, 1961), pp. 74–82.

[1]"Pace of General Dynamics," *Fortune,* July, 1957, p. 125; see also Robert Sheehan, "General Dynamics vs. the U.S.S.R.," *Fortune,* February, 1959, p. 87.

[2]*Wall Street Journal,* April 23, 1957, p. 9; see also *Philip Morris Incorporated Report to Shockholders, Year 1957,* p. 6.

[3]*Wall Street Journal,* September 6, 1960, p. 24; see also "Francis of Studebaker-Packard (Businessmen in the News)," *Fortune,* November, 1960, p. 83.

corporate acquisitions during recent years. Specifically, here are several typical ones:

1. An electronics firm acquired a company in a related field for about $9 million. It was estimated that to build up a similar business, the company would have had to invest over $12 million and six years' work. The firm which it acquired already had a solid reputation in the field.
2. The major stockholders in a closely held plastic products corporation faced the problem of obtaining additional capital because of rapid sales expansion. These stockholders were of an age where it was not prudent for them to assume the burden of substantial long-term borrowing.

   Accordingly, they accepted an attractive offer from a national manufacturing company seeking diversified product lines and sold out at an approximate gain of $6 million over an original investment of $200,000. This gain was taxed at a maximum rate of 25 percent (capital gains) compared with normal personal income tax rates ranging up to 91 percent which would have applied to dividend income.
3. The stockholders of a closely held corporation had seen their business expand substantially in fifteen years from a modest beginning. Feeling they had too many eggs in one basket, they arranged a merger with a large company in the construction field which was seeking to diversify. Exchanging their capital stock for that of the larger company not only gave them a more secure investment but also postponed any taxable gain until they disposed of the stock received, which had a market value of $15 million. The principals continued in executive positions in the larger company.

The current wave of acquisitions and mergers involves large as well as small companies in virtually every industry. This trend is unlike the merger movement in the early part of the century, which involved expansion and integration within a given industry (e.g., steel). Nor can it be compared with the pre-World War II movement, when merger activity was largely generated by relatively few companies in the public utility, drug and chemical, food-processing, and retail store fields.

The advantages of many of these corporate acquisitions and mergers are apparent, but there are serious problems involved in such business combinations. Acquiring a company is not like buying an automobile or a refrigerator at a competitive price. A fair price for a going organization is not easily determined. Accordingly, questions like the following are important for top management:

1. How should an acquisitions committee be set up?
2. What information should be secured about prospective acquisitions?

3. What methods of valuation should be used?
4. What accounting, SEC, and federal income tax problems need to be borne in mind?

In discussing these and other questions in this article, I shall draw heavily on a good deal of recent experience of both large and small companies. Most of my emphasis will be on the financial, accounting, and legal considerations. The problems of new management relationships are obviously important, too, but must be treated elsewhere.

## Question of Motives

First, let me make a few very general comments about how management's objectives in contemplating an acquisition or merger affect the purchase and valuation problem.

As I have indicated, these objectives may vary greatly. They may range from expansion of capacity, product diversification, improvement of competitive position, and extension of market outlets to integration of operations, acquisition of management or technical personnel, and a need to invest excess funds. But in any case the urgency with which these aims need to be attained will affect the price offered and the method of accomplishing the business combination. For example:

1. A company with a tax-loss carry-over dating back several years may need to acquire one or more profitable enterprises with dispatch and in such a way that its tax credits can be utilized.
2. Similarly, a management replacing an overly conservative predecessor group in a declining industry may be under pressure to effect a business combination which would quickly improve its profit position.

In recent boom years the prospective purchaser, or dominant company, has usually made the first move in a proposed business combination. Many larger enterprises are constantly searching for companies to acquire or absorb, resulting in spirited competition for the seemingly more desirable of the medium-size and smaller companies. For this reason, purchase prices have been generous in relationship to either current earnings or net tangible assets.

This situation is reversed during depression periods, or for companies in depressed industries. Then the prospective seller, or company to be absorbed, is likely to take the initiative to salvage its position rather than be forced into bankruptcy. The price paid in such circumstances may be quite low. In some instances, it has even been less than the selling company's net current assets.

# Organizing to Act

Whenever a company plans to buy or merge with other companies, its first step should be to form an acquisitions committee. Depending on the size of the firm and its acquisitions program, this committee may include one or more full-time members, or it may consist entirely of executives who devote only a portion of their time to this activity. This aspect of form does not, in my opinion, make so much difference.

However, at least one member of the board of directors should serve on the committee; and in certain cases, he should be an "outside" director. There are times when the interests of the stockholders may not coincide with the personal interests of all of the management group with regard to a proposed acquisition or merger. For instance, it may be quite apparent that one or more members of a management team would be eliminated or downgraded in position if a proposed business combination were affected, yet the merger might be highly advantageous for the owners.

When an acquisitions committee is established, the company's board of directors should advise it of general objectives, policies, and types of mergers and acquisitions which should be considered. Such advice need not be detailed, but should indicate broad goals similar to those mentioned in the previous section. Also, the committee should be instructed about the desirability of cash deals as against exchanges of capital stock or combinations of stock and cash.

## *Information to Be Obtained*

Rather than limiting itself to certain companies which happen to come to the attention of the directors, an acquisitions committee should study all companies which may be considered good prospects. This can be done by:

1. Reviewing the classified industries section of *Moody's Industrial Manual* or similar directories.
2. Encouraging suggestions from officials in the sales and operating divisions with respect to unlisted companies.
3. Confiding in bankers and others who often know of companies which might be interested in a sale or merger.

Systematic investigation by an acquisitions committee has often turned up a prospect whose management had previously given no thought to business combination possibilities.

Before making any overtures, it is desirable to obtain as much information as possible on all prospects and to assemble these data in an orderly manner. A check list will be of considerable aid in carrying out such a comprehensive study. The list should include questions on financial position and results, manufacturing operations, personnel, sales, marketing, research, and other pertinent areas (see Appendix [p. 578]).

The use of such an outline will help to avoid many unpleasant surprises which tend to develop when negotiations have been concluded without benefit of an adequate investigation. In some instances, companies have found that the cream has been skimmed off the market in a particular product of an acquired company and that future profits would be much lower than those of the several years prior to acquisition. In others, they have had to supply considerably more working capital than was planned, or they have found facilities so inadequate that extra funds were needed for expansion or for new facilities at a different location. Also, companies that have planned on retaining management and key technical personnel often find, after closing a transaction, that such persons either do not fit into the revised organization or do not desire to remain in it.

## Evidence of Value

When both companies are in the same line of business and their capital stocks are activtly traded, market prices may be fairly persuasive evidence of value. But if the firms are in different lines of business, the market quotations may not be indicative of relative values at all. For example, during any period there are companies in "glamor" industries (e.g., electronics, as this article goes to press) whose stocks are priced so high relative to earnings that buyers appear not only to have discounted the future but also the hereafter! This lack of realism may be canceled out if *both* firms are in the industry, but otherwise it throws trading prices out of perspective.

Actually, we might go further than this and argue that in almost *any* circumstance management should regard stock prices with some suspicion. There are too many instances of capricious market action like this:

> The public relations counsel of a company announced development of a device for transmitting handwritten messages instantaneously by telephone. Although the company expected an operating loss for the year and officials of the nation's largest telephone system had thus far approved such a device only for a rival firm, the market price of the stock trebled in ten days.

In other words, current market prices of stock are not by any means conclusive measures of relative value (which is the important thing in exchanging shares) even when buyer and seller operate in the same general field of industry.

Among the other factors to be considered, the most significant are (1) potential earnings, (2) dividend-paying capacity, and (3) net assets. For operating companies whose worth is largely dependent on continuance as going concerns, potential earnings generally are the most important factor. On the other hand, for companies with substantial holdings of disposable assets, such as securities or real estate, over-all valuation might be related more closely to the fair market values of such underlying assets.

## *Potential Earnings*

Where two companies entering a business combination are in the same industry, their financial statements may be compared without much difficulty. In the absence of any unusual conditions affecting future profits of either company, agreement may be reached readily as to the period or periods for which earnings should be averaged as a valuation factor. Thus:

1. A five-year historical period is most common for this purpose, having the general sanction of the Internal Revenue Service for federal estate and gift tax purposes, of investment bankers for security underwritings, and of the SEC for registration and reporting purposes.
2. Where a Company's business is expanding, as in the electronics industry, and its capacity has increased considerably during a recent period, more weight should be given to earnings in the latest period of, say, one to three years.
3. In companies subject to cyclical variations, as in the steel, heavy machinery, construction, and steamship industries, historical earnings may be considered for a period longer than five years.

Regardless of whether both companies entering into a business combination are in the same or different lines of business, their earnings should be determined substantially on the same basis of accounting. This basis must be fairly specific. Even within the framework of "generally accepted accounting principles" and permissible accounting methods under the internal Revenue Code, divergent practices can produce considerable differences in operating results and net asset valuations.

One of the pitfalls to be avoided is that of overestimating the savings in expenses expected to result from the elimination of duplicate functions. These savings should be estimated on a conservative basis, since they often do not materialize. Acquiring companies frequently find that many expenses increase because of their higher compensation scales and more liberal benefits, which are extended to personnel of the company absorbed.

A factor that is often difficult to assess is the effect on future earnings of newly developed products, of the impending expiration of patents, and of the loss of exclusive manufacturing know-how which becomes a matter of common knowledge. For instance, in the pharmaceutical industry the greatest profit margins are generally realized on a product immediately following its introduction. When sales reach a respectable volume and competitors become interested in the product, unit prices are reduced, often drastically, as a result of competition.

Dividend capacity is often considered in valuing a company. But dividends actually paid in the past may have no relation to dividend-paying *potential,* particularly in a closely held company. If this factor is considered, it should be based on indicated capacity rather than on the historical record.

## Comparative Assets

Net asset values of the acquiring company and of the company to be acquired or merged should be determined, as closely as possible, on a comparative basis. In some cases, companies go so far as to have appraisals made of various assets. In other cases, book figures are adjusted to allow for differences in accounting practices (just as earnings may be adjusted).

Any disposable assets not used in a business, such as security investments and nonoperating land and plant, should be taken in at fair market values rather than at the book figures at which they are carried. If there is a presumption that nonoperating assets will be disposed of, the income tax effect of disposition should be considered in arriving at fair valuation.

## Weighting Factors

Many experts regard the price-earnings ratio (the relationship of the market price of a firm's capital stock to its annual earnings per share) as the sole evidence of value of a going industrial concern. In the absence of a market price, the price-earnings ratio of similar companies having listed securities or an industry ratio is sometimes applied to a company's earnings.

But while the price-earnings ratio is important, there are many instances where other factors should also be considered. Published data on a number of recent acquisitions and mergers show that astute managements have looked at these other factors in arriving at the purchase or exchange price:

1. Estimated future earnings
2. Plants and properties to be acquired
3. Net asset values
4. Accumulated losses deductible for income tax purposes
5. Benefits from anticipated operating economics

Various formulas used by courts in federal estate and gift tax cases are worth noting. For purposes of acquisition or merger, values would be generally higher than for tax appraisals, so one should not adhere rigidly to the formula approach. Nevertheless, three factors used by the courts and agencies should be considered in valuing the capital stocks of closely held corporations for any purpose:

1. "Earning power basis," "dividend basis," and "book value basis" were given weights, respectively, of 50 percent, 25 percent, and 25 percent in a U.S. District Court case in 1959 in valuing, for estate tax purposes, the capital stock of a closely held corporation.[4]
2. In a revenue ruling, also in 1959, the Internal Revenue Service outlined the approach, methods, and factors to be considered in valuing shares of capital stock of closely held corporations for estate and gift tax purposes. The same three factors were included in this ruling, as were a number of other items which are generally difficult, if not impossible to evaluate. Regarding the averaging of factors, the ruling concludes as follows:

   "Because valuations cannot be made on the basis of a prescribed formula, there is no means whereby the various applicable factors in a particular case can be assigned mathematical weights in deriving the fair market value. For this reason, no useful purpose is served by taking an average of several factors (for example, book value, capitalized earnings, and capitalized dividends) and basing the valuation on the result. Such a process excludes active consideration of other pertinent factors, and the end result cannot be supported by a realistic application of the significant facts in the case except by mere chance."[5] [But this does not mean that the three factors generally should not be the *primary* ones considered.]

## *Special Circumstances*

There is no great problem in arriving at net asset values and average adjusted historical earnings for a specified period or for a weighted combination of periods. Actual dividends are also readily compiled but are less significant than dividend-paying capacity. Note, however, that the latter may be difficult to determine for a company whose stock has been held closely, for there is every tax incentive to keep dividend pay-

[4]Revenue Ruling 59–60, *Internal Revenue Bulletin,* No. 1959–9, p. 8.
[5]*Bader, Clair B., Executor* v. *U.S.,* 172 Fed. Supp. 833 (1959).

ments to a minimum and finance operations through the retention of earnings. So in many cases, dividend-paying capacity should be excluded as a factor, and either 25 percent or 33⅓ percent weight should be given to adjusted net asset values, the remainder being assigned to earning power.

If this combination is utilized, any assets not used in the business and any income applicable to them should be excluded from the initial computation. *After* the weighted values have been computed, these assets should be added at their fair value. This gives added weight to net asset values in the total result; but it is fair, for there is no better evidence of value than the price at which an asset can be sold.

The gift tax regulations in the Internal Revenue Code define fair market values as the price which would change hands between a willing buyer and a willing seller when neither is under any compulsion to buy or sell, both parties having a reasonable knowledge of the facts. This general dictum has an air of profundity, but the cases are rare wherein both parties to a corporate acquisition or merger have the same desire and willingness to consummate a deal and have a full knowledge of all pertinent facts.

Some companies embarked on ambitious programs of acquisition and merger use a general yardstick in price determination which is based upon historical or adjusted historical earnings. That is, for the price paid, the company must acquire sufficient earnings not to dilute its per share earnings. Also, a similar determination may be made that net equity per share is not diluted as a result of the transaction. Of course, where a reasonably accurate forecast can be made for the year or two following consummation of a transaction, prospective earnings may be of greater significance and may justify a price that *would* lead to some dilution of per share earnings on a historical basis.

## *Method of Payment*

Before a price is finally determined, consideration must be given to to the method of payment. Is the price substantially above the federal income tax base of the seller? If so, it is generally desirable from the standpoint of the purchaser to pay cash or a combination of cash and securities so that a new tax basis may be established. But from the standpoint of the seller, it is usually advantageous to receive payment through exchange of capital stock. Take this example:

If a sole stockholder whose investment is $200,000 receives $6.2 million in cash for his company, he will pay a capital gains tax of $1.5 million on the transaction, leaving $4.7 million. On the other hand, if he receives capital stock having a fair market value of $6.2 million in exchange for the stock of his company, the transaction will not be subject to federal income tax unless he sells the newly acquired stock.

Assuming that these proceeds constitute his net estate, that he dies, and that the maximum marital deduction is applied, the difference in estate tax between a net estate of $6.2 million and one of $4.7 million will be only about $400,000. In other words, the estate will be worth some $1.1 million more, after all taxes, if the seller receives capital stock rather than cash in exchange for his original shares.

Thus an astute purchaser will pay a lesser price in an exchange of securities where the tax basis of the seller is lower than the purchase price, since he will take into consideration prospective tax savings to be gained by the seller.

There are circumstances in which the seller may obtain some cash and some securities. For example, if there are several corporations involved in a sale, it is possible to arrange that cash be paid for one or more firms and securities exchanged for the others, so that only part of the over-all transaction will result in a taxable gain to the seller.

Although the accounting treatment under a "pooling-of-interests" concept will not reflect the fair value of securities issued in an exchange, management should bear in mind that the "purchase" price is the aggregate market value of such secuities. Its astuteness in negotiating a deal should be judged with this thought in mind.

## Tax Aspects

The taxable status of acquisitions, mergers, or other business combinations under federal law is covered by specific rules in Subchapter C of the Internal Revenue Code. Without getting into the technicalities of these rules, a business combination may be "tax-free" in:

1. A "statutory" merger or consolidation
2. The exchange of voting capital stock of one corporation for that of another
3. The exchange of voting capital stock of one corporation for substantially all of the properties of another corporation

"Tax-free" means that the stockholders of the selling company, or the company that is being merged, will not be required to recognize any gain or loss on the securities received from the purchaser or surviving company in the merger. Such securities will have a substituted tax basis equivalent to the basis of the securities surrendered immediately or in liquidation as a result of the business combination. On the other hand, when a transaction *is* taxable to the selling stockholders, a new tax basis is created. The acquiring company allocates the purchase price, whether in cash or a combination of cash and securities, to the tangible and intangible net assets received.

In a nontaxable transaction the federal income tax basis of assets should always be ascertained by the acquiring company. It is not safe to assume that the basis is the same as the book amounts at which assets are carried by the selling company.

Under the reorganization provisions of the Internal Revenue Code (especially Sections 351, 354, and 368), an advance ruling is usually requested from the Internal Revenue Service to the effect that no gain or loss shall be recognized as a result of the transaction.

## Accounting Problems

For accounting purposes, a business combination will fall into one of two categories: (1) a purchase or (2) a pooling of interests. According to the American Institute of Certified Public Accountants:

> A *purchase* is described as a business combination of two or more corporations in which an important part of the ownership interest in the acquired corporation or corporations is eliminated or in which other factors requisite to a pooling of interests are not present.
>
> A *pooling of interests* is described as a business combination of two or more corporations in which the holders of substantially all of the ownership interests in the constituent corporations become the owners of a single corporation which owns the assets of the constituent corporations either directly or through one or more subsidiaries. The Institute's bulletin describes certain other conditions which should be met so that a business combination may qualify as a pooling of interests.[6]

In accounting for a purchase, the assets acquired are recorded on the books of the acquiring corporation as *cost,* which is measured in cash or other consideration at the fair value of such total consideration or at the fair value of the property acquired, whichever is more clearly evident. If the consideration is more than the fair value of the property acquired, then the item of goodwill must be reflected in the accounts of the acquiring company. This should be considered in determining potential earnings. In most cases, goodwill must be amortized against future earnings, with no tax benefit being derived therefrom.

By contrast, when a combination is deemed to be a pooling of interests, a new basis of accountability does not arise. The assets and liabilities of the constituent corporations (assuming they are in conformity with generally accepted accounting principles and on a reasonably uniform basis) are, in effect, combined, and their earned surpluses

---

[6]American Institute of Certified Public Accountants, Committee on Accounting Procedure, *Business Combinations,* Bulletin No. 48 (New York: January, 1957).

and deficits are combined and carried forward. Adjustments are made through capital and surplus accounts to reflect appropriately the capital stock outstanding in the combined enterprise after consummation of the transaction. In a pooling of interests, no recognition is given to goodwill.

There may be cases where the net assets and the business of several corporations of common ownership are acquired partly by pooling and partly by purchase. Then, too, if a company acquires a capital stock interest in another company for cash and later acquires the remaining capital stock in exchange for its own capital stock, the initial transaction may be treated as a purchase and the subsequent exchange as a pooling of interests.

## Filing Requirements

It is most important that a company consult with legal counsel and its independent public accountants regarding filing requirements with the SEC as the result of a corporate acquisition or other business combination. Without going into the many and varying circumstances under which reports must be filed, a corporate purchase or business combination may require (1) a registration statement under the Securities Act of 1933 or (2) a proxy statement under Regulation X–14 of the Securities Exchange Act of 1934. In either case, summaries of earnings for a period of years and one or more balance sheets must be furnished.

In other cases, neither a registration statement nor a proxy statement may be required. But a current report under the Securities Exchange Act of 1934 *is* required if an acquisition (which, under SEC definition, is a purchase, exchange, merger, consolidation, or the like) is deemed to involve a significant amount of assets, or if the gross revenues of the acquired company exceed a specified percentage of the gross revenues of the acquiring company and its subsidiaries.

Even though the assets and revenues of the acquired company may be below such specified percentages, if the amount of securities outstanding of the acquiring company is increased in excess of a specified percentage as a result of the transaction, a current report is still required. The current report instructions specify that a balance sheet and profit and loss statements for certain periods of the acquired company must be furnished to and certified by independent public accountants where a "significant" acquisition is involved.

It is essential to investigate carefully whether a company is or is not subject to the various filing requirements of the SEC. It is desirable to confer with SEC personnel when any doubt exists as to the necessity of filing, or to obtain their agreement regarding the type of data to be filed if unusual problems are involved.

Even though a company may not be subject to SEC filing requirements, there still are other obligations to be met. If its securities are listed on a national exchange, for example, it is required to file a stock list application for any new securities issued in the transaction. Also, it is prudent at times to obtain stockholder approval of a business combination to forestall later criticism, whether or not such approval is legally required.

## Conclusion

To most companies, a corporate acquisition or business combination is far from a routine matter. Accordingly, it is vital that company officers and directors have all the facts to enable them to reach an informed decision on the merits of a proposed transaction. Although imagination and enthusiasm are important ingredients in the successful operation of a business enterprise, when it comes to planning and negotiating for a corporate acquisition or merger, careful investigation and evaluation of pertinent factors are of even greater importance. To help businessmen make this effort, I have outlined in the Appendix the most important categories and items of information that I think a firm should try to acquire.

*Appendix*

# *Information to Be Obtained on a Prospective Corporate Acquisition or Merger*

## *Accounting-Finance*

The latest audited balance sheets and income statements for a number of years should be obtained and reviewed to determine:

1. Whether the accounting practices of the company are conservative or otherwise.
2. If the business appears to be on the upturn or decline.
3. How per share earnings of common stock, price-earnings ratios, net assets, dividends paid, and so forth, compare with similar data of the acquiring company.

Also, comparison should be made of the data customarily shown in *Moody's Industrial Manual* as to the percentage of annual depreciation to gross properties, inventory turnover, and return on net worth, with similar data for the acquiring company. If a company's stock is listed on a national exchange, information—in addition to that shown in the published annual report—may be obtained from the Form 10–K annual report on file with the SEC regional office and from copies of prospectuses, if the firm has had a recent public offering.

The accounting-finance members of the committee should also ascertain if possible, the amounts of outstanding common stock held by large stockholders. This information is found in the annual proxy statements to stockholders, for listed companies, and in Dun & Bradstreet reports, for unlisted companies.

## *Operations*

The following data should be obtained regarding operations:

1. The company's productive facilities including (*a*) the location of plants and warehouses and (*b*) the age and condition of plants and major equipment.
2. The productive capacity of the plants (e.g., if the company is operating on only a one-shift basis, would it be feasible to operate two or three shifts).

3. Whether the company manufactures for stock or against specific orders, and what proportion of its business is in various product lines. The operations member of the committee may have to work with the sales member to obtain this information.
4. The sources of supply of the company's major raw materials, if this can be determined.

## *Personnel*

The following should be obtained with reference to personnel:

1. The number employed, broken down into operating, office, and sales, or in some other appropriate way.
2. Unions the company has dealings with in its various plants, and how their wage scales compare with other companies in the area and with those of the acquiring company. If the company has operating personnel in some areas which are nonunionized, the increase in compensation and fringe benefits resulting from the unionization of such employees should be estimated.
3. The ages and length of service of top personnel, and judgments about how such personnel would fit into a combined enterprise. The data regarding executive personnel usually may be obtained from Dun & Bradstreet reports and from *Poor's Register of Directors.*
4. Particulars of the pension, stock option, and other similar plans.

## *Sales*

Sales information should include the following:

1. The principal products sold by the company as shown in catalogues or sales literature, the annual volume of each of the principal products, and the company's position in the industry wherein it markets its major products.
2. The method of marketing the company's products, i.e., whether distribution is through distributors, dealers, manufacturers' agents, direct consumers, or some other channel or combination of channels. Generally, if the marketing methods of the company are very different from those of the acquiring company, consideration may be given to coordinating such distribution methods with those of the acquiring company.
3. In appropriate cases, the proportion of the company's volume consisting of items sold for repair purposes.
4. To the extent practicable, data showing whether any appreciable volume of a company's sales are made to a few large customers or whether it sells large quantities of goods directly or indirectly to the U.S. government.

## *Accounting Adjustments*

It makes no sense to compare many assets and liabilities of two parties to a merger unless the figures are based on comparable accounting policies. In examining the need for accounting adjustments, the following items should be considered:

1. *Differences in Methods of Valuing Inventories.* For example, is one company inventorying all overhead applicable to finished goods and work in

process, while another company, because of conservative practices or low standard cost rates, is inventorying a much lesser portion of such overhead? Or is one company using the Lifo method for valuing a portion of its inventory and the other company using one of the other conventional methods? Similarly, practices regarding the write-down or write-off of slow-moving and so-called "obsolete" stocks should be reviewed to ascertain that both companies are on a comparable basis in this regard.

2. *Differences in Depreciation Practices.* For example, is one company using accelerated methods while straight-line depreciation is used by the other company? And even when both companies are using accelerated methods, if one has expended substantially more in recent periods for property, plant, and equipment than the other has, adjustment should be made to place both companies on the straight-line basis during the period under review.

3. *Practices with Regard to Inventorying Small Tools and Supplies.* Many companies write off to expense small tools, maintenance supplies, and spare parts, while others inventory such items. If the amounts of such items purchased annually are significant, it would be necessary to place both companies on a comparable basis of accounting therefor.

4. *Deferred Research and Experimental Expenses, Unamortized Debt Expense, Goodwill and Trademarks, etc.* Where such items are material, the accounts of both companies should conform to reflect a common practice.

5. *Reserves and Other Liabilities.* Policies of companies with regard to vacation pay, pension plans and commitments, and other similar items should be considered in computing adjusted earnings.

6. *Nonrecurring Charges and Credits.* Any substantial charges and credits resulting from transactions which are unlikely to recur in the foreseeable future should likewise be considered in adjusting earnings.

7. *Commitments.* The effect of recent actions which may not be reflected in earnings for the full period under review should be taken into consideration in determining normal earnings. Such items would include pension plans adopted during the period, sales price changes, increases or decreases in basic wage rates and in the cost of raw materials and supplies, and so on.

8. *Federal Income Taxes.* Some companies make it a practice to be generous in their accruals for federal and other income taxes, while others provide reserves on the basis of the tax computed in returns filed. Where practices vary between the companies, adjustments should be made for apparent overaccruals or for possible additional assessments, if material. Also, account should be taken of any income taxes that arise from adjusting prior earnings in the ways earlier described.

*Chapter 33*

# *The Place of Scientific Techniques in Mergers and Acquisitions**

By Roger R. Crane

IN CONSIDERING a merger or acquisition, management faces one of its most difficult decisions. There is much potential risk involved because of the long-term implications of such a move. An ill-advised acquisition can be the turning point in a company's history—from profit to loss, from prestige to failure. On the other hand, a carefully planned acquisition can lead to success for both parties, open entirely new product areas, and provide a basis for a good profit and for healthy growth opportunities.

In recent years, many companies have chosen the acquisition route for expansion and have been faced with the difficult decision of selecting a company or companies with which to merge. Naturally, many different methods are used for determining the best candidate for acquisition. However, such planning generally includes a great deal of detailed analysis. Volumes of information may be gathered concerning the prospect's plant, its personnel, its products, and many other aspects of its profit potential. All available financial data are usually gathered and interpreted. This analysis often must be carried out under considerable secrecy, particularly in the event that competitors are interested in the same companies.

However, when the decisions are finally made, frequently they seem to be based largely on politics or on "feelings" about certain companies, rather than on sound, logical considerations. The detailed analysis may not be used adequately in the final decision at the board of directors level because of the natural difficulty of digesting the volume of paper

*Reprinted by permission from *Controller,* Vol. XXIX (July, 1961), pp. 326–29, 340, 342.

In the preparation of this article, the author was assisted by Alvin E. Wanthal.

and untangling the many interlaced decision elements in relatively infrequent and brief board meetings.

A certain amount of initial screening of merger candidates can be accomplished quite readily once basic guidelines have been established. Some companies which are obviously unsuitable can be immediately discarded without further consideration. There normally remains a residue of three or four almost equivalent companies, some strong in one desirable aspect and weak in others, and vice versa. Accordingly, the difficult problem of weighting and balancing the different factors to make the best decision is created.

Although the comparison of companies according to these factors can be done intuitively through the exercise of judgment based on experience, the greater the number of factors involved, the more confusing the situation becomes. As the confusion increases, the possibility of a serious error and an unprofitable acquisition also increases.

Scientific techniques can be applied to assist in the evaluation of these factors just as they have been applied to more specific management problems such as inventory management and production scheduling. By providing a structure for the decision and a quantitative view of the intangible factors involved, the application of the scientific method can aid management in better making this critical decision.

To show how scientific methods can be applied, let us consider a typical acquisition decision problem. We shall assume that the typical voluminous staff analyses have been made. Many different prospects have been investigated in great detail, and the "easy" eliminations have been made. Three companies, which we shall call A, B, and C, remain as top prospects. All three of the companies are eligible, and any one of them would be acceptable for a merger. The usual evaluations have been made, but it is still difficult to choose among the three companies or to establish priorities for approaching them. In the following sections, we shall explore an approach to the solution of this problem.

## *Defining Objectives*

The most important requirement of any major decision of a company, and hence of an acquisition, is that it satisfy the objectives of the company. While many companies get along rather well without ever expressing explicitly their objectives, it is certainly helpful if these objectives are expressed in writing. In most cases, this much can be accomplished without much help from science. However, it would be even more helpful in many instances in reaching the most effective over-all decision if the relative importance of each of these objectives were also known. It is highly probable, for example, that each prospective acquisition satisfies all the objectives to some extent. The next step is to rank and weight the objectives if possible.

If the company executives have never bothered with a formal definition of objectives at all, this process can be quite revealing and will be a valuable exercise to perform. It is a basic prerequisite of any intelligent planning process. The determination of relative importance can be made in a number of ways, but perhaps can best be illustrated in the context of a group meeting of key executives, such as the board of directors. Here the executives are asked to rank the given objectives and compare them in various ways.

Suppose, for example, that a vote were taken to start this process and it was established that the most important objectives were the following, listed in order of importance:

$0_1$—Growth rate of at least 15 percent of sales annually
$0_2$—Ability to return at least 20 percent on investment (before taxes)
$0_3$—Continual improvement of management personnel
$0_4$—Stable union relations (no major strikes, minimum turnover)
$0_5$—Maintenance of high standards of product quality

In the mathematical evaluation which follows, we assume that the objectives are mutually exclusive, that is, attainable independently of each other, and that the values of these objectives are additive.

It is highly probable that each executive will have a different opinion of the relative importance of these objectives. Following is a method for obtaining the best consensus of the relative values of each of these objectives.

## *Weighting Objectives*

All objectives must be numerically weighted in order to quantify the various opinions about their relative importance and to use them in further evaluations. One method which can be used to weight the objectives is the "Relative Theory of Value" which was introduced by Professors Churchman and Ackoff in the May, 1954, issue of the *Journal of the Operations Research Society of America*. In general, this method consists of assigning tentative relative values to each alternative, testing these values by successive combinations of the various alternatives, reviewing all values for logical consistency, and normalizing the results. The evaluation can be accomplished fairly efficiently in a group meeting by independent voting, accompanied by free discussion among the participants. An arbitrary scale of values, such as 0 to 10 as is used in our example, must first be established. Or perhaps more easily, each member of the group can note his own evaluation of each objective, and averages can be taken to obtain initial values of the objectives.

The remaining steps in the process can be illustrated as follows:[1]

1. The most important objective according to the original ranking ($0_1$) should be given the highest value (in this case, 10 unless the average method is used). Each of the other objectives should be given a tentative value in relation to the most important one. For example:

$$0_1 = 10$$
$$0_2 = 7$$
$$0_3 = 5$$
$$0_4 = 3$$
$$0_5 = 2$$

2. The assigned values should first be tested by considering whether the value for $0_1$ is greater than the sum of $0_2$, $0_3$, $0_4$, and $0_5$. If, for example, $0_1$ is considered to be 25 percent more valuable than the sum of the other objectives, the relative values of the others should be adjusted downward accordingly, as follows:

$$0_2 = 4.0$$
$$0_3 = 2.5$$
$$0_4 = 1.0$$
$$0_5 = 0.5$$

3. Then the value assigned to $0_2$ should be tested by considering whether $0_2$ is more valuable than the sum of $0_3$, $0_4$, and $0_5$. If it is 25 percent more valuable, the other values should be adjusted as follows:

$$0_3 = 1.5$$
$$0_4 = 1.0$$
$$0_5 = 0.5$$

4. Next the value of $0_3$ should be tested by considering its relation to the combination of $0_4$ and $0_5$. If the values should be about equal, as they are, the valuation is correct.
5. All values should then be rechecked for consistency with the original evaluation. If the two are inconsistent, an error in logic has been made, and the entire process should be repeated, beginning with the original ranking. In our example, this comparison is as follows:

| *Original* | *Final* |
|---|---|
| $0_1 = 10$ | $0_1 = 10.0$ |
| $0_2 = 7$ | $0_2 = 4.0$ |
| $0_3 = 5$ | $0_3 = 1.5$ |
| $0_4 = 3$ | $0_4 = 1.0$ |
| $0_5 = 2$ | $0_5 = 0.5$ |

[1]In this process, it is easiest to think of executives carrying out the process one by one, although group action has a great deal to offer provided a strong, experienced moderator is available to assure progress.

6. Since both evaluations are consistent and thus logically correct, the final results should be normalized by dividing by the sum of all values (17). Thus:

$$0_1 = 0.59$$
$$0_2 = 0.23$$
$$0_3 = 0.09$$
$$0_4 = 0.06$$
$$0_5 = 0.03$$

By this sequential evaluation process, each objective of the company has been given a relative value based on the combined judgment of the management personnel. These values can now be applied to the prospective acquisitions.

## *Matching Acquisitions Against Objectives*

To determine the extent to which each prospective acquisition satisfies the company's objectives, scientific techniques can again be employed to quantify the judgment of management and clarify the decision problem. The purpose of matching acquisitions and objectives is to determine the over-all value which might be expected from each prospective acquisition, considering it in relation to each of the major objectives. This comparison can be facilitated by the use of a mathematical model.

TABLE 1

| *Five-Year Corporate Objectives* | $0_1$ | $0_2$ | $0_3$ | $0_4$ | $0_5$ | |
|---|---|---|---|---|---|---|
| | *15% Annual Growth* | *20% Return before Taxes* | *Better Management* | *Good Labor Relations* | *High-Quality Product* | *Expected Value if Acquired* |
| *Associated Value* | *0.59* | *0.23* | *0.09* | *0.06* | *0.03* | |
| *Description of Prospective Acquisition* | | | | | | |
| A Large company Poor management | 8 | −9 | −6 | −4 | 4 | 1.99 |
| B Medium company Good management | 7 | 2 | 0 | 4 | 6 | 5.01 |
| C Small company Excellent management | 5 | 7 | 8 | 9 | 7 | 6.03 |

The model can be filled in by placing a value in each box which represents the extent to which each acquisition satisfies each objective.

The interpretation of these values must be established before they are determined. An arbitrary scale of values must first be established such as the $-10$ to 10 which we chose. In our illustration, $-10$ indicates that the acquisition seriously threatens the objective, 0 indicates that the acquisition has no effect on the attainment of the objective, and $+10$ indicates that the acquisition virtually guarantees the objective.

To demonstrate how a particular value was chosen, consider company A and objective $0_2$. Company A is a large company with poor management personnel. It would be very unlikely that our company would be able to secure a 20 percent return before taxes by acquiring company A because of the size of the investment required and the associated shortcomings of the personnel. Therefore, this alternative was given the value $-9$. The logic behind the other values is similar in nature. The completed model with all values is shown in Table 1.

Again, the values can be established by independent voting of the executives and discussion of the resulting rows and columns, or they can be individually established and the results averaged. The expected value can be calculated for any particular acquisition by multiplying the value in each box of that row by the normalized value associated with the corresponding objective, and taking the sum of the five products. For example, the expected value of company B is:

$$7(0.59) + 2(0.23) + 0(0.09) + 4(0.06) + 6(0.03), \text{ or } 5.01$$

## *Matching Prospective Acquisitions Against Possible Conditions*

One of the most important risk factors which should be considered is the consequence of making the acquisition under various possible conditions of the market. In order to evaluate this factor, it is necessary to prepare some quantitative data concerning the probabilities that certain future events will occur. The use of probability is not so complicated as it sounds. In fact, once the concept is understood, the application is fairly simple, and the results will contribute significantly to the structure of the basic decision problem.

The most significant characteristics of the acquisitions should first be identified, to serve as guides for thinking about the effect of future events. These characteristics might include the size of the company facilities, the quality of the management personnel, or other similar factors.

The market (or markets, in the case of a diversified company) must be identified and analyzed to forecast the probable future behavior. The market for the entire company's product (including the acquisition) should be considered, and it should be determined if the acquired company's product will be similar or identical to the parent company's product. If there is a diversification motive involved, the market for both companies' product lines must be considered when assigning values within the model. Therefore the diversification model would be similarly constructed but more complicated than the single-product model. It is assumed that normal market research techniques will be (or have been) used to develop information on these product markets.

A probability of occurrence can be attached to different market conditions by observing past trends. However, this should be adjusted for the future outlook if significant changes are predicted. To estimate this probability, consider the sales trend at any point in time and the outlook for a future period (perhaps one to three months). Then, note the behavior at the end of the period as one occurrence in a frequency distribution: By considering successive points on the same time axis in this manner, the complete frequency distribution can be obtained, from which the reasonable range of possible conditions can be determined. These probabilities must add up to 1.0, because they should cover the entire range of possible alternatives.

After estimating the probability of any possible future market condition, the initial comparison of acquisitions and conditions can be made. However, this comparison can be improved significantly if the probability of making any prospective acquisition is also determined.

To estimate this probability, we must consider the peculiar situation of each prospective acquisition individually. The following factors should be evaluated: The attitude of the prospect's executives toward mergers in general and toward our company in particular; the financial condition of the prospect, with all associated factors; the potential competition for the prospect as a merger candidate; and the nature of the bid which we intend to make for the prospect (financial or political limitations). Thus the probability of acquiring each prospect will be determined mainly by judgment of our management personnel who are making the decision; but this is a judgment which can be isolated and made fairly easily, within reasonable limitations. These probabilities should fall within the range of 0 to 1.0, with 0 representing no possibility of acquiring, 1.0 representing certain acquisition, and 0.5 representing a "toss-up" situation.

All these probabilities, factor analyses, and market studies can now be employed and considered in a model of the combined company situation relative to various market conditions. This model can be constructed as shown in Table 2.

Although our model is shown with values already included, the

TABLE 2

| *Possible Market Conditions* / *Probability of Occurring* / *Prospective Company Acquired (Significant Factors)* / *Probability of Acquiring* | | *Drop 10% or More* | *±10% of Present* | *Increase 10% or More* | *Expected Value of Each Acquisition Considering Market Only* | *Expected Value of Each Acquisition Considering Market and Probability of Acquiring* |
|---|---|---|---|---|---|---|
| | | *0.1* | *0.3* | *0.6* | | |
| Company A<br>Large plant<br>Poor management | 0.5 | −10 | 2 | 7 | 3.8 | 1.9 |
| Company B<br>Medium plant<br>Good management | 0.8 | − 2 | 5 | 6 | 4.9 | 3.9 |
| Company C<br>Small plant<br>Excellent management | 0.5 | 3 | 6 | 6 | 5.8 | 2.9 |

matrix should originally be furnished to the executives in its blank form with only the alternatives and probabilities noted. The values should then be filled in by a group discussion process. The arbitrary scale which we chose for the values ranged from −10 to +10. Each value should be determined by considering the question: *If we acquired company Y, what is its value if the market does X?*

To illustrate how a typical value was determined, consider company A relative to an increase in the market of 10 percent or more. This acquisition would be particularly desirable in such a situation because of its capacity, but the shortcomings of its management personnel reduce the potential value from the maximum attainable. Therefore, this combination was given the value +7. The values for the other combinations were determined in a similar fashion.

After all values have been assigned, the expected value of acquiring each company relative to the probable market conditions can be evaluated. This evaluation can be made by summing for each company the product of each market condition and the value associated with it. For example, the expected value of company B is:

$$0.1(-2) + 0.3(5) + 0.6(6) = 4.9$$

The conclusion that can be drawn from these values is that company C would be the best acquisition, considering the market behavior only.

The expected values can be adjusted to consider both the probable outcome of the acquisition attempt and the market trend. The calculation is elementary; the product of the previously calculated expected value should be multiplied by the probability of acquiring each company. The effect of this calculation is to include a consideration of both factors in the new values. In our example the calculation results in company B, rather than company C, being considered the best candidate for the acquisition attempt.

## *Optimum Acquisition Strategy*

If the acquisition desires of our company become known to a competitor, the competitor may review his own position and decide to pursue the same prospects; or he and others may already be doing so, particularly in a single-product situation where certain companies are considered to be particularly desirable merger candidates. In the event that this situation occurs, mathematical techniques can again be employed to determine the optimum competitive strategy. The particular technique involved is the Theory of Games. It is applicable to any situation which involves opposing forces, each of which has an identical set of alternative moves. Analytical techniques are now available for many simple varieties of games; but unfortunately, the mathematics of solving more interesting and difficult games becomes quite cumbersome as the size of the games increases.

Many business situations can be analyzed as competitive games to improve the insight of the executives involved and possibly increase the probability of a favorable outcome. By viewing a situation as a game, competitive moves can be anticipated and countered. Thus, even though game theory is still in its infancy with respect to problem-solving capability, when applied as an analytical tool, it can still contribute significantly to the outcome of important decisions.

In the previous analysis of our example, it became apparent that companies B and C were both fairly equal as desirable candidates for merger, while company A was eliminated from consideration. In the event that a principal competitor had reached the same conclusion, an ideal game situation would result. The conflict situation is readily apparent, consisting of two persons opposing each other, with each person having the same three alternatives or moves: (C), (B), or (B and C). It might be desirable to approach either company B or company C individually; but once one was chosen and approached, the likelihood of getting the other would be reduced in the event that the first approach was unsuccessful. The advisability of making either one of these two choices will be evaluated in our game, together with the alternative of approaching both companies at the same time. It would be possible, of course, to test a large variety of alternatives; but from our previous analysis, these three appear to be the most interesting.

Essentially, by playing this game, we are trying to determine the best strategy to pursue in competing for the companies. For the purposes of the game, the best strategy will be the one which guarantees us the maximum payoff over the long run. Since each player will probably only have one move in our game, the possibility of playing various moves according to the odds, which would insure our maximum long-run gain, is not available to us. However, studying the game may still be a valuable exercise.

In the normal technical terminology, this game would be called a two-person, zero-sum game. One of the prerequisites of such a game is that any payoff to one of the opponents (persons) must be at the direct expense of the other. Our objective will be to maximize our gain in terms of payoff, while our opponent will attempt to minimize his losses. Assuming that the most favorable alternative for both persons would be to acquire both B and C, it is not difficult to understand the zero-sum definition—what one person gains, the other must lose.

The first step is to assign values to each combination of moves. To select these values, we must consider nine questions similar to this one: *If we choose company C and our competitor chooses company B, what is the payoff to us?*

In our example, such a move would probably allow us to realize the full value of company C, which was calculated in the previous example as about 6. The result of our move B versus their move C could be calculated as 5 in the same manner. If we had chosen C and B with the objective of getting both and our competitor had chosen either C or B, our payoff might be slightly higher than the payoff for choosing either one individually, because we would almost certainly get one acquisition and have an equal chance of bidding for the other. Accordingly, these payoffs were each judged as 7. The diagonal payoffs, representing the three moves where each opponent is bidding directly against the other, have been set at low values to reflect the obvious uncertainty and undesirability of such situations. The other values were placed on the arbitrary scale of 0 to 10 by similar judgments, which are not too difficult to make, particularly in real situations where more detailed knowledge of the competitor and the situation is available.

The game matrix, with all values filled in, is shown in Table 3.

To realize the full value of the game analysis, after all payoffs have been determined, we must calculate the optimum strategy for each opponent and the theoretical value of the game. By careful examination of our game, we can see that there is no single move which is always best for either of the two players. Such a condition would be called a "saddle point" and would greatly simplify the play if it were present, because the best strategy for either player would be always to play this one move.

TABLE 3

| | | *Competitors' Moves* | | | |
|---|---|---|---|---|---|
| | | *C* | *B* | *C and B* | *Odds (see text)* |
| Our Moves | C | 3 | 6 | 5 | 4 |
| | B | 5 | 2 | 4 | 4 |
| | C and B | 7 | 7 | 3 | 1 |
| Odds (see text) | | 1 | 0 | 2 | |

However, since our game is not one of these most simple cases, we conclude that the best strategy for each player will be a "mixed" strategy, i.e., to play various moves alternately, depending on the odds associated with each move. The method for calculating the odds to be used in these mixed strategies can be found in various books on game theory. The original development work on the theory was performed and published by Von Neumann and Morgenstern. Later works have explained the basic elements of the theory in less mathematical terms which can easily be followed.

If we examine the odds that have been calculated for the game, we can see that the best strategy for our company is 4:4:1, while the best strategy for our competitor is 1:0:2. If each player follows his best mixed strategy, he will insure that over the long run the results will be as favorable as possible to him (maximum gain or minimum loss), and that the net value over the long run will be the value of the game from the odds and the payoffs, the value of our game can be calculated at $4\frac{1}{3}$. Because this value is greater than zero, the game is plainly unfair to our competitor.

As we have already discussed, a mixed strategy is of little value to us because the game will probably only consist of one move. Thus the solution does not tell us exactly which move to choose. However, it does tell us that if our competitor chooses company B, he will be making his worst possible move, because it does not enter into his best mixed strategy. This knowledge will be significant if we are playing against an unenlightened competitor. We can only hope that he did not read this paper.

To summarize, let us consider what the application of scientific methods and mathematics contributed to the acquisition decision problem that we have illustrated. It is apparent that the scientific method did not solve the problem or make the decision itself, contrary to the fears of many thinking businessmen. However, it did aid in structuring the decision, clarifying the relationships involved, and revealing the sensitivity of pertinent factors. By measuring values in a quantitative manner and introducing the concept of probability, the scientific method helped to bring logic and insight into this otherwise intangible decision problem.

*Chapter* 34

# *Depreciation and Enterprise Valuation**

By Walter J. Blum and Wilber G. Katz

WHAT FUNCTION should prospective depreciation of assets serve in valuing an enterprise, especially for purposes of constructing a fair plan of corporate reorganization?

The anwswer which in the past gained wide acceptance in legal literature can be stated rather simply. Value of an enterprise is to be arrived at by estimating its earnings[1] in future years, on the basis of its assets and prospects as of the time of reorganization, and capitalizing the projected earnings at an appropriate rate. If the firm is viewed as having an earnings capability for an unlimited time, the estimate of annual earnings is to be capitalized in perpetuity. The projection of earnings then must reflect the need to replace major operating assets where it is foreseen that they will lose value through use and that at some predictable date their retention by the firm will become uneconomic in the sense that in operation their worth to the firm will be less than their resale or scrap value. Replacement in this common situation has to be presumed in order to validate the basic assumption that the estimated annual earnings will continue undiminished in perpetuity. The projection of an annual charge for depreciation adjusts estimated earnings to accommodate such replacement in valuing an enterprise.

---

*Reprinted from *University of Chicago Law Review,* Vol. XXXII (Winter, 1965), pp. 236–42, by Walter J. Blum and Wilber G. Katz, by permission of the *University of Chicago Law Review*. Copyright, 1965, by the University of Chicago.

[1]In describing the generally accepted formula for valuing an enterprise, there is no need at the outset of this comment to be more specific about the meaning of "earnings." Refinement is added later when required by analysis of the depreciation problem.

Under the generally accepted approach to valuation, the total of depreciation charges over the forecasted life of an asset reduces estimated earnings by the expected diminution in the value of that asset resulting from its consumption. The total usually has no connection with the foreseeable cost of replacing the asset with a new or better model. The main reason for tying depreciation to existing asset values is that earnings estimates are usually geared to assets of the firm as of the time of reorganization. It would be incorrect to reduce such estimates by the anticipated cost of higher quality replacements inasmuch as, all other things being equal, these improvements can be expected to enhance the earnings picture.[2]

In placing a value on a perpetual firm, the accepted approach usually entails calculating depreciation charges on the simple straight-line annual basis—that is, dividing the total foreseeable charges for an asset by its estimated life. For some assets a case might be made for using an accelerated or retarded pattern of annual charges. But it is sufficient to observe that in reaching valuations, there is a strong pull toward using a constant charge. In the typical situation the estimate of earnings, which is to be capitalized, takes the form of a constant figure that represents the most probable annual earnings for the foreseeable future. The quest for a constant annual estimate of earnings tends to be served by constant depreciation and to be thwarted by other patterns.

For purposes of valuing a perpetual enterprise, nothing turns on whether depreciation is thought of as reflecting anticipated declines in values or as reflecting costs which are to be amortized by charges against future operations. The two conceptions produce like results because in valuing an enterprise, the total cost of depreciable assets to be amortized is, as previously stated, equal to the total anticipated deterioration in value.

Not all firms are viewed as perpetuities; in various situations, it is anticipated that the enterprise will be liquidated at some foreseeable future date, and it is not contemplated that major assets are to be replaced. In arriving at valuation in these cases, the prescription which has gained general acceptance is different. Estimated values obtainable on liquidation and estimated annual earnings for the finite period of predicted operation are to be discounted to present value without depreciation being taken into account in computing those earnings. Depreciation can be ignored because the prediction of earnings does not turn on replacing

---

[2]To be distinguished are situations in which it is assumed that certain assets will be replaced immediately after reorganization. If the estimate of earnings is predicated on such a development, the projection of depreciation for the asset to be acquired would be based on its anticipated cost—which presumably would be equal to its value at the time of acquisition.

the existing assets of the enterprise. It is only necessary to take account of the estimated cost of maintaining and operating the existing assets until the date assumed for liquidation of the firm.

These principles for valuing perpetual and limited-life enterprises were given official expression in corporate reorganization proceedings in the late thirties and early forties.[3] They appear still to receive general acceptance in reorganization literature. However, a reconsideration of the treatment of depreciation seems to be in order. More recent trends in financial analysis suggest that the old standard way of handling depreciation in valuing enterprises viewed as perpetuities is too simple and often leads to incorrect results.

The clue to the source of oversimplification is found in the accepted treatment of an enterprise of limited life. Assume for purposes of analysis that an enterprise is composed of a single asset, a commercial building, which was completed today at a total cost of $1 million; assume further that it is estimated to have a 40-year useful life and no scrap value thereafter, and that it is expected to produce an annual net cash inflow of $105,000 before depreciation; and finally, assume that no working capital is required in running the enterprise, that there is no income tax, and that all agree that 8 percent is the appropriate rate for converting the projected net cash inflow into a statement of present value. If the venture is treated as a perpetuity—meaning that it is assumed that every 40 years the structure will be replaced by an identical building costing $1 million—the standard approach would operate as follows: Straight-line depreciation of $1 million spread over 40 years would call for an annual charge of $25,000; this would bring net cash inflow down to $80,000 a year; and capitalizing that amount in perpetuity at 8 percent would result in a valuation of $1 million. Suppose, however, it is assumed that the enterprise has a life limited to 40 years and that the building will not be replaced. Under the accepted approach, depreciation would not be taken into account, the $105,000 of estimated net cash inflow would be valued as a 40-year annuity on an 8 percent basis, and the result would be a present value of not $1 million but $1,252,084.

Why, against all the dictates of common sense, is the same profitable enterprise found to be worth more as one of limited duration than as a perpetuity? A moment's reflection will point to the treatment of depreciation in the perpetuity calculation as the root of trouble. The straight-line asumption produces an improper timing of earnings and therefore an understatement of value. Depreciation covered by earnings can be

[3]What is referred to as the generally accepted approach is well illustrated in *Matter of Atlas Pipeline Corp.*, 9 SEC 416 (1941) (Corporate Reorganization Release No. 42).

thought of as capital which has been disinvested from the depreciated asset and which is now available for other purposes: It can be left at risk generally in the operation of the enterprise, it can be accumulated in a savings account type of sinking fund for replacing the building, or it can be used to reduce outstanding indebtedness of the firm. Under any of these programs the value of the $25,000 a year taken as depreciation would at the end of 40 years exceed $1 million. If the savings account rate of interest were 4 percent per annum, the sinking fund would accumulate to $2,375,638 in 40 years; and if the business were to succeed in earning its rated 8 percent per annum, the added value attributable to the earnings retained by depreciation for general use in the business during that same period would be $6,476,413.[4] Obviously, in either case the allowance for depreciation is far too generous. What is needed is not $1 million in total charges over 40 years, but charges which, compounded at the proper earnings rate assigned to the disinvested amounts, will grow to a total of $1 million in that time. Depreciation is thus like an annual annuity. At a 4 percent earnings rate on disinvested sums, the yearly depreciation annuity for the building would be $10,523; the net cash inflow after depreciation would then be $94,477; and the capitalized value of the enterprise, at 8 percent in perpetuity, would be $1,180,962. At 8 percent on disinvested sums the depreciation annuity would be $3,860; the net cash inflow after depreciation would be $101,-140; and the capitalized value of the enterprise, at 8 percent in per-

---

[4] If the disinvested capital is used to retire indebtedness, the appropriate computation might seem to be somewhat different. Assume, by way of illustration, that the firm had outstanding $1 million principal sum of 4 percent debentures which could be called at any time at par plus accrued interest; assume further that the debentures always sell in the market at their call price. If the same amount of debentures is to be retired each year, and if the final retirement is to occur at the maturity date, the constant annual retirement would have to be $25,000 ($1,000,000 ÷ 40). In this situation, if debt retirement is thought of as being financed out of disinvestment by way of earned depreciation, the required amount of depreciation would appear to be $25,000 a year, or $1 million in total—thus seeming to contradict the position taken in the text.

The contradiction, however, is only superficial. The effect of retiring the debt is to hold in the firm the amounts which otherwise would have been paid out in interest on the debt. The "savings" in the second year would be $1,000 (4 percent of $25,000); in the last year, it would be $39,000 (4 percent of $975,000). The total savings is the sum to which the savings in the particular years ($1,000 in year 2, and $1,000 plus $1,000 for each year after year 2) will grow in 40 years when compounded at the appropriate rate. If the appropriate rate is 4 percent, the situation can be viewed as though the firm at the end of each year bought $25,000 of its own debt as an investment yielding 4 percent a year. The interest on the investment would cumulate to $1,375,638 in 40 years at 4 percent. (The similarity to putting $25,000 annually into a savings account sinking fund should be apparent.) If investment in the firm is rated at 8 percent, that rate, rather than the 4 percent interest rate on the debentures, is the proper one for compounding the investment attributable to the "savings" in interest payments.

petuity, would be $1,264,250. It is to be noted that the value of the enterprise treated as an 8 percent perpetuity exceeds its value of $1,252,084 as an 8 percent venture with 40 years of life. This is an obviously correct relationship in view of the assumption that annual net cash inflow after depreciation is positive and not negative. The excess of $12,166 is the present value of a deferred perpetual annuity of $101,140 starting 40 years from now.

It might now be asked whether the straight-line approach to depreciation on the basis of existing values always results in an incorrect valuation of the firm. Further reflection on the commercial building example is helpful. The reason why the straight-line approach is inappropriate is that it fails to take account of the time schedules for disinvestment and reinvestment. In the illustration, the $1 million of anticipated disinvestment spread over 40 years through earned depreciation of course has a higher present value than anticipated reinvestment of $1 million in a lump sum 40 years from date. A disparity of sufficient proportions between time of disinvestment and of reinvestment always causes straight-line depreciation on existing values to produce distorted results; and this is equally true where reinvestment is expected to take place earlier than disinvestment through earned depreciation. Only where such disinvestment and reinvestment are expected to occur on substantially the same schedules—so that the two are in equilibrium—will straight line-depreciation based on existing values produce a proper result in valuing the enterprise.

These reflections suggest that an enterprise can be valued without taking *annual* depreciation into account. It should be noted that the old generally accepted approach to depreciation imports a degree of circularity into the valuation process: Value of the enterprise turns on earnings after depreciation, while the total amount of depreciation depends on the present value of certain existing assets of the firm. This circularity is especially troublesome where the present value of particular assets turns on their estimated earning power rather than on independent market data. Thus, in the commercial building example, how can one estimate earnings after depreciation without knowing the current value of the building on which to base depreciation charges? And once that value has been determined, is not the whole problem of valuing the firm thereby solved? If these questions are answered in the affirmative, as they must be, it would seem advisable to find a route by which depreciation can be dispensed with entirely in the valuation of enterprises.

So long as elementary straight-line depreciation continues to be applied in inappropriate situations—where the anticipated schedule of annual reinvestment does not match the anticipated schedule of annual disinvestment through earned depreciation—the omission of annual depreciation from the valuation computation would make a difference in the result reached. But such a difference reflects only the improper handling of depreciation. Were depreciation to be figured correctly, in accordance with the analysis presented earlier, an alternative approach would produce the same valuation of an enterprise without working through an accounting for annual depreciation. The alternative would treat the cost of anticipated asset replacements merely as cash outflows and would offset their negative present values against the valuation otherwise obtained by capitalizing anticipated positive annual net cash inflows. The commercial building case can be used as an illustration once again. The estimated annual net cash inflow of $105,000 (ignoring depreciation) would be capitalized in perpetuity at 8 percent, giving a present value of $1,312,500; the negative present value of $1 million to be spent every 40 years to keep the enterprise operating in perpetuity is $48,250; combining the two components results in a valuation of $1,-264,250—the same figure reached when depreciation is taken into account on a proper annuity basis in valuing the firm as a perpetuity.

It should be clear that the skip-depreciation approach to enterprise valuation consists of finding the present positive value of all anticipated net cash inflows and the present negative value of all anticipated investments to produce and maintain those inflows. Hence, in essence, it values a perpetuity on the same principle as that which underlies the generally accepted method for valuing an enterprise of limited duration.

One can now easily see why use of this approach to a perpetuity produces the same valuation as does application of a proper depreciation pattern. The present value of anticipated investment to replace assets is equal to the total present value of all depreciation charges that would be projected under annuity depreciation.[5] A final look at the commercial building example will show why this relationship exists. Depreciation on an 8 percent annuity basis to accommodate the first replacement at the end of 40 years would, as noted, call for annual depreciation of $3,860, which on an 8 percent assumption has a present value of $46,030. The present value of a reinvestment of $1 million in 40 years, discounted at 8 percent, is likewise $46,030. This equivalence of present values will hold 40 years from now in regard to the contemplated second building replacement at the end of 80 years; it will also hold then in regard to the third replacement at the end of 120 years, and so on through infinity. The present values today of the disinvestment side and

[5]The present value of anticipated investment to replace assets would be equal to the total present value of all projected depreciation charges called for by elementary straight-line depreciation in the case of a firm expected to be in disinvestment-reinvestment equilibrium.

the reinvestment side of each replacement in the series will also be exactly equal. It must follow that this equivalence will hold whether the enterprise is viewed as a finite series of limited duration ventures or as a perpetuity. Annual depreciation therefore can safely be ignored in valuing the firm.

It need only be added that the skip-depreciation approach—that of arriving at present values for all anticipated cash inflows and outflows of the firm—is equally applicable where net cash inflows or investments are expected to follow an irregular pattern. It can be employed where earnings estimates at the time of valuing the firm are predicated upon ownership of assets which are to be acquired in the future. And it also can accommodate situations in which the risks associated with various classes or strata of anticipated earnings or of investments are different.[6]

[6]Henry B. Gardner, Jr. "The SEC and Valuation Under Chapter X," University of Pennsylvania Law Review, Vol. XCI (January, 1943), p. 440.

# Index

# *Index*

*This book has been set in 10 and 9 point Times Roman, leaded 2 points. Display faces are Times Roman and Caslon True Cut. The size of the type page is 26 by 44 picas.*